TELLA DALLAS DAYS OF OUR LIVES THE EDGE
F NIGHT ALL MY CHILDREN JUST PLAIN BILL
HE ROMANCE OF HELEN TRENT MARY NOBLE,
ACKSTAGE WIFE MA PERKINS THE GUIDING
GHT YOUNG DOCTOR MALONE LIFE CAN BE
EAUTIFUL VIC AND SADE GENERAL HOSPITAL
LL MY CHILDREN MYRT AND MARGE PORTIA
ACES LIFE WOMAN IN WHITE AS THE WORLD
URNS ONE MAN'S FAMILY ALL MY CHILDREN
HEN A GIRL MARRIES ONE LIFE TO LIVE DARK
HADOWS THE YOUNG AND THE RESTLESS THE
ECRET STORM RYAN'S HOPE JUST PLAIN BILL
OVE OF LIFE THE GUIDING LIGHT LIFE CAN BE
EAUTIFUL YOUNG DOCTOR MALONE VIC AND
ADE MYRT AND MARGE ONE MAN'S FAMILY

SOAP WORLD

Also by Robert LaGuardia
MONTY

Soap WORLD

by Robert LaGuardia

ARBOR HOUSE   New York

To Hugh J. Lynch Jr.,
a good friend and a good advisor

Library of Congress Catalogue Card Number 83-72889
ISBN: 0-87795-482-8
MANUFACTURED IN THE UNITED STATES OF AMERICA

This book is printed on acid free paper. The paper in this book meets the guidelines
for permanence and durability of the Committee on Production Guidelines for Book
Longevity of the Council on Library Resources.
Design by Antler & Baldwin, Inc.

CONTENTS

Acknowledgments

Part One   THE HISTORY

Introduction—SOAPS ENTER A NEW AGE	3
THE RADIO SOAPS	9
THE FIRST TELEVISION SOAPS	24
THE MODERN SOAP WORLD	36
SEX IN THE SOAPS	52

Part Two   CURRENT SOAP OPERAS: BACKGROUNDS AND COMPLETE PLOT SUMMARIES

Introduction	59
ALL MY CHILDREN	61
ANOTHER WORLD	79
AS THE WORLD TURNS	105
CAPITOL	130
DAYS OF OUR LIVES	134
THE EDGE OF NIGHT	154
GENERAL HOSPITAL	174
THE GUIDING LIGHT	210
LOVING	235
ONE LIFE TO LIVE	238
RYAN'S HOPE	257

SEARCH FOR TOMORROW   268

THE YOUNG AND THE RESTLESS   293

Part Three PAST FAVORITES

Introduction   310

LOVE OF LIFE (1951-1980)   311

THE BRIGHTER DAY (1954-1962)   329

THE SECRET STORM (1954-1974)   332

FROM THESE ROOTS (1958-1961)   341

THE DOCTORS (1963-1982)   344

LOVE IS A MANY SPLENDORED THING (1967-1973)   353

TEXAS (1980-1982)   357

APPENDIX

A.   Casts and Credits for Selected Radio Soaps   363

B.   Casts and Credits for Canceled Television Soaps Lasting
     Under Ten Years   374

C.   Courses in Soap Opera   390

Bibliography   391

Index   393

ACKNOWLEDGMENTS

OVER the course of ten years this book itself has almost become a continuing serial. Its antecedents were *The Wonderful World of TV Soap Operas* (1974, revised in 1977) and *From Ma Perkins To Mary Hartman* (1977). After they went out of print around 1980, I began hearing from many people that the two books had become a kind of underground fare. Because they were the only sources of long-term plot summaries of all the soaps and had historical details that could not be found elsewhere, every soap opera fan magazine editor had his own copy for reference and refused to lend it out. Actors, producers, head writers of soap operas kept their copies under lock and key. (When he was writing *Another World,* Harding Lemay recommended that all his sub-writers acquire *The Wonderful World* to gain background on their own show.) During a period of about six months, around the time that the Luke-and-Laura mania was beginning, I started receiving phone calls from people around the country anxious to acquire copies of the books: they had been to every out-of-print book store in their area. Among them were two college teachers who wanted to use them for courses on soap opera. When was I going to get them back in print?

And so I began planning this present volume. It would have to incorporate the historical elements of the original books, yet needed a complete metamorphosis; for I didn't want mere updates of the story line summaries or simple revisions of the backstage histories, but a thorough renovation of the project so that the emphasis would now be on reference and permanence rather than on the star-heavy quality of the previous books.

The considerable task of this volume, which really began in the early seventies, could not have been done without the help of many people. For their help with early story lines, I wish to thank: Bud Kloss (*All My Children*); Mary Bonner, Jacquie Courtney, Val Dufour (*Another World*); Eileen Fulton, Don MacLaughlin, Rosemary Prinz, Helen Wagner (*As the World Turns*); H. Wesley Kenney (*Days of Our Lives*); Hugh McPhillips, Jim Pritchett, Joseph Stuart (*The Doctors*); Teri Keane, Mandel Kramer, Maeve McGuire, Erwin "Nick" Nicholson (*The Edge of Night*); Jim Young, Kylie Masterson (*General Hospital*); Charita Bauer (*The Guiding Light*); Larry Auerbach, Audrey Peters, Ron Tomme (*Love of Life*); Doris Quinlan (*One Life To Live*); Mary Stuart, Mary-Ellis Bunim (*Search for Tomorrow*); Jada Rowland (*The Secret Storm*); and Karen L. Palmer, (*The Young and the Restless*).

I wish to express my deep appreciation to John Kelly Genovese for his extraordinary knowledge of soap opera (he began watching soaps when he was ten) and for his tireless assistance on behalf of this book. He compiled the cast lists which appear in this volume from his extensive library, and helped with many other projects including storyline updates. He also helped with the exhausting process of photo verifications and dating, and contributed his recollections of the early *General Hospital* as well as other shows.

Among the people who granted interviews and

helped enormously with the historical sections (other than story line summaries) were Charita Bauer, Mart Hulswit and Bruce Cox, for *The Guiding Light*; Don MacLaughlin, who painted vivid images of a bygone era; Val Dufour, who told great stories; Virginia Dwyer, who recalled the radio days; Helen Wagner, Pat Bruder, Joe Willmore and Eileen Fulton, who made the backstage events of *As The World Turns* throb with life; Tom Donovan, Allen Potter, Agnes Nixon and Jacquie Courtney, who made their experiences on *Another World* seem like an adventure; Irna Phillips, who talked with me from Chicago only months before she died; John Beradino, Leslie Charleson, Lieux Dressler, Mathilde Ferro, Anthony Geary, Marlena Laird, Emily McLaughlin, Doug Marland, Kylie Masterson, Gloria Monty, Pat Falken Smith, Lucille Wall, and Jim Young, who portrayed the backstage saga of *General Hospital*; Harding "Pete" Lemay, with whom I talked many times while he was writing *Another World*; Joe Behar and Ken Corday, who told me about the early *Days of Our Lives*; and Leonard Valenta, who has been a director on most of Procter & Gamble's shows and who has inspired me time and again with his incisive understanding of the past.

Throughout the course of all these soap opera books, Bob Short, former head of Procter & Gamble Productions in Cincinnati, has been gracious and co-operative. I'd like to express my appreciation to him. Much thanks, too, to John Valente, of the same office, for a Hollywood lunch in which he helped expand my understanding of contemporary trends in the soaps, and for being generally helpful.

I would like to thank the photo departments of ABC, CBS and NBC for supplying the photographs for this book. Individuals in those departments spent hours on photo research.

A special thank you to Diane Dalby and Daytimers magazine, which opened its files to me and was of tremendous help; also to Soap Opera Digest and two of its staffers, Jody Chester and Ellen Howard, who prepared first drafts of the recent story line summary updates on *General Hospital, The Doctors, Texas* and *Capitol.* Others who helped with recent updates were: Connie Passalacqua (*Ryan's Hope*); Linda Susman (*Search for Tomorrow*); Tony Rizzo (*The Young and The Restless*); John Genovese (*Another World, As the World Turns, Days of Our Lives, The Edge of Night, The Guiding Light*—new material on the show's first few years, *Love of Life* and *Loving*); Leena Titenus, of the *One Life To Live* production office; and Candice Earley, who remembered everyone else's storylines on *All My Children,* including her own.

Part One

THE HISTORY

INTRODUCTION—SOAPS ENTER A NEW AGE

WEBSTER's *New World Dictionary* defines soap opera as a daytime serial drama of "a highly melodramatic, sentimental nature." That doesn't seem quite right, for if the definition holds not all soaps would be soaps, an impossibility. Some have only occasional melodrama, and others are far from being sentimental. The entire first year of one soap during the fifties had hardly any drama let alone sentiment.

But we need a definition and it is here in this book—the summaries of the story lines from the first day the soaps began, with their heroines and love triangles and perpetual quests for happiness; the history of the medium, going back more than fifty years to Depression Chicago, when the first radio soap operas took hold; the scores of soap operas, each with its own special theme, that have come and gone on television.

This book is a definition of "soap opera."

Somewhere during the course of reading through the story line summaries, looking at the photographs, reading backstage histories, you may also discover what soap operas are *about*. That is even more difficult to define than what they are. They often appear to be about families. It was Irna Phillips who invented soaps about families (adding her special touch of always including doctors, ministers and lawyers as key characters), which still exist in one form or another on today's shows. But *General Hospital* is about the activity in a busy urban hospital. The early Hummert soaps were fantasies. In the end, you may decide that soap operas are merely elaborate love stories—with the word "love" meaning primarily love between a man and a woman (although *The Young and The Restless* has broached lesbianism), but also love between mother and daughter, father and son, best friends: that is, the gamut of intimate personal relationships.

This book tells what soap operas are about.

But, however defined, the soaps attract a television audience in the multi-millions. Networks, sponsors and advertising agencies are still in a state of confusion about what has happened to daytime drama in the past six years. When it was announced that the wedding of Luke and Laura on *General Hospital* in 1982 had attracted fourteen million viewers, there were many in the soap opera industry who began to throw away the rule books. At least fifty million people watch soaps at different times in any one week, but because of the vast number of teenagers who have become serial addicts, there may now be as many as seventy million people who tune in weekly.

At one time sponsors knew they were appealing to housewives over thirty-five, but today's monster audience is made up of both sexes and many different age groups. What has happened is that the stories are now split into parts, with each part appealing to a different audience group. It's like hunt and peck typing with a blindfold on.

Daytime television dramas have never before

3

been as elaborate or well honed. At a cost of $100,000 to $200,000 per week (twenty times the weekly budget of the fifties), they involve fanciful location shootings in places like Madrid, Rome, Jamaica and the Greek isles, and now use costly nighttime filming techniques. A full ten hours of daily soaps are watched devotedly, sometimes clandestinely (hurriedly switched off when the doorbell rings), sometimes with the greatest abandon. Sometimes the soaps are viewed close up, hands clasped in laps, tears and laughter alternating; or they are watched from a sickbed, or the kitchen table, or from behind ironing boards and potato peelings or in groups in college dormitories. Sometimes viewers show as much interest in their favorite actors as in the story line itself. The actors are frequently objects of unbelievable involvements on the part of viewers—involvements that sometimes lead to hate or love mail, or long distance phone calls to offer advice (during murder trials, for instance), or the sending of handmade gifts to characters who are ill. Viewers have been known to stage large wedding parties in their homes (complete with wedding cake) when characters marry, and they have even, though rarely, physically attacked or harassed actors. Several years ago, a woman left her television set in the midwest, traveled to Hollywood, walked into the *General Hospital* production office and found an unattended Rolodex with Denise Alexander's home address. The woman then parked herself in front of the actress's door, determined to become part of her life. A stunned Denise Alexander spent days talking the woman out of her obsession.

It is always a surprise to learn who watches soap operas. Tallulah Bankhead used to call production offices to offer her advice on story lines. ("Why doesn't she shoot the bastard!" she once yelled at a production assistant of *The Edge of Night*.) Bette Davis and Judy Garland both loved *Another World*. Judy almost went to pieces at one of her concerts when she spotted Constance Ford (Ada) in the audience. Learning that Tennessee Williams was a fan of *From These Roots*, the writers found themselves producing more literary dialogue and employing numerous references to the theater world. These days famous fans need only pick up the telephone and they can walk right onto their favorite shows. When Christina Crawford became ill in 1968 and couldn't appear on *The Secret Storm*, her mother, Joan Crawford, filled

in for her for two days, even though she was thirty years too old for the part. More recently, Carol Burnett let the word out that she wouldn't mind appearing on her family's favorite soap, *All My Children*. Soon she was playing a patient (and quite charmingly) for a day at Pine Valley Hospital. Elizabeth Taylor took to *General Hospital* while she was touring with *The Little Foxes*, called producer Gloria Monty, and the writers worked up an important role for her in the Luke and Laura wedding plot. (It was a great victory for the soap world, for obvious reasons.) Sammy Davis, Jr., has appeared on no less than three soap operas: *Love of Life*, *General Hospital* and *One Life To Live*. By the time Barbra Streisand and Ryan O'Neal take parts on *The Young and The Restless*, it will almost be old hat.

But years ago no actor with a reputation dared appear on a soap opera for fear of the stigma of the medium. In the early days of soaps there were only examples of actors who became big stars *after* leaving their soap roles. From radio soaps came Orson Welles, Macdonald Carey, Don Ameche, Van Heflin, Agnes Moorehead, Mercedes McCambridge, Art Carney, Gary Merrill, Paul Ford, Anne Frances, Richard Widmark. And from televised daytime fare have emerged Jack Lemmon, Eva Marie Saint, Tony Randall, Hal Holbrook, Efrem Zimbalist, Jr., Sandy Dennis, Roy Thinnes, Beverly Garland, David Birney, Richard Thomas, Tom Selleck, Roy Scheider, David Hasselhoff, Jill Clayburgh, Ellen Burstyn, Dyan Cannon, Larry Hagman, Lee Grant, and many others. You will come across most of these names in this book.

We are living through an interesting sociological period, in which television soap operas are beginning to play a more than peripheral role. One reason is the escalating divorce rate and the subsequent rise in alienation. Millions of young people, many of whom are the products of divorced parents, are reliving their prior ordeals through the endless rites of love, marriage and divorce on daytime serials. There is a kind of healing process involved. The key is that the dramas are so drawn out and detailed that the reliving is done with a microscope, for one can peer at evolving relationships as closely as entomologists watch specimens. In a world that has become confusingly fast, the soaps slow the action down, enabling uprooted people to study a world-like prototype, to find their place again with others.

Along similar lines, the soaps can teach whole life processes. Numerous experiments involving them are going on all over the country. For several years doctors have been using daily soap operas as part of their treatment of terminally ill patients. The idea is that the dying patient watches an ongoing story line about a dying character (there are a handful of such stories every year) and learns to cope with his or her own illness. Sociologists and psychologists also use soaps as a teaching/learning tool and write articles about their experiences in the various professional journals.

With all this talk of watchers, we must not forget the non-watchers, who no longer frown at the addicts because of fundamental changes in social attitudes in the past ten years. But the soaps are still treated as a comical symbol of an over-sentimental world scorned by sophisticates. Writers, by poking fun at the soaps, often find some truth about human behavior in them. Norman Lear's *Mary Hartman, Mary Hartman*, which premiered in 1976, functioned this way, as a kind of gag about soaps which then used the form to convey the superficiality of our hyped, Madison Avenue culture. The nighttime show, *Soap*, which wasn't one, took the *Mary Hartman* gags to preposterous extremes, using pseudo soap plots to ridicule the baseness of human beings. There are sequences on sitcoms where some he-man sits in front of a television and pretends that he has just gotten hooked on something called "All The Doctors," while we hear absurd, breathy dialogue coming from the tube. The point is supposed to be that we are all vulnerable to emotion.

And then there are live soap opera parodies in carbarets, jokes in magazines, takeoffs in movies. Dustin Hoffman used the ancient "washboard weeper" joke in the movie, *Tootsie*. No real soap opera director in his right mind would have hired the mad creature that Hoffman played, but the audience buys the joke because there is a time-honored ridiculous aura around soaps.

This is all by way of what daytime serials mean to different people. To Hollywood writers of the above, they are not funny in and of themselves (script writers don't burst into hysterics the moment *Guiding Light* comes on), but the idea of them is funny. To our grandmothers and other devotees of *Stella Dallas*, they were deadly serious. Radio soaps went to the heart of women and the softer side of men, so synchronizing with their needs that there was an alarming disregard for the barrier between fact and fiction. On-air weddings, births and deaths inspired an out-

pouring of mail from listeners to the characters. After a character gave birth, shows would be so deluged with rattles, pink or blue baby bonnets, whole layettes, that the production staffs would have to respond to the gift-givers with printed thankyous.

One New York psychiatrist, Dr. Louis Berg, misunderstanding the relationship between listeners and their radio soaps (which in 1942 comprised almost all of the daytime broadcast hours), went on a campaign to stop the madness. In a widely publicized report he wrote: "Pandering to perversity and playing out destructive conflicts, these serials furnish the same release for the emotionally distorted that is supplied to those who desire satisfaction from a lynching bee, lick their lips at the salacious scandals of the *crime passionnel*, and who in the unregretted past cried out in ecstasy at witch burnings." Dr. Berg also accused the serials of causing such physical symptoms as "tachycardia, arrhythmias, increase in blood pressure, profuse perspiration, tremors, vasomotor instability, nocturnal frights, vertigo and gastrointestinal disturbances."

The campaign, of course, failed, as did many others, for what Dr. Berg was up against was a form of entertainment so infectious that it stopped being mere entertainment; it was as much a part of listeners' lives as their own families. Tuning in to radio soap opera was a compulsion of magnitude. Our grandmothers felt a deep down chill when Gil Whitney and Helen Trent kissed, thrilled when the Grosvenors had to admit once again that Stella Dallas was right about her daughter Laurel's virtue, sighed when widow Ellen Brown once again accepted the proposal of Dr. Anthony Loring. And grandmother shared the grief of fictional families when anyone died on one of her favorite shows.

There's a story about how Minnesota Vikings halfback William "Chuck" Forman got his name. When little Chuckie, Meta's boy, died on *The Guiding Light*, after having been mistreated by his father, William Forman's mother was so touched that she decided to call her own son William, "Chuck," so that the dead boy could live in him. So, for as long as he can remember, William Forman has always been called Chuck.

When Don MacLaughlin was playing the title role on *Chaplin Jim, U.S.A.* on radio, he received a harried long distance phone call from a farmer who said he had a problem. His son had deserted the Army and he was hiding him in the coal bin; he wanted Don's advice on what to do next. Don MacLaughlin tried to tell the farmer that he wasn't a chaplain, just a hard-working actor, but then, hearing the real desperation in the man's voice, he tried to comfort him by saying, "I'm sure they won't execute your son," and then asked him to talk to his own priest.

That kind of fierce acceptance of the reality of soaps carried over to television, which was supposed to be a more sophisticated medium than radio. During the first decade of television soaps, the one that seemed to please viewers most was *As The World Turns*, which had actors sitting, sipping coffee and talking at length about seemingly trivial problems. The madness that appeared to overtake our grandmothers now overwhelmed our mothers, who had to get their daily fix of Oakdale and Penny, Ellen, Grandpa Hughes, Nancy, Chris and all the others. Viewers sent truckloads of mail to the characters, especially Nancy—always played by Helen Wagner—who would often be in the mesmerizing process of cooking a real meal (housewives watched every detail of her movements from stove to refrigerator to counter) while discussing family troubles. Not our mothers, maybe, but there was a multitude of angry women who sent death threats (once a dead fish) to the actress who played the young femme fatale who had married wonderful Bob Hughes for convenience. Eileen Fulton had to have a guard escort her to the television studio for fear of harm to her person.

Each generation discovers soaps anew. To the generation of the sixties, shows like *Days of Our Lives, Another World* and *General Hospital* had the electric pulse of a restless world which seemed to be coming apart. Oddly, on the very day that President Kennedy was shot, executives at Young & Rubicam were plotting the first series of deaths and tragedies on *Another World*. While in the real world young people went to anti-Vietnam rallies and took drugs, in the soap world, the inner-reflected world, a young girl fell in love with her own father, then fell in love with an older man who was in love with her stepmother, and finally took LSD and died in a frightful accident. *Days of Our Lives* was even stranger—so weird, that to read the early story line is to understand the underlying social frenzy that this show communicated.

The depth and severity of the emotions aroused by *Days of Our Lives* is still hard to believe. Years ago, while editing a soap opera magazine, I received a letter from a woman in Oregon about the show suddenly killing off Julie's mother, Addie, in a street accident. The show's writer, William Bell, had intended to have Addie die months earlier from leukemia, but had been persuaded by tons of protesting letters to save her life. He finally decided he really did need to have her die. Viewers became furious. The letter said:

> We immediately got to work here in this small town. I came in contact each week with over 300 women. I had cards printed with every sponsor of *Days of Our Lives* listed, and in two days I had seventy-five signed pledges from my friends not to watch the show any more, and not to buy any of those sponsors' products. I have notified each sponsor why we are not buying his product any more. We are putting it very simply: as long as that idiot, Mr. Bell, continues to write *Days of Our Lives*, we will forget it ever existed. He pulled a fast one on us. A relative from Santa Rosa, California, who has been visiting me, has gone home to put the same plan in operation. She took the list of sponsors that I had and was sure that her friends in Santa Rosa would stop watching also. She has sisters in Salt Lake, Phoenix, Twin Falls and Bountiful, Utah, and she is writing to them to do the same thing.

My correspondent and her friends in Oregon were showing the kind of spirit that was making the soap world into an empire. The emotions of these women over the Addie story were volcanic and their connection with *Days of Our Lives* inseparable, despite all the talk of cutting off the show. What would Dr. Louis Berg, soap opera's greatest enemy, have said about the groundswell of horror, grief and anger over Addie's death?

The daytime fan magazines began in 1968, first with Afternoon TV and then Daytime TV, for the first time catering especially to viewers of soaps. What had occurred was that so many new soap opera lovers were accumulating with each succeeding generation that specialty publications had to emerge. Then, close on the heels of the early soap fan magazines, came the appearance of daytime stars on talk shows: Mike Douglas, David Frost, Merv Griffin and numerous local shows. Soon after came articles on the soaps in Life, The New Yorker, Show, Pageant, People, After Dark, Cosmopolitan, Time, Ms. and the New York Times Magazine. All the interest was being sparked by the existence of the fan magazines and Agnes Nixon's new, topical dramas for ABC, *One Life to Live* and *All My Children*. The public was developing a fixation on daytime serials.

In the seventies a wave of young people began watching the soaps—their own, of course, aimed at their own problems. For the most part these were the children of the men and women of the fifties who had married, moved to the suburbs, bought tract houses and lawn mowers, had two jobs and often wound up divorced. The seventies generation became the young liberated housewives, the uprooted college kids with cars and parents living in two places, young people who had been touched by the Vietnam war. They were a group who badly needed a sounder structure for their personal lives. The show that they discovered was *All My Children*, which was about emotional wars among young people in love and which had references to peace marches, fighting for various social causes such as women's rights, talk of teenage prostitution, even open discussions about pap smears. For those young people, *All My Children* offered small-town family security, as an antidote for the spreading rootlessness of their lives. While students took computer courses on campuses, they dreamed of living in the peace of Pine Valley, where relationships, not microchips, were king.

College courses on the soaps sprang up all over the country almost simultaneously late in the seventies. College students had taken to soap opera, but in a special way—together. They watched in groups, in dormitories, discussed plots and fictional relationships as if talking about some short story they had all read in freshman comp. These were not the Depression housewives who listened alone and quietly to *Our Gal Sunday*, the women who ironed and suffered along with Joanne's problems on *Search for Tomorrow*. These were the children of all the people who had joined encounter groups in the early sixties. These were Marshall McLuhan's electronic tribe, not the least embarassed about their relationship to a television screen, openly admitting their involvement with fictional families, unwanted pregnancies and endless love triangles.

In 1978 a new generation, starting at an even younger age than the preceding one, joined soap opera lovers. They were the youngsters with perfect teeth; fed since the cradle on a diet of slick, fast-paced, action-oriented, expensively produced night-time shows served on color consoles. The first soap opera they chose was the one that most closely resembled prime-time television, *General Hospital*. The big attraction for six million new teenage addicts was that the show dealt with two teenagers who were like themselves and in love but who had serious sexual difficulties with other people. That was the compelling point: the story dealt with their own sexual lives, *their* needs and fantasies, and was psychologically up-to-date in their world. This was indeed the first soap opera for teens. The young girl in the story, Laura, was later permitted to leave her young husband and run away with an older man without being punished, as would have invariably happened a decade earlier on all soaps. While the Laura character caused burning interest on the part of millions of boys and girls, a new morality was taking place on daytime television. The censors did not object to Laura's story; the families of young viewers did not protest and in fact applauded the story; other soaps instantly began similar stories.

That new morality had really been taking place throughout the seventies, and the summaries of the current soaps in this volume reveal remarkable change in sexual attitude that occurred in the soap world, especially toward the end of the last decade. Prostitutes and pimps have been causing havoc in those small soap towns; married heroines have taken on lovers; a mother and daughter discovered they were sleeping with the same lover; and characters have talked about doing each other "sexual favors." Most of the rules governing the television serial world of the fifties have disappeared, as soaps seek to become more contemporary and appeal to as wide an audience as movies and nighttime television. One almost sheds a tear for those viewers of *Love of Life* and *Search for Tomorrow* who were reassured by their favorite soaps of right and wrong in their personal lives. Daytime serials are less like a guidebook for living these days and more a reflection of popular mores.

This has indeed become a new age for the soap world. The desires and lifestyle of young people are now controlling the medium on an equal footing with older viewers. A new soap, *Loving*, has been created with youth appeal in mind, stealing a little bit of the thunder from those pay TV serials about smooth, appealing bodies and the rites of early adulthood. But this is all quite new. No one knows how much of daytime television will eventually cater to the very young. Meanwhile, soap budgets head higher, crews will possibly be setting out on location for Africa next, Marlon Brando may be making arrangements to appear on his favorite serial, and producers are already setting the table for the next generation of soap lovers.

THE RADIO SOAPS

It was certainly an event-filled afternoon. Helen, the beautiful and much-desired dress designer, had been sentenced to the gas chamber after weeks and weeks of an agonizing murder trial. But today the real murderer confessed! Bill, the barber, just prevented another marriage from breaking up, but they're still threatening to take Ma's lumberyard away from her. Pretty Joan Davis's husband doesn't know who he is or what town this is; in fact, there have been a great many amnesia cases lately. The nice inventor finally sold his first patent on a foot warmer, but his wife can't remember where she put the money he made. Lord Henry simply will not stop being jealous of his low-born wife, the one from a little mining town. Laurel was just kidnapped again, and her seamstress mother, a humble woman, is going all over town asking questions; Laurel's suspicious in-laws, the Grosvenors, aren't much help in this new crisis, to say the least. Lady lawyer Portia might lose her first case to the D.A., who is in love with her. And Dr. Rutledge, the minister, comforted a hysterical couple after their little boy died of meningitis. . . .

S O went the fictional day of the average woman at home. Each weekday during the twenty-five years following the start of the Great Depression, approximately forty million housewives had their lives eased and enriched by tuning in to the fifteen-minute continuing dramas on radio known as soap operas—

about twice the number of people who now watch television soaps. By the end of the thirties, soap opera was radio's most economically powerful product, and by the early forties there were thirty-three serials on the air, beginning at ten in the morning and ending at six in the evening.

Most of them inspired fanatical devotion rather than casual addiction, although there were always those sane outsiders who were perplexed by the repetitive fabric of radio soaps: the churchy organ music, the purple epigraphs, the humorlessness, the endless parade of sicknesses and sadness. They were the paperback romance novels of their day, to be absorbed in personal isolation, away from husband, children and neighbors—with the difference that radio serials, unlike novels, claimed to be utterly real, "true to life," happening at the moment that they were heard. Radio soaps were quite the opposite, as we shall see; but the fact that daytime stories of heroines and fictional families lasted over a period of many months and often years, enhanced the illusion of ongoing reality and occasionally led to a good deal of confusion on the part of listeners.

Soap opera was born at one moment in time. Back in 1930, listeners had had some experience with open-ended, or continuing, serials on nighttime radio, with shows like *Amos 'n' Andy, The Goldbergs, Clara Lu, 'n' Em,* and *Myrt and Marge*. But these were all comedies, a far cry from personally involving dramas. Daytime radio was a wasteland, offering housewives nothing meatier than live stock reports, and

9

information on diet and mouth hygiene. What finally filled those daytime radio hours, soap operas, was not really based on anything that came before, did not slowly or haphazardly evolve in the early days of radio as many writers seem to believe. Soap opera was an ingenious, highly complicated, intellectual invention. It was the result of a deliberate creative act on the part of a few highly sensitive individuals, and it worked almost immediately.

The invention of the soaps came at the beginning of the Depression in Chicago. In some ways this was a peculiar starting place for the serials. New York City had been the radio capital, for financial as well as artistic reasons. Because of a complicated system of broadcasting along telephone wires rather than air waves, New York was the cheapest locale from which to originate a network program. In addition, the most experienced radio artists resided in New York, aspiring toward Broadway roles. But this highly paid talent made New York the worst place for experimentation. In Chicago, on the other hand, aspirations were lower,

Betty and Bob, starring Betty Churchill and Don Ameche, was the only true soap among the original four 1932 daytime serials. It was the continuing story of a humble secretary, Betty, who marries her wealthy boss, Bob Drake, and the struggle of the Drakes to surmount their marital difficulties.

Vic and Sade, starring Art Van Harvey and Bernadine Flynn, was one of the first four network daytime serials presented on the NBC Blue Network in 1932. In this episodic comedy, married couple Vic and Sade Gooks went on and on about their wacky neighbors and friends.

Marie, The Little French Princess, 1933, was CBS's first radio soap, starring Ruth Yorke and James Meighan. About a one-time wealthy princess who must now find love and happiness as an ordinary American girl, it was too grim for housewives during the Depression and went off the air after two years.

Just Plain Bill, *the first smash hit soap, was moved by Frank and Anne Hummert from nighttime radio, where they began it in 1932, to daytime in late 1933. The show, written by Robert Andrews, ran twenty-three years and featured Arthur Hughes (right), as the town's problem-solving barber, Bill; Ruth Russel as his daughter; and James Meighan as her trouble-prone husband, Kerry Donovan.*

Ma Perkins, *1933, was intended by the Hummerts as a female* Just Plain Bill, *and lasted 27 years with Virginia Payne in the lead. Miss Payne was an attractive young woman in her twenties when she started the role, but she was usually photographed in heavy make-up to look 40 years older. The show was written for many years by Orin Tovrov.*

with local talent often working for free, hoping to break into radio. If a youngster walked into a Chicago producer's office with a terrific idea for a fifteen-minute radio show, he might just walk out with a small check and permission to write and act in his own radio program.

That was how Irna Phillips, a young Dayton, Ohio, schoolteacher, happened to create the nation's first daytime radio soap opera, *Painted Dreams*, about Mother Moran, her children and their problems. It was broadcast in 1930 on WGN, a local station owned by the Chicago *Tribune*, and starred Ireene Wicker and Irna herself.

Although Irna created the first bona fide soap, and three years later wrote a network serial, *Today's Children*, based on *Painted Dreams*, it was only late

The Romance of Helen Trent, *1933, was an ingenious Hummert soap which offered millions of Depression housewives a syrupy, breathy world of romantic entanglements. It ran for twenty-seven years. Pictured are Julie Stevens (left,) who played the title role; David Gothard as constant suitor Gil Whitney; and Mary Jane Higby as the malevolent Cynthia.*

in the thirties that she became an influential force in soap opera. Eventually she would become the greatest soap creator of them all, when she brought her special talents to television in the fifties.

The actual invention of soap opera as a widely imitated form must be credited to two advertising executives named Frank and Anne Hummert. In 1933 they created and introduced, through the Blackett-Sample-Hummert advertising agency of Chicago, the three network shows that were to define soap opera for the next several decades: *Just Plain Bill*, *The Romance of Helen Trent*, and *Ma Perkins*. There had been other domestic dramas in the preceding two years, like *Vic and Sade* and *Betty and Bob*, but none of them contained that special wish-fulfilling fantasy which was to make hits out of daytime dramas. The Hummerts followed their initial three successes with *David Harum*, *John's Other Wife*, *Our Gal Sunday*,

Pepper Young's Family, *1936, had been an evening radio comedy for four years under the title* Red Davis. *When it switched to daytime, it became a complicated drama of family dilemmas. Here, the show's creator, Elaine Carrington, helps the cast celebrate its fifteenth anniversary. From left, seated: Betty Wragge (Peggy Young Trent), Marion Barney (Mary Young), Thomas Chalmers (Sam Young), Elaine Carrington. Standing: organist William Meeder, Greta Kvalden (Hattie), Blaine Cordner (Andy Hoyt), Jean Southern (Edie Hoyt), John Kane (Nick Havens), Madeline Pierce (who did baby cries for little Hal Trent) and Euncie Howard (Linda Young).*

The Story of Mary Marlin, *1935, was one of many serials about valiant wives trying to keep their weaker husbands afloat. In this group shot, taken in 1945, Anne Seymour was the new Mary Marlin (Joan Blaine was the first); the occasion was a visit to the studio by Mrs. Stewart, a fan from Denver who never missed a broadcast. From left: John Seymour, Carlton Brickett, Margaret Fuller, Anne Seymour, Mrs. Stewart, Nelson Chase, Lawson Zerbe and Phil Clarke.*

Lorenzo Jones, *Valiant Lady*, *Young Widder Brown*, *Stella Dallas*, *Houseboat Hanna*, and *Front Page Farrell*, titles that are synonymous with radio soap opera.

"True to life" is what radio soaps, especially the Hummert shows, claimed to be, which was part of the mesmerizing fantasy, the reason for their huge success. Take *Ma Perkins*. Like most radio heroines Ma was supposed to be true to life and therefore compelling. However, a moment's reflection is enough to realize that she wasn't at all real. The miracle that kept her breathing from 1933 to 1960 was sheer invention on the part of creators Frank and Anne Hummert, writer Orin Tovrov, and actress Virginia Payne—"Oxydol's Own Ma." Ma Perkins, somewhat like Lamont Cranston and his secret counterpart, The Shadow, was one sort of person pretending to be another: in her case, a young and vital genius masquerading as an old, folksy lumberyard owner who baked a lot of pies for her workers, Willy and Shuffle and the others. She had to be a genius—who else could solve so many human dilemmas per month? Although she tried to hide her natural speech with a veneer of the ordinary, she spoke eloquently. Ma was the den mother of our dreams—a pie-baking Sherlock Holmes with an I.Q. of 180. For twenty-seven years, youthful and sophisticated Virginia Payne played Ma Perkins with complete understanding of this fantasy.

Most radio soaps were much the same: pretending to offer slices of life while serving a very different dish of fantasy. The pretense of real life was necessary for complete listener identification with the characters, but the fantasy was the true payoff, both as reward and as escape—which housewives urgently needed during the Depression.

For women then had hard lives. Mid-century time-saving appliances had not yet appeared. The whole morning or afternoon could be spent rubbing a big bar of soap across a washboard, lifting a heavy scalding-hot iron, cooking budget foods from scratch. There were often too many children. Divorces were neither afforded nor tolerable. Men were the undisputed masters of their homes.

Is it any wonder that so many women became almost religiously involved with *The Romance of Helen Trent?* Even though the heroine of this long-running soap was endowed with perhaps the dullest personality the Creator could muster, she lived, inex-

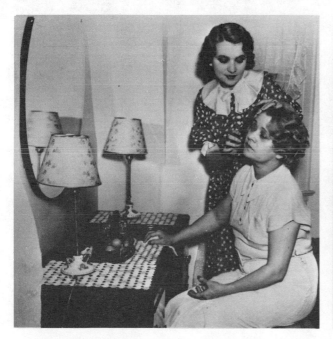

Myrt and Marge, an ongoing evening feature since 1931, became a daytime show in 1937. Myrtle Vail and her daughter Donna Damerel played two vaudeville performers who talked about their adventures every day. When Donna Dameral died in childbirth in 1940, her mother tried but failed to keep the serial going.

Aunt Jenny's True Life Stories, 1937, originally starred Edith Spencer, sitting to the right of Emily Post and the show's director. Aunt Jenny spun hundreds of tales, featuring different actors, during her nineteen years on daytime. Before each episode began announcer Dan Seymour would drool over her pies and pastries, prepared with Spry, a product of the show's sponsor, Lever Brothers.

plicably, a spectacularly glamorous life as a Hollywood dress designer who attracted one handsome devil after another with her invisible charms. At thirty-five, Helen had romance and no husband, and no children, and no drudgery. That was the fantasy reward, like Ma's hidden genius. But although her life was a fantasy, Helen herself was real enough for women to feel that, just possibly, they could be living as she was living.

The long epigraph told it all. "And now *The Romance of Helen Trent:* the real-life drama of Helen Trent, who, when life mocks her, breaks her hopes, dashes her against the rocks of despair, fights back bravely, successfully, to prove what so many women

The Guiding Light, 1937, Irna Phillips' most important radio creation—still going strong on television—contained all the qualities that would help to define the soap opera philosophy for generations to come. The Guiding Light *originally focused on the life of a minister named Dr. Rutledge and his family; the Bauer family was introduced in the forties. Mercedes McCambridge, second from left, played Mary Rutledge.*

Our Gal Sunday *began in 1937. By the 1950s, Vivian Smolen played the famous orphan girl from Silver Creek, Colorado, and Alistair Duncan was her wealthy, titled and extremely jealous English husband.*

Lorenzo Jones, *1937, was a Hummert soap about a half-baked but lovable inventor whose get-rich-quick schemes amounted to more laughs than cash. From left, seated: Colleen Ward, Lucille Wall (Belle Jones), Karl Swenson (Lorenzo), Nancy Sheridan. Norman Sylvester and John Brown are among the men standing.*

The Road of Life, *1937, the first successful hospital soap, starred Don MacLaughlin as Dr. Jim Brent, who always had to call "surger-eee," and Virginia Dwyer as his wife, Jocelyn McCleod Brent. It was written by Irna Phillips.*

long to prove, that because a woman is thirty-five, or more, romance in life need not be over, that romance can begin at thirty-five."

Virginia Clark played Helen from 1933 to 1944, during the show's first decade in Chicago. When the Hummerts took Helen to New York, and Virginia Clark decided to remain in the Windy City with her family, Julie Stevens took the role. Julie was a mere twenty-two, and fresh from playing the starring role of *Kitty Foyle,* when she won the part of the thirty-five-year-old romance-smitten dressmaker; she remained in it until the show's cancellation in 1960.

"I always assumed that Helen Trent was patterned after Edith Head," said Julie Stevens in a telephone interview. "Here was Helen Trent, who it seemed had it all with this glamorous Hollywood life she led, and yet women could identify with her. The funny thing about Helen, though, is that she was supposed to find romance at thirty-five, but she never did. She never married and never had lovers. But she did

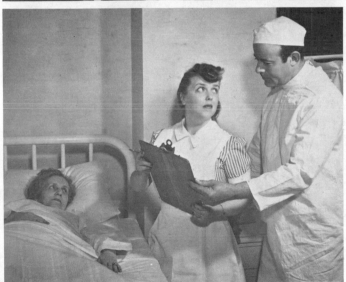

Woman In White, *1938, another Irna Phillips hospital soap, starred Sarajane Wells as nurse Eileen Holmes and Ken Griffin as Dr. Paul Burton. Radio actors wore costumes only for photographs and appearances, never in front of the microphones.*

Irna Phillips was the greatest, most prolific soap opera writer of all, becoming even more powerful on television than on radio. Most of today's soaps are based on concepts she dramatized some fifty years ago. She died in 1973.

have a lot of suitors, because she was terribly fascinating to men. I always imagined her as a tall, startling brunette. I was short and blonde, and so they tried to suppress my identity—and rightly so, I think, for the good of the show. I loved Helen. I always played her with a soft, lolling voice, and David Gothard played Gil Whitney—Helen's main beau—almost the same way. It wasn't an acting choice on our parts. We were supposed to be breathy, to suggest all the romance. But Helen was a pretty boring lady even though she had all of this glamor in her life. We used to kid her a lot. Ernest Ricca, our director for many years, let us fall around and scream with laughter during rehearsals. We had to keep our sanity. By air time we had gotten it all out of our systems and could be dead serious about the story. But we weren't as bad as some actors on other shows, with pranks like pulling actors' pants off on air and things like that."

So many soaps claimed to be true to life. The writers of *Stella Dallas* even used the phrase in the show's opening epigraph: "We give you now—*Stella Dallas!*—a continuation on the air of the true-to-life story of mother love and sacrifice in which Stella Dallas saw her beloved daughter, Laurel, marry into wealth and society and, realizing the difference in their tastes and worlds, went out of Laurel's life. These episodes in the later life of Stella Dallas are based on the famous novel of that name by Olive Higgins Prouty and are written by Frank and Anne Hummert."

The original Prouty novel and the movie with Barbara Stanwyck attempted to be somewhat realistic, albeit sentimental, focusing on an intimidated mother who finally realizes that she must leave her daughter to a better life. But the radio soap made Stella into a superwoman, who solved more problems with her one daughter than the old woman who lived in a shoe ever encountered. Those problems? For

Joyce Jordan, Girl Interne *was highly innovative for 1938, when the idea of female medics was not as readily accepted as it is today. Ann Shepherd, as Joyce, is shown here with Raymond Johnson. Ann Shepherd was also the first Bert Bauer on radio's* The Guiding Light.

Stella Dallas, *1938, the popular saga of mother love and sacrifice, starred Anne Elstner (right) as Stella and Vivian Smolen as Laurel. It was based on the novel by Olive Higgins Prouty, although the story was made famous by the Barbara Stanwyck movie.*

some reason Lollie Baby (Laurel) drove Arabian sheiks mad with lust, caused criminals to kidnap her ad nauseum, and generally stimulated male juices, inspiring wild seduction schemes by sundry scoundrels. Lollie Baby was (understandably) under constant suspicion by her husband's (Dick Grosvenor's) family on grounds of unfaithfulness. Stella had to come continually back into Laurel's life to help her.

Anne Elstner, who played Stella with haunting sincerity from 1938 to 1955, recalled one long plot sequence in this true-to-life story: "Lollie had been captured by a sheik and became part of his harem, so I had to go to the Sahara Desert to try to save her. On the way I saved a lot of people from a train wreck. Then I was trapped in a submarine at the bottom of the Suez Canal. When I finally got to the desert, there was confusion about the fact that I was called Laurel's 'mummy' and so was a real Egyptian mummy. I remember that I had to huff and puff a lot because I was going through all these Sahara sandstorms, which were created by our one sound-effects man."

No wonder Anne Elstner's most famous line in all her years as Stella was: "Lollie Baby, I ain't got no time for nothin' but trouble." And no wonder Olive Higgins Prouty disliked the show: It had nothing to do with her novel. But the story of the original novel, lacking the fantasy of the radio show, would not have generated such a popular soap.

Just about every famous radio heroine or hero of the "we're just folks" genre of soap opera played similar two-faced games with the millions of devotees. *Just Plain Bill* was about as plain as Jesus Christ walking on water, even though the epigraph told listeners that this was: "The real-life story of a man who

Life Can Be Beautiful, *1938, featured Ralph Locke as the voice of radio's wisest man, Papa David Solomon, and Teri Keane as his ward, Chichi. Papa David was always teaching Chichi, as well as other characters, and listeners, that life was indeed precious—in case there was any doubt about it.*

Young Dr. Malone, *1939, was probably the most famous of all hospital soaps. It starred Alan Bunce in the title role and Elizabeth Reller as his wife Ann. The soap was one of the last four radio soaps to be cancelled in 1960.*

might be your next-door neighbor . . . a story of people we all know." Barbers usually cut hair and talk about the weather, but "just plain" Bill Davidson spent most of his time out of his barber shop, miraculously keeping people from going off the deep end, patching up marriages, holding the town together with his sophisticated philosophy of life. Arthur Hughes did a splendid deep and crawling voice for Bill, never forgetting that Bill, whatever he did or said, was supposed to be plain. The same could be said of Karl Swenson's *Lorenzo Jones,* except that Swenson exaggerated the pauses, the stuttering, and the high-pitched voice which was *de rigueur* for the folksy male hero—probably because this was intended as a comic soap. "We all know couples like lovable, impractical Lorenzo and his wife, Belle," went the epigraph. "Their struggle for security is anybody's story . . ." Exactly how many screwball inventors were running around in the thirties is hard to say. But whatever the epigraph told us, *Lorenzo Jones* was in fact an imaginative situation comedy that featured clever routines rather than ordinary domestic events.

The last line of the epigraph of *Our Gal Sunday*—"The story asks the question: Can this girl from a mining town in the West find happiness as the wife of a wealthy and titled Englishman?"—has been responsible for countless jokes and takeoffs. But *Our Gal Sunday* was actually a top-notch serial which featured utterly believable characters. Vivian Smolen's Sunday was unforgettable. Vivian played her, not like Ma Perkins or Stella, with all their grammatical mistakes and deliberate nonsophistication, but with a plaintive coolness and a dignity that made you feel that no man, let alone the boorishly jealous Lord Henry Brinthrope, was really worthy of her. While Stella and Ma and Bill tended to steamroll you with their homely posing, Sunday dreamily confronted all her marital problems and could make even the most critical listeners comfortable with the fantasy. She lasted from 1937 until 1959: pretty much the full term for radio's most beloved soaps.

Other creators followed Frank and Anne's brilliant lead with soaps that used the same concept, like Jane Cruisinberry's *The Story of Mary Marlin,* but the formula was never quite as clearly felt with other writers, who often forgot, perhaps deliberately, that the idea was to transfigure the mundane surreptitiously. The Hummerts understood the great need of the Depression-enslaved housewife, and as a result their interest in character per se was minimal. What they

Portia Faces Life, *1940, starred Lucille Wall (right) as the indomitable lady lawyer whom men desired outside the courtroom but feared inside it. Lucille Wall, here in a scene with Allison Skipworth, later became famous to television viewers as nurse Lucille Weeks on* General Hospital.

The Second Mrs. Burton, *1941, about the struggle of Terry Burton to take the place of Stan Burton's first wife, was a serious melodrama in the forties, but later became a light comedy. Alice Frost (left) and Larry Haines, as Marcia and Lew Archer, played out a courtship with lots of funny one-liners.*

aimed for, always, was the spectacle and glamor beneath the plain words their writers wrote, bringing dreams to life for adult women much as comic-book heroes did for children. In fact, years later Frank Hummert admitted that the original inspiration for his in vention was the serialized comic strips of his day.

The Hummerts' "best-sellers" certainly made them the wealthiest people in radio. After the Blackett-Sample-Hummert agency folded, the Hummerts formed their own production company, Air Features, which could only be described as a writing factory. Frank and Anne went into seclusion to write the outline of an original story plus five or six episodes; then they hired writers to create dialogue for the show.

Since Frank and Anne were advertising people, they ran Air Features like an ad agency. Writers and actors—even stars—couldn't talk to the Hummerts directly; they went through copy chiefs and other executives who supervised the work. Many saw Frank and Anne as totally wrapped up in themselves and living in an ivory tower; the Hummerts were accused of underpaying their stars and stifling creativity by being too rigid about their formulas. However, after the initial shock of receiving half the money non-Hummert stars received, many an actor soon learned that working for the Hummerts had its compensations. "My heart sank when I saw my contract for *Helen Trent*," says Julie Stevens. "But the Hummerts' lawyer assured

Perry Mason, *1943, a daytime serial based on the Erle Stanley Gardner stories, was written by Irving Vendig, who later wrote* Search For Tomorrow. *The stars were John Larkin as Perry and Joan Alexander as Della Street. Larkin was later to star in Vendig's thinly disguised answer to* Perry Mason— The Edge of Night.

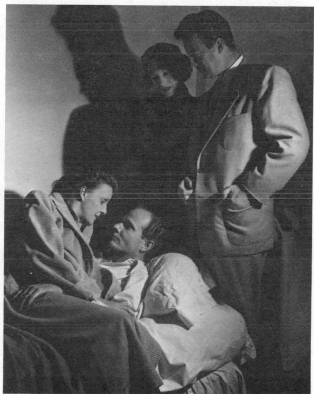

This Is Nora Drake, *1944, concerned nurse Nora, assistant to the head of a mental clinic, and her many professional and personal problems. From left: Elspeth Eric, Leon Janney, Joan Tompkins as Nora Drake and Grant Richards.*

me that I would wind up working on every one of their serials and I would be making good money. I did." Says Anne Elstner, "I didn't earn a fortune on *Stella Dallas*, but I did so many other serials—sometimes ten a day—that my weekly income was good. I never complained about the money."

The big difference between radio and television acting was the lesser amount of work required by radio. "You did a Hummert show in an hour and fifteen minutes," said Anne. "I never looked at my script until I arrived at the studio. We'd rehearse for an hour and then go on air. That left time to do a lot of other shows the same day." If you had a good vocal delivery and could change your voice to suit a part, then you had it made on radio, since there was no memorizing and no physical acting. If a kiss was called for in the script, for instance, you simply kissed the back of your hand. The sound-effects man took care of the very passionate clinches (which were sparse), as well as falls and knocks and just about every other sound but the human voice. The only props actors ever had to deal with were their own mimeographed scripts. Because of the easiness of radio, many former radio actors today refer to the medium as the "gravy train."

The charge that the Hummerts killed creativity by making their serials a factory product may in part be true. The Hummerts did not want their original concepts tampered with (and neither did listeners), so they ran their shows by rules rather than inspiration. Actors had to speak every word in the script with unnatural clarity, and often weren't permitted to change poorly written passages. Writers were allowed to create only within the confines of the initial fantasy. The only justification for the whole system appears to be that the Hummert shows remained among the most popular. Who is to say that another procedure might not have wrecked Frank and Anne's near-perfect inventions?

Irna Phillips, less a fantasist and more of a realistic writer than the Hummerts, ran her soap world in a totally different way. Her radio creations, which included *The Guiding Light* and *The Road of Life* in 1937, *Woman in White* in 1938, *The Right to Happiness* in 1939, and *The Brighter Day* in 1948, reflected her deep interest in character rather than in story fantasy, and it is doubtful whether her great success could have come earlier than the end of the Depression. All her shows featured a new breed of character: the professional. *The Guiding Light* and *The Brighter Day* had ministers, Dr. Rutledge and the Reverend Richard Dennis; *The Road of Life* had Dr. Jim Brent; and *Woman in White* had nurse Karen Adams and various doctors. With the interesting lives that doctors, nurses and ministers led, Irna did not have to superimpose fantasy plots upon her characters. Her stories grew out of the characters themselves and the built-in life-and-death melodrama of their working lives. She was the first writer to use such people, and her wisdom in this creative choice was confirmed years later when doctors, lawyers and nurses became the dominant television soap characters. In fact, daytime television today is much more the offspring of Irna Phillips's brand of radio soap than of the Hummerts'. With the exception of *The Young and The Restless*, which seems to incorporate Irna Phillips's family structures with appealing Hummert-like fantasies, television soaps focus more on realistic character

The Brighter Day, *1948, was about the Rev. Richard "Poppa" Dennis and his family. From left: William Redfield (Grayling), Pat Holsky, (Patsy) Jay Meredith (Althea), Lorna Lynn (Babby). Standing (right): Margaret Draper (Liz). The show went on television in 1954, two years before it left radio.*

portrayal than on the old-style wish-fulfilling super-heroines.

Irna Phillips is credited by many as having invented the amnesia story. With so many doctor characters, she was naturally interested in unusual and colorful illnesses. Mary Jane Higby, who played Joan Davis on Elaine Carrington's *When a Girl Marries*, says that the first amnesia victim was Joe Marlin on *The Story of Mary Marlin*, but, whatever the case, Irna used amnesia constantly, as did other writers. There was a kind of quasi-myth that whenever ratings were sagging, a spicy case of memory loss would bring back the listeners. Amnesia, of course, was fantasy disguised as medical phenomenon, for even Irna was not above Hummert tricks when they suited her purposes. Today, while amnesia isn't used quite as much on television, head writer Tom King recently had Dr. David Stewart of *As the World Turns* become so angry at another character that he suffered a nervous break-

down and lost his memory, and took up life in another city; and the writers of *Capitol* gave amnesia to heroine Julie Clegg, just before she was to marry her great love, Tyler McCandless, as a device to prolong their love story. It all comes from the radio soaps of the forties.

* * *

If the average person recalls anything about the old daytime radio serials, it's probably those peculiar but familiar opening thematic statements, or epigraphs. After a few strains of "Red River Valley," came the opener: *"Our Gal Sunday*—the story of an orphan girl named Sunday from the little mining town of Silver Creek, Colorado, who in young womanhood married England's richest, most handsome lord, Lord Henry Brinthrope. The story asks the question: Can this girl from a mining town in the west find happiness as the wife of a wealthy and titled Englishman?"

One Man's Family had been a nighttime serial for many years before it came to daytime radio in 1955. Carlton E. Morse's serial is considered a novel more than a soap, since it built its structure with "books" and "chapters" rather than with the typical subplot storylines. It was written with great skill and broadcast from Hollywood. Seated on the sofa, from left: J. Anthony Smythe (Father Barbour), Minetta Ellen (Mother Barbour), Michael Rafetto (Paul). Holding the triplets: Page Gilman (Jack) and Jean Rouverol (Betty). Standing against the wall, from left: Bob Dwyer (Nicky), Ann Whitfield (Penny), Barbara Fuller (Claudia), Mary Lou Harrington (Joan), Conrad Binyon (Hank), Bernice Berwin (Hazel), Dawn Bender (Margaret), Bill Boucher (Dan). Seated on far right: Jeanne Bates (Teddy) and Barton Yarborough (Clifford).

These were wordy radio openers, but then words, not visual images, were what made the radio serial work for listeners. Today's television serial listener learns the events of yesterday's episode (which he may have missed) through a sophisticated device in which characters discuss what has happened in the story—but for the radio listener of yesterday, the announcer recapitulated the story. So, with the epigraph and the announcer's recap, and a lot of theme music, the audience always had to wait some time before the actual story began.

For instance, hear how one radio episode of *Mary Noble—Backstage Wife* started out: *"Mary Noble—Backstage Wife!*—the story of Mary Noble, a little Iowa girl who married Larry Noble, handsome matinee idol, dream sweetheart of a million other women, and her struggle to keep his love in the complicated atmosphere of backstage life."* . . . Commercial . . . "And now, *Mary Noble—Backstage Wife!* . . . Mary has been the victim of a false friend, Armand Delubec, who took her diamond engagement ring with the promise of having it repaired. But instead Armand pawned the ring and tried to blackmail Mary and Larry. And when Marsha Mannering tried to make it appear that Mary was in love with Armand and had given the ring to him, she turned Larry violently against her. And thereupon Marsha conspired with Armand to get even with Mary and Larry. When Mary and Larry later discover that the ring has disappeared from the shop, Mary is heartbroken, and Larry is determined to notify the police."

By today's standards the epigraph was an obvious device, but it served its purpose well. It told listeners exactly what a show was all about; it was a boon to new serial listeners, and a good reminder to the old ones. Even the earliest daytime television serials used epigraphs, albeit much shorter. *Days of Our Lives* still does.

There were, of course, many outrageously silly things connected with the old radio soaps. None were sillier than the jewelry giveaways that were awkwardly worked into stories and then offered to listeners at the end of the program by some terribly embarrassed actor in the show. Listeners were required to send in a box top or two and at least a quarter for a piece of costume jewelry "worth many times that amount." Other sorts of premiums were offered, but jewelry was chosen most often because it could be worked more easily into the script—some brooch that Ma Perkins was especially fond of, or some pin "with real simulated-gold flashing" that Lollie Baby had been given by her wealthy husband. Actors always dreaded the incursion of saccharine phrases that surrounded the introduction of a piece of jewelry in a story, for this invariably meant that they'd be forced to sell the cheap, horrible thing to the audience at the end of the show. James Thurber heard a young actress give this rehearsal dialogue reading: "I am happy to meet you, Mrs. Nelson, and where in the world did you get that perfectly stunning orchid clip? Why, it gleams like virgin gold, and just look at those gorgeous colors— exactly like a rainbow and sunset coming together in a resplendent display of almost unimaginable beauty. For heaven's sake, do I have to read this glop?" The director assured her that if she didn't they'd both be out of a job.

*   *   *

In the late thirties and early forties, the soaps left Chicago and came to New York, where the big advertising agencies took them over. But, with few exceptions, most serials remained a Chicago product—that is, the characters remained Midwestern in nature. In fact, it can be assumed that most fictional towns on today's television soaps exist in the Bible belt—the place where it all started.

During and after the war years in the forties radio soaps flourished. Stronger and more popular than ever, the daytime shows seemed as if they would last forever. The establishment of AFTRA in 1937 created decent minimum salaries ($10 per fifteen-minute daytime broadcast), and daytime actors, with this mandatory minimum and so many shows to work on, never had it so good. Because of AFTRA rules, the networks and ad agencies had to announce the daytime actors' names at least once a week. In the end, all caution was flung to the wind and big afternoon stars were given massive personal publicity, making the actors even happier.

It was too hot not to cool down; in fact, it all just suddenly froze and cracked. The Great Soap Plotter up on high was planting signs of doom all over the blithely onrushing gravy train. Someone hung a big poster on the wall of a radio rehearsal hall: HELP STAMP OUT TV! It was that way all through the early fifties. Some soap actors, figuring radio couldn't lick the new kid in town but could at least make friends, went over to the other side and tried to become television soap stars. Larry Haines, who became Stu Bergman on *Search for Tomorrow* in 1951, was among the few who succeeded. Other actors, like David Gothard of *The Romance of Helen Trent*, saw the end coming and ran off to Hollywood to start afresh. Most, however, hung on tightly to their radio soap roles, hoping TV would just go away, like a stubborn case of amnesia.

By the mid-fifties there was no more hoping. Not only was television wrecking daytime radio's audience ratings, local radio stations were demanding autonomy and the right to put on their own shows for bigger profits. In better times the networks could have afforded to pay off the small-fry locals, but not now. Advertising revenue continued to fall, partly because of a drop in ratings, but mostly because sponsors were losing faith in radio's future and thought that television would be better for sales by improving their products' image. Wasn't it worth the extra cost to show what your soap flakes looked like in action?

Like a star going into supernova, the first explosion of network panic, in the fall of 1955, blew off *Just Plain Bill, Lorenzo Jones, Stella Dallas* and *Young Widder Brown*. By now everyone knew it was over. Some of the actors had been preparing themselves. Anne Elstner and her husband, Jack Matthews, had already bought a luxurious restaurant in Lambertville, New Jersey, and joyously concentrated on cuisine when Stella's true-to-life journey reached its end. Karl Swenson (Lorenzo Jones) and his actress wife, Joan

Tompkins, worked in television a while, then rushed off to work in Hollywood.

But as the radio soaps left the air, many actors, terrified of cameras and live audiences and comfortable only with vocal acting, had to cope with oblivion. The sadness of it all was expressed by Anne Hummert, who wrote to Frankie (*Tom Corbett, Space Cadet*) Thomas: "What's to become of all my actors?" The Hummerts themselves had no interest in television, on whose channels they obviously could never recreate their vast empire.

Irna Phillips, however, *was* interested. She continued to write *The Guiding Light* for both radio and television, and in 1956, when the show left radio, Irna was firmly established in the new medium. She was, in fact, the only radio soap writer to become a success in television and to maintain herself in it over the years.

With true-to-life grimness, radio soaps now died whole blocks at a time. In 1959 CBS killed *Mary Noble—Backstage Wife, Our Gal Sunday, Road of Life*, and *This Is Nora Drake*. In early November of 1960 *Helen Trent* bit the dust. Two weeks later, on November 25, the organ music went up and out for the last time on *The Right to Happiness, Ma Perkins, Young Dr. Malone* and *The Second Mrs. Burton*. That was the end of them. The most colorful era in soap opera's history had died, after a full thirty years of blazing afternoon fantasy.

THE FIRST TELEVISION SOAPS

TO work in daytime drama in the early years of television you had to be young and gutsy, or else extremely desperate. In the hastily rebuilt radio studios, the lights were so bright and hot that the heavy makeup dripped from actors' faces; at station breaks the perspiration had to be wiped from brows, and aspirins were doled out in abundance. Scenery, shaken by the vibrations of cameras moving awkwardly in poorly arranged rooms, fell during passionate love scenes. Many an actor found himself holding up a cardboard wall while delivering his lines. The video cameras themselves, only slightly more reliable than ordinary light bulbs, were forever blowing out, whereupon the director would frantically signal the actors to reposition themselves toward another camera. Horror stories of microphone-trained actors suddenly freezing on their lines were legion. Mona Bruns, in her *By Emily Possessed,* relates the oft-told story of radio actor Ralph Locke, who was supposed to be in a plane in the TV version of *One Man's Family.* He suddenly "went up" on his lines—there were no teleprompters in those days—and told his fellow actor that he had nothing more to say. He then fled the plane set, apparently, in terms of story logic, falling thousands of feet to his death.

One Man's Family, however, premiered in 1954, when daytime serials had already gained a solid footing in television. But well before afternoon TV drama had advanced to the five-across-the-board format, as with the radio soaps, there was drama in the daytime. Len Valenta, a director of numerous Procter & Gamble soaps, relates the astonishing fact that he appeared in a late-afternoon television series as early as 1942! Called *Last Year's Nest,* it was aired from Philadelphia on station WPT (which was owned by Philco, obviously to give the few owners of Philco television sets something to watch). Each episode was a different story with different characters, and it came on only once a week, but it did give viewers a sense of being a serial by having the same actors in each story.

The show's scenery was minimal. Len had to play Abraham Lincoln against a painted cardboard backdrop so narrow that if the camera moved a foot viewers would see stagehands. A few years later Len appeared in a series called *Action in the Afternoon*, for which the cameras, actors and crew went outdoors to enact such interesting affairs as shootouts in the Old West while airplanes roared overhead. Viewers, fascinated by the new idea of movies at home, didn't seem to mind all the mistakes which were largely due to the shoestring budgets of the early programs. The underpaid actors and directors, as fascinated by the new medium as viewers, were dogged in their sincerity and hard work.

The first real television soap opera came from New York's Dumont Studios in Wanamaker's department store in 1947 and was called *A Woman to Remember.* It was written by John Haggert and produced by Bob Steele, and starred John Raby, Patricia Wheel, Ruth McDevitt, Mona Bruns and her son Frankie Thomas. Mona remembers that at Dumont Studios facilities were so primitive that the actors dressed in the lavatories and had to remain stationary in scenes because of the tiny sets. Right after his debut, John Raby went back to his radio co-star, Mary Jane Higby, pale and shaking. He had played a scene on *A Woman to Remember* with an actress who simply panicked under the pressure of live cameras and tried to run off the set. He had to grab her, push her into a chair, and say her lines as well as his own. After the show, he threw up. The terrified actors made a mere $100 a week, less than they would have made on a similar fifteen-minute radio soap, which required no memorizing and a fraction of the work. The show lasted only a few months.

The first network soap was actually a continuing comedy serial called *The First Hundred Years*, presented in 1950 on CBS. The stars were James Lydon and Anne Sargent, as Connie and Chris Thayer, newlyweds who were embarking on their "first hundred years" of married life. It was sponsored by Procter and Gamble, and was canceled after a year and a half.

Big-time TV soaps, however, didn't appear until late 1951, when writer/advertising executive Roy Winsor—a kind of Frank Hummert of early daytime television—started *Search for Tomorrow* and *Love of Life* through the now defunct Biow advertising agency. When CBS also added *The Guiding Light* in 1952 and another Winsor-Biow soap, *The Secret Storm*, in 1954, that network became the undisputed leader in soap opera programming and ratings. NBC's only successful serial had been the expensively produced *Hawkins Falls* (which featured wonderful live outdoor scenes).

Just as Frank and Anne Hummert had invented exactly the right kind of fifteen-minute soap for Depression housewives, Roy Winsor created precisely what the TV-watching housewife needed in the early fifties. All of the characters on his *Search for Tomorrow*, *Love of Life*, and *The Secret Storm* had problems stemming from marriage, children and family. The situations were indeed real, for the housewife of the fifties, unlike the Depression housewife, was prepared to identify and suffer along with people whose

One of the first continuing television serials was the space opera Captain Video, *which premiered at the old Dumont studios in 1949 and was aired late in the afternoon so that kids could watch. The stars were Don Hastings, (left), as the Ranger, Al Hodge in the title role, and Nat Polen as Agent Carter.*

The first bona fide network soap was CBS's The First Hundred Years, *a comedy concerning the ups and downs of wedded life, launched in late 1950, and sponsored by Procter & Gamble. The main characters were young marrieds Chris and Connie Thayer. At the show's first anniversary party were, from left: Valerie Cossart (Mrs. Thayer), Don Tobin (Mr. Thayer), James Lydon (Chris), Anne Sargent (Connie), Mary Linn Beller (Margy Martin), Robert Armstrong and Nana Bryant (Mr. and Mrs. Martin).*

motivations were much like hers. *Search for Tomorrow's* widowed Joanne Barron had to struggle to make ends meet for herself and her little girl, Patti. She also had to battle her late husband's interfering in-laws for the custody of her child. While romance was a part of her life, duty to friends and family always came first. *Love of Life's* Vanessa Dale fought her sister Meg over questions of morality and tried to give her nephew Beanie, Meg's son, the love his mother withheld because of her selfishness. The whole Dale family suffered because of Meg's continual involvement with unethical people. The Ameses in *The Secret Storm* were wracked with grief when Ellen, Peter's wife and the mother of his three children, suddenly died in an auto accident. Viewers were shown, in realistic detail, every effect of such a grim tragedy on a large family which could easily have been their own. On television, for the first time soap opera became true to life.

The old fantasies were there, too, but they were not part of the main idea. In its first years, *Love of Life* had both Meg and Van tried for murder, and on *Search for Tomorrow* Joanne was charged with murder. On *The Secret Storm* Peter's romance with the housekeeper was broken up by Aunt Pauline, who found the

Hawkins Falls *aired in 1951 from Chicago on NBC and was a great success, lasting four years. People liked it because it was lively—outdoor scenes were filmed in Woodstock, New York—had good Americana and good sets, and offered a variety of stories about local folk. Pictured are Russ Reed as Spec Bassett and Elmira Roessler as Elmira Cleebe.*

The Egg and I, *1951, was based on the famous novel about city slickers who move to the country to run an egg farm. The romantic leads were John Craven and Pat Kirkland, at left. Others in the cast were Doris Rich and Frank Twedell. The show was CBS' second try and was short-lived.*

Flora Campbell was Helen Emerson in Valiant Lady, *a 1953 CBS soap about a widow and her three children in a mythical suburb, Middlebury. Child actress Bonnie Sawyer was featured.*

Follow Your Heart, *1953, which ran for six months on NBC, was written by Elaine Carrington, who based the show on her successful radio soap,* When A Girl Marries. *It featured Sally Brophy (left) as Philadelphia society girl Julie and Nancy Sheridan as her mother, who wanted her to "marry well."*

The Road of Life, *a CBS Soap in 1954, was a remake of the famous radio show and starred the same leads: Don MacLaughlin (left) as Dr. Jim Brent and Virginia Dwyer as his wife, Jocelyn McLeod Brent. Supporting players were Barbara Becker as Sybil Overton (in wheelchair) and Charles Dingle as Conrad Overton.*

housekeeper's long-lost husband—thought dead, but actually marooned on a desert island. These colorful but farfetched plot devices were introduced to glamorize the realism a bit, not to replace it, and they were almost always duplications of the clichés of radio soaps.

Roy Winsor, the genius who first introduced these first successful CBS soaps on television for American Home Products (later Procter & Gamble purchased *Search for Tomorrow*), had also created and produced many of the old radio serials that originated in Chicago. It is no accident that the themes of his shows were as clear and easy to follow as those of

One Man's family *lasted for more than twenty years at the radio microphones but only a few before NBC's television cameras in 1954. Mary Adams and Theodor Von Eltz played Mother and Father Barbour. Carlton E. Morse wrote the television version as well.*

radio soaps. One even began with an epigraph: "*Love of Life*—Vanessa Dale's search for human dignity." *Love of Life* was so clearly defined that it was almost a morality play. Viewers knew that Van was pure of heart and would always fight for the right to happiness of others around her; like Stella Dallas, she was monumentally good, unlike her sister Meg, who was irresponsible and bad. However, Winsor's *The Secret Storm* didn't need an epigraph (although in the sixties it acquired one); its title was enough to suggest all the desperate inner conflicts and hidden desires of the family of Peter Ames. Viewers always knew that every episode would concern the nerve-wrenching story of a family so shocked by the death of a wife and mother, that each member began to retreat into his own shell of suffering and, because of his torment, never to find happiness. *The Secret Storm* was one of the most popular of the early soaps and was quite advanced for its time, despite the strict adherence to one theme. Says Winsor, "The audience could always follow what we were doing in the stories. I'm not so sure they can now. The themes of soaps aren't clear any more."

Golden Windows, *1954 on NBC, had to do with the romantic troubles of classical pianist Juliet Goodwin, played by Leila Martin, who co-starred with Grant Sullivan.*

Constance Ford starred as New York fashion designer Lynn Sherwood in Woman With A Past, *a 1954 CBS attempt.*

First Love, *1954, was a delightful love story whose stars were Patricia Barry as Laurie and Val Dufour as Zack James. The show aired from Philadelphia for two years on NBC.*

Louise Albritton was imported from Hollywood in 1954 to play opposite John Raby on NBC's Concerning Miss Marlowe. *Maggie Marlowe was an actress who had to choose between her career and true love. The show gave Efrem Zimbalist Jr. his start.*

The casts of these successful soaps were, by and large, not from radio, but young people from the theater, and in a few instances from Hollywood. Mary Stuart, the brilliant young actress whom director Charles Irving and producer Roy Winsor hired to play Joanne Barron, had been an MGM starlet for several years. The one exception to this was *The Guiding Light,* whose actors came from radio because the show simply continued from radio to television (with simultaneous broadcasting for four years in both media) without change of cast or story line. Charita Bauer (Bert) practically grew up on radio.

All these shows were broadcast from CBS's Liederkrantz Hall, an attractive red-brick turn-of-the-century building, at Fifty-eighth Street and Park Avenue, which had been used originally as a clubhouse for German singers. Video moved awkwardly into its once-comfortable four-story innards with swirling cameras, bright lights, and anxious people. Hildy Parks, who played Ellie Crown on the original *Love of Life,* described those early days at Liederkrantz Hall: "There was so little room there to move and work that if you ended a scene with 'I'll never see you again,'

The Greatest Gift—*that of medical knowledge and talent—was possessed by Phillip Foster (Dr. Phil Stone) and Anne Burr (Dr. Eve Allen) in this late 1954 NBC offering. It was short-lived, like most NBC soaps of this period.*

With The Seeking Heart, *1954, CBS tried to capture the interest of male viewers. The soap had both romance and gunplay. Included in the cast were Scott Forbes, Flora Campbell, Dorothy Lovett, Judith Braun and James Yarborough.*

you'd go right out a door and find yourself up against a studio wall. The cameramen were always worried about shooting off the sets during scenes because they were so cramped. The sets themselves were usually just angles, with a sofa, a chair, a table and a black velour backdrop, and most scenes would be shot with two cameras instead of three because of the space problem." At Liederkrantz Hall there was no such thing as a star's dressing room; the women had a single large communal one, as did the men. *Search for Tomorrow* and *Love of Life* had to stagger their rehearsal hours so that the actors from both shows could use the same small makeup room.

Yet almost every actor who recollects his soap opera work at the old Liederkrantz experiences a shiver of delight at the memory of all the fun. Jada Rowland, who was little Amy Ames on *The Secret Storm*, remembers: "The people and the enthusiasm made it all great. We used to do shots on the back stairs of Liederkrantz—where people would be found

murdered or something—and we all thought that was very arty. I guess the crowded conditions were a pain for the technical people, but it also meant that you got to be friends with actors on the other shows. Things were always happening! *Captain Kangaroo* was right next door. An elephant ate my purse, a llama spat at Virginia Dwyer, and a cow chased our director, Gloria Monty, into the studio."

Most CBS soaps now originate from Hollywood or from the network's Broadcast Center on Fifty-seventh Street between Tenth and Eleventh Avenues. It is large, sterile, and quite uncolorful compared to Liederkrantz Hall. "You rehearse in these air-conditioned rooms without a single window," says Jada. "At Liederkrantz we rehearsed on the top floor and could look out onto the street. Richard Avedon had his photographic studio across the street, and we'd all go to the windows and have fun watching him work with high-fashion models."

Gloria Monty, as director of *The Secret Storm*,

Modern Romances, *1954 on NBC, was an anthology soap, presenting a different story each week. This one featured Georgann Johnson and John Kellogg.*

Date With Life, *1955, was another NBC anthology series. One of the stories concerned schoolteacher Jennifer, played by June Dayton, and her suitor David, played by Miss Dayton's real-life husband, Dean Harens.*

Hotel Cosmopolitan *was a kind of* Grand Hotel *serial, which CBS began in 1957 and quickly withdrew. The romantic leads were Dinna Smith (in the background) and Donald Woods (far left); Woods was also the narrator. Others in the cast, to the right of him, were John Holm, Walter Brooke and Tom Shirley.*

was the most powerful woman executive in daytime television. Like most directors in the early days, she virtually ran her show. (Most soaps today are run by the producers, and in some cases by the writers.) Gloria, who stayed with *The Secret Storm* until the late sixties, remembers some of the fun herself. "There was no such thing as stopping the tape if there was a major goof. The show was live, and if you made a mistake millions of viewers saw it. Once, Haila Stoddard, as Aunt Pauline, had to say to her mother, Marjorie Gateson, 'I always thought she was a bit of a witch.' I didn't realize that this was a tongue twister for Haila—otherwise we would have changed the line. On air Haila came out with, 'I always thought she was a whit of a bitch.' You just didn't use that word in those days! Instead of just going on with her lines, Marjorie said, 'Oh, dear, Pauline, you didn't mean to say that.' It got more and more confused. We had a lot of explaining to do after the show. Then another time there was a scene with Peter Hobbs, as Peter Ames, Jim Brod-

Kitty Foyle *was NBC's 1958 soap opera revival of the famous story, with Judy Lewis (left) as Molly Scharf and Kathleen Murray in the title role.*

Today is Ours, *1958 on NBC, involved the audience in the problems of a divorced young mother, Laura Manning, played by Pat Benoit. Laura was an assistant principal in a school. Peter Lazar played her son Nicky.*

erick, and another actor. Peter and Jim had their backs to the cameras, and this third actor was supposed to say, 'Are you calling me a crooked cop?' On air it came out, 'Are you calling me a crooked cock?' Peter and Jim broke up, with their shoulders just shaking. Then the camerman became hysterical, and you could hear it on air. When we broke for commercial, I kept saying to them, 'He didn't say it! He didn't say it!' The commercials were live in the beginning, and Don Hancock, the announcer, couldn't stop laughing in the middle of this serious commercial. It all got out of hand. The actor who said the line wasn't aware of what he had said, and he became furious with Peter and Jim. Calls came in from our sponsor, American Home Products, and the only thing I could tell them was that it was just a mistake."

Since these were fifteen-minute shows, they re-quired far less time for rehearsal and broadcast than today's half-hour and hour soaps, and gave actors a chance to audition for Broadway shows and even do matinees when it was necessary. Scale was $50 per broadcast, but most principals got more than that. Mary Stuart started *Search for Tomorrow* at $500 per week, which at that time was top soap money for television.

Love of Life's schedule was typical. An actor arrived at Liederkrantz at 8:00 A.M., rehearsed in the room across from Richard Avedon until 9, came out of makeup at 10, had his scenes blocked on the actual set with the cameras until 11, finished dress rehearsal at 11:30, broke for lunch, went on air in one of the four fifteen minute soap spots, which began at noon, and then hurried off to an audition. "Because of the schedule," says Hildy Parks, "it wasn't your whole life. It was a little like having a grocery store on the side."

Young Dr. Malone *was still a radio show when NBC began its television version in 1958, with John Connell (left) as Dr. David Malone, and William Prince and Augusta Dabney as his fosterparents. The program went off radio in 1960 and lasted on television until 1963—it was the last soap to air in both media. Mr. Prince and Miss Dabney met on the program and were later married in real life.*

The House on High Street, *1959, was a half-hour NBC series based on actual cases from the files of domestic relations courts. Phillip Abbott played probation officer John Collier. By now viewers were losing interest in serials with episodic formats and continually changing casts.*

NBC struggled to compete with these strong CBS soaps, presenting one unsuccessful serial after another. It wasn't a question of money, however. Such NBC soaps as *The Bennetts, Follow Your Heart, Three Steps to Heaven, A Time to Live, Golden Windows, First Love, Concerning Miss Marlowe, The Greatest Gift, Modern Romances, Miss Susan* and *Date with Life* had generally higher budgets and better sets than did *Search for Tomorrow, Love of Life* and *The Secret Storm,* the Roy Winsor-Biow serials. The trouble was that the NBC soaps were too romantic, and the days of Helen Trent were over. Housewives wanted to see the realistic dilemmas of other housewives, not the troubled love involvements of glamorous actresses like Maggie Marlowe.

This NBC notion that soaps had to be romantic came from radio. In fact, network executives—those of CBS included—tried transplanting a number of old radio soaps to the channels. *The Guiding Light,* which is still on, and *The Brighter Day,* which lasted eight years, were the only successful ones. The failures on CBS were *Valiant Lady, Portia Faces Life* (later called *The Inner Flame*) and *Road of Life,* and on NBC *Follow Your Heart* (Elaine Carrington's TV remake of her old *When a Girl Marries*), and *One Man's Family.* After the mid-fifties, television abandoned radio as a source for soaps.

And yet, it was a veteran radio soap writer who was soon to revolutionize, with an amazing creation, the nature, impact, and economics of daytime serials.

* * *

Irna Phillips was already a wealthy woman in 1952, when she brought her radio creation, *The Guiding Light,* to television—and she was to grow much, much richer. Thoroughly adaptable to new situations,

For Better or Worse, *1959, had Dyan Cannon and Ronald Foster playing newlyweds in one of the show's weekly stories. This CBS anthology series featured tales of marital troubles taken from the files of a prominent sociologist.*

Dyan Cannon, like many famous performers, got her start on the soaps. In CBS's Full Circle, *1960, she played opposite Robert Fortier in a story about a wanderer who finds romance and intrigue in a small Virginia town.*

Irna quickly learned how to write for the visual medium. By 1954—when it was obvious from the growing popularity of both nighttime and daytime television fare that video soaps were here to stay—Irna had decided that it was time for her to break new ground. She suggested to Procter & Gamble, sponsor and owner of *The Guiding Light*, that the show be lengthened to a full half-hour.

P&G was astonished. Soap operas, almost by definition, were creatures of fifteen-minutes per day. There had never been a half-hour soap, and the detergent company's initial response was that the plan was far too risky. How much of any one show could the ladies at home take? And, brilliant as Irna was, could she really make the Bauer family interesting for thirty minutes a day? The great Queen of Soap Opera insisted she could. She kept on insisting for two full years, until P&G finally relented and told Irna that, although she couldn't change the format of *The Guid-*

ing Light, she could create a new thirty-minute soap.

On April 2, 1956, P&G premiered the most historically important soap opera in modern times: *As the World Turns*. Irna's new show wasn't just an expanded fifteen-minute serial, but a fresh approach to a twenty-six-year-old invention—a totally visual approach. She slowed time down to a near halt, and had the cameras peer at length into the faces of actors whom she and director Ted Corday had picked with assiduous care. The Lowells and the Hugheses simply pondered family problems, and gradually, ever so gradually, increasing numbers of viewers were drawn to the show, fascinated by its realism. Never before had a soap probed its characters so deeply and so thoroughly. There were no murders, no amnesiacs, no mysterious people popping up from desert islands, no villains. There weren't even flawless heroines, such as Vanessa on *Love of Life* and Joanne on *Search for Tomorrow*. The situations were as real and as slowly observed as in

The Clear Horizon, *on CBS, was remarkable as the first futuristic soap. The setting was Cape Canaveral and the story was about astronauts and their brave but jittery wives. Featured in the cast were Craig Curtis, Denise Alexander and Jimmy Carter.*

Our Five Daughters, *begun in 1962 on NBC, starred fifteen-year-old Jacquie Courtney as one of the daughters in a story about the Lee family. Edward Griffith played her on-screen beau. Miss Courtney went on to fame a few years later in* Another World.

life. *As the World Turns* was not only the most visual but also the most adult drama yet televised in the afternoon.

By 1957, after *As the World Turns* and P&G's other half-hour serial, *The Edge of Night*, had become top-rated, daytime television was changed forever. It was far cheaper to produce one half-hour serial than two fifteen-minute ones, and so the existing soaps quickly started expanding, and every new one was a half hour.

After the success of these two half-hour shows, CBS had a virtual monopoly on daytime drama. It tried only a handful of new ventures after that: *Hotel Cosmopolitan*, a lavish anthology series; *The Verdict Is Yours*, a courtroom series featuring real judges and lawyers; *For Better Or Worse*, another anthology series, about newlyweds; and *The Clear Horizon*, a daring serial about astronauts. They all failed.

NBC tried every sort of approach to break CBS's grip on daytime. *From These Roots* (owned by Procter & Gamble) was the most remarkable of all the net-work's efforts of the late fifties, lasting three and a half years, but its ratings were never good. *Young Doctor Malone*, a radio transplant, lasted a bit longer. Other attempts ended more quickly, including *Kitty Foyle, Today Is Ours, The House On High Street* and *Our Five Daughters*. Infant ABC tried its first one in 1960, *Road To Reality*.

The most prominent figures of the fifties had been Roy Winsor and Irna Phillips. Roy Winsor gave soaps their true start on television, while Irna, years before during the era of radio soaps, had already given them the form that would eventually endure on television. She had invented family-centered radio soaps like *The Guiding Light*, which led to her revolutionary *As the World Turns*. She also created the first radio soap about hospital life, *The Road of Life*, and followed that with other memorable ones. Irna's families and her hospitals and doctors would soon define the soap world's upcoming decade and cement her unbreakable link with modern daytime viewers.

THE MODERN SOAP WORLD

THE sixties was a time of great turmoil in the soap world, which was now passing its thirtieth birthday. Television executives, increasingly aware of the huge potential profits of the new half-hour daytime serials, grew restless in their search for the right themes and formats to attract daylight viewers. Hospital shows, like *Dr. Kildare*, were already hits on nighttime television. Both NBC and ABC, determined to break CBS's afternoon ratings death grip, premiered medical soaps on the same day in 1963. *The Doctors* on NBC was an effective anthology series about hospital life, and soon became a full-fledged serial. ABC's *General Hospital* was similar. Although there had already been hospital soaps on television, like *The Greatest Gift* in 1954 and *Young Dr. Malone* in 1958, these new medical shows, because of higher budgets and technical advances in serial production, were the first successes. They were able to offer viewers much more authentic atmospheres. Realistic operations were staged, often under the supervision of hospital professionals. Actual medical settings, such as therapy rooms and intensive-care units with modern gadgetry, were shown. Writers carefully researched the progress of different diseases before presenting them in story lines. Overwhelmed by the realism, many viewers began to write to the doctor characters for medical advice.

General Hospital also offered viewers a bit more. The head writers, Frank and Doris Hursley, had created a story for two of their main characters, nurse Jessie Brewer and her husband, Dr. Phil Brewer, of blatant and repeated infidelities, sandwiched between the usual hospital crises. After Jessie first learned that her young husband was sleeping with another woman, she refused to have relations with him, whereupon he raped her and she became pregnant. There was a fundamental difference between how the Hursleys were writing the popular story of the Brewers and the romantic problems described in the soaps of the fifties—a difference which began to pervade the sixties soap world. Sex, especially rape and extramarital sex, began to appear in story after story in this new decade. Later we'll take a closer look at the history of sex in the soaps and why such changes occurred.

NBC was quite happy with *The Doctors*, but it wasn't until 1964, with its premiere of Irna Phillips's *Another World*, that the network was able to begin a solid competitive afternoon lineup. The fact that it took Irna to create one of NBC's first few successful serials, after television soaps had been around for fifteen years, demonstrated once again her thorough understanding of the modern woman at home and what she wanted to see.

Another World was in some ways like Irna's previous creation on the rival network, *As the World Turns*. It concerned two family groups—actually two branches of the Matthews family—one rich, one middle-class. It was also fairly slow-plotted and dependent on the evolution of fluid characters. But *Another World* was distinctly different from *As the World Turns* in that it was intended as psychological melodrama

36

rather than a day-to-day account of ordinary events. Murder, villainy, and tense romantic entanglements served as catalysts for the surfacing of the complex inner lives of characters. Through extraordinary happenstance, one character's happiness could be gained only by causing another's misery. The title referred to the "other world" that all the Matthewses of Bay City, along with their friends and enemies, hoped for. There was even a thematic epigraph: "We do not live in this world alone, but in a thousand other worlds."

The show was the most complicated of Irna's creations to date, and somewhat out of her league, for she lacked the skill to execute a melodrama. She had too many major characters, like Grandma Matthews and lawyer Mitchell Dru, sitting around quietly discussing trivia, the way her characters did in *As The World Turns*, instead of measuring up to the dire events around them. *Another World* had to wait three years for viewers finally to take to it, after Agnes Nixon became the head writer in 1968. But what is significant is not that Irna had failed but that she had accurately read the spirit of the times and had imbued her new serial with psychological undercurrents, much as the highly advanced *The Secret Storm* had done years before. For many years after Irna stopped writing it, until the mid-seventies, *Another World* adhered to Irna's original concept of a drama of people imprisoned and made unhappy by their own private worlds of existence, worlds they secretly wished to leave.

In 1965, newly enlightened NBC introduced *Days of Our Lives*, the most important soap opera of the sixties. Created by director Ted Corday, Irna Phillips and Allan Chase, it was all about the Hortons, a family of doctors. In the beginning it had a conventional setup, like Irna Phillips's other soaps, and began quite as *Another World* had, with an out-of-wedlock pregnancy, a murder and an elaborate trial. But after a few years the show evolved into a bold combination of intense family suffering, medical and psychiatric melodrama, and continuous story lines emerging from sexual catastrophes, such as rape and near-incest; that incendiary mixture could not have been presented on daytime television before the mid-sixties. Gifted writer William Bell, who had been apprenticing as a sub-writer for Irna Phillips, had taken over as the new head writer in 1967 and transformed *Days of Our Lives*, which had only fair ratings, into an endlessly

fascinating high-rated drama of modern expressionism. Bell threw most of the show's original realism out the window and began to engage viewers in one stunning adult fantasy after another. A sister falls in love with a stranger that her brother brings home, and then, when she later discovers that he is their own brother, transformed by plastic surgery, she hears the call and becomes a nun; two women friends fall in love with the same man, become bitter enemies and later have sexual relations with men as a way of hurting each other; a man rapes his brother's wife, becomes the father of her son, and enters into a conspiracy with her to keep the child's parentage a secret; and so on. These exotic mosaics from the mind of William Bell and his sub-writers (including Pat Falken Smith, who was later to become a head writer herself, carrying on the tradition) brought the art of soap opera to a new height, finally combining the old romantic fantasies of radio, the preoccupation with family life of Irna Phillips, and the hysteria, sexual confusion and violence of America in the sixties.

*   *   *

After its surprising success with *General Hospital*, once conservative ABC turned its daytime broadcasting hours into a soap opera laboratory. Believing that there were millions of young people who would tune in to soaps with younger formats, the network began *The Young Marrieds* in 1964 and *Never Too Young* the following year. Also, *Flame In The Wind*, in 1964 (later retitled *A Time For Us*), dealt with class conflict that involved young lovers. With *The Nurses* in 1965, ABC was attempting to generate another hit hospital soap. All these new ventures were noble but short-lived. Then, in 1966, ABC's daytime laboratory cooked up the right potion.

Dark Shadows, a tongue-in-cheek serial about vampires, witches and weird Gothic doings, became the new rage among teenagers, lasting four high-rated years. Jonathan Frid was featured as Barnabas, the resident vampire-who-wouldn't (but usually did). The show had so many science fiction-like switches in time that the actors themselves couldn't tell where they were in the wickerwork of plot. *Dark Shadows* had every device ever employed in horror-supernatural movies since the old *Phantom of the Opera*. There were live burials, living corpses, strange bedeviled young men, unknown ailments and nutty conjurers. Apart from teenagers home from school, fans of all the mock fright included young housewives, "camp" lovers and Jackie Onassis. During the phenomenon, the public and the media began to see ABC as an important force in daytime broadcasting.

During the last three years of the sixties, because daring ventures such as *Days of Our Lives* and wholly experimental ones such as *Dark Shadows* had quite accidentally increased the size of the afternoon viewing audience, the networks began to glut the channels with innovative serials in hopes of attracting these millions of mysterious new viewers. Expensive new soap opera ratings wars resulted in increased media publicity. Newspapers, magazines and talk shows began to discuss the soaps in terms of sex, vampires, budgets, ratings and the two new soap cults or themes which began to emerge between 1967 and 1970 and which would help make the soaps "fashionable" in the seventies: Young Love and Relevancy.

The history of those three years is vitally important for an understanding of the modern soap world. In the latter part of 1967, CBS introduced a serial which, quite unintentionally, inaugurated one of the two cults.

Love Is A Many Splendored Thing was supposed to be a soap about interracial love, and as such was another shot-in-the-dark experiment. Loosely based on the novel and movie of the same name, the initial story had an American, Dr. Jim Abbott, in love with a Eurasian girl, Mia. Less than a year after the show's premiere, CBS (perhaps bombarded by too many protests from conservative viewers) became frightened of the subject matter and forced the writer, Irna Phillips, to abort the interracial love story between Jim and Mia. Furious, Irna immediately quit the show.

But then something odd happened. Many of Irna's lesser characters—meant to enhance the main love story—were young. Irna Phillips is dead now, and cannot tell us what she intended to do with these young people, but after Irna, and her character Mia, left the show, the new writers—Jane and Ira Avery—needing to do something with the remaining characters, involved young Mark Elliott with two of the young incidental characters, Iris and Laura Donnelly (played by Leslie Charleson and Donna Mills). When David Birney replaced Sam Wade as Mark Elliott, the show's ratings began, inexplicably, to skyrocket. Although serial writers had always used Young Love (Penny Hughes and Jeff Baker on *As the World Turns*, for instance), the special focus these young characters received and the unusual attractiveness of the three

The Young Marrieds, *1964, one of ABC's first soaps, was a story of four suburban couples. Floy Dean (left) played new bride Liz Forsythe Stevens, and Peggy McCay was Susan Garrett.*

Flame In The Wind, *1964 on ABC, was about class conflict in a small town. Among the show's many stars were Maggie Hayes as Roxanne Reynolds, and Walter Coy as Jason Farrel, her wealthy publisher father.*

performers gave *Love Is a Many Splendored Thing* a new young look, and a new popularity. Until then, the going theory had been that because viewing housewives were usually over thirty, they wanted to see soaps primarily concerned with people of a similar age. That idea was now instantly shattered.

The birth of the cult of Relevancy came with the premiere of *One Life to Live* in 1968 on ABC. Agnes Nixon, the show's creator, had been Irna Phillips's dialogue writer for years and had, at different times, been head writer of nearly all the Procter & Gamble serials. Tired of the soaps' media image of being behind the times, Agnes decided to create a "relevant" soap—that is, one which was topical and dealt with contemporary life. In *One Life to Live* she had various ethnic types—Jews, Blacks, Poles, Irish—struggling for identity in a WASP-dominated culture. In addition, her highly publicized story lines dealt with drug addiction, VD, sexual repression, prejudice and child abuse. These were occasional concerns, however, not part of the mainstream of events. In general, Mrs. Nixon's realistic ethnic people were primarily involved in solid romantic stories and fairly conventional soap fantasies: amnesia, split-personality (a variation on the amnesia fantasy), unwitting bigamy. From the beginning the show was popular with viewers.

Meanwhile, NBC departed from these main trends and introduced *Hidden Faces*, a crime melodrama in the mold of CBS's *Edge of Night*, in 1968. The show was well conceived, but the network made the fatal mistake of programming it at 1:30 P.M. opposite CBS's high-rated *As The World Turns*, and it lasted a mere six months. What is remembered about the show today is its extraordinary cast: Conard Fowkes as lawyer Arthur Adams, Gretchen Walther as Kate Logan, a former surgeon in love with him; Nat Polen as a corrupt businessman; Rita Gam as the wife of a senator; a very young Linda Blair as their daughter; and Tony LoBianco, who became a movie star in *The French Connection*.

Where The Heart Is, which came in 1969 on CBS, was clearly a sixties soap with its theme of sexual entanglements within and around members of the same family, the wealthy Hathaways. But where its predecessor, *Days of Our Lives*, had seemed like an abstract comment on the times, *Where The Heart Is* appeared tedious and at times unwholesome. A father and son in the story had become sexual rivals

Moment of Truth, *1965, starred Douglass Watson as college professor Dr. Robert Wallace. It was made in Toronto, Canada, and briefly shown on NBC. Douglass Watson later became well-known to* Another World *devotees in his role as Mac Cory.*

A Time For Us, *1965, was ABC's new title for* Flame In The Wind, *which lasted only another six months. Conard Fowkes played director Paul Davis and Joanna Miles was Linda Skerba, who wanted to be an actress.*

not over just one woman, but two; and the most common affliction in the town of Northcross was pregnancy—unwanted, illicit or plotted. The network received many angry letters from viewers who claimed they were offended but continued to watch, and for the first few years the ratings weren't bad. Two weeks after the premiere, NBC countered with its *Bright Promise*, a vehicle for movie star Dana Andrews, who played college dean Thomas Boswell. Although the campus setting at first allowed the show to focus on young characters, after six months the town of Bancroft became central and *Bright Promise* went back to early sixties material.

The real action was happening at ABC, where the next decade of soaps was being born. Agnes Nixon's second soap, *All My Children*, premiered in January 1970, with Rosemary Prinz ending her self-imposed exile from daytime television to play Amy Tyler, a woman with a shady past that included an illegitimate birth. Her present was filled with a desire to go off on peace marches, work for the environment and pursue other such social causes which were on the minds of young people all over the country. Mrs. Nixon wrote the character that way because the much sought after Rosemary Prinz made it a condition of her playing Amy Tyler. But well after Rosemary Prinz left the show, Mrs. Nixon continued to write sequences dealing with war protest—such as Ruth Brent's famous speech against all war after young Philip was reported killed in Vietnam—child abuse, abortion, even the new interest in face lifts. It was the same pattern as with her *One Life To Live*, imposing topical issues on what Ruth Warrick (who plays Phoebe Tyler) calls "classical soap opera," that is, the kind of drama that Agnes and Irna Phillips used to write together, such as *As The World Turns* and *The Guiding Light*. At its heart, *All My Children* was pure classical soap opera, about two families, one rich, one middle-class, and the romantic problems of all the various children. It was a contemporary continuation of a wonderful old form, with its own special appeal, including a well-written love triangle involving three very young characters. The show quickly gained a responsive younger audience.

Right after the premiere, there was a great deal of publicity surrounding Agnes Nixon and her shows. But the media saw both *All My Children* and *One Life To Live* differently from viewers. Relevancy—in other words, topical elements introduced into the form—was considered sensational, revolutionary, worthy of many words. The housewife now was seen as being "educated" rather than entertained. Many of these media impressions were exaggerated, but the overall impact of this publicity on the world of the soaps was positive. It amounted to saying that critics should give it a second look and that people working in that world deserved more respect. Relevancy sold the soaps to the media and the public at large, while Young Love, the more durable of the two trends, continued to increase the size of the afternoon audience.

* * *

On the same day, March 30, 1970, three more soaps were added to serial blocks. It was the first time since radio that there had been so many soaps, now twenty of them, all running a full half hour. The three new shows were ABC's *The Best of Everything*, based on the Rona Jaffe novel about career girls working for a magazine in New York, starring Susan Sullivan and Geraldine Fitzgerald; the same network's *A World Apart*, written by Katherine Phillips, with an assist from her mother Irna Phillips, loosely based on Irna's own life as a soap opera writer; and *Another World— Somerset* (later called *Somerset*), a spinoff of *Another World* on NBC which, when written by *The Edge of Night*'s head writer, Henry Slesar, later turned into a crime melodrama. The first two were quickly canceled.

The networks were by now glutted with afternoon serials, a full ten hours of daytime fiction. Viewers were confused by the hodgepodge assortment, each network's afternoon serial block being destroyed by the incursions of the other two networks. Ratings and advertising revenues began to shrink while the writers of the twenty serials suffered an understandable slump in creativity. Irna Phillips, called back to rescue *As The World Turns* from its sudden dip in ratings, told the New York *Daily News*: "The daytime serial has been destroying itself. The people responsible for the shows have lost sight of the most important element in them—their humanness. NBC recently got a call from a viewer who wanted them to know that one of the CBS serials was stealing their plots. It wasn't theft. It was just lack of imagination. Why, at one point last year, CBS had murder trials going on all four of its house-produced serials. No wonder they can't keep an audience."

This was a time in the soap world when the

stakes had grown high, with millions of dollars of ad revenues on the table. Although the total viewing audience had more than doubled in just a few years, no one format seemed to be succeeding. Most of the older shows from the fifties were in serious trouble, as were some of the once-popular sixties soaps, like *General Hospital*. Nervous network executives, scrambling for the formulas that would win the ratings game, began interfering with the creativity of daytime writers and producers. Roy Winsor, who had produced *The Secret Storm* and *Love of Life* until 1969, says: "I had been working on a fixed budget from American Home Products to do those shows. I got their money and they got their shows. For a long time they were very popular. I always worked on sound principles of theme and story, the same principles that dictate great novels, and they worked for my shows. Then, when the ratings competition got heavy, CBS kept pressuring me for fancier sets, better trimmings, and with the money spent there we had to lower our acting budget and the story suffered."

The networks, up against the unknown, tinkered with the writing as well. "It got to a point," says Winsor, "where if a show had slipped half a point in the ratings shares, the poor writer would be given orders to make someone pregnant to get the numbers back up." During this era, there were quite a few characters killed off on all the shows—desperation strategies to attract viewers with all the new sadness.

After Roy Winsor left *The Secret Storm* and *Love of Life*, both shows deteriorated badly, losing their clear-cut themes, their most beloved characters and audiences. As one head writer after another took over the helm of *The Secret Storm*, the show grew less and

Paradise Bay, *a picturesque California beach town, came to NBC in the fall of 1965 and left the next summer. Keith Andes played Jeff Morgan, the owner of a radio station, and Marion Ross played his wife.*

Morning Star, *1965 on NBC, starred Elizabeth Perry as Katy Elliot, a fashion designer who fled personal tragedy to pursue a career in New York, and Ed Mallory as Bill Riley. The drama departed with* Paradise Bay.

less continuous. Each of the writers, anxious to put his own stamp on it, indifferent to its past, systematically eliminated the important Ames family. Eventually only Amy Ames (Jada Rowland) was left and only diehard viewers continued watching a story that seemed to have little purpose. *The Secret Storm* had been one of the most brilliant efforts of the fifties, but in 1974 CBS, after trying for years to revive it with different producers and writers' concepts, had no choice but to cancel it. *Love of Life* floundered similarly and was able to last only six years longer.

The true problem with both of these historic soaps is that, twenty years after they began, there was no one executive in any position of power who could remember why they were done in the first place. No executive had any reason to fight for their original integrity, for they were products of other minds and another era. *Search for Tomorrow* and *The Guiding Light* survived because they were owned by Procter & Gamble, which employed executives like Bob Short, who knew exactly what those soaps were like in the fifties and fought to maintain continuity for older viewers.

The Nurses, *1965 on ABC, starred Mary Fickett as nurse Liz Thorpe and Pat Polen as Dr. John Crager, colleagues at Alden General Hospital. The show lasted eighteen months.*

A kind of cancellation panic began in 1972-73, when CBS killed two of its house-produced soaps, *Love Is A Many Splendored Thing* and *Where The Heart Is*, and NBC removed *Bright Promise*. The general mood at the networks was that longevity and old viewer loyalties were less important than immediate ratings. The demise of *Love Is A Many Splendored Thing* was especially remarkable, in light of the show's once-high ratings and promise. Most observers blamed the network for not trying harder to hold on to David Birney, Donna Mills and Leslie Charleson, whose appeal for viewers was at least half the reason for the show's success. After the three actors departed for nighttime television, the show's fans became weary of the succession of actors hired to replace them and finally abandoned *Splendored Thing* for a trip to the supermarket.

NBC replaced *Bright Promise* with *Return To Peyton Place*, an afternoon continuation of the sizzling nighttime series about infidelities and other peccadillos in the famous New England town. Stories that were left unresolved in the mother series were featured in the new soap, along with some of the original actors. The performers were all young and quite attractive, but housewives weren't prepared for the show's string of boudoir situations. Without the use of some sort of family structure for the story, as most soaps had, it appeared that the new soap was parading sex for its own sake. Many viewers wrote angry letters to the network and boycotted the show, which was finally canceled in January 1974. Said Gail Kobe, its assistant producer: "Of course it was the ratings. We were counterprogrammed against *One Life To Live*, which was a story about family relationships, while ours was that 'dirty little town.' Viewers would have bought us if we had been a story of interrelationships within families. Instead of just canceling, I think NBC should have allowed us the opportunity to change our format."

In the same time slot the network began *How To Survive A Marriage*, its first foray into Relevancy. The show was the brainchild of NBC's then vice-president in charge of daytime, Lin Bolen—a young woman who, as the show's star, Rosemary Prinz, put it, "knew and believed in all the modern jargon concerning sexual liberation. She speaks it like a native." At the time of the premiere, Ms. Bolen described *How To Survive A Marriage*: "It's a very contemporary dramatization of a problem which confronts so many couples in today's society—separation and impending divorce. The heroine of the story, Chris Kirby, is a thirty-two-year-old woman who has separated from her husband, Larry, after twelve years of marriage. She finds herself faced with the challenge of making a new life for herself, and she must cope with situations she has never before faced—job hunting, apartment hunting and serving as mother and father to her young daughter. Both husband and wife must adjust to their new lifestyles as they try to learn to live apart from one another . . . They must learn to date again in a new singles society from the one they knew twelve years ago."

It all sounded wonderful, but the actual show, for the most part, was so grimly intent on presenting contemporary issues—psychiatry, sexual liberation, the merits of single versus married life, how to divorce, feminism and improving one's lifestyle through improving one's interpersonal relationships—that the serial began to sound more and more like an extended talk show. It had far too little story to hold viewers' interest. By the time Dr. Julie Franklin (Rosemary Prinz) gave her umpteenth lecture on the self-fulfilling prophesy, there was no place for *How To Survive A Marriage* to go. Cancellation came after little more than a year.

Although NBC took a beating with *Marriage*, the show was a noble experiement and valuable in that it showed how far any soap could take Relevancy, which wasn't very far. The underlying drama could not be a mere excuse for a soap box.

The Young and The Restless, which premiered on March 23, 1973, brought CBS into the contemporary serial field and was a wildfire ratings success. It was written and created by William Bell, whose talents had kept *Days of Our Lives'* viewers on tenterhooks for six years. Within a few years, Bell had made of his show the single greatest influence in the soap world of the seventies. Once again, there was the "classical soap opera" setup, with two families, one upper middle-class and one poor, and the focus was on the romantic lives of the children. But the difference was that Young Love was given preference

Dark Shadows *premiered on ABC on June 25, 1966, and lasted four ghoulish years, to the delight of millions of teenagers. It was ABC's first success in the afternoon. Jonathan Frid played the vampire, Barnabas Collins.*

Hidden Faces, *1968, was NBC's answer to* The Edge of Night. *The crime melodrama featured (from left): Stephen Joyce, Tony LoBianco, and Conard Fowkes as attorney Arthur Adams, the show's main character. It lasted only a few months; CBS had suicidally programmed it opposite* As The World Turns.

to the "thirty-five or more" variety, and sex had come out of the closet; in fact, in the show's first year, sex was the major topic of conversation among all the characters. Young Chris and Snapper had endless discussions over whether they should have intercourse before marriage. Snapper had conversations with his mother about his choosing Sally McGuire as a sex partner while he was engaged to Chris. Snapper and Chris later had many talks about her feelings after she was raped by a stranger. Viewers felt that they were part of the intimate lives of these young people, who were at heart family-centered, conservative types, and therefore understandable to a daytime audience.

Bell, who loves to write sophisticated fantasy, made of his show a psychedelic dream of beauty. With the help of clever producer John Conboy, all the parts were cast with suntanned and glamorous Hollywood actors. Bell employed these young billboards in one grown up fairy tale after another. A plain girl turns into a beautiful world-famous concert pianist through the power of love. A handsome millionaire falls in love with a gorgeous poor girl, whose fondest dream had always been one of wealth and glamor. It was Hummert radio soap opera fantasy all over again, with a good deal more added.

As the show progressed, a certain style of production emerged. John Conboy called for shadowy movie-type lighting, easily supplied in the show's Hollywood studio; special camera angles; ingenious short teasers before commercials; singing and dancing by the young performers to a full orchestra amid shimmering candelabra. The earlier frank sexual talk soon melted into the lavish romance of a perpetually moonlit world of Young Love. There was much Relevancy, too, such as long sequences concerning realistic rape trials involving two sisters, their mother's mastectomy, frigidity, impotence and even lesbianism, but these elements were subservient to the main entertainment, which was always in the grand style.

* * *

If half-hour soaps were better than fifteen-minute

Where The Heart Is, *1969, had a conventional structure, a story about two families, the wealthy Hathaways and the Prescotts—but was filled with steamy sexual situations, putting it ahead of its time. The show featured (from left): Diana Walker as Mary Hathaway, Robyn Millan as Vicky Lucas and Diana Van Der Vlis as Kate Hathaway. CBS cancelled it after three and a half years.*

A World Apart, *1970 on ABC, was written by Irna Phillips' daughter, Katherine Phillips, and was loosely based on Irna's own life. Elizabeth Lawrence (left) played a successful soap opera writer, Betty Kahlman, and Susan Sarandon was her adopted daughter, Patrice.*

ones, what about full hour soaps? That was what Paul Rauch, executive producer of *Another World*, asked his Procter & Gamble bosses in mid-1974. Rauch gained great clout with the company after he and head writer Harding Lemay rescued *Another World* from oblivion and brought its ratings to nearly first place, just behind *As The World Turns*. Believing he knew whereof he spoke, the soap company, on January 6, 1975, made the historic expansion of the show to a full hour.

The changeover could not have been more chaotic. As an outcome of unfortunate backstage politics,

Another World's two main romantic stars, George Reinholt and Jacquie Courtney (Steve and Alice) were dismissed at the time of the expansion, creating a disruption in the story line. Viewers were likewise upset by the sudden introduction of many new characters intermixed in three or four simultaneous love triangles, and unnecessarily long and repetitive scenes. Procter & Gamble and the many onlookers quickly began to see the pitfalls of the hour soap. It was much more difficult to write and produce than its predecessor.

Nevertheless, *Another World* held its audience

The Best of Everything, *1970, was based on the Rona Jaffe novel about four career girls trying to make it in New York. The ABC serial featured (from left): Julie Mannix, Kathy Glass, Patty McCormack and Rochelle Oliver.*

and soon afterward *Days of Our Lives* followed suit. P&G similarly expanded *As The World Turns* and *The Guiding Light*, pouring millions of dollars into new facilities, better and bigger sets and more colorful trappings. ABC, suffering from the increased competition and the poor ratings of *General Hospital* and *One Life To Live*, expanded those shows to forty-five minutes each, trying to create a block that would keep viewers from switching to the P&G competition. The network even hired George Reinholt and Jacquie Courtney for *One Life To Live*, attempting to encourage fans of *Another World*'s Steve and Alice romance to change soaps. The ploy didn't work. P&G soaps only got bigger audiences.

Daytime economics had been changed forever, now that viewers showed no reluctance to sit through hour soap operas. Obviously, the hour soap made much more money than two half-hour ones, since production expenses were consolidated, and ratings on the second half-hour were always guaranteed. There may also have been another reason for expanding shows. *The Guiding Light*, for instance, had not

Somerset was a 1970 "spinoff" from Another World *and was supposed to take place in the town of Somerset, to the mother show's Bay City. The shows were placed back to back on NBC and characters would travel from one to the other. Dorothy Stinnette and Paul Sparer played a wealthy couple, Laura and Rex Cooper. It ran six years.*

been doing well before it went to an hour in 1977. Under the same head writers, Jerome and Bridget Dobson, the new hour show's ratings suddenly shot up. The writers had obviously been inspired by the longer format and bigger budget. At least one network did not fail to notice that expansion might be good medicine for a floundering soap.

Fighting all these new trends, ABC introduced the thirty-minute *Ryan's Hope* in 1975. Writers Claire Labine and Paul Avila Mayer chose not to do a soap with lots of sex, pretty faces and topical issues. Instead, their new soap had a modified Irna Phillips recipe: Take one big closely knit family, have the grown up children strive for happiness in romance and work, add generous portions of marital strife and infidelity, throw in a dash of villainy from outsiders, simmer the whole thing in a hospital atmosphere and serve realistically five times a week. The title referred to the aspirations of the show's main family, the Irish-American Ryans of New York City. *Ryan's Hope* was quite successful, mainly because of Labine and Mayer's excellent scripts.

Ryan's Hope was the exception, for the whole of the soap world was still under the spell of *The Young and The Restless*. All the expanded shows introduced young people facing sexual dilemmas, often appearing partially clad or in bathing suits. All the old restrictions, especially on P&G shows, about not showing an unmarried man and woman in bed together, were gone. Every show had ongoing affairs which continued in the bedroom at his or her place. Sexual mores on the soaps had changed well before the seventies, as a glance at past story lines will show, but the effects before 1975 had never seemed as pronounced.

Procter & Gamble paired its successful writer-producer team from *Another World*, Harding Lemay and Paul Rauch, on its new soap, *Lovers and Friends*, which premiered in 1977 on NBC. The advance publicity led insiders to believe that it was going to be P&G's answer to *The Young and The Restless*, about sexual yearnings among beautiful young people. *Lovers and Friends* turned out to be an attempt to update Irna Phillips with a slower, grander approach to the two-family structure. There were a few young characters, but in the first months the show was burdened by so much expository dialogue on the backgrounds of all the characters, that the audience had a hard time sensing a true story. After four months P&G

withdrew the show, reworked it into a faster moving drama, and presented it again as *For Richer, For Poorer*, with equally dismal ratings results, and the show was canceled.

* * *

Throughout the seventies, a fascinating phenomenon had been developing, known mostly to the demographics experts at the soap-producing advertising agencies. The viewing audience had gradually been getting younger as it grew bigger. Apparently young housewives, who would never have watched soap operas their mothers may have watched, were drawn by the newer, younger shows like *All My Children*. Some teenagers as well watched the soaps after school, and their numbers were increasing. Also, a soap fad had caught on in the colleges. The diminishing age of the audience delighted networks and sponsors: younger people buy more soap for their new families and generally consume more goods. Younger people also have many more years ahead in which to become loyal fans of their favorite shows.

In the seventies most soaps dealt with this pleasant surprise by doctoring their story lines a bit and adding a few young characters. They were written mainly by writers whose sympathies were with the

Return to Peyton Place *made its "return" in 1972 on NBC. It was a daytime continuation of the popular nighttime series, and even featured some of the original players. The story of sexual frustrations in a small town offended some viewers, but it reflected the public's growing desire for franker soaps. Attending the wedding of Dr. Michael Rossi and Selena Cross were (from left): Joe Gallison (as Steven Cord), Ron Russell (Norman Harrington), Yale Summers (Rodney Harrington), Guy Stockwell (Dr. Michael Rossi), Margaret Mason (Selena) and Julie Parrish (Betty Harrington).*

older characters. What was wrong with this approach, as time would reveal, was that the nature of the soaps themselves was not changing nearly enough to accommodate this powerful new audience.

A great cataclysm suddenly shook the soap world in 1978. ABC was getting ready to cancel *General Hospital*, which had become so slow and worn out that it was at the bottom of the Nielsens. In a final maneuver to save the show, the network expanded it to an hour, hired Gloria Monty as producer and former *Doctors* head writer Douglas Marland as writer. Marland continued the main story lines, but instead of

following the lead of most other head writers and tacking on a few young characters, he took two teenagers already in the story and put their romance "on the front burner"; that is, he made their story more important than any other. Meanwhile, producer Gloria Monty speeded up the pace of scenes, so that the entire production began to have a nighttime television feel. She began calling for elaborate movie-like setups, such as crowd scenes and location shootings. The network held its breath. Within a few months the ratings leaped. The Laura Vining-Scotty Baldwin love story was all the rage among teenage viewers. After a

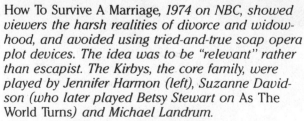

How To Survive A Marriage, *1974 on NBC, showed viewers the harsh realities of divorce and widowhood, and avoided using tried-and-true soap opera plot devices. The idea was to be "relevant" rather than escapist. The Kirbys, the core family, were played by Jennifer Harmon (left), Suzanne Davidson (who later played Betsy Stewart on* As The World Turns) *and Michael Landrum.*

Lovers and Friends, *1977, was about the interrelationships of two families, the rich Cushings and the middle-class Saxtons, in a wealthy Chicago suburb. Written by Harding Lemay, the NBC soap had fine characterizations but became bogged down in expository dialogue in its first few months. Procter & Gamble, after giving the show a second try with a new title,* For Richer, For Poorer, *withdrew it in 1978. Richard Backus, Vicky Dawson (center), and Patricia Englund played Jason, Tessa and Josie Saxton.*

year the show was top-rated and eventually, during its two-year Luke and Laura love story which swept the whole country, *General Hospital* became number one. A great watershed had just been passed. (See the backstage story of *General Hospital*, which begins on page 00.)

Every other soap quickly felt the impact. The message was sharp and clear. Some shows responded timidly by casting Luke-and-Laura look-alikes, adding characters rather than revamping the major focus. However, a number of soaps, including *All My Children* and *The Young and The Restless*, immediately began long-term major stories involving teenagers who were appealing, three-dimensional and as well conceived as the older characters—stories capable of holding teenage viewers over a period of years.

Doug Marland's portrait of the Laura Vining character caused an important new trend, whose end is still not in sight. Laura was a teenager who was allowed to have as elaborate a sex life as any older character and who was portrayed as having affairs with older, more experienced men. The stunning moral implications of presenting such a story did not create the kind of censorship problems that networks imagined. After Laura, a number of soaps began stories of teenagers sexually involved with much older adults. These were essentially teenage fantasies, just as *The Romance of Helen Trent* had been a house-wife's fantasy.

The era of the eighties soap world had clearly begun. The new trend wasn't simply a continuation of the decade-old youth trend of the seventies, but a new way of seeing and portraying young people, and appealing directly to their psyches. The new paths of the present also involved elaborate production values, similar to nighttime television shows (but still much cheaper), all paid for by the added advertising revenues generated by the new audience. Expensive location sequences in places like Hong Kong, Spain and Jamaica became commonplace.

Procter & Gamble expanded *Another World* once again, in March 1979, this time to ninety minutes. Since the show's ratings had been unimpressive before the change, the decision seemed perverse; but so had Fred Silverman's decision to expand *General Hospital* to an hour when it was on the brink of cancellation. *The Guiding Light* also fared much better as an hour show. Such reasoning notwithstanding, the

new ninety-minute *Another World* became an un-wieldy daymare. Head writer Harding Lemay found it virtually impossible to keep five stories going simultaneously, with twenty actors on screen every day, and still hold viewers' interest. As the show became harder and harder to follow, the Nielsens dropped and Lemay gladly gave his task to other writers, who fared no better. While *Another World* continued to suffer, P&G launched a spinoff soap in 1980, *Texas*, and soon after brought *Another World* back to its hour format, ending the ninety-minute notion for a while. *Texas* was all about Iris Carrington, who had left Bay

Texas, *1980, was another spinoff soap from* Another World, *with that show's star, Beverlee McKinsey, as Iris, who suddenly moves to Houston to marry wealthy Alex Wheeler and begin a new life. The new P&G soap lasted two and a half years. Members of Iris Wheeler's new family included (from left): Lily Barnstone (as Lacey Wheeler), Gretchen Oehler (Vivien Gorrow), Jim Poyner (Dennis Carrington) and, to the right of Beverlee McKinsey, Donald May (Grant Wheeler).*

City to live and marry in Houston, where she soon became involved with her new husband's family and friends. The sponsor had hoped that Beverlee McKinsey, whom viewers had loved on *Another World* as Iris, would create audience interest in the new show. In fact, there was very little audience interest; the ratings of the NBC shows before and after it weren't high enough to give the new soap a good start. The show was canceled late in 1982.

During the early period of *General Hospital*'s miraculous rating turnabout, ABC poured much money into its soaps, promoting them more heavily than any network had ever done in the past. Since ABC, unlike CBS and NBC, owned all its soaps except *The Edge of Night* (a P&G show; CBS and NBC own none), it was able to quickly upgrade all of its shows to catch the spillover of *General Hospital*'s huge new teenage audience. *All My Children*, still with Agnes Nixon as head writer, experienced a profound change. A good show, but one with flaws, turned into one of the best written dramas in all of television. Mrs. Nixon not only installed a major young story line, but wrote in fascinating Dickensian characters, like Opal Gardner (played by Dorothy Lyman, who won an Emmy), and Langley Wallingford. Group scenes were wonderfully directed. Under Mrs. Nixon's guidance, *All My Children* became consistently top-rated, creating for ABC an afternoon drama block so strong that its advertising revenues doubled that of CBS's.

ABC led the daytime movement in other ways. Like the old Hollywood movie studios, it began a talent development program, encouraging gifted young actors to take roles in ABC soaps, for possible later transfer to prime-time shows. In the past, soaps (like *Another World*) had experienced a drastic turnover in its young actors, who were frightened of becoming too comfortable on daytime and quickly fled to Hollywood. With ABC's new approach, there was less reason for young actors to fear being lost in the medium.

Procter & Gamble did not give up its many years of soap opera leadership to ABC without a brilliant fight. It matched ABC dollar for dollar and kept its time-tested success, *As The World Turns*, in the top three. Head writers Bridget and Jerome Dobson kept it dramatically unified during their regimes in the early 1980's, managing not to jar loyal viewers with the many new sequences focusing on Young Love. Similarly, P&G's *Guiding Light* has entered the eighties

with a smooth new razzmatazz look under the helm of Doug Marland. The show's new logo tells it all; a carnival montage of quickly changing clips: one showing a fight, one showing a horrible screaming death, one of smiling Bert Bauer and so on. It's as if *Guiding Light* were telling its audience: "We're new, we're fast, we're exciting . . . but we also have the Bauer family you've loved for years." Contrast that logo with *Days Of Our Lives*'s opening hourglass shot, with Macdonald Carey's voice intoning as always, "Like sands through the hourglass, so these are the days of our lives." It's as if *Days* were likewise telling its fans: "We're the same show you've always loved and relied upon." Viewers are now being confronted with both messages from old, beloved shows in a modern environment that has turned fast-moving, slick and highly dangerous to survival.

The network whose afternoon dramas seem to be in a somewhat precarious position is NBC. After *The Doctors* was canceled late in 1982, the network did not announce plans to replace it with another serial. Among its few remaining soaps are P&G's *Another World* and *Search for Tomorrow*, which was switched to NBC in 1981; both have been in trouble for several years, although *Another World* has a history of being able to fight its way back from disastrous Nielsens. Some executives at NBC have indicated that the network may not be willing to compete with the other two networks' soap operas, but may in the future put more emphasis on other kinds of afternoon fare.

Among the very newest soaps on the airwaves is *Capitol*, which premiered on CBS in March 1982, a story about two warring Washington matriarchs and the romances of their politically ambitious sons. Produced by John Conboy, who had helped give *The Young and The Restless* its dressed-to-the-nines look, *Capitol* has been faring well with viewers. In June 1983, there was much ado at ABC about its new soap, *Loving*, co-written by none other than Agnes Nixon herself and Doug Marland, whose writing of *General Hospital* from 1978 to 1980 helped make that show a legend. *Loving* had to do with lots of what the title suggested, and of the youngest kind. There was also much talk around the network of Gloria Monty doing a spinoff of *General Hospital* itself, called *The Young Loves of General Hospital*.

As the soap world enters its fifty-fourth year, its future seems bright, with clear byways leading forward in several directions. Cable TV seems to have discovered soap opera and has adapted it to a serialized form of its own. (Although serials like Showtime's *Loving Friends and Perfect Couples* are not true soaps because they lack the same emotional appeal, they nevertheless presage a future growth of the form on cable TV. In the future we may also see more of the past. Interest in this popular kind of entertainment has been mounting, while a number of college teachers, students, researchers and other academics have grown interested in a serious study of soap opera history. We are sure to see more college courses, books, articles and television programs on the subject. Also, the actual structure of daytime drama could change. The success of Gloria Monty's *General Hospital* has proven that soaps do not have to concentrate on one or two families to do well, but can have other sorts of stories, as long as they remain about love and strong relationships. It is even remotely possible that sex alone may dominate soap operas to the exclusion of family life. But the Irna Phillips brand of classical soap opera, featuring families, so pervades the form, fulfilling so many of viewers' deepest needs for stronger ties with parents and other relatives, that there will probably never be a wholesale deviation from her kind of show, even though all the externals may change. Soap operas, after all, are, and will always be, not about mere momentary needs but the joys and sorrows of long-term involvements with others.

SEX IN THE SOAPS

SOMETHING odd happened one afternoon in 1948. During what seemed an ordinary broadcast of *The Romance of Helen Trent*, Gil Whitney once again pleaded for the tender but unattainable love of Helen. He had been trying for more than a decade (and would continue trying for yet another) to convince the woman he worshipped to walk down the aisle. As usual Helen responded with bewildered and reluctant sighs. "Ah, for chrissakes, lay the dame and get it over with!" came another voice right on the air. A man— perhaps some unwitting technician?—began giving specific advice on what Gil should do to Helen, with no graphic terms spared. Millions of housewives were listening. In shock, CBS control booth personnel frantically tried to track down the origin of the advice giver's voice on the complicated Round Robin system, but with no success. The expletives continued.

Radio soap star Mary Jane Higby told this story in her entertaining biography, *Tune In Tomorrow*. After Helen's hermetically sealed off world of virginal romance had been violated by a member of the male sex there were surprisingly few protests from presumably easily offended housewives. One can only guess that listeners refused to verbally acknowledge even a hint of the truth that they implicitly understood: the last thing their favorite dressmaker wanted was to get in the sack with any man.

The Romance of Helen Trent was one of dozens of Hummert daytime fantasies which were designed to exclude sex from romance. The unmarried hero-ines, like Helen and Ellen Brown (of *Young Widder Brown*), found every excuse to avoid the marriage bed, or the writers would invent sudden plot events to help them avoid it, while a sexless romance pervaded their lives with a dreamlike quality. The married Hummert heroines, such as Sunday, Mary Noble and Laurel Grosvenor (*Stella Dallas*), spent a good deal of their time trying to prove to their mates that they hadn't had improper relations with other men. The nature of their own love lives with their husbands was left quite unspecific. For all of these afternoon ladies, sex was one of the major threats to their happiness.

On other radio soap operas, such as those by Irna Phillips and Elaine Carrington, family life was stressed more than romantic fantasy. Female characters were allowed to marry, become pregnant and even, in the stories of the late forties, divorce their husbands. The progressive Irna Phillips had Meta Bauer, of *The Guiding Light*, have an illegitimate child by Ted White. But that was a cautionary tale with a negative message about the effects of loose living. None of the events on these family soaps were in the least bit provocative, and all occurred within the serious framework of family relationships.

Intercourse, when it occurred on certain radio dramas of the thirties and forties, could only be surmised by a resulting pregnancy, but did not exist as an event in the story. The rare prolonged kiss was as far as writers would go.

There had always been a great disparity between

the content of movies and novels, and radio soaps. When Clark Gable was trying to be proper by putting up "the walls of Jericho" between his bed and Claudette Colbert's in the 1934 film *It Happened One Night*, there was no equivalent urbanity in the afternoon. By 1946, when moviegoers watched Lana Turner and John Garfield act out James M. Cain's explicit drama of desperate clinches, *The Postman Always Rings Twice*, the daytime airwaves were still dominated by those harmless Hummert romances, which seemed to have come out of a time capsule. Daytime audiences were ready for more sex in soaps.

It came, of course, on television. Raymond William Stedman, in his well-researched book *The Serials*, observes: "On the same day that Helen Trent was resisting the advances of Kurt Bonine, [the character] Vicky Harcourt, on TV's *Love of Life*, was teasing a producer into giving her a part by touching the top button of her blouse and laughingly threatening to 'call for help and say you were molesting me.'" After network television soaps began in 1950, radio soap heroines began to look like cloistered mother superiors in comparison with their visual counterparts. But Stedman's example is a bit misleading. In the early fifties there may have been a few Vicky Harcourts on daytime soaps, but by and large the writers were extremely circumspect about erotic content. On *Love of Life*, for example, the only character who was permitted to have a continuing story line which involved sexual behavior was Meg, the bad sister. Meg's affairs with underworld paramours like Miles Pardee were suggested by chitchat over a few quick drinks, some provocative smiles, a dance or two, a light kiss. The affair was established in conversations between Meg and Van or other characters.

While Meg was merely drinking and chatting and barely kissing, Burt Lancaster and Deborah Kerr were wound around each other's bodies in the famous 1953 bathing suit scene in *From Here To Eternity*. Soaps were making progress, but they were still light years away from the permissiveness of movies. But so were nighttime programs, which were controlled in the early days by an extreme industry-wide attitude of self-censorship. Moreover, people in the fifties were ambivalent about sex. A big part of the adult population was still recoiling from the results of the Kinsey Reports, especially the idea in *Sexuality In The Human Female* that women had almost as much premarital and extramarital intercourse as men. At the same time, young people were beginning to experiment with promiscuous behavior. Soap opera viewers then, and for a decade following, were housewives over thirty. In such an environment the only safe route for sponsors was to present sex from the point of view of the conservative older viewer. What she wanted was reinforcement of the sanctity of her family role in a world of rapidly shifting moral values.

These days soaps are so ruled by the goddess of love that it may be hard for some young people to imagine the soap operas of the fifties. Romance was important, but it did not control story structure. *Search for Tomorrow*'s Joanne and Arthur Tate were in love, but the story in the early years had to do with the mob's attempt to take over the Motor Haven by discrediting her. Vanessa on *Love of Life* likewise loved Paul Raven, but was preoccupied by the exploits of her corrupt sister and the sudden appearance of Paul's ex-wife. Both shows used crime melodrama, not romance, to move the story. The heroines, in fact, put off their sex lives for the greater good of their families. Viewers were not encouraged to see them as sexual women.

Irna Phillips was already beginning to change things on *The Guiding Light*, which was now (1952) broadcast on television as well as radio. In the tale of Kathy Roberts, she portrayed a young woman who suddenly found herself pregnant by a dead husband, then married Dr. Dick Grant without telling him about the baby. When he discovered the truth, he divorced her. The story was tame, but was one of the first to use pregnancy as a symbol for a woman's sexual behavior. What the characters were really worried about was the completeness of a woman's commitment to her new marriage bed.

In 1956 Irna caused afternoon eyebrows to raise with her story of Aunt Edith, the "other woman" on the new *As The World Turns*. Irna had unhappily married Jim Lowell begin an affair with Edith Hughes, and was planning to have Jim divorce his wife to marry his lover when the conservative sponsor stopped the story. But the genie was already out of the bottle. Writers were dying to write such stories; audiences were eager for them. A year later *Search for Tomorrow* introduced Jo's sister, Eunice Gardner, who seduced Jo's husband, Arthur Tate. The tale was deliberately made brief to test the waters; but soon the theme of the infidelity of weak husbands came regularly to Henderson and replaced the show's old melodramas.

Other shows did similar things, although actual affairs between a husband or wife and an outsider were kept minimal and the outsider was always quickly disposed of.

In the late fifties daytime serials were becoming preliminary introductions to the Kinsey Reports, at least the parts that would interest women. New soaps that ignored the famous sex researcher died terrible deaths. But afternoon fare was still quite mild compared with what was now beginning to happen in novels and movies. All the indecision over Kinsey was resolving in movies like *Freud*, 1961, which told of the unconscious sexual preoccupation of all humans; *Peyton Place*, 1957, which mired a small New England town in one sexual scandal after another; *Suddenly Last Summer*, 1959, about all manner of perversions committed by a homosexual poet, using insectivorous plants, savage birds and young boys as erotic images. James Gould Cozzens's *By Love Possessed* and Sloan Wilson's *A Summer Place* were novels that told readers all about the obsessive sexual nature of people in modern society. The movies made from those books revealed the well-kept secret that teenagers also had complex sex lives.

Much of this frankness was reflected in the soap world of the sixties. Those early brief stories of unfaithfulness developed into the most important soap opera invention of the decade: the love triangle.

The love triangle, as used by soap opera writers in the middle of the decade, was a special sort. It always involved an unwanted pregnancy and a marriage to an unloved partner. There were such story lines on almost every serial: Steve-Rachel-Alice, 1967, on *Another World*; Susan-David Martin-Julie, 1966, and Mickey-Laura-Bill, 1967, on *Days of Our Lives*; Dan Stewart-Susan-Elizabeth Talbot, 1969, on *As The World Turns*; and Mike-Leslie-Ed, 1967, on *The Guiding Light*. In all of these stories, there was a complex arrangement of one person loving another but unable to marry that person because of a pregnancy and the secret of paternity. The soaps had sporadically used love triangles in the late fifties and early sixties, but not nearly as successfully as this type. The big change was that by the mid-sixties writers were permitted to use illegitimate pregnancy as the focus of the triangle, which created added interest and gave stories long-term appeal. A seven-year war among three or four characters, with an illegitimate child (or one not knowing his real father) at the center, was common.

These stories don't need much analysis, except to say the obvious, that extramarital or premarital sex between two characters had started them. Under certain circumstances, viewers were told by their soaps, good people can find emotional/sexual fulfillment with compatible partners, even if it means breaking some of the rules. But viewers were warned that if those rules were broken, there would always be lasting heartaches. It was Kinsey interpreted by a reasonable though ultimately moralistic mind.

The social tensions of the sixties had crept into the soaps and affected the way they portrayed sex. The Gil Whitneys had long since disappeared from daytime. Heroines were suffering rape and violence. On *General Hospital* Jessie became pregnant after being raped by her unfaithful younger husband. Laura Horton on *Days of Our Lives* was raped and made pregnant by her brother-in-law Bill Horton. Interestingly, these women were not secretaries attacked by strangers as they walked home from work, but professional women (a nurse and a psychiatrist) attacked by professional men (doctors) whom they really loved—a convoluted interpretation of the dangerous times in which viewers lived. (Some years later *The Young and The Restless* featured major story lines about young women who were raped by strangers.)

The seventies explored and deepened the intricacies of the love triangle, or quadrangle, for often a fourth person was involved. One of the most interesting quadrangles occurred on *The Young and The Restless* in 1978. Leslie, abandoned by her husband Brad, had relations with Lance, who eventually married Leslie's sister Laurie. Leslie became pregnant by Lance, but married Lance's brother Lucas, even though she loved Lance. There were many variations of this kind of story.

But by the seventies, while the love triangle dominated story structure, the psychology of sex on the soaps was once again moving forward. Moviegoers were flocking to see nudity in movies like *Last Tango In Paris*, 1973, and daytime viewers watched love scenes between attractive young men and women who were sometimes partly undressed. The message now was that sex was not only a serious, isolated phenomenon which caused years of heartache when the rules of sex were broken, but one of the pleasures of life. Viewers were encouraged to see young people in a sexual way. Eroticism had come to daytime. By the late seventies no soap dared not have it.

Viewers of the serials of the fifties wouldn't recognize today's soaps as soaps, partly because the sexual point of view has changed so drastically. Afternoon drama used to be a haven for older housewives from the wrenching uncertainties of human relationships, from Kinsey and from what the movies were beginning to present. In the present afternoon environment, the sexuality and sensuality of young people must co-exist with the libidos of older characters. A recent study in the *Journal of Communications* by Bradley Greenberg confirmed what everyone was beginning to suspect, that there is now more sex in the daytime than on nighttime television—at least two "intimate sexual acts" per hour. He found a great emphasis on "heavy petting" between unmarried people, which is what Burt Lancaster and Deborah Kerr were doing in that beach scene in *From Here To Eternity*. And there is as much heavy petting on soaps as on celluloid.

Until recently, Procter & Gamble, which owns five network soap operas, had an unbreakable rule that unmarried people could never be shown in bed—even though a story might imply that two unmarried people have had relations. The sponsor also expected that all of its performers use modesty and discretion when appearing in other media. All or most of those caveats have gone by the wayside. Every soap now has beds populated mainly by unmarried people. When several P&G actresses (one from *As The World Turns*) posed nearly nude for a magazine layout, executives gnashed teeth but did not retaliate. As Bob Short, head of Procter & Gamble Productions, said with a frustrated sigh: "What can you do? Everything's changed."

Permissive as they are, daytime dramas still hesitate to get into certain areas, such as homosexuality.

Two shows, *The Young and The Restless* and *Days of Our Lives*, began story lines about lesbianism but quickly aborted them. Harding Lemay tried to introduce daytime's first story about a male homosexual around 1977 on *Another World*. He had planned to have young Michael Randolph return home from college and announce to his parents, John and Pat Randolph, that he was gay. Lemay was going to keep Michael's lover away from Bay City to avoid the problems the love scenes might cause. Procter & Gamble became fearful and refused to approve the story. But a few years later, *Dynasty*, one of those nighttime "soap operas" that have based their continuing story lines on the techniques of daytime dramas, told the story of young Steven Carrington, who announced to his wealthy father Blake Carrington that he was in love with a man. For two years *Dynasty*'s ratings have soared as gay Steven has fought the Punic wars with his homophobic father. In late summer 1983, Blake was planning to sue Steven for custody of Steven's son, based on Blake's hardened belief that a homosexual man should not raise a child.

When daytime writers begin to exhaust their conventional love triangles and quadrangles, it is more than probable they will turn to similar stories. They will likely turn to many other untapped areas as well. They have already, for example, explored teenage sexuality, used prostitutes and pornographers, sold their young characters into white slavery, given a pretty young girl a venereal disease, suggested a bondage-humiliation situation between a husband and his wife's lover, and portrayed a murderous drag queen. What will they do next? And what would Helen and Sunday and Mary and Stella say about all those "intimate sex acts" per hour? That is, if they are even still speaking to us.

Part Two

CURRENT SOAP OPERAS: BACKGROUNDS AND COMPLETE PLOT SUMMARIES

INTRODUCTION

BECOMING a new viewer of a soap opera has its problems. It's a little like walking into a movie theater in the middle of a feature that has thirty characters and four simultaneous plots. References are made to strange people and unknown past events. You hear (hypothetical) dialogue like: "Betsy is angry with Kim. If Kim were Betsy's natural mother, she couldn't have been a better parent. But it's been hard—with the deaths of first Dan, then Nick. Kim believed she was doing the right thing by discouraging Betsy's relationship with Steve." The kind of background required to understand this recap information (How did the relationship between Betsy and Kim come about? Who are Dan and Nick? How did they die? Who were Betsy's real parents?) might take the new viewer many months to acquire, if ever.

Long-term regular viewers have an advantage over recent converts not only because they are more familiar with current story lines but because their recollections of past events in the story add greater richness to their viewing pleasure. That is in fact the appeal of any serial. When Ellen Stewart on *As The World Turns* was recently accused of murdering John Dixon, millions of the show's fans recalled the time many years ago when she stood trial for killing her housekeeper. The effect was a kind of *déjà vu*. On *Ryan's Hope* the writers deliberately invoked this effect by putting Frank, Jill, Seneca and Delia in a repeat of an original love quadrangle, reminding viewers of the show's early years. Most soaps have romantic story lines involving young adults who are the children of characters who played out dramas of their own in preceding decades. The new stories therefore remind viewers of the old ones. There is a satisfying generational continuity.

This section is meant as a briefing for serial viewers—new or old—on the stories and backstage histories of the various current daytime dramas. There are also complete chronological cast and credit lists, which begin on a soap's premiere date and become progressively more recent, rounding out the picture of what came before. An asterisk (*) next to an actor's name indicates that he played his part longer than any other actor. The (P) next to a name indicates that the performer was in the premiere cast. The actors' names under each role are arranged chronologically. The term "Packager" is an old term, which indicates the company ultimately responsible for the production and content of each show.

In the summaries of story lines, all the attention is on major plots and characters, while untold numbers of short-term subplots have been eliminated for brevity. Also, a warning. The summaries are only that; they are not meant to reveal the stories in complete detail or in the exact order in which plot points were made. A year's complex story line involving a group of characters may be boiled down to a few lines and may appear in a discussion of other story line events which took place at a different time and in a different order. The true purpose of these summaries is to provide helpful backgrounds, not to become a substitute for day-to-day viewing.

The summaries are up-to-date as of July 1983. For supplementary updates, the author highly recommends that the reader consult monthly issues of Soap Opera Digest or Soap Opera World.

One can write volumes about the story lines: how they changed from decade to decade (see the *Love of Life* and *The Secret Storm* summaries in the next part); how they reflected either the mores of the times in which they were written *or* the mores of the group of viewers to whom they were aimed; how, in a disguised way, they told the story of women's progress in our society. Some of these ideas have already been discussed. There are many other observations one could make. One example: note the numerous stories that deal with the phenomenon of amnesia, and also the stories about twins and the sudden appearance of a previously unknown relative. All of these seemingly different story twists actually have a similar psychological function. They are fantasies of identity change. When Leslie on *The Young and The Restless* lost her memory and wandered off to another town, where the handsome owner of a lowlife tavern fell in love with her, the fantasy of identity change was much the same as in Marco Dane's saga on *One Life To Live*. Marco was a vicious pimp who later, as penance for causing the death of his twin doctor-brother, took his dead brother's identity and began practicing medicine. In both stories, as in many others going back to the first years of the radio soaps, characters became different people, satisfying an ancient desire in all of us. Such stories began in the Great Depression years, when many people longed to escape the harsh reality of the times.

Brian Rose, in an article in *Journal of Communication* (see bibliography), makes the point that most soap opera stories revolve around secrecy, but of a special kind. The audience almost always knows the secret that only one or two of the characters know. As the plot unfolds, more and more characters discover the secret, creating a dramatic change in their relationships. These days, the secrets are often ones involving pregnancy and parentage.

One point about the summaries: they will often reveal a kind of theme for each show, which may not be apparent to new viewers. All soap operas begin their lives *about* something, even if only a philosophy or a way of looking at life. The backgrounds preceding each summary offer historical details that elucidate the themes. It is extremely helpful to know how Irna Phillips created *As the World Turns* and *Another World*, and how the story lines of each show reflected their creator's attitude toward her audience. It also helps to know that William Bell created brilliant fantasies for *Days of Our Lives* before inventing *The Young and The Restless*, which had very different story lines but, in the end, a related philosophy; that *Days of Our Lives* originally came from the mind and career of Ted Corday, who for years had a close working relationship with Irna Phillips. One can still sense some of the early *Days of Our Lives* in today's show.

The idea behind the following section is to bring soap opera's past into the present. Using the plot summaries, you should be able to unravel the existing complex relationships that are the basis of all the daytime dramas: how Phoebe Tyler came to rub so many people the wrong way on *All My Children*; why Mike Bauer and Alan Spaulding on *Guiding Light* have often been at each other's throats in the past; what past desperate situation between Monica and Lesley on *General Hospital* now causes them to stay at arm's length; what events on the same show brought about Scotty's perpetual meanness; how Mac and Rachel married and divorced two times on *Another World*; how the entire Matthews clan of Bay City disappeared around Liz Matthews; what biographical details account for beautiful Julie Williams's frequent bouts with insecurity, despite the deep love of her husband Doug on *Days of Our Lives*. In other words, you can walk into the theater, in the middle of the movie, and not feel quite as lost.

ALL MY CHILDREN

SOAP opera is not a literary medium as the theater often is, but a class in playwriting could benefit from a study of selected episodes of *All My Children*. Fourteen years after its premiere, *All My Children* still has many of the same core characters: Ruth and Joe Martin, Phoebe Tyler, Erica, her mother Mona. But the show's creator and guiding force, Agnes Nixon, now surrounds them with an array of characters that are not at all the usual television types and nothing less than marvelous. Often they are pure Dickensian, such as Opal Gardner and Langley Wallingford; or British theatrical, such as Palmer and Daisy Cortlandt; or tongue-in-cheek, like the late Ray Gardner. The show's directors combine them all into beautiful ensemble scenes, with a bigger-than-life feel that remind one of sophisticated theater. One clearly sees why *All My Children* frequently comes in top rated, and why it may well be the best written of all daytime dramas.

BACKGROUND

All My Children officially began on January 5, 1970, but it actually started years before in the mind of Agnes Eckhardt Nixon. This extraordinary woman had been raised in Nashville, of Dutch-Irish parentage, and later attended Northwestern University, where she majored in drama with such later luminaries of the screen as Patricia Neal and Charlton Heston. Agnes Eckhardt was so determined to become a writer that her father, after she graduated Northwestern in 1946, set up a meeting in Chicago between his daughter and the era's most celebrated writer of daytime drama, Irna Phillips. Mr. Eckhardt, who had wanted his daughter to join his burial garment business, was half-hoping that Irna Phillips would turn his daughter down, but instead she hired the talented and pretty Agnes on the spot to write dialogue for her established radio soap, *Woman In White*.

Agnes got along well with the great writer but after six months felt the need to move away from Chicago to New York, where she began writing for the live television shows of what we now call "The Golden Age": *Studio One*, *Philco Theater* and *Robert Montgomery Presents*. She also wrote the first scripts for Roy Winsor's *Search for Tomorrow*. After she married Chrysler executive Bob Nixon and began raising a family in Philadelphia, Irna Phillips contacted her from Chicago and asked her to do dialogue for *The Guiding Light*, which had just gone to television. Before long Agnes became that show's head writer, and later co-writer of Irna's masterpiece, *As the World Turns*, conferring with Irna continually by long-distance telephone.

In 1958, Agnes began her first successful head-writership on *The Guiding Light*, and until the mid-sixties continued to write the dramas created by Irna

Phillips, with great adherence to Irna's concepts and themes. It was surely time for Agnes to begin her own serial and so in her spare time she invented a new show, mostly about young love. The first characters she delineated were older teenagers with the names Tara, Phil and Chuck: friends who were to become involved in a heartbreaking triangle which would shatter a long-standing friendship and enmesh their families in misunderstandings. These young people and their relatives lived in a town Agnes called Pine Valley, which was supposed to be only an hour's drive from New York and was probably patterned after Agnes's own community of Bryn Mawr, Pennsylvania, a posh suburb of Philadelphia. In the original proposal of this show, which Agnes titled *All My Children*, she described Pine Valley as "almost as important in our story as are the characters themselves. A settlement whose roots go deep into prerevolutionary soil, the valley has a distinct personality and charm which affects all who live in or near it."

In 1965 Agnes took the "bible," consisting of the proposal plus five completed scripts, to St. Croix and finished the editing and rewriting process. When she and her family arrived back in Bryn Mawr, tragedy struck: she discovered that the suitcase containing the only copy of her *All My Children* prospectus was missing. She held her breath. After a few days the suitcase turned up. She gave the proposal to Procter & Gamble, whose executives loved the new serial and optioned it, but later said they had to turn it down for lack of air time. It may have been the worst single decision that P&G ever made, not only because *All My Children* would eventually become so popular and famous, but because its theme of Young Love was ahead of its time.

Mrs. Nixon, greatly disappointed, quietly put *All My Children* into a drawer and went on with her writing career. In 1967 her next big success in daytime television came when she replaced Irna Phillips as head writer of Irna's *Another World*, which was failing badly in the Nielsens. Within a short time, Agnes had brought *Another World* into the number two spot (see the background to *Another World* beginning on p. 79), achieving in a mere matter of months what Irna couldn't do for three years. Agnes now had a reputation. ABC, taking advantage of P&G's failure to give Agnes the show she deserved, approached her in 1968 and asked her to create a new serial, which became *One Life to Live*, premiering on July 15 of that year.

Agnes left *Another World* and the Procter & Gamble fold for her new home on ABC.

Some months later, on the heels of Agnes's success with *One Life To Live*, the network asked her to create another serial. At first Agnes was reluctant to give them the proposal to *All My Children*. It had been stashed in a drawer for years and was by now a half-forgotten remnant of a rejected creative effort. It was also a product of Agnes's connection to her more youthful self, possessing an honesty and vulnerability that Agnes was not anxious to see turned down again. But in fact ABC was delighted. The new serial focused on youth and intergenerational problems, which the network had been thinking about for its daytime shows for years.

One only has the highest praise for the way Agnes Nixon performed in the latter part of 1969 during the crush of preparations for the premiere of the new serial right after New Year's Day. With uncanny sensitivity, she chose the actors for the premiere cast, almost perfectly matching their abilities to the parts. Many of them were personally known to Agnes and were all, with one exception, the sort of actors who would not leave their roles at the first sign of restlessness. Mary Fickett, Hugh Franklin, Ruth Warrick and Ray MacDonnell had all had long-term parts on soaps before. Rosemary Prinz was that "one exception." Agnes had known her when she played Penny on *As the World Turns* for eleven years and knew that she had sworn to everyone in the industry that she would never do another serial. But Rosemary was still loved by millions of daytime fans. Agnes offered her a special deal: she could leave the show after six months. Rosemary wanted to play in a Relevant soap, and so Agnes agreed to have her character, Amy Tyler, involved in peace marches and movements to clean up the environment. The two women shook hands on the deal.

During *All My Children*'s critical first six months, the time in which most soaps are made or destroyed, Agnes proved her mastery of daytime drama. Instead of leaving the short-term role of Amy Tyler dangling, as most writers would have done, given the certain departure of the leading player, she carefully made the character the center of several major plots that could exist for years after the character left the show. Agnes Nixon also went out of her way to keep her characters and major plots to a minimum, to draw and intertwine them so carefully that they would warrant longevity. Her previous experience told her which "key" characters to emphasize: the brash male newcomer who provoked all the action, Nick Davis, similar in function to her Steven Frame on *Another World*; the ambitious, trouble-making young girl, Erica, who was originally written as that show's Rachel. But there were many characters, like Ann Martin, her snobbish mother Phoebe Tyler and all the characters in her first Young Love story line, that were simply in Agnes's unused creative repertory. The first year worked beautifully. A study of those early scripts could probably give other writers pointers on how to launch a daytime serial.

Within a few years the show's focus on the problems of Young Love, seen in the context of a real town, real family environments and the occasional use of Relevant topics, such as a beautiful, in-depth handling of a sequence on abortion, brought the show to the attention of young people all over the country. In one of the most surprising outcomes of the soap world of the seventies, college students on many campuses adopted *All My Children* as their own, becoming so infatuated with it that at a number of schools courses on soaps were offered. What college students saw in *All My Children* was a different way of looking at themselves: as members of caring families, as young people involved in old-fashioned, long-term romantic dilemmas rather than as figures in the kaleidoscope of modern-day campus life.

In August 1974, *All My Children* for the first time became the top-rated soap opera, finally bringing ABC's daytime lineup back to a competitive position. Contrary to what has often been written about the show, it does not owe its great success to its use of young characters or frequent stories involving a social message, but to the sheer excellence of its writing. In the early days of the show, most viewers were attracted to Agnes's manner of contrasting rather stable, sympathetic characters, such as Ruth and Joe Martin, with flamboyant near-caricatures, like Phoebe Tyler and Erica Kane. It was a writing technique that had never been seen before in daytime drama. In recent years, Mrs. Nixon has toned down her popular Phoebe Tyler, mellowed Erica and introduced a host of other characters who are far more complex in their theatricality and can appeal to highly intelligent minds. The script changes have coincided with a significant upgrading of production values, including foreign location shootings.

Mrs. Nixon works with head writer Wisner Washam, who has been of great help in establishing the excellence of *All My Children*.

THE STORY

When the story began PHOEBE TYLER (Ruth Warrick) was Pine Valley's prime matriarch, wed to the town's leading physician, DR. CHARLES TYLER (Hugh Franklin). She was a snobbish, wealthy, and often overbearing woman, who was always worrying needlessly about appearances, especially where her children's conduct was concerned. Phoebe, nonetheless, always meant well. Their children were ANN (last played by Gwyn Gilliss) and LINCOLN (last played by Peter White); Charles's grandson, CHUCK (currently Richard Van Vleet), had been living with them ever since he was orphaned in infancy.

The other important family in Pine Valley has DR. JOSEPH MARTIN (Ray MacDonnell) at its head. His wife, Helen, had died and left Dr. Martin a widower with two children, TARA (Karen Gorney played the part the longest) and JEFF (last played by Jim O'Sullivan).

AMY TYLER (originally played by Rosemary Prinz and now out of the story), the serial's first real protagonist, was described in a network press release as a "liberal political activist dedicated to the peace movement, who marries into a conservative family with considerable wealth and stature in the community." Amy married Lincoln Tyler. Phoebe, however, did not approve of Lincoln's marriage to Amy because she was beneath him socially.

Everyone thought that young PHILLIP BRENT (Richard Hatch, Nicholas Benedict) was the son of Amy's sister, nurse RUTH BRENT (Mary Fickett), and her husband TED BRENT (Mark Dawson). However—unbeknownst to the Tylers, to Phillip or to anyone else in Pine Valley—it was revealed, when NICK DAVIS (Larry Keith) first came to town, that Amy was Phillip's real mother. Years before, Amy had had an affair with Nick Davis, now a dancing instructor, and Phillip was born illegitimate. In secret, Amy asked her sister, Ruth, and her brother-in-law, Ted, to adopt Phillip, who grew up believing that the Brents were his real parents.

The newly wealthy Amy kept the secret but ERICA KANE (Susan Lucci), a young and beautiful trouble-maker in Pine Valley, learned the whole story and made sure everyone else in the town found out, including Phillip. Ted, believing Nick to have gone back on his word never to tell Phillip who his real mother and father were, drove toward Nick Davis's place, intending to have it out with him. Instead, Ted crashed his car and was killed, leaving Ruth Brent a widow.

Phillip was horrified by the accident and by the knowledge that "Aunt Amy" and Nick Davis were his real mother and father. As self-protection against all this unhappiness, Phillip's mind rebelled, and he developed amnesia. He wandered off to New York, forgetting his vow of love to his high school sweetheart, Tara Martin.

Everyone's finding out about Phillip so humiliated Amy that she left her husband, Lincoln, and Pine Valley. Ann came back to Pine Valley and together with a friend, SYDNEY SCOTT (Deborah Solomon), opened a chic boutique, which became an instant success. Lincoln, now alone, fell in love with Sydney and followed her to New York.

Ruth Brent, however, didn't have to think twice about accepting Joe Martin's proposal of marriage. Ruth, who had never been happy with her now dead husband, Ted Brent, finally found happiness with Joe.

Beautiful but dangerous Erica Kane set her designing sights on naive but hard working Jeff Martin, a fine young doctor. Jeff succumbed, and they later eloped. When she became pregnant, Erica had a secret abortion, which nearly killed her because she did not consult her doctor when dangerous symptoms later appeared.

By now, Phillip's psychosomatic amnesia had lifted, and he remembered that he had once been in love with Tara. But Tara was still in a state of shock because of the way Phillip had treated her before his amnesia, and she decided to spurn his affections for those of Chuck Tyler.

Ann Tyler, meanwhile, was falling in love with Nick Davis despite her mother's predictable objections to a bottom-of-the-social-ladder dance instruc-

The first six months of All My Children, which began on January 5, 1970, were filled with high drama and stunning revelations, triggered by the sudden appearance in Pine Valley of a mysterious dancing instructor named Nick Davis (Larry Keith). Rich and snobbish Phoebe Tyler (Ruth Warrick) was at first charmed by him.

Amy Tyler (Rosemary Prinz) and her sister Ruth Brent (Mary Fickett) harbored a terrible secret: young Phillip Brent was really Amy's illegitimate son by Nick Davis, and not Ruth's son as everyone supposed. Amy was married to Lincoln, the son of Phoebe Tyler.

tor marrying into her family. Ann and Nick eloped but their happiness, however, was marred by Nick's obsession that he was sterile and could never father Ann's children. Fearing that Ann would discover his inadequacy, he asked her for a divorce. Ann—horrified and feeling that Nick had simply stopped loving her—gave him the divorce. Shortly afterward, Ann learned she was pregnant by Nick—Nick, of course, wasn't sterile—but by the time he found out about Ann's pregnancy, she had already married Joe Martin's younger brother, PAUL MARTIN (William Mooney), a brilliant lawyer. She was fond of Paul, but she didn't love him.

On the day of Tara's wedding to Chuck Tyler—a grand, elaborate affair, in the best tradition of the wealthy Tyler family—there was a melodramatic turn. Before the couple could say "I do," Nick shouted out from the audience that the marriage couldn't take place because Tara still loved his son. Chuck keeled over—not from shock at the announcement, but from a grave kidney affliction.

Chuck went into the hospital, leaving Phillip and Tara to reestablish their old relationship. Because of Chuck, however, they restrained themselves physically—until Phillip was drafted and learned that he was going to Vietnam. No longer willing to keep their relationship platonic, they eloped just two days before Phillip was to leave for the war. A violent snowstorm prevented them from getting to a justice of the peace, so they stopped at a roadside chapel and got "married" by exchanging vows by themselves.

Tara couldn't bring herself to tell Chuck about her union with Phillip. Chuck recovered and Phillip was reported missing in action.

By now Jeff was having serious problems with Erica, who was told by a New York modeling agent, JASON MAXWELL (John Devlin), that she could become a glamorous, successful model in New York. She began making forays from Pine Valley to New York for modeling assignments, and in so doing was slowly destroying her marriage to Jeff. Erica found herself falling in love with Jason Maxwell and the way of life he represented. Jeff turned to MARY KENNICOTT (Susan Blanchard), an attractive nurse who had loved Jeff from afar.

Tara found out that she was pregnant with Phillip's baby and told Chuck, who said he didn't care and still wanted her to marry him. She later gave birth to a baby boy, whom she called Little Phillip.

* * *

Phillip Brent (Richard Hatch) and Tara Martin (Karen Gorney) were in love and planned to marry. When he found out the truth—that his "Aunt Amy," not Ruth—was really his mother, he suffered a breakdown and spurned Tara.

Chuck Tyler (Jack Stauffer), Phoebe's orphaned grandson, offered to marry Tara when Phil rejected her and she accepted, even though she still loved Phil. On the day of Tara and Chuck's wedding, in 1971, he collapsed of a grave kidney infection. Susan Blanchard played nurse Mary Kennicott. The Tara-Chuck-Phil story went on for years and attracted a wide, youthful audience.

Nick Davis, believing he had lost Ann for good, turned to a fellow dancing instructor, KITTY SHEA (Francesca James). They had a brief affair, which ended in Kitty's becoming pregnant. Not wanting to father another illegitimate child, Nick agreed to marry Kitty—especially since Kitty, a self-pitying neurotic woman, had tried to commit suicide when she discovered that Nick was still in love with Ann. Kitty lost the baby and was put under the care of a psychiatrist. Nick vowed that after she was cured he would divorce her and try to get Ann back.

Meanwhile, Erica asked Jeff for a divorce and continued to see Jason Maxwell in New York. Jason, one day, came to Pine Valley, registered in a hotel and then phoned Jeff, asking him to come visit him there that night. Before Jeff arrived, someone murdered Jason. Jeff had to stand trial and was defended expertly by his uncle, Paul Martin. Destructive Erica again made Jeff's situation worse by asking to be paid off by Joe Martin, Jeff's father, in return for telling the jury the truth—that Jeff had harbored no hostility against Jason Maxwell. Erica's mother, MONA KANE (Frances Heflin), and MARGO FLAX (Eileen Letchworth), Erica's friend from New York, were both skeptical of Erica's real motives. In fact, *everyone* soon became suspicious that conniving Erica was the real murderess.

After many agonizing months of the murder trial, Jason's real killer was exposed. Under the influence of sodium pentothol, Mona Kane, Erica's mother, revealed that it was she who shot Jason Maxwell to death! On the night of his death Mona had come to his hotel room to ask him to stop seeing Erica. She wound up struggling with him over a gun left behind by Margo Flax. The gun accidentally went off, killing Jason! Afterward, Mona had blocked the whole incident from her mind. Jeff Martin was freed.

* * *

During all this, Tara was dumbfounded on learning that Phillip, presumed killed in Vietnam, was really alive. When he returned home, he was shocked to learn that his "wife" had married his best friend, Chuck Tyler. Although still deeply in love with her high school sweetheart, Tara decided that, for the

In early 1972, Ruth Brent married Dr. Joe Martin (Ray MacDonnell, center), the father of Tara and Jeff Martin (Charles Frank, second from right). Ken Rabat (second from left) was the original Paul Martin, the younger brother of Joe Martin.

Ann Tyler (Judith Barcroft) had married Nick Davis, divorced him, and then discovered she was pregnant by him. She married lawyer Paul Martin (now William Mooney), even though she still loved Nick. Thus began the show's second major triangle.

good of her baby and for Chuck's sake, she would keep her marriage intact and not tell Phillip that her son was really his son too. Out of loneliness, Phillip allowed himself to be seduced into a minor romance with Erica, who—now that she was losing Jeff to Mary Kennicott—found him irresistible.

When Ann Martin finally learned the truth of why Nick had divorced her—because he thought himself to be sterile—she grew haunted by a mirage of the happiness that they could have had together; soon she was torn between her husband Paul and an ardent Nick. When Ann went on a buying trip for her boutique, Nick pursued her there. Finally Ann realized whom she loved and told Nick, while they were driving back to Pine Valley in a violent snowstorm, that it was Paul. Seconds later the car crashed, and its passengers brought home in critical condition. Nick, who regained consciousness first, lied and led everyone to believe that Ann fully intended to divorce Paul to marry him. Crushed, Paul began seeking comfort in the arms of Margo Flax. Meanwhile, Ann—who was now recovering and thought Paul knew it was he, not Nick, she loved—was dazed by her husband's lack of fidelity, and simply got up from her hospital bed and wandered out of the hospital to parts unknown.

* * *

Despite the warnings of those who cared for him, Phillip persisted in seeing Erica. When she became pregnant with his baby, he did the honorable thing and married her, following her divorce from Jeff. But Phil was still deeply in love with Tara. Erica became unbalanced when she suffered a miscarriage and had to be temporarily committed. Not long after, the secret Tara had been hiding for so long was revealed to Phil. Little Phil was injured and needed a blood transfusion, and when it was Phillip's, not Chuck's, blood type that matched the boy's, Phil finally knew that he was Little Phil's father! Phil forced Tara to admit that she still loved him, and she planned to ask Chuck for a divorce. But Tara, realizing that she simply couldn't hurt Little Phillip by separating him from the only father he had ever known, couldn't go through with it. It was finally Chuck who, upon learning that Tara and Phil had had physical relations, demanded that Tara divorce him. But Tara and Phillip were still kept apart. Erica, newly released from the asylum, was not eager to grant Phil a divorce. Also Little Phil's separation from his "father," Chuck, was causing the boy to suffer asthma attacks, and Tara feared the shock of her remarriage would aggravate the boy's condition.

* * *

Charles Frank and Susan Blanchard played out the ill-fated romance of Jeff Martin and Mary Kennicott, starting in 1972. Erica had seduced him into marriage. After he finally gained his freedom and married Mary, she was murdered by escaped convicts.

Susan Lucci, left, has grown famous in the role of Erica Kane, the beautiful troublemaker of Pine Valley. Her mother, Mona Kane (Frances Heflin, the sister of Van Heflin), has always tried to curb Erica's meanness.

Ann Martin turned up alive and well, residing with her brother, Lincoln Tyler, in Seattle. After both she and Linc came back to Pine Valley—much to everyone's relief—she learned the truth about the misunderstanding between her and Paul that had made her run away in the first place. Before Ann and Paul could talk it out, Margo Flax, frantic to keep her new romance with Paul, went to Ann and convinced her that Paul had finally become happy now that Ann was out of his life. Ann knew that it was true that she had caused him much grief, and decided to divorce him without telling him the truth—*because* she loved Paul so.

Margo, fearing the onset of middle age, secretly went to New York City to have a face lift. When she returned to Pine Valley a younger and far more attractive woman, Paul married her. But Margo, suspecting that she could never replace Ann in her new husband's life, became difficult to live with. When her daughter, CLAUDETTE MONTGOMERY (Paulette Breen,

Susan Plantt Winston), came to Pine Valley, Margo had to keep telling lies to cover up the original one that she had been visiting Claudette (when she had really been having the face lift). Claudette, a schemer, attempted to blackmail her own mother by threatening to tell Paul the truth.

Ann was amazed to learn that she was carrying Paul's child. Reluctant to confront him with the truth, she considered accepting Nick Davis's proposal of marriage. But it was Paul she loved, and when Paul found out about all of Margo's deceptions and demanded a divorce, Paul and Ann made plans to remarry. Driven temporarily insane by the loss of Paul, Margo tried to murder Ann by trapping her in the boutique, which was filled with deadly carbon monoxide from a leaking furnace. But Ann was saved, and Margo left Pine Valley to wed a wealthy plantation owner. At long last, Ann and Paul were wed. Gloom, however, hung over their remarriage when Ann learned that she had toxoplasmosis, a disease that

In 1975, the cast of All My Children *included, from left, back row: Chris Hubbell (Chuck Tyler), Susan Blanchard, Charles Frank, Susan Lucci, John Danelle (Dr. Frank Grant), Ray MacDonnell, Stephanie Braxton (Tara), Hugh Franklin (Dr. Charles Tyler), Ruth Warrick, Peter White, Judith Barcroft, William Mooney, Paulette Breen, Larry Keith, Francesca James. Front row: Eileen Letchworth, Nick Benedict (Phillip), Mary Fickett, Kay Campbell (Kate Martin) and Frances Heflin.*

Lincoln Tyler (Peter White) came back to Pine Valley in 1975, fell in love with Kitty Shea Davis (Francesca James), and planned to marry her against Phoebe's wishes. Kitty later died of a neurological disorder, which so upset viewers that the show brought back Francesca James as Kitty's twin, Kelly Cole.

could have damaged her unborn child. When the child—Beth—did eventually die, Ann and Paul faced the tragedy bravely.

* * *

Jeff Martin, after the ordeal of his murder trial, wed sweet nurse Mary Kennicott. Except for the fact that Mary could not have children because she suffered from a circulatory disorder, she and Jeff had an ideal marriage. Then one day a pair of ruthless ex-convicts broke into their home, holding poor Mary hostage. When little TAD GARDNER, a boy Jeff and Mary considered adopting came to the door, Mary bravely ran to him and told him to run for his life. The boy's life was saved, but Mary was shot by the convicts and later died. Depressed by his overwhelming loss, Jeff Martin left Pine Valley. He returned many months later.

* * *

Ann's brother, Linc Tyler, proposed marriage to Kitty Shea, much to the distress of Phoebe Tyler, since Kitty was socially beneath Lincoln. To thwart the marriage, Phoebe hired a drunken old woman, MYRTLE LUM (Eileen Herlie), to pose as Kitty's long-lost mother, Mrs. Lucy Carpenter. The plan was for Mrs. Lum to tell Kitty that she was ill and lure her away from Pine Valley—and Linc. Briefly taken in, Kitty later learned the truth about Myrtle, who began to think of Kitty as a real daughter, while Kitty returned her affections, much to Phoebe's dismay. Then tragedy struck: it was learned that Kitty was dying of a rare neurological disorder. Linc and Myrtle vowed to make her last months happy ones.

Phoebe simply couldn't bear the loss of the control she'd once had over her family, and was now making grievous errors in judgment—such as her self-destructive scheme with Myrtle. Another error was her insistence that her husband Charles fire his longtime secretary and comforting friend, Mona Kane. When Phoebe finally said, "Either she goes or I go," Charles abruptly moved out of the house and into

Eileen Letchworth, left, played Margo Flax, who wanted Paul and schemed to keep him and Ann apart. To attract him, Margo had a secret facelift done in New York, while in real life the actress had an actual facelift performed. The character's post-operative look was quite genuine.

Robin Strasser, right, played Dr. Christina Karras in 1976 and Lisa Wilkinson was social worker Nancy Grant. Robin left Children *in 1978 to play Dorian Cramer on* One Life to Live.

his club, after suing for divorce. Mona did quit her job, thinking that she was breaking up Charles's marriage, but she and Charles grew closer while he was living apart from Phoebe. When Charles got his divorce, he and Mona married and became a contented pair in Pine Valley. Phoebe turned to liquor.

Chuck Tyler became concerned about a mysterious young patient at Valley Hospital named DONNA BECK (Francesca Poston, Candice Earley), a teenaged prostitute dominated by a black pimp, TYRONE (Roscoe Orman). In trying to get Donna to go straight and break away from Tyrone and the pimp's dangerous henchmen, Chuck put himself in danger. Chuck was obviously feeling more than friendship for Donna. Torn by guilt over what she believed she had done to Chuck's life, Tara began to involve herself with Chuck's problems with Donna, much to Phil's dismay.

It seemed that Erica was getting ready to divorce Phil and he wanted to marry Tara as soon as the divorce came through. But Tara's guilt and Little Phil's asthma were still causing troubles. Tara, who finally came to her senses, married Phil in a beautiful ceremony. Happiness was at last theirs.

After continual arguments over Chuck, Tara and Phillip, Ruth and Joe Martin became estranged. Ruth found herself turning for understanding to a physicians' assistant named DAVID THORNTON (Paul Gleason), who wanted her to move with him to his isolated cabin, where they would know nothing but love. When Joe found out about Ruth's growing attachment to David Thornton, Ruth moved into Jeff Martin's old apartment. Ruth's feelings for David increased when she learned that he was once a doctor but his inability to save the life of his brother made him give up the

Erica's half-brother, Mark Dalton (Mark LaMura), came to Pine Valley in 1977 and had a May-December romance with Ellen Shepherd (Kathleen Noone), the mother of a grown daughter. They each eventually embarked on a rocky marriage.

Phoebe and Dr. Charles Tyler (Hugh Franklin) began having marital problems, mostly concerning her meddling in the lives of everyone around her. After she recovered from a paralysis, Charles divorced her to marry Erica's mother, Mona Kane. Phoebe was scandalized and took to drink.

practice of medicine to become a lowly assistant. But Ruth still loved Joe. After he nearly died of appendicitis she reconciled with him.

* * *

David Thornton, now practicing medicine again, soon found himself growing closer to CHRISTINA KARRAS (Robin Strasser), a new doctor at the hospital who was tormented by strange ESP experiences. David Thornton and Christina Karras were on the verge of marriage when David's ex-wife, EDNA THORNTON (Sandy Gabriel), showed up with their epileptic daughter, DOTTIE THORNTON (Dawn Marie Boyle), and claimed that they were still legally married. So distraught was David over Edna's breaking up his love affair with Christina Karras that he turned maniacal and attempted to poison Edna's wine. Fate tricked

him when their daughter Dottie switched wine glasses, without realizing, and he died—by his own hand. By then Christina Karras had already fallen in love with widower Jeff Martin, but their two-career marriage failed and they left town separately. Edna Thornton also left Pine Valley, after falling in love with Louisiana oil millionaire HANK FERGUSON (Jay Devlin).

Meanwhile, Phoebe Tyler's newly arrived niece, BROOKE ENGLISH (Julia Barr), a brash girl, was torn between a comically rough hoodlum named BENNY SAGO (Larry Fleischman, Vasili Bogazianos) and the late Mary Kennicott's sweet brother, DAN KENNICOTT (Daren Kelly). Benny, who became Phoebe's chauffeur, thought he prized money most of all. But when he met ESTELLE LA TOUR (Kathleen Dezina), Donna Beck's best friend and a former prostitute herself, he realized that it was really love he sought. But Estelle

Erica and ex-athlete Tom Cudahy (Dick Shoberg) honeymooned in 1978 on the island of St. Croix, where actual sequences were filmed. Erica's new career as a model for a cosmetics company brought her wealth and fame but eventually destroyed her marriage.

By 1978, the Chuck-Tara-Phil story was eight years old and nearly played out. Tara (now Nancy Frangione, sitting) finally wed Phil (Nick Benedict, standing). Chuck (Richard Van Vleet) married ex-prostitute Donna Beck (Candice Earley).

was still under the influence of her pimp, BILLY CLYDE TUGGLE (Matthew Cowles), who forced her to marry him. A discouraged Benny briefly married Edna Thornton. Benny, however, continued to love Estelle and when Billy Clyde eventually turned insane, kidnapping and raping poor Estelle, it was Benny who rescued her. After Billy Clyde went to jail, Estelle learned she was carrying his baby. Benny married her anyway and adopted her little girl, EMILY ANN, as his own. Later, Benny and Estelle's marriage was almost destroyed by his newly acquired gambling fever. When that subsided, Benny and Estelle found happiness, but all too briefly, for she was killed in a car accident. Benny had to raise their little girl alone.

* * *

Soon after they reconciled, Ruth and Joe adopted fourteen-year-old Tad Gardner, once again left homeless after Mary Kennicott was killed. It was then that the vicious criminal, RAY GARDNER (Gil Rogers), came to Pine Valley and would become like a figure in a nightmare to the Martins. Ray Gardner, who was Tad's natural father, offered to allow Ruth and Joe to keep Tad in return for money. After the Martins went to the police to press charges against him, Ray raped Ruth out of revenge, then took hostages in a desperate attempt to stay out of prison. When Ray Gardner was finally convicted, he vowed that he would kill Ruth and Joe.

Some months after Kitty Shea died, a woman who looked very much like her, called KELLY COLE (Francesca James), showed up in town. She was Kitty's twin sister! As hard as Kitty was sweet, Kelly Cole sang at the Chateau and was addicted to pills, supplied to her by her corrupt manager, EDDIE DORRANCE (Warren Burton). Naturally Linc was attracted to Kelly, since she was the mirror image of Kitty. Through the power of his love Kelly became sweeter and more lovable. Suddenly, Eddie was found shot to death and Kelly was charged with his murder since her fingerprints were on the gun. But the real killer turned out to be Margo's wayward daughter, Claudette

College student Wally McFadden (Jack McGee) married Devon Shepherd (Tricia Purseley) after he made her pregnant in 1979. They had the sort of serious troubles usually reserved for older characters. She had an extramarital affair and then became an alcoholic.

The 1979 romance between Dr. Cliff Warner (Peter Bergman) and Nina Cortlandt (Taylor Miller) grew extremely popular. Petite Nina's domineering father, Palmer, tried all sorts of tricks to break them up.

Montgomery, who, on her deathbed after an auto accident, confessed that she had been involved with Eddie Dorrance and had murdered him. Kelly was released from jail and married Linc. Eventually the happy couple left Pine Valley.

* * *

After losing Phil to Tara, Erica began seeing Nick Davis. They even set a wedding date, but Nick came to his senses, none too soon, and realized that he could never find happiness with one so self-obsessed. He sold the Chateau to a firm called Unirest and moved to Chicago to work for them. Erica was depressed until she met robust TOM CUDAHY (Dick Shoberg), an ex-football player who was running a restaurant called the Goal Post. They wed and began to run the restaurant together, with Tom, a devout Irish Catholic, hoping to have children with Erica. But she still had hopes of a modeling career. One day, debonair BRANDON KINGSLEY (Michael Minor) spotted Erica in a print ad with Tom and signed her on as the main model for Sensuelle Cosmetics. Seen in television commercials and print ads all over the world, Erica

became a fabulous overnight sensation as a high-fashion model. Tom became deeply upset by her long absences in New York and especially when he discovered that she had been taking birth control pills behind his back. Erica soon divorced Tom to concentrate on the affections of Brandon Kingsley, who said he wanted to marry her, without admitting that he was already married to SARA KINGSLEY (Tudi Wiggins), who lived in Connecticut with their daughter, PAMELA (Kathy Kahmi). However, hardly had Erica fallen into Brandon's arms when she was lured by one with even greater wealth. During a modeling assignment in New Orleans, Erica received luxurious presents, sapphire

Nurse Sybil Thorne (Linda Gibboney) and Sean Cudahy (Alan Dysert) were helping Palmer with his schemes against Nina and Cliff. When Sybil threatened to tell all, Sean killed her and Cliff was tried for her murder.

Monique Jonvil (Gillian Spencer, left) arrived in Pine Valley in 1981 and turned out to be Daisy Cortlandt, Nina's mother, long thought dead. She and wealthy Palmer Cortlandt (James Mitchell) revived their old relationship, even though he was married to Donna Beck. Elizabeth Lawrence played Nina's grandmother, Myra Murdoch.

earrings, a diamond necklace and the like, from a secret admirer, who turned out to be none other than KENT BOGARD (Michael Woods, then Lee Godart). Kent's power-wielding father, LARS BOGARD (Robert Milli), owned an even bigger cosmetics firm than Brandon's. Selfish and opportunistic Erica quickly switched her affections once again to dashing Kent, while Brandon went to Tokyo and reconciled with his wife Sara.

Meanwhile, Erica learned that she had a half-sister on her father's side called SILVER KANE (Deborah Goodrich). At first Silver appeared to be Erica's complete opposite: a mousey type who wore sack dresses and horn-rimmed glasses. Acting as her sister's assistant, she willingly took all sorts of abuse from Erica. But underneath the drab facade there was a raving beauty and a scheming mind. Silver, whose true glamor emerged slowly, began to usurp important modeling assignments from Erica and, worse,

to attract Kent, with whom Erica was madly in love.

* * *

Newly divorced ELLEN SHEPHERD (Kathleen Noone), an attractive fortyish divorcée, came to Pine Valley with her rebellious daughter, DEVON (Tricia Pursley). Ellen became involved with the much younger MARK DALTON (Mark LaMura), a music professor who taught at Pine Valley College. Erica had fallen for Mark until discovering he was her half-brother on her father's side. After surmounting numerous obstacles, including Devon's objections to Mark, Ellen's fear of the social implications of marrying a much younger man and a brief liasion between Ellen and Paul Martin, Ellen accepted Mark's proposal. But, after Mark had a one-night stand with Pamela Kingsley, Ellen separated from Mark.

Her restless daughter Devon became pregnant by a staid, square college student WALLY MC FADDEN (Jack McGee) and entered into a loveless marriage with him for the sake of the baby. Some time after it was born, she met Tom Cudahy's caddish younger brother, SEAN CUDAHY (Alan Dysert), who seduced her into an affair and soon after dropped her like a spent toy, causing Devon to turn to liquor for comfort. But a truer source of comfort turned out to be her husband Wally, who

Famous and glamorous Erica set her sights on rich cosmetics baron Kent Bogard (Lee Godart), but her half-sister, Silver Kane, was also determined to win handsome Kent.

Vasili Bogazianos became the new Benny Sago. He is shown with Robert Morse as gambler Harry in 1982. Benny had fallen in love with ex-prostitute Estelle LaTour, saved her from her pimp, then married her. Just when it seemed that he and Estelle had found happiness, she was tragically killed in an auto accident.

forgave her, helped her quit the bottle and took her and their baby to St. Louis to start a new life.

* * *

A new arrival in Pine Valley was wealthy and meddling PALMER CORTLANDT (James Mitchell), a widower who doted on his fragile, diabetic daughter NINA (Taylor Miller) and harbored secret sexual yearnings toward her. When Nina fell in love with handsome DR. CLIFF WARNER (Peter Bergman), Palmer grew obsessed with keeping them apart. One of his schemes was to convince Nina that she was going blind with her diabetes and that for her to marry Cliff was selfish. When Nina and Cliff finally wed, Palmer refused to accept defeat and conspired with Cliff's old paramour at Pine Valley Hospital, nurse SYBIL THORNE (Linda Gibboney), to name Cliff as the father of her newborn baby. Nina, distraught, left her husband.

Palmer's schemes also helped ruin Chuck and Donna Tyler's marriage, which had been an insecure one from the start. Her background as a teenage prostitute, her childlessness and her fears that Chuck still loved only Tara had caused continual marital frictions. One night, after an argument with Chuck, Donna met Palmer Cortlandt at the Chateau. He was attracted to her youth and the same vulnerability that had enabled him to manipulate his daughter Nina for so many years. Donna was overwhelmed by Palmer's manners and wealth. To win her over, he bought her expensive clothes and jewels and took her to Haiti, all the while convincing her that he could give her the self-respect she could never find with Chuck. Meanwhile, a lonely Chuck began seeing CARRIE SANDERS (Andrea Moar), a sympathetic girl whose father had been a cruel wife-beater. Chuck divorced Donna, who now turned to Palmer completely and married him.

But fate threw Chuck and Donna together again. While Donna and Palmer were on a skiing trip in Switzerland, they ran into Chuck. A quirky accident trapped Donna and Chuck all night in a cave. Fearing they would meet their deaths within hours, they made love. After they were rescued, they vowed not to tell anyone about their night of bliss. Chuck then married Carrie and not long afterward Donna found herself pregnant—by Palmer, she assumed. But Palmer knew

Con man Langley Wallingford (Louis Edmunds) had married Phoebe Tyler for her money but became interested in outspoken Opal Gardner (Dorothy Lyman), who was seriously wanting in some of the social graces. All My Children has become a standout in its proficient use of such roguish characters.

Teen favorites Laurence Lau and Kim Delaney played sweethearts Greg Nelson and Jenny Gardner. Jenny, horrified to learn that her father was a base criminal, couldn't face Greg and ran off to New York. She eventually came back to Pine Valley and Greg.

differently: he was sterile.

Sybil Thorne, the young nurse who was being paid by Palmer Cortlandt to destroy his daughter Nina's marriage to Dr. Cliff Warner, was suddenly found murdered! Cliff, who had every reason to kill Sybil, including the desire to have custody of their illegitimate son BOBBY, was charged with the murder. Cliff was nearly convicted but at the eleventh hour a mysterious newcomer, MONIQUE JONVIL (Gillian Spencer), came forward to confess that she knew the killer: Sean Cudahy. Monique had been having an affair with Sean and learned that he and Sybil Thorne had been friends and had been conspiring with Palmer Cortlandt to break up Nina and Cliff's marriage. Sean, who had been madly in love with Nina's money, was aghast when Sybil threatened to reveal all their schemes to Cliff. Sean only meant to scare Sybil with a gun but accidentally killed her. Monique also confessed that her real name was Daisy Cortlandt, Nina's supposedly dead mother who had been banished to exile in Europe by Palmer years before after he had discovered that she was having an extramarital affair. And MYRA MURDOCH (Elizabeth Lawrence), Palmer's stern housekeeper, turned out to be Daisy's mother! Sean went to prison, Cliff was exonerated, finding happiness once again in Nina's arms, and Palmer Cortlandt was drenched in shame by the public exposure of his deceptions.

* * *

In the worst tragedy ever to hit Pine Valley, Ann Martin was blown to bits by a bomb placed in Paul Martin's car. Paul had been investigating a drug mob and the bomb was meant for him. For months he was stricken by guilt and remorse over Ann's death and, unable to face his memories of Ann in Pine Valley, he accepted a job in Washington, D.C. PEG ENGLISH (Patricia Barry), Brooke's mother, was revealed to be the mob head, but Brooke weathered the storm thanks to her new husband, the understanding Tom Cudahy.

Tara Brent, too, had to face life alone when Phil Brent was suddenly killed in the Caribbean in a helicopter crash. His death was particularly cruel since he and Tara had only just found happiness as a family with Little Phil. In time Tara let go of her grief and married a child psychologist, JIM JEFFERSON (Paul Falzone), who had been treating Little Phil—now called "Charlie"—after his father's untimely death. They all left Pine Valley.

After Ray Gardner went to prison for raping Ruth Martin, his ex-wife, OPAL GARDNER (Dorothy Lyman), came to town with their daughter JENNY (Kim Delaney). Opal, an unsavory and lazy woman, painted her nails while she forced Jenny to work all day to support them. Jenny became best friends with a streetwise black kid called JESSE HUBBARD (Darnell Williams), who was the nephew of Chuck Tyler's friend DR. FRANK GRANT (John Danelle) and his social worker wife, NANCY (Lisa Wilkinson). Having no idea that her father was an ex-convict, Jenny was utterly shocked when he was released from prison and returned to Pine Valley seeking revenge on Ruth and Joe Martin. Jenny had fallen in love with wholesome GREG NELSON (Laurence Lau) but now felt so ashamed upon learning the truth about her father that she broke off with Greg and ran off to New York, although in time she returned to Pine Valley and Greg. Meanwhile, her mother Opal opened a beauty salon called Glamorama. Her maniacal father, Ray Gardner, was at last killed, by a bomb intended for Ruth and Joe Martin.

Phoebe, after a long bout with liquor, met a foppish con man named LANGLEY WALLINGFORD (Louis Edmunds), who pretended to have money along with his manners but was only after hers. Vain and foolish Phoebe succumbed to her loneliness and married him. Predictably, Langley's roving eye soon sought out younger women for liaisons while he gambled away much of Phoebe's wealth. He became particularly attracted to flamboyant Opal Gardner.

* * *

Petite Nina Cortlandt continued to be happy with her new husband, Dr. Cliff Warner, but a new emotional complication arose when her co-worker, wildly handsome lawyer STEVE JACOBI (Dack Rambo), began to spend an inordinate amount of time with her. Nina found herself torn between the comforting love of her husband Cliff and the excitement of Steve. Her father, Palmer, became bored with his wife Donna and sought love in the arms of his ex-wife, Daisy, although his fear of scandal made him keep the affair secret. He also continued to keep from Donna the fact that her baby had to be Chuck's; he wanted another child to carry on his name, and the child was christened, PALMER JOHN CORTLANDT. Donna, still in love with Chuck, was pleased when he offered to be the baby's godfather. Then Phoebe discovered Chuck had fathered the child and told Donna, who by now was on good terms with Phoebe. Donna left Palmer, relieved to be rid of her, and Carrie deserted Chuck and Pine Valley. But only time would tell if Donna and Chuck would at long last find happiness together.

CAST

ALL MY CHILDREN
ABC: January 5, 1970

Ruth Brent Martin	Mary Fickett (P)
Dr. Joe Martin	Ray MacDonnell (P)
Phoebe Tyler Wallingford	Ruth Warrick (P)
Dr. Charles Tyler	Hugh Franklin (P)
Mona Kane Tyler	Frances Heflin (P)
Erica Kane	Susan Lucci (P)
Nick Davis	Lawrence Keith (P)
Amy Tyler	Rosemary Prinz (P)
Lincoln Tyler	James Karen (P)
	Paul DuMont
	Nicholas Pryor
	Peter White*
Anne Tyler Martin	Diana De Vegh (P)
	Joanna Miles
	Judith Barcroft*
	Gwyn Gilliss
Kate Martin	Kate Harrington (P)
	Christine Thomas
	Kay Campbell*
Tara Martin Jefferson . .	Karen Gorney* (P)
	Stephanie Braxton
	Nancy Frangione
	Mary Lynn Blanks
Phillip Brent	Richard Hatch (P)
	Nicholas Benedict*
Dr. Chuck Tyler	Jack Stauffer
	Gregory Chase
	Chris Hubbell
	Richard Van Vleet*
Ted Brent	Mark Dawson (P)
Lois Sloane	Hilda Haynes (P)
Dr. Marcus Polk	Norman Rose*
	John Michael King
	William Roerick
	Bernie McInerney
Sydney Scott	Deborah Steinberg Solomon
Clyde Wheeler	Kevin Conway

	William Ade
Dr. Jeff Martin	Christopher Wines
	Charles Frank*
	Robert Perault
	James O'Sullivan
Paul Martin	Ken Rabat
	William Mooney*
Edie Hoffman	Marilyn Chris
Bill Hoffman	Michael Shannon
Mary Kennicott Martin .	Jacqueline Boslow
	Susan Blanchard*
Margo Flax Martin	Eileen Letchworth
Harry Flax	Biff McGuire
Jason Maxwell	Tom Rosqui
	John Devlin
Kitty Shea Tyler	Francesca James
Tad Gardner	Matthew Anton
	John E. Dunn
Dr. Frank Grant	Don Blakely
	John Danelle*
Nancy Grant	Lisa Wilkinson*
	Avis McCarther
Claudette Montgomery .	Paulette Breen
	Susan Plantt Winston*
Hal Short	Dan Hamilton
Stacey Coles	Maureen Mooney
Wyatt Coles	Bruce Gray
Jamie Coles	Jason Lauve
Caroline Murray Grant .	Patricia Dixon
Dr. David Thornton	Paul Gleason
Dan Kennicott	Daren Kelly
Brooke English Cudahy	Elissa Leeds
	Julia Barr*
	Harriet Hall
Donna Beck Cortlandt .	Francesca Poston
	Candice Earley*
Benny Sago	Larry Fleischman
	Vasili Bogazianos
Estelle LaTour Sago . . .	Kathleen Dezina
Tyrone	Roscoe Orman
Lettie Jean	Delphi Harrington*
	Judith Anna Roberts
Myrtle Lum Fargate	Eileen Herlie
Nigel Fargate	Alexander Scourby
	Sidney Armus
Charlie Brent	Brian Lima
Dr. Christina Karras . . .	Robin Strasser
Mark Dalton	Mark LaMura
Ellen Shepherd Dalton .	Kathleen Noone

Devon Shepherd McFadden	Tricia Pursley Hawkins	Suzanne Robbins	Tracy Fitzpatrick
Harlan Tucker	William Griffis	Nelson Manning	Rudolph Willrich
Maureen Teller	Rosemary Murphy*	Jim Jefferson	Paul Falzone
	Valerie French	Eugenia Robard	Georgann Johnson
Carl Blair	John K. Carroll		Audrey Peters
	Steven James*	Rick Kincaid	Stephen Parr
Tom Cudahy	Richard Shoberg	Melanie Sawyer	Carol McCluer
Edna Thornton Sago	Sandy Gabriel	Jesse Hubbard	Darnell Williams
Dottie Thornton	Dawn Marie Boyle	Opal Gardner	Dorothy Lyman
Billy Clyde Tuggle	Matthew Cowles	Jenny Gardner	Kim Delaney
Ray Gardner	Gil Rogers	Greg Nelson	Laurence Lau
Maggie Flanagan	Paula Trueman	Enid Nelson	Natalie Ross
Kelly Cole Tyler	Francesca James	Liza Colby	Marcy Walker
Eddie Dorrance	Ross Petty	Kent Bogard	Michael Woods
	Warren Burton*		Lee Godart*
Wally McFadden	Jack Magee	Lars Bogard	William Blankenship
	Nigel Reed		Robert Milli*
	Patrick Skelton	Harry	Robert Morse
Aunt Bessie	Minnie Gentry	Judith Sawyer	Gwen Verdon
	Frances Foster	Silver Kane	Debbie Goodrich
Dr. Russ Anderson	David Pendleton	Stephen Jacobi	Dack Rambo
	Charles Brown*	Jasper Sloane	Ronald Drake
Betsy Kennicott	Carla Dragoni	Angie Baxter	Debbi Morgan
Langley Wallingford	Louis Edmonds	Les Baxter	Antonio Fargas
Dr. Cliff Warner	Peter Bergman	Pat Baxter	Lee Chamberlain
Nina Cortlandt Warner	Taylor Miller	Amanda Cousins	Amanda Bearse
Palmer Cortlandt	James Mitchell		
Myra Murdoch	Elizabeth Lawrence		
Sybil Thorne	Linda Gibboney		
Hank Ferguson	Jay Devlin		
Adrian Shepherd	Robert Hover		
Carl Grant	Billy Mack		
Sean Cudahy	Alan Dysert		
Daisy Cortlandt	Gillian Spencer		
Carrie Sanders Tyler	Andrea Moar		
Leora Sanders	Lizbeth MacKay		
Kurt Sanders	William Ferriter		
Jerry Benson	Steve Rankin		
Peg English	Patricia Barry		
Ed English	James Hawthorne		
Brandon Kingsley	Michael Minor		
Sara Kingsley	Tudi Wiggins		
Pamela Kingsley	Kathleen Gene Kamhi		

Creator: Agnes Nixon

Head Writers: Agnes Nixon and Wisner Washam

Executive Producer (first few months): Doris Quinlan

Producers: Bud Kloss, Jorn Winther, Jacqueline Babbin

Directors: Jack Wood, Del Hughes, Henry Kaplan, Jack Coffey, Peter Andrews, Robert Myhrum, Dino Narizzano, Bruce Minnix, Sherrell Hoffman, Jorn Winther, Robert Scinto, Larry Auerbach

Musical Direction: Aeolus Productions, James Reichert, Sid Ramin

Packagers: Creative Horizons, Inc., ABC-TV

P indicates premiere cast member
* indicates longest in role

ANOTHER WORLD

THE backstage history of *Another World*, which has been on television for twenty years, is a veritable adventure story. No other soap opera has had more behind-the-scenes joys and agonies, ratings declines and triumphs, and general turmoil than this show, sponsored by conservative Procter & Gamble. Perhaps the internal agitation has been caused by the fact the *Another World* was initially a failure, then later saved by strong writers, producers and actors, giving the show a certain air of a frontier that could be conquered by only the heartiest and most competitive. Adding to that feeling, the show was produced in a Brooklyn warehouse, miles away from the influence of Manhattan civilization. The show's acting has always been extraordinarily good, but that maverick Brooklyn-warehouse spirit has often led to temperamental flareups and angry flurries between actors and management, or writer and producer, or writer and actors. In the mid-seventies, such disputes not only began to characterize *Another World*'s backstage life, but determined the course of its story lines.

Procter & Gamble, probably quite wisely, has always remained in the background, allowing the battle to rage in Brooklyn, stepping in to make judicious decisions only when absolutely necessary. During most of the seventies, the *Another World* wars led to splendor and excellence, keeping the show removed from the dangers of daytime competition. Late in 1977, it began a prolonged period of decline from which it is only just now beginning to emerge. But declines have happened several times before in its history and the show has always rebounded following a change in dynasty.

BACKGROUND

Irna Phillips came up with the idea for her new soap while she was still writing *As the World Turns*, which was so successful that Irna conceived of her new serial—as yet untitled—as a spin-off. Bay City was supposed to be only a stone's throw from Oakdale; in the original scripts and story outline Irna even had various friends and members of the Hughes family coming to Bay City to visit the Matthews family. Irna had used the spin-off technique once before, on radio, when she created *The Right to Happiness*, based on characters, the Kranskys, who were friends of characters on her already successful *The Guiding Light*.

Although the great sponsor in Cincinnati, P&G, was all for the idea of a sister serial, CBS regretfully had to turn down Irna's brainchild because their afternoon lineup was already full. NBC, in desperate need of better ratings in the daytime, happily took Irna and her new show. Having lured success-infected Irna into their fold, NBC execs saw dollar signs hastily strewn over their late-afternoon soap structure. There was breathless anticipation all over the soap world. Sponsors rushed to their phones to buy time on the presumed new blockbuster.

Irna knew she had to live up to her reputation as the number-one "best-selling" soap-opera author, and wasn't about to take any chances with a prolonged wait for ratings. Although she could no longer link Bay City's new characters with the old Oakdale ones, since the show was to appear on a rival network, she still exploited the success of *As the World Turns* by wryly calling her new show *Another World*. The daily episodes would begin with the announcer briefly telling the philosophy of the program: "We do not live in this world alone but in a thousand other worlds." This was a rather high-sounding rationalization for the initial nature of her program: pure melodrama.

Irna had already planned *Another World* to open with a terrible family tragedy, soon followed by an out-of-wedlock pregnancy, a septic abortion, a murder, a murder trial and a story of young love between a gorgeous orphan and a rich boy thwarted by the villainous mother who tries to break them up. There was not the least hint in these exotic doings of the philosophy of daily living that was typical of all of Irna's other serial creations on radio and television. Irna was totally out of her element with this sort of material. Why did she even consider it? Notes Allen Potter, the first producer of the show: "Irna just didn't want to take a chance on waiting for the ratings. She felt that with this kind of showy story she could build an audience more quickly."

Before the premiere on May 4, 1964, there was a big talent hunt. Irna, who had always felt somewhat of an outcast in her own family, spent a great deal of her emotional energy in creating the orphan girl, Missy Palmer. She was to represent the disconnection and vulnerability that Irna had always felt. The big search for Missy Palmer ended one day when Tom Donovan, the show's director auditioned sixteen-year-old Carol Roux. After Carol's audition, Tom and the other executives—who included Allen Potter and his associates, Doris Quinlan and Bud Kloss—hired Carol on the spot, without the usual procedure of sending the audition tape to Irna. In a rare move, Irna agreed to trust their judgment. When she finally saw Carol in the part as the waif who was found living alone in a garret in Bay City, and then "adopted" by the Matthewses, she was beside herself with delight. Carol's big, wistful eyes seemed to fill the whole TV screen with their haunting reticence. For the first few years Missy Palmer was the show's sincerest and best-articulated character.

But many of the other characters on the original *Another World* seemed to be clichéd adaptations from Irna's *As the World Turns*, peculiarly assembled into a plot that revolved around flashy and colorful, rather than real, events. Says Tom Donovan, "In construction Irna was attempting to follow the structure of *As the World Turns*. Irna would never conceive of a story not based on a family. But the story and characters didn't always work together. Irna had Virginia Dwyer, as Mary Matthews, playing a kind of Nancy Hughes. But Mary never had the same importance as Nancy and tended to stagnate, mostly because Irna's melodrama didn't allow Mary Matthews the same range as Nancy Hughes."

Irna could never solve the problem of trying to reconcile the large Matthews family setup, borrowed from *World Turns*, and her desperate melodrama. Toward the end of the first year, Irna realized her mistake and Vera Allen, who was Grandma Matthews, was eventually written out. The days in Bay City weren't quiet enough to allow the Matthews family to honor their elders as the Hughes and Lowells could in Oakdale. (However, Geoffrey Lumb, as older attorney Mitchell Dru, hung on for several years. Lumb had played the same character on both *As the World Turns* and *The Brighter Day*.)

During the first months of her soaps Irna, partly out of fear of failure, tended to behave quixotically. *Another World* was no exception. After the first episode the competent John Beal was let go as Jim Matthews and replaced by Leon Janney. Then, a week later Sarah Cunningham was fired as Liz Matthews and replaced by Audra Lindley.

Jacquie Courtney already had a fine reputation as a good teenaged actress and was hired to play the incidental character of Alice Matthews, the sister of the older and more important Pat Matthews. Irna's habit of firing actors on sudden, trumped-up excuses was well known. Says Jacquie: "In the first months of the show there was this tremendous panic about who would be fired next. We were always hearing that Irna wasn't happy about this actor or that one. Irna was axing like crazy. Susan Matthews [Liz's daughter and Bill's sister] lasted only a year, and three actresses—Fran Sharon was the first—played the part. Irna wasn't happy about any of them and sort of kept the character doing nothing."

On the other hand, Irna was ecstatic over Susan Trustman's Pat Matthews, and concentrated heavily on the story of Pat's pregnancy by, and murder of, Tom Baxter. According to Jacquie, Susan was kept working every day for a year and a half, and it was killing her. She finally asked to be let out of her five-year contract, and Beverly Penberthy took the role.

* * *

For the two years that Irna wrote *Another World* the ratings were ghastly, and everyone connected with the show knew it. Says Tom Donovan, "We did so poorly while Irna was writing that at the end of the second year Bob Short's boss at Procter and Gamble said, 'You're going to cancel it, of course.' Bob said, 'Oh, no! Give it a chance. It's got great possibilities!' "

The problem was Irna's plotting and dialogue. As Allen Potter says, "She was from another era, still writing kids going down to the malt shop. She believed that her audience was tremendously conservative, and she would write dialogue and scenes on that level." Meanwhile, however, to shock viewers into watching, she was plotting a very unconservative story, and *Another World* just didn't gel. Adds Tom Donovan, "Irna wasn't comfortable writing *Another World* because her story didn't allow her characters to just sit around and philosophize, which was the kind of dialogue she did best. Also, don't forget, there was a big abortion story and murder trial for Pat. Irna, who was a stickler for authenticity, used to pay doctors and lawyers for their advice. It was harder for Irna to incorporate all of these technical things into her dialogue, which she never wrote at the typewriter but always dictated to her secretary, Rose Cooperman. Irna would lower her voice: 'Pat, you can't tell that to your mother.' And then raise it: 'Well, John, if I don't . . .' Rose would interject occasionally, 'Irna, are you sure you want Pat to say that . . . ?' This way of writing just didn't work well with *Another World*'s story."

Irna couldn't live with the failure of *Another World* and left the show. James Lipton became head writer and thought that the way to save the show was to introduce his own characters and get rid of some (or all) of the Matthewses. As Jacquie remembers, "He brought in a new family played by Ellen Weston, James Congdon and Mark Lenard, and one by one was sending the Matthewses off to different places. Our ratings only got worse—I think we were at the bottom of the list by now."

Then brilliant Agnes Nixon took over the writing. Before Agnes became head writer in 1967,

Another World was a cliché-ridden, slow, often unbelievable story without theme or guts. In the first year of her reign, Agnes made one spectacular decision after another. She immediately killed all of James Lipton's new characters in a plane crash and brought the exiled Matthewses back into prominence. She saw Alice sitting on a shelf and decided to do something with Jacquie's character. She sent her to nursing school and quickly made her a nurse. Meanwhile, she spiced up Missy's tale with the, as Tom Donovan calls it, "*Who Killed Danny Fargo?* story." Agnes arranged events so that Missy would be lured into a marriage with the villainous Danny Fargo (Antony Ponzini) and then be tried for his murder. While Bill Matthews (Joe Gallison) was defending her, Walter Curtin (Val Dufour) was brought into the story to act on behalf of the prosecution. Meanwhile, Agnes was already making good use of socialite Lenore Moore (Judith Barcroft), who had been attempting to steal Bill away from Missy. The trial story was immensely popular, not just because of itself but because of all the fascinating characters Agnes had introduced to complicate Missy's dilemma. The ratings soared to an unbelievable 10, putting it ahead of the popular *General Hospital. Another World*, three years after its premiere, had become a winner.

Agnes Nixon's imagination bloomed even more splendiferously after the Missy story was over and Missy and Bill left Bay City. She paired her volatile new district attorney, Walter Curtin, with materialistic Lenore Moore, and began a new love story for Alice Frame. It was to become daytime television's most powerful romance.

George Reinholt was brought on to play a new character, Steven Frame, a self-made young businessman, in 1967. For almost a year the character floundered while Agnes searched for romantic possibilities for him. George Reinholt was a little shy, not quite sure of himself. Agnes tried him out in a few scenes with Jacquie Courtney, who, as Alice, also seemed to lack forcefulness. Then, noting how well George and Jacquie worked together, the idea came to Agnes. She fashioned a romantic triangle between Alice, Steve and Alice's scheming, upwardly-mobile sister-in-law Rachel.

Agnes says: "I envisioned Steven Frame as a young Cash McCall. I may have been thinking of a football hero here in Philadelphia who would have attracted the beautiful Alices and the beautiful

Rachels. I patterned Rachel after Erica Kane, since I wrote the original story of *All My Children* years before. Rachel was a character with doom potential—meaning that she is destructive but was ultimately a greater threat to herself than to other people." By creating a love triangle—involving a selfish and handsome *nouveau-riche* bachelor, a destructive young girl with an equally knockabout background who appealed to the young man's baser sexual feelings and another young girl with "good" upbringing—Agnes fired the imaginations of viewers with a drama that for the first time fulfilled Irna Phillips's original promise of a story concerning different psychological "worlds."

In 1968 Agnes Nixon left as *Another World*'s head writer to create *One Life To Live*. Although Bob Cenedella did a fine job of writing the show for the next year, the show's high ratings began to drop. Murder (Walter Curtin committed a murder, for which his wife, Lenore, was tried) and other elements of melodrama were again resorted to in order to raise the Nielsens. They stubbornly remained low. In 1970, Jacquie Courtney took an extended leave of absence after marrying Dr. Carl Desiderio—causing further ratings problems.

* * *

Procter & Gamble hired the new head writer, Harding ("Pete") Lemay, in 1971 as an experiment. He had only minimal television writing experience but had written a prestigious autobiography which had won him several awards. P&G asked the question: Could a good writer who had no experience with daytime soaps bring freshness and better ratings to a show that was on the skids? They hired Lemay but insisted he first apprentice with Irna Phillips for six months. He would write outlines and scripts; she would look over them, criticize, give tips. For a while Irna seemed pleased with his work, until Pete did something that horrified her: He broke up Pat and John and turned Pat into an alcoholic. Irna immediately called P&G and complained, "He'll wreck the show! Pat and John *have* to stay together. Our viewers identify with their happiness." What Pete instinctively knew and Irna forgot was that tentpole characters were not as important on *Another World* as on the more structurally stable *As the World Turns*. As a romance rather than a family story, *Another World* did not have to live up to ethical marital standards.

Pete Lemay, when finally released from Irna's yoke, did as much for *Another World* as Agnes Nixon had. He took her Steve-Rachel-Alice love triangle (Jacquie Courtney had returned to her part) and deepened it with wide-ranging psychological ramifications. Rachel—now played by Victoria Wyndham—became less a force of pure destruction than a real person caught in the vise of her self-predetermined fate. Pete refused to distinguish between Rachel's and Alice's tears, reminding viewers in scene after scene that both characters were suffering because of events out of their control.

Said Pete, "I didn't feel it was necessary to keep Rachel a black-and-white character. I didn't see her as a villainess. I saw her instead as a person who had always had bad breaks and who defeats herself because she is so used to failure. I wanted the audience to feel her pain as I felt it. I wanted the audience to feel her tears."

Pete also gave Steven Frame a background, a family and a framework in which to deepen the two sides to his nature: the coarsely sexual and the intellectual. It became clear that for Steven, Alice and Rachel were but fantasies of love, at war with each other; since humans often fall in love with their images and their fantasies, rather than real people, Steven, as the audience was forced to see, was being no less destructive than Rachel in his yearnings for unfulfillable fantasies. The writer had Mary Matthews turn against Steven, because she alone could see that he was a man susceptible to his dreams of two separate loves rather than the realities of her daughter Alice's needs. No writer of a daytime serial had so profoundly explored the relationship between surface human behavior and that "other world" of fantasy and yearning. Pete quickly eliminated all melodramatic devices from the story.

The ratings once again soared.

For the next five years, *Another World*, under the helm of Harding Lemay and the show's strong executive producer, Paul Rauch, became a leader in the soap world. Without melodrama the show was able to stay top-rated, despite the incursions of new trends from soaps like *The Young and The Restless*. On January 6, 1975, P&G, at the urging of Paul Rauch, expanded *Another World* to a full hour, and it flourished with continued healthy ratings.

Nevertheless, serious internal problems developed. Just before the show went to an hour, George

Reinholt was fired (over alleged flareups of temperament) and his character, Steve Frame, was killed off. At almost the same time, Lemay, feeling less sentimental about the Matthews family than viewers, gave Mary Matthews, the show's mother figure from the beginning, a fatal heart attack. Some months later Jacquie Courtney, who had become a sort of Our Gal Sunday to millions of the show's devotees, was dismissed as Alice.

To fill the added half-hour and the void caused by the loss of three of the show's most prominent actors, Pete Lemay introduced a number of new characters and stories. He had already begun refocusing the show on the newly rehabilitated Rachel and her love story with rich, middle-aged Mac Cory. Lemay now pitted her against the show's new villainess, Mac's scheming daughter, Iris Carrington. Although the writer had some difficulty with organizing a full-hour daily serial (there were no precedents; it had never been done before), on the whole the show was well-written, albeit a little slow, and the audience held for several years. But big problems developed. Since Harding Lemay's original orientation had been in the theater, he and Paul Rauch tended to choose New York theater actors for most of the new characters they introduced. Theater actors are notoriously restless and one by one they left their *Another World* roles for Hollywood or other pastures. Lemay and Rauch also dismissed a number of actors because they seemed unsuitable and eventually wrote out their characters. In short, the show was being written and produced in such a way as to leave *Another World*'s devotees with no other continuity besides the story of Mac, Rachel and Iris. By 1977, the audience, which at first had been fascinated by the first full-hour soap, became less than thrilled with an hour of characters and stories that seemed to come and go every few months.

The ratings remained poor through 1979, when Procter & Gamble, once again following the recommendation of the producer, expanded *Another World* to ninety minutes. The sponsor had some reason to believe that expansion might be the answer to *Another World*'s troubles. Faced with having to outline and script five ninety-minute episodes per week, and under continual pressure from the sponsor in Cincinnati to improve the ratings, Harding Lemay left his post as head writer shortly after the premiere of the ninety-minute format. Two years later Atheneum published his book, *Eight Years In Another World*, a riveting account of his years as head writer of the show. In it he gave a unique view of how a soap opera writer lives and works, and why the drama he had made so compelling for five years began to decline under his own authorship. One of his most astonishing admissions is that he finally realized, when it was too late, that Irna Phillips was correct in her obsession with continuing the characters, themes and especially the families of her shows. Pete was surely overworked toward the end, and too inexperienced to know how to delegate more responsibility to other writers, which contributed to his problems; but one senses that his greatest mistake in handling *Another World* was destroying the Matthews family and agreeing to the dismissal of Jacquie Courtney as Alice, which undermined the historical foundation of the show.

Procter & Gamble, realizing that longer was surely not better, brought *Another World* back to sixty minutes in 1980. The same year, the show's beloved villainess, Iris Carrington Bancroft (Beverlee McKinsey), was written out to become the main character of *Texas*, P&G's brand new daytime spinoff from *Another World*, premiering on NBC on August 4, 1980 and also produced by Paul Rauch (see p. 357). Needless to say, the loss of Iris did not help the parent show. *Texas*, which had story problems similar to *Another World*'s, was canceled in 1982.

Rauch remained as executive producer of *Another World* for four years after Harding Lemay resigned, until mid-1983, during which time numerous writers and sub-writers were hired to give the show a more solid foundation, but succeeded only in wearing out the core characters of Mac and Rachel. In a reprise, Allen Potter, the show's first producer, now became the new producer. In the spring of 1983 the show was exhibiting miraculous signs of recovery. Viewers were taken, especially, with the strong de Poulignac story, which Paul and his writers had developed several years before.

THE STORY

Two deaths in succession caused turmoil for the huge Matthews family. William Matthews, wealthy brother of accountant JIM MATTHEWS (played longest by Hugh Marlowe), had just died, leaving his snobbish widow, LIZ MATTHEWS (Audra Lindley, currently Irene Dailey), and their two children. Then Jim and his wife, MARY MATTHEWS (Virginia Dwyer), were horrified when their daughter PAT (Beverly Penberthy) was accused of murdering TOM BAXTER (Nicholas Pryor), the boy who caused her pregnancy and talked her into having an illegal abortion, which Pat thought had left her sterile. Jim and Mary hired the best lawyer they could afford, JOHN RANDOLPH (Michael Ryan), who not only got her off with a plea of temporary insanity (it was proved that the murder was accidental), but managed to fall in love with her.

Pat and John's marriage should have been happy, but there were snags. LEE RANDOLPH (Barbara Rodell), John's grown-up daughter from a previous marriage, resented Pat for taking her place as the lady of the house. However, when John was struck by a car and wound up paralyzed, Lee and Pat called a temporary truce. Then handsome lawyer MIKE BAUER (Gary Pillar) showed up in Bay City with his daughter, Hope, after

his wife had committed suicide. Trying to start a new life, he was helping the crippled John Randolph with his cases when, despite himself, he fell in love with Pat, who one day had to admit that she also returned his love. Lee, however, was desperately in love with Mike. When she overheard Pat and Mike talking about their mutual love, she lost control of herself and ran away from home. She fell in with a sleazy criminal, LEFTY BURNS (Lawrence Keith), who introduced her to LSD. Meanwhile, realizing that he was causing trouble in Bay City, Mike Bauer returned with Hope to Springfield.

ADA DOWNS (Constance Ford) and her second husband, ERNIE DOWNS (Harry Bellaver), were simple, hard-working people. Ernie owned a garage, where Ada's brother, SAM LUCAS (Jordan Charney) was employed while studying for his law degree. Sam fell in love with Lee Randolph and wanted to marry her, but Lee was terrified because she believed her bouts with LSD would cause any children she bore to be genetically damaged. Finally, under the influence of LSD, Lee crashed her car and was killed. Sam married model LAHOMA VANE (Ann Wedgeworth) and they moved to Somerset, when he got his law degree. Pat and John (now fully recovered and able to walk), settled down to a happy life together and eventually became the parents of twins.

At the premiere of Another World *on May 4, 1964, Jim and Mary Matthews (John Beal and Virginia Dwyer) heard the news that Jim's wealthier brother William had just died. Jim and Mary represented the more middle-class half of the Matthews clan.*

Young Joey Trent played the first Russ Matthews, a bystander in the extreme melodrama of the show's first years. Joey Trent stayed in the role until 1967. Virginia Dwyer played Mary Matthews until the character was killed off in mid-1975.

While all this was happening to Jim Matthews's clan, the family of his dead brother was having problems of its own. Lawyer BILL MATTHEWS (Joe Gallison), son of William and Liz Matthews, fell in love with MELISSA "MISSY" PALMER (Carol Roux), a beautiful, sensitive girl who was tormented by the fact that she had spent her life in foster homes. To add to her misery, she discovered, just before she was to become Bill's bride, that she was illegitimate. Too ashamed to marry Bill, she ran away to Chicago.

Missy—alone, distraught and wandering the streets of a big, frightening city—soon became involved with a small-time crook named DANNY FARGO (Antony Ponzini). After convincing her to enter into a platonic marriage with him—only for protection—he raped her, and she became pregnant. Later, Danny's old girl friend, FLO MURRAY (Marcella Martin), hysterically jealous over his marriage to Missy, killed him with a knife during a tussle. Since Missy had mistakenly picked up the knife and left her fingerprints on it, she was put on trial for Danny Fargo's murder.

Bill had been searching furiously for her, but by the time he located Missy she was already being tried for first-degree homicide. Defending her himself during the emotional trial, Bill was able to track down the real killer, and Missy was set free. Bill and Missy married—despite the objections of his mother, Liz, who thought no woman was good enough for him—and the two of them moved to California with Ricky, her baby by Danny Fargo. Their happiness, however, didn't last long. Bill Matthews drowned in a terrible accident.

* * *

While rich Bill Matthews was courting Missy, RUSS MATTHEWS (David Bailey, but for years played by Sam Groom), scion of the poorer Jim Matthews clan, fell under the spell of RACHEL DAVIS (Victoria Wyndham, earlier Robin Strasser), a beautiful and calculating young girl who was a patient at the hospital where he was an intern. Rachel, who had known poverty all her life with her mother, Ada Downs, felt this was her chance to marry into a respectable, well-off family. Ambition, not love, made her marry Russ.

But young interns' wives must economize and live simply, which was not Rachel's cup of tea. Bored with Russ, Rachel's eyes began to wander in the direction of handsome, virile STEVEN FRAME (George Reinholt), who had come into his own after a life-

Liz Matthews (Sarah Cunningham) was William's widow and Susan (Fran Sharon, hired shortly after the premiere) was their daughter.

Only weeks after the premiere, Audra Lindley became the new Liz Matthews. Now without a husband, she turned fanatically possessive of her son Bill, played by Joe Gallison until 1968. "Aunt Liz," as she was known for years, has recently mellowed.

time of poverty quite like Rachel's. His company, Frame Enterprises, was becoming phenomenally successful. At every possible juncture she would arrange on-purpose chance meetings with him. Steven wasn't at all interested in Rachel, but one night she threw herself at him in his penthouse and he took advantage of the opportunity. He regretted the mistake when Rachel later became pregnant. Then he fell in love with ALICE MATTHEWS (played longest by Jacquie Courtney), Rachel's sister-in-law. He knew the Matthews's middle-class mores would prevent him from marrying Alice if the truth ever got out.

It did—Rachel made sure of that. It was a moment of intense drama. An engagement party was being held in honor of Steven and Alice, and a vituperative Rachel got Alice alone in a room and told her who was really the father of the child she was carrying. Alice, hurt beyond belief but too considerate of the feelings of her brother, Russ, to tell him the

truth, canceled her engagement to Steven and took an extended tour of Europe. When she returned to Bay City, she forgave Steven his transgression with Rachel, and became Mrs. Steven Frame.

* * *

The problems of selfish and temperamental Liz Matthews were exacerbated when her daughter, SUSAN MATTHEWS (last played by Lynn Milgrim), began competing with her for the affections of handsome attorney FRED DOUGLAS (Charles Baxter).

After the confrontation between mother and daughter ended in the younger woman's marrying Fred Douglas—then divorcing him, and finally finding happiness by marrying DR. DAN SHEARER (John Cunningham, later Brian Murray)—wealthy Liz turned to corrupt playboy WAYNE ADDISON (Robert Milli) for her new romance. At the time, Addison was involved in dishonest dealings with Bay City's once greatly re-

Original members of the Matthews family included, from left: Jacquie Courtney as Jim and Mary's daughter Alice—a minor character when the show started; Vera Allen as Grandma Matthews; Liza Chapman as Janet Matthews, Jim's sister; and Susan Trustman as Pat, the older of Jim and Mary's two daughters. Vera Allen (wearing old age makeup) was on the show for a year. Liza Chapman remained on a bit longer.

The early plot of Another World *centered around the ill-fated romance of Pat Matthews (Susan Trustman) and Tom Baxter (Nicholas Pryor). Tom was spoiled and unwilling to take responsibility for Pat's pregnancy. He talked her into having an abortion. Later, she killed him in a rage.*

spected district attorney, WALTER CURTIN (Val Dufour). Fortyish and insecure, Walter felt he needed more money than he could earn as D.A. to provide for his new young bride, the former LENORE MOORE (Susan Sullivan, previously played by Judith Barcroft). So he quit his job as D.A. to become Wayne Addison's partner in shady deals, while putting up a good front as a partner in John Randolph's law firm.

Liz Matthews began secretly to hate Lenore Curtin, whose mother, HELEN MOORE (Murial Williams), was her good friend. Wayne Addison, to rid himself of Liz, had lied and said he was having an affair with Lenore behind Walter Curtin's back. Then Walter killed Wayne Addison in a fit of rage. Lenore, seen leaving Wayne Addison's apartment on the night of his death, was accused of his murder. With the help of the vindictive Liz Matthews, the state was able to get an indictment. Ironically, Walter Curtin himself defended his wife, and Lenore was acquitted. Some time later, Walter confessed the murder to her and promised to tell the authorities, but on his way to his lawyer's office he was killed in an auto accident, leaving Lenore a widow and his little son WALLY fatherless. To protect her husband's memory, Lenore vowed that she would never reveal Walter's crime.

* * *

Rachel called her new infant baby boy JAMIE (played as an adult by Richard Bekins), and for a time Russ was a proud father and husband—until he learned that Steven was the real father. After Russ divorced his unfaithful wife, he became interested in CINDY CLARK (Leonie Norton), a young nurse at the clinic where he worked. Her brother, TED CLARK (Steven Bolster), was simultaneously falling in love with the forlorn and husbandless new mother, Rachel.

Bill Matthews met orphan Missy Palmer (Carol Roux) in 1965 at the Copper Kettle Inn, a teenage hangout, and fell in love with her. Liz tried to break up the romance. The Missy-Bill story was extremely popular for two and a half years.

Liz brought Missy's mother, Cathryn Corning (Ann Sheridan, left), to Bay City to prove that the girl was illegitimate so that Missy would be disgraced and Bill would not marry her. Horrified, Missy fled to Chicago, but eventually married Bill.

Again Rachel married a man for convenience, rather than for love.

Rachel, however, was still scheming to get Steven for herself, using their illegitimate son Jamie as the excuse to continue to see Steven. One day, Alice overheard Rachel saying that she and Steven were together the day that Alice lost her own baby, and she imagined the worst. She left him flat and ran off to New York.

Meanwhile, Pat Randolph discovered that her husband, John, was seeing another woman and she began drinking out of self-pity. Pat became so devoted to the bottle that none of the Matthewses would tell her that Russ's fiancée, Cindy, was dying of a heart ailment. When she learned that Russ had married Cindy only hours before she died in the hospital—believing to the end that she and Russ would live a happy, full life together—Pat began to realize that her own problem was cutting her off from others. John's extramarital affair ended when his paramour, Wayne

Addison's ex-wife BERNICE (Janis Young), was accidentally pushed off a terrace and killed by a second lover, lawyer MARK VENABLE (Andrew Jarkowsky), and he and Pat came together again.

Steven was mystified and hurt by Alice's running off suddenly. After waiting months for her to return, he finally allowed Rachel (now divorced from Ted Clark) to reenter his life, for the sake of his son, Jamie. From New York, where she was working for writer ELIOT CARRINGTON (James Douglas) as his son's governess, Alice granted Steven a divorce so he could marry Rachel. But when Eliot Carrington convinced Alice to return to Bay City because her brother, Russ, was now treating his invalid son, DENNIS (played by Mike Hammett, later as an adult by Jim Poyner), she and Steven finally confronted each other and realized that their divorce had been a mistake. Steven vowed that he would find some way to free himself from Rachel so he could remarry Alice.

Eliot's wealthy, estranged wife, IRIS CARRINGTON (Beverlee McKinsey), was all too happy to see Steven and Alice marry because she still loved Eliot and feared he would marry Alice. But after suffering a nervous breakdown, Iris divorced Eliot and took up

Pat married the lawyer, John Randolph (Mike Ryan), who gained her an acquittal on a charge of murder. She and his daughter, Lee Randolph (Gaye Huston), became rivals for his attentions. Then, in 1966, John developed Meniere's syndrome and had to be confined to a wheelchair for many months.

Teenagers Lee Randolph and Alice Matthews met their boyfriends at the Copper Kettle Inn. With Jacquie Courtney is Alex Canaan. Joe Bennett is with Gaye Huston.

life in Bay City. Meanwhile, when Steven finally discovered why Alice had left him, he seized the opportunity to sue Rachel for divorce on the grounds that their marriage was based on a fraud. He was so desperate to remarry Alice, he bribed Rachel's father, GERALD DAVIS (Walter Mathews), to falsely testify at the divorce hearing. The divorce was granted, but John Randolph, Steve's lawyer, found out about the bribe and felt compelled to tell the court—over the frantic objections of his wife, Pat. Steve remarried Alice only days before being sentenced to prison for six months. John Randolph—blamed by Pat for Steve's "betrayal," and deprived of Steve's legal business—quickly took to drink. Divorce seemed likely. About the only really *happy* event happening in Bay City now was the brand-new infant Ada and her new policeman husband, GIL MCGOWAN (Dolph Sweet), were shortly expecting.

* * *

It was just too much for insecure Alice to bear.

Steve's imprisonment and the secret she was keeping, that she could never bear a child, caused her to go into a deep psychotic depression. After Steve was released, she refused to see him. Rachel, believing that this was her chance to win Steve back, showed him medical records indicating that Alice knew she was barren. Rachel's information made Steve suddenly realize why Alice was refusing to see him—even though her acute schizophrenic-withdrawal symptoms were disappearing. Steven went to Alice and forced her to see that, children or no children, life without her was meaningless for him.

Rachel was in a sorry state after she realized, at long last, that she had lost Steve for good. With most of Bay City against her, she was friendless, and now loveless. It was a bizarre twist of fate that MACKENZIE CORY (Douglass Watson)—Iris Carrington's millionaire father, newly arrived from New York City—took a romantic interest in forlorn Rachel, despite everyone's warning him about her scheming nature. Somehow, Mac saw something good beneath her seemingly ruthless exterior—and he married her! Iris,

Constance Ford joined Another World *as husbandless beautician Ada Davis and wed garage owner Ernie Downs (Harry Bellaver) in 1968.*

Attractive Micki Grant played secretary Peggy Harris, one of the few blacks seen on soaps in the midsixties. She is seen here with Judith Barcroft, as socialite Lenore Moore, and Barbara Rodell, who became the new Lee Randolph in 1968.

who had been raised in Swiss boarding schools and had always been deprived of her father's love, became insanely jealous of Mac's love for Rachel.

While couples Steve and Alice, Rachel and Mac, and Ada and Gil were all happy, architect ROBERT DE-LANEY (Nicolas Coster) and his new bride, widow Lenore Curtin, were quickly drifting apart. Robert objected to his wife's spending so many hours at her job at Frame Enterprises, feeling that she should be more of a wife and mother. Fellow architect, beautiful CAROL LAMONTE (Jeanne Lange), became attracted to Robert and took advantage of his problems with Lenore. Carol slept with him, making sure that Lenore found out about the affair, then began tormenting Lenore by dropping hints that she knew *something* about the deceased Walter Curtin. Frantic that if she stayed in Bay City any longer Wally would find out that his father had been a murderer, Lenore fled Bay City and later divorced Robert. Robert turned to liquor for solace.

John, who had also hit the bottle and was separated from his wife, was helped to get back on his feet by Rachel. Steve, realizing that he had been wrong to blame John for his conviction, gave him back the legal business of Frame Enterprises. Pat and John once again reconciled and appeared happy—for a while.

* * *

A monstrous double tragedy suddenly struck Bay City. While on a second honeymoon with her husband, Jim Matthews, Mary Matthews died of a coronary seizure, leaving Jim a distraught widower. Then Steven was suddenly killed in a helicopter crash in Australia! Alice went into convulsive shock. A big part of her had died in that helicopter crash. She and Steven had made such tender plans. They were going to adopt a child. Suddenly, with uncanny bravery, Alice put her grief aside and adopted little SALLY SPENCER (now Mary Page Keller), whose parents had just been killed in an auto accident. Alice was now a rich widow, which made her vulnerable to golddiggers.

Marriage to rich Mac Cory had changed Rachel's nature. She was no longer the devil she had once

Jordan Charney played Ada's brother, Sam Lucas, a law student who was in love with Lee Randolph. After she was killed in an auto crash, following an LSD hallucination, he married Lahoma Vane (Ann Wedgeworth), a girl with a shady past who was willing to change. (In 1970, Sam and Lahoma Lucas were the central characters in Somerset, *a spinoff serial from* Another World.*)*

Doris Belack played Madge Murray, the sister of the girl who murdered Danny Fargo. In Chicago Madge was involved with a waiter named Charlie (Ralph Oliver). Then she moved to Bay City when Missy was exonerated. She became Ada Davis's confidante and tried to help her with her difficult daughter, Rachel. Eventually she went back to Charlie in Chicago.

been, but now a sensitive and sympathetic person. When Steve died, Rachel even felt sorry for Alice! Iris, however, continued to hate Rachel for marrying her father, and staged a scenario to make Mac think Rachel was cuckolding him. She paid playboy PHILIP WAINWRIGHT (James Luisi) to seduce Rachel, and when that failed, Iris simply told her father that Rachel had been unfaithful, and showed him a ring that Rachel had supposedly given Philip for his "services." Mac refused to believe Rachel when she denied Iris's charges, forcing Rachel to leave him. But when Philip's ex-girl friend, a sympathetic, pretty waitress named CLARICE HOBSON (Gail Brown) finally revealed the truth to Mac, Mac disowned his daughter and pleaded with Rachel to take him back.

Russ Matthews had been engaged to Iris, but broke off with her when he, too, discovered the truth. Afraid to face life alone, Iris turned to lonely Robert Delaney, who had been having a romance with Clarice Hobson. Never quite the same since Lenore left him, Robert—commissioned by Iris to design a guest house—allowed himself to be charmed by Iris and her wealth. Before Clarice could tell him that she was pregnant by him, Robert had self-destructively married serpentine Iris Carrington! Iris found out about Clarice's baby but never told Robert. Stunned at Iris's deception, Robert turned to drink and left town. Clarice, fearful of Iris's threats to take away her child, moved in with sympathetic Ada McGowan and Gil—who was later tragically killed in the line of duty. Ada became a widow once again.

* * *

The younger brother of Steven Frame, WILLIS FRAME (John Fitzpatrick, Leon Russom), turned out to be unscrupulous, interested only in snatching control of Frame Enterprises from Alice, who naively trusted him. He and Carol Lamonte, his new lover, soon were in cahoots to take over the company. After Robert Delaney took to drink and left town, Alice's only real protector against conniving Willis and Carol was lawyer RAYMOND GORDON (Ted Shackelford, Gary Carpenter), the son of Rachel's housekeeper, BEATRICE GORDON (Jacqueline Brookes). Raymond was falling in

For four years viewers were involved in the story of Walter and Lenore Curtin. In 1967, Lenore Moore (Judith Barcroft), had come into the story as an unsympathetic socialite who was trying to split up Missy and Bill to get Bill for herself. In 1969, she wed Walter Curtin (Val Dufour), a much older man. His insecurities because of their age difference eventually drove him to criminal behavior.

George Reinholt came to Bay City as successful businessman Steven Frame in 1968, but his romance with Alice Matthews didn't start until the following year. Phenomenally popular, Steve and Alice were the Luke and Laura of their day, keeping Another World*'s ratings high for nearly seven years.*

love with Alice. Fearing that Raymond would warn Alice about his ulterior motives, Willis paid Raymond's troublemaking ex-wife, OLIVE GORDON (Jennifer Leak), to come to Bay City to divert his attentions from Alice and Frame Enterprises. After Alice, learning of Willis's schemes, dismissed him, he was shocked into realizing the error of his ways, and tried to resume his old romance with co-worker ANGIE PERRINI (Toni Kalem, Maeve Kinkead). Olive, however, continued to make trouble.

Iris and her father were reconciled, but again Mac threw her out of his life when it appeared that she was the cause of Rachel's losing her baby. This time, however, Iris did not have to plot to break up the Corys. They were having domestic problems unrelated to Mac's insidious daughter. Mac felt that Rachel was neglecting him and Jamie for her new interest in

sculpture, as well as her sculpture instructor, KEN PALMER (William Lyman), and Rachel became jealous of Mac's intense new working relationship with Pat Randolph, who had split with John for good this time. But it was DAVE GILCHRIST (David Ackroyd), a doctor from New York in whom Pat was really interested, much to the bitter disapproval of Pat's daughter, MARIANNE RANDOLPH (last played by Beth Collins), who wanted her parents to reconcile. In time Dave moved back to New York where he had built his practice.

Russ, never very good at picking lovemates, married SHARLENE WATTS (Laurie Heineman), one of Steve's sisters. Sharlene had a past as a prostitute, which broke up the marriage. Then Russ had a string of unsuccessful romances. He became torn between GWEN PARRISH (Dorothy Lyman), a strong-willed and volatile architect, and COUNTESS ELENA DE POULIGNAC (Christina Pickles, Maeve McGuire), Iris's good friend. Unlike Iris, Elena had a gentleness and sincerity which was never ruined by her social status. Neither relationship worked out so Russ moved to Texas.

Russ Matthews (Sam Groom, who replaced Joey Trent) wed poor but cunning Rachel Davis (Robin Strasser). She made a fool out of him and tormented sensitive Alice when she seduced Steve Frame and became pregnant with his baby. That triangle, begun in 1969 by Agnes Nixon, was the key to all future developments on Another World.

Hugh Marlowe became the fourth Jim Matthews in 1970 and Nancy Wickwire (center) became the third Liz when Audra Lindley left for Hollywood. Nancy Wickwire died of cancer in 1974. When Hugh Marlowe died in 1982, the character also died.

Around this time, Ada took her fourth husband, CHARLIE HOBSON (Fred J. Scollay), Clarice's father. When he first came to Bay City, Clarice resented him for leaving her years before to raise her two brothers, but she was eventually won over by his gentle simplicity and was happy when he and Ada wed.

✳ ✳ ✳

Suave BRIAN BANCROFT (Paul Stevens), the new legal counsel for Cory Publications, had his hands full when he decided to wed hard-to-handle Iris. They acted out a kind of *Taming of the Shrew* story, with Iris finally giving in to the stronger, more mature Brian, vowing that she would stop her scheming and reform. For a while, serious trouble erupted in their marriage when Iris discovered that her old friend Countess Elena de Poulignac and Iris's teenaged son, Dennis, were having an affair. Brian was aghast at the machinations Iris devised to break up the lovers and briefly left her.

Alice and Ray Gordon, her lawyer, became engaged. They were both stunned when they learned that Ray's mother, Beatrice Gordon, was the grandmother of Alice's newly adopted daughter, Sally. After Alice and Ray married, Beatrice suddenly kidnapped Sally, believing that her son Ray was far too weak a man to be a good father to her. At the urging of Jim Matthews, with whom Beatrice had been in love, she returned her granddaughter to Alice and Ray. Beatrice felt such guilt over what she had done that she left Bay City. But she turned out to be right about Ray. After taking over Frame Enterprises, he ran it to the ground, and his marriage along with it. Alice dismissed him from the company and he, too, left town. Afterward, Alice became briefly engaged to the once-hateful Willis Frame.

The Randolphs endured a series of tragedies, culminating in the worst ever to strike their family. John Randolph, after his divorce from Pat, made the

The cast in 1970 included, back row from left: Jordan Charney, Harry Bellaver, George Reinholt, Beverly Penberthy, Val Dufour, Micki Grant, Hugh Marlowe, Virginia Dwyer, Geoffrey Lumb (Mitchell Dru), Mike Ryan, Constance Ford. Front row: Ann Wedgeworth, Charles Baxter (Fred Douglas), Lisa Cameron (Susan Matthews), Nancy Wickwire, Judith Barcroft, Jacquie Courtney, Robin Strasser and Sam Groom.

Susan Sullivan (left) was the new Lenore Curtin in 1972 the year her husband Walter was killed in a car accident while on his way to the authorities to confess to the murder of Wayne Addison. Murial Williams (center) had played Lenore's mother, Helen, since 1967. In the same year Beverly Penberthy (right) had become the new Pat Randolph.

mistake of marrying viper Olive Gordon, who was only interested in his money. She soon began a steamy extramarital affair with EVAN WEBSTER (Barry Jenner), a handsome but sly architect. After the twins, MICHAEL (Lionel Johnston) and Marianne, became suspicious of Olive, John found out what was going on and confronted Evan. There was a terrible fight during which John gave Evan a blow to the head in self-defense and Evan was killed! Before John could be tried for murder he suffered a complete mental breakdown and had to be institutionalized. Eventually he recovered, divorced Olive and tried to pick up the pieces of his life.

Pat Randolph also experienced a desperate drama. Marianne had become engaged to GREG BARNARD (Ned Schmidtke), John's new law partner. At first he appeared moral and idealistic, until he suggested to Pat, Marianne's own mother, that he and she have an affair. Greg then convinced Marianne that her

mother had attempted to seduce him. Pat finally confronted Greg about the terrible thing he was doing to her family. His response was to try to rape her. In fighting him off, she struck him on the head and killed him. She was forced to relive that horrible night, many years before, when she had killed her lover, Tom Baxter. Once again, Pat had to stand trial and was acquitted, this time on the grounds of self-defense.

Then, Liz Matthews's daughter, Susan Shearer, came back from Boston to set up a psychotherapy practice in Bay City. Susan had separated from her husband, Dan. Still interfering in her children's lives, Liz brought Dan to Bay City hoping that Susan and he would reunite. After Susan refused a reconciliation, Dan became interested in Alice. But Olive had already fallen for him. When Alice announced her engagement to Dan, Olive became so enraged that she set fire to Alice's rented vacation house. Bravely, John Randolph rushed into the flames to save Alice, only to

Beverlee McKinsey came to Bay City in 1973 as Iris Carrington, the spoiled and wealthy ex-wife of Eliot Carrington. When writer Harding Lemay began to turn Rachel into the story's new heroine, he used Iris as Bay City's main scheming villainess. The switch was peculiar but worked. For a while she and Russ (now David Bailey) were engaged.

The Steve-Alice story raged on, now (1973) in its fourth year. Alice mistakenly believed that Steve was having an affair with Rachel and so ran off to New York, where she took a job with Eliot Carrington (James Douglas) as governess to his son Dennis. Eliot fell in love with her.

die himself. All of Bay City was devastated by the tragedy. The Randolphs could only be comforted by the fact that John died a hero. Soon after, Alice and Dan broke their engagement. Dan and Susan realized they still loved each other and moved back to Boston.

* * *

Rachel had suffered a miscarriage. Now, after several failed attempts to become pregnant by Mac, she worried that they would never have a child together. Through medical tests, however, Mac learned that he had become infertile but, out of manly pride, kept the news from his wife. When Rachel later learned the truth she believed the bond of trust between them had been broken and left him. Mac then became the indirect victim of another one of his daughter's schemes. Iris had hired a surly Scandinavian named SVEN PETERSEN (Roberts Blossom) to pose

as Mac's butler and spy on the Corys. Sven, however, began to conjure his own gruesome schemes against Mac, in an effort to acquire Mac's house and fortune. He drugged both Mac and his own illegitimate daughter, REGINE LINDEMAN (Barbara Eda-Young), placing them together in bed. When they awakened they believed that they had had relations in a drunken stupor. Later, Regine learned that she was pregnant and Mac learned that he was *not* infertile, causing Mac to think that he had fathered Regine's child. Mac asked Rachel for a divorce so that he could marry Regine to give her baby his name. She refused. Meanwhile, Iris's faithful servant, LOUISE GODDARD (Anne Meacham), was being courted by Mac's hulking chauffeur, ROCKY OLSEN (John Braden). When Rocky caught on to Sven's schemes, Sven murdered him, hacked his body to pieces and shoved them under the floorboards of the Cory stables. Suspicious of Sven, Rachel amassed

All misunderstandings between Steve and Alice were cleared up in 1974 when they remarried in the house he built for her. From left: Irene Dailey (the new Liz), David Bailey, George Reinholt, Hugh Marlowe, Jacquie Courtney, Nick Coster (Robert Delaney), Chris Allport (Tim McGowan) and Victoria Thompson (Janice Frame, Steve's sister). Steve was killed off the show the following year.

Mackenzie Cory (Douglass Watson), Iris's wealthy father, came to Bay City in 1975 and married Rachel (played by Victoria Wyndham since late 1972). Rachel's love for Mac made her stop her scheming and become considerate of the feelings of others. There was a new triangle now between Mac and Rachel and Iris, who was unnaturally possessive of her father.

enough evidence against him to have him arrested for murder. Then Mac learned that the father of Regine's child had been womanizing CLIFF TANNER (Tom Rolfing). The expectant Regine and Cliff decided to leave town. Rachel and Mac reunited—for a while.

Another result of the fury at the Cory mansion was the breakup of young Michael Randolph's marriage to MOLLY ORDWAY (Rolanda Mendels), the daughter of Steve and Willis's sister, EMMA (originally Beverlee McKinsey, later Tresa Hughes). Bored by Michael, who spent much time at his law studies, Molly had also slept with Cliff Tanner. After Michael found out and divorced her, she left Bay City.

The whole Perrini family, Italian Americans, came to Bay City. The first to arrive had been Angie Perrini, who had become involved with destructive Willis Frame. Prodded by her mother, ROSE PERRINI (Kathleen Widdoes), to break up with Willis, Angie married his newly arrived brother, VINCE FRAME (Jay Morran), a far more easygoing man. Too late she realized that it was Willis she really loved and divorced

Vince to pursue him. But Willis had found someone else and so Angie left Bay City. Rose stayed in town with her son, JOEY PERRINI (Ray Liotta, Paul Perri), who fell in love with pretty EILEEN SIMPSON (Vicky Dawson). Meanwhile, much to Alice's dismay, her adopted daughter Sally had become wildly incorrigible now that she was in her mid-teens. Infatuated with Joey Perrini, Sally conspired with her new friend, PHIL HIGLEY (McLin Crowell), to break up Joey and Eileen. Phil, a member of a prostitution ring, tried to have Eileen kidnapped and imprisoned in white slavery. Joey saved Eileen and had Phil arrested. Then it was discovered that Eileen had a fatal blood disease. Joey wed her in a quiet ceremony and the next day she died. Alice, who had been driven to a near nervous breakdown by Sally's behavior, took a nursing job in Chicago, temporarily separating from the girl.

* * *

Rachel's old scheming nature suddenly reappeared when Jamie, now in his late teens, married

Steve's sudden death in a helicopter crash made Steve's brother Willis Frame (John Fitzpatrick) a key figure in Frame Enterprises in 1975. He began to devise ways of usurping the company from his brother's widow, Alice. Roberta Maxwell played lawyer Barbara Weaver.

Beatrice Gordon (Jacqueline Brookes), Rachel's housekeeper, was really the grandmother of Sally Spencer, Alice's newly adopted daughter. Her son, Raymond Gordon (Ted Shackelford), fell in love with Alice and tried to protect her from Willis.

BLAINE EWING (Laura Malone). In this gorgeous Wyoming farm girl, Rachel saw herself at Blaine's age, looking for a meal ticket. Determined to rid Jamie of his new wife, she bribed Blaine's redneck ex-boyfriend, BUZZ WINSLOW (Eric Conger), to come to Bay City and win Blaine away from her son. Both Mac and Jamie were horrified when they discovered what Rachel had done; Mac separated from Rachel, but only briefly.

But then Mac did something almost as dreadful. Rachel had become pregnant by Mac and they were now the happy parents of little AMANDA. In front of Iris, Mac called Amanda his "first child," negligently revealing the secret that Iris had been adopted. Feeling lied to and rejected, Iris separated from her husband, Brian Bancroft, and searched constantly for her natural mother. She turned out to be SYLVIE KOSLOFF (Leora Dana), a New York based designer of cut-rate women's clothing. Initially Iris thought her mother a crude, classless type, but soon formed a warm bond with her. Sylvie came to Bay City with her business associate, KIRK LAVERTY (Charles Cioffi). With his myriad development plans he swept Iris off her feet, but he had a wife and was only interested in Iris's money. Kirk was eventually murdered by his lawyer, JEFF STONE (Dan Hamilton). Clarice's new policeman husband, LARRY EWING (Robert J. Porter), Blaine Ewing's good-hearted brother, put Jeff Stone behind bars. Sylvie left Bay City and Iris reconciled with Brian.

The pattern of breakups and reconciliations between Mac and Rachel continued. Steve's sister, JANICE FRAME** (Christine Jones), came back to Bay City, colder and more calculating than ever. Taking a job working for Mac in his publishing firm, she began to lure him into a romantic tryst, purely for his money. Foolishly, Mac did not suspect her motives but Rachel

**Janice Frame had come to Bay City years before while Steve was alive. Played by Victoria Thompson, she had tried to win Robert Delaney away from Lenore, then left town.

By 1976, Susan Harney replaced Jacquie Courtney as Alice and Gary Pillar (now known as Gary Carpenter) became the new Raymond Gordon. (Ten years earlier Gary Pillar had played Michael Bauer, who had come to Bay City from The Guiding Light.*) After Alice married Raymond, he ruined her business affairs and she divorced him.*

Sympathetic waitress Clarice Hobson (Gail Brown, the sister of Karen Black) was one of those "mood" characters on the new hour-long show. Harding Lemay stressed her personality rather than her involvement in a sustained plot. With her in 1977 is Burt McGowan (William Russ), the son of Ada's third husband Gil. She and Burt wed briefly.

did and began to quarrel with him, not only over Janice's designs on him, but over Jamie's marriage to Blaine. Before long, Rachel and Mac were divorced. He set up housekeeping with Janice and, rather cruelly, had his little daughter Amanda kidnapped from Rachel to live with him and Janice. She had a secret lover, MITCH BLAKE (William Gray Espy), who came to Bay City and began to help her carry out her sinister plan to acquire Mac's money. At Mac's publishing offices, she had read a murder mystery called *Harry Must Die!*, and now began to use it as a model for killing Mac. Meanwhile, Pat, who also worked for the publishing company, became suspicious when she found pages of that mystery novel missing. Because of the novel and other evidence, Rachel felt sure Jan-

ice was planning to kill Mac. In a dazzling turn of events, Mac, Janice, Rachel and Mitch all wound up on the island of St. Croix. To learn the details of Janice's plan, Rachel slept with Mitch, who decided to help her foil Janice. Janice poisoned Mac but then, in a violent struggle in a swimming pool, Rachel stabbed Janice to death in time for Mac to get medical help. Mac and Rachel were happily remarried, this time, oddly, with Iris's blessing.

Not long after, Iris left Bay City for Houston, since her son Dennis had gone there to open an art gallery. There she met ALEX WHEELER (Bert Kramer), a Boston oil magnate. He had had an affair with Iris many years before when he was a poor seaman and had been Dennis's real father. Iris divorced Brian Bancroft to

On March 5, 1979, Another World *inflated to an unwieldy ninety minutes and then deflated back to an hour some months later. The enormous cast then included, foreground, from left: Mike Ryan, Beverly Penberthy, Paul Stevens, Beverlee McKinsey, Douglass Watson, Victoria Wyndham, Constance Ford, Tim Holcomb, Anne Meacham, John Tillinger, Robert Lintner. Back row, from left: Adrienne Wallace, Irene Dailey, Lionel Johnston, Hugh Marlowe, Susan Harney, Lynn Milgrim, Jennifer Leak, Christina Pickles, Jim Poyner, Leora Dana, Vicky Dawson, Ray Liotta, Kathleen Widdoes, Trish Hawkins, Laura Malone, Jay Morran, Maeve Kinkead, Leon Russom, Eric Conger, Dorothy Lyman, Christine Jones, Rick Porter, Fred J. Scollay, Margaret Barker and Gail Brown.*

rediscover love with Alex in Houston. (Actually, Iris and Dennis had moved to *Texas*, the new spinoff serial from *Another World*. See page 358.)

* * *

Joey Perrini eventually recovered from the loss of Eileen Simpson and became attracted to a soft-spoken young nurse named KIT FARRELL (Bradley Bliss). Right after Joey married her, he was stunned when he learned that Kit Farrell's actual last name had been Halloway and that she was quite wealthy and had at one time been kidnapped by Italian terrorists. Kit had kept her identity a secret to avoid publicity. Joey accepted that. His conservative mother, Rose, however, couldn't and became so upset at Kit's deception that she alienated her own beau, blue collar worker PAUL CONNELLY (Stephen Joyce). Rose decided to leave Bay City. Kit and Joey had marital problems stemming from the clash of very different backgrounds, and they had their marriage annulled. But they were still in love and some time later they remarried and left Bay City.

Members of Kit's family came to town, including her understanding father, TAYLOR HALLOWAY (Ron Harper); Kit's elder sister, AMY DUDLEY (Deborah Hobart), a divorcée who was jealous of the attention Kit always had; and RICK HALLOWAY (Tony Cummings), Kit's brother, a hardworking doctor.

Meanwhile, Jamie had divorced Blaine and Blaine remarried JERRY GROVE (Michael Garfield, Kevin Conroy, Paul Tinder), a struggling lawyer, and hoped to make a better life for herself. But she soon became ensnared in Bay City's crime syndicate. The syndicate was about to kill her husband's mother, MARGO GROVE (Judy Cassmore), since she had recognized its members earlier in Las Vegas. To save her mother-in-law, Blaine told Jerry that their marriage was over and went undercover, becoming the mistress of the leading syndicate figure, JORDAN SCOTT (J. Kenneth Campbell).

The lives of many in Bay City, even that of innocent Russ Mathews, would soon be touched by the same crime mob. Russ had returned to town, as did TRACY DE WITT (Caroline McWilliams, Janice Lynde), Iris's old society friend. Russ and Tracy fell in love and married, but JASON DUNLAP (Warren Burton), who was managing Tracy's new singing career, wanted Tracy for himself. He paid mob figure ILSA FREDERICKS (Gwyda DonHowe) to have Russ annihilated in a car explo-

In an elaborate 1981 tale concerning Rachel's attempts to save Mac from being murdered by his new wife, Janice Frame, Rachel, seduced shady Mitch Blake (William Gray Espy) in order to gain information about the murder. The story took place in St. Croix. Most soaps were now taping sequences in such exotic places.

Jennifer Runyon played the important character of Sally Frame (here with James Horan as Denny Hobson) in 1982. As Alice's adopted daughter, she represented the tail end of the Frame clan, along with Steve's illegitimate son Jamie.

Steve Frame suddenly turned up alive in 1982 (with David Canary as the lead) and married Rachel after the two were trapped by an explosion. In shock over losing him again, Alice left Bay City. The show had come full circle, resolving its original plot line. Early in 1983 Steve was killed, this time for real, leaving Rachel to reunite with Mac.

sion. But, because of a mistake, it was poor Tracy who was blown up and killed. Russ was beside himself at the loss of his new wife.

For several months, Mac and Rachel had found happiness. Mac had become quite ecstatic when he learned that Rachel was finally pregnant. But Rachel harbored a terrible secret: she knew that the baby was Mitch Blake's. Mitch also knew that the baby was his and pressured Rachel almost daily to divorce Mac so that they could become a family. Then, when the Cory stables burned to the ground, a dead body was found in the remains and assumed to be Mitch's, since it bore his identification and Mitch himself was missing. Rachel was tried for his murder. During the trial, the cunning D.A., ZACHARY COLTON (Curt Dawson), proved that Rachel's baby was Mitch Blake's and tried to show that Rachel had murdered Mitch to cover up her secret. Mac was demolished and swore he would cut Rachel out of his life. She was found guilty and sent to prison, while still with child.

Jordan Scott became suspicious of Blaine's motive in taking up with him. When he tried to rape her, she shot him in self-defense and then stood trial for his murder. But Jordan's killer turned out to be Blaine's own prosecutor, Zachary Colton, the same district attorney who prosecuted Rachel. He was in the mob's pocket and had shot and killed Jordan after Blaine had shot him. Jason confessed to his plot to kill Russ, turned state's evidence and was granted immunity. Blaine was released.

When Ada's husband, Charlie Hobson—the father of Clarice—died peacefully in his sleep, Rachel was released for a day to attend his funeral. But instead of returning to the prison, she escaped to look for Mitch, whom Mac and some others still believed to be alive. When Rachel finally found him, he was suffering from amnesia. He had been struck on the head and a *prowler* had been killed, his body put in the stables! After Mitch came back to Bay City, Rachel was absolved of any wrongdoing and returned to Mac, who was deliriously happy to have her back with him and Amanda. But by now it was clear to Rachel and everyone else that she was now in love with Mitch, the father of her new baby boy, MATTHEW. She left Mac to live with Mitch and little Matthew, but in a bitter custody battle lost baby Amanda to Mac.

Beautiful young heiress CECILE DE POULIGNAC (Susan Keith, Nancy Frangione), the niece of Countess Elena de Poulignac, arrived in Bay City. Sophisti-cated on the surface, Cecile was no lady when it came to affairs of the heart. Handsome PHILIP LYONS (Bob Gentry), an editor at Cory Publications who had been a gigolo in the past, had at first courted the rich Cecile for her money. When he realized that he was losing his zeal for golddigging, he became sincerely interested in co-worker Pat Randolph, whose old drinking problem had been plaguing her again. Cecile tried to win Philip back from Pat by becoming a sensationalistic, aggressive editor at Cory, working closely with Philip. Soon she and Pat were also professional foes on a new women's magazine, Brava. Pat conquered her drinking problem and successfully fought Cecile back for Philip. But after Pat and Philip had a brief sexual relationship, Pat felt she had become too dependent on him and ended it to concentrate on her publishing career.

Cecile went on to marry Jamie Frame, who had now grown into a fine looking young man, and thereby Cecile established strong ties to the Cory empire. Meanwhile, Mac Cory became friends with tall, blond SANDY ALEXANDER (Christopher Rich), who had been the prize stud in the syndicate's nationwide "escort service" (for older female clients). Sandy wanted more out of life than to be a prostitute, and so with Mac's help he began a promising career at Cory. Cecile was instantly attracted to gorgeous Sandy. Then she looked at Sandy's birth certificate and realized that the young man was Mac's illegitimate son! She decided that she would undermine her own marriage to Jamie to marry him, keeping Mac unaware that she had caused the divorce.

Jamie worked at Cory Publications, too, and drove himself hard in order to prove himself to Mac. Obsessed with work, Jamie began to take "uppers," or pep pills, to get through the day—totally unaware that his wife had her eyes on his good friend Sandy Alexander. Marianne Randolph, now a nurse at the hospital, sensed Jamie was driving himself too hard and began counseling him. Marianne, despite her ongoing romance with Rick Halloway, Kit's doctor brother, found herself becoming more and more emotionally attached to Jamie. To her rival Pat and others, cunning Cecile began claiming that Jamie's involvement with Marianne, as well as his addiction to pills, was breaking up their marriage. She even drugged Jamie several times while he was trying to lick his habit! Eventually Cecile divorced Jamie and married Sandy, soon giving birth to their child, MAGGIE. When Sandy had finally freed himself of all connections to the mob, he told a delighted Mac that he was his illegitimate son.

*   *   *

Alice and Sally returned to Bay City from Chicago, still at odds over Sally's youthful sexual involvements. Now hoping to marry a man who could provide material luxuries for her, Sally became interested in DENNY HOBSON (James Horan), Clarice's business-minded young brother. Sally was delighted when Denny obtained a big position with Black Hawk Enterprises, a firm of nebulous nature headed by a mysterious "Mr. Black." Denny wondered when his boss, this Mr. Black, would show himself. Mr. Black finally did come to Bay City. His real name was Steven Frame!

He had not died in a helicopter explosion in Australia, as everyone thought, but instead had been thrown from the burning aircraft and had suffered prolonged amnesia. By now Alice had become engaged to Mac and Rachel believed that she had a future with Mitch. Steve's reappearance destroyed all these new romantic ties. Rachel broke off with Mitch, who promptly hired an unethical organization dedicated to preserving fathers' rights to kidnap Matthew away from Rachel. Steve, who was beginning to grow close to Rachel again, helped Rachel grab Matthew away from the men. Alice broke off with Mac to become engaged to Steve but became more and more insecure over his newfound admiration of Rachel as a mature woman with a conscience.

Jamie was quite happy to be reunited with his father Steve, whom he hadn't seen since he was a child. Still, Jamie was fairly sickened by the romantic merry-go-rounds and the hypocrisy which surrounded him. He began work on a scandalous novel, *A View From The Bay*, based on the lives of the people of Bay City. Marianne fell in love with Jamie and left her new husband, Rick Halloway, to live with him. She peeked at the contents of Jamie's manuscript and saw that it described in detail the Greg Barnard murder story. Quite upset, she left Jamie, reconciled with her husband Rick and told Pat about the novel. Pat, who had been on the brink of accepting Brian Bancroft's proposal of marriage, was so horrified that Jamie would publish her story that she left Bay City. Marianne and Rick left town as well, leaving Jamie to bask alone in the ill-gotten glory of his phenomenally successful novel, which was made into a movie.

While Ada and Steve sympathized with Jamie, Rachel and Mac became furious at his vindictiveness.

Sandy Alexander finally saw his wife, Cecile, for what she was, and left her for Blaine Ewing, with whom he had fallen in love. But Cecile was determined to get him back any way she could. She hired ALMA RUDDER (Elizabeth Franz), the sister of Blaine's old criminal boyfriend, Buzz Winslow, to drive Blaine mad. Then Buzz kidnapped Blaine but, fortunately, fell off a cliff to his death. Alma escaped the authorities. Simultaneously, Cecile's father, LOUIS ST. GEORGE (Jack Betts), had arrived in town and had begun art transactions with Rachel's new art gallery. He was being pursued by a gang of Nazi art smugglers, while Cory lawyer Brian Bancroft was investigating suave Louis and the smugglers. Brian convinced Sandy to renew his relationship with Cecile in order to get information on Louis St. George. Meanwhile, Cecile was still trying to adjust to the fact that Elena de Poulignac was not her aunt but, by her own admission, Cecile's mother!

*   *   *

Steve Frame, while engaged to Alice, brought DIANA FRAME (Anne Rose Brooks), to Bay City. She was the daughter of his recently deceased British wife, PAMELA. A stubborn girl, she fell in love with Steve's stable boy PETE SHEA (Christopher Mercantel) and married him, despite Steve's and her parents' objections. Denny Hobson, who still worked for Steve, married Sally with Steve's approval, but Steve was unaware that Denny was playing double agent with crooked union leaders who murdered LORETTA SHEA (Anita Gillette), Pete Shea's mother, by blowing up her car. After Sandy and Blaine got to the bottom of the union corruption, which touched Steve's operation, Denny was sent to prison.

On the eve of Alice and Steve's wedding, Steve and Rachel were trapped in a crumbling building which had been purposely engineered to collapse in order to ruin him financially. During this shared, desperate moment, Steve and Rachel realized they belonged together. Steve's love for Alice, he now thought, had been a mere fantasy. Rachel, who represented his passionate and truer side, had finally won out. After they were rescued, Steve broke off his engagement to Alice. Then Alice was struck by a second mortal blow: word came that her father, Jim Matthews, had died of a heart attack in Helsinki while doing business for Steve! With most of her family now dead or out of town, Alice decided to leave Bay City for good.

Steve, who moved in with Rachel, went bankrupt and had to rely on her for financial support until he was hired by Ilsa Fredericks to redecorate Mitch's old discotheque, the Connection. Ilsa was still very much involved with the mob. Steve and Jason Dunlap, who had turned state's evidence after he had tried to get Ilsa Fredericks to kill Russ Matthews, teamed up to secretly investigate Ilsa and wipe the mob out of Bay City. Steve at last married Rachel but, tragically, as they were driving on their honeymoon, they suffered an auto accident and Steve was killed. Rachel was grief-stricken for months, but later, in a double ceremony, Rachel and Mac once again exchanged wedding vows, as did Sandy and Blaine.

Jamie called himself "James Frame" these days and became a professor of writing at Bay State University. After returning to the good graces of his family, he became involved with the older Susan Shearer, once again separated from her husband Dan, while being pursued by JULIA SHEARER (Kyra Sedgwick, Janna Leigh), Susan and Dan's adopted teenage daughter. She had begun an acting career in the movie that they made right in Bay City from Jamie's scandalous novel. However, Susan reconciled with Dan in Boston, and Julia got over her infatuation with Jamie. Jamie then fell in love with competent woman attorney STACEY WINTHROP (Terry Davis).

Alma Rudder returned to Bay City in disguise to blackmail Cecile! Cecile's lover, Stacey's ambitious brother, CASS WINTHROP (Stephen Schnetzer), was caught up in the scheme. Cass was also having an affair with FELICIA GALLANT (Linda Dano), Louis St. George's ex-wife, a strong-willed romance novelist. The outcome: Alma was murdered!

CAST
ANOTHER WORLD
NBC: May 4, 1964

Liz Matthews	Sarah Cunningham (P)
	Audra Lindley
	Nancy Wickwire
	Irene Dailey*
Jim Matthews	John Beal (P)
	Leon Janney
	Shepperd Strudwick
	Hugh Marlowe*
Mary Matthews	Virginia Dwyer (P)
Pat Matthews Randolph	Susan Trustman (P)
	Beverly Penberthy*
Dr. Russ Matthews	Joey Trent (P)
	Sam Groom
	Robert Hover
	David Bailey*
Alice Matthews Frame	Jacqueline Courtney* (P)
	Susan Harney
	Wesley Ann Pfenning
	Vana Tribbey
	Linda Borgeson
Bill Matthews	Joseph Gallison (P)
Missy Palmer Matthews	Carol Roux (P)
Dr. Susan Matthews Shearer	Fran Sharon (P)
	Roni Dengel
	Lisa Cameron
	Lynn Milgrim*
Grandma Matthews	Vera Allen (P)
Janet Matthews	Liza Chapman (P)
Ken Baxter	William Prince (P)
Laura Baxter	Augusta Dabney (P)
Tom Baxter	Nicholas Pryor (P)
Ann Fuller	Olga Bellin (P)
John Randolph	Michael M. Ryan
Lee Randolph	Gaye Huston
	Barbara Rodell*
Alex Gregory	James Congdon
Karen Gregory	Ellen Weston
Dr. Ernest Gregory	Mark Lenard
Mitchell Dru	Geoffrey Lumb
Michael Bauer	Gary Pillar (a.k.a. Carpenter)
Hope Bauer	Elissa Leeds
Emily Hastings	Mona Bruns
Kathryn Corning	Ann Sheridan
Danny Fargo	Antony Ponzini
Flo Murray	Marcella Martin
Madge Murray	Doris Belack
Charlie Rushinberger	Ralph Oliver
Helen Moore	Murial Williams
Lenore Moore Delaney	Judith Barcroft
	Susan Sullivan
Walter Curtin	Val DuFour
Ada Davis Hobson	Constance Ford
Rachel Davis Cory	Robin Strasser
	Margaret Impert

	Victoria Wyndham*
Sam Lucas	Jordan Charney
Lahoma Vane Lucas	Ann Wedgeworth
Ernie Downs	Harry Bellaver
Peggy Harris Nolan	Micki Grant
Lt. Dick Nolan	Lon Sutton
Fred Douglas	Charles Baxter
Lefty Burns	Lawrence Keith
Steven Frame	George Reinholt*
	David Canary
Jamie Frame	Seth Holzlein
	Aiden McNulty
	Brad Bedford
	Robert Doran
	Tim Holcomb
	Richard Bekins
Wayne Addison	Edmund Hashim
	Robert Milli*
Bernice Robinson	Janis Young
Dr. Dan Shearer	John Cunningham
	Brian Murray
Cindy Clark Matthews	Leonie Norton
Belle Clark	Janet Ward
Ted Clark	Stephen Bolster
Caroline Johnson	Rue McClanahan
Michael Randolph	Christopher Corwin
	Glen Zachar
	Tim Nissen
	Tom Ruger
	Tom Sabota, Jr.
	Christopher J. Brown
	Lionel Johnston*
Marianne Randolph Halloway	Tracey Brown
	Tiberia Mitri
	Loriann Ruger
	Jill Turnbull
	Ariane Munker
	Adrienne Wallace
	Beth Collins
Wally Curtin	Scott Firestone
	Jason Gladstone
	Dennis McKiernan
Gerald Davis	Walter Mathews
Robert Delaney	Nicolas Coster
Gil McGowan	Charles Durning
	Dolph Sweet*
Dr. David Rogers	Walter McGinn
Janice Frame Cory	Victoria Thompson
	Christine Jones
Linda Metcalf	Vera Moore
Emma Ordway	Beverlee McKinsey
	Teresa Hughes*
Iris Carrington Bancroft	Beverlee McKinsey
Eliot Carrington	James Douglas
Dennis Carrington	Mike Hammett
	Jim Poyner
Louise Goddard Brooks	Anne Meacham
Mackenzie Cory	Robert Emhardt
	Douglas Watson*
Dr. Kurt Landis	Donald Madden
Vic Hastings	John Considine
Carol Lamonte	Jeanne Lange
Therese Lamonte	Nancy Marchand
Dr. Dave Gilchrest	David Ackroyd
Willis Frame	John Fitzpatrick
	Leon Russom*
Sharlene Watts Matthews	Laurie Heineman
Angie Perrini Frame	Toni Kalem
	Maeve Kinkead*
Tim McGowan	Christopher Allport
Barbara Weaver	Roberta Maxwell*
	Kathryn Walker
Philip Wainwright	James Luisi
Clarice Hobson Ewing	Gail Brown
Sally Spencer Frame	Cathy Greene
	Julie Philips
	Jennifer Runyon
	Dawn Benz
	Mary Page Keller
Beatrice Gordon	Jacqueline Brookes
Raymond Gordon	Ted Shackelford
	Gary Carpenter
Olive Gordon Randolph	Jennifer Leak
Ken Palmer	Kelly Monahan
	William Lyman*
Tracy DeWitt Matthews	Caroline McWilliams
	Janice Lynde*
Molly Ordway Randolph	Rolanda Mendels
Jeff Stone	Dan Hamilton
Rocky Olsen	John Braden
Leonard Brooks	Joseph Maher
	John Horton
	John Tillinger*
Gwen Parrish Frame	Dorothy Lyman
Evan Webster	Barry Jenner
Brian Bancroft	Paul Stevens
Ted Bancroft	Eric A. Roberts
	Richard Backus

Burt McGowan . . . . William Russ*
Joseph Hindy
Sven Petersen . . . . Roberts Blossom
Helga Lindeman . . . . . . Helen Stenborg
Regine Lindeman . . . . . Barbara Eda-Young
Cliff Tanner . . . . Tom Rolfing
Elena de Poulignac . . . . Christina Pickles
Maeve McGuire
Greg Barnard . . . . Ned Schmidtke
Charlie Hobson . . . . Fred J. Scollay
Vince Frame . . . . Jay Morran
Rose Perrini . . . . Kathleen Widdoes
Joey Perrini . . . . Ray Liotta*
Paul Perri
Eileen Simpson Perrini . Vicky Dawson
Vivien Gorrow . . . . Gretchen Oehler
Blaine Ewing Grove . . . . Laura Malone
Larry Ewing . . . . Richard J. Porter
Buzz Winslow . . . . Eric Conger
Sylvie Kosloff . . . . Leora Dana
Karen Campbell
Randolph . . . . Laurie Bartram
Leueen Parrish . . . . Margaret Barker
Paul Connelly . . . . Stephen Joyce
Phil Higley . . . . McLin Crowell
Mimi Haines Frame . . . . Trish Hawkins
Kirk Laverty . . . . Charles Cioffi
June Laverty . . . . Geraldine Court
Cecile de Poulignac
Cory . . . . Susan Keith
Nancy Frangione
Philip Lyons . . . . Bob Gentry
Mitch Blake . . . . William Gray Espy
Jason Dunlap . . . . Warren Burton
Alex Wheeler . . . . Bert Kramer
Kit Halloway Perrini . . . Bradley Bliss
Taylor Halloway . . . . Ron Harper
Dr. Rick Halloway . . . . . Tony Cummings
Amy Dudley . . . . Deborah Hobart
Miranda Bishop . . . . Judith McConnell
Jerry Grove . . . . Michael Garfield
Kevin Conroy
Paul Tinder
Jordan Scott . . . . J. Kenneth Campbell
Zachary Colton . . . . Curt Dawson
Ilsa Fredericks . . . . Gwyda DonHowe
Sandy Alexander Cory . Christopher Rich
Melissa Needham . . . . . Taro Meyer

Dr. Olivia Delaney . . . . . Tina Sloan
Leigh Hobson . . . . Christopher Knight
Denny Hobson . . . . James Horan
Quinn Harding . . . . Petronia Paley
Diana Frame Shea . . . . . Anne Rose Brooks
Pete Shea . . . . Christopher Marcantel
Harry Shea . . . . Edward Power
Loretta Shea . . . . Anita Gillette
Julia Shearer . . . . Kyra Sedgwick
Janna Leigh
Lt. Bob Morgan . . . . Robert Christian
Henrietta Morgan . . . . . Michelle Shay
R. J. Morgan . . . . Reggie Rock Blythewood
Ed Harding . . . . Howard E. Rollins, Jr.
Milo Simonelli . . . . Louis Zorich
Alma Rudder . . . . Elizabeth Franz
Louis St. George . . . . . . Jack Betts
Cass Winthrop . . . . Stephen Schnetzer
Stacey Winthrop . . . . . . Terry Davis
Felicia Gallant . . . . Linda Dano

Creator: Irna Phillips
Head Writers: Irna Phillips and William Bell, James
Lipton, Agnes Nixon, Robert
Cenedella, Harding Lemay, Tom King,
L. Virginia Browne, Corinne Jacker,
Robert Soderberg and Dorothy Purser
Assistant Head Writer: Douglas Marland (for
Harding Lemay)
Executive Producers: Lyle B. Hill, Paul Rauch,
Allen Potter
Producers: Allen Potter, Doris Quinlan, Paul Robert,
Mary Harris, Lyle B. Hill, Sid Sirulnick,
Joe Rothenberger, Mary S. Bonner,
Joseph D. Manetta, Gail Kobe, Joe
Willmore, Robert Costello, Robert
Calhoun, James A. Baffico, Kathlyn
Chambers
Directors: Tom Donovan, Leonard Valenta, David
Pressman, Ira Cirker, Joseph L. Scanlan,
Cort Steen, Richard T. McCue, Melvin
Bernhardt, Peter Levin, Art Wolff, Kevin
Kelly, Paul Lammers, Jack Hofsiss, Robert
Calhoun, Tony Giordano, Barnet Kellman,
Andrew D. Weyman, Ron Lagomarsino
Organists: Clarke Morgan, Chet Kingsbury
Musical Direction (later): Score Productions
Packager: Procter & Gamble

AS THE WORLD TURNS

IN modern times *As the World Turns* remains the most historically important soap opera. Although college students and teenagers now seem to prefer ABC soaps, those very soaps which are the darlings of college courses owe a debt to Irna Phillips's greatest creation. For many years it had a special, groundbreaking style and dominated daytime television. Let us journey back twenty-eight years.

BACKGROUND

A sleepy Nancy: "Good morning."
A sleepy Chris: "Good morning, dear."

With such deathless dialogue, spoken in the kitchen of Oakdale's Nancy and Chris Hughes, drowsily began the first episode of *As the World Turns* on April 2, 1956. The words with which the happily married couple continued their morning conversation—as well as the dialogue of succeeding scenes with daughter Penny Hughes, her best friend Ellen Lowell, Judge Lowell, Grandpa Hughes and all the other members of the Hughes and Lowell families—were naturally more substantial, though hardly more dramatic.

The activities on *As the World Turns* were very, *very* slow. The majority of scenes did not advance the plot, what little there was. Often the action seemed to stop entirely as the TV cameras, like curious eyes closely scrutinizing alien beings, studied the geography of faces. Lines were delivered with numerous pauses and introspective glances. Characteristic scenes involved Nancy and Chris discussing rather ordinary family dilemmas either in their kitchen or seated on the sofa of their living room; Penny and Ellen talking in their bedrooms about their plans for college, ideas about boyfriends, reactions to their parents; and unhappily married Jim and Claire Lowell individually seeking advice from Jim's wise father, Judge Lowell. The one "plot" character was Edith Hughes ("Aunt Edie"), who was having an affair with Ellen's father, Jim, much to the distress of the two families. Other than Edith, all the others in the story were simply existing, as most people do, seemingly unconcerned with the day-to-day story interest they projected to viewers.

Would anyone bother watching this non-story story? Was it even a bona fide soap opera?

Only the creator of *As the World Turns*—neurotic, stormy, insecure and unquestionably brilliant Irna Phillips—had been convinced that the answer to both those questions was a resounding yes. She felt she knew what women wanted and needed to watch in the afternoon.

As the World Turns started with an exceptionally low rating point of four (about four million people) and had hardly any ratings growth for about a year. Casual dial turners apparently didn't take to its slow pace and the time, 1:30 P.M. E.S.T., was such a poor one in those days that it used to be known as the "graveyard." With great foresight Irna had expected this turn of events and had insisted in her P&G contract that no matter how poor the ratings, her new show could not be canceled for at least a year. Despite the bad Nielsens, Irna slaved with director Ted Corday, her sidekick in the venture from the first day, to keep *As the World Turns* true to her original concept. The ratings began to increase, gradually as more and more housewives discovered what was happening in the "graveyard." But by the end of its second year, *As the World Turns* was television's highest-rated soap opera. For most of its history it has stayed in that same position or close to it.

* * *

Irna Phillips was ahead of her time when she invented the iconoclastic *As the World Turns*. Irna saw daytime drama in terms of time and character, rather than story. She understood something that only loyal soap fans truly know: that people want to become involved with the lives of other people; that viewers follow soaps not just to see what happens next, but to experience the characters, almost as if they lived in viewers' homes. Story to Irna was simply a vehicle; it was from the moment-to-moment emotions of her characters, expressed to each other in quiet scenes, that viewers derived true vicarious pleasure. Understanding this essential truth about the viewer, Irna needed more television time—a full half-hour—for the camera to eavesdrop on long "coffee cup" conversations, showing every facial reaction in utmost detail. Obviously, such probing scenes required the most exquisite sort of cameo acting, so Irna and partner Ted Corday—one of the great directorial talents in serials, from the days when they were all broadcast from Chicago radio studios—chose their actors with painstaking care. Each performer had to be capable of totally absorbing the viewer with his or her personality, and of handling Corday's extreme emphasis on closeups.

Irna and Ted individually chose the two actors for the central characters of Nancy and Chris Hughes. Ted picked Don MacLaughlin because he knew his work so well from radio. Irna picked Helen Wagner because she had seen her play a convincing mother on *The World of Mr. Sweeney* for several years. After a pro forma audition, Don and Helen were signed. As Helen Wagner recalls, "I was fired after the first thir-teen weeks of the show over a guarantee dispute. Irna said she didn't like my hair, the way I wore my clothes and a lot of other little things as an excuse to fire me. Irna would often invent trivial gripes about an actor in order to fire him, when it was just a case of Irna's being angry. I left the show, not too upset, and went immediately into a play. I think Irna had Nancy go off on a vacation. After she had cooled off and realized that she had made a mistake, she offered to renegotiate my contract with my husband [producer Bob Willey, who acts as Helen's manager] and was told that she couldn't get me back immediately because I was in a play. Irna loved being at my mercy and wanted me back on the show all the more."

There were a few other firings in the beginning. Billy Lee, the first Grandpa Hughes, was let go after three episodes and replaced by Santos Ortega, who remained in the part until his death on April 10, 1976. Hal Studer (husband of Billie Lou Watt), the first Donald Hughes, was let go because Irna thought he was too short, and replaced by Richard Holland.

In the rest of the cast there was extraordinary stability. The regulars included Rosemary Prinz as Penny, Bobby Alford as little Bob Hughes, Ruth Warrick as Aunt Edie, Les Damon and Anne Burr as Jim and Claire Lowell, Wendy Drew as Ellen Lowell and William Johnstone as Judge Lowell.

For the first few years, *As the World Turns* was aired from the old Grand Central Television Studio; the show later moved to the old Dumont Studios; then, in 1963, to the Himan Brown Studio, and finally, in recent years, to CBS's West Fifty-seventh Street broadcasting megalopolis—all spacious broadcasting centers, and quite a far cry from the overcrowded, smallish Liederkrantz Hall, where most of CBS's soaps had been jammed in during the early fifties.

Countless executives had been involved in the creation and day-to-day progress of *As the World Turns*, but the show was really controlled by only two people: Irna and Ted Corday. Ted was called executive director, but could just as easily have been called head man. A strict and humorless disciplinarian, Ted handled his actors with an invisible whip. He expected every actor to show up at rehearsals knowing every word of dialogue and in a somberly professional mood. You waited for Ted in the rehearsal hall as if waiting for the Second Coming.

Yet everyone respected him. Unlike the majority of directors of daytime serials, who have little time during their hectic days to give actors detailed instructions on matters of interpretation, Ted always did find the time. He had an uncommon understanding of every personality in Oakdale. He put himself in complete command of the unusual pacing that he and Irna had worked out well before the premiere, the delicate interrelationships that his three cameras would catch in startling closeups, the defiance of normal dramatic time. Until Ted left *As the World Turns* in the mid-sixties to create his own show, *Days of Our Lives*, no one worked harder than he did to keep Irna's Oakdale the very special place it remains today.

While Ted minded the store in the actual locale of broadcast in New York City, Irna kept an eye on the doings from her Chicago apartment *cum* writing factory. Daily at 1:30 her secretaries and assistant writers would lapse into silence while she watched the globe turn on her television screen, followed by the day's episode. One or two minutes after the live broadcast, an assistant of Ted's at the New York studio received a call from Irna. A typical taking-an-Irna-call-after-the-broadcast was fraught with tension, frosted over with a bit of polite sickly sweet goo on both the Chicago and New York ends. Sometimes the call was placed from the New York end and the underling might say, "Hello, Irna. This is *As the World Turns* . . ." She'd snap, "Not today it didn't!" before going into her criticisms of what had gone wrong. When speaking to anyone besides Ted Corday, whom she respected, she used an interesting speaking technique, which she had probably learned during her early years as a schoolteacher: She would speak softer and softer, until the listener was nearly mesmerized. It was her way of controlling the conversation. It was rather frightening, even when one caught on to her method. Among some of the less-intimidated executives, a running joke to Irna was: "Irna, please don't lower your voice to me!" Once she replied, "Oh, you figured it out." But not many had the guts to joke with her honestly once that cleverly paced Midwestern voice began droning on the other end of the line.

Often Irna's calls were four- to six-party conference tie-ins, bordering on the surrealistic. There would be one or two executives on lines at the New York studio end, someone tied in from the advertising agency (for years it was Benton & Bowles, then Young & Rubicam, and currently Benton & Bowles again), one or two people tied in from Procter & Gamble Productions in Cincinnati, and of course Irna, totally and regally in charge of the proceedings from her Chicago home. To hear all of these lofty executives kowtow to soft-spoken Irna seemed absurd. Yet there was the inescapable fact that *As the World Turns* was her private vision, which, not inconsequentially, was making P&G the absolute leader in daytime programming and lots of money. It was this money which gave Irna the power.

In her early fifties when *As the World Turns* premiered, Irna Phillips was a strange and complex genius. She appeared to have a far greater comprehension of the millions of women for whom she wrote than she did of herself—as evidenced by her typically uningratiating posture in a world of other people. Outside of her pleasant blue eyes, Irna was not an especially attractive woman. She had been a late baby and had grown up with the feeling that she was an "accident" in her family, an unwanted child. These problems may have been the key to her insecurities, which prompted a lifelong quest for success in a man's world, kept her from the fulfillment of marriage (although, as a single woman, she adopted and raised two fine children) and appended to her personality, as she grew older, a stinging cruelty.

The day-to-day placidity, warmth, and sense of family involvement that she added to the lives of viewers of *As the World Turns* has never been duplicated on any other serial, not even in her last major creation, *Another World*. Yet behind the scenes of the show that exalted the joys of love and small-town peace, Irna created a tense, fearful atmosphere. She habitually called most of the show's regular actors and addressed them by their character names, "Penny" or "Chris," never their own names. In these calls she would make exasperating comments on what she thought the actor should do to improve himself, either personally or professionally, for the good of the show. It was quite as if for Irna Oakdale was a real place—far more real than New York or Chicago, and far better. From Irna's point of view, the least deviation from her idea of Oakdale—whether it was something as minor as a change of wording that an actor made in her original dialogue—was an assault on the reality of Oakdale.

A number of actors were too frightened of Irna's power to argue with her when the inevitable call came, and that would infuriate her. Although she didn't outwardly invite it, she wanted people to talk with her on a one-to-one basis, even attempt to dominate her if they could. An actor often found himself fired after having politely agreed to all of Irna's suggested changes—simply because Irna would have preferred more of a challenge. Don MacLaughlin learned quite early in his career as Chris Hughes how to handle her. Don comments: "Irna was talented and neurotic. The content of her scenes was brilliant, but her dialogue was terrible. Many actors, including myself, would change her lines, and later she would call from Chicago to complain about the changes. Now, some people could stand up to Irna and she'd love it, and some people would just get the ax. I happened to get along well with Irna. In the first year of the show she told me flatly she didn't want me rewriting her lines, and I just told her: 'Irna, I'll say what you've written and I'll follow the content of your script. But if you want me to say your lines word for word, you'd better get yourself another actor.' " That approach didn't always save one's job, but it was safer than saying nothing. Helen Wagner also openly argued with Irna about matters of interpretation. "I constantly fought with Irna about Nancy's possessiveness. I think Irna was trying to make Nancy like her own mother. Anyway, I tried to make Nancy's sins understandable—so that even if the audience disapproved of her possessiveness, they at least saw that Nancy *believed* she was helping her children."

Yet, the only talent connected with *As the World Turns* who could truly stand up to Irna was Ted Corday. She would come to the broadcasting studio during her incessant trips to New York, often when a new actor was being cast for an important role. Irna would watch the audition and, knowing full well that Ted liked the performer, immediately afterward stun Ted with "I don't think that actress will do." Ted would say, matching the challenging power play with an equivalent sally, "What do you mean? She's terrific." Ted and Irna didn't have quiet little conferences out of earshot of cast and management. They had shouting fights in the halls outside the rehearsal rooms and executive offices. It was quite a sight and sound: big, paunchy, terribly imposing Ted and the quietly calculating Midwestern queen of soaps, openly at each other's throats in an attempt to gain full control of the show. The hearty competition was thoroughly enjoyed by Irna, who needed to fight in order to feel her power. Ted was good therapy for her. She would never have dreamed of severing her enjoyable relationship with him. Besides, Irna knew that Ted was making her

initial concept stronger and stronger each year, conditioning the cast to understand the peculiar psychology which was Oakdale, keeping her ratings at the top.

Mighty as Irna was, even she couldn't break certain strict rules which P&G enforced on its serials. One of them concerned the handling of extramarital affairs in story lines. P&G allowed a writer to delineate an adulterous affair, but not to reward the adulterers in any way. During *As the World Turns*'s first year, Irna showed an involvement between unhappily married Jim Lowell and Chris's sister, Edith. The story was expertly handled, with Les Damon capturing the audience with his portrayal of a businessman tortured by an untenable personal situation. Viewers were torn between their sympathy for Jim and their desire to see Jim and Claire patch up their marriage. All the other members of the Hughes and Lowell families were distressed and confused by the complexity of Jim and Claire's plight—which was the essential scenario for an Irna story. In any given personal dilemma, she showed a variety of opposing responses in the observers, forcing the audience, ultimately, to grieve over the heartbreak of the human condition rather than to hang on to a fixed value judgment. Irna wanted to resolve this particular story by having Jim divorce Claire and marry Edith. P&G, which did not generally like divorce resolutions, in this case permitted Irna to break up the couple, but absolutely refused to allow Jim to marry Edith. It would have looked too much as if the show were rewarding adulterous Jim with happiness. Irna was furious with P&G, and did what she always did when she was angry with her benefactors—she began killing off popular characters. She sent Jim Lowell on a business trip to Florida, where he suddenly died in a boating accident. It was mean (but characteristic) of Irna to have evaporated Jim in this sudden way, without at least giving Jim some sort of "death" story for the satisfaction of loyal fans. Afterward, when their calls and telegrams of grief flooded the production office, Irna decided to console them by sending them back part of her own poignant message about life and death: "As the world turns, we know the bleakness of winter, the promise of spring, the fullness of summer, and the harvest of autumn . . . the cycle of life is complete. . . . What is true of the world, nature, is also true of man. He too has his cycle."

In 1970 Irna left *As the World Turns*, severing her

contract with P&G for health reasons; but it was rumored that her main reason for leaving was to help her daughter, Katherine Phillips, write the new serial Katherine had created for ABC, *A World Apart*. About a soap opera writer and her adopted children, *A World Apart* appeared to be based on Irna's own life. The soap lasted only fifteen months. By 1972 *As the World Turns* had a serious ratings setback and P&G asked Irna to come back as head writer. What she found when she returned to her creation repelled her: brothers Dan and Paul Stewart were in love with the same girl, Elizabeth Talbot, and Dan had fathered not only a daughter by his wife, Susan, but also a daughter by Elizabeth. Irna found this tangle of love and pregnancy all quite immoral (even though most other soaps were using such stories), and quickly began to cut out characters. She gave Paul a brain tumor and had him die off camera, had Elizabeth die from a fall on a staircase, sent Dan to England and annulled Susan's new marriage to Dr. Bruce Baxter on the grounds that he was sexually impotent. These coarse, catastrophic events were badly handled and so upset viewers that the show plummeted to as low as seventh place in the ratings, a low not seen by *As the World Turns* since its first difficult year.

Irna, however, did do one extraordinarily vital thing for viewers: she invented Kim Reynolds, one of the strongest characters that *As the World Turns* has ever introduced. In a telephone interview Miss Phillips said, in the raspy voice which had begun to characterize her later years: "Everyone asks me how I got the idea for Kim Reynolds on the show, because she certainly is an unusual character. She's really me—at a much younger age. She's fiercely independent, as I was, and she won't settle for second best. She looks in the mirror and refers to herself as 'the lady in the mirror.' Well, that was her other self, which no one knew about: the true me, the person that I always hid from the world. She's having a child out of wedlock, which will be only hers. I adopted two children— Cathy and Tommy—without having a husband. We're both the same. And she's going to have that child to prove that a woman can do it alone." One might also add that Kim, as Irna delineated her, was aloof, almost cold, in her intelligent selfishness—suggesting to the audience a magnificent intrigue beneath the beautiful gloss. Whatever Kim said, it was almost oracular: verbal insights that Irna was perversely denying to the other inhabitants of Oakdale. It was clear

from the start that Kim was much too liberated (in the most modern sense of the word) to marry except for love—the kind of love that comes only rarely to any person's life. Irna deliberately had Kim become involved with Bob Hughes, her brother-in-law, a man that she could never marry. Irna herself, it is said, had been involved with one man for years but couldn't or wouldn't marry him.

However, the show's deeply conservative viewers were upset and angered by Bob Hughes's extramarital involvement with Kim. The audience was accustomed to seeing Bob as flawless in his relations with women; he was the show's White Knight. Years before, Irna would have known better than to mutilate Bob's image, but at this juncture the only character she seemed interested in preserving was Kim. A wave of angry letters from viewers splashed into the production office. The ratings dropped again. P&G abruptly fired Irna in mid-1973.

It was a terrible blow, to be fired as the writer of her most important work. She retreated to her Chicago home to write her autobiography, with various tentative titles like *The Lady In The Mirror* and *The Ivory Tower*, all suggestive of an emotionally unfulfilled life. There was some indication that she was severely depressed. On the evening of December 22, 1973, her personal secretary, Alice Shea, peeked into her bedroom and found Irna propped up in bed spryly at work on her life story. The next morning Alice Shea again looked into Irna's bedroom. She had died in her sleep.

* * *

Robert Soderberg and his wife, Edith Sommer, had already taken over as head writers, and soon brought the show back to its old position. In the process they insisted on changing Irna's concept of Kim and remaking her into a traditional long-suffering heroine. For the most part they did preserve Irna's old style of writing and kept the continuity intact.

As the decade progressed, *As the World Turns* remained slow and conservative, pleasing its loyal fans, although its stories now concentrated on love triangles, each containing some sort of unwanted pregnancy, as a belated concession to trends on other soaps. The female characters became glamorous and younger. Toward the end of the seventies, Procter & Gamble came under tremendous pressure to speed up the pacing of the show, emphasize younger characters at the expense of some of the older ones and generally revamp *As the World Turns* so that it would attract younger viewers. Bridget and Jerome Dobson, who had done such a splendid job of changing *The Guiding Light* to a contemporary program without offending older loyal viewers, were made head writers of *As the World Turns* in 1980. In the story line you are about to read, they introduced most of the major new characters from Brad Hollister on, including James Stenbeck. (The Dobsons left, then returned, and left again in mid-1983). The painful decision was also made to reduce the once-major characters of Nancy and Chris to cameo walkons; thus Helen Wagner and Don MacLaughlin are still seen, though infrequently and on a non-contract basis. As part of all the change, Kim has become a supportive "recap" character, while Betsy—the baby who caused all the turmoil between Dan, Paul, Elizabeth and Susan—is now a young woman and the focus of a romantic story line.

As the World Turns, which is high in the Nielsens, still has most of its old fans because in the past it had been meticulously careful in the way sex was presented, in the conservative way relationships were shown, in its responsiveness to viewers sensibilities. The old fans remember and they hang on, half hoping that the old days of the live show will come back, but also pleased at the elaborate and absorbing show they are watching now.

* * *

THE STORY

Wealthy JIM LOWELL (Les Damon) kept after his law partner and good friend CHRIS HUGHES (Don Mac-Laughlin) to join the town country club with his wife,

The Hugheses of Oakdale were one of the two prominent families of As the World Turns. *They were middle class, believed in togetherness and were clearly a wholesome family. Several months after the premiere (April 2, 1956), the Hughes family were, from left, Rosemary Prinz as daughter Penny, Helen Wagner as Nancy, Richard Holland as oldest son Donald and Don MacLaughlin as benevolent father Chris. Little Bob Hughes (not pictured) was played by Bobby Alford.*

The Lowell family had more status than the Hugheses, but were plagued by personal troubles. In the first year, Jim Lowell (Les Damon, right), who headed a law firm with his father, Judge Lowell (William Johnstone), had an unhappy marriage to Claire Lowell (Anne Burr).

NANCY HUGHES (Helen Wagner), but Nancy and Chris were much too down-to-earth to want that sort of thing. Unlike the well-fixed Lowells, they believed in the old-fashioned virtues, so they were understandably upset when they discovered that Chris's sister, EDITH HUGHES (Ruth Warrick), was having an affair with Jim, who was already married to CLAIRE LOWELL (played by Anne Burr, and later by Nancy Wickwire and Barbara Berjer). JUDGE LOWELL (William Johnstone), Jim's father and Chris's kind boss, strove to keep Jim on the straight and narrow.

Chris always worried about his sister, Edith, because of his guilt feelings toward her. His parents had worked a farm in Illinois and put Chris through law school, with the provision that he would pay his parents back by helping to send Edie to college. But Chris didn't. He had fallen in love with Nancy, a former schoolteacher, and had to start supporting his own family. When the show started, Nancy and Chris had already been married more than a decade and a half. Chris's father, WILL ("PA") HUGHES (Santos Ortega), was already a widower.

Nancy and Chris's teenaged daughter, PENNY HUGHES (Rosemary Prinz), and her friend, Jim and Claire's daughter, ELLEN LOWELL (Wendy Drew, and later Patricia Bruder), were both deeply disturbed by the relationship between Edith Hughes (Penny's aunt) and Jim Lowell. Ellen was further haunted by the lack of love her parents felt for each other, and Penny by the feeling that her mother, Nancy, loved her sister, Susan, more than her.

Confused, Ellen became infatuated with married DR. TIM COLE (William Redfield), by whom she became pregnant. After she had her child out of wedlock, she gave it up for adoption. After her son was adopted by research physician DR. DAVID STEWART (Henderson For-

Ruth Warrick played Edith, Chris Hughes's sister. Both families became upset when they found out that she was having an affair with Jim Lowell. Young Penny admired her liberated aunt and was influenced by her.

Joyce Van Patten was Janice Turner in 1957, with Leona Powers playing her mother. Donald fell in love with Jan and became engaged to her, but Nancy didn't approve of Jan and succeeded in breaking them up.

sythe) and his wife, BETTY (Pat Benoit)—and named DAN STEWART (Jeff Rowland, John Colenback, who played the part the longest, John Reilly, then John Colenback again)—Ellen became desperate to have her son back and took the matter to court. After a long, drawn-out battle, Ellen realized that it would be best for her son's happiness if she let him stay with his new parents. However, by a twist of fate, Betty Stewart and Tom Cole both died, and David, now all alone, came to Ellen for advice on how to take care of Dan and his natural son, Paul. Before long they fell in love. A wedding would have taken place quickly but for the troublemaking of David Stewart's insanely jealous housekeeper, FRANNY BRENNAN (Toni Darnay), who threatened to tell young Dan of his illegitimacy if Ellen went through with her plans to marry David. In an ensuing struggle with Ellen, Franny was accidentally killed. Ellen was sent to prison. Upon her release, she and David finally married.

Penny also had a string of problems. Her disillusionment with her family pushed her into a relationship with wild JEFF BAKER (Mark Rydell), with whom she eloped. A stunned Nancy and Chris were for-

tunately able to have the marriage annulled. With the passage of time, Jeff straightened himself out, and this time Nancy and Chris gave glowing approval to the marriage of Jeff and their daughter. Penny was shocked to discover that she could never have children, but nonetheless, she and Jeff were happy—until he was tragically killed in a car crash. Distraught, Penny tried to pick up the pieces of her life, and fell in love with handsome NEIL WADE (Michael Lipton), a doctor who for personal reasons could no longer face practicing medicine. Together they started the Wade Bookshop, and were going to adopt a child when again Penny's hopes were dashed. Neil, going blind, was hit by a car and killed. Shattered, Penny vowed she'd never marry again, and later left Oakdale for England. When last heard from, she had married a European racing champion and had finally succeeded in adopting a little Eurasian girl by the name of Amy.

* * *

While Penny's brother BOB HUGHES (Don Hastings) was attending college, he was ensnared by a

In 1958, the popular story of Penny and Jeff Baker (Mark Rydell, left) began. After the couple eloped, Nancy and Chris had the marriage annulled, but Penny and Jeff continued to meet in the local ice cream parlor. Here hot-tempered Jeff confronts Donald Madden as Al James while Jean Mowry, as James's girl friend, watches. Mark Rydell has since become a famous Hollywood film director.

Ellen Lowell (Wendy Drew) had an unhappy love affair with a married man, Dr. Tim Cole (William Redfield), by whom she became pregnant. After her baby was born, she gave it up for adoption. That story slowly and ingeniously evolved into the story of her later, happier years.

designing young girl named LISA MILLER (Eileen Fulton, currently Betsy Von Furstenberg) from Rockford, Illinois. Nancy and Chris were stunned when they learned from Lisa that Bob and she had eloped, but this time they could not annul the marriage, because Lisa had become pregnant. So Nancy and Chris offered to let the couple live in Bob's old bedroom. This was kind of them, but at the same time it caused a strained domestic situation when Lisa became pregnant, and especially when newborn infant TOM HUGHES (played now as an adult by Justin Deas) joined the family.

Lisa was a poor wife and a neglectful mother; she would let Nancy do all the work of taking care of her child while she tried to end her own boredom by continuing school, and later having an extramarital affair with a shoe tycoon named BRUCE ELLIOTT (Jim Pritchett). She saw a chance to become the well-to-do Mrs. Elliott and divorced Bob Hughes. Though she tried to put on airs, Lisa could not hide the fact that she was just a lost and confused farm girl at heart, and Elliott would have no more to do with her. At the same time, little Tom became seriously ill and almost died. Ashamed, the once self-confident Lisa begged Bob to take her back, and when he refused, she begged Nancy to get him to remarry her. Finally, after much self-pity, Lisa left young Tom with the Hugheses and fled to Chicago.

After Jim Lowell's death, Claire, a rather elegant woman, married DR. DOUG CASSEN (Nat Polen), who eventually died. Later, she became interested in a much younger man, DR. MICHAEL SHEA (Roy Shuman), who was full of charm but really interested only in himself and in gaining money and power. Claire, blinded by love and upset by her own oncoming middle age, married him, not realizing that he didn't love her in return.

After some months, Lisa returned from Chicago a

Widowed Claire Lowell met Dr. Doug Cassen (Nat Polen) in 1959, with the saga of their romance and marriage lasting nearly a decade. Claire is usually remembered as Claire Cassen.

The day before Christmas of 1959, Penny and Jeff Baker were wed in an affecting ceremony which stirred many viewers to write letters of approval. Those same viewers were shocked when, the following year, Irna Phillips had Jeff killed in a car crash, since Mark Rydell wanted to leave the show.

totally changed woman. In Chicago she had married a wealthy man, whom she later divorced with a good settlement. The newly glamorous Lisa and Michael Shea were immediately attracted to one another, and an affair between them took place behind Claire's back. When Lisa got pregnant, Michael Shea became furious. A social climber, he was worried that Claire would find out and ruin his glorious plans. He turned a deaf ear to Lisa, who begged him to divorce Claire and marry her. Eventually Claire did find out, and she divorced him. From then on, Claire's daughter Ellen Stewart was resentful of Lisa. Claire was later hit by a car and killed. As his and Lisa's son, CHUCK, grew older, Shea became fond of the boy and offered to marry Lisa, but this time she turned *him* down.

Lisa's other son, Tom Hughes, had already returned from the war in Vietnam—an experience which had shaken him. He began to seek refuge in drugs, and one day even tried to steal some from Dr. Shea's cabinet. The unscrupulous Shea caught Tom and forced a written confession from him. He used the confession to blackmail Lisa into marrying him.

* * *

Back at the Hughes household, Bob Hughes hadn't been sitting on his hands all this while. After his marriage to Lisa had ended, he married SANDY MCGUIRE (Dagne Crane, Barbara Rucker), a beautiful girl whom Ellen had met in prison. When she was paroled, Ellen introduced her to Bob. Sandy married him mostly because she wanted security for herself and her son, Jimmy. The basis of the marriage was shaky, and it soon collapsed. Sandy went off to New York to try to become a professional model.

Lisa and Michael Shea's marriage was a farce—with Lisa prancing before him in sexy nightgowns and then locking her door, just to torment him. Angered, Shea announced that he was going to prove her an unfit mother in court. Frightened by the possibility of losing her son, Lisa fled with Chuck to Mexico.

Eileen Fulton, in 1960, played a young schemer from Rockford, Illinois, named Lisa Miller, and Don Hastings began playing Bob Hughes. Lisa talked innocent Bob into eloping with her and later caused all sorts of trouble for Nancy and Chris. Over the years, Miss Fulton's portrayal of the character has been fascinating and complex.

Ellen Lowell's life first became intertwined with Dr. David Stewart's in 1961, when Ellen sued him to regain custody of her son, Dan, whom David and his wife had adopted. Pat Bruder took the role from Wendy Drew the year before.

Hearing that her mother, ALMA MILLER (Ethel Remey), was ill, Lisa secretly returned to Oakdale, only to discover that her son Tom was on trial for the murder of Michael Shea. She rushed to the courtroom in a panic, just in time to hear her son confess to Shea's murder—to protect her. Lisa fainted on the spot and developed amnesia; she couldn't remember if she was the murderess or not. It was soon revealed, however, that a former paramour of Shea's had snuffed out his life. Lisa and Tom—and everything else in Oakdale—returned to normal.

Like Tom, the two Stewart boys had grown up, and all three had problematic love affairs. Dan Stewart—Ellen's son by the late Dr. Tim Cole—had become a fine doctor and was already married to SUSAN STEWART (Marie Masters) when he fell in love with an English girl by the name of ELIZABETH TALBOT (Jane House). Susan refused to give him a divorce; later both she and her rival, Liz, became pregnant at the same time. Susan had a miscarriage, but Liz's

baby girl lived and was named Betsy. Also in love with Liz, PAUL STEWART (Dean Santoro)—Dan's adopted brother and David Stewart's natural son from his former marriage—offered marriage, and Liz accepted in order to give her baby a name. That marriage, however, broke up; Paul later died of a brain tumor. When Susan at long last divorced Dan to marry another doctor, Liz and Dan wed and were able to find happiness—if for only a few days. Right after their wedding, Liz fell on a staircase and fatally ruptured her liver. Feeling that his life in Oakdale was wrecked by all this tragedy, Dan took his daughters, Betsy and Emily, and went to live in England.

In 1962, Millette Alebander (left) joined the show as Sylvia Hill, a nurse dying of lupus and in love with Bob. Sylvia was supposed to die in the original story. But so many people with the disease (which is only sometimes fatal) called the show to ask if they too were going to die that the writers cured Sylvia and married her off to avoid frightening anyone. Also pictured is Joan Anderson, who played nurse Mary Mitchell.

James Broderick portrayed Jim Norman, one of Ellen's suitors before she became seriously involved with David Stewart.

Tom Hughes fell in love with a beautiful and rich runaway named MEREDITH HALLIDAY (Nina Hart) when he should have been paying more attention to the call of true love, in the person of pretty, down-to-earth CAROL DEMING (Rita McLaughlin). Meredith's wealthy guardian, SIMON GILBEY (Jerry Lacy), stormed into Oakdale, where he had learned his daughter was hiding. After a brief but passionate romantic interlude with Tom's mother, Lisa, Gilbey took Meredith away, leaving the path clear for a healthier romance to develop between Tom and Carol, who were soon married.

* * *

After a number of disastrous marriages and affairs, the now worldly Lisa Shea began to realize what a wonderful man her first husband, Bob Hughes, had been in comparison with the men she had known. So she again set her sights for him; but Bob's own sights were set on JENNIFER RYAN (Gillian Spencer), a widow of a brilliant surgeon who had gone through school with Bob.

Lisa was blocked with Bob, but not with Bob's older brother, DONALD HUGHES (played longest by Peter Brandon), a man with almost as many marital mishaps and romantic false starts as Lisa. Lisa fell in love with Don, who was fascinated by Lisa but in the end refused to marry her.

Bob Hughes married Jennifer Ryan, but trouble started immediately when her son, DR. RICK RYAN (Con Roche, Gary Hudson), who worshipped his father, openly displayed his resentment toward Bob. When Jennifer, torn between her son and her new husband, left Bob, he and Jennifer's sister—KIM REYNOLDS (Kathryn Hays)—beautiful, utterly independent, and totally sympathetic—fell in love and had a brief affair in Florida. Jennifer returned to Bob when she learned that she was pregnant. Ironically, Kim also learned that she was pregnant from her affair with Bob. DR. JOHN DIXON (Larry Bryggman), a devious social climber who wanted Kim—and always got what he wanted—eventually convinced her to marry him for the sake of the baby. Jennifer eventually discovered

The Hugheses and the Lowells got together, on November 1, 1963, for a portrait on the occasion of Grandpa's seventieth birthday. Back row, from left: Michael Lipton, who was Dr. Neil Wade; Walter Burke brought in for a few days to play John Hughes, Chris's brother; Henderson Forsythe; Ruth Warrick, brought back to play Aunt Edie again for the reunion; Nat Polen; Eileen Fulton; Jone Allison, who briefly played Claire Cassen; Don Hastings; and William Johnstone. Front row, from left: Pat Bruder, Rosemary Prinz, Santos Ortego as Grandpa Hughes, Jerry Schaffer as Tom Hughes, Helen Wagner and Don MacLaughlin.

Beginning in 1966, Bob became involved with model Sandy McGuire (Dagne Crane) and her ex-husband, Roy McGuire (Konrad Matthaei). Sandy married Bob mostly for security and the marriage broke up.

whose baby Kim was really carrying, but confronted neither her sister nor her husband, and forgave them. Kim lost Bob's baby and bravely tried to make a go of a marriage with a man she didn't love, but it was hopeless. When she asked John Dixon for a divorce, he blackmailed her into staying with him by threatening to reveal her affair with Bob to Jen—who, of course, already knew. Further tragedy threatened Kim and Bob's lives when Bob alone discovered that Jennifer had a terminal neurological disease. At first he kept the awful secret to himself.

Meanwhile, Lisa Shea was, as usual, being pursued by a number of suitors. One, a minister-turned-doctor, WALLY MATTHEWS (Charles Siebert), attracted Lisa's eye for a while. Then a strange young man by the name of JAY STALLINGS (Dennis Cooney) appeared in Oakdale and took the empty apartment next to the Wade Bookshop—managed by Lisa for her former sister-in-law, Penny Hughes, still living in England. When mysterious attacks were made on Lisa's life, many thought Jay responsible because of his moodiness and shady past. Among those who tried to save Lisa from her unseen assailant was GRANT COLMAN (Konrad Matthaei, James Douglas), a new lawyer in Chris Hughes's firm who found the temperamental Lisa irresistible. Lisa's pursuer was discovered to be Jay Stallings's stepfather, GIL STALLINGS (Edward Grover) who eventually tried to murder his stepson and Lisa together as part of a plot to acquire Jay's inheritance, and to make it look as if Jay had killed Lisa himself after numerous attempts on her life. Fortunately, Grant Colman arrived at the Wade Bookshop just in time to save Lisa and Jay. Jay's stepfather was killed by the police.

After Kim and Bob finally confessed their past affair to an understanding Jen, Kim thought she was finally free of John Dixon and his blackmailing. But John, faced with losing Kim, had a fit, rushed down

John Colenback took over the role of Dan Stewart in 1969 and played it the longest. His unhappy marriage to fellow doctor Susan (Marie Masters) gave rise to years of deeply engrossing love triangles involving Dan, a bitter Susan and the women with whom he fell in love.

Michael Hawkins became the new Paul Stewart after Steven Mines. Elizabeth Talbot (Jane House) had an illegitimate child, Betsy, by Dan, but married his half-brother Paul to give her baby a name. In 1969 this sort of plot was innovative and effective.

the stairs to try to reach Jen, fell, and was seriously injured. After surgery, John suffered a depression that threatened his recovery, possibly even his life, and Kim dared not attempt leaving him until he was better. Sensing that his illness was a ring in Kim's nose, John faked a much longer recovery period than he really needed. What he didn't know, however, was that Kim was being drawn to someone new—his name: Dr. Dan Stewart!

* * *

All those years of immaturity and insecurity were over for Lisa. She had acquired integrity. Grant Colman had proposed marriage and Lisa accepted and was indeed happy—until Grant admitted that he was married and still had to get his estranged wife, JOYCE COLMAN (Barbara Rodell), to agree to a divorce. Lisa patiently waited for Grant to rid himself of this confused and often childish woman, who came to Oakdale and kept delaying the divorce through a series of mishaps and deliberate maneuvers: a burst appendix,

a murder trial during which Grant was her attorney, pleas to Grant for a reconciliation. After a year she gave him a divorce. But on his and Lisa's wedding day he received a note from Joyce claiming that three years earlier she had given birth to their son and was now with him somewhere out of Oakdale. Grant *had* to find out if Joyce's story was true. Lisa's patience was being sorely tested.

Jay Stallings, now wealthy, began to take a great deal of interest in Carol Hughes, whose marriage to Lisa's son Tom was running into trouble. Carol objected to Tom's continually seeing a new client named NATALIE BANNON (Judith Chapman), which led to continual arguments and finally to a divorce. Carol married Jay almost immediately afterward, and Tom would have married Natalie—but right after his pro-

Dr. John Dixon (Larry Bryggman) and Kim Reynolds (Kathryn Hays) came on in 1972 and would become World Turns' *most memorable villain and heroine for more than a decade. Their relationship began when he married her to give her baby (and Bob's) a name, and evolved into exquisite and innumerable twists and turns of love and hate.*

On July 26, 1973 Tom Hughes (Peter Galman) married Carol Deming (Rita McLaughlin) in one of the show's most elaborate wedding ceremonies. The marriage broke up three years later.

posal of marriage she fled Oakdale, telling Tom in a note that her past sins had made her unworthy of him. In reality she went back to Kilborn, to resume her affair with LUKE PORTER (Ted Agress), a married man. Weeks later, after things went sour with Luke, she came back to Oakdale and married Tom. Lisa was fearful that her son was making a terrible mistake.

New storm clouds were forming over the Stewart family. Dan Stewart, who had fled to England with his girls to keep Susan from getting custody of baby Emily, decided to risk a court action and return to Oakdale. Predictably, Susan filed a custody suit—but only as a ploy to get Dan back. Susan knew that if Dan wanted to visit his daughter, he would also have to see Susan. Susan did win custody of their daughter but then lost it when, through her negligence, Emmy wandered off one night and was later found in a delivery truck on the other side of town. The shock of losing both Emmy and Dan made Susan turn to alcohol. She lost her job at the hospital. Oddly enough, her only real friend, John Dixon—a fellow "compulsive"—told her, in his vituperative way, that she was a pathetic

drunk. Angered, Susan shot back that she had seen Dan and his precious Kim in each other's arms.

It was true. Dan and Kim had fallen passionately in love. They were really so right for each other. Marvelous Kim had made motherless Betsy feel like the happiest little girl in the world, for Kim loved Betsy as if she were her own child. (Betsy really was Dan's daughter by the late Liz Talbot—but Dan never revealed this. Everyone still believed Betsy's father to be Dan's late half-brother, Paul Stewart.) Kim asked John for a divorce, planning to marry Dan, but John reminded Kim that Susan loved Dan and would probably die of alcoholism if Kim married him. Dan and Kim delayed their wedding, but when Susan started overcoming her drinking problem, Dan pressured Kim to set a date. Unsure of whether Susan might be hurt, Kim went to a nearby town to think things out. While writing to Dan to tell him that she had finally decided to marry him, she was struck on the head during a tornado and developed amnesia. Once back in Oakdale, she no longer knew whom she loved, Dan or John Dixon! She allowed John to take care of her

John Reilly became the new Dan when the character returned from England in 1974. Dan loved Kim but Kim feared that if she married Dan, his ex-wife Susan would drink herself to death out of self-pity. It was the kind of story, replete with nobility and self-sacrifice, that made As the World Turns *the top show for years. The acting was pinpoint sharp.*

Another triangle that year involved Lisa, lawyer Grant Colman (James Douglas) and his estranged scheming wife Joyce, played by Barbara Rodell, who was a standout in the role.

and in time had sexual relations with him. Depressed, Dan decided to take a job in South America. Just before he was about to leave, Kim regained her memory and called Dan twice, each time leaving a message on his answering machine saying that she remembered everything about their romance. Susan got to the machine before Dan, heard the taped messages, and quickly hid the tapes. Dan's failure to return Kim's calls made Kim believe that he no longer loved her, when in fact he still adored her; and her failure to call him after he came back from South America and learned that she had regained her memory and was now pregnant with John Dixon's child made Dan believe that Kim no longer loved him. The romance was tragically foiled, but secretly Dan and Kim continued to care.

* * *

Jen was suddenly killed in an auto accident! For a while Bob was inconsolable, but he kept repeating a prayer that Jen had once taught to him: "Look to this day,/For it is life,/The very life of life."—and he was able, but just barely, to resume his life. Soon afterward, Bob had to face possible dismissal from Memorial for supposedly arguing with a heart attack patient, Sandy Hughes's estranged husband, NORMAN GARRISON (Michael Minor), causing his death. When John Dixon found out that it was TINA RICHARDS (Toni Bull Bua), Garrison's girl friend, who had argued with him, John told her not to tell anyone else at the hospital that she had done it. John wanted Bob to suffer! But the truth did surface, and it was cruel John, not Bob, who was fired from Memorial. Kim was so distressed by what John had tried to do to Bob that she demanded a divorce from John, who gave it to her. He then turned to liquor.

Joyce's story was true. There was a son—Grant's—adopted three years before by a couple named MARY and BRIAN ELLISON (Kelly Wood and Bob Hover), who lived in Laramie, Wyoming. Joyce was now suing these good people for custody of the boy, TEDDY ELLISON, but Grant believed that they were good

Dan and Kim finally wed in late 1976. The wedding party included, back row, from left: Helen Wagner, Don MacLaughlin, Marcia McClain (Dee Stewart), Henderson Forsythe, Dennis Romer (Doug Campbell), Martina Deignan (Annie Stewart) and Wayne Hudgins (Beau Spencer). Front row, from left: William Johnstone, Pat Bruder, John Colenback (who returned to the role of Dan), Kathryn Hays, Phil Sterling (Rev. Booth), Ethel Remey (Alma Miller), Rita McLaughlin and Dennis Cooney (Jay Stallings).

After Dan died in 1979, Kim fell in love with a Greek-American named Nick Andropolous (Michael Forest), whose own wife, presumed dead, suddenly turned up quite alive and ready to make trouble.

parents for Teddy and agreed to represent them against Joyce. After Joyce lost, she went temporarily insane and deliberately cracked up her car, seriously injuring herself. Once again, Grant rushed to Joyce's side at Memorial. Lisa, up until now, had shown great patience with Grant's persistence in continually going to Joyce whenever she was in trouble, which was often. Fed up with both Grant and Joyce, Lisa threw him out of the apartment. She began dating lawyer DICK MARTIN (Ed Kemmer), an old flame of hers, which threw Grant into convulsions of drunken jealousy. When the Colmans finished their game playing, however, they reconciled. Weeks later, Grant received the tragic news that Mary Ellison's husband, Brian, had been killed in an accident on a construction site. Widowed Mary came to Oakdale to work in Grant's office and was soon at loggerheads with Joyce, who insisted on paying frequent visits to Teddy.

Lisa had been right: Natalie *was* bad news for Tom. After the truth came out, that Natalie had had an affair with her own husband's brother and had been the cause of her husband's suicide, Tom was ready to forgive her. But his marriage to her was over when he learned that she had just slept with Jay Stallings! Jay, one of Tom's clients, was terrified that Carol would find out. But Tom, now falling in love with Carol all over again, was not about to tell her the truth and see her hurt the way he had been. Jay began living on the edge when Natalie chose to stay in Oakdale and threatened to tell Carol everything unless Jay helped her overcome her "loneliness." Then the big shock came: Natalie was pregnant with Jay's baby.

* * *

Two new arrivals in town were VALERIE CONWAY (Judith McConnell) and KEVIN THOMPSON (Michael Nader). One-time playgirl and playboy, they were both now attempting to seek a serious life for themselves. Kevin fell in love with Susan Stewart and tried to make her aware of the terrible thing she had done to Dan

Justin Deas was the new Tom Hughes and Margaret Colin played policewoman Margo Montgomery. In an elaborate 1981 sequence, taped in Jamaica, the two sought out the evil genius, "Mr. Big," and later became engaged.

Dee Stewart (Jacqueline Schultz) sued her own husband, John Dixon, for rape. Under questioning by John's attorney Maggie Crawford (Mary Linda Rapeleye), Dee had to admit that she willingly had sex with John, but only because she thought he was Brad—her sister's husband.

and Kim and tell them the truth finally. Valerie, the sister of Kim's deceased first husband, Jason Reynolds, held a grudge against Kim for once having helped Jason break up a destructive love affair that Valerie had when she was young and immature. To get even with Kim, she began dating Dan, because she had heard that Dan and Kim had been in love. Later, Valerie grew more serious about Dan.

After the joyous birth of Kim's baby, whom she called ANDREW, Dan was about to marry Valerie Conway—but just before the wedding Susan at long last went to him and revealed the dreadful trick that she had played with his answering machine tapes to keep him and Kim apart. Naturally he broke off his marriage to Valerie, then set a date with Kim. Destructive Valerie blamed Kim and tried to spread lies about her all over Oakdale. But the greater threat was from far more destructive John Dixon, who became obsessed with acquiring custody of his and Kim's son, Andrew. With nurse PAT HOLLAND (Melinda Peterson), who was in love with John, he concocted an elaborate plot to kidnap Andrew and hide him on the outskirts of Oakdale with Pat. Kim suffered desperate anguish while Andrew was missing, never suspecting that John Dixon had kidnapped him. But Dan did suspect, and soon followed John to where he and Pat were hiding Andrew, and Kim recovered him. Emotionally disturbed, John took his gun and went after Dan—only managing, though, to shoot himself accidentally, later claiming Dan had shot him. Dan was charged by the police but cleared when Pat Holland finally told the truth. Soon after, she fell down a staircase and died.

* * *

Carol immediately filed for divorce when she discovered the affair Jay and Natalie had been having. Tom hoped to remarry Carol. Carol, however, was shattered after Andrew had been kidnapped—since it happened while she was looking after him in a supermarket—and allowed herself to be comforted by Jay, whose ardor won her back. Then Natalie, who was pregnant by Jay, had a baby girl and left it on Carol and Jay's doorstep, before leaving Oakdale. Carol was delighted finally to be a mother and called the baby AMY.

Meanwhile, ANNIE (currently Mary Lynn Blanks) and "DEE" (DAWN) STEWART (currently Vicky Dawson) —the daughters of David and Ellen Stewart—now young women attending the local college, fell in love with the same young graduate student, BEAU SPENCER (Wayne Hudgins). For a long time Annie tried to hide her love for Beau, to protect Dee, but in time everyone knew that Beau and Annie were in love. While Dee forgave them, David Stewart would not give his blessings; he thought Beau irresponsible for having pretended interest in Dee while simultaneously making passes at Annie. But in time David accepted Beau when he realized how hard Beau was working for his law degree. Annie and Beau married.

After Kim and Dan wed, Dan developed anxieties which led to impotence. He turned to none other than Susan Stewart for sex, but soon realized that he loved Kim and went back to her. Once again, Susan was left alone and distraught. There was, however, one other thing that Dan had to do before he and Kim could settle down to a happy marriage. He told Betsy the truth: he was not her uncle but her father. Confused, Betsy bitterly turned away from Dan at first, but with Kim's help she was able to accept her new relationship with him.

Donald Hughes once again chose the wrong mate. He married scheming Joyce Colman! Blindly in love with her, he began taking on sensational divorce cases in Judge Lowell's firm to pay for their new house and Joyce's massive decorating bills. She began an extramarital affair with RALPH MITCHELL (Keith Charles), a playboy realtor who had once been involved with Valerie. After he became friends with Don through his business, Ralph felt sorry for Don and insisted that Joyce tell her husband the truth about their affair. Joyce then plotted to kill Ralph. She intended to shoot him in her house, and then claim that she thought he had been a prowler, but by mistake wound up shooting and paralyzing Don! When Ralph was able to prove to everyone that Joyce had really intended to kill him, Joyce fled Oakdale. Word came later that she was killed in a car accident.

Kevin Thompson realized that he was wasting his time with Susan Stewart, who would never love any other man but Dan. He fell in love with Sandy Hughes and married her. Then Sandy found out something startling about Kevin: he had been a secret "periodic" alcoholic—that is, he went on binges for days at a time, then stopped drinking completely. His drinking and his new friendship with Carol Stallings was destroying their marriage. Finally, Sandy and Kevin were involved in an auto accident and Kevin was killed. Sandy rejoined her son Jimmy outside of Oakdale.

Kevin's friend, Valerie Conway, in time forgot her hurt after Dan married Kim, and wed DR. ALEX KEITH (Jon Cypher), a volatile but dedicated physician. They also left Oakdale.

A new arrival, however, was young, pretty, but very calculating MELINDA GRAY (Ariane Munker). She said she was the illegitimate daughter of Kim's late sister, Jennifer Hughes, and Dan and Kim took her in. Soon Melinda began causing a great deal of trouble. She nearly broke up Carol's marriage by having an affair with Jay; then she did break up the marriage of Annie and Beau Spencer. JANE SPENCER (Georgann Johnson), Beau's domineering mother, had resented Annie's independence and so helped Melinda, now Beau's secretary, woo Beau away from Annie. Annie divorced Beau, who left Oakdale along with his malicious mother. Some time later, Melinda drowned in a lake.

* * *

Just when Dan and Kim had finally found happiness in each other's arms, Dan contracted a fatal blood disease and died! Kim, along with Dan's parents, Ellen and David, who had lost Paul only several years before, mourned Dan. In her grief and confusion, Betsy fell in with a group of delinquents, but with Kim's firm but loving guidance Betsy came to terms with Dan's death and straightened out.

Not long after Dan's death the Stewarts had a financial windfall. A cheerful but extremely clever geologist named BRAD HOLLISTER (Peter Brouwer) secretly discovered silver on land owned jointly by the Stewarts and the Hugheses. Brad talked the Stewarts into letting him mine silver from their half of the mine. To refine the silver, Brad brought mysterious JAMES STENBECK (Anthony Herrera), heir to a Scandinavian fortune, to Oakdale. Meanwhile, BARBARA RYAN (Colleen Zenk*), Jennifer Hughes's daughter, came back to Oakdale. Years before, during Bob and Jen's marriage, Barbara had dated the very young Tom Hughes. Now, with Lisa's encouragement, she became engaged to Tom. But somehow Barbara was in a state of turmoil about brooding James Stenbeck, who began arranging strange meetings with her. It turned out that years before they had had an affair and conceived a child, PAUL. James's family had pressured him into giving the child up to another couple. Now, when

*The character had been played years before by Judi Rollin, Barbara Stanger and Donna Wandrey.

James told Barbara that he wanted her and his son back, she was torn between her old love for James and her fear of hurting Tom. Then, just before she and Tom were to exchange vows in front of the minister, Barbara called off the wedding and ran from the church. Soon afterward, she married James Stenbeck and began living with him and Paul.

At the same time, NICK ANDROPOLOUS (Michael Forest), the handsome Greek owner of the Plaka restaurant, rescued Carol Stallings and Melinda Gray from a fire at the Wade Bookshop. Nick's gentle way and solid sense of values impressed everyone, especially Betsy Stewart, who anxiously encouraged a romance between Nick and widowed Kim. They fell in love and were planning to marry when word came that Nick's wife ANDREA (Patricia Mauceri), thought to have died years ago, was alive in Greece. Andrea came to Oakdale and made life miserable for Kim as she waged a campaign to win Nick back. Then Nick discovered a terrible truth: his hotheaded younger brother, STEVE ANDROPOLOUS (Frank Runyeon), and Andrea had been lovers while Nick had been married to Andrea. Nick also learned that Andrea and Steve had together stolen the famous Green Fire necklace. With her past fully exposed, Andrea was forced to divorce Nick, who married Kim soon after.

A seemingly unrelated chain of events began to unravel, then burst into an explosion that would hurt almost everyone in Oakdale. Dee Stewart, who had grown into a desirable, cool blond, became an assistant to composer IAN MCFARLAND (Peter Simon). Dee fell in love with him. In Rome, where they went for one of his concerts, the two were in the midst of consummating their love when suddenly Ian had a heart attack and died! John Dixon, of all people, had been in Rome, too, as Ian's doctor. He became Dee's sole confidant, promising not to tell anyone but David and Ellen how Ian had died. Once back in Oakdale, Dee was courted by Brad Hollister. She loved him but was so frightened by sex, after what had happened to Ian, that she rejected him. Then, on the rebound, he married her sister Annie. Now emotionally dependent on John, who understood why she was afraid of sex, Dee married him, to the absolute shock and bewilderment of David and Ellen Stewart.

John Dixon, meanwhile, brought nurse LYLA MONTGOMERY (Veleka Gray, Anne Sward) to Oakdale to work at Memorial Hospital. Years before they had had an affair in Chicago. A divorcée, Lyla had two daughters, brassy MARGO MONTGOMERY (Margaret Colin) and nubile CRICKET (Lisa Loring). Lyla became engaged to Bob Hughes, but was fearful Bob would discover her less than pure background in Chicago.

Little by little, the darkly dishonorable character of James Stenbeck became apparent to his new wife, Barbara Ryan. After she discovered that he was having an affair with Lyla's daughter, Margo, whom James had hired to tend his stables, Barbara demanded a divorce. But James, for a very special reason, would not give it to her. From the very start, James's whole motivation in seeking to reunite with Barbara and his son Paul had been strictly financial. Little Paul, as a Stenbeck heir, was to inherit a fortune! James, who needed his son's money, became desperate to reconcile with Barbara and Paul.

Right after Dee married John Dixon she began to realize why her family had disliked him so. John would go into jealous rages over Brad, with whom Dee worked in his silver mining office. The truth is, John and Dee hadn't yet consummated their marriage because of her fears about sex, while it was Brad that she now really wanted. But Brad was married to Annie! Dee separated from John after another one of his rages. One night, John stole back into their apartment and forced his way into Dee's bed. Dee brought rape charges against her own husband and hired Tom to represent her, while aggressive MAGGIE CRAWFORD (Mary Linda Rapeleye), Lyla's younger lawyer sister, represented John. During the scandalous trial two bombshells were dropped. Dee was forced to admit that she willingly made love to John, mistaking him for Brad! Then Lyla admitted that John had been her lover and had fathered Margo! The Stewarts were shattered, Annie left Brad and Bob broke off his engagement to Lyla; all of Oakdale was in an uproar. Then, before the rape verdict could be decided, John was run over by a hit-and-run driver in a parking garage. The accident injured his optic nerve and left him blind.

* * *

After Donald Hughes, paralyzed from the waist down, fell in love with sweet Mary Ellison, his spirits revived and his paralysis lifted. He now knew how he had been lied to and abused by Joyce and was trying to have her declared legally dead so that he could marry Mary. But Joyce returned to Oakdale very much alive, causing Don and Mary much grief, and lied her way back into Grant Colman's life. She faked a doctor's letter which led him to believe that she had a terminal brain tumor. Feeling pity for Joyce and in great need of companionship since Lisa had left him, he became engaged to her. After Lisa, always suspicious of Joyce, uncovered her sham, Joyce left Oakdale for good. Grant tried to reconcile with Lisa, but when she refused, he moved to Laramie, as did a happy Mary and Donald.

Jay Stallings was killed in an explosion at one of Brad's mines! Carol mourned him but after a while began seeing Nick's younger brother, Steve Andropolous. Steve was making a conscious effort to reform, for the sake of his brother Nick and for Carol. He therefore returned the Green Fire necklace, which he had stolen with Andrea, to its rightful owner, movie mogul ARI TRIANDOS (Richard Council). By coincidence, Triandos's new wife and partner turned out to be Natalie, who briefly came back to Oakdale to make sure that Carol and Steve, now married, were good parents to her daughter Amy.

The turmoil surrounding John Dixon's rape trial and hit-and-run accident only grew worse. Everyone thought that Dee's father, David Stewart, had run John down. When David suddenly left Oakdale, so that he could deal with his deep hatred of John Dixon, David looked even guiltier. Ellen became frantic with worry. Meanwhile, Margo Montgomery now knew that John was her father and moved in with him, since he was blind and couldn't care for himself, while still trying to continue her affair with James Stenbeck. John soon discovered who the hit-and-run driver was: James Stenbeck himself! James, fearful that John would tell his wife Barbara about his continuing affair with Margo, had tried to kill John in the parking garage. After James talked his way back into Barbara's arms, Margo tried to forget him and attended the police academy.

Around that time, there was a great deal of policing to do in Oakdale. Barbara and Lisa had opened up a dress shop called Fashions Ltd., which greedy James began secretly using as a front for his new illicit dealings in cocaine, in partnership with an insidious dope ring. The organization was also using Steve Andropolous's trucking business to run the cocaine. In the end, James and Steve turned state's evidence to stay out of jail. But the head of the ring, code-named "Mr. Big," was still unknown. Policewoman Margo teamed up with lawyer Tom Hughes to nab "Mr. Big." He turned out to be BERNARD GRAYSON, (Brent Collins), a snarling dwarf who held them hostage in an *Alice in Wonderland* type house of horrors he had erected in Europe. By the time Tom and Margo escaped and landed "Mr. Big" in jail, they were engaged.

Tom's father, Bob Hughes, also finally found the right woman, exotic MIRANDA MARLOWE (Elaine Princi). She had been involved with the dope ring but had reformed. Bob waited for her to finish a prison term and married her.

Amidst all of this romance, a terrible tragedy struck Kim's family. Carol and Steve had begun to have chronic marital troubles and separated. Then Steve began to romance young Betsy Stewart in secret. When Kim and Nick found out, Kim was upset but Nick became enraged—and had a massive heart attack and died! Kim once again had to face widowhood. Guilt-ridden, Betsy broke off with Steve. Carol, however, found happiness with handsome REV. NORMAN FRAZIER (Norman Walter) and married him.

* * *

For months Ellen Stewart and Annie and Dee hadn't heard a word from David since he suddenly disappeared. Then Dee found him living in the town of Flatrock. He had amnesia! His emotional torment had been so acute over what John had done to his daughter, that at first he simply couldn't remember if he had run John Dixon down, and then he lost his memory completely. Calling himself "Donald Saunders," he got a job as a pharmacist, working for attractive widow CYNTHIA HAINES (Linda Dano), and then became engaged to her. Cynthia's daughter, KAREN HAINES (Kathy McNeil), was painfully insecure and looked up to David as a father. After Ellen brought David back to Oakdale, he regained his memory under sodium pentothal and returned to Ellen, but it was clear to everyone that he was still fond of Cynthia. Both she and her daughter, Karen, had accompanied David to Oakdale, although Cynthia soon left. David finally realized that he had never stopped loving Ellen. But Ellen had learned to become her own person during David's absence and decided to divorce him to find her own way in the world. Soon, however, Ellen tired of a single's existence and admitted she needed David. They remarried happily.

After an embittered Annie had divorced Brad over the revelations in John Dixon's trial, Brad left

Oakdale. Annie began seeing DR. JEFF WARD (Robert Lipton), who had always been interested in her, and finally married him. They became the proud parents of Oakdale's first quadruplets.

Lisa went to Europe and came back with WHIT MC COLL (Robert Horton), her new husband! He was the egomaniacal head of a newspaper empire. His ambitious assistant, Lyla's son CRAIG MONTGOMERY (Scott Bryce), courted Betsy Stewart, who was to come into a huge trust fund left to her by her father. Despite the fact that she and Steve Andropolous were still very much in love, she suddenly married Craig. The way Nick died still made her fell guilty about her love for his brother, Steve. To complicate matters, DIANA MC COLL (Kim Ulrich), Whit's spoiled daughter, made overt plays for both Steve and Craig. And just as Betsy decided to leave Craig for Steve, she became pregnant! Although she tried to pass the child off as Craig's, David—who discovered Craig was sterile—knew differently.

Barbara and James were happy for a while, but soon James had more extramarital affairs. Then Barbara was bewildered by dreams involving James, Dee and a blond male stranger in a sixteenth-century setting. The stranger showed up one day as GUNNAR ST. CLAIR (Hugo Napier), James's orphaned cousin. Gunnar was a professional balloonist, adventurous and romantic, everything that Barbara wanted and James was not. Meanwhile, John Dixon had recovered from his blindness and became rich from an exploitative novel he had written about his marriage to Dee. He met and married ARIEL ALDRIN (Judith Blazer), the grasping daughter of GRETA ALDRIN (Joan Copeland), James's former nanny. However, Ariel became far more interested in James Stenbeck, until her mother told her the shocking truth: James and Ariel were half-brother and -sister! Greta had given birth to James but, determined that he be given the rights of a Stenbeck, switched the infant James with the legitimate heir, who wound up in an orphanage. That heir was Gunnar! Through Ariel, James found out who he was, and so did John, while surreptitiously tape recording Ariel and James. Predictably, James tried to stop the truth from slipping out. He promised Ariel a lot of money for keeping quiet, then tried to murder John Dixon after John blackmailed him for $100,000. Fearful that Barbara and Gunnar were becoming romantically involved, James talked Barbara into believing that she was going insane and placed her in a corrupt dungeon-like institution, until Gunnar, with the help of BILAN MARLOWE (Kathleen Rowe McAllen), Miranda Marlowe's young daughter, saved her. James and John then began to compete furiously for the affections of Dee Stewart. Ellen discovered that John wanted Dee back and went to confront him, only to find him wounded from a gunshot. When she returned with the police, the body was gone! John was presumed dead, but months later he revealed himself in a courtroom, when Dee was accused of his murder! John had faked his own death in order to frame James. The authorities sentenced John to work part-time at the prison hospital, and Dee left Oakdale to start anew.

Beautiful Karen Haines also discovered that Gunnar, not James Stenbeck, was the rightful Stenbeck heir and blackmailed James into marrying her—after he gave Barbara a divorce. But then both Ariel and Karen suspected that the true heir to the Stenbeck fortune was young DUSTIN DONOVAN the son of James's stableman BURKE DONOVAN (David Forsyth), since Dustin's real father may have been Gunnar. Greedy Ariel and Karen soon began a ruthless competition for Burke's affections.

CAST
AS THE WORLD TURNS
CBS: April 2, 1956

Dr. Bob Hughes	Bobby Alford
	Ronnie Welch
	Don Hastings* (P)
Nancy Hughes	Helen Wagner (P)
Chris Hughes	Don MacLaughlin (P)
Edith Hughes Frye	Ruth Warrick (P)
Penny Hughes Wade ...	Rosemary Prinz* (P)
	Phoebe Dorin
Donald Hughes	Hal Studer (P)
	Richard Holland
	James Noble
	Peter Brandon*
	Martin West
	Conard Fowkes
Pa Hughes	William Lee (P)
	Santos Ortega*
Judge Lowell	William Johnstone (P)
Ellen Lowell Stewart ...	Wendy Drew (P)
	Patricia Bruder*
Claire Lowell Cassen ...	Anne Burr (P)

	Nancy Wickwire
	Gertrude Warner
	Jone Allison
	Barbara Berjer*
Jim Lowell	Les Damon (P)
Janice Turner Hughes ..	Joyce VanPatten (P)
	Virginia Dwyer
Mrs. Turner	Leona Powers (P)
Carl Whipple	Rod Colbin
John Hughes	Laurence Hugo
	Walter Burke
Dr. Doug Cassen	Nat Polen
Jeff Baker	Mark Rydell
Grace Baker	Selena Royle
	Frances Reid
	Grace Matthews
	Murial Williams
Dick Baker	Carl Low*
	Court Benson
Al James	Donald Madden
Tom Pope	Hal Hamilton
	Charles Baxter
Mitchell Dru	Geoffrey Lumb
Dr. George Frye	George Petrie
Dr. Tim Cole	William Redfield
Louise Cole	Mary K. Wells
Greg Williams	Robert Readick
Julie Spencer	Lisa Howard
Lisa Miller McColl	Eileen Fulton*
	Pamela King
	Betsy von Furstenberg
Alma Miller	Joanna Roos
	Ethel Remey*
	Dorothy Blackburn
Henry Miller	Luis van Routen
Dr. David Stewart	Henderson Forsythe
Betty Stewart	Patricia Benoit
Dr. Dan Stewart	Paul O'Keefe
	Jeffrey Rowland
	John Colenback*
	John Reilly
Dr. Paul Stewart	Alan Howard
	Ed Gaynes
	Doug Chapin
	Steven Mines
	Michael Hawkins
	Marco St. John
	Dean Santoro
Tom Hughes	James Madden

	Jerry Schaffer
	Frankie Michaels
	Richard Thomas
	Paul O'Keefe
	Peter Link
	Peter Galman
	C. David Colson
	Tom Tammi
	Justin Deas
Bill Abbot	Patrick O'Neal
Jim Norman	James Broderick
Meg Blaine	Teri Keane
Bruce Elliott	James Pritchett
Linda Elliott	Bonnie Toman
	Beverley Owen
Debbie Whipple	June Harding
	Kimetha Laurie
Alice Whipple	Jean McClintock
	Leslie Charleson
Dr. Chuck Ryan	Michael Ebert
	Don Chastain
	Bob Baliban
Mary Mitchell	Joan Anderson
Sylvia Hill Suker	Millette Alexander
Dr. Al Suker	Michael Ingram
Martha Suker	Ann Hegira
Helene Suker	Jerrianne Raphael
Dr. Neil Wade	Michael Lipton
Judith Wade Stevens ...	Connie Lembcke
Dr. Jerry Stevens	Stephen Elliott
	Roy Poole
Franny Brennan	Toni Darnay
Dick Martin	Joe Maross
	Edward Kemmer*
Ann Holmes	Augusta Dabney
Bill Holmes	William Prince
Amanda Holmes	Deborah Steinberg Solomon
Dr. Jerry Turner	James Earl Jones
Dr. Bellows	P. Jay Sidney
	Brock Peters
Sandra McGuire Thompson	Dagne Crane
	Jill Andre
	Ronnie Carrol
	Barbara Rucker*
Roy McGuire	Konrad Matthaei
Martha Wilson	Anna Minot
Carl Wilson	Martin Rudy

Jack Davis	Martin Sheen
Sara Fuller	Gloria DeHaven
Dr. Susan Burke Stewart	Diana Walker
	Connie Scott
	Jada Rowland
	Leslie Perkins
	Marie Masters*
	Judith Barcroft
Julia Burke	Fran Carlon
Dr. Michael Shea	John Lasell
	Jay Lanin
	Roy Shuman*
Karen Adams	Doe Lang
Elizabeth Talbott Stewart	Jane House*
	Judith McGilligan
Ronnie Talbott	Peter Stuart
	Curt Dawson*
Hank Barton	Peter Burnell
	Paul Falzone
	Gary Sandy
Peter Kane	Arlen Dean Synder
Dr. John Dixon	Larry Bryggman*
	Robert Elston
Carol Deming Frazier ..	Rita McLoughlin Walter
Miss Thompson	Jacqueline Brookes
Simon Gilbey	Jerry Lacy
Meredith Halliday	Nina Hart
Miss Peterson	Nancy Andrews
	Margaret Hamilton*
Ellie Bradley	Swoosie Kurtz
Dr. Annie Stewart Ward .	Carman Schreider
	Jean Mazza
	Barbara Jean Ehrhardt
	Ariane Munker
	Shelley Spurlock
	Martina Deignan
	Julie Ridley
	Randall Edwards
	Mary Lynn Blanks
Dee Stewart Dixon	Simone Schachter
	Glynnis O'Connor
	Marcia McClain
	Heather Cunningham
	Jacqueline Schultz*
	Vicky Dawson
Betsy Stewart Montgomery	Tiberia Mitri
	Maurine Trainor

	Suzanne Davidson*	Dr. Jeff Ward	Robert Lipton
	Lisa Denton	Dr. Doug Campbell	Dennis Romer
	Meg Ryan	Marcia Campbell	Cynthia Bostick
Jennifer Ryan Hughes . .	Geraldine Court	Bennett Hadley	Doug Higgins
	Gillian Spencer*	Hester Pierce	Ann Stanchfield
Dr. Rick Ryan	Con Roche*	Dana McFarland	Deborah Hobart
	Gary Hudson	Ian McFarland	Peter Simon
Barbara Ryan Stenbeck	Judi Rolin	Brad Hollister	Peter Brouwer
	Barbara Stanger	Eric Hollister	Peter Reckell
	Donna Wandrey	James Stenbeck	Anthony Herrera
	Colleen Zenk*	Nels Andersson	Einar Perry Scott
Kim Reynolds		Nick Andropolous	Michael Forest
Andropolous	Kathryn Hays*	Steve Andropolous	Frank Runyeon
	Patty McCormack	Lyla Montgomery	Veleka Gray
Dr. Bruce Baxter	Steve Harmon		Anne Sward*
	Ben Hayes*	Margo Montgomery	
Dr. Wally Matthews	Charles Siebert	Hughes	Margaret Colin
Grace Burton	Eugenia Rawls	Cricket Montgomery . . .	Lisa Loring
Peter Burton	Christopher Hastings	Bart Montgomery	Jim Raymond
Marion Graham Burton	Laurie Heineman	Maggie Crawford	Mary Linda Rapeleye
Amy Hughes	Irene Yaah-Ling Sun	Andrea Korackas	Patricia Mauceri
Dr. Eric Lonsberry	Douglas Marland	Sofia Korackas	Robin Leary
Jay Stallings	Dennis Cooney	Hayley Wilson Hollister	Dana Delany
Gil Stallings	Edward Grover	Cody Sullivan	Beau Gravitte
Grant Colman	Konrad Matthaei	Ari Triandos	Richard Council
	James Douglas*	Connie Wilson	Debbie McLeod
Joyce Colman Hughes .	Barbara Rodell	Cynthia Haines	Linda Dano
Natalie Bannon Triandos	Judith Chapman*	Karen Haines	Kathy McNeil
	Janet Zarish	Stan Holden	W. T. Martin
Norman Garrison	Michael Minor	Ernie Ross	Marshall Watson
Tina Richards	Toni Bull Bua	Miranda Marlowe	
Luke Porter	Ted Agress	Hughes	Elaine Princi
Margaret Porter	Kathleen Noone	Lydia Marlowe	Zsa Zsa Gabor
Mary Ellison	Kelly Wood	Bilan Marlowe	Kathleen Rowe McAllen
Brian Ellison	Robert Hover	Gunnar Stenbeck	Hugo Napier
Pat Holland Dixon	Melinda Peterson	Ariel Aldrin Dixon	Judith Blazer
Marion Connelly	Clarice Blackburn	Greta Aldrin	Joan Copeland
Kevin Thompson	Michael Nader*	Suz Becker	Betsy Palmer
	Max Brown	Craig Montgomery	Scott Bryce
Valerie Conway Keith . .	Judith McConnell	Bernard Grayson ("Mr.	
Beau Spencer	Wayne Hudgins	Big")	Brent Collins
Jane Spencer	Georgann Johnson	Madame Koster	Marilyn Raphael
Melinda Gray Spencer .	Ariane Munker	Dr. Ben Forrest	David Bailey
Ralph Mitchell	Keith Charles	Brian McColl	Robert Burton
Rev. Booth	Philip Sterling		Frank Telfer*
Dr. Alex Keith	Jon Cypher	Whit McColl	Robert Horton
Karen Peters	Leslie Denniston	Diana McColl	Kim Ulrich
Nick Conway	Douglas Travis	Burke Donovan	David Forsyth
Tina Cornell	Rebecca Hollen	Dustin Donovan	Brian Bloom

Kirk McColl .... Christian Le Blanc

Creator: Irna Phillips
Head Writers: Irna Phillips, Kathryn Babecki, Joel
Kane, Winifred Wolfe, Katherine L.
Phillips, Robert Soderberg and Edith
Sommer, Ralph Ellis and Eugenie
Hunt, Douglas Marland, Bridget and
Jerome Dobson, K. C. Collier, Tom
King, Caroline Franz and John Saffron
Assistant Head Writers for Irna Phillips: Agnes
Nixon,
William J.
Bell
Executive Producers: Ted Corday, Joe Willmore, Joe
Rothenberger, Fred
Bartholemew, Mary-Ellis Bunim

Producers: Charles Fisher, Allen Potter, Lyle B. Hill,
Mary Harris, Robert Driscoll, Arthur
Richards, Susan Bedsow Horgan, Robert
Rigamonti, Michael Laibson
Directors: Ted Corday, Walter Gorman, Bill Howell,
James MacAllen, Carl Genus, Tim Kiley,
Cort Steen, Leonard Valenta, Paul
Lammers, John Litvack, Robert Myhrum,
Richard T. McCue, Paul Davis, Allen
Fristoe, Alan Skog, Heather H. Hill, Paul
Schneider, Bruce Barry, Richard Dunlap
Organist: Charles Paul
Musical Direction (later): Charles Paul, Elliot
Lawrence Productions
Packager: Procter & Gamble

CAPITOL

HOW a daytime serial begins, its initial concept and cast, is the major factor determining its success or failure. With *Capitol*, executive producer John Conboy and creators Stephen and Elinor Karpf made all the right moves. Their idea of a modern-day *Romeo and Juliet* set within the political intrigue of Washington, D.C., was dramatically correct. John Conboy's casting of movie star Carolyn Jones and stage star Constance Towers (wife of the American ambassador to Mexico, John Gavin) for the story's main warring matriarchs was perfect. CBS's decision to air the premiere episode, March 26, 1981, at night was also right. The result of all these well-conceived moves was good ratings for the first six months and ever-increasing viewer loyalty.

The guiding force for *Capitol* is John Conboy, whose creativity had previously helped William Bell make *The Young and The Restless* into one of the strongest soap operas on television. His taste for beautiful faces and bodies is as evident on *Capitol* as on *The Young and The Restless* although he doesn't indulge himself quite as much in dark lighting and odd camera angles.

Capitol is an excellent story, pitting the powers of hate and ambition against the glory of love. One could suggest, however, that the show have more detailed descriptions of the actual workings of Congress, the White House, and the process of government and foreign service as a service to viewers.

Capitol already has some but not nearly enough of this sort of realism.

BACKGROUND

Like the Montagues and Capulets of *Romeo and Juliet*, two Washington, D.C. families have become bitter enemies because of past hurts. Thirty years before, a socially accomplished, wealthy debutante named MYRNA CLEGG (Carolyn Jones, Marj Dusay) had met and fallen in love with the man of her dreams, the late BAXTER MCCANDLESS. Her best friend had been another Washington debutante from a well-to-do family, beautiful CLARISSA TYLER (Constance Towers). When Clarissa married Myrna's great love, Myrna swore revenge against Clarissa and her family. Myrna today is a willful, vindictive, manipulative woman who is married to SAM CLEGG (Richard Egan), a monied, high-echelon government employee with considerable power. Myrna is always interfering in the lives of her children, attractive JULIE CLEGG (Kimberly Beck-Hilton), teenagers JORDY (Todd Curtis) and BRENDA (Leslie Graves), and Sam's grown son from a previous marriage, TREY CLEGG (Nicholas Walker).

Clarissa, now widowed, is a wonderful mother to four sons and a daughter and clearly doesn't deserve Myrna's hatred. Some time ago, during the Senator McCarthy hearings, Myrna had Clarissa's father,

JUDSON TYLER (Rory Calhoun), framed as a Communist sympathizer and cast out of Washington. While Clarissa today fears her rival—indeed Myrna is dangerous—she and her family refuse to cower.

THE STORY

At first Julie Clegg tried to hide her love for TYLER MCCANDLESS (David Mason Daniels), a returning Air Force hero and one of Clarissa's sons. She feared the wrath of her mother, Myrna, who held nothing but contempt for all the McCandlesses. Julie was also under pressure to end the romance from her half-brother Trey, Tyler's main political rival, a young man obsessed with the idea of one day becoming Presi-

dent. After Tyler proposed marriage, Julie announced to her family that she intended to become his wife, despite the objections of her mother and brother. Trey, a decent young man, relented and gave Julie his blessings, but to no avail—for suddenly Julie was in a boating accident that resulted in almost complete amnesia. Her mother, Myrna, soon took advantage of the situation. While Julie recovered in the hospital, Myrna made Julie believe the elaborate lie that Julie had consented to marry Myrna's young aide, LAWRENCE BARRINGTON (Jeff Chamberlain), whom Myrna believed to have wealth and social connections. In reality, Lawrence Barrington's true identity was Gordon Hull, a mysterious and penniless man who was only interested in Julie for the money and prestige of the Clegg name. Julie had no memory of her past love for Tyler

Capitol, *which began on March 29, 1982, focused on two young star-crossed lovers, each from feuding political families in Washington, D.C. The lovers were college student Julie Clegg (Kimberly Beck-Hilton) and returning Air Force hero Tyler McCandless (David Mason Daniels).*

Taking orders from Julie's scheming mother, Frank Burgess (Duncan Gamble) began a dirty tricks campaign to smear Tyler McCandless, using prostitute Shelley Granger (Jane Daly), who later went straight. The actors Duncan Gamble and Jane Daly became man and wife in real life.

McCandless and agreed to marry conniving Lawrence Barrington/Gordon Hull.

Julie's younger brother, Jordy, had been badly spoiled by his mother, and was prone to drinking and violence. However, he loved Julie and was stunned when he saw his parents conspiring to end Julie's happiness with Tyler. When Jordy finally stood up to Myrna and Sam, Sam threw him out of the house. Jordy, for the first time in his life, found a job and began living on his own and liking it.

Meanwhile, brave Clarissa stood solidly behind her son Tyler's love for Julie as well as his decision to run for Congress against Trey Clegg, the son of her dangerous enemy. Tyler also had the complete support of SENATOR MARK DENNING (Ed Nelson), an old friend of the McCandlesses. Mark was hopelessly in love with Clarissa, although he was already married to a mysterious woman named PAULA (Julie Adams), who had not left their house in years. Mark wanted nothing more than for his beautiful, headstrong daughter SLOANE DENNING (Deborah Mullowney) to wed Tyler. Ambitious Sloane, an investigative reporter for a Washington, D.C. television news show, was really only interested in becoming a future First Lady. Since she believed that either Trey or Tyler would eventually sit in the White House, she cunningly flirted with both.

* * *

The four McCandless brothers lived in and coped with the cutthroat political atmosphere of Washington, D.C. Tyler's youngest brother, WALLY MCCANDLESS (Bill Beyers), had always felt intimidated by Tyler's achievements. Wally had tried to win the love and attention of their father, while he was alive, but was only ignored. After Wally fell in love with Julie Clegg and then lost her to his older brother, he developed a self-destructive gambling habit, which forced him deeply into debt and into the hands of a loan shark, DANNY DONATO (Victor Brandt). Donato invented a blackmail scheme that would seriously damage the middle brother, MATT MCCANDLESS (Shea Farrell, now Christopher Durham), a football hero. The fourth brother, THOMAS MCCANDLESS (Brian-Robert Taylor, Tom Catlin), was a hardworking doctor, handicapped since birth and forced to walk on crutches. He had always been insecure with women, because of his disability, until he fell in love with LISBETH BACHMAN (Tonja Walker), a college friend of his sister,

GILLIAN MCCANDLESS (Kelly Palzis). But beautiful Lisbeth was also attracted to Jordy Clegg and especially to the kind of life his wealth could offer her.

Determined to have her son Trey beat Tyler in the congressional election, Myrna Clegg schemed with former FBI agent FRANK BURGESS (Duncan Gamble) to destroy Tyler's public reputation. Tyler was a member of the Joint Committee for Intelligence, a top secret government organization. Myrna and Frank learned that one of the members of the committee, PHIL DADE (Anthony Eisley), often went to prostitutes, and tricked him into believing that he had murdered a hooker named SHELLEY GRANGER (Jane Daly). Once they had him in their pockets, they tried to have him leak vital government secrets, but making it appear as if Tyler had done the leaking. Meanwhile, Shelley Granger realized that she had been used for dirty political tricks and changed her name to Kelly, taking a job with Tyler's rival Trey. Before long, unsuspecting Trey and Kelly fell wildly in love.

Tyler became frantic with worry when his beloved Julie suddenly became ill and was taken to an undisclosed hospital by her father. Before Tyler could find her, he was called away by the military to a foreign country called N'shoba to effect a special rescue. In N'shoba, he and Sloane Denning, who flew to the country to get a big scoop for her television show, were arrested and detained as political prisoners. Once rescued themselves from N'shoba, Sloane and Tyler returned home, and none too soon, for Julie was just about to marry Lawrence Barrington. Just as the minister began the service, Tyler rushed into the church, brought the ceremony to a halt, knocked Lawrence out, and carried a bewildered Julie off, explaining to her that she would soon understand everything. In time her memory came back and, much to Myrna's ire, Julie planned once again to marry Tyler.

CAST

CAPITOL
CBS: March 26, 1981

Clarissa McCandless ...	Constance Towers (P)
Judson Tyler	Roy Calhoun (P)
Sen. Mark Denning	Ed Nelson (P)
Myrna Clegg	Carolyn Jones (P)
	Marla Adams
	Marj Dusay

Sam Clegg	Robert Sampson (P)
	Richard Egan*
Trey Clegg	Nicholas Walker (P)
Julie Clegg	Kimberly Beck-Hilton (P)
Tyler McCandless	David Mason-Daniels (P)
Wally McCandless	Bill Beyers (P)
Gillian McCandless	Kelly Palzis (P)
Dr. Thomas McCandless	Brian-Robert Taylor (P)
	Michael Catlin
Sloane Denning	Deborah Mullowney (P)
Frank Burgess	Duncan Gamble (P)
Lawrence Barrington	Jeff Chamberlain (P)
Bob Simpson	Donald Neal (P)
Maggie Brady	Julie Parrish (P)
Annie	Mary Gregory (P)
Jordy Clegg	Todd Curtiss
Brenda Clegg	Leslie Graves
Lizbeth Bachman	Tonja Walker
Matt McCandless	Shea Farrell
	Christopher Durham
Danny Donato	Victor Brandt
Roger Avery	Todd Starks
Shelley Granger	Jane Daly Gamble
Phillip Dade	Anthony Eisley
Joan Dade	Corinne Michaels
Jeff Johnson	Rodney Saulsberry
Haley Dodd	Patti Jerome
Veronica Angelo	Dawn Parrish
Joe Luck	Tony Dale
Col. Amir	Paul Picerni
Kurt Voightlander	Wolf Muser
Ian Bankhead	Peter Bailey Britton
Paula Denning	Julie Adams

Creators: Stephen and Elinor Karpf
Head Writers: Stephen and Elinor Karpf, Joyce and John William Corrington, Peggy O'Shea
Executive Producer: John Conboy
Producer: Stockton Briggle
Directors: Corey Allen, Jeffrey Hayden, Alan Cooke, Rick Bennewitz, Bob La Hendro, Richard Bennett, Bill Glenn
Musical Direction: Score Productions
Packager: John Conboy Productions

DAYS OF OUR LIVES

LAST spring Susan Seaforth Hayes gave a stirring speech when she received an award for achievement in daytime television during a gathering of the Academy of Television Arts and Science.

"I practically grew up with you," she said, addressing members of *Days of Our Lives*, tears streaming from her eyes. "You were there during the most important moments of my life. Mac and Frances, you were like my second mother and father. I fell in love with my leading man. Wes Kenney, our producer, came to my wedding. You beautiful people—you are my family!"

It was an emotional moment as Susan summed up what *Days of Our Lives* has always been for the core cast: a place to call home, a family. Countless viewers feel the same way about the show and could also burst into tears at the very thought of it, especially the way it was during its ragingly successful years, the late sixties and early seventies. *Days* was and still is the epitome of old-fashioned family soap opera, but with unique elements that enable it to appeal to the modern soap opera viewer.

BACKGROUND

Days of Our Lives had its roots in radio and early television soap opera, in the dramas of Irna Phillips, like *The Guiding Light* and *As The World Turns*, which

Ted Corday had directed for years and controlled in partnership with Irna. Ted Corday was not a writer but had an extraordinary instinct for the look and feel of a genuine soap. His concept for *Days of Our Lives* was an accurate, creative statement summing up all of his years behind the scenes of bestselling soaps.

When Betty and Ted Corday first came to Hollywood in 1964, they set up a production company with Columbia Pictures and created and produced their first soap opera, *Morning Star*. That show failed after six months, but Ted and Betty were already devising his next Corday Productions soap for NBC, with some assistance from his old partner Irna Phillips and writer/director Allan Chase. An hourglass motif was invented and Irna Phillips came up with an epigraph: "Like sands through the hourglass, so are the days of our lives"—a clever way of incorporating the show's title into a statement. During those months Ted Corday worked hard to develop the kind of show he wanted and was the main creative force behind it. "I remember Irna Phillips came to California once to meet with us all, but I don't think she had much more to do with the show," says Joe Behar, who directed the pilot and has been with the show ever since. "As far as I knew, Ted was the man who made all the decisions."

Ted Corday was very much the authoritarian male, which is probably why *Days of Our Lives* had a *One Man's Family* feel about it and why Dr. Tom Horton was his most important character. The part went to Macdonald Carey, who was at that time the first movie star to join the cast of a television soap. (Interestingly, his career had begun on radio on soaps such as *Stella Dallas*.) Ted cast the other parts and conducted the first rehearsals with characteristic meticulousness and an obsessive love for realism. Joe Behar recalls that one of Ted's suggestions in the early days was for everyone to call the actors by their character names rather than their real ones, undoubtedly an idiosyncrasy that Ted inherited from Irna.

Days of Our Lives premiered on November 8, 1965, and suffered from poor ratings for more than a year. Ted, who had been seriously ill for some time, persevered against the burden of failing health and what appeared to be an indifferent audience to his show. Less than a year after the premiere, not knowing if the program would succeed, Ted Corday died. He left behind him not only the legacy of *Days of Our Lives* but one of the most brilliant careers in broadcasting. His widow, Betty, had to take over as executive producer of the show while caring for their two sons fourteen-year-old Kenneth and sixteen-year-old Christopher. Things couldn't have been worse. The network was beginning to talk about cancellation.

In 1967, Betty Corday hired William Bell as the new head writer. Like Ted, Bill Bell's roots also went back to Irna Phillips and Chicago; in fact, Bell still lived there. He had written dialogue with Irna for a number of her soaps, including *The Guiding Light* and *As The World Turns*, and collaborated with her on *Another World*. The problem with *Days of Our Lives*, when Bell first became head writer, may have been that it was too mild at a time when audiences were discovering sex and bizarre psychology in other media. What William Bell did was to bring the sexual rage of the novels and movies of the time to Ted Corday's new Oakdale of the sixties, then include special fantasies of his own. Bell's vision of *Days of Our Lives* was exactly right. The new show went high in the Nielsens and stayed there for the next eight years. (See p. 37.)

After William Bell left *Days* to create *The Young and The Restless* in 1973, his former sub-writer, Pat Falken Smith, took over as head writer for several years. On January 12, 1976 Time magazine put Susan Seaforth Hayes and Bill Hayes on its cover and in the story on the soaps ("Sex and Suffering In The Afternoon") called *Days of Our Lives* the best soap. It was a wonderful morale boost for the cast and good for the soap world in general but, ironically, for the first time in years *Days* had already begun to lose its hold on the audience. The fault seemed to be NBC's; after *Days of Our Lives* had expanded to an hour in 1975, the network had counterprogrammed it against the newly expanded *As The World Turns*, whose viewers had always been fiercely loyal, but the truth is that *Days* was having the same problem as other soaps which originated in the sixties: the demographic makeup of the audience itself was changing. The show now had to face a quandary: how much of the old show, if any, did it have to discard (along with some of its loyal fans) in order to attract the millions of new and younger viewers out there?

Days of Our Lives is still a family soap opera run by a family (Ken Corday has recently joined the show as one of the producers)—a family that cares deeply about its own roots and its creation, carried on from generation to generation. It is therefore unlikely that the Cordays will ever drop the Horton family and the core themes, abandoning millions of older fans, and do what ABC did with *General Hospital*. But they have nevertheless chosen a middle ground of moderate change. For the past six years *Days* has been speeding up the pace of scenes, introducing many new young characters and spicing the story lines with more action. The Hortons are still the true heart of the show, and a great tradition has been intelligently maintained. Now numberless viewers still receive reassurance from the sands of time in the opening hourglass introduction, which still seems to say something about the importance of continuity in families, fiction and life itself.

THE STORY

Nineteen years ago, the Hortons of Salem were a happy family, all still living together—with the exception of the oldest son, TOMMY HORTON (later played by John Lupton), who was missing in action in Korea.

DR. TOM HORTON (Macdonald Carey), Chief of Internal Medicine at University Hospital, and his wife ALICE (Frances Reid), had four other grown children: ADDIE (Pat Huston, later Patricia Barry), Tommy's twin; MICKEY (John Clarke), a lawyer; BILL (Edward Mallory), a brilliant young surgeon attempting to follow in his father's footsteps; and the youngest, MARIE (Marie Cheatham, currently Lanna Saunders).

When Addie married wealthy banker BEN OLSON (Robert Knapp) and moved to Europe with him, Tom and Alice felt little joy at their daughter's sudden departure. But they did have consolation in that Addie and Ben left their daughter, JULIE OLSON (now Susan Seaforth Hayes), to be raised by her grandparents. The Olsons reared their other child, STEVE OLSON (Flip Mark, now Stephen Schnetzer), in Europe. Young Julie, however, never forgave her mother for deserting her.

Julie became the tortured and motherless young girl searching for love and friendship wherever she could find them. Unfortunately she tended to find both in all the wrong places.

Her one-time best chum from high-school days, SUSAN HUNTER (Denise Alexander, Bennye Gatteys), eventually became her bitter rival and the cause of many of her heartaches. The friendship was first severely strained when Julie found out that Susan was carrying the child of DAVID MARTIN (Steve Mines, Clive Clerk), to whom Julie was then secretly engaged. Julie, however, stepped aside and let the two marry, even stoically agreeing to become Susan's maid of honor, but bitterness raged between the two women when Susan, after the birth of her child, refused to divorce David so that Julie could marry him.

While the two rivals steamed, Dr. Bill Horton, a brilliant young surgeon attempting to follow in his father Tom's footsteps at University Hospital, met and fell in love with a fellow interne, DR. LAURA SPENCER (played longest by Susan Flannery), who was specializing in psychiatry. They became engaged, but when Bill discovered that he could no longer operate because of an infirmity in his hands, he suddenly left Salem.

As if fate were punishing Susan and David for their sins, tragedy engulfed them. Shortly after their son, Richard Martin, was born, his father, David, was playing with him on a swing and the child was killed accidentally. Susan went out of her mind and shot David Martin!

The Hortons of Salem were the main family of Days of Our Lives when the show began on November 8, 1965. Tom and Alice Horton (Macdonald Carey and Frances Reid) had five grown children. Tom was chief of internal medicine at University Hospital; today he is chief of staff.

Marie Cheatham played Marie, the younger of the two Horton daughters, and Dick Colla played her romantic interest, Tony Merritt. A deeply sensitive girl, she was always hurt in her relationships with men. In the late sixties she became a nun after unwittingly falling in love with her own brother.

Susan was put on trial for his murder. Since she was a patient of Laura Spencer's and was being defended by MICKEY HORTON (John Clarke), Bill's brother, Laura and Mickey had to spend a great deal of time together. Laura, distraught over Bill's continued absence from Salem, began to return Mickey's affections. The outcome of Mickey's defense was Susan's acquittal on the charge of murder on the basis of temporary insanity—established during the trial by Laura's expert psychiatric testimony. Laura married Mickey, and Bill returned to Salem—heartbroken to find that his brother and fiancée had wed.

Shattered though he was, Bill had to turn his attention to a young doctor MARK BROOKS (played by John Lupton) whom he had brought home with him. Burned and tortured during the Korean War, the young doctor had undergone extensive plastic surgery, which completely changed his appearance, and was still suffering from the amnesia inflicted by shell shock. MARIE HORTON (Marie Cheatham, Lanna Saunders), the Hortons' youngest daughter, was instantly attracted to Mark and fell in love with him. Later, when the young man was revealed to be her missing brother, Tommy Horton, Marie was able to retain her sanity only by becoming a nun. KITTY HORTON (Regina Gleason), to whom Tommy was married before leaving for Korea, had returned to Salem with their daughter, SANDY HORTON (Heather North), and she immediately began causing trouble for everyone.

Meanwhile, Bill couldn't forget Laura. The thought of the woman he loved being married to his own brother haunted him day and night. Having to work with her every day at the hospital made it even worse for him. One night at the hospital the pressure became too much for him, and he raped her. Soon after, she became pregnant and knew that it had to be Bill's child. By then Tom Horton knew that Mickey was sterile and could never father his own child, and so confronted Laura with this knowledge. She was forced to admit that Bill had raped her. Tom was be-

Charla Doherty played the first Julie Olson, Addie's daughter, and Clive Clerk was David Martin in 1966. Julie and David were secretly engaged, until Julie learned that her best friend, Susan Hunter, was carrying his baby. The story that evolved was ingeniously melodramatic and highly popular.

Susan Hunter (Denise Alexander) was put on trial in 1967 for murdering her husband, David Martin, after he caused the accidental death of their son. Mickey Horton (John Clarke, right), Tom's next-to-oldest son, defended her and gained Susan an acquittal on the basis of temporary insanity.

side himself but dared not say anything for fear someone would tell Mickey the truth about himself.

After Bill's son, MICHAEL HORTON (played longest by Wesley Eure), was born, the interfering Kitty Horton got hold of a tape recording of a conversation between Laura and Tom Horton that proved Michael's true parentage. She threatened Bill with revealing the truth to the whole world. A struggle between the two of them took place, and Kitty, who already had a heart condition, died on the spot. During Bill's trial for supposedly killing her, he repeatedly refused to say what caused the struggle in order to protect Mickey from the truth, and was finally sentenced to six months in prison for manslaughter.

* * *

Julie Olson, pregnant with the murdered David Martin's baby, gave birth to an infant boy, and on the advice of the family and against her better judgment, Julie put him up for adoption. SCOTT BANNING (Mike Farrell, Ryan McDonald) and his wife, JANET (Joyce Easton), adopted the baby, calling him Brad Banning. Soon, however, fate began to weave a sinister web. Susan became the Bannings' next-door neighbor, never suspecting that their adopted baby was really the son of her old nemesis, Julie Olson. After Scott's wife died of a brain tumor, Susan began helping him raise his little boy, and the two started falling in love.

Tormented by the loss of her baby and also by the thought that her hated rival, Susan, might soon become her son's mother, Julie sued to win back custody of the boy. Since Scott was no longer married, the court gave the baby back to Julie, who renamed him DAVID BANNING (played longest by Richard Guthrie, now by Gregg Marx), after his father. But Scott, meanwhile, had grown so attached to the child that he agreed to marry Julie in order to remain the boy's father. Julie's only interest in marrying Scott, however, was to settle the score with Susan, who she knew loved Scott.

Julie Olson (now Susan Seaforth) married Scott Banning (Mike Farrell) in 1968 to spite her enemy, Susan Martin; Scott wed Julie to keep from losing custody of her son, David, whom he had adopted. Another long-term triangle appeared when psychiatrist Laura Spencer (Susan Flannery, center) married Mickey Horton although she was still in love with his younger brother, Bill.

None of the Hortons recognized the young doctor, brought home to Salem in 1968 by Bill, as his son, Tommy Horton (John Lupton). He had suffered extensive wounds in Korea and had undergone plastic surgery, which changed his face, and also suffered from amnesia. He and Marie fell in love without knowing they were brother and sister. When his memory came back, Tommy went back to his trouble-making wife, Kitty (Regina Gleason).

While still in prison, Bill Horton met a singer named DOUG WILLIAMS (Bill Hayes). An adventuresome con man, Doug was excited by Bill's revelation that Salem's Susan Martin had inherited $250,000 after the death of husband David Martin. When Doug was released from prison he immediately came to Salem in order to win over Susan and her money. Not a bit interested in his love patter, Susan tried to get Doug interested in Julie in an effort to destroy her marriage to Scott. Susan even offered Doug money for his trouble. It was indeed little trouble on Doug's part, for he and Julie fell madly in love almost at once.

Julie's happiness with Doug was interrupted by the sudden reappearance in Salem of her mother, Addie Olson. Her husband (and Julie's father), Ben Olson, had died of a heart attack while they were living in Paris, where she decided to leave her second child, STEVE OLSON (most recently Stephen Schnetzer), to finish his education. From the very start, Julie did not attempt to hide her hostility toward her mother. After all, not only had Julie been abandoned by Addie as a child, but she had been rejected by her a second time when the young girl, pregnant with David Mar-

tin's child, had gone to Paris to seek her mother's help. With Addie, Julie became secretive about all her affairs, including the one with Doug Williams.

Addie, however, found out about Julie's involvement with Doug through a private investigator. Although she despised Doug at first for the bon vivant small-time opportunist he seemed to be, as time went by Addie became unexplainably attracted by Doug's charm and easygoing manner. Doug seemed to make Addie realize that her life with her dead husband, Ben Olson, had been a shell, a façade for his business life. In a desperate maneuver to discover the true meaning of life and love, Addie suddenly asked Doug to marry her—on the very night he and Julie had had a bitter quarrel. Doug, also acting on a mad impulse, agreed and eloped with Addie. Later, although happy with his new wife, he suffered many months of soul-searching, realizing that Julie, who blamed herself for causing her break with Doug, was willing to make amends with him at any cost—even the happiness of her mother or that of her husband, Scott Banning.

Addie, despite the ever-present threat of Julie, was able to strengthen her marriage to Doug by buy-

Bill Hayes joined the cast in 1969 as con man-troubadour Doug Williams. Susan offered him money to make love to Julie, in order to break up her marriage to Scott. Instead of playacting, Doug really did fall in love with Julie—and Bill Hayes fell in love with Susan Seaforth and married her. They became one of daytime's top romantic twosomes.

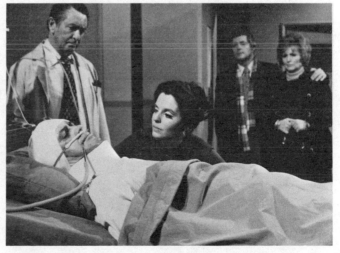

In 1973 Scott Banning (now Ryan MacDonald) was seriously hurt in a construction site accident and died before Julie could serve him with divorce papers. She was still in love with Doug, who married her mother Addie (Patricia Barry, in far background).

ing the club in which he was singing, Sergio's, and renaming it "Doug's Place." She then offered it to him. Later she became pregnant with his child.

Julie, realizing that her heart belonged only to Doug and that her life was becoming a sham, began to make secret preparations to divorce Scott Banning. On the day she was filing divorce papers, Scott was tragically killed at the construction site where he was designing a structure for wealthy contractor BOB ANDERSON (Mark Tapscott). He died without realizing that his wife belonged to another. Meanwhile, Bob Anderson and his wife, PHYLLIS ANDERSON (Nancy Wickwire, Corinne Conley, Elizabeth McRae), an older couple, were shocked by Scott's death and allowed Julie, torn by guilt over Scott, to lean on them and make them substitute parents. However, Bob, feeling the pangs of

middle age, began to have mixed emotions about the luscious young Julie. Added to Bob's secret affection for her, Julie's lawyer, DON CRAIG (Jed Allan), also began falling in love with her. But Julie continued loving only one man—who belonged to her mother.

* * *

Susan Martin's own melodrama hadn't subsided one bit. The night that Scott Banning had left her for Julie, Susan had relations in a park with a young stranger. Later she convinced herself that it was rape. After a few weeks of emotional shock, Susan finally snapped out of it by involving herself in running the free clinic she had bought with her inheritance. After handsome DR. GREG PETERS (Peter Brown) began to help her run the clinic, Susan began to fall in love

After Scott's untimely death, the Anderson family gave Julie the love she never had from her mother. But things, as usual, grew complicated. Handsome older man Bob Anderson (Mark Tapscott, left) found himself falling in love with Julie, while his wife Phyllis (Nancy Wickwire, center), remained Julie's unsuspecting best friend. Karin Wolfe played the Anderson's daughter Mary; James Carroll Jordan, standing, played Julie's brother Steve Olson.

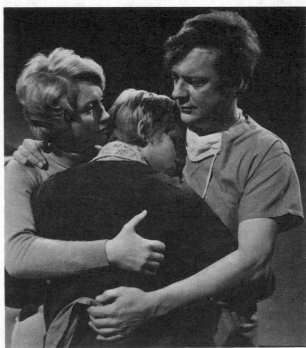

Young Michael Horton (Stuart Lee) blamed himself after Mickey, whom he believed to be his father, suffered a near-fatal heart attack during an argument with the boy. Michael's real father, however, was Bill Horton (Ed Mallory), Mickey's brother. Laura and Bill kept the dreadful secret for years.

with Greg. But, to her horror, she discovered that she was pregnant from her encounter in the park. Considering having an abortion, Susan was told by Dr. Tom Horton that she had cancer of the uterus and the child she was carrying would be her last. Susan, realizing that she had to keep the baby, forced herself to tell Greg the truth—or what she believed to be the truth—that she had been raped one night. Although shocked, Greg still agreed to marry Susan, since he believed her story.

When Susan Martin met Greg's younger brother, a novelist by the name of ERIC PETERS (Stanley Kamel), it was her turn to be shocked: He was the man in the park! Suffering from a near breakdown, Susan was made to realize, in therapy sessions with Laura Horton, that what had happened in the park was a willing act on her part as a result of losing Scott and young David all at the same time. However, Greg soon

learned that Eric was the father of Susan's child. An episode in Eric's new novel, *In His Brother's Shadow*, told the whole story of Eric, Susan and Greg in thinly veiled terms. Greg, furious at Eric, assaulted his brother so badly that he had to be put in the hospital. Susan, shocked by Greg's unjust treatment of his brother, told Greg the truth she had learned in therapy with Laura. After an apology to his brother and much soul-searching, Greg realized that, despite everything, he still loved Susan and soon made her Mrs. Greg Peters. The memory of her night with Eric, however, along with his constant presence, began to haunt Susan and cause trouble in her marriage.

The lives of Bill, Laura and Mickey continued to sink deeper into a morass of trouble and confusion. After Bill returned from prison and Laura learned why he had refused to tell the court the real reason for his struggle with Kitty Horton, Laura was filled with com-

When Addie Williams (Patricia Barry) was stricken with terminal leukemia in 1974, she encouraged her daughter Julie to become a family with her husband Doug and little daughter Hope, after her death. Addie had a miraculous remission but was later killed trying to save Hope from the wheels of a car, causing thousands of letters of protest from grief-stricken viewers.

An interracial romance began in 1977 between young David Banning (Richard Guthrie), Julie's son by the late David Martin, and Valerie Grant (Tina Andrews).

passion and love for him; she made sure that his medical license was reinstated by testifying in his favor at a formal board hearing.

Laura and Bill were in love, but both had too much regard for Mickey Horton, who still believed himself to be the father of Michael, to carry on behind his back. But Mickey began to unjustly suspect Bill and Laura of having an affair, and to pay them back he had an affair with LINDA PATTERSON (Margaret Mason), his secretary. Finding out, Laura threatened divorce, but eventually decided against it when young Michael, hearing his distraught mother and "Uncle Bill" declare their love, rushed out into the street in a panic and was hit by a car. After his recovery, Laura tried to make a go of it again with Mickey, who by now

had developed a serious heart condition and needed her more than ever.

After this storm had seemingly passed, another one developed. Young Michael found out about Mickey's affair with Linda and turned against the man whom he believed to be his father. Mickey, in the ensuing struggle with his son, suffered a serious heart attack. It was his brother, Bill, who then performed a brilliant piece of heart surgery on Mickey—a triple bypass—and returned him to near normal. However, his despondency over his health, over Laura and Bill and young Michael, and his fear of never again being a complete man because of his heart condition, caused him to have a stroke, resulting in total amnesia. Alone in the hospital while everyone was attending Greg and Susan's wedding, Mickey quietly dressed, left the hospital and disappeared. Later he began working on a small farm, some distance from Salem, owned by a lovely young girl, MAGGIE SIMMONS (Suzanne Rogers), who was crippled by a car accident which had resulted in the death of her parents. All the

Scheming Linda Phillips (Margaret Mason) married Bob Anderson for his money in 1978, while his best friend, Chris Kositchek (Josh Taylor) looked on. Linda came into the story in 1972 as Linda Patterson, in love with Mickey Horton.

Sister Marie Horton (Lanna Saunders) returned to the story in 1978 after an absence of seven years. Alex Marshall (Quinn Redeker), who had been Marie'e lover in New York before she became a nun, was still in love with her and began pressuring Marie to leave her order to marry him.

Hortons and the police back in Salem frantically began following every lead in an attempt to find him. However, Laura and Bill, although worried sick about Mickey's whereabouts, were also falling more and more in love each day that Mickey was gone, and finding it increasingly difficult to keep from living together. Mickey himself seemed to have found happiness with Maggie Simmons, whom he finally married—still remembering nothing of his past life. Laura and Bill, meanwhile, were also married, since everyone assumed Mickey to be dead. Only Maggie knew who her "Marty Hansen" really was in his former life—but she vowed never to reveal the truth lest she lose him for good.

* * *

Addie and Doug, happy in their marriage and excitedly awaiting the birth of their child, were both stricken by the news that Addie had leukemia. Although she vowed not to tell anyone that she was dying until the birth of the child, the whole family eventually found out—with the exception of Julie—and began giving the moribund Addie all of their support.

Julie, ignorant of her real mother's distress, was finding mother love elsewhere, in the form of Phyllis Anderson. Phyllis herself was beginning to need Julie's friendship more than ever now, for her husband, Bob Anderson, had left her. Little did Phyllis suspect that it was Julie herself who unwittingly caused the breakup of her marriage.

After Addie gave birth to HOPE (now Kristian Alfonso), Julie found out that her mother was dying and rushed to her bedside. Addie made Julie promise to

The cast in 1981 included, from left, sitting: Meg Wyllie (Flora Chisholm), Jean Bruce Scott (Jessica Blake), Frances Reid, Macdonald Carey, Suzanne Rogers, Patty Weaver. From left, standing, foregrounds: Gregg Marx (David Banning), Lanna Saunders (Marie Horton), Quinn Redeker (Alex Marshall), Brenda Benet (Lee Dumonde), Gloria Loring (Liz Chandler), Bill Hayes, Joseph Gallison, Susan Seaforth Hayes, Jed Allan, Diedre Hall, Dianne Harper (Leslie James). From left, rear: Paul Keenan (Tod Chandler), Charles Bateman (Max Jarvis).

take care of Doug and Hope when she was gone. Julie, still in love with Doug, broke off her forthcoming marriage to Don Craig, believing that she and Doug and Hope would soon become a family. But Addie didn't die; instead she had a miraculous remission which enabled her to resume her life with her husband and newborn daughter. Poor Julie—torn between happiness over her mother's recovery and despair at losing Doug once again—suddenly became cynical, deciding that love wasn't important, only material wealth. She married Bob Anderson after he impulsively asked her to be his bride. Phyllis Anderson was shattered that her best friend would do such a thing to her. Already emotionally disturbed by her divorce from Bob, Phyllis grew even sicker and tried to murder Julie. But she mistook for Julie her daughter, MARY ANDERSON (Karin Wolfe, Barbara Stanger), and to her dread realized that she had shot her own flesh and blood! Mary recovered, but another tragedy soon followed: Addie was struck by a car and killed while

bravely saving her daughter Hope's life from its wheels. Once again Julie, married to Bob, and Doug, now a widower, had to confront the possibility of finally finding happiness together as the ironical outcome of Addie's sad fate.

* * *

The lives of Susan and Greg Peters became strangely interwoven with those of two deeply flawed people: AMANDA HOWARD (Mary Frann), a widow disturbed by persistent nightmares involving her dead husband, and her physician, DR. NEIL CURTIS (Joe Gallison), a compulsive gambler. Amanda's psychiatric problems were rooted in her having had an affair with Neil Curtis while her husband was on his deathbed. The ensuing guilt reaction was being treated by Laura Horton; but Neil only made Amanda's condition worse by insisting that she not tell Laura about her affair with him. Neil was a society doctor, worried about scandal. Self-involved, Neil had no intention of

Tod Chandler (Paul Keenan) had a fling with flirtatious Renee Dumonde (Philece Sampler) in 1981. Tod had been involved in several desperate dramas: he had accidentally shot and killed his evil father, Kellam Chandler, and then was sent to an institution after he was mistakenly thought to have murdered his girl friend.

Jed Allan had played perennial bachelor-lawyer Don Craig since 1974. In 1981 he married Tod's half-sister Liz Courtney (Gloria Loring), after a previous marriage to Marlena Evans. By 1982, he was a bachelor again.

marrying Amanda—until mounting gambling debts forced him to propose to her for her money. On the night before their wedding, Amanda found Neil in the arms of a prostitute, and then tried to kill herself. Of course, the wedding never took place. Greg Peters, Neil's associate, found himself responding to this beautiful woman's urgent need for love—because Susan was turning into a nagging wife. Soon, Greg and Neil Curtis were at odds over Amanda's welfare (and affections), and Susan was beginning to suspect that her husband was not just taking Amanda's blood pressure every night.

A seemingly unimportant newspaper photo of a man who had just won a farming prize in a town near Salem caused eyebrows to raise in the Horton clan. Julie thought the man in the local paper looked vaguely like Mickey and showed the item to Tom Horton, who was sure that it wasn't his son—but he decided to go to the farm of Maggie Hansen in Brookville anyway. When Tom found "Marty Hansen" the happiness was almost too much for Tom to bear. All the Hortons cried with relief—except perhaps Laura and Bill, who now, of course, couldn't marry. But the Hortons were not quite so elated when Mickey couldn't remember any of them and treated his mother and father like strangers. Young Michael, who worshipped his dad, was destroyed when all Mickey could do was shake his son's hand. Tom told Mickey that his memory could be restored with an operation, but after finding out what his other self had been like—a jealous, vindictive, unfaithful husband—Mickey would have nothing to do with an operation that would make him the same way again. He apologized to all the Hortons for all the trouble he had caused, granted Laura her divorce so that she could marry Bill and went back to Brookville to resume his quiet, peaceful life as crippled Maggie Hansen's trusting, affectionate husband.

Following Addie Horton's tragic death, Doug Williams wallowed in grief for months. It had been Addie's wish that if anything should ever happen to her, Doug and Julie would marry and take care of little Hope together. But not only was Doug too grief-

Diedre Hall joined the show as psychiatrist Dr. Marlena Evans in 1977. Several years and dramas later, in 1981, Marlena had a brief friendship with mysterious Joshua Fallon (Stephen Brooks).

Tammy Taylor (here pictured with Jack Coleman) played Hope Williams, Doug Williams' daughter by the late Addie. In the story today, Hope is fully grown and involved in a whole new generation of heartaches on Days of Our Lives.

stricken to consider a life with Julie, he wouldn't even see his daughter, who was being taken care of by Tom and Alice.

Julie's materialistic marriage to Bob Anderson had been bad from the start. At first Bob's guilt over having divorced Phyllis for a younger woman had made him impotent. Then a combination of Bob's inordinate attention to his ex-wife—who needed constant emotional support from him after having almost murdered her daughter—and Bob's suspicions that Julie was making it with younger men behind his back became too much for Julie to bear, and she filed for a divorce.

When at last Doug's wounds were healing and he was able to consider marrying Julie, she found out that she was pregnant with Bob Anderson's child. Doug discovered the secret, without telling Julie he knew, and told her a lie that hurt them both: that he didn't love her, and that the best thing she could do would be to return to Bob.

* * *

Salem saw the beginnings of several young love involvements. Michael Horton, terribly disturbed by his father's refusal to have an operation that would restore his memory and by Laura's marriage to "Uncle Bill," sought comfort in a platonic relationship with teenager TRISH CLAYTON (Patty Weaver), a girl with a brooding mother named JERI CLAYTON (Kaye Stevens) and a brutal, "overaffectionate" stepfather named JACK CLAYTON (Jack Denbo). Neither Trish nor Michael wanted to live with either of their families, so they took an apartment together—but were afraid to have sexual relations, since each had seen what anguish sexual involvements had brought to the adults they were closest to. Another young couple were David Banning—Julie's long-estranged, playboy son, who had come to Salem seeking an inheritance—and BROOKE HAMILTON (Adrienne LaRussa), a loose girl with whom David had been living before they came to Salem. Jealous of Julie, Brooke spread ugly rumors to the effect that Julie was carrying Doug's child and not Bob's. David, who accidentally overheard Julie and Doug discussing their love for each other, bought Brooke's vicious lie, became completely disillusioned with the mother he was just beginning to love, and took Doug's car and drove it off a bridge, intending to kill himself. In fact, everyone believed he was dead—although no body was ever found—and there was

even a funeral service for him. Then, blaming herself for it all, Brooke tried to kill herself! She was really a sad case, seeking to make up for a loveless childhood through sex rather than real love. Her mother, ADELE HAMILTON (Dee Carroll), was a penniless alcoholic, of whom Brooke was ashamed. Years before, Adele and Bob Anderson had had an affair—and eventually Brooke found out that Bob was her real father. Adele died—but just before passing on, told Bob that Brooke was his own daughter, and that he must keep it a secret. Bob began to flood Brooke with gifts and attention, making his other daughter, Mary Anderson, suspicious.

During David's prolonged absence, he began living with a black family named Grant. David fell in love with beautiful VALERIE GRANT (Tina Andrews, Diane Sommerfield), beginning a tempestuous interracial romance.

* * *

As an act of the conscious mind that betrayed his subconscious desire to have a child with Julie, Doug decided that his daughter, Hope, needed a brother or sister. He donated his sperm to Dr. Neil Curtis, who was supposed to find an anonymous surrogate mother to bear Doug a second child. But Neil chose Doug's beautiful housekeeper, REBECCA NORTH (Brooke Bundy), since she wanted the substantial sum that Doug was paying to send to her boyfriend JOHNNY COLLINS (Paul Henry Itkin), living in Paris. When Rebecca became pregnant with Doug's semen, everyone (but Neil) thought that Johnny was the father. ROBERT LE CLAIRE (Robert Clary), a singer at Doug's Place, fell in love with Rebecca and offered to marry her for the sake of her baby. But Rebecca was still in love with Johnny and waited for his return. But when Johnny did come back to Salem and then deserted her on the day of their planned wedding, Rebecca agreed to marry Robert, who still believed her baby to be Johnny's and not Doug's.

Neil Curtis and Greg Peters called a shaky truce in their war of male egos over Amanda Howard when Amanda's terrible secret was revealed: She had a brain tumor and had only six months to live! She refused to have a spectacularly dangerous operation that could have left her without memory or speech; but she was also condemning herself to certain death. Neil wed aging Phyllis Anderson only for her large settlement from Bob, in order to pay off his gambling debts. But Neil had reformed, and had he known of Amanda's plight he would have married her instead of Phyllis—because he truly loved Amanda. Greg loved Amanda, too, and after divorcing Susan (who eventually left Salem) he begged Amanda to marry him, but she wouldn't; she still loved Neil. Both doctors finally persuaded Amanda to have the operation, and when it was over her life was saved, but she was almost a vegetable: no memory, no speech. There was some improvement, and one day she wrote on a piece of paper: "Which man do I love?" Neil proved his mettle when he allowed Amanda to be lied to, for her own good, because Neil was married: "Greg Peters." Greg and Neil eagerly awaited her further recovery. As Amanda slowly regained her memory, it was Neil, not Greg, she was drawn to, and Neil eventually responded, even though Phyllis was having his baby. NATHAN, the infant, died after birth.

The whole Horton family was thrown into turmoil when Marty Hansen suddenly began remembering his past as Mickey Horton. It happened in the most upsetting way possible. After Michael had been in an accident at the Brookville farm, and needed a blood transfusion, Marty naturally donated his, since he believed himself to be the boy's father. When it was Bill's blood type, and not Marty's that matched Michael's, Marty realized that Bill was Michael's father! The whole ghastly, ugly past now came flooding back to Mickey. His mind snapped. He grabbed a gun and tried to murder his brother, but fortunately only wounded Bill in the arm. When Mickey went into total hysterics, his father, Tom Horton, had to make the tortured but necessary decision to commit his son. The only people who objected were Michael, who simply couldn't believe his father was insane, and Linda Patterson, who had come back into Mickey's life and was trying to steal him away from Maggie, who had several operations on her legs and could now walk. Mickey was quite dangerous. At the sanitarium he tried to strangle two blond nurses who reminded him of Laura. But the insanity was only temporary, and Mickey was about to be released. Linda made a point of being on Michael's side in everything concerning his father, and even asked Michael to live with her, as a tactic to gain Mickey's sympathy and lure him away from Maggie. Maggie realized that since she could walk now she could not rely on her handicap to hold on to Mickey. She had to find another way to show Mickey—who was no longer her

"Marty"—that she was more worthy of his love than Linda.

When Michael confessed to Linda that he feared he was homosexual because he couldn't have relations with Trish, Linda slept with him, à la *Tea and Sympathy*. Michael soon fell in love with Linda who became increasingly distraught now that Maggie was winning Mickey back. Linda confessed to Michael that every time she had sex with him she closed her eyes and made believe he was his father Mickey.

* * *

When word came that her son was alive, Julie, in her anxiety to rush to David, tripped and fell down a flight of stairs. The baby she was carrying was lost. After she divorced Bob Anderson, Doug realized how much he loved Julie and they made wedding plans. But a Polynesian princess, KIM DOUGLAS (Helen Funai), suddenly showed up in Salem claiming to be Mrs. Brent Douglas—"Brent," as Doug admitted, was his real name. Doug said yes, it was true that he had once married her, but he had divorced her years ago—but Kim came up with the little bombshell that she had never signed the divorce papers, and his marriage to Addie had never been legal. After making Julie and Doug suffer for months, she admitted that indeed the divorce had been finalized. Doug and Julie were at last wed in a lavish ceremony that thrilled all of Salem.

Shortly after Julie and Doug were wed, an artist friend of hers, SHARON DUVAL (Sally Stark), showed up in Salem with her wealthy husband KARL DUVAL (Alejandro Rey). Sharon was dominated by the suave Karl, who flirted with Julie. One day Sharon told both Julie and Karl that she had lesbian feelings toward Julie. Quite upset by the admission, Julie dropped the couple as her friends and the Duvals moved to Europe. Much more problematical for the Williamses was LARRY ATWOOD (Fred Beir), a rival club owner who had the liquor license of Doug's Place revoked and had raped Julie. When Atwood was suddenly murdered, Julie had to stand trial. But the killer turned out to be ARLO ROBERTS (Nathaniel Christian), Atwood's henchman. Doug and Julie settled down to a happy marriage.

After losing Julie forever, Don Craig fell in love with DR. MARLENA EVANS (Diedre Hall), Mickey's brilliant psychiatrist. Don and Marlena were a perfect match, both possessing rapid-fire wit and professional dedication. Hardly had their romance gotten off the ground, when Marlena's twin sister SAMANTHA (Andrea Hall-Lovell) came to Salem. Although Samantha, an unemployed actress, didn't show it, she was severely unbalanced, resenting Marlena's romantic and professional success. She stashed Marlena away in Lakeview Sanitarium, impersonated her and even treated Marlena's patients! Mickey, Laura and Don suspected something and soon uncovered the truth. Samantha was institutionalized and eventually cured. A month after Don and Marlena had gotten back together, they were visited by LORRAINE TEMPLE (Francine York), an old affair of his. Lorraine proved that Don had fathered her confused teenage daughter DONNA (Tracy Bregman), then left town. For a while Donna schemed against Don and Marlena's romance, but truly came to love both of them. Don and Marlena were finally married.

When Neil Curtis realized that Amanda had developed a good marriage with Greg Peters, he tried to strengthen his bonds with his own wife, Phyllis, whom Neil had originally married for money. But the union had been a poor one from the start and was ripe for problems. Weak Neil had allowed himself to be seduced by Mary Anderson, Phyllis's own daughter! They began an affair. One day Phyllis learned the awful truth when she walked in on them making love. She divorced Neil and soon after left Salem to go on a world tour. Later Mary became involved with CHRIS KOSITCHEK (Josh Taylor), a charming self-made inventor who worked for her father Bob Anderson at his company, Anderson Manufacturing. Mary and Chris began living and working together. Taken with Chris, Bob hoped he would become his son-in-law; but Chris, an independent soul, insisted on working out of a garage, and the affair with Mary collapsed. Bob and Chris, however, remained good friends.

Amanda and Greg did have a strong marriage for a while. But after Greg was appointed chief of staff at University Hospital, he developed an obsession with power and prestige which alienated Amanda. When he later took another position in Chicago, Amanda, feeling neglected, returned to Salem alone and started a passionate love affair with Chris Kositchek, who found Amanda wonderful after his many stormy months with strong-minded Mary Anderson. They planned on marrying, but then Greg came to Salem and talked Amanda into going back with him to Chicago. Alone again, Chris had a romance with an am-

bitious Anderson employee, LESLIE JAMES (Dianne Harper), but she proved far too overpowering and Chris broke up with her.

Linda Patterson was still intent on winning Mickey Horton back from Maggie, with whom he was now happily married and living in Salem. After Mickey set up a thriving law practice with Don Craig, Linda became their secretary, to be near Mickey. Other men, however, found her quite desirable, including rich Bob Anderson, who was Mickey's star client, lonely Tommy Horton and JIM PHILLIPS (Victor Holchak), a former suitor of hers. When she became pregnant by Jim Phillips, she married him to give their baby daughter, MELISSA (now Lisa Trusel), a birthright. But to lure Mickey away from Maggie, Linda began claiming that Melissa was Mickey's daughter. When Jim Phillips found out about the ruse he went into a rage while driving a car, and crashed it. During Linda's visit to him at the hospital, he had a seizure and, to get rid of him, she left him to die! Soon after, however, Mickey and Maggie proved that Jim had fathered Melissa. Having lost Mickey again, widowed Linda married Bob Anderson for his money. Tommy Horton left Salem.

Mickey and Maggie's problems weren't over. Mickey was sterile and Maggie wanted children, so they adopted a little orphan girl named JANICE (Martha Nix). Then JOANNE BARNES (Corinne Michaels), the child's real mother, showed up in Salem and wanted custody. Maggie, for years a teetotaller, buckled under the pressure of a custody hearing and turned to drink. The judge ruled on a shared custody arrangement whereby Joanne and the Hortons would each have Janice for six months out of the year. But during Janice's first stay with her mother she wrote Mickey and Maggie a heartbreaking letter in which she told them that she wanted to remain with Joanne. Nevertheless, Maggie conquered her alcoholism and again became a good wife to Mickey.

Mickey and Maggie were also involved with the serious problems of their neighbors, JEAN and FRED BARTON (Jocelyn Somers and John Lombardo). Fred was beating Jean brutally, and finally Jean attended a therapy group for battered wives. Marlena Evans treated Fred and he was able to shake his problem, but it was too late: Jean told Fred she was leaving him. Destroyed, Fred tripped over her suitcase and fell down a stairway, ending up paralyzed after Bill Horton performed emergency brain surgery. Jean realized that Fred was not evil but rather a sick man in need of help, and decided to stay married to him and care for him.

Meanwhile, the marriage of Laura and Bill Horton almost broke up. Laura had become so involved with her practice and with helping friends in trouble—such as Marlena Evans, who was distraught after her release from the sanitarium—that Bill felt he had lost Laura. So he had a brief affair with DR. KATE WINOGRAD (Elaine Princi), a darkly attractive anesthesiologist at the hospital. Bill and Laura reconciled when Kate departed Salem. Soon after, however, Laura was haunted by visions of her mentally ill mother, and had a complete breakdown. Bill found Laura only seconds before she was about to hang herself in their bedroom on "orders" from her mother. Bill had her committed to Lakeview Sanitarium. Once cured, Laura was released and she and Bill left Salem.

* * *

Michael Horton and Trish Clayton had been in love but were really too young to know how to cope with their feelings. Trish, who had had a platonic living arrangement with Michael, was deeply hurt when she learned of his brief affair with Linda. Then, after Mickey told a shocked Michael that his brother Bill was his real father, Michael turned bitter and confused and shut Trish out of his life. Feeling worthless, Trish turned to David Banning, who was still on the rebound from his relationship with Valerie Grant, and the two made love. Trish became pregnant by David! When her ghoulish stepfather, Jack Clayton, tried to rape her, Mike attacked him and, in the scuffle, Jack was killed. It was all too much for fragile Trish, who had a breakdown and developed a multiple personality. After she recovered from the schizophrenia, she married David and then gave birth to their son SCOTTY (named after David's late father, Scott Banning). But Trish still loved Michael, who was now forging ahead with his own life. In reaction to all the lies he had been told by Bill and Laura, and their middle-class values, he became a mechanic. He married MARGO ANDERMAN (Suzanne Zenor), an uneducated but loving young woman, fully knowing she had a terminal blood disease. In time Margo died, once again leaving Michael embittered. Meanwhile, Trish, still confused about her feelings toward Michael and her husband, abandoned David and little Scotty to begin a Hollywood acting career. She became involved with a

crime syndicate which also employed Julie's brother, Steve Olson. After the mob was caught, Steve escaped prosecution, and Trish went back to David. She and Mike settled for a friendship which neither was able to define.

* * *

Ever since Bob Anderson had divorced his first wife, Phyllis, he had sought love from the wrong women and wound up in unhappy marriages. Linda Patterson was no exception. Newly rich but bored, Linda argued constantly with Bob's daughter Mary and his good friend Chris over the running of Anderson Manufacturing, and had a sordid extramarital liaison with irresponsible Neil Curtis. Both Bob and Mary discovered Linda's treachery and Bob divorced her, although he left Melissa, Linda's little girl, a large legacy in his will. Meanwhile, Phyllis came back to Salem with her new fiancé, a handsome fortyish cad named ALEX MARSHALL (Quinn Redeker), who was only interested in the Anderson fortune. Acting out old competitive patterns, Phyllis's daughter Mary became attracted to Alex, who broke his engagement to Phyllis and married Mary, with Bob's reluctant blessing. As a *coup de grace* to unsavory events in the Anderson family, Bob suffered another in a string of heart attacks, this time his last. As he lay dying he learned the stunning news that his new young helpmate at Anderson Manufacturing, captivating STEPHANIE WOODRUFF (Eileen Barnett), was really Brooke Hamilton, his illegitimate daughter! She had been presumed dead several years before but had now returned to Salem intent on winning her father's affection and respect. Bob died in peace. Not long after, Brooke tragically died in a car crash.

No one knew that Alex Marshall had a secret past connection to Marie Horton, which made Sister Marie try to avoid him at almost every turn. Years earlier, before Marie had become a nun, she had been a drug addict in New York. Alex had also been an addict there, and the two had carried on a sado-masochistic sexual relationship which produced an illegitimate daughter. Marie gave the infant up for adoption. Before Marie severed ties with Alex, she had witnessed his struggle with his brother, HARLEY, which ended in Harley's fatal fall off an outdoor balcony. Now, years later, Marie was a practicing nurse at University Hospital, as well as a nun, and Alex, whose marriage to Mary was insincere, was once again deeply attracted to Marie. At first Sister Marie only wanted to hide from the past as well as Alex, even after Alex and Mary divorced. Finally, after Alex spent many months trying to convince Marie that he loved her and wanted to marry her, she admitted to herself that she still loved him and began thinking about leaving her convent order.

Rebecca North, who had given birth to DOUGIE (Doug Williams was the father), had run off with her boyfriend Johnny and left Dougie with her husband, Robert Le Clair. Rebecca wrote Doug that he was the father of her little boy, just before she was killed in a car crash, and soon Robert Le Clair and Doug were in a bitter conflict over possession of Dougie. Robert finally placed Dougie in a private school and went to Paris to sort out his feelings toward his old friend.

Simultaneously, insidious events began systematically to destroy Doug and Julie's hard-earned marriage. Doug was reunited with his estranged elder half-brother BYRON CARMICHAEL (also Bill Hayes, in a dual role), who died after a lingering illness, leaving a fortune to Doug. Then a tragedy occurred: Julie's face was terribly scarred in an oven grease fire at Maggie Horton's ranch! Afraid that Doug would no longer be attracted to her, Julie obtained a quick Mexican divorce. Doug was hurt by Julie's obvious mistrust of him and allowed himself to be seduced by LEE DUMONDE (Brenda Benet), his late brother's golddigging widow, and married her. Plastic surgery restored Julie's face, but Doug's emotional scars remained; so at first he refused to reconcile with Julie. However, when Doug and Julie realized that they were still in love and wanted to remarry, Lee refused to grant him a divorce and secretly hired her ex-boyfriend BRENT CAVANAUGH (Frank Ashmore) to kill Julie! But just as Brent was about to murder Julie, Lee had second thoughts and killed him instead with a blow to the head. Lee granted Doug his divorce and he and his "fair lady" were joyfully remarried.

* * *

Incredibly wealthy, corrupt politico KELLAM CHANDLER (Bill Joyce) moved into his new mansion in Salem. He fell in love with Marlena Evans Craig, who separated from her husband Don Craig after their newly-born son D.J. suddenly died. Kellam hired both Don and Marlena for his campaign staff, then plotted to win Marlena from Don permanently. He pushed Don together with his strong-willed daughter LIZ COURTNEY (Gloria Loring), a divorcée who detested her father, and the plan worked perfectly: Marlena divorced Don, who hastily married Liz, despite warnings that Liz had skeletons in her closet. A young man named JOSHUA FALLON (Stephen Brooks, Scott Palmer), the son of one of Kellam's ex-wives, found evidence that Kellam had had his mother murdered. Joshua also learned that spoiled TOD CHANDLER (Paul Keenan), Kellam's son, and he had the same mother. In a dramatic denouement, Kellam went insane and raped Marlena, had a furious struggle with Joshua and was shot dead by his own son Tod.

Sister Marie Horton and Alex Marshall suddenly discovered that Tod's girl friend, a shy nursing student named JESSICA BLAKE (Jean Bruce Scott) was their long-lost illegitimate daughter. Alex adopted Jessica and Marie, moved by the fact that Jessica was her daughter was on the verge of leaving the convent to marry Alex. But scheming Mary Anderson wanted Alex back and seduced him, arranging for Sister Marie to catch them *in flagrante delicto*. Then Mary found out that Jessica was really their daughter, forcing Alex and Marie to tell Jessica the ugly truth about her birth. Jessica became so consumed with hatred over this strange revelation that she developed a split personality. By day she became the pure side of her mother, joining a convent to escape her problems; by night she became her vision of Marie's old self, a cheap slut named "Angel" who walked the streets.

Some time before, David Banning had become overly ambitious at Anderson Manufacturing and had allowed Alex Marshall to use him as an instrument in company sabotage. After he was found out David deserted Trish and fled Salem with little Scotty. Now, a year later, he returned as an honest, successful businessman, and tried to convince Trish to take him back. David also brought his tycoon boss STUART WHYLAND (Robert Alda) to Salem. Stuart purchased the local radio station and hired Marlena to emcee a psychiatric call-in show. One of the callers was a strange young man pleading for help for his urge to kill cheap-looking women. For a while everyone believed the young man was Tod Chandler, who had already been accused of murdering a girl named CASSIE BURNS (Deborah Dalton). But after Tod was institutionalized, there were more phone calls—and strangulations.

Meanwhile Jessica, as her bar-hopping persona "Angel," became attracted to JAKE KOSITCHEK (Jack Coleman), Chris Kositchek's womanizing young brother. While Marlena was curing Jessica of her schizophrenia, Jake came to truly love her and proposed marriage. He was determined to shelter Jessica from the dread Salem Strangler, who soon killed both Samantha Evans, Marlena's twin, and poor Mary Anderson! Don Craig, who had become the new district attorney, joined forces with police sergeant ROMAN BRADY (Wayne Northrop) to nab the killer. Diamond-in-the-rough Roman Brady was attracted to Marlena Evans and appointed himself her protector. Finally the madman revealed himself to Marlena: it was Jake Kositchek! Just as he tried to murder Marlena, Roman shot Jake dead. Roman and grateful Marlena began a wonderful romance and married.

* * *

Debonair COUNT ANTHONY DI MERA (Thaao Penghlis), Liz Courtney's ex-husband, suddenly showed up in Salem with proof that his divorce from Liz had never been finalized! Don Craig, whose marriage to Liz had not been a good one anyway, suddenly discovered that he wasn't married to Liz after all. Neil Curtis had been in love with her from the start and Liz would have gone to him had not Anthony DiMera's father, STEFANO DI MERA (Joseph Mascolo), the head of a crime syndicate, come to Salem. The DiMera family threatened to harm Neil if Liz didn't remain under their roof. Stefano, who turned out to be Stuart Whyland's boss, had Stuart and his son EVAN (Lane Davies) murdered, and plotted to take over Anderson Manufacturing. After Doug and Julie learned that Stefano also wanted to take over their club for mysterious purposes, they went undercover to get the goods on him.

Alex Marshall was shot! Suspected of the crime, David Banning went on the run and was sheltered by RENEE DUMONDE (Philece Sampler), Lee Dumonde's flirtatious younger sister. Alex's assailant turned out to be a mob figure and David was cleared. He still wanted Trish back. Trish, still torn between David and Mike, finally had relations with Mike—but Mike felt that she still loved David and left Salem. Trish decided not to take David back after all and left town to further her singing career. Alex Marshal lived to return to his scheming ways. Right afterward Lee Dumonde revealed that she was not Renee's sister, but her mother! And her father was crime boss Stefano DiMera! Renee and Tony DiMera had been in love, but now had to part because they were brother and sister. Renee married David Banning, but a few months later Tony discovered that Stefano was not his biological father. Neither he nor Renee knew what to do next. Matters became even more complicated when Liz became pregnant by Tony, her legal husband, while still very much in love with Neil. Evil Stefano finally died of a stroke.

Chris Kositchek and Melissa Anderson, Linda's daughter, inherited Anderson Manufacturing following the deaths of Bob and Mary Anderson. Linda had tried to get her hands on the company, but Mickey and Maggie prevented it by gaining custody of Melissa, and Linda left Salem. Maggie had just given birth to a baby girl, SARA, through artificial insemination, with Mickey's approval. Don Craig became involved with GWEN DAVIES (Ann-Marie Martin). Gwen was secretly the sister of OLIVER MARTIN (Shawn Stevens), Mellissa's new boyfriend, and WOODY KING (Lane Caudell), an egotistical country singer who sang at Tony DiMera's new nightclub, Shenanigans. However, when Mickey was held hostage by Stefano's underlings and falsely presumed dead, Don fell in love with Maggie—his best friend's wife. Also, Marie's daughter, Jessica Blake, and Joshua Fallon were married.

CAST
DAYS OF OUR LIVES
NBC: November 8, 1965

Dr. Tom Horton	MacDonald Carey (P)
Alice Horton	Frances Reid (P)
Mickey Horton	John Clarke (P)
Marie Horton Curtis	Marie Cheatham (P)
	Kate Woodville
	Lanna Saunders*
Julie Olsen Williams	Carla Doherty (P)
	Catherine Dunn
	Catherine Ferrar
	Susan Seaforth Hayes*
Addie Olson Williams	Patricia Huston (P)
	Patricia Barry*
Ben Olson	Robert Knapp (P)
Steve Olson	Flip Mark (P)
	James Carroll Jordan
	Stephen Schnetzer*
Craig Merritt	David McLean (P)
	Harry Lauter
Tony Merritt	Richard Colla (P)

	Ron Husmann	David Banning	Chad Barstad
Detective	Robert Stevenson (P)		Jeffrey Williams
Jim Fisk	Burt Douglas (P)		Steve Doubet
Dr. Bill Horton	Paul Carr		Richard Guthrie*
	Edward Mallory*		Gregg Marx
Dr. Laura Spencer		Dr. Greg Peters	Peter Brown
Horton	Floy Dean	Eric Peters	Stanley Kamel
	Susan Flannery*	Anne Peters	Jeanne Bates
	Susan Oliver	Dr. Phil Peters	Herb Nelson
	Rosemary Forsyth	Mary Anderson	Brigid Bazlen
Susan Hunter Peters ...	Denise Alexander*		Karin Wolfe
	Bennye Gatteys		Nancy Stephens
Diane Hunter	Jane Kean		Carla Borelli
	Coleen Gray*		Barbara Stanger*
Richard Hunter	Terry O'Sullivan		Susan Keller
David Martin	Steven Mines		Melinda Fee
	Clive Clerk*	Bob Anderson	Mark Tapscott
Helen Martin	K. T. Stevens	Phyllis Anderson Curtis	Nancy Wickwire
John Martin	Robert Brubaker		Corinne Conley*
Scott Banning	Robert Carraway	Dr. Neil Curtis	Joseph Gallison
	Mike Farrell	Amanda Howard Peters	Mary Frann
	Robert Hogan	Don Craig	Jed Allan
	Ryan MacDonald	Maggie Simmons Horton	Suzanne Rogers
Janet Banning	Joyce Easton	Jeri Clayton	Kaye Stevens
Dr. Tommy Horton	John Lupton	Jack Clayton	Jack Denbo
Kitty Horton	Regina Gleason	Trish Clayton Banning .	Patty Weaver
Sandy Horton	Heather North*	Melissa Phillips	
	Martha Smith	Anderson	Kim Durso
Dr. Mel Bailey	Richard McMurray		Debbie Lytton*
Peter Larkin	Gene Peterson		Lisa Trusel
Claire Larkin	Catherine McLeod	Hope Williams	Natasha Ryan*
Sarah Fredericks	Kay Peters		Tammy Taylor
Janene Whitney	Mary Wilcox		Kristian Alfonso
	Pat Hornung	J. R. Barnett	Mark Miller
	Joan Van Ark	Rebecca North LeClair .	Brooke Bundy
Doug Williams	Bill Hayes	Johnny Collins	Paul Henry Itkin
Robert LeClair	Robert Clary	Brooke Hamilton	Adrienne LaRussa
Linda Patterson			Eileen Barnett
Anderson	Margaret Mason	Adele Hamilton	Dee Carroll
Cliff Patterson	John Howard	Nathan Curtis	Tom Brown
Jim Phillips	Victor Holchak	Valerie Grant	Tina Andrews*
Michael Horton	Bobby Eilbacher		Rose Fonseca
	Eddie Rayden		Diane Sommerfield
	Alan Decker	Danny Grant	Michael Dwight-Smith*
	John Amour		Roger Aaron Brown
	Dick DeCoit	Helen Grant	Ketty Lester
	Stuart Lee	Paul Grant	Lawrence Cook
	Wesley Eure*	Rosie Carlson	Fran Ryan
	Paul Coufos	Janice Horton	Martha Nix

Jim Stanhope	William Traylor
Kay Stanhope	Doris Singleton
	Sandy Balson
Ginny Stanhope	Janet Wood
Sharon Duval	Sally Stark
Karl Duval	Alejandro Rey
Dr. Marlena Evans	Deidre Hall
Barbara Randolph	Elizabeth McRae
Kim Williams	Helen Funai
Jean Barton	Jocelyn Somers
Fred Barton	John Lombardo
Larry Atwood	Fred Beir
Dr. Kate Winograd	Elaine Princi
Samantha Evans	Andrea Hall-Lovell
Chris Kositchek	Josh Taylor
Toni Johnson	Chip Fields
Lorraine Temple	Francine York
Donna Temple Craig . . .	Tracy Bregman
Margo Anderman	
Horton	Suzanne Zenor
Arlo Roberts	Nathaniel Christian
Joanne Barnes	Corinne Michaels
Theresa Harper	Elizabeth Brooks
Dr. Jordan Barr	George McDaniel
Scotty Banning	Erick Petersen
	Dick Billingsley*
Mimi Grosset	Gail Johnson
Byron Carmichael	Bill Hayes
Lee Dumonde	Brenda Benet
Alex Marshall	Quinn Redeker
Kathy Breton	Cindy Daily
Stan Kositchek	Thomas Havens
Leslie James	Dianne Harper
Flora Chisholm	Meg Wyllie
Joshua Fallon	Stephen Brooks
	Scott Palmer
Jessica Blake Fallon . . .	Jean Bruce Scott
Kellam Chandler	Bill Joyce
Liz Chandler	Gloria Loring
Tod Chandler	Brett Williams
	Paul Keenan*
Maxwell Jarvis	Charles Bateman
Cassie Burns	Deborah Dalton
Brent Cavanaugh	Perry Bullington
	Frank Ashmore
Carol Welles	Tyler Murray
Kyle McCullough	Richard Hill
Renee Dumonde	
Banning	Philece Sampler

Jake Kositchek	Jack Coleman
Stuart Whyland	Robert Alda
Dr. Evan Whyland	Lane Davies
Count Antony DiMera . .	Thaao Penghlis
Stefano DiMera	Joseph Mascolo
Sgt. Abe Carver	James Reynolds
Sgt. Roman Brady	Wayne Northrop
Kayla Brady	Catherine Mary Stewart
Lorie Masters	Cynthia Leake
Gwen Davies	Ann-Marie Martin
Woody King	Lane Caudell
Oliver Martin	Shawn Stevens
Esther Kensington	Dorothy Jones
Anna Brady DiMera	Leann Hunley
Nikki Wade	Renee Jones
Preston Wade	Jason Bernard
Mitzi Matuso	Livia Ginise
Johnny	Jeremy Schoenberg
Bo Brady	Peter Reckell
Shawn Brady	Frank Parker
Caroline Brady	Peggy McCay
Daphne DiMera	Madlyn Rhue

Creators: Ted Corday, Irna Phillips, Allan Chase

Head Writers: Peggy Phillips and Kenneth M. Rosen, William J. Bell, Pat Falken Smith, Ann Marcus, Elizabeth Harrower, Ruth Brooks Flippen, Nina Laemmle, Michele Poteet-Lisanti and Gary Tomlin, Margaret DePriest and Sheri Anderson

Executive Producers: Ted Corday, Betty Corday, H. Wesley Kenney, Jack Herzberg, Al Rabin

Producers: Gene Banks, Ken Corday, Lynne Osborne, Patricia Wenig

Directors: Joseph Behar, Ira Cirker, Livia Granito, Richard Sandwick, Herbert Kenwith, Frank Pacelli, H. Wesley Kenney, Al Rabin, Alan Pultz, Ken Herman, Jr., Byrle Cass, Edward Mallory, Rudy Vejar, Richard Dunlap, Susan Orlikoff Simon, Herb Stein, Arlene Sanford

Musical Directors: (together) Tommy Boyce, Bobby Hart, Barry Mann and Charles Albertine

Packager: Corday Productions for Screen Gems and Columbia Pictures Television

THE EDGE OF NIGHT

THE EDGE OF NIGHT isn't a true soap opera but what used to be called a "melodrama": a show which depends upon catastrophic events, such as murder and other heinous crimes, for its main interest. During most of its colorful twenty-eight-year history, it has occupied a late afternoon time slot, attracting men and teenagers home from school as well as housewives. That has been one key to its great success. Another has been the skill with which it has been written and produced.

BACKGROUND

The Edge of Night began almost as an afterthought. For several years in the early fifties, Irna Phillips had been hectoring Procter & Gamble to let her expand her fifteen-minute television show, *The Guiding Light*, to a full half hour. The sponsor considered the idea of a half-hour soap, which had never been done before, odd and chancy, and refused to let her change her show. But in November 1955 P&G finally permitted Irna, through the Benton & Bowles advertising agency, to film a pilot of a new half-hour serial with the title, *As the World Turns*. There had been a great deal of skepticism but, strangely, as the premiere date of April 2, 1956, began to draw close, a number of people at Benton & Bowles grew sanguine about the prospects of half-hour soaps. Two years of uncertainty over Irna's proposal had in the end gener-

ated so much added enthusiasm that someone at the agency came up with the idea of doing another half-hour serial with a cops-and-robbers theme. The enthusiasm became pervasive. P&G then attempted to negotiate for the rights to *Perry Mason*, which the soap company had sponsored as a daytime radio serial. But when *Mason's* creator, Earle Stanley Gardner, refused to allow his character love entanglements in the soap opera mold, his radio *Mason* writer, Irving Vendig, created a new show. It became *The Edge of Night*, premiering on exactly the same day as *As the World Turns*—April 2, 1956. Both shows were the first half-hour television soaps.

There were other connections between the old *Perry Mason* radio show and its new television counterpart. John Larkin, who had played Perry, was now the lead crook-catching character on *The Edge of Night*, assistant district attorney Mike Karr. Perhaps Teal Ames's Sara Lane may also have reminded people of Della Street, although the character was delineated differently. In the first story line, Sara was a member of the large Lane family and was touched by corruption through her brother Jack (played by Don Hastings, who spoke the first words in the opening live episode), and her evil uncle, Harry Lane (Lauren Gilbert). But *Edge* also incorporated romances, such as the one between Mike and Sara, giving the show more of continuing feel than the old *Perry Mason*.

From the very beginning, *The Edge of Night* was a great success, with nine million viewers before its first year was over. It was in fact the number one television soap for four years until *As the World Turns* moved up. Producer/director Don Wallace brought daytime television to new heights when he began staging live shootouts between John Larkin and fictional criminals in warehouses and on the roofs of the studio, keeping action-oriented viewers sitting on the edge of their seats. But there were also a great many "sob sisters" out there, as the show discovered in 1961 when Sara Karr was killed while saving her little girl from an onrushing bus. Shocked and grief-stricken viewers tied up the CBS switchboard for hours, registering complaints.

It was during these early days that the most famous live television blooper of all time occurred. John Larkin, who died in 1965, remained endlessly embarrassed about the scene in which he came through a door and yelled at the cameras: "Hello, all you folks out there in TV land!" and then started cutting up and dancing around. He wondered why none of the other actors were laughing along with him. When the commercial break came, he discovered that he had mistaken the live broadcast for the dress rehearsal and that ten million people had watched the whole charade. John passed out and the episode continued without him.

For many years *The Edge of Night* enjoyed uninterrupted high ratings, until Procter & Gamble made a questionable maneuver in late 1972. Since its own CBS soaps had better ratings than CBS's house-produced soaps, P&G wanted all of its shows together in one block and asked that *Edge* be moved from 3:30 P.M. to 2:30 P.M. E.S.T. The new time period removed the men and older schoolchildren from the audience, thereby pulling down the show's ratings. After two years of bad Nielsens, CBS requested the removal of *The Edge of Night* (as it did, later on, of *Search for Tomorrow*). On December 1, 1975, ABC gladly took it, returning it to 4:00 P.M., and thereafter the ratings rose considerably. But sadly, when the show switched networks it ceased being live, ending an era: *Edge* had been the last live soap.

As you will see from the following story line summary, it is the logical rather than the emotional that governs the world of *The Edge of Night*—especially since Henry Slesar became head writer years ago. He has a rare imagination that can develop the most convoluted plots, filled with Byzantine twists and turns, and keep them going for several years. Slesar has

wonderful idiosyncrasies. (He is drawn, for instance, to borderline women's names, like Raven and Brandy, which to some ears sound like the names of well-bred airedales.) For the most part, Slesar's work for *Edge of Night* could easily have served as the basis of a sophisticated series of murder mystery novels. In 1983 he left the show and was replaced by Lee Sheldon, writer of many nighttime series.

In the current story line, the main long-term characters are Mike and Nancy Karr, former political figurehead Geraldine Whitney Saxon and police chief Derek Mallory. Mike, a longtime crime fighter, left his law practice a couple of years ago to become D.A. of Monticello. Nancy, his second wife, is a crime reporter for the Monticello *News*. Geraldine, once an interfering matriarch, has mellowed since the gradual annihilation of most of her family at the hands of criminals, and is now an executive at the WMON-TV television studio.

The Edge of Night's manner of employing victims or villains for only a year or two before killing them off or sending them away has put the show in the enviable position of being able to hire vast numbers of talented actors through the years. "Graduates" of the show have included Larry Hagman, Ruby Dee, Tony Roberts, John Cullum and Barry Newman.

THE STORY

The gentleness and quiet simplicity of SARA LANE (Teal Ames) immediately attracted Assistant D.A. MIKE KARR (originated by John Larkin, later played by Larry Hugo and currently by Forrest Compton). His gang-busting work was tough. When she became Mrs. Mike Karr, Sara's sympathetic, understanding nature always helped ease the emotional burdens of his work. With the birth of their daughter, LAURIE ANN KARR (played longest as an adult by Emily Prager, later by Jeannie Ruskin, Linda Cook), Mike became the happiest crook-catcher alive. But when Laurie was only two, tragedy, with one of its cruelest blows, struck the Karrs. Sara, rushing into the street to shove Laurie Ann away from the wheels of an onrushing car, was killed.

Mike thought he would never recover, but he had

little Laurie to think about, so two years later he married a young reporter named NANCY POLLOCK (Ann Flood) in a big, elaborate wedding. Nancy has always been a fine mother to Laurie and a great help to Mike in his work.

When Mike Karr quit being D.A. to go into law practice for himself, his main link with the police department was its chief of police, BILL MARCEAU (Mandel Kramer). Widowed Bill Marceau—he had a neurotic daughter, JUDY (Joan Harvey), who later left Monticello after causing everyone much grief—began working with an efficient police secretary, MARTHA SPEARS (Teri Keane), and slowly the two fell in love, and were married a few years later. They weren't young enough to have a child of their own, so they adopted fifteen-year-old PHOEBE SMITH (originated by Heidi Vaughn, later Johanna Leister). At first Phoebe was a "bad seed" type, causing all sorts of trouble for Monticello residents, but she later straightened out.

Tall, attractive lawyer ADAM DRAKE (Donald May) arrived in town just in time to give Mike Karr some badly needed help in catching some elusive murderers, and to simultaneously frustrate all the ladies by his perpetual bachelor's standoffishness. One of those ladies was Nancy Karr's young sister, COOKIE POLLOCK (Fran Sharon) who, unable to get anywhere with Adam, fell in love with New York public relations man RON CHRISTOPHER (Burt Douglas) and later married him.

Beautiful, wealthy and spoiled NICOLE TRAVIS (played longest by Maeve McGuire) arrived in Monticello from Capital City after being forced into a divorce by her ex-husband, DUANE STEWART (Richard Clarke). Embittered by the loss of Duane, Nicole tried to get even with the world by attempting to seduce happily married Mike Karr, and, of course, she failed. Meanwhile, she began running McGrath's dress shop with her friend, SUSAN FORBES (Bibi Besch), who had her own sights set for Adam Drake. Adam, however, found Nicole much more interesting than Susan Forbes, but—*c'est la vie*—Nicole simply found Adam boring.

The Edge of Night *has always been a combination of soap and mystery story. When it began on April 2, 1956, John Larkin played the crook-catching assistant D.A., Mike Karr, and Teal Ames played sweet Sara Lane, with whom Mike fell in love. They were wed in 1958 after a drawn-out story involving her family.*

Sara's widowed mother, Mattie Lane (Peggy Allenby), married Winston Grimsley (Walter Greaza), Monticello's leading citizen and a good friend of Mike Karr. Mattie and Winston were important "tentpole" characters during Edge's first decade. Mattie was also important as the matriarch of the Lane family, central to the show's early crime plots.

Nicole's father, BEN TRAVIS (Bill Prince, later Cec Linder), was a corrupt senator, who headed a vicious loan-shark ring. Among the victims of Ben Travis's organization were the husband and daughter of STEPHANIE MARTIN (Alice Hirson), both of whom were killed in an auto "accident" arranged by the mob. Both Stephanie and her other remaining daughter, DEBBIE (Ellen Hansen), consequently became mentally ill, but in different ways: Debbie became autistic, and Stephanie swore a secret vendetta against Nicole Travis, because, with twisted logic, Stephanie saw Nicole as just as evil as her father (who was arrested and sent to prison). Stephanie began to send Nicole poison chocolates, spiders, quotes from *Macbeth* dealing with blood and murder, and would creep around in man's clothing with a stocking over her face, just to try to scare Nicole out of her wits. At the same time, Stephanie was pretending to be Nicole's friend, and even got a job in her dress shop. Adam Drake, who by now had gained Nicole's affection somewhat, became suspicious of Stephanie.

Adam finally gathered evidence to prove to Nicole that Stephanie was the culprit. Before Adam could warn Nicole about it, though, Duane Stewart showed up in Monticello, intent on winning her back. In a jealous fury, his new wife, PAMELA STEWART (Irene Dailey), tried to kill Nicole, but instead mistakenly murdered Stephanie Martin. When Nicole walked onto the scene and saw Stephanie lying on the ground with a knife sticking out of her back, she was horrified—and so was Stephanie's daughter, Debbie, who happened to be there. "Pull it out!" Debbie screamed. Shocked because autistic Debbie Martin had uttered her first words, Nicole didn't stop to think, and she pulled the knife out of Stephanie's back, of course leaving her fingerprints on it. Nicole was charged and tried for the murder. Adam pled and won her case, causing Nicole to fall more deeply in love with him, but in the end Adam wouldn't give up his bachelorhood to marry her. However, the experience of being tried for murder caused a dramatic personality change in Nicole Travis. Her spoiled, haughty

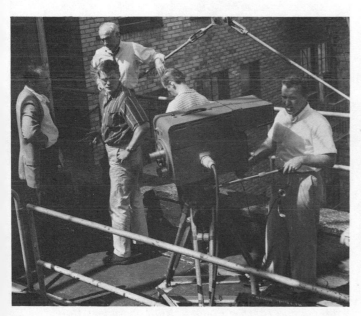

In the show's early days, shootout sequences were staged on the roof of the CBS studio, completely live. Edge *was an instant success with viewers.*

Mandell Kramer, left, came on in 1959 as Bill Marceau, Monticello's chief of police, and remained in that role for more than twenty years. Joan Harvey was Judy Marceau, Bill's troublemaking daughter, who married lawyer Ed Gibson, played by Larry Hagman, in 1961.

nature had been knocked out of her.

* * *

Then began the bizarre saga of the wealthy but tragic Whitney family. Though influential and powerful himself, ex-senator GORDON WHITNEY (Allan Gifford) always seemed to stand in the shadow of his domineering wife, GERALDINE WHITNEY (Lois Kibbee). They had two sons: one a hard-working junior senator, COLIN WHITNEY (Anthony Call), and the other a devilishly handsome but schizophrenic young man, KEITH WHITNEY (Bruce Martin). Colin Whitney was so dedicated a politician that his wife, TIFFANY (Lucy Martin), felt perpetually neglected and was driven to having affairs. One of her extramarital flings was with Ron Christopher, the husband of Nancy Karr's sister, Cookie. When Cookie found out about the affair, she had a complete breakdown and had to go into a mental institution, of course causing Nancy and Mike much grief. The Karrs' lives were also deeply affected by the Whitneys in another way. Their daughter Laurie became infatuated with a bearded-hippie type by the name of Jonah Lockwood—who was really Keith Whitney in disguise. Keith was a vicious multiple-murderer! Adam Drake, growing suspicious of Jonah's true identity and of Keith's shady past, visited a tropical island where Keith had lived and discovered that he had murdered his native-girl wife. Adam then rushed back to Monticello to warn Laurie. But by then the murderous Keith was about to push Laurie off a high turret, but fortunately, in the last moments of high melodrama, Keith slipped and fell to his death and Laurie was saved. Much later, both Gordon and his son, Colin Whitney, were killed in a tragic accident. Geraldine and Tiffany, the sole survivors of the ill-fated family, were left to live with their haunted

Larry Hugo, standing, took over as lawyer Mike Karr in 1962. Phil and Louise Capice, played by Ray MacDonnell (sitting) and Mary K. Wells, were an important couple on the show for a decade. Louise was Winston Grimsley's daughter, originally a rich, spoiled debutante. Phil was a successful businessman often involved with Mike Karr's detective work.

Mike Karr married reporter Nancy Pollock (Ann Flood) on April 22, 1963, following Sara Lane's tragic death in 1961. Cast members at the wedding were, beginning at left, back row: Mandel Kramer, John Gibson (as Joe Pollock, Nancy's father), Ronnie Welch (Lee Pollock, Nancy's brother), Ann Flood, Larry Hugo, Walter Greaza, Ray MacDonnell, Nancy Pinkerton (Beth Anderson), Conard Fowkes (John Paul Anderson); front row: Fran Sharon (Cookie Pollock, Nancy's sister), Ruth Matteson (Rose Pollock, Nancy's mother), Kathleen Bracken (Laurie Ann Karr), Peggy Allenby and Mary K. Wells.

memories. Cookie, recovered from her breakdown, and Ron Christopher were eventually reunited, and they left Monticello.

LIZ HILLYER (Alberta Grant), who first came on the scene as the daughter of wealthy ORIN HILLYER (Lester Rawlins), fell in love with DR. JIM FIELDS (Alan Feinstein), a resident psychiatrist in the home for disturbed children where she was doing volunteer work. After their marriage, her lonely father, Orin, recently injured in a plane crash and confined to a wheelchair, convinced Liz and Jim to move into the family mansion, Claybank, with him. Liz became pregnant, and the conniving ELLY JO JAMISON (Dorothy Lyman), a relative of Orin's dead wife, arrived at Claybank to "help out," but what she really was interested in furthering was the demise of Orin and Liz so that she would get his money. But when Elly Jo tried to kill Liz and her unborn child in a speeding automobile, she fell out and was killed herself in a dramatic finale. Liz and

Jim then had a beautiful baby boy, the new Hillyer heir. Orin moved to Europe for his health.

Liz's former boyfriend, lawyer VIC LAMONT (Ted Tinling), joined the Mike Karr–Adam Drake team and fell in love with Mike's daughter, Laurie Ann Karr. After Vic risked his life by letting himself get sent to prison to get evidence to break up a Monticello narcotics ring, Laurie Ann and Vic were married in an elaborate wedding. Although the two were in love, their marriage did not go smoothly. Vic, ambitious to do well as a lawyer, worked hard and long hours, and he had little energy to devote to his bride. Laurie Ann, bored, insisted on taking a job despite Vic's male-chauvinist objections and began working at the New Moon Café, owned by ex-convict JOHNNY DALLAS (John LaGioia), who started falling in love with her.

Meanwhile, trouble was brewing for Adam Drake and Nicole Travis. Adam made his long-awaited proposal of marriage to Nicole, which infuriated lawyer

Elizabeth Hubbard played Carol Kramer, who was involved with Emory Warren (Philip Abbott), a con man who was trying to extort money from Winston Grimsley.

Widower Bill Marceau married his secretary, Martha Spears, played by Teri Keane, in 1965. Martha became the best friend of Nancy Karr, giving her moral support during crisis. Teri Keane stayed in the part until the character was written out in 1975.

JAKE BERMAN (Ward Costello), Nicole's new employer, who had fallen in love with her himself. To get Adam convicted on an attempted-murder charge, Jake Berman arranged for Johnny Dallas to wound him in the arm and make it look as if Adam had done it. Instead, Jake was murdered and Adam was tried! Then, JOEL GANTRY (Paul Henry Itkin, Nicholas Pryor), Kevin's detective friend, was revealed as Jake's stepson. Joel had amassed evidence proving Jake had killed his wife, who was Joel's mother, EDITH BERMAN (Pat Bright), and murdered Jake in a fit of revenge! Adam was freed and he and Nicole were married in a big ceremony on Mike and Nancy's patio, and at last settled into quiet married life.

Vic and Laurie Lamont were not so fortunate.

Their marital troubles worsened when it was revealed at the trial that Laurie had had a brief extramarital affair with her boss, Johnny Dallas. Vic sued Laurie for divorce, and he soon became involved with one of his clients, a wealthy divorcée named KAY REYNOLDS (Elizabeth Farley). The rejected Laurie took up again with Johnny Dallas, despite the disapproval of her parents, Mike and Nancy, who suspected that, in some way, Johnny was involved with "the mob." They had, in fact, infiltrated Johnny's New Moon Café.

The mob was Monticello's huge crime syndicate, which little by little seemed to be invading the lives of not only Nancy and Mike, through their daughter's involvement with Johnny Dallas, but also Bill and Martha Marceau and Adam and Nicole.

Martha, who had never had a child of her own, became obsessed with the idea of adopting an infant.

Bill and Martha adopted fifteen-year-old Phoebe Smith (Heidi Vaughn). In 1968, Rick Oliver (Keith Charles), a disc jockey, became interested in young Phoebe. When Rick Oliver was suddenly murdered, all the evidence tended to incriminate Martha Marceau, who was put on trial.

Society woman Laura Hillyer (Millete Alexander, in her second role on the show) had been in love with Rick Oliver and was revealed as his murderer. When the truth came out, Laura, dressed in a sable coat, drove off a cliff to her death. Later, Millette Alexander returned to the show as Laura's look-alike, Julie Jamison (depicted in photo). Adam Drake (Donald May), Mike Karr's new law partner, defended Julie Jamison in another murder trial. She was exonerated just before she was to be hanged.

Eventually she and Bill adopted little JENNIFER, but, unknown to them, the child came through a black-market baby-adoption ring—one of the mob's "franchises." With the town's leading law-enforcement officer in their vise, the syndicate began to tighten the screws. Bill now had to choose between blackmail payoffs or losing the little girl, who was giving Martha the first real happiness she had known in many months. Bill's whole career seemed on the brink of disaster.

Adam was delighted when wealthy Geraldine Whitney—morbidly seeing in Adam the image of her dead son, Colin Whitney—offered to back his campaign if he ran for state senator. The mob was already devising means for keeping him out of the election race. They made arrangements for Ben Travis—now dying of cancer—to be released from prison in the custody of his daughter, Nicole Drake. The plan was for Ben to try to dissuade Adam from running for senator by convincing Nicole that she'd be unhappy as the wife of a politician. Ben's male nurse, MORLOCK SEVINGY (Jay Gregory), planted by the mob in Adam's house, was to make sure that Ben kept Adam out of the race. When it looked as if Ben was failing with his task, Morlock arranged for Adam's murder. The mob tried to sink the boat that he and Nicole were on during a Caribbean cruise—and Nicole was reported drowned.

Meanwhile, Geraldine Whitney had made of young reporter KEVIN JAMISON (Dick Shoberg, John Driver) a permanent house guest. Just as Adam reminded her of Colin Whitney, Kevin reminded her of her other dead son, Keith.

Rather than continue to let the mob manipulate

Maeve McGuire began the role of the rich, spoiled divorcee, Nicole Travis, in 1968. A year later she was arrested for the murder of Stephanie Martin, but later freed with the help of Adam Drake, who fell in love with her. Donald May remained in the part until the character was killed off in 1978.

After the failure of her first marriage, Liz Hillyer (Alberta Grant) fell in love with psychiatrist Dr. Jim Fields (Alan Feinstein), in 1970. Liz and Jim Fields were important characters until 1974, when they were both written out.

him like a puppet because of Martha's attachment to Jennifer, Bill Marceau made the tough decision to resign as chief of police in Monticello. Fearful that he would now turn against them, the syndicate set up an elaborate *mise en scène* of terror, death and blackmail. As part of the plan, TAFFY SIMMS (Mari Gorman), the mother of Jennifer, regained custody of the little girl. Martha tearfully confronted Taffy, who refused Martha's request to see Jennifer. There was a gun lying on a table; Martha picked it up, threatening Taffy. The gun somehow went off, and Taffy fell. Martha fled; later the police found Taffy dead of a gunshot wound. With Jennifer's mother now dead, the Marceaus were awarded legal custody of the child; Bill became chief of police again. Only Martha and the mob knew what had happened in the apartment that day, and they threatened to reveal that she had murdered Taffy unless Martha persuaded Bill to release Morlock, who

was caught red-handed trying to kill Adam Drake. Instead Martha bravely confessed all and was charged with premeditated murder.

* * *

Adam had by now quit his political campaign to concentrate on his one obsession: finding Nicole's killers. Ben Travis was racked with guilt over his daughter's death, and was about to tell Adam his employer's names when Morlock killed him. A beautiful assistant district attorney by the name of BRANDY HENDERSON (Dixie Carter) became involved with Adam— and quite attracted to him—in his quest for his wife's murderers.

DANNY MICELLI (Lou Criscuolo), Johnny Dallas's closest friend and a bartender at the New Moon Café, wed loving waitress BABS (Leslie Ray). After she unwittingly overheard a conversation that implicated spe-

Laurie Ann Karr (Emily Prager), Mike's daughter by the late Sara, had a stormy romance with Lawyer Vic Lamont (Ted Tinling), in 1971. Later, she married reformed mobster Johnny Dallas. Laurie Ann had a nervous breakdown in 1978 and left the story.

Forrest Compton became the new Mike Karr in 1971 when a simultaneous change in story dynamics took place. Mike, who had always been the main crook-catching character, now shared the limelight with Adam Drake, the detective with perpetual marital and romantic problems.

cific members of the mob in Nicole's death, Morlock had her killed. Devastated by his best friend's grief, Johnny Dallas began working as an undercover agent against the mob. When Laurie found out that Johnny had turned straight, all of her suspicions about his underworld connections vanished, and she married Johnny with the blessing of her parents, the Karrs.

Vic Lamont's marriage to Kaye Reynolds eventually cost him his life. Johnny had no idea that her wealthy father, WALTER LE PAGE (William Post, Jr.), was the *head* of the syndicate. When Laurie, standing up for Johnny's character, told Vic that her husband was now working against the syndicate, Vic innocently told the same to his father-in-law, Walter Le Page. Then Vic learned that because of his mistake Johnny was about to be bumped off. He rushed to save Johnny and caught the bullet himself. Vic died a hero.

Through a spectacular piece of forensic deduc-

tion, Adam figured out how Taffy Simms was actually killed. The syndicate planted a loaded gun in Taffy's apartment the day Martha came there, and as planned, it went off in Martha's hands. But the bullets had been blanks, and Taffy was only pretending to be dead, so that the syndicate could blackmail Martha. After Martha left the apartment, fully believing that she had killed Taffy, the mob knocked off Taffy themselves just to make sure they would "own" Martha.

While Adam was stunning the courtroom with this elaborate reconstruction of the crime, Danny Micelli accused Morlock of killing Babs. A gun was pulled, and there was a tussle, then a shot, and then Morlock fell. Thinking he was about to die, Morlock made a full confession to the police: He had a fellow gangster plant the bomb which killed Nicole during Adam and Nicole's Caribbean cruise; he had Babs Micelli and Ben Travis murdered; he had sent the

A whole new set of story lines evolved by 1978, two years after The Edge of Night *moved to ABC. Widow Nicole Drake (Jayne Bentzen) and Dr. Miles Cavanaugh (Joel Crothers) fell in love. Miles's dying wife, Denise (Holland Taylor, standing), devised a plot to kill herself to make it look as if Miles and Nicole had murdered her.*

Lovely April Cavanaugh (Terry Davis), Miles' sister, wed lawyer Draper Scott (Tony Craig) in 1978. Not long after, Draper was accused of murder and developed amnesia.

gunman to kill Johnny Dallas (he wound up killing Vic Lamont by accident); and he killed Taffy Simms as part of an elaborate scheme to blackmail the Marceaus. The Monticello mob was soon apprehended. Martha was acquitted and went away with Jennifer for a happy rest.

* * *

Before this complicated story was resolved, one important relationship ended and another began. Liz Fields left her psychiatrist husband flat to take care of her sick father, Orin Hillyer, in Italy, and Jim Fields also left Monticello, to take a new post in Canada. TRACY DALLAS (Pat Conwell) came to work for her brother Johnny at the New Moon Café, and grew close to Danny Micelli. Tracy was obviously disturbed by her mysterious past. Unknown to Danny, who eventually married her, Tracy had once been a call girl.

Corrupt NOEL DOUGLAS (Dick Latessa) married Tiffany Whitney for her money, while having an affair with Tracy Dallas. Geraldine found out about Noel and Tracy, threatened to tell Tiffany about the affair, then was found near death, in a coma, at the bottom of the stairs. Soon after Tracy's marriage to Danny, Tracy believed that she would go to prison, because she had pushed Geraldine down the stairs, so she ran away to become a prostitute again. But Adam found out that it was Noel who had actually caused Geraldine's coma, by attacking her after Tracy left the house. Noel was afraid that Geraldine would tell Tiffany that he was a two-timing golddigger.

When Geraldine went into a prolonged coma, Kevin Jamison traveled to Paris to locate a doctor specializing in amnesia cases who had helped a woman recover consciousness after she had spent months in a coma. This doctor, CLAY JORDAN (Niles McMaster), introduced Kevin to this woman. It was Nicole Drake! Soon, Dr. Clay Jordan—who was more than just professionally interested in Nicole—and his patient returned to Monticello, where Adam was thrown into an emotional storm. He and Brandy had resumed their relationship, and were close to marriage; now here was Nicole. Which woman did Adam really want?

Nicole, feeling that she was not the same woman Adam had married, proposed that they divorce. At

Lee Godart (right) came on the show as Eliot Dorn, the leader of a far-out religious cult who later became a gigolo. Beautiful Yahee played Star Wilson, a nightclub singer who was one of Dorn's cult followers. She married policeman Calvin Stoner (Irving Lee, left) in 1979.

Flirtatious Raven Alexander (Sharon Gabet) married politically ambitious D.A. Logan Swift (Joseph Lambie, left) in 1979. Girl crazy lawyer Cliff Nelson (Ernest Townsend, right) worked in Mike Karr's law office.

first Adam agreed. Then the horror started. Nicole began to have nightmares of a terrible, laughing native, whom she called "Billy," coming at her with a spear. The nightmares turned partly real—for Nicole was suddenly involved in a series of bizarre accidents that nearly took her life.

A seemingly unrelated tragedy occurred. Tiffany Whitney, finally wise to Noel Douglas's deceptions, went to see her lawyer about a divorce. His office was many stories up, and before she could see him she fell, or was pushed, from one of the high windows to her death. Noel had already left town. Later, after Adam realized that Nicole was being pursued by someone with homicidal intentions, he deduced that this mysterious person, seeing Tiffany in Nicole's raincoat, had pushed Tiffany out the window thinking that she was Nicole! Nicole, before the onset of her coma—following the ship's explosion—had apparently learned a secret so dreadful that not only did

someone wish to kill her for it, but she had blocked it out of her conscious mind. Clay wanted to administer hallucinogenic drugs to help Nicole remember. Frightened of them, Nicole at first refused.

The fantastic SERENA FARADAY (Louise Shaffer) story took place during the early part of Nicole's ordeal. Serena, divorced from MARK FARADAY (Bernie McInerney), was Adam's cousin. Mark sued for custody of their son, TIMMY FARADAY (Douglas McKeon) claiming that quiet, charming Serena led a profligate life, neglecting her son while she slept around with strange men. Then JOSIE FARADAY, a loose woman who was more like Mark's description of Serena, came to live with Serena; Josie said she was Serena's sister. Josie and Serena turned out to be the same woman—two sides of a split personality. During the custody hearing, Serena (or Josie) suddenly shot Mark Faraday to death on the steps of the courthouse while TV newsmen filmed the whole event! Serena

Policewoman Deborah Saxon (Frances Fisher) and fellow cop Steve Guthrie (Denny Albee) had a wonderful romance until Deborah learned that her father, Tony Saxon, was the kingpin of a crime syndicate. She then broke up with Steve. They helped supply Edge *with the kind of young love story that viewers had come to expect on all soaps by 1980.*

Stage and screen actress Kim Hunter played Nola Madison, a fading, alcoholic actress who was still in love with her estranged filmmaker husband, Owen Madison (Bruce Gray, seated). Their children, Brian and Paige (Stephen McNaughton and Margaret Colin, standing) enacted a love story which teased the audience by hinting at incest.

was put on trial, but Adam cleverly proved that Josie had completely taken over Serena's personality. Both members of the prosecution team—Brandy Henderson and DRAPER SCOTT (Tony Craig)—were forced to settle for Adam's plea of insanity for his client, and Serena was committed. Her son, Timmy, came to live with Nancy and Mike Karr. Nancy, attached to the boy, became upset when Serena's *real* sister, JOSEPHINE HARPER (Judith McGilligan), showed up and wanted custody of the boy.

Kevin Jamison and Phoebe Smith were finally married. But their first year of marriage was not a happy one. Kevin felt neglected, and wanted Phoebe to give up her job as assistant to psychiatrist QUENTIN HENDERSON (Michael Stroka), Brandy's brother. Brandy still carried a torch for Adam, while Draper Scott was falling in love with her. Johnny Dallas once again began doing undercover mob-fighting work for Bill Marceau and Mike Karr, using the New Moon Café as a "setup" meeting place for gangsters from all over the state. However, the lives of Johnny, Laurie and their new baby boy, John Victor Dallas, were put in great danger. Meanwhile, Tracy Dallas had come back to town, wanting to return to Danny as his wife. Terribly hurt when he found out what his wife's profession had been, Danny threw her out of his life. But after he saved her from a suicide attempt, Danny realized that he still loved Tracy and took her back, and they left Monticello.

* * *

Slowly, all of Monticello's horrible mysteries—the haunting of Nicole, murders, deceptions—began to congeal into one gigantic war by the syndicate, headed by TONY SAXON (Louis Turenne), against a man who had embezzled millions from it, GILBERT DARCY, alias CLAUDE REVENANT (Scott McKay). Many months before, Darcy had been in the Caribbean hiding from Saxon. After the explosion on the yacht—on which Nicole and Adam had been staying—Darcy rescued Nicole and took her to his secret hiding place, the mysterious Limbo Island. Nicole was later rescued, but developed amnesia. Terrified that she would reveal all to Tony Saxon, Darcy hired Clay Jordan to

Nancy's nephew, Kelly McGrath (Allen Fawcett) romanced teenage dancer Jody Travis (Lori Loughlin), Nicole's half-sister, in 1980. Jody lived with Miles and Nicole and became involved with all of Edge's main villains.

Raven wed Schuyler Whitney (Larkin Malloy) in an elaborate ceremony at the mansion of Sky's rich aunt, Geraldine Whitney (Lois Kibbee, left), in 1981. In one of Edge's typically Byzantine plot twists, it turned out that Raven had married an imposter lookalike.

pose as her psychiatrist and drug her into admitting all she knew! It was fiendish Clay who attempted to murder Nicole, then murdered psychiatrist Quentin Henderson—*and* Phoebe Jamison, with a bomb planted in her car! Finally Clay, when evidence of his deeds began to mount, kidnapped Nicole and gave her sodium pentothol to make her tell the truth. Clay was apprehended, as was Darcy, and Nicole was safe—but the child she now carried by Adam may have been damaged by the drug. The frightened Drakes awaited further medical tests on the unborn fetus.

Tony Saxon's syndicate tried to foil Mike Karr's attempts to uncover its leaders through Nancy and her attachment to little Timmy Faraday. Handsome, slick and dangerous BEAU RICHARDSON (David Gale) had Timmy taken away, and then told Nancy he would be killed unless she secretly went through Mike's files and fed Beau information on what Mike knew about the syndicate. Nancy was torn; rather than destroy Mike's career, she abruptly left him to put distance between herself and his files. Soon Mike began to believe that she was having an affair with Beau Richardson. Then Beau was murdered and Mike Karr, who appeared guilty, had to stand trial. The Karrs reconciled. Suddenly, Monticello's worst tragedy ever occurred: Adam Drake was shot in the back and killed while typing an exposé on the syndicate! Mike Karr was exonerated when the killer of both Beau and Adam turned out to be RAYMOND HARPER (Dick Callinan), the syndicate-linked husband of Timmy's aunt, Josie Harper. Mike and Nancy were tearfully reunited with Timmy before he went away to boarding school. The prolonged ordeal of the Karrs caused Laurie to suffer a mental breakdown and she had to be institutionalized. Her husband Johnny Dallas joined his friend Danny Micelli and sister Tracy out of town, after gaining custody of little John Victor. Syndicate head Tony Saxon was later killed in a police shootout.

* * *

After the brutal murder of her husband, Nicole was heartbroken. Later, she gave birth to a healthy baby boy, ADAM JR. The dedicated physician who saw

Lisa Sloan took over as Nicole Cavanaugh in 1981, playing opposite Joel Crothers as Miles. Nicole was killed off in 1983.

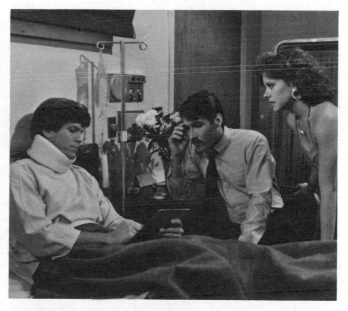

Eligible bachelor Derek Mallory (Dennis Parker, center) became the new chief of police when Bill Marceau was forced into retirement in 1978. Fellow policeman Damian Tyler (Christopher Jarrett, left) started a romance in 1982 with Poppy Johnson (Karen Needle), who had been one of the mob's secretaries before going straight.

her through her precarious pregnancy, DR. MILES CAVANAUGH (Joel Crothers), was beginning to fall in love with the lonely Nicole. Miles had a shrewish wife, DENISE (Holland Taylor), who realized that she was losing her husband. After Denise discovered that she had a fatal disease, she concocted a morbid plot to kill herself and then make it look as if Miles and Nicole had murdered her! Meanwhile, Draper Scott had fallen in love with Miles's appealing young sister, APRIL CAVANAUGH (Terry Davis). When April found her sister-in-law Denise murdered, she was accused of the crime, but was freed when the killer was revealed to be Denise's own father, DR. GUS NORWOOD (Wyman Pendleton). He had discovered his daughter's plan and didn't want her to go ahead with it. Gus died of a stroke and two happy couples were wed: April and Draper, and Miles and Nicole, who set up housekeeping in Monticello with little Adam Jr.

Despite the tragic losses that Geraldine Whitney had suffered, she remained spirited to the last and delighted in the arrival of a young flirt named RAVEN ALEXANDER (Sharon Gabet). Raven had come from a wild affair with New York lawyer ANSEL SCOTT (Patrick Horgan), but for image's sake Ansel married NADINE ALEXANDER (Dorothy Stinnette), Geraldine's friend and Raven's own mother. Raven and pretty April became fast friends. One of Raven's first romantic conquests in Monticello was LOGAN SWIFT (Joseph Lambie), a good-humored young district attorney. But Raven knew that Geraldine was grooming Kevin Jamison for the governorship and so ambitious Raven married Kevin, but continued her affair with Logan. Kevin was suddenly killed in a car which had been rigged to murder Draper! Logan became Geraldine's next political protégé and of course Raven, now pregnant by him, married Logan.

Neither April nor her brother Miles knew much about their dead parents and clung to what few memories they had. After April took a job at Monticello's television station, WMON-TV, the hard-nosed station owner MARGO HUNTINGTON (Ann Williams) confessed to April that she was her mother! Life around Margo suddenly became chancy. Her associate, WADE MEECHAM (Dan Hamilton), began blackmailing WINTER AUSTEN (Stephanie Braxton), who had started an affair with Logan Swift when Logan's marriage to Raven began falling apart. Winter tried to hide from Logan the fact that she had been a porno queen and prostitute and eventually murdered blackmailing Wade. She fell

to her death from a studio catwalk while escaping the authorities.

At this time a virile opportunist named ELIOT DORN (Lee Godart) came to Monticello. He led a far-out religious cult called Children of the Earth, but disbanded the sect to marry Margo Huntington for her money. The marriage was a farce and he soon became a kept man to NOLA MADISON (Kim Hunter), a fading, alcoholic actress. Nola talked her estranged filmmaker husband OWEN MADISON (Bruce Gray) into letting her make a comeback in the horror movie he was making in Monticello called *The Mansion of the Damned*. It was aptly named, for people connected with the movie started dying. Meanwhile, Owen began a romance with policewoman DEBORAH SAXON (Frances Fisher), the daughter of the late Tony Saxon. Dangerously insecure, Nola still loved Owen and set out to try to kill Deborah. When Miles discovered her plot, Nola slipped him a mind-altering drug that turned him into an insanely jealous husband to Nicole! He had some moments of lucidity, then would suddenly fly into uncharacteristic rages. He became convinced that Nicole was sleeping with the new chief of police, DEREK MALLORY (Dennis Parker), who had replaced the retired Bill Marceau. In fact, Derek loved Nicole but she cared only for Miles. The situation reached its crest when Margo was found murdered in her penthouse apartment! Ever since Margo had revealed herself to be April's mother, she had interfered with her daughter's marriage to Draper, who hated her. Draper was tried and convicted of the murder. Derek and young policeman STEVE GUTHRIE (Denny Albee) proved that the killer was none other than exotic Nola. She had demanded that Margo divorce Eliot, and when Margo refused Nola murdered her. She was sent to an institution.

Nola and Owen had two children, BRIAN (Stephen McNaughton) and PAIGE (Margaret Colin), who were half-brother and -sister (Paige was the product of Owen's second marriage). Brian broke the ancient laws against incest when he fell in love with his sister, who became so confused that she fell in with a gang of terrorists. Later, Paige and Brian discovered that Owen was not Brian's father after all, and they married and left Monticello.

* * *

Only hours before he was exonerated of Margo's murder, Draper was on a train taking him back to prison. The train plummeted down an embankment and Draper lost his memory! Dazed, he found himself in a small town, given shelter by an unstable young girl, EMILY MICHAELS (Margo McKenna). Emily's maid and protectress, MOLLY SHERWOOD (Laurinda Barrett), feared for Emily's sanity when Emily mistook Draper for her estranged husband, Kirk. Having no memory at all, Draper began to believe that he was Kirk too! After Draper regained his memory and told Emily that he was not Kirk, she lost her mind and had to be committed. Meanwhile, Draper went back to April and their new baby JULIA in Monticello. Soon after Emily escaped the mental home and took an apartment in the same building as the Scotts, while Molly Sherwood worked as Draper and April's maid. Draper and April felt a responsibility to Emily, who began driving a wedge between them.

Raven abandoned her marriage to Logan in favor of a liaison with Eliot Dorn, who now owned a nightclub called the Unicorn, given to him by his late wife Margo. Derek Mallory also began an affair with manipulative Raven. After Logan sued for divorce and won custody of their son JAMIE, Raven discovered that her mother, Nadine, had willed an astronomical sum to her grandson. For the sake of the money, Raven tried desperately, once again, to gain custody of Jamie. Before anything was resolved, Nadine drank poisoned tea at Raven's apartment and was killed in a car crash!

Several new young people arrived in Monticello and became involved in this developing web: KELLY MCGRATH (Allen Fawcett), Nancy's happy-go-lucky nephew who harbored a mysteriously violent past in Italy, and Nicole's half-sister JODY TRAVIS (Lori Loughlin). Kelly fell in love with Jody, who took a job working for Eliot Dorn at the Unicorn. Kelly also took a job there with an offbeat puppeteering act. One night Eliot tried to rape Jody but Kelly pried the lascivious Eliot loose. Moments later Eliot was stabbed in the back and killed by a hand manipulating one of Kelly's puppets. Raven was suspected, but so was Kelly. Then April's life was threatened by someone who confessed to the murders of both Nadine Alexander and Eliot Dorn: sweet little Molly Sherwood! Molly had meant to poison April, in order to free Draper for Emily, but Nadine had taken the tea. Molly killed Eliot when he suspected the tea, not the car, caused Nadine's death. Just as Molly was ready to kill April, Raven arrived and Molly tumbled down a

stairway to her death.

Emily continued to remain a thorn in the side of April and Draper, who were anxious to obtain evidence that Emily needed to be recommitted. They sensed a strange connection between Emily and MATT SHARKEY (Chris Goutman), an orderly who had helped her escape from the mental home. Nancy Karr used her investigative reporting ability to finally trace Sharkey to the Rexford Clinic, a creepy hospital where criminals paid one million dollars for plastic surgery to make them unrecognizable. Nancy was held captive at the clinic by Sharkey and his boss, DR. KENNETH BRYSON (James Hawthorne), who wound up falling in love with her! After Draper went undercover as an orderly and saved Nancy, Bryson was sent to prison, where he later died. Draper and April Scott moved to Europe to investigate Bryson's other criminal connections.

* * *

SCHUYLER WHITNEY (Larkin Malloy), Geraldine's wealthy black-sheep nephew, was a ballet impresario with mysterious connections to two ballet dancers. One was MARTINE DUVAL (Sonia Petrovna), whom Schuyler, or "Sky," was blackmailing into remaining his mistress with the information that she had helped her lover, COLLIER WELLES (Albert Owens), steal precious jewels in Europe. Sky had brought Martine out of a life of crime and made her a great dancer. The other dancer, GAVIN WYLIE (Mark Arnold), who had been one of Martine's lovers, hated Sky because years before Sky ordered his menacing bald servant, GUNTHER WAGNER (David Froman), to break both of Gavin's legs so that he could never dance again; now he could only teach dancing. Sky set up a dance troupe in Monticello and made Jody Travis his principal dancer. Soon Jody fell in love with Gavin Wylie, her teacher, and her old boyfriend, Kelly McGrath, fell for VALERIE BRYSON (Leah Ayres), the daughter of the late Kenneth Bryson.

Meanwhile, Raven did not spend much time grieving for Eliot Dorn. She took up with lethal Sky Whitney, who was a perfect match for her double-dealing greed, and married him in an elaborate ceremony at the Whitney mansion. After she spotted an old photograph of Sky with Valerie Bryson, Raven investigated and discovered that her husband was not Schuyler at all, but JEFFERSON BROWN, an associate of the real Sky! He had left Sky for dead after a Swiss plane crash, gone to Kenneth Bryson's other clinic in Switzerland to have his face redone to match Sky's and assumed Schuyler's identity and vast fortune. Valerie had been in love with both the old and the new Sky. Sky now feared that Raven would uncover even more of his criminal past and devised a plot to kill her. After wily Gunther, Sky's servant, found out about his intention to murder his wife, and blackmailed Sky, Sky murdered him and framed Gavin! He then spirited Raven off to a vacation in the Swiss Alps, where he intended to push her to her death. Instead, a masked assailant shot and killed Sky! In the end, the real Sky surfaced—he had survived the original plane crash—and fought his imposter's widow, Raven, for his rightful fortune. The real Sky's servant turned out to be the *real* Gunther. The menacing "Gunther" in Monticello had actually been Bruno, Gunther's twin brother. Gavin was freed when Mike Karr proved that Jefferson Brown had killed Bruno. The real Sky settled in Monticello. Martine Duval had already left Monticello with her old lover, Collier Welles.

* * *

When Kelly McGrath left Monticello, Valerie Bryson became involved with JIM DIEDRICKSON (David Allen Brooks), an attractive trickster who had come to Monticello and told Valerie various lies about his past to gain her affections. Jim formed an acting troupe and tried, but failed, to convince Raven to let him use the new Whitney Theater. Two of his friends—HECTOR WILSON (John Rensenhouse) and his impressionist brother, SMILEY (Frank Gorshin)—devised an elaborate plan to get the theater for Jim. Hector and Smiley made Raven believe that she had killed an actress, JINX AVERY (Susan McDonald), after a struggle. The Wilsons abducted Raven, convincing her that they were helping her escape a murder charge! But the Wilsons ended up murdered by other associates. Raven, now safe, let Jim use the theater. Jinx Avery, who had pretended to be dead, married Derek Mallory and then really did die from a fatal illness a few days later.

The real Sky Whitney made his mark in Monticello by purchasing the Monticello *News* and station WMON-TV. A shrewd businessman, he thrilled Raven anew with his charm and money, although he was now interested in Valerie Bryson. Raven waged a campaign to pry him loose from Valerie. Sky, more ethical than Jefferson Brown, nevertheless harbored a dan-

gerous entourage. His methodical assistant, SPENCER VARNEY (Richard Borg), kept Sky's secret that the murderer of Jefferson Brown was LIBBY WEBSTER (Marion Lines), Sky's ex-wife. Libby moved to Switzerland. Spencer, Gunther and Gunther's girl friend, NORA FULTON (Catherine Bruno), had worked on the estate of wealthy CAMILLA DEVEREAUX (Mary Layne). Spencer and Camilla had been lovers and Camilla's brother, IAN DEVEREAUX (Alan Coates), was a suspected spy who was falling for Raven.

Nora Fulton worked for Miles and Nicole, but when they realized she was unbalanced they fired her. She took a job at the Whitney mansion as a housekeeper, spreading rumors about Miles and other women to get back at him. Also, to keep Gunther in line, she lied to him that she was pregnant with his child. She was frantically insecure about Gunther's attraction to MITZI MARTIN (Lela Ivey), a comically dizzy waitress who was herself in love with a girl-crazy lawyer named CLIFF NELSON (Ernest Townsend). Nora tried to kill Mitzi but in due course it was Nora who wound up murdered!

Miles and Nicole were both suspects, but the killer turned out to be DAVID CAMERON (Norman Parker). A double agent, Cameron had wanted to foil Nora's attempts to interfere with an espionage plot he concocted in order to frame Ian. Ian left town, as did Camilla and Spencer who absconded with all of Sky's fortune! Sky and Raven married and set up a detective agency. Miles and Nicole, however, were not so fortunate. Just as they were relieved of possible prosecution, Nicole was killed on her TV news program by poisoned makeup!

Although still in love with Gavin Wylie, Jody Travis was convinced by mob front man DWIGHT ENDICOTT (Alfred Drake) to become a martyr for an obscure foreign country called Eden. But Mike and Derek, with the help of young police investigator DAMIAN TYLER (Christopher Jarrett), proved that Eden was "owned" by the Monticello mob and vanquished the operation. In the meantime, handsome Damian had a romance with POPPY JOHNSON (Karen Needle), one of the mob's secretaries who finally went straight. Damian and Poppy left Monticello happily.

CAST

THE EDGE OF NIGHT
CBS: April 2, 1956 to November 28, 1975
ABC: December 1, 1975

Mike Karr	John Larkin (P)
	Laurence Hugo
	Forrest Compton*
Sara Lane Karr	Teal Ames (P)
Mattie Lane Grimsley . .	Betty Garde (P)
	Peggy Allenby*
	Katherine Meskill
Winston Grimsley	Walter Greaza (P)
Louise Grimsley Capice	Lisa Howard (P)
	Mary K. Wells
Jack Lane	Don Hastings (P)
Harry Lane	Lauren Gilbert (P)
Cora Lane	Sarah Burton (P)
Sgt. Charley Brooks	Ian Martin (P)
Grace O'Keefe	Maxine Stuart (P)
Walt Johnson	Mark Rydell (P)
Bob Anderson	Bob Dixon (P)
Marilyn Bollon	Mary Alice Moore (P)
Lt. Victor Rhodes	John Raby (P)
George Murray, Jr.	Charles Taylor (P)
Rose LaTour	Henrietta Moore
Willie Bryan	Edward Holmes
Martin Spode	Eric Dressler
	Henderson Forsythe
Hester Spode	Helen Shields
Bebe Spode	Kimetha Laurie
	Beverly Lunsford
	Betty Sue Albert
Phil Capice	Robert Webber
	Earl Hammond
	Ray MacDonnell*
Betty Jean Battle Lane .	Mary Moor
Dr. Hugh Campbell	Wesley Addy
Gail Armstrong	Millette Alexander
Sybil Gordon	Doris Belack
Clayton Pike	Leon Janney
Liz Pike	Ann Loring
Dick Appleman	Michael Strong
Mary Appleman	Joan Copeland
Big Frank Dubeck	Michael Conrad
Ruth Hakim	Ann Jones
Bill Marceau	Carl Frank
	Mandel Kramer*
	Frank Campanella
Judy Marceau Gibson . .	Joan Harvey
Ed Gibson	Larry Hagman
Victor Carlson	Charles Baxter
	Byron Sanders
Jennings Carlson	Jeff Harris
Teresa Vetter	Rebecca Sand
George Vetter	Vincent Gardenia
Cynthia Purcell	Doe Lang
Sally Smith	Mary Fickett
Manny Smith	Frank Marth
Viola Smith	Jacqueline Courtney
Austin Johnson	Lawrence Weber
Constance Johnson	Elizabeth Lawrence
Margie Gibson	Karen Thorsell
Leo Magagnoli	Frank Campanella
Gigi Magagnoli	Chevi Colton
George Holmen	Gene Peterson
Casey Reno	Richard McMurray
Scofield Killborn	Logan Ramsey
Dr. Ursula Bower	Rita Morley
Lyn Wilkins Warren . . .	Gillian Spencer
John Lambert	Ray MacDonnell
Helen McCabe	Marion Brash
Barbara Barnett	Audra Lindley
Nancy Pollock Karr	Ann Flood
Laurie Ann Karr Dallas .	Victoria Larkin
	Kathleen Bracken
	Kathy Cody
	Emily Prager
	Jeanne Ruskin
	Linda Cook
Joe Pollock	John Gibson*
	Allen Nourse
Rose Pollock	Frances Reid
	Ruth Matteson
	Kay Campbell*
	Virginia Kaye
Lee Pollock	Ronnie Welch
	Sam Groom
	Tony Roberts*
Cookie Pollock	
Christopher	June Carter
	Fran Sharon*
Ted Grant	Douglas Rodgers
	Paul Sparer*
Judge Grant	Hal Burdick
Toby Marshall	Rita Lloyd
Betsy Brown	Carolyn Groves
Nate Axelrod	Robert Mandan
Beth Anderson Barnes .	Nancy Pinkerton
John Paul Anderson . . .	Conard Fowkes
Emory Warren	Bill Berger
	Philip Abbott
Carol Kramer	Elizabeth Hubbard

Clinton Wheeler	Dana Elcar
Irene Wheeler	Barbara Berjer
Capt. Lloyd Griffin	James Mitchell
Kate Griffin	Priscilla Gillette
Martha Spears Marceau	
....	Teri Keane
Elizabeth McGrath	Ludi Claire
	Nancy Coleman
Gerry McGrath Pollock .	Penny Fuller
	Joanna Miles
	Millee Taggart
John Barnes	Barry Newman
Malcolm Thomas	Edward Kemmer
Kitty DeSena	Valerie French
Eve Morris	Constance Ford
Andre Lazar	Val DuFour
Tony Wyatt	Antony Ponzini
Roy Cameron	Allen Nourse
Abby Cameron	Margaret DePriest
	Patricia Allison
Liz Hillyer Fields	Alberta Grant
Orin Hillyer	Lester Rawlins
Laura Hillyer	Millette Alexander
Rick Oliver	Keith Charles
Phoebe Smith Jamison .	Heidi Vaughn
	Renne Jarrett
	Laurie Kennedy
	Johanna Leister
Ken Emerson	Alan Manson
Jeanne Culpepper	Frances Chaney
Pete Quinn	George Petrie
David Gideon	John Cullum
Angela Talbot	Ann Wedgeworth
Lonnie Winters	Peter Kastner
Ephraim Webster	Nat Polen
Jessica Webster	Rita Lloyd
Paul Koslo	Roy Poole
Alex Gura	Norman Rose
Roy Sanders	Martin Sheen
Adam Drake	Donald May
Susan Earle	Micki Grant
Steve Prentiss	Conard Fowkes
Julie Jamison Hillyer ...	Millette Alexander
Harry Constable	Dolph Sweet
Bart Fletcher	James Ray
Willie Saffire	Jackson Beck
Ron Christopher	Burt Douglas
Eric Barrington	Leon Janney

Ben Travis	William Prince*
	Cec Linder
Nicole Travis Cavanaugh	Maeve McGuire*
	Jayne Bentzen
	Lisa Sloan
Susan Forbes	Gretchen Kanne
	Bibi Besch*
Sara Capice	Christopher Norris
Lydia Holliday	Jane White
Calvin Brenner	Scott Glenn
Dr. Jim Fields	Alan Feinstein
Vic Lamont	Ted Tinling
Stephanie Martin	Alice Hirson
Debbie Martin	Ellen Hansen
Duane Stewart	Richard Clarke
Pamela Stewart	Irene Dailey
Mrs. Castermore	Minerva Pious
Roger Castermore	Lawrence Pressman
	Roy London*
Geraldine Whitney	
Saxon	Lois Kibbee
Gordon Whitney	Alan Gifford
Sen. Colin Whitney	Anthony Call
Tiffany Whitney Douglas	Lucy Martin
Keith Whitney	Bruce Martin
Kate Sloane	Jan Farrand
Frank Sloane	Sam Gray
Johnny Dallas	John LaGioia
Angela Morgan Hillyer .	Valerie French
Jake Berman	Ward Costello
Edith Berman	Pat Bright
Elly Jo Jamison	Dorothy Lyman
Kevin Jamison	Richard Shoberg
	John Driver*
Joel Gantry	Paul Henry Itkin
	Nicholas Pryor
Kay Reynolds Lamont ..	Elizabeth Farley
Walter LePage	William Post, Jr.
Morlock Sevingy	Jay Gregory
Taffy Simms	Mari Gorman
Danny Micelli	Macintyre Dixon
	Lou Criscuolo*
	James Catusi
Babs Werner Micelli ...	Leslie Ray
Tracy Dallas Micelli ...	Patricia Conwell
Lt. Luke Chandler	Herb Davis
Brandy Henderson	Dixie Carter
Dr. Quentin Henderson .	Michael Stroka

Noel Douglas	Thom Christopher
	Dick Latessa*
Timmy Faraday	Doug McKeon*
	Andrew McMillan
Serena Faraday	Louise Shaffer
Mark Faraday	Bernie McInerney
Clay Jordan	Niles McMaster
Claude Revenant	Scott McKay
Draper Scott	Tony Craig
Ansel Scott	Patrick Horgan
Nadine Alexander Scott	Dorothy Stinnette
Raven Alexander	
Whitney	Juanin Clay
	Sharon Gabet*
Steve Guthrie	Denny Albee
Deborah Saxon	Frances Fisher
Tony Saxon	Louis Turenne
Beau Richardson	David Gale
Josephine Harper	Judith McGilligan
Raymond Harper	Dick Callinan
Raney Cooper	Kiel Martin
Dr. Miles Cavanaugh . . .	Joel Crothers
Denise Cavanaugh	Holland Taylor
April Cavanaugh Scott .	Terry Davis
Dr. Gus Norwood	Wyman Pendleton
Logan Swift	Joseph Lambie
Winter Austen	Lori Cardille
	Stephanie Braxton
Wade Meecham	Dan Hamilton
Margo Huntington Dorn	Ann Williams
Eliot Dorn	Lee Godart
Calvin Stoner	Irving Lee
Star Wilson Stoner	Yahee
Cliff Nelson	Ernest Townsend
Nola Madison	Kim Hunter
Owen Madison	Bruce Gray
Paige Madison	Margaret Colin
Brian Madison	Stephen McNaughton
Derek Mallory	Dennis Parker
Emily Michaels	Margo McKenna
Molly Sherwood	Jane Hoffman
	Laurinda Barrett*
Matt Sharkey	Christopher Goutman*
	Norman Snow
Kelly McGrath	Joey Alan Phipps
	Allen Fawcett*

Jody Travis	Lori Loughlin
Gavin Wylie	Mark Arnold
Martine Duval	Sonia Petrovna
Schuyler Whitney	Larkin Malloy
Gunther Wagner	David Froman
Dr. Kenneth Bryson	James Hawthorne
Valerie Bryson	Leah Ayres
Damian Tyler	Christopher Jarrett
Collier Welles	Albert Owens
Spencer Varney	Richard Borg
Nora Fulton	Catherine Bruno
Mitzi Martin	Lela Ivey
Jinx Avery Mallory	Kate Capshaw
	Susan MacDonald
Libby Webster	Marion Lines
Jim Diedrickson	David Allen Brooks
Smiley Wilson	Frank Gorshin
Hector Wilson	John Rensenhouse
Didi Bannister	Mariann Aalda
Troy Bannister	Keith Grant
Poppy Johnson	Karen Needle
Dwight Endicott	Alfred Drake
Ian Devereaux	Alan Coates
Camilla Devereaux	Mary Layne
David Cameron	Norman Parker

Creator: Irving Vendig

Head Writers: Irving Vendig, Lou Scofield, James Lipton, Henry Slesar, Lee Sheldon

Executive Producers: Lawrence White, Don Wallace, Erwin Nicholson

Producers: Werner Michel, Charles Pollacheck, Charles Fisher, Erwin Nicholson, Rick Edelstein, Robert Driscoll, Jacqueline Haber

Directors: Don Wallace, Fred Bartholemew, Allen Fristoe, Richard Sandwick, Leonard Valenta, Joseph K. Chomyn, Ted Mabley, John Sedwick, Joel Aronowitz, Andrew D. Weyman, Joanne Goodhart, Richard Pepperman

Organist: Paul Taubman

Musical Direction (later): Paul Taubman, Elliot Lawrence Productions

Packager: Procter & Gamble

GENERAL HOSPITAL

STARTING in the first half of 1978, six million teenagers became fervently preoccupied with the psychosexual entanglements of a handful of young people who lived in the fictional town of Port Charles. All over the country *General Hospital* fever spread. In living rooms and dormitories, teens would huddle in front of color sets and later discuss the problems of Scotty and Laura and Lesley and Rick and David and Bobbie. To those millions of new soap addicts, and perhaps to a few older ones as well, it may have seemed that *General Hospital* had recently premiered as a revolutionary soap meant especially for them.

BACKGROUND

It was, in actuality, on April 1, 1963, some fifteen years earlier, that the audience, mostly housewives in those days, caught their first glimpses of nurse Jessie Brewer and Dr. Steve Hardy ministering to the sick and sick at heart on the famous seventh floor (internal medicine) of General Hospital. The only young people seen were the orderlies, and a mere four or five actors carried the intensely personal melodramas in sets that were drabber than most.

The original network concept of the series, far from being revolutionary, was meant to mirror the highly successful medical shows then being aired at nighttime, such as *Dr. Kildare*. "I want a daytime *Ben Casey*," said Armand Grant, ABC's head of daytime

programming in New York, to Selig J. Seligman, the executive producer who was to package the show for ABC in Hollywood. Seligman, an affable ex-lawyer who had not a shred of interest in the current vogue of medical dramas, hired nighttime television writer Elizabeth Lewis to script the anthology series that Armand Grant had outlined, to be called *Emergency Hospital*. She came up with a pilot which Miss Lewis remembers as starring four actors who played a nurse, a doctor, an ambulance driver and a policeman, and featured a new medical emergency every day.

But by now, early 1963, ABC surely knew that rival NBC was planning another anthology hospital series in the daytime (which became *The Doctors*) and which was to premiere on the same day. ABC axed *Emergency Hospital*. Armand Grant now hired two experienced and talented soap opera writers, Frank and Doris Hursley, to devise a full-fledged soap called *General Hospital* (the title reminiscent of *Dr. Kildare*'s Blair General and *Ben Casey*'s County General Hospital). At the time, Frank and Doris Hursley had been the successful head writers for the highly rated *Search For Tomorrow*. Busy with that show, they hired another married couple, Theodore and Mathilde Ferro, to write *General Hospital* while the Hursleys guided the story during weekly conferences. As Kylie Masterson, the first associate producer, notes, the Hursleys at first were not even mentioned on the show's scripts or credit scrolls.

When the new producer-director, Jim Young, saw

General Hospital's absurdly low budget, most of which went to pay actors' salaries, he had serious doubts whether the show could get off the ground. Before the premiere he asked John Beradino to take a cut in his previously negotiated $1500 a week salary, so that more money could be spent on sets.

In those early days few people seemed to have faith in the long-term possibilities of *General Hospital*. ABC, for years thought of as a poor relation to the other two big networks, had never had a network success in the afternoon, so there was little reason to suppose that this venture would be any different from all its other quickly aborted soaps. Kylie Masterson recalls telling Seligman, before the premiere, that she didn't want to work on it; and John Beradino remembers blithely signing away five years of his life because his agent assured him "it will be canceled in six months, so take what you can get now."

But within months it was clear that *General Hospital* wasn't following the usual ABC pattern of failure. The show was quickly catching on, primarily because of Jim Young's expertise, the Hursleys' excellent story sense and casting that was nothing less than brilliant.

* * *

The first black-and-white show took an excruciating twenty-two hours to tape, as Jim Young nervously set up artful camera shots while the sponsors watched him work. The shows that followed were nearly as exhausting.

John Beradino and Emily McLaughlin today both swear they would not want to relive the nightmare of that first year. Because of the tiny budget and small cast for a half-hour show, the writers had to have both actors on camera every day to carry the major story lines. Forty pages of script had to be memorized five times a week and there was endless recapitulation of the previous day's dialogue. The show was "live tape"; that is, the tape was never stopped no matter what mistakes were made, and John, overworked and overwrought, would lie awake nights worrying about the mistakes he had made. Emily found herself rising in the middle of the night from a fitful sleep, wandering around her bedroom and crying. Both actors developed ulcers, Emily's so severe that she had to be hospitalized.

All that intensity was apparent to viewers, who became mesmerized by John and Emily and by the strong characters the Hursleys had developed for

them. Lieux Dressler, who played Alice Grant until recently, was an early fan of the show and says, "The thing that got me hooked was that every one of the characters was distinctive. By comparison, we are more like vanilla today. Jessie was a wonderful, warm woman with a backbone. Steve Hardy was the Rock of Gibraltar but with feet of clay." The Hursleys gave their characters intricacies of behavior which went over well with viewers. Stalwart Steve, played by an Italian ex-baseball star, had a passionate nature which was forever in conflict with his sense of professionalism. Jessie, who knew how to handle patients and doctors, had the sort of vulnerability that would always lead her to the wrong man. (Viewers became obsessed with pairing the two of them romantically, which would have been impossible as story material but which underscored the magnetism of the new show. "I used to throw my arms around him and cry on his shoulder," says Emily. "It was all very platonic, but there was always the intimation that something could happen. We were both washing dishes in my apartment one evening. I was single and Audrey was in Vietnam, and Steve said, 'Jessie, we're both free . . .' Just then the phone rang. Afterward we got tons of mail.")

Jessie had already married the wrong man well before the story started. The story of Jessie and Phil Brewer was fairly advanced for daytime, since soaps usually took their stories from the movies of the forties. It may have been suggested to the Hursleys by the popular novel of the day, *Not As A Stranger*, the story of a nurse who supports her younger husband through medical school and later must face his infidelities. (Olivia de Havilland and Robert Mitchum played the leads in the movie version.) Not only did Phil torture Jessie with his unfaithfulness with a younger patient, Cynthia Allison, but he enmeshed her in his own professional jams at the hospital. The story was the show's strongest for several years, for any woman over thirty-five could identify with the trap Jessie had fallen into. An unknown Roy Thinnes believably played the part of the lovable cad for two and a half years, before he left for nighttime stardom.

After six months the Hursleys left *Search for Tomorrow* to become *General Hospital*'s new head writers (and were, a few years later, correctly identified as the creators). Their gift for characterization and melodrama helped capture the ratings, although the melodrama they used became fairly relentless. "Rachel

Ames and I had to cry every day," says Emily. Soap opera expert John Kelly Genovese remembers those early daily dramas in which Audrey would shout in one scene, "Oh, Steve! No! You can't!" and slam a door while in the very next scene Jessie would break down in tears over still another of Phil's extramarital indiscretions.

Every half-hour episode, for years, was interrupted only three times for commercials, rather than the usual five, allowing the writers to create much longer scenes. Jim Young developed a fascinating, almost avant-garde method of shooting them. Rather than cutting from one conversation to another on the seventh floor of the supposed hospital, he would, instead, show Steve and Jessie talking in his office, follow them out into the corridor with his camera, leave them and then move the camera into the waiting room where, say, Tom and Audrey were having it out, and then pan down the corridor to yet another couple. By envisioning each scene as a series of small encounters, Young's pacing was always lively and helped to distract the viewer from the boredom of the constricted sets and small cast.

All soaps of the day had operating room hospital scenes, but *General Hospital*'s were far more advanced, with the whole story circling around doctors, nurses and patients. Before the first air date, the Hursleys painstakingly researched the setup of a modern hospital and suggested the hiring of Dr. Franz Bauer as medical consultant. He remained with the show for years, organizing the elaborate operating rooms and helping the Hursleys come up with real diseases. Under the Hursleys's the show never used fictional diseases.

Lucille Wall's debut on June 3, 1963, as the head of student nurses, ushered in the new mood of bald humor which saved the show from the effects of unrelieved melodrama. For thirteen years Lucille Wall played the rough and ready disciplinarian, whom the student nurses called "Sarge" but who had a heart of gold. Lucille's portrayal was filled with warmth and hidden compassion, making her one of the most popular people on the seventh floor.

Mae Clark, the famous actress who got a grapefruit smashed in her face by James Cagney in *The Public Enemy* first appeared in a role similar to Lucille Wall's head nurse "Marge." Understandably, she wanted a contract, which the show couldn't afford, and so Lucille Wall took her place, but only as an "under five" in the beginning. Lucille had been a big star on radio, playing the leads on *Portia Faces Life* and *Lorenzo Jones*, but had done very little television. "She was scared to death of television," says Kylie Masterson. "She just walked around here and there, gradually got lines, and her confidence came in no time."

She created the fun at the nurses station "out of frustration. I just didn't know what else to do with the role." The Hursleys and Jim Young quickly picked up on what she was doing and began to add little skits of mock meanness, together with bouncy music and sometimes elaborate props. After a while, everyone had a hand in creating the fun at the nurses' station. Typical was the charade with the balloon: "One of the kids [who played a student nurse] brought in a balloon, I don't know why, and drew an awful face on it with the word 'Sarge.' Jim loved the idea and had the student nurses fool with the balloon in the medicine room. Well, when they heard me coming they hid it in the refrigerator. She didn't know why they were all in the medicine room and she said, 'Isn't there any more work to do in Ward A? Okay, McGinnes, you go over there and I want to see every bed made.' Well, she opened the refrigerator and out came the balloon. She thought she was seeing things at first and then frustration really set in. It was very funny."

Offscreen, Lucille was even funnier, cracking up the other actors and the people in the control booth with antics that gave everyone a daily lift. When she decided to retire from the show in 1977, her character left the hospital to run a farm in upstate New York where, from time to time, as it suited the story and vacation schedules, various nurses and doctors from General Hospital would visit her.

* * *

Five years after *General Hospital* began, it became the top-rated soap and put ABC's daytime lineup on the map. The long drawn-out drama of Steve Hardy's supposed sterility and his wife Audrey's secret artificial insemination had been extremely popular. The show finally catapulted to the top, for a period of months, when Audrey was put on trial for the murder of the wicked nurse who had kidnapped her baby.

For the next five years, during which the Hursleys continued to write and Jim Young to produce, there was status quo. All the original leads—Emily, John,

Lucille, Rachel Ames (who came on as Audrey March after the first year), Craig Huebing and Valerie Starrett (who played the Taylors for many years) and Peter Hansen (as attorney Lee Baldwin)—remained loyally in their roles, which they all acted with great sincerity. The Hursleys, like Irna Phillips with her *As The World Turns*, created and then guided their show carefully for many years, insuring continuity by gradually adding new characters.

But as time went on the melodrama became extreme and cliché-ridden. The strong Phil and Jessie story deteriorated into the old soap story line of a wife, believing her husband to be dead, marrying another man, only to find out that her husband was still alive and had a drastically changed personality. (See the summary of the long-term story line.) Other clichés, like frequent murder trials, began to accumulate.

Although the show had gone to color in 1966 and was more expensive to produce, the budget was still not what Jim Young needed. He became frustrated at the look of the show. Shaking his head, he would say to Kylie, "Steve's apartment is looking pretty shabby." Steve Hardy was head of the hospital but appeared to be living on an intern's salary. Most of the other sets Jim had to work with had been used for years.

Predictably, the ratings had begun to fall. In the early seventies, when the network daytime wars for ratings became fairly ruthless, ABC grew increasingly restive about *General Hospital*, but still kept it on a tight budget. After the Hursleys left as the head writers, they tried to hold on to continuity by having their daughter, Bridget, and her husband, Jerome Dobson, take over as head writers. (As the creators, the Hursleys would naturally have a special interest in *General Hospital*, which would provide them with a generous weekly income for as long as it ran.)

Jim Young had to contend with the persistent low budget and eventually the intrusion of the network itself. ABC, anxious to compete in the ratings wars, hired Denise Alexander away from *Days of Our Lives* for *General Hospital*. As Susan Martin on *Days*, Denise had been voted the most popular actress in all the fan magazine polls, and the network hoped her fans would watch her on *General Hospital*.

Jim Young left *General Hospital* in 1976. While he refuses to say why he left, Kylie says he simply wasn't happy with the way the show was going. Tom Donovan, who had produced *Another World*, was asked

to come from New York to replace him. Around that time Procter & Gamble began to expand its soaps to one hour and ABC's new programming head, Fred Silverman, decided to fight back by expanding *General Hospital* and *One Life to Live* to forty-five minutes each, hoping to make it uncomfortable for viewers to switch from an ABC show to one of the rival hours. After Jim Young left, other writers took over, including Richard and Suzanne Holland, Eileen and Robert Mason Pollock, Irving and Tex Elman, and once again the Hollands. Through all the changes in writers along with the expected drastic changes in approaches to story and dialogue, the show's ratings and quality began to skydive.

Tom Donovan and the Pollocks attempted to revamp the show, writing out some twenty characters, including the beloved Lee Baldwin (Peter Hansen)—and with him went the whole Chandler family. (Some time later Lee Baldwin came back to the show with his brother Tom, then played by Don Chastain.) Donovan changed Jim Young's directorial approach. Instead of long, flowing scenes, with the camera drifting almost extemporaneously from one hospital compartment to another, the scenes became individual set pieces.

The Pollocks, who introduced the Webbers and the Dantes, were excellent writers and their Webber story would eventually lead to all sorts of rich complications and excitement. But the ratings during this period only worsened. There was rampant talk of cancellation by 1977 when the show's audience share fell to a calamitous 16 percent. Donovan asked ABC for more money for better sets and a bigger cast, but network executives, apparently believing, as always, that money alone wouldn't make the difference, turned him down. The show's demise was almost a certainty.

What was the real problem with *General Hospital*? Was it a question of money? Jim Young? Tom Donovan and the Pollocks? We have seen elsewhere how easy it is for soaps to burn themselves out. The regular characters grow long in the tooth, the audience that grew up with them is older, the original story themes are lost in a maze of different writers with differing talents responsible to new managements. Medical soaps are even more vulnerable to the aging process because of their formats. Both *The Doctors* and *General Hospital*, which began on the same day, fell prey to the same sort of ratings and story problems simultaneously, even though they were carried by different networks.

The appeal of a hospital soap is, as Jim Young puts it, that "anyone can walk out of an elevator." The drawback is that the hospital setting becomes a trap in which operating rooms, doctors' offices, nurses' stations, hospital garb, oscilloscopes, waiting rooms, diseases, the perpetual facing of death, romances between doctors and nurses, becomes such a daily claustrophobic occurrence that the burnout effect is certain, in spite of efforts by producers and writers.

General Hospital was not at all mismanaged—Jim Young and the Hursleys, especially, had been marvelous for the show; it was slowly undergoing a natural dying process caused by the original limited format. The only way to keep the show alive was to do something extravagantly unorthodox, like revivifying a very old person by replacing all of his organs with microprocessors.

* * *

"When I saw the show, the only thing I could think of doing was to put you all on a plane and crash it," Gloria Monty told an actor shortly after she became producer on January 1, 1978. Under Gloria Monty's watershed reign, previous values in the soap world of the seventies would fall apart and the revolutionary, metamorphosed soap world of the eighties would emerge with the impact of, indeed, a plane crash.

Several months earlier, the Pollocks had left the show as writers (and were temporarily replaced by the Hollands) and Tom Donovan, who was not especially happy with *General Hospital*, announced his imminent departure. Fred Silverman had already decided that *General Hospital* would be canceled in six months if the ratings did not improve by at least two points: the show, along with *The Doctors*, was virtually at the bottom of the Nielsens. "Things looked pretty bad," says Emily. "Most of us were out auditioning for new jobs."

Jackie Smith, ABC's canny head of daytime in New York, may have been the first person at the network to sense what had to be done. Impressed that her daughter preferred *The Doctors* over *General Hospital* because it had younger story lines, she called the former head writer, Douglas Marland, to find out what he thought he could do and to ask him to write a few outlines. That was desperation tactic number one. Number two was calling Gloria Monty who had,

years before, as the director of *Secret Storm*, gained for herself the reputation of being a strong, self-contained type who knew how to handle actors and fight for long-term success. Jackie Smith hired Gloria as the new producer, even though Gloria hadn't directed a soap, let alone produced one, for ten years. The assignment to both Doug Marland and Gloria was the same: sit home, watch the show and decide how to save it.

"I was paid to watch the show for about two months," says Doug Marland. "I read all the breakdowns—hours and hours and weeks of reading, boxes of outlines all out of continuity. They were taken from ten different writers' story submissions. The show was so boring that I couldn't sit in the room and watch it for forty-five minutes, which made me feel guilty because I was being paid rather handsomely. I'd fidget, get up, leave the room, come back. On the show they had people sitting on opposite sides of a desk, just talking for an entire scene; two people in a cafeteria sitting and talking; two people in a kitchen. No movement, just talk, and there wasn't much to talk about, because there wasn't much happening. Lesley had just married Rick, Monica and Alan Quartermaine were arguing a lot, Scotty and Laura were talking a lot. I couldn't figure out whether Scotty and Laura had been to bed together or even if they were attracted to each other. ABC said they didn't know either. So many people had had their fingers in the pie: the Elmans, the Pollocks, the Hollands and A. J. Russell, who had been helping the Hollands."

Doug understood that he was considered too untried to be hired instantly as head writer. He had, after all, only started writing for soaps just a few years before, when he was an underling dialogue writer for Harding Lemay on the hour-long *Another World*. What Doug didn't know is that there was behind-the-scenes panic at *General Hospital*. The production mechanism had wound down to a point where shows were being taped barely a week after they were written. Agnes Nixon, who acts as consultant on all of ABC's soaps, took one look at Doug's daily outlines and told Jackie, "Hire him!"

"I took over as head writer that Friday and there wasn't time for me even to edit the scripts which the Hollands were writing from my outlines," Doug said.

Meanwhile Gloria Monty was making notes. "I knew what I wanted to do right away," she said. "The show needed faster pacing. I thought *General Hospital* was doing everything in a 1950's style."

While Gloria was preparing to fly out to California to produce the show, Doug had already introduced a much younger story line, with Scotty and Laura, mere teenagers, now put in the spotlight ahead of the older characters. No soap writer had ever done that before. ABC, anxious to try anything new that could work, had no objections.

Gloria had a round of lunches, first with the head writer in New York (she agreed with everything he was doing), then with the actors in California (Emily was thrilled to learn she was going to be given a story line). The pattern was quickly established: lunches, coast-to-coast telephone calls, endless discussions at the studio, after-hours telephone calls and meetings, absolute personal and obsessive involvement in every phase of the show. Almost from the start on *General Hospital*, Gloria became Irna Phillips and Ted Corday rolled into one: fearsome in her determination to succeed. But could she?

Just before Gloria Monty arrived in Hollywood, Fred Silverman made what seemed at the time a crazy decision: to expand the show to a full hour. When Doug Marland asked him, "Why would you take a sick forty five minutes and turn it into an hour?", Silverman couldn't explain; it had been one of those seat-of-the-pants maneuvers he had been famous for. In any case, the financial loss of an hour show would be staggering if the ratings didn't improve.

When Gloria took over she was shown the first four hour-long shows, which had been taped and were ready to be aired. She found them tediously slow and ordered them thrown out and reshot. The budget had always been slim pickings and here $100,000 or more was being thrown down the sink! The temerity was shocking.

Eyebrows continued to raise. To her delight Gloria found tape editing machines at the Desilu studio, where the show had been done, and in an instant abolished the concept of "live tape," which by now all soaps had been using. She ordered the shows to be shot in many disconnected pieces, which would later be viewed, spliced and reconnected by her directors on the tape editing machines. She had learned the technique during her ten years as a nighttime television director (mostly of ABC's Wide World Mystery specials) and knew that it would enable her to speed up the pacing and break her shows up into twice as many scenes as before.

General Hospital had not been set up to be shot like a nighttime show and her overnight transformation of it caused great wails of pain. It was a terrifying process of rebirth. The whole cast and crew had to work from early morning until eleven at night, and often until two in the morning. The cameras would stop and start again, as Gloria balked over the least bit of motionless staging, even the tiniest reversion back to those long soap pauses. She would walk from set to set, snapping her fingers with the same words for everyone: "Pick up the pacing! Pick up the pacing!" Often the studio would ring with exhortations with Gloria's voice booming like the Wizard of Oz's over the loudspeakers. The egos of some actors took a drubbing.

"Those were difficult days," says Lieux Dressler. "We were all very tense. Gloria made such demands of everyone." The tension turned the studio into a mass of nerves. All the demands, the starting and stopping of the cameras until midnight or later, and the edginess of knowing that failure would mean cancellation, caused extremes of emotions that no one would ever forget. "Some nights," says Marlena Laird, the show's director and Gloria's good friend, "I would just come home and break down crying."

Reactions among the fatigued crew were divided. Some people exclaimed, "Oh, my God! It's like making a movie every day!" while others complained, "What does she think she's doing?" Emily responded once with a remark that quickly became the general feeling among the actors: "Do you want to do it her way or would you prefer the unemployment lines when we're canceled?" This was Last Chance Gulch for *General Hospital* and almost everyone understood what Gloria was doing.

A superb director in her own right, Gloria Monty took the normal working energies of actors on a daily soap, usually quite high, and escalated them even higher. She would beg, badger and cajole until she got better performances. She would have one-to-one conferences with actors, discuss long-term motivations, improvise with them. Leslie Charleson, who plays Monica Quartermaine, said that she has never worked harder in her life and that Gloria opened new doors for her. Emily says that she used to look forward to Gloria's acting notes. "She would come in with that little touch or perception and transform the whole scene."

Throughout this travail, Gloria made the greatest demands on herself and was the most exhausted of all. She amazed everyone with her night-and-day dedication to saving the show. Doug Marland says that she would make phone calls to him in the middle of the night to discuss scripts. When she became briefly ill a closed circuit TV monitor was set up in her hospital room so that she could view the show being made. (After noticing that her blood pressure would rise whenever she viewed the monitor, her doctor ordered it removed from the room.) No soap producer had ever worked so hard.

(But it wasn't all humorless, unrelieved hard work. "Gloria wears hard-heeled shoes," says Emily. "When she's coming across the stage, you can always hear her: 'Click, click, click.' Someone got a shot of her doing that and showed the clip at a Christmas party with a bunch of outtakes. She got a big kick out of that.")

Doug Marland was thrilled at the miracle Gloria had performed on the shows he had written and he soon began to write twice the number of scenes per episode. By March, 1978, the show looked much faster than other soaps. All the long pauses of the old show were sliced out, leaving only quick back-and-forth camera cuts, as dazzling to the viewer as any nighttime action series. Gloria's three directors were now staging scenes so that, instead of simply sitting and talking, the actors continually moved about as they spoke.

The ratings doubled by that summer, with the prominent Scotty Baldwin-Laura Vining story drawing considerable teenage interest, helped by the show's being aired just as teenagers were returning home from school. It had been the first time in years that *General Hospital* had shown the least sign of attracting new viewers, thus enabling Jackie Smith to pry loose the ABC pursestrings.

The money flowed for new sets and costumes. Set designer Bill Mickley, fresh from the East Coast, moved Steve and Audrey Hardy out of Audrey's skimpy three-room apartment into their own spacious home. Jessie also got lovely quarters, along with the rest of the regulars, who now had much more lavish hospital rooms in which to discuss their heartaches. It was all very expensive. Some of the new sets cost $80,000 apiece. Costume designer Bob Anton, also flown in from New York to help refurbish the show, dressed the ladies exquisitely in high-priced Neiman-Marcus outfits, even replacing the old hospital garb with designer-fitted nurses' uniforms. There was new

money for elaborate location exteriors, for which Jim Young had fought in vain for so many years.

Doug Marland continued to introduce young characters. His creation of student nurse Bobbie Spencer was one of the most remarkable of 1978. "More than anything, that year, I needed vitality. I needed an actress who would move through that hospital like a dose of smelling salts and wake everybody up—I needed a Jackie Zeman." The big-eyed, firm-breasted actress was a dramatic miracle for the show: her Bobbie Spencer excited all the men and upset the women. And the ratings kept going.

Other soaps weren't just sitting on the fence while *General Hospital* sprinted ahead in the ratings by using such scintillating new tactics. Most soaps that could afford it upgraded their costumes and sets, paced their scenes a bit faster and, in the summer of 1978, at least four shows introduced very young characters in prominent story positions. The average soap viewer probably noticed that his favorite soaps were getting younger and moving faster but without knowing why.

By the end of the first year of Gloria's stewardship, word came that ABC was spending a million dollars on a new home for *General Hospital*. For years the show had been housed at the ABC lot, and then for a year put in the Desilu Studios, an old structure with fireproofing hanging from the walls. The new Gower Studio (at Gower and Fountain in Hollywood) was more than just breathtaking—awe-inspiring would be closer. "When we walked onto the stage at the Gower for the first time," says Emily, "we just gasped. It was immense!" It was by far the largest studio ever devoted to one soap. With all the sets and lights in place, it reminds one today of the building described by Isaac Asimov in his *Foundation* trilogy that is so huge, with a ceiling so high that the people within it no longer knew that they were indoors. The vast new sets were constructed so that Gloria's cameras could always catch actors in motion, with plenty of room for the five cameras that her directors often employ in complicated scenes.

The actors were starting to see the results of all the hard work. For one thing, they were making more money. Leslie Charleson hired a full-time secretary to handle her increased fan mail and was able to buy a luxurious West Hollywood condominium. Stuart Damon, her co-star as Alan Quartermaine, bought a fabulous house. Each actor on the show now had his own dressing room which, unlike before, could not be used by any other actor. Upon Gloria's insistence, ABC built an outdoor patio at the Gower Studio for all of *General Hospital*'s stars, rescuing them from the unhealthful effects of having to spend the whole day underground under artificial lighting.

* * *

At their first meeting in her office, Anthony Geary told Gloria Monty: "I hate soap opera."

She replied, "Honey, so do I. I want you to help me change all that."

Gloria Monty may border on genius, but she would have to have been supernatural to know that the specialized character actor she was hiring would turn out to be daytime television's answer to Tom Selleck and Burt Reynolds. She did know, from having worked with him on a Wide World Mystery special called *Sorority Kill* that he played underworld types with absorbing intensity and could add a certain lowlife intrigue to her show.

At first they talked about his playing a crooked politician named Mitch Williams (Chris Pennock was later cast), but Tony wasn't right for that.

Around that time Bobbie Spencer was behaving viciously toward pretty teenager Laura Vining, because Laura was her rival for the affections of noble Scotty Baldwin. Jackie Zeman played the role so effectively that many viewers became confused and believed she was vicious herself. Various angry letters, including frightening death threats, began to come to Jackie. Television production offices must turn over all such threatening letters to the FBI which, in turn, investigates them. The show found itself with a sackful of evil letters, a frightened actress and the FBI buzzing around the production offices. The only answer seemed to be to introduce another character who could take over some of Bobbie's meanness toward Laura and thereby lighten Jackie's part. So Gloria had a brainstorm and hired Tony Geary as Bobbie's underworld brother.

Luke Spencer, in the beginning, wasn't supposed to have been an elaborate invention. For months Tony played him on one or two shows a week as, he says, "a real lowlife working for the Mafia. Mainly I was just Bobbie's runner, to do whatever she wanted." Naturally, Bobbie wanted her brother Luke to hurt Laura. "I was a secondary villain, just color."

Nevertheless, the character showed great prom-ise, mainly because Gloria allowed Tony to work it out himself, to take liberties with the script that occasionally bordered on improvisation. "I had control over my wardrobe and I suggested music and I could rewrite my dialogue. Gloria was very open to my suggestions. I had played a rapist on *The Young and The Restless* for six months and I knew streetwise characters. Fourteen years in show business puts you in the streets and I knew I could speak the jargon better than the writers, who were also writing Doctor Hardy."

Marlena Laird recalls: "The audience loved him because he wasn't Ken and Barbie Doll good looking. He was spontaneous and had a fascinating body language and carriage about him. People who worked in the Las Vegas nightclubs used to watch just because of him. The dialogue didn't seem as though it was written. It was, but he added the street handles. People would tune in just to find out what he would say."

Teenagers, especially, loved those "handles," which were sometimes downright risqué. Apparently the network censors did not object to such insertions as "The line is busy. Oh, Amy's probably on the phone just yackin' off."

Although Tony wasn't aware that bigger things were in store for his gifts, others certainly were. "Gloria was grooming him," says Marlena, who loved to direct Tony. "We would stage him and then she would go out and give him the directions she wanted the character to go in. From that the writers would pick up on what he was doing and write for him."

Millions of young people, meanwhile, continued to be addicted to the wonderfully wrought Laura-and-Scotty story, long after the high point of David Hamilton's death by Laura's hand and Lesley's exoneration of his supposed murder. As scripted by Doug Marland, Laura and Scotty kept having obstacles thrown in the path of their getting married. The first was vicious Bobbie Spencer, who claimed to be carrying Scotty's child, followed by the schemes of Luke Spencer. But finally, in mid-1979, they were married, and Bobbie and Luke had lost much of their story line function. At story conferences there was talk of killing Luke off.

For the first time since they began working together, trouble arose between writer and producer over what to do next. The turbulent Laura-Scotty story had helped bring the show to an astonishing first to third place among all soaps, and Gloria was reluctant to see the couple put on the back burner as just another happy couple on the show. Happiness does not generate ratings on a soap opera. Doug remembers: "I was afraid we would burn out the characters. I kept saying, 'Let Genie Ann have a breathing space. She's married to Scotty, so let her be happy for a while.' But Gloria wanted Scotty and Laura to be perpetually unhappy and the network sided with Gloria during story meetings."

Doug and Gloria violently disagreed over whether to have the newly married Laura fall in love with Luke Spencer, and early in 1980 a final eruption between them led to Doug's departure as head writer. (He subsequently became *The Guiding Light*'s new head writer.) One cannot take sides, for these two highly gifted and dedicated individuals had already done wonders for the show. Nevertheless, had Gloria not prevailed, the world's most popular soap opera story line might never have been aired.

A decade earlier, the romantic pairing of the wholesome teenager Laura, played by a fifteen-year-old actress, and the underworld Luke Spencer, played by a thirty-four-year-old actor, might have caused serious censorship problems, especially since it would involve a rape that the young girl apparently subconsciously desired. The fact that the show became a must-see for every teenager in America, who was tuning in just for Luke and Laura, is clear proof that soaps had changed forever. *General Hospital* was leading the way.

How did the Luke and Laura story come about? Gloria says she was a great lover of Frank Capra's *It Happened One Night* and blended that with a touch of Hitchcock's films. "One day we had put a blanket in the room between the two beds. Tony and Genie said, 'Gloria, how did you ever think of that? It's wonderful.' I thought they were putting me on. They were too young to have seen *It Happened One Night*." (In the film Claudette Colbert and Clark Gable play a rich girl and an earthy reporter on the run, having adventures and falling in love.) The actual rape scene was suggested to Pat Falken Smith, the new head writer, by Jackie Smith. "Jackie Smith told me, 'Pat, you're famous for rape stories. Why don't you do one?' I had done one with Bill and Laura Horton on *Days Of Our Lives* and it lasted for seven years. I said this time I wanted to do a rape story which really isn't rape. Laura would yell 'rape!' because she couldn't cope with the fact that she had been seduced."

In fact, many writers worked out the details of the Luke and Laura story, with Pat Falken Smith writing the main romance, New York story consultant A. J. Russell writing "Luke and Laura On the Run" and the island story, and Gordon Russell writing the story of Hutch befriending Luke and Laura.

Gloria was extremely fond of Genie Francis, who at fourteen, had been hired by Tom Donovan to play the ingenuous Laura several years before, and saw tremendous possibilities between her and the far more experienced, looser Tony Geary. Genie had already been heavily worked in the David Hamilton and Scotty Baldwin stories. "It was hard on Genie," said Marlena Laird. "She was up to forty pages a day and she was scared to death. Tony had been nervous himself about playing with her, since she was underage. Tony was just wonderful with her. He would guide her through everything. He'd say, 'It's all right. I'm scared too. Now let's play it together.'"

The chemistry between these two actors was wonderful from the start. These days people still wonder what it was exactly about Luke and Laura that held so many glued to their sets. Some feel that the real magic occurred in the eyes of the actors. "They had a good time together," says Marlena, "and the audience really saw love in those two people's eyes for each other. When I directed them, I'd get hung up in their scenes, because I never knew what I was going to get on tape. All of a sudden we'd get into a love scene where tears would be coming from Genie's eyes, and then we'd all be hushed." Others saw the true power in the relationship itself. Laura, at first, could not consummate sexual relations with Luke. But instead of Laura's simply saying no, for months both he and she would discuss whether or not they should, and would decide, mutually, not to. The relationship, which gave both partners equal sexual say, was extremely modern. When they finally did have sexual relations, viewers could see their great pleasure.

Still other observers found the answer to the immense popularity of Luke and Laura in the possibilities for identification: any young girl, no matter what her station in life, could see herself as the object of attention by someone like Luke, who didn't look like Burt Reynolds but who cared greatly in his own fascinating way.

The characters were so true and strongly individual that the audience began to sense that in some way real life was happening on the TV screen. Tony Geary found that Luke "became more psychodrama than acting" and experienced great strains on his own psyche. Genie Francis found herself not really acting in front of the cameras at all, but growing up, going through the process of maturation for millions to view. "Young people went nutty because they weren't getting a twenty-five-year-old faking it, they were getting a real kid," she told Newsweek. "I couldn't remember my lines because I was afraid of the sex. I hadn't gone through those things yet. All of a sudden, I had to find the woman inside of me and bring her out in front of America. It was very, very scary."

Many viewers believed that these actors just made up the words they spoke, which in fact, did happen. Tony says: "Genie Francis and I once did a six-minute scene that was totally improvised. We had taken the script into Gloria's office and she agreed that it didn't make any sense. She said, 'You both know who you are. Here are the four points that need to be covered in this scene, and at the end of the scene—some kind of kiss. Move anywhere you want. I'll be in the booth and we'll cover it.' It turned out to be one of our best scenes."

Young love had never been portrayed like this before. Neither Tony nor Genie had been prepared for the storm of attention from millions of fans.

* * *

Encouraged by the ratings and Gloria's proven abilities, the network authorized expensive and elaborate location settings for Luke and Laura's flight from the Frank Smith mob. Then, for two years, *General Hospital* looked more like a soap that should really have been called *The Saga of Luke and Laura*. Every episode was dominated by either the two characters themselves or other characters discussing them as, week after week, America became mesmerized by the couple. The show became *the* top-rated soap opera.

There had never been a phenomenon like it in the history of soaps. *General Hospital* fever became pandemic. The actors couldn't move on the streets without being mobbed. "It was just all around us," says Lieux Dressler. "Stores would tell me that they could not hire help between two and three P.M. and one store had to create a two-to-three P.M. lunch hour." "I love *General Hospital*" T-shirts and cups were suddenly popping up everywhere.

ABC was making millions on the show, while at rival networks there was much gnashing of teeth. At a restaurant a CBS executive peevishly called out to Gloria Monty: "Why don't you take a vacation and give the rest of us a chance?"

The demographics experts at the advertising agencies tell us that about six million teenagers tuned into Port Charles in those years, with the teen cult clearly beginning after Laura and Scotty were paired, and culminating in the second year of the Luke and Laura story. Doug Marland remembers receiving letters similar to the one signed by 175 girls from one high school. "They would tell me how much they liked the show and how they would all meet in the morning and the ones who saw it would fill in the ones who hadn't." Gloria says that she gradually became aware of all the teenage fans along with the adult ones. "I got one letter from a man who said, 'Thank you for giving me back my family.' His whole family watched *General Hospital* and began talking over the intergenerational problems at the dinner table."

Writing and producing a soap that would appeal to teenagers as well as adults was utterly unknown territory and led to a good deal of experimentation. The only hard and fast rule was that Luke and Laura had to be at the center of the show. Up until 1981 all of the sequences involving Laura, and later Luke, were based on the presumed psychosexual fantasies of older teenagers; i.e., Laura's affair with the worldly David Hamilton, her brief involvement in a prostitution ring, her "rape seduction" by the older Luke Spencer, spending the night locked up with him in a department store, running away with him from a boring marriage to work in places like a farm and a diner. It all worked flawlessly and kept the show at the top.

In 1981 Gloria and her writers decided to try a far younger comic book fantasy by putting Luke and Laura in an action mystery story which climaxed on an exotic island ruled by an evil genius named Mikkos. While the show, to ABC's relief, did not budge from its position in first place, those six million teenagers, who had begun watching a few years before, shifted in age from about eighteen years old to about thirteen, and became more like "the Saturday morning crowd." That is not the most desirable change, notes Doug Marland, because thirteen-year-olds are more fickle in their viewing habits.

Before the Ice Princess story even began, head writer Pat Falken Smith warned Jackie Smith: "You do this story and it's the beginning of the end of this show. It's science fiction and you will break the empathy." The mixing of something like *Spiderman* with the intense adult personal problems in Port Charles did seem a bit weird: the regular actors who remembered the old show found themselves tittering. After the opening credits, with the usual shot of the ambulance rushing toward General Hospital, the show would open on an island where Luke, Laura and undercover man Robert Scorpio (played by new daytime heartthrob Tristan Rogers) were frantically trying to stop the maniac Mikkos (John Colicos) from using his vile machine to freeze the world, starting with Port Charles. Poor Jessie, who had suffered through trials, rapes and romantic dilemmas, now had to sit and freeze in her blue sweater through a science fiction story line. For her, the soap world *had* changed!

None of it, however, was meant to be taken seriously. Gloria and her stalwarts were, as always, just experimenting with new modes for daytime, as when she permitted Pat Falken Smith to invent a murderous transvestite character. The risk was only moderate; as one observer says, "If Luke and Laura had gone to the moon, the show would have stayed on top." But whenever Gloria Monty sneezed the rest of the soap world caught a cold. Other shows soon had young main characters running off to have exotic adventures on islands, and one even had a weird evil genius.

For a year and a half, the frenzy of young and old fans continued, as *General Hospital* stayed solidly number one in daytime ratings. Yet the average non-soap watcher barely knew that the show existed. Outside of daytime fan magazines, *General Hospital* remained an "insider's" happening. All that changed by the fluke of an actors' strike. "The media didn't have anybody to write about," says Lieux Dressler, "and they looked around and here we were." Newsweek, in September, 1981, ran a cover story entitled "General Hospital—Television's Hottest Show." It told America what much of America had not known, that *General Hospital* had become the big new fad in the daytime, much as *Dallas* had been for nighttime viewers. The article made instant celebrities of Gloria Monty, Tony Geary, Genie Francis and the rest of the cast, all of whom were pictured and their characters described in detail. Gloria and Tony appeared on The Merv Griffin Show to tell all about the new mania, and People magazine began running a series on the soap, even devoting a two-page article to Gloria herself, unheard of personal publicity for a producer. (Only writers Irna Phillips and Agnes Nixon had received such treatment in the past.) Newsstands and television talk shows came down with *General Hospital* fever. Even business publications were running stories on how much money the show was netting for ABC.

Then a great hue and cry shook the entertainment world when ABC announced that Elizabeth Taylor would be making a week's appearance on her favorite show, *General Hospital*. Media writers rushed to their typewriters. Was there no barrier that Gloria Monty could fail to break? The unthinkable had happened to not one show but to the whole of the soap world.

Elizabeth Taylor, who had been appearing in Los Angeles in her first play, *The Little Foxes*, had actually called Gloria Monty directly to ask to be on the show. Gloria quickly had her new writers (Pat Falken Smith and the old team of subwriters had just left) write in the character of Helena Cassadine, widow of evil Mikkos, to appear just prior to Luke and Laura's wedding. Mrs. Cassadine was to put a curse on Luke and Laura as retribution for their dispatching Mikkos on the island—a clever plot to justify Laura's sudden disappearance a few months hence, since Genie Francis intended to depart.

There was much ado around the Gower Studios as the most famous actress of modern times was about to sanctify soapdom. Tony Geary went into shock when he discovered that he and Elizabeth had no scenes together. "Genie and I had put as much time, energy, blood, sweat and guts in the show as anyone else, and I felt cheated." After triggering complaints to management, he ordered enough roses for a football parade delivered to the stage for Elizabeth's first day, along with a note explaining how sorry he was that they did not have a scene together. But the writers had already caught the oversight and wrote in a marvelous scene for the famous pair, which began with Tony walking in a door and saying to Elizabeth: "There's one thing that I want to tell you—I'm up! My God, it's Elizabeth Taylor!" She fell down laughing and the tension around her broke like shattered glass.

"She has the loudest laugh I've ever heard—it's sort of a cackle, and it's infectious," says Emily, who was so nervous about her one line at the nurses' station with Elizabeth that she was shaking like a leaf. But Elizabeth was equally nervous. "She had to have the big cue cards," recalls John Beradino, "and she looked straight into the camera to see them, she never looked sideways. On one long speech she kept blowing her lines, and it took six or seven takes. Everybody, including Elizabeth, was laughing about it."

What thoroughly surprised everyone was that Elizabeth knew all the actors by their real and character names, turning gracious and cute with her favorites, like Emily. She had become a great fan of the show during the years she spent in Washington, D.C., as the wife of Senator John Warner, and this was obviously a great treat for her.

Elizabeth could not make a move without new romantic myths emerging, especially between husbands. People, *The National Enquirer* and countless fan magazines decided that she was desperately in love with Tony Geary, to the point of wanting marriage. Elizabeth was not at all incensed but terribly amused. After her week on *General Hospital* (taped in three days) was over, she left front row center complimentary tickets to *The Little Foxes* for the whole cast. But more than that, she left behind glittery myths and truths of her own that no one on the show can ever forget.

Besides Elizabeth Taylor, Gloria hired other celebrities, including rock star Rick Springfield to play the steady role of Dr. Noah Drake (although she had no idea he was a rock star when she cast him), and Richard Simmons to play himself. When he came on *General Hospital* to lead a campy diet-exercise class at the Disco (as one more colorful backdrop for the developing Luke and Laura romance), Richard Simmons was virtually unknown. His appearances on the show aided his sudden leap to fame as America's best-known diet guru. The show has also helped Rick Springfield rekindle the embers of his pop musical career by giving him wide television exposure among teenagers.

Luke and Laura's wedding, after two years of adventures in unlikely locales which fairly dominated the new hour show, had an audience of fourteen million people, a 52 percent share, and outdrew Prince Charles and Lady Diana's wedding. No soap opera episode had ever before achieved that kind of rating, which would have been exceptional for any nighttime show. Students on campuses dropped everything to see the elaborate show (as, indeed, the writers had all of Port Charles, including the mayor, turn out). Taverns served beer with the wedding. Teenagers rushed home from school. "I was in a restaurant," says Emily, "and the owner ran over and said, 'You're missing the wedding. I'll bring a television set to your table.' "

Later, when Emily congratulated Gloria over the ratings, Gloria replied: "Do you realize I have nowhere to go now but down!"

General Hospital had indeed come far from where it began twenty years before. No one but a crystal gazer could have guessed, then, where destiny would eventually take the Hursleys' creation. However, the show, as transformed, doesn't seem to have much relationship to its origins. I suggested to Gloria that instead of saving *General Hospital* from cancellation what she had done was to "cancel" the show, at least in spirit, and begin a new show, one that did not live and breathe in a hospital. She said that the show still had John Beradino, Emily McLaughlin, Peter Hansen, Rachel Ames and Susan Brown. "But I look back at the lives and loves, at the people who had been on the show and I say, 'you mean he's so and so's father?' There were just so many murders and trials."

The real connection between the old and the new *General Hospital* is the handful of actors who have appeared on it for two decades, yet none of whom have any dramatic function left. For long-term aficionados it is very sad. Actors who were once the core of *General Hospital* were now coming to the Gower Studio a few times a week to say four or five lines about Luke or some other young character yet were obviously not needed for any of the stories.

"I don't know what the function is of Steve Hardy and Jessie and Audrey and Lee Baldwin and Tommy," says John Beradino, "except that we're the backbone if something might happen to the show."

But the shelving of the older regulars isn't just a *General Hospital* happening; it is part of a sea change that has overtaken all of daytime soaps. On most other soaps "tentpole" characters, like Nancy Hughes on *As the World Turns*, have either been written out or relegated to the limbo of reduced parts, in favor of younger actors. To Gloria's credit, she did not sweep away all vestiges of the old show. Emily says that she is lucky to have her job: "We know it's the turn of the younger actors now."

Shortly after the brouhaha caused by the Newsweek article and the round robin of talk show appearances, Genie Francis left *General Hospital* and then signed a contract with CBS to appear in a series of made-for-TV movies, beginning with *Bare Essence*, a sexy mini-series. The great reward for ABC, Gloria and all of the soap world was not just that Genie Francis was starred and had a cover article in TV Guide, but that CBS promoted her as "*General Hospital*'s Genie Francis." It was an acknowledgment by nighttime television that daytime soaps were its equals in the entertainment world.

Now, at the height of *General Hospital*'s greatest success, the show had a serious problem. With the Luke and Laura story suddenly over, what could the writers come up with to fill the void? Tony Geary was still daytime's heartthrob, but in the minds of millions of viewers he was Laura's mate. Gloria and her staff knew that the show's abnormally high ratings were in jeopardy. The solution they came up with was wonderfully imaginative, if not wholly effective. Minutes after Laura wandered off into the night fog, never to return (fulfilling Mrs. Cassadine's curse), Luke spotted another young woman who resembled Laura—in fact, her name was Laura! The story of Luke's search for the old Laura, and his involvement with the new Laura lookalike (played by Janine Turner), went on for months. It never quite worked, but it did help new head writer Anne Howard Bailey to buy time until a new romance could be found for Luke, which finally emerged in the character of Holly Sutton (Emma Samms), a beautiful young girl who was entangled with her criminal family. Gloria's choice of Emma Samms was excellent. The audience took to her magnetic, photogenic appeal. The only problem is the problem on any soap, especially an hour show that focuses so much of its attention on one couple for several years. After the big romance ends there are bound to be severe withdrawal symptoms as the show scrambles to find new themes, interests and story lines.

As of this writing, *General Hospital* had not fully recovered from the loss of Laura. Many of the six million teenagers who had been hooked on Luke and Laura had simply stopped watching, although no one realistically expected the teen phenomenon to last. Tony Geary, who has threatened to leave the show by the end of 1983, may yet play Luke for years to come, but Gloria Monty and her staff still have the task of reforging whole structures and moving the show away from the Luke cult hero.

* * *

Nothing remotely like what has happened to *General Hospital* since 1978 has happened to any other soap opera. As images from the show's past rush by our mind's eye—the young Jessie and Steve on their first day in Internal Medicine; the laughable barking of head nurse Lucille March; the illnesses, the melodramas, the murder trials, the day-after-day appearances in hospital white of a handful of dedicated actors for almost two decades—somehow there is intense sadness at the loss of the old show.

But it was going to die, leaving us without even the aging faces of Jessie and Steve and Audrey to help us recall time gone by. Gloria Monty, like one of the show's highly skilled surgeons, came on the scene to give it a face lift and an infusion of youth and energy that will keep it alive for a long, long time.

The success of the show has been the dream of a lifetime for her. "I always hoped that daytime would get the attention that I thought it deserved. I don't think there's a finer group of actors." She created huge stars of her cast. She made every actor in the business aware of the importance of her show. An actor was recently overheard at a local Hollywood gym telling another: "I've been trying out for *General Hospital* and Gloria Monty. You know, that's the one to get on, but it's hard." Before Gloria's dynasty began, that was the one to get off.

As for Gloria Monty in a larger context, her achievement in the soap world is enormous but perhaps too remarkable to be assessed accurately at such close historical range. It is clear that she did not herself create the new elements of the soap world of the eighties—these had been on the way for years—but she had the brilliance to envision, before anyone else, what the new daytime look could and should be like.

THE STORY

JESSIE BREWER, R.N. (Emily McLaughlin), everybody's friend and confidante on the seventh floor (Internal Medicine division) of General Hospital, had met and married DR. PHIL BREWER (originally Roy Thinnes, then Ricks Falk, Bob Hogan and lastly Martin West), a handsome young intern seven years younger than she, and sacrificed to help him become a practicing cardiologist. Phil returned Jessie's love, but, having a willful, less-than-noble character, he also sought the excitement of an illicit romance. Jessie found out and sued for divorce. While she awaited the final papers, Phil, drunk and frustrated, assaulted her one night, and she became pregnant. The child was born with a serious heart ailment, and cardiologist Phil Brewer was helpless to prevent his own baby's death. The tragedy ended when Phil and Jessie were finally divorced.

Trouble didn't stop there for the two of them. Feeling pity for the dying DR. JOHN PRENTICE (Barry Atwater), Jessie married him, and when he finally died of an overdose of drugs by his own hand, Jessie had to stand trial for his murder. Phil and Jessie were reunited during that terrible episode, ending with her acquittal and their remarriage. But the reunion was short-lived. Phil, now himself accused of murdering John's daughter POLLY PRENTICE (Jennifer Billingsley), with whom he had had an affair, ran away and was later reported killed in a plane crash.

Jessie's closest friend and ally in the daily encounters with death, despair and hope at the hospital was, and has always been, DR. STEVE HARDY (John Beradino). Reserved and wise, Steve, the son of a missionary family and born and raised in China, was devoted to his work at the hospital. But he also needed love. That need was fulfilled, for a while, in his marriage to one-time swinging airline stewardess AUDREY MARCH (Rachel Ames), sister of LUCILLE MARCH (Lucille Wall), the good-hearted senior nurse. Audrey had gotten tired of all the men and all the parties and had wanted children with Steve. When she failed to become pregnant, Audrey mistakenly believed Steve to be sterile and became pregnant through artificial insemination. But the unborn child died in an auto accident when Steve was at the wheel, and their marriage subsequently ended in divorce. Audrey, ever obsessed with motherhood, went to Vietnam to care for orphans.

* * *

With Phil out of the picture, Jessie found temporary happiness in a marriage to psychiatrist DR. PETER TAYLOR (Craig Huebing), a quiet and undemanding type, about as different from Phil Brewer as imaginable. But, unwittingly, Jessie was committing bigamy, for Phil was still alive. To be near Jessie, whom he still loved, Phil assumed a new identity—"Harold Williamson"—and began working as a dishwasher in a restaurant near General Hospital. Afraid to tell Jessie he was still alive, Phil—as Harold—soon was diverted by an involvement with beautiful DIANA MAYNARD (Valerie Starrett, Brooke Bundy), who worked at

When General Hospital *began on April 1, 1963, the three bastions of the show were John Beradino as Dr. Steve Hardy, Emily McLaughlin as Nurse Jessie Brewer and Roy Thinnes as Dr. Phil Brewer. Viewers saw the three stars in every half-hour episode.*

Lucille Wall began playing rough and tough Lucille March several months after the premiere. As head of student nurses she was the first of a handful of humorous characters. (Here shown with one of her nurses, Sharon McGillis, played by Sharon DeBord.)

the restaurant as a waitress. However, when Jessie and Phil finally confronted each other one day, when he was brought into the hospital after an auto accident, Jessie was forced to annul her marriage to Dr. Peter Taylor and try to find happiness again with Phil. Diana Maynard faded into the background.

Meanwhile, Audrey March returned from Vietnam to become a nurse at General Hospital and marry DR. TOM BALDWIN (Paul Savior, Don Chastain), whom she married just to prove to herself that she didn't love Steve. Audrey realized she didn't love Tom, a self-destructive loser type, and wouldn't have sexual relations with him, but he forced himself on her anyway, and she became pregnant. When Audrey realized that she still loved Steve Hardy, she sued Tom Baldwin for a divorce and left town to have her child. When she returned to the hospital she told everyone that the baby had died, in order to keep Tom from invalidating their divorce. After Audrey and Steve decided to remarry, Audrey had to keep spinning a bigger web of deceit, hurting their relationship. The remarriage between Steve and Audrey never took place, because Tom did find out about his son, whom Audrey was secretly hiding at home, and Audrey had to return to him to keep her child. But of course a loveless marriage can't work, so Tom, threatened himself this time with the loss of his son in a divorce action, kidnapped young Tommy—with the help of adult babysitter FLORENCE ANDREWS (Maida Severn) and ran away, leaving Audrey in shock.

Tom Baldwin's handsome, fortyish attorney brother, LEE BALDWIN (Peter Hansen), had once fallen in love with Jessie Brewer, but after losing her to Phil he married MEG BALDWIN (originally Pat Breslin, later Elizabeth MacRae), a nurse with a young son and a problem stepdaughter, BROOKE CLINTON (Indus Arthur). After her mastectomy, Meg had a mental breakdown and was committed to a sanitarium. Later, she was cured but developed high blood pressure, for which beautiful and independently single DR. LESLEY WILLIAMS (Denise Alexander) began treating her. Meg finally died, leaving Lee a widower with a stepson, SCOTTY BALDWIN (Don Clarke, currently Kin Shriner), to care for.

Steve Hardy had romantic ties to nurse Audrey Marcy, played by Rachel Ames, from the time she entered the story early in 1964. They've had countless personal dramas, including a divorce and a remarriage.

Martin West became the fourth Phil Brewer in 1968. Phil cheated on Jessie once again with Polly Prentice (Jennifer Billingsley), just before she was killed in an auto accident caused by Phil.

Again, Jessie and Phil Brewer's reunion for the umpteenth time turned into utter disaster, especially when Phil found out that Diana Maynard, with whom he had been living before coming back to Jessie, had married Dr. Peter Taylor in order to give her unborn son (Phil's) a name. However, after Phil's breakup with Jessie, Diana informed Phil that she was now in love with Dr. Taylor. Diana gave birth to Phil's child while still married to Peter, who knew that it wasn't his. But Phil, who previously thought he was permanently impotent, forced himself on Diana in her apartment and raped her, which caused another pregnancy. Diana became frantic with worry that her husband, Peter, would discover that this child, too, wasn't his.

Jessie, meanwhile, found herself another young "Phil" by the name of TEDDY HOLMES (John Gabriel). Teddy, a recklessly handsome newspaperman and an adventurer in the worst sense of the word, first came to General Hospital as a hepatitis patient. He imme-

diately saw a way to exploit Jessie and her money, to give him the independence he needed to get to the top of the literary world. Lonely and vulnerable, unsuspecting Jessie invited Teddy to stay at her home during his recovery.

With the death of Jessie's widowed brother, she became the guardian of his two children, CAROL MURRAY (Anne Wyndham) and KENT MURRAY (Mark Hamill). Teddy, learning that Jessie's niece, Carol, was to come into a large inheritance on her eighteenth birthday—and his eyes now burning with dollar bills—told Carol he was in love with her and not Jessie, and Carol took the bait. When they ran away together Jessie was in shock, especially since she had cosigned a $25,000 loan for Teddy, supposedly for an investment in a motorcycle shop, and was stuck for the money. She turned to Lee Baldwin for help in paying off the burdensome loan.

Audrey Baldwin was also dangling by a string, waiting for her husband to bring back their son, TOMMY BALDWIN (currently David Walker), whom he kidnapped just before the boy was to have vital heart surgery by DR. JAMES HOBART (James Sikking). While Audrey worried for her son's safety, Dr. Hobart, ob-

Nurse Jane Harland (Shelby Hiatt) married irresponsible Howie Dawson (Ray Girardin). Jane would confide her marital frustrations to her nursing friends on the seventh floor.

Life was always dealing harsh blows to sensitive Meg Baldwin (Elizabeth McRae), who was married to lawyer Lee Baldwin (Peter Hansen). Before marrying Lee, her own stepdaughter stole her fiance. Meg would later suffer a mastectomy, then a complete mental breakdown.

viously attracted to her, was relieving her anxiety somewhat by his attention. Later, the boy was found. Audrey was told that Tom Baldwin had been killed in Mexico.

Diana Taylor soon gave birth to MARTHA, still concealing the fact from husband Peter that Phil Brewer was the real father. With Phil trying to coerce Diana into leaving her husband for him, Peter inevitably discovered the child's parentage. He refused to have further sexual relations with his wife, whom he felt he could no longer trust. Even after Phil realized that his pursuit of Diana was hopeless and once again left General Hospital, Peter was not to be appeased. Depressed over his prolonged rejection of her, Diana reluctantly sued for divorce. Ironically, Peter admitted to friends that he was still in love with his wife.

Dr. Lesley Williams was now treating an ulcer patient by the name of FLORENCE GRAY (Anne Collings), wife of a former college professor, GORDON GRAY (Howard Sherman). Florence's ulcers, it turned out,

were caused by her feeling that her husband didn't love her. She revealed to psychiatrist Peter Taylor that she was disturbed over the fact that her husband had left her years before to have an affair with one of his students; he returned to her only when the girl left him. Unbeknownst to Florence, the woman was Dr. Lesley Williams herself! In fact, Lesley had become pregnant by Gordon, but the child died at birth, or so Lesley thought. Now Gordon begged her to marry him. The old feelings were still there. Lesley was filled with guilt because of her patient and asked Steve Hardy to take her off the case.

*   *   *

At first it was Audrey Baldwin who needed comforting; later, it was Audrey's suitor, Dr. James Hobart, who needed support. An automobile accident caused by his alcoholism left his hands damaged, and the possibility existed that he would never be able to operate again. Jim's drinking worsened. To rescue

Nurse Sharon McGillis (Sharon DeBord) secretly married a bumbling but lovable intern named Henry Pinkham (Peter Kilman), who defied his domineering uncle by marrying her.

Howie's mother, Mrs. Dawson (Phyllis Hill), lived with her son and daughter-in-law Jane. During the couple's continual marital spats, Mrs. Dawson initially took her son's side until seeing him for the child-man he really was.

him, Audrey became his wife—more out of pity than love. After they married, Audrey was uneasy about their lovemaking. The marriage seemed destined for trouble.

Nurse JANE HARLAND and HOWIE DAWSON (Shelby Hiatt and Ray Girardin), embarked on a problemmatical marriage. Howie, not wanting the responsibility of children, had had a vasectomy without Jane's consent. After many arguments over Jane's insistence that they adopt a child, Howie moved into a hotel. Later, after being promoted to assistant to the administrator of General Hospital, Howie asked to come home again. Jane took him back, despite her suspicions that he came back to her only because his new job necessitated the appearance of marital stability. The vasectomy, however, was constantly on Jane's mind and caused sexual difficulties between her and Howie. After he began having affairs with other women, Jane divorced him. Howie went to New York City to accept a job.

Another unhappy spouse was DR. HENRY PINKHAM (Peter Kilman) whose wife, nurse SHARON PINKHAM (Sharon DeBord), had left him for another man. In his loneliness, Henry turned to the newly divorced Jane Dawson and they fell in love.

While mutual hurt pride continued to keep Diana and Peter apart, each was pursued by an attractive new member of the seventh-floor staff: DR. JOEL STRATTON (Rod McCary) and nurse AUGUSTA MC LEOD (Judith McConnell). Ravishing Augusta, never popular with her fellow nurses because she flaunted her sexiness, seduced Peter into an affair. Diana was just about to divorce him when she suddenly saw how close he and her little daughter, Martha, were becoming; there was a brief reconciliation. Then Dr. Joel Stratton begged Diana, because she was a nurse, to care for his brother OWEN STRATTON (Joel Marston), stricken with a terminal heart ailment. Misunderstanding Di-

Jessie married Dr. Peter Taylor (Craig Huebing) in 1970 after she learned that her husband, Phil Brewer, had been killed in a plane crash. But Phil was indeed alive and came back to town disguised with a beard.

The cast in 1972 included, from left, front row: Rachel Ames, John Beradino, Emily McLaughlin, Shelby Hiatt, Lucille Wall, Tony Campo (Scotty Baldwin). Middle row: Indus Arthur (Brooke Clinton), Peter Hansen, Anne Helm (Mary Briggs), Ray Girardin, James Westmoreland (Teddy Holmes), Anne Wyndham (Carol Murray), Mark Hamill (Kent Murray), Paul Savior (Tom Baldwin). Back row: Elizabeth McRae, Peter Kilman, Martin West, Sharon DeBord, Jim Young (producer), Valerie Starrett and Craig Huebing.

ana's relationship with her new private patient, Peter once again left his wife and resumed his affair with eager Augusta McLeod. Owen fell in love with compassionate Diana. She knew he had only a few more weeks of life left, and, determined to make him happy by marrying him, she reinstituted divorce proceedings against Peter. But Owen suddenly died. Peter, finally learning the truth, rushed back into Diana's arms.

Phil once again showed up at General Hospital, seeking to win Diana back. Augusta had written to Phil in Nairobi informing him that she was carrying Peter's baby, but now she begged Phil not to tell Peter because of her pride. Caring only for himself, Phil went to Peter and told him that he was soon to be a new father, casting a new cloud over the Taylors' marriage.

One night, nurse Jane Dawson found Jessie Brewer hugging Phil's limp body. "I'm sorry," Jessie kept saying, over and over. Phil had been murdered!

Who did it? At least five people had reason to want to see him dead. It was Jessie who was finally charged with Murder One—although the blunt instrument that had cracked Phil's skull was never found. Before Phil's death Jessie had come down with San Joaquin Valley Fever, but had courageously refused to leave her nursing chores to recuperate. Jessie now had to face two imperiling crises.

Dr. Lesley Williams was relieved when her old flame, Gordon Gray, reassured his psychosomatically ailing wife, Florence, that he no longer loved Lesley but loved her, and the Grays left General Hospital. Lesley soon fell deeply in love with Dr. Joel Stratton, who, although he loved her, mysteriously refused to marry her. What Lesley didn't know was Joel's secret, a hereditary heart condition (the same one that took his brother's life), which made it impossible for him ever to consider marriage. Lesley, heartbroken, ended her relationship with Joel.

Wealthy CAMERON FAULKNER (Don Matheson), became a patient of Lesley Williams's and fell in love with her. Joel, still in love with her, was hurt when she responded to Cameron's attentions—but bravely put

Diana Maynard (Valerie Starrett), a waitress turned nurse, had an affair with Phil Brewer, believing that he was someone called "Harold Williamson," and became pregnant by him. When Phil went back to Jessie, who had to divorce Peter Taylor, Peter married Diana. Phil later raped Diana, also becoming the father of her second child. By 1973, many soaps were mixing the classic triangle with pregnancy dramas.

Denise Alexander came on the show in 1973 as Dr. Lesley Williams, becoming involved with Dr. Joel Stratton (Rod McCary) the following year. He had a hereditary heart ailment which he kept secret from her.

his feelings aside after a crazed patient of Lesley's shot Cam, and operated on him, saving Cam's life. Grateful, Cameron financed a new free clinic that Lesley had proposed, and soon Lesley and her benefactor were wed. Joel hung around long enough to help Lesley start her humanitarian free clinic, but couldn't bear to see the woman he loved sleeping with another man and went to Boston to practice.

* * *

Just before Jessie Brewer was to be tried for the murder of Phil Brewer, Diana Taylor suddenly confessed that she was the murderess! To make sure that she was believed, she turned over a blood-stained geode, the murder weapon, to the police. She was tried, convicted and sentenced. Frantic Peter Taylor was convinced that Diana had confessed only to protect him, and he pleaded with her to believe that he wasn't the killer. Peter and lawyer Lee Baldwin went over and over the details of the night of the killing. Dr. Jim Hobart had already told the police that he had

been with Phil that fateful night, but he had been too drunk to remember who else he had seen or what had happened. Finally Jim remembered—he had seen Augusta with Phil that night. Badgered by Peter, Augusta confessed to killing Phil! It had been in self-defense. He had been striking her during an argument, and, terror-stricken that he would harm the baby she was carrying, she struck him on the head—so hard that he died. Augusta went to prison, had her baby, which was placed in a foster home, and, upon release, left town. Peter told Diana that the baby was his, and she forgave him.

Lesley Williams's marriage to Cameron Faulkner, on the other hand, was in deep trouble. The difficulty stemmed from Lesley's sudden discovery that the illegitimate daughter by Gordon Gray who she had thought died at childbirth was still alive. A dying patient at General Hospital, nurse DORIS ROACH (Meg Wyllie), had revealed to Lesley the whole incredible tale. Years before, just after Lesley gave birth to her illegitimate baby, Lesley's father had plotted with nurse

Lee Baldwin, a widower by 1975, married Caroline Chandler (Augusta Dabney), whose grown son Bobby (Ted Eccles) developed terminal Melenkoff's disease. In 1976, writers Eileen and Robert Mason Pollock sent them all to New York and out of the story.

Laura Vining first entered the story in 1975 as a child played by Stacy Baldwin. Barbara Vining (Judy Lewis) thought she was Laura's mother, until Lesley found out that there had been a baby switch years before, making Laura her own child. There was a bitter custody fight.

Roach to switch Lesley's healthy baby for the dead baby of a couple called the Vinings—making Lesley believe her baby was dead. Obsessed with finding her daughter, Lesley located the Vinings after an investigation. BARBARA VINING (Judy Lewis) and JASON VINING (Jonathan Carter) were shocked when they were told that young LAURA VINING (Stacy Baldwin, later Genie Francis) was really Lesley Williams's daughter. Lesley launched a custody suit, and the judge, realizing that all parties had been wronged, put off making a decision until Laura got to know her real mother and could voice her own feelings. Laura was to live with Lesley and Cameron for a one-month trial period. Of course, Laura was terribly fascinated with the Faulkners' glamorous way of life—plane trips to exciting places, luxurious restaurants—but during an illness Laura called out for her "real" mother, Barbara Vining. Cameron and Lesley now knew the truth about Laura's feelings, but Lesley pleaded with him not to tell the judge. Cameron was growing tired of Lesley's ceaseless preoccupation with her daughter. It was obvious to Cameron that his marriage to Lesley,

which never really got off the ground, would soon fail—unless he took drastic steps, however dishonest.

Jim and Audrey Hobart's marriage was also coming apart. Jim was growing weary of Audrey's mothering. After Jim lost his job at the hospital, he began seeing psychiatrist Peter Taylor, who helped Jim decide to stop drinking once and for all. A new man, Jim became a success as a college professor, had an affair with one of his students, glamorous SALLY GRIMES (Jenny Sherman), and then left Audrey, claiming that she was "old and burned out." He then promptly left town. Distressed, Audrey tried to kill herself with an overdose, but Dr. Steve Hardy helped restore her self-confidence. After taking his new post as hospital chief of staff, Steve made Audrey the superintendent of student nurses.

Nurse Jane Dawson became grief-stricken when her daughter, Joann, took sick and died. Jane couldn't bear General Hospital, with all of its painful memories of a failed marriage and a dead daughter, and left

Lesley's new husband, wealthy Cameron Faulkner (Don Metheson), became bored with Lesley's obsession with Laura and in 1976 had an affair with his secretary, Peggy Lowell (Deanna Lund). He was killed in an auto accident the following year.

By 1978, Laura and Lee's son Scotty Baldwin were daytime's most important teen sweethearts. Played by Genie Francis (age fourteen) and Kin Shriner (Herb Shriner's son), their story was given prominent focus on the show and proved, for the first time, that teenage love could skyrocket ratings.

town in a state of heartbreak. Henry Pinkham, in love with her, went with Jane.

New arrivals in town (now called Port Charles) were CAROLYN CHANDLER (Augusta Dabney) and her son, BOBBY CHANDLER (Ted Eccles). Widower Lee Baldwin fell in love with Caroline and married her. Her son, Bobby, married nurse SAMANTHA LIVINGSTONE (Marla Pennington), then found out that he was dying of Melenkoff's disease, for which there was no cure. Bobby's main concern was that Samantha, who had just become pregnant, would have to raise their child alone after his certain death. Then Steve Hardy heard from a New York City hospital, which had been conducting further tests, that Bobby, in reality, had something called Farrier's syndrome, which *could* be cured, providing Bobby came to New York for treatment. Lee Baldwin, Carolyn, Bobby and Samantha all happily left for New York for Bobby's cure—without announcing any intention of returning to General Hospital.

The Webbers then came to General Hospital. Steve's old colleague Dr. Lars Webber and his wife had been killed in an auto accident many years ago. Their oldest child, TERRI WEBBER ARNETT (Bobbi Jordan), gave up her plans for a singing career in order to care for her two younger brothers, RICK WEBBER (Michael Gregory, currently Chris Robinson) and JEFF WEBBER (Richard Dean Anderson). Terri had married a General Hospital psychiatrist, Dr. David Arnett, who died. Rick, a promising young surgeon, had been engaged to an insecure but beautiful interne named MONICA BARD (Patsy Rahn, currently Leslie Charleson), who had grown up in a foundling home. Rick had gone to Africa and was later presumed killed. The day that the Webbers had found out about Rick's supposed death, Monica had received a letter from Rick breaking off their relationship, and on the rebound Monica had married Rick's younger brother, Jeff, also an intern. Monica never told Jeff that Rick had broken up with her.

All this occurred before the Webbers were first seen at General Hospital. As their story began, Terri had just opened up a new nightclub, called Terri's Place, and invited her lifelong friends at General Hos-

William Bryant came on as millionaire Lamont Corbin and Frank Maxwell played his right hand man, Dan Rooney. Lamont schemed to keep his wife Katie and Mark Dante apart. Dan was interested in Jessie and later became administrator of General Hospital.

Monica Webber schemed for years to marry her brother-in-law, Rick Webber. By 1979 the roles were played by Leslie Charleson and Chris Robinson.

pital to attend the opening. Cameron Faulkner had financed the restaurant, and for that Terri vowed her eternal gratitude to Cam. Jeff and Monica, Steve's experimental "Mr. and Mrs. Intern" team at the hospital, were facing serious problems. Jeff doubted his ability to get out of his older brother's shadow, and even had a nightmare in which everyone at the hospital was calling him "Rick." Then just as Jeff was gaining self-confidence, Rick turned up alive! Monica was still in love with Rick and began an extramarital affair with him, hurting Jeff so terribly that he began to take amphetamines to gain confidence. After Jeff, under the influence of pills, shot himself, Rick broke off with Monica—since he saw her as the destructive and vicious schemer she was. Still, Monica continued to lie to Jeff and Rick to win Jeff back.

* * *

Dr. Steve Hardy and nurse Audrey Baldwin once again attempted a marriage—since, after all these years, they had never stopped loving each other. The day after their wedding, while they were honeymooning in Hawaii, they received the shocking news that Tom Baldwin, who was thought to have died in Mexico, arrived in Port Charles. This meant that Au-drey and Steve might not have been legally married. Even though their son, Tommy, insisted that Audrey and Tom reconcile, Tom Baldwin did grant Audrey a divorce and left town. A relieved Steve and Audrey settled happily into their new Port Charles house.

DR. MARK DANTE (Gerald Gordon), a brilliant neurosurgeon who had come to General Hospital to operate on Steve Hardy after a head injury that nearly killed him, found himself becoming entangled with the Webber family. Although he fell in love with Terri, he couldn't marry her because he was still married to MARY ELLEN or "MELLIE" (Lee Warrick), newly released from a sanitarium and under Dr. Peter Taylor's psychiatric care. Mark feared that if he asked Mellie for a divorce she would have another breakdown. When the deranged Mellie spotted Mark with Terri, she began a series of plots to murder poor Terri. Mellie was put back into an institution, but Mark still wouldn't marry Terri because he couldn't abandon his sick wife. Heartbroken, Terri left town. Some time afterward, Mellie died in an auto accident.

Mark also saved the life of Jeff Webber, Terri's brother, with his neurological skills, and found him-

Spoiled rich girl Tracy Quartermaine (Jane Elliot) worked hard to land and keep married politician Mitch Williams (Chris Pennock).

Bryan Phillips (Todd Davis) and Claudia Johnston (Bianca Ferguson) were originally friends of Scotty and Laura in 1979. Bryan was a reformed alcoholic who helped Lee Baldwin climb back on the wagon. Bryan and Claudia later married.

self trying to keep Monica from further hurting his patient Jeff. Meanwhile, a dangerously neurotic young girl, working as a domestic for Peter and Diana—named HEATHER GRANT (Georgann LaPiere, currently Robin Mattson)—fell in love with Jeff, and seduced him. After Jeff's recovery, Heather told him that she was carrying his child, but Jeff refused to consider divorcing Monica, with whom he was still passionately in love.

Desperate to be free of her situation, Heather at first tried to sell her baby, Steven Lars, to Peter and Diana Taylor; and then, when that failed, headed for New York with her baby, with dreams of becoming a model. When Jeff sued for custody of little Steven Lars, Heather, in need of money, again tried to sell her baby to Diana and Peter, this time anonymously. The Taylors had no idea that their newly adopted little son, whom they called P.J., was really Heather and Jeff's little boy. Heather told the unforgivable lie to Jeff that

his son had died! Newly drawn to Heather over the presumed loss of their son, Jeff, after divorcing Monica, asked Heather to come back to Port Charles with him as his wife.

Attempting to save his marriage to Lesley, Cameron Faulkner bribed the Vinings out of Port Charles. But Lesley's relationship with Cam began to deteriorate despite all of his plots. Unable now to win his wife's love back through further deceit, Cam forced himself on Lesley, then began to drive with her toward his cabin retreat. Lesley struggled with him and the car crashed, killing Cameron. Lesley later located her daughter Laura in a commune in Haverland, Canada, where a Charles Manson-type character sexually abused the girls.

Shortly after Cam died, Lesley discovered she was pregnant with his baby. In her hour of distress, Rick comforted her and the two fell in love. Monica had always loved Rick Webber and schemed to break up the relationship. However, after she became the cause of Lesley's tragic miscarriage, she promised to stop interfering. Rick and Lesley were finally wed and settled down with her daughter Laura.

DAVID HAMILTON (Jerry Ayres), an old college

The Luke and Laura frenzy started in late 1979 and continued for two years, making General Hospital *the top-rated show. Tony Geary and Genie Francis were idolized by six million teenagers.*

Gorgeous Jackie Zeman played trouble-making nurse Bobbie Spencer. She fell for her brother Luke's best friend, Roy DiLucca (Asher Brauner), who was involved with Luke in the underworld.

buddy of Rick's, moved in with Rick, Lesley and Laura. Secretly he hated Rick because David's late wife had loved him. He made advances to Lesley. When she rejected him, he turned to Laura, a teenager enchanted by the older, worldly man and let herself become entangled in a torrid love affair. When Rick found out about it, he ordered David to leave town. Laura, who had given her body to David, begged him to take her with him. Then she overheard him tell Lesley that he had only made love to Laura to make Lesley jealous. Laura was stunned. Confronting David, she threw a statue at him, causing him to hit his head on the hearth. A horrified Laura fled the apartment. Minutes later Lesley found David on the floor—dead! To save her daughter from jail, Lesley confessed to the murder and was indicted. Laura was so distressed that she blocked the whole death scene

Richard Dean Anderson played Rick's sensitive brother, Jeff Webber, who always made the wrong romantic choice. While his wife Heather was in an asylum, he took up with Audrey Hardy's niece, Anne Logan (Susan Pratt).

Richard Simmons headed a 1979 diet-exercise class in the Disco, as a backdrop for Luke and Laura's story. (He's shown here with Vanessa Brown as Mrs. DeFreest and Louise Hoven as Beverly De-Freest.) Simmons's appearances on Hospital *aided his sudden rise as America's number one diet guru.*

By 1980 Robin Mattson had the role of self-destructive Heather and Lieux Dressler played her ever-concerned mother, Alice Grant. Heather had to be committed after accidentally taking LSD.

from her mind and later ran away to New York without testifying at her mother's trial. Lesley was sent to prison.

Young Scotty Baldwin had been in love with Laura before her affair began with David and now, frantic with concern for her whereabouts, Scotty and his friend, BRYAN PHILLIPS (Todd Davis), went to New York to look for her. They found Laura involved in a drug and prostitution ring! Posing as street hustlers,

Scotty and Bryan rescued her and brought her back to Port Charles, where she finally confessed to killing David. Lesley was freed.

The whole Webber family suffered unendingly. Unable to rid herself of her guilt over lying to her husband Rick for so many months about David's true killer, Lesley could not have sexual relations with him. And Laura, who was sentenced to six month's probation under her mother's watchful eye, felt like a

The full 1980 cast included, from left, kneeling: Phillip Tanzini (Jeremy Hewitt Logan) and Bradley Green (Tommy Baldwin). Front row: Shell Kepler (Amy Vining), Eileen Dietz (Sarah Abbott), Bianca Ferguson (Claudia Johnston), Brooke Bundy (the new Diana Taylor), Genie Francis, Gail Rae Carlson (Susan Moore), Susan Pratt (Anne Logan), Emily McLaughlin, John Beradino, Rachel Ames, Loanne Bishop (Rose Kelly), Denise Alexander and Bob Hastings (Capt. Burt Ramsey). Second row: Todd Davis (Bryan Phillips), Lisa Lindgren (Kathy Summers), Frank Maxwell (Dan Rooney), Lieux Dressler (Alice Grant), Robin Mattson (Heather Webber), Richard Dean Anderson (Dr. Jeff Webber), Doug Sheehan (Joe Kelly), Pat Renella (Dr. Bernard Nelson), Tristan Rogers (Robert Scorpio), Chris Robinson (Dr. Rick Webber) and Richard Sarradet (Howard Lansing). Third row: Rick Moses (Hutch), Tony Geary (Luke Spencer), Anna Lee (Lila Quartermaine), Norma Connolly (Ruby Anderson) and Cherie Beasley (Shelly Vernon) [the row stops at Anderson]. Back row: Jacklyn Zeman (Bobbie Spencer), Susan Brown (Dr. Gail Baldwin), Stuart Damon (Dr. Alan Quartermaine) and David Lewis (Edward Quartermaine).

prisoner in her own home. Her only source of comfort was Scotty, who was still in love with her even though he had been having an affair on the rebound with a vivacious but golddigging student nurse named BOBBIE SPENCER (Jackie Zeman). To take up with Laura again, Scotty ended his affair with scheming Bobbie, only to be told that she was pregnant by him. That turned out to be a lie. Bobbie was determined to make Scotty marry her and she enlisted the aid of her brother, LUKE SPENCER (Tony Geary), a brash and street-wise young man with underworld connections but who was devoted to his family. In one vicious scheme after another, Luke helped his sister Bobbie in causing a rift between Scotty and Laura. Before long, however, Luke began to take an interest in Laura himself.

* * *

New arrivals in town were BEATRICE HEWITT (Anne Seymour) and her eleven-year-old orphaned grandson, JEREMY HEWITT (Philip Tanzini). Soon an epidemic of a fatal disease, Lassa Fever, swept through Port Charles, killing Mrs. Hewitt and many other residents, but mostly affecting the General Hospital staff. When Steve Hardy contracted the disease, Audrey, fearing he would die, told Jeff Webber the truth: that Steve, not Lars Webber, was his real father! Years ago Steve and

Helene Webber had had an affair and their child Jeff was born. Both Jeff and Rick were stunned by the news that they were only half-brothers. Steve eventually recovered and in time Jeff accepted Steve as his father. Meanwhile, the hospital was placed under quarantine, trapping Monica and Rick together for weeks until the disease carrier, who turned out to be young Jeremy, was discovered.

Monica had already married insecure and jealous DR. ALAN QUARTERMAINE (Stuart Damon), the son of wealthy EDWARD QUARTERMAINE (David Lewis) and LILA QUARTERMAINE (Anna Lee). Sensing that his wife Monica had been unfaithful with Rick, whom she had always loved, Alan Quartermaine undermined Rick's career at the hospital at every turn. Meanwhile, Rick Webber, still frustrated by Lesley's frigidity, returned Monica's interest and they had an extramarital affair. But just as he was about to leave Lesley for Monica, Rick learned that Lesley's daughter Laura had been in a serious car accident. Rick saved Laura's life and the emotional experience brought Rick and Lesley together again, while a frustrated Monica was forced to return to the sham of her marriage with Alan Quartermaine.

Monica soon learned that she was pregnant—

Grasping Monica married Alan Quartermaine (Stuart Damon), scion of wealthy Edward Quartermaine (David Lewis), for money and social position. For months Rick Webber was thought to be the father of Alan Jr. (Eric Kohl).

Rock star Rick Springfield originated the role of Dr. Noah Drake in 1981. Bobbie Spencer, in love with him, pretended to be blind to gain his sympathy.

with Rick's baby, she believed. One day, while Monica and Lesley were trapped by a blizzard, Monica deliriously shouted that the baby was Rick's. A shattered Lesley told Rick that she planned to divorce him. Rick now wanted to marry Monica and start a family with her and their baby. But Alan swore that if Monica ever tried to divorce him and embarrass him in the eyes of the world, he would use the Quartermaine fortune to take her child away from her.

Alan's spoiled and money-hungry sister, TRACY QUARTERMAINE (Jane Elliot), had wanted nothing better than for her brother and Monica to break up, for she wanted the Quartermaine fortune to go to her own son NED, not Alan and Monica's baby. Now Tracy began to try to prove that Monica's newborn baby, ALAN JR., was really fathered by Rick. As brother and sister battled each other, their mother Lila discovered an interesting fact: Alan Jr.'s birthmark looked exactly like Alan's. Monica was stunned! Further medical tests proved that Alan was really the father. At first Monica tried to keep the truth a secret from both Alan and Rick, but the truth came out and Rick, realizing that Monica was a heartless manipulator, went back to Lesley. Again, Monica had to face boredom with Alan.

* * *

Heather schemed to get her son back from the Taylors by driving Diana insane! Without realizing the danger, Diana had named Heather and Jeff baby P.J.'s legal guardians should anything happen to Diana and Peter. Heather began by making anonymous threatening phone calls to poor Diana. Peter hired private detective JOE KELLY (Doug Sheehan) to discover the caller's identity. At the same time, Steve Hardy also hired Joe Kelly to locate Steven Lars (P.J.!), who was, after all, his grandson. Still trying to drive Diana crazy, Heather spiked her drink with LSD, but accidentally ingested the drug herself. Now Heather went insane! Unable to bear Heather's cruel deceit any longer, her mother, ALICE GRANT (Lieux Dressler), told Peter that his son was none other than Steven Lars. The shock was too much for Peter, who suffered a heart attack and died. Dreadful Heather, now institutionalized, was responsible for the tragedy.

The widowed Diana became frantic that she would lose P.J. to his real father, Jeff Webber, and so began a campaign to try to marry him. Meanwhile, Heather, coming out of her LSD-induced psychosis, became suspicious that her husband was involved with another woman and fled the asylum. She spotted Jeff kissing nurse ANNE LOGAN (Susan Pratt), Audrey

Pretty Rose Kelly (Loanne Bishop) had been married to the late father of Joe Kelly (Doug Sheehan). The two shared a close relationship.

Conspirators three: Renee Anderson as Alexandria Quartermaine, Andre Landzaat as Anthony Cassadine and Thaao Penghlis as Victor Cassadine. They coveted the Ice Princess statue in 1981 as part of a strange plot to take over the world.

Hardy's pretty young niece, and swore to get even.

Diana Taylor was found murdered! On the floor beside her, written in her own blood, was scrawled the name "Anne." Jeff believed that unstable Heather had committed the heinous crime, intent on framing Anne. At first Jeff refused to let Heather near their son, and then finally he divorced Heather and left Port Charles with Steven Lars.

Heather was being investigated by detective Joe Kelly, who found strong evidence connecting her to Diana's murder. Finally Heather admitted that she had indeed intended to kill Diana the night of the murder, but she couldn't remember actually pulling the trigger of her gun. Joe Kelly, who was falling in love with Heather, now believed her innocent and eventually discovered that Heather's mother, Alice Grant, had killed Diana. It turned out that Alice had followed Heather to Diana's that awful night, saw Heather point a gun at Diana, then saw Diana pull out her own gun. Fearful that her daughter would be killed, Alice shot Diana. The judge senteced Heather to six-month's probation for attempted murder and, citing extenuating circumstances, set Alice free.

Teenagers Laura Vining and Scotty Baldwin were wed, but Laura soon realized that she had made a

Elizabeth Taylor made a week's appearance as Helena Cassadine and had a memorable scene with Tony Geary. Tabloids and fan magazines were sure the two would marry. In fact, Elizabeth and Tony did date.

mistake. She was really attracted to the far more interesting Luke Spencer and his unconventional life-style and offbeat friends. Luke, too, was drawn to Laura and her wholesomeness and innocence. Taking a job at the Campus Disco, which Luke managed for the mob, Laura had at first become wonderful friends with Luke. But soon their story took a dramatic turn when the mob elected Luke to perform a hit job on Tracy Quartermain's new husband, MITCH WILLIAMS (Chris Pennock), the corrupt assistant D.A. who was now running for governor and campaigning to crack down on organized crime. Luke surmised that he was soon about to die himself; if he didn't assassinate Mitch Williams the mob would kill Luke, and if he did kill Mitch he would hang for it. Tormented by his fate, Luke confessed to Laura the secret of his love for her and began kissing her passionately, tearing at her clothes, until she resisted. Then, on the floor of the disco, he raped her.

Afterwards, for reasons Laura didn't understand herself, Laura refused to name Luke as her attacker; while Luke, sensing her deep distress, begged her to name him as her rapist. Scotty, who knew only that his wife had been raped by a stranger, felt hurt when Laura refused to make love to him.

Back at the disco, the night of the hit arrived. It was to take place at Mitch Williams's election headquarters. When Laura finally learned what Luke was about to do, she tossed his car keys over the cliff. Hearing that Luke would be delayed, his best friend, ROY DI LUCCA (Asher Brauner), decided to take Luke's place, and was himself killed instead of Mitch. Luke's sister, Bobbie Spencer, had fallen in love with Roy and was shattered by the news.

Laura became personally implicated in these underworld doings. She was spotted overhearing a conversation between Luke's boss, FRANK SMITH (George Gaynes), and his henchmen. Laura now knew too much and was being watched by Frank's men. Meanwhile, Frank's daughter, JENNIFER SMITH (Lisa Marie), was attracted to Luke, who, pressured by Frank, was forced to propose marriage. Disheartened, Laura decided she had to make the best of her marriage to Scotty. But on the day of Luke and Jennifer's wedding aboard the Smith yacht, Scotty read a letter Laura had written to Luke and found out who her rapist was. Minutes before the wedding ceremony, Scotty beat up Luke, who fell overboard and was presumed drowned. Later, Laura discovered him on shore and the two fled Port Charles.

Frank Smith found out that Luke and Laura, before they left town, had stolen Smith's coded black book which, once uncoded, would detail all of his criminal activities and put him in jail for good. Frank became desperate to get the couple back into his clutches and tried one scheme after another to force them to return. He even severely beat Luke's kind-hearted aunt, RUBY ANDERSON (Norma Connolly), but failed to bring Luke out into the open. Finally, Frank sent a hit man named HUTCH (Rick Moses) after him. Meanwhile, Luke and Laura were having a glorious time while running for their lives. Although he was ready, she wasn't sure whether she wanted to break her marriage vows and make love to him, so Luke good-naturedly agreed to hold off.

The hit man Hutch found Luke and Laura and befriended them, secretly waiting for the right moment to dispatch the two. The three secured jobs in a local tavern, little suspecting that the owner of the tavern, SALLY (Chris Morley), was really a hit man named MAX in drag, sent by Smith to kill all three of them.

Luke decoded the black book—at last he had the goods on Smith and he and Laura could return to Port Charles. Suddenly, Laura was kidnapped by Sally Max, the hit man in drag. A shootout took place in which Hutch was critically wounded and Max killed. The black book was turned over to the police, the organization was broken up and Frank Smith was jailed. With the nightmare over, Luke and Laura returned to the farm where they had spent their happiest moments. Luke made advances to Laura and this time, sure of her feelings for him, she made love to him.

They returned triumphantly to Port Charles, but the sight of the reporters brought back the David Hamilton affair all over again. Pressed for a statement about her involvement with Luke, Laura blurted out that she was still Mrs. Scott Baldwin and had been faithful to her husband. Laura regretted what she said and was ready to ask Scotty for a divorce, but Luke, destroyed by her outburst, decided to part with Laura.

Scotty's father, Lee Baldwin, heard that his wife Caroline had died in a boating accident in Florida. He became involved with Monica's sympathetic confidante, DR. GAIL ADAMSON (Susan Brown), but turned to liquor again when she could'nt shake the memory of her late husband. With the help of Alcoholics Anonymous, Lee licked the problem and eventually married Gail. Lee also had problems with Scotty, who suddenly turned cynical and dishonest as a reaction to

Genie Francis is shown here in a scene with Sharon Wyatt as Tiffany Hill and Milton Berle, making a guest appearance as Mickey Miller in 1981. Tiffany had been the mistress of the deceased evil genius, Mikkos Cassadine.

Demi Moore, left, and Janine Turner played the Templeton sisters, Jackie and Laura in 1982. The Laura Templeton character was introduced as a kind of Laura lookalike to tease viewers after Genie Francis left the show.

his wife Laura running off with another man. Lee wanted Scotty to give Laura a divorce, but Scotty refused to let her go.

* * *

Edward Quartermaine's shrewd, beautiful niece, ALEXANDRIA QUARTERMAINE (Renee Anderson), arrived in town to work on a business deal with her uncle. However, she was really interested in locating an ugly little abstract black statue known as the Ice Princess, and she hired Luke Spencer to find it. Luke certainly didn't know what Alexandria knew, that the Ice Princess was not only the world's largest uncut diamond, but also contained the secret formula for the manufacture of synthetic diamonds. At the same time Laura began working as a receptionist at the Edward Louis Quartermaine Industries, where Luke also worked, although he wasn't ready yet to resume their affair. As Luke started digging for information on the Ice Princess, he was thwarted at every turn by several sinister characters, including TONY CASSADINE (Andre Landzaat) and ROBERT SCORPIO (Tristan Rogers). Soon Luke and Robert Scorpio, who secretly worked for the World Security Bureau, became good friends. Robert told Luke the truth about the statue and the formula

and that if the formula for synthetic diamonds fell into the hands of the infamous Cassadine Brothers, the Cassadines could control the world. Luke also learned that Alexandria Quartermaine had been in cahoots with them. A second Cassadine brother, VICTOR CASSADINE (Thaao Penghlis), arrived in Port Charles, and it was Victor who finally wound up with the statue.

Robert Scorpio found out that the Cassadines were about to set sail with the Ice Princess, and he and Luke stowed away on their yacht, the *Haunted Star*. Once on board they found another stowaway—Laura! She would not be parted from Luke. The yacht brought them all to the Cassadine's lush, tropical private island. The Cassadine brothers and their guests were lodged in a huge underground cavern, where they were joined by the eldest Cassadine brother, the evil genius MIKKOS CASSADINE (John Colicos). The stowaways, meanwhile, managed to find a hiding place on the island. Mikkos revealed his master plan: with the formula now in his possession, he could manufacture a substance with the ability to alter the climates of the world! Back on the surface, Luke and Laura were enjoying their tropical paradise, while Scorpio found his way underground with the help of Victor's mistress,

An interesting outcome of the Luke and Laura romance was that Scotty Baldwin (still Kin Shriner) became a bearded villain. After Laura abandoned him for the older Luke, he turned toward insidious greed instead of love. He plays opposite Leonard Stone as Packy Moore.

Luke's new 1982 romance, after Laura disappeared into a fog, was with Holly Sutton (Emma Samms), who was at first in cahoots with her father, Charles Sutton (Mark Roberts, left) to con Luke and his friends. Warwick Sims played henchman Basil Durban, alias Basil Corso.

beautiful actress TIFFANY HILL (Sharon Wyatt). She was horrified by Mikkos's plan. As the four concocted a way to stop the Cassadines, Mikkos gave the head of the World Security Bureau an ultimatum: surrender to him now or he would freeze the major cities of the world, starting with Port Charles! To do just that, Mikkos had invented a terrifying machine. In the end, Luke and Scorpio were able to turn the evil freezing machine back on Mikkos himself, freezing Mikkos, Alexandria Quartermaine and Tony Cassadine all to death! Victor was jailed, and the world was now safe from the Cassadines.

Luke, Laura and Robert Scorpio returned to Port Charles, along with Tiffany Hill, who found Robert quite attractive. Laura learned that Scotty, now living in Mexico, had agreed to give her an uncontested divorce and so she and Luke were free to marry at last. All of Port Charles turned out for Luke and Laura's storybook wedding, even the mayor. The happy occasion was marred, however, by the appearance of Mikkos Cassadine's vengeful widow, HELENA CASSADINE (Elizabeth Taylor), who put a curse on Luke and Laura for having killed Mikkos. Scotty also showed up at the wedding and tried to spoil things, but to no avail. The couple, deliriously happy, were wed. After their honeymoon, Luke and Laura settled down to a quiet life aboard *The Haunted Star*, the Cassadine yacht which had been given to Luke as a gift. Soon, though, their idyll ended when Laura won the title of Miss Star Eyes, which made her the representative of a cosmetics firm and required that she shuttle back and forth between Port Charles and a photographer's studio in New York. During those journeys, she became uncomfortably aware of a strange man named DAVID GRAY (Paul Rossilli) who wore a bewitching sapphire ring and seemed to be following her. One night Laura returned to Port Charles earlier than expected and found the yacht empty. Alarmed, Laura ran onto the foggy dock. She suddenly noticed David Gray following her. As he held up his sapphire ring, Laura screamed and ran off into the night. She had disappeared! Helena Cassadine's curse had worked.

Luke returned to the dock and began a frantic search for Laura. For a moment he thought he saw her standing there, but when the girl turned around he saw that it was someone who only looked like her, named LAURA TEMPLETON (Janine Turner). Soon the second Laura disappeared! Laura Templeton's sister, JACKIE (Demi Moore), arrived in Port Charles and teamed up with Luke and Scorpio to locate the missing two Lauras. Eventually they found out that Laura Templeton and her photographer boyfriend, MEL WILSON (Dawson Mays), were mixed up in a bizarre plot concocted by the sinister David Gray. A priceless exhibition was coming to Port Charles and David Gray planned to steal the most valuable pieces from the collection, using Mel's invention, a holistic lens which beamed three-dimensional images of seeming real objects. These exhibition pieces were vital to his plan to overthrow the government of a small (fictional) foreign country, Malkuth. Meanwhile, a pendant Luke had given his Laura turned up in Port Charles as part of the wreckage of a small cabin cruiser that was lost at sea. A raincoat was also found, which Lesley identified as her daughter Laura's. Luke now believed that Laura had died on the cruiser and held David Gray responsible. In a life and death struggle with him, Luke finally recovered the stolen treasures of Malkuth and David was killed.

* * *

Lucille Wall came back to the show for a one-day appearance in 1982, greeting fellow "regulars" Emily McLaughlin, John Beradino, Peter Hansen and Rachel Ames. Her character, Lucille March Weeks, has retired to a farm in upstate New York.

Pretty Bobbie Spencer fell in love with DR. NOAH DRAKE (Rick Springfield), a quiet young man to whom women were attracted. Constantly jealous of Noah, who was unable to tell Bobbie he loved her, Bobbie pretended to be blind, hoping to arouse his love. The deception backfired and a depressed Bobbie left town. Then, many months later, she returned, only to find that Noah was involved with Tiffany Hill, Victor Cassadine's ex-mistress. Tiffany smoldered as Noah began to see more of Bobbie, but the cat fight was to no avail—Noah left *General Hospital.*

Heather's social-climbing, scheming cousin, SUSAN MOORE (Gail Rae Carlson), tried to break up several of Port Charles's wealthiest marriages in her relentless pursuit of money. Tracy Quartermaine learned of her husband Mitch's affair with Susan, and used her money and power to win him back. They moved to Albany, out of Susan's reach. Then Susan won the favor of rich and very married Alan Quartermaine. In return for becoming his mistress, Alan agreed to help her purchase the Campus Disco. When Susan learned that she was pregnant with Alan's child, she ran off to New York to have her baby in secret. Alan pursued her, brought her and her baby Jason back to Port Charles and moved in with them. However, he was afraid to sue Monica for divorce for fear she would gain custody of their son, Alan Jr. Alan's love tryst with Susan Moore abruptly ended when Alan found himself impotent, for Alan had simply become bored with Susan. After Alan moved back with Monica, Susan enlisted unscrupulous Scotty Baldwin as her lawyer and sued Alan, winning a million dollars. Alan, however, remained unscathed, for he now had Monica's love for the first time; but Susan had nothing but her money and turned to alcohol. Meanwhile, her vicious cousin, Heather, slept with Scotty and plotted with him to take control of little Jason's inheritance. Attempting to have Susan declared an unfit mother, they encouraged her drinking. Scotty, as part of the plan, made Susan believe he loved her, while he was really interested in Laura Templeton, who resembled his first wife. When Susan spotted Scotty and Laura Templeton together, she tried to commit suicide. Scotty saw this as his chance to control Jason's inheritance. While Susan lay fighting for her life, Scotty married her! Laura Templeton left town and soon Scotty and Heather fought a desperate battle over Jason's wealth. Finally, Alice Grant gained custody.

Trying to forget his Laura, Luke went on an extended vacation and became attracted to an exquisite English girl named HOLLY SUTTON (Emma Samms). As he made passionate love to her, Luke had no idea that she was setting him up as a mark in a big oil scam, planned by CHARLES SUTTON (Mark Roberts), her father, and the DURBAN family, a small-time crime ring who were also Holly's blood relatives. With Luke's help, Holly and her father got most of Port Charles to invest in a bogus oil well. But after the Durbans, Holly's own people, had tried to commit murder, Holly had second thoughts about her involvement, especially since she had fallen in love with Luke. Holly confessed all to him and soon after that the Durbans had her kidnapped. Playing detectives again, best friends Luke and Scorpio tracked her to British Columbia and rescued her, but her peril continued when, after she came back to Port Charles, Holly was arrested as an accessory to attempted murder. All seemed grim until her father, Charles Sutton, confessed on his deathbed to his own guilt and his daughter's innocence. Holly was free.

Dr. Mark Dante had discovered that the wife of a wealthy new patient of his, LAMONT CORBIN (William Bryant), was none other than his old childhood sweetheart, KATIE (Maggie Sullivan). Mark and Katie fell in love again and when Lamont found out, he threatened Katie with ruining Mark's medical career unless Katie gave him up. Katie had no choice. But then Lamont died, and she and Mark were wed at last and left the country. Some time afterward, Mark, now a widower, came back to General Hospital and fell in love with pretty young ROSE KELLY (Loanne Bishop), who had been married to Joe Kelly's late father, PADDY KELLY (Frank Parker). The May-December relationship seemed headed for trouble. Meanwhile, Joe Kelly, who had fallen out of love with Heather when he realized that she was compulsively promiscuous, left Port Charles to take a job in Albany.

CAST

GENERAL HOSPITAL
ABC: April 1, 1963–

Dr. Steve Hardy	John Beradino (P)
Jessie Brewer	Emily McLaughlin (P)
Dr. Phil Brewer	Roy Thinnes (P)
	Robert Hogan

	Craig Huebing
	Ricks Falk
	Martin West*
Angie Costello Weeks ..	Jana Taylor (P)
Eddie Weeks	Craig Curtis (P)
	Doug Lambert*
Al Weeks	Tom Brown (P)
Mrs. Weeks	Lenore Kingston (P)
Mike Costello	Ralph Manza (P)
Janet Fleming	Ruth Phillips (P)
Fred Fleming	Simon Scott (P)
Priscilla Longworth ...	Allison Hayes (P)
Peggy Mercer	K.T. Stevens (P)
Philip Mercer	Neil Hamilton (P)
Dr. Ken Martin	Hunt Powers (a.k.a. Jack Betts) (P)
Cynthia Allison	Carolyn Craig (P)
Roy Lansing	Robert Clarke (P)
	Liam Sullivan*
Lee Baldwin	Peter Hansen*
	Ross Elliott
Lucille March Weeks ...	Lucille Wall*
	Mary Grace Canfield
Audrey March Hardy ...	Rachel Ames
Randy Washburn	Mark Miller
Dorothy Bradley	Susan Seaforth
Meg Bentley Baldwin ..	Patricia Breslin
	Elizabeth McRae
Brooke Bentley Clinton	Adrienne Hayes
	Indus Arthur
Noll Clinton	Ron Husmann
	Dean Harens
Dr. Tom Baldwin	Paul Savior*
	Don Chastain
Scotty Baldwin	Johnnie Whittaker
	Teddy Quinn
	Tony Campo
	Don Clarke
	Johnny Jensen
	Kin Shriner*
Polly Prentice	Catherine Ferrar
	Jennifer Billingsley*
Dr. John Prentice	Barry Atwater
Chase Murdock	Ivan Bonar
Judy Clampett	Robin Blake
Jane Harland Dawson ..	Shelby Hiatt
Howie Dawson	Ray Girardin
Mrs. Dawson	Maxine Stuart
	Phyllis Hill*

Sharon McGillis Pinkham	Sharon DeBord
Dr. Henry Pinkham	Peter Kilman
Hank Pinkham	Maurice Manson
Iris Fairchild	Peggy McCay
Denise Wilton	Julie Adams
Beverly Cleveland	Sue Bernard
Dr. Tracy Adams	Kim Hamilton
Dr. Peter Taylor	Paul Carr
	Craig Huebing*
Diana Maynard Taylor ..	Valerie Starrett*
	Brooke Bundy
Mary Briggs	Anne Helm
Dr. Lesley Williams Webber	Denise Alexander
Dr. Jim Hobart	James Sikking
Teddy Holmes	James Westmoreland
	John Gabriel
Carol Murray	Anne Wyndham
Kent Murray	Mark Hamill
Mark Simpson	Gary Frank
Augusta McLeod	Judith McConnell
Gordon Bradford Grey .	Howard Sherman*
	Eric Server
Florence Grey	Anne Collings
Wyatt Chamberlain	Edward Platt
Dr. Joel Stratton	Barry Coe
	Rod McCary*
Kira Faulkner	Victoria Shaw
Cameron Faulkner	Don Matheson
Mai-Lin	Virginia Ann Lee
Ling Wong	George Chiang
Hayes Colman	Frank Aletter
Owen Stratton	Joel Marston
Ross Jeanelle	Tony Dow
Beth Maynard	Michele Conaway
Margaret Colson	Betty Anne Rees
Felix Buchanan	Mark Travis
Mac McLoughlin	Bert Douglas
Carolyn Chandler Baldwin	Augusta Dabney
Bobby Chandler	Ted Eccles
Samantha Livingstone Chandler	Kimberly Beck
	Marla Pennington*
Laura Vining Spencer ..	Stacy Baldwin
	Genie Francis*
Barbara Vining	Judy Lewis
Jason Vining	Jonathan Carter

	Richard Rust	Tracy Quartermaine	
Amy Vining	Cari Ann Warder	Williams	Jane Elliot
	Shell Kepler*	Dan Rooney	Frank Maxwell
Dr. Kyle Bradley	Daniel Black	Bobbie Spencer	Jacklyn Zeman
Kate Marshall	Monica Gayle	Howard Lansing	Richard Sarradet
Pat Lambert	Laura Campbell	Susan Moore	Gail Rae Carlson
Sally Grimes	Jenny Sherman	Bryan Phillips	Todd Davis
Terri Arnett	Bobbi Jordan	Claudia Johnston	
Dr. Rick Webber	Michael Gregory	Phillips	Bianca Ferguson
	Chris Robinson*	Capt. Burt Ramsey	Bob Hastings
Dr. Jeff Webber	Richard Dean Anderson	Cal Jamison	Larry Block
Dr. Monica Webber		Beatrice Hewitt	Anne Seymour
Quartermaine	Patsey Rahn	Jeremy Hewitt Logan . .	Philip Tanzini
	Leslie Charleson*	Anne Logan	Susan Pratt
Peggy Lowell	Deanna Lund	Coleen Middleton	Joyce Jameson
Heather Grant Webber .	Georganne LaPiere	Mitch Williams	Christopher Pennock
	Mary O'Brien	Luke Spencer	Tony Geary
	Robin Mattson*	Spence Andrews	Dan Travanti
Alice Grant	Camila Ashland	Jonelle Andrews	Mary Ann Mobley
	Lieux Dressler*	Roy DiLucca	Asher Brauner
Elizabeth Maynard	Joan Tompkins	Beverly DeFreest	Louise Hoven
Dr. Mark Dante	James York	Mrs. DeFreest	Vanessa Brown
	Michael Delano	Joe Kelly	Doug Sheehan
	Gerald Gordon*	Ruby Anderson	Norma Connolly
Mary Ellen Dante	Lee Warrick	Zelda Bernstein	Sarah Simmons
Dr. Gina Dante Lansing .	Anna Stuart*	Frank Smith	George Gaynes
	Brenda Scott	Jennifer Smith Spencer .	Lisa Marie
	Donna Bacalla	Stella Fields	Jeff Donnell
Dr. Adam Streeter	Brett Halsey	Pop Snyder	Milton Selzer
Jill Streeter	Karen Purcil	Rose Kelly	Loanne Bishop
Dr. Gail Adamson		Paddy Kelly	Frank Parker
Baldwin	Susan Brown	Mike	David Mendenhall
Tommy Baldwin Hardy .	David Comfort	Hutch Hutchins	Rick Moses
	Bradley Green*	Sarah Abbott	Eileen Dietz
	David Walker	Kathy Summers	Lisa Lindgren
Larry Joe Baker	Peter D. Greene	Dr. Noah Drake	Rick Springfield
	Scott Mulhern	Alexandria	
	Hunter Von Leer	Quartermaine	Renee Anderson
Jason Craig	Ivor Francis	Robert Scorpio	Tristan Rogers
Dr. Gary Lansing	Steve Carlson	O'Reilly	Billie Hayes
Dorrie Fleming	Angela Cheyne	Slick Jones	Eddie Ryder
David Hamilton	Jerry Ayres	Emma Lutz	Merrie Lynn Ross
Lana Holbrook	Janice Heiden	Charles Lutz	Ken Smolka
Kathryn Corbin Dante .	Maggie Sullivan	James Duvall	Arthur Roberts
Lamont Corbin	George E. Carey	Anthony Cassadine	Andre Landzatt
	William Bryant*	Victor Cassadine	Thaao Penghlis
Dr. Alan Quartermaine .	Stuart Damon	Mikkos Cassadine	John Colicos
Lila Quartermaine	Anna Lee	Helena Cassadine	Elizabeth Taylor
Edward Quartermaine .	David Lewis	Mickey Miller	Milton Berle

Tiffany Hill	Sharon Wyatt
Dr. Arthur Bradshaw . . .	Martin E. Brooks
Delfina	Nita Talbot
Dr. Vivian Collins	Marie Windsor
Jackie Templeton	Demi Moore
Laura Templeton	Janine Turner
Blackie Parrish	John Stamos
Johnny Morrissey	Miles McNamara
Packy Moore	Leonard Stone
David Gray	Paul Rossilli
Mel Wilson	Dawson Mays
Ambassador Tabris	Henry Darrow
The Magus	Peter Breck
George Durnley	Paul Comi
Anthony Hand	John Warner Williams
Holly Sutton	Emma Samms
Charles Sutton	Mark Roberts
Basil Durban	Warwick Sims
Reginald Durban	George Lazenby
Eddie Phillips	Sammy Davis, Jr.
Flora Johnston	Fran Bennett
Harve Johnston	Vince Howard
Louisa Swenson	Danielle von Zerneck
Constance Townley	Jeanna Michaels
Jimmy Lee Holt	Steve Bond
Celia Quartermaine Putnam	Sherilyn Wolter
Dr. Grant Putnam	Brian Patrick Clarke
Natalie Dearborn	Melinda Cordell
Jake Meyer	Sam Behrens
D.L. Brock	David Groh
Shirley Pickett	Roberta Leighton
Gregory Malko	Joseph Lambie
Ralph Fletcher	Edwin Owens
Dr. Hector Jerrold	Booth Colman

Creators: Frank & Doris Hursley

Head Writers: Theodore & Mathilde Ferro, Frank & Doris Hursley, Bridget & Jerome Dobson, Richard & Suzanne Holland, Eileen & Robert Mason Pollock, Irving & Tex Elman, Douglas Marland, Pat Falken Smith, Robert J. Shaw, Joyce & John William Corrington, Anne Howard Bailey

Story Editors: A.J. Russell, Gordon Russell

Executive Producer (first few months): Selig Seligman

Producers: Gene Banks, James Young, Tom Donovan, Gloria Monty

Co-Producer (for Monty): Jerry Balme

Directors: James Young, Ken Herman, Jr., Phil Sogard, Lamar Caselli, Ross Bowman, Peter Levin, Marlena Laird, Alan Pultz, Jim Drake, Rudy Vejar

Organist: Kip Walton, George Wright

Musical Directors (later): Jack Urbont, Charles Paul

Packagers: Selmur Productions, ABC-TV

THE GUIDING LIGHT

THE GUIDING LIGHT has been on daytime television for thirty-two years, making it one of the oldest soaps in the medium. But if one takes into account its early years on radio, the show would today be forty-seven years old and *the* longest currently running soap opera. Although the tendency for most soaps that are more than twenty years old is to lose their audiences to younger, newer shows, *The Guiding Light* regained its vitality in 1977 when it went to a full hour and is today Procter & Gamble's second most popular soap. (*As The World Turns* has usually been the sponsor's highest rated.) That is quite fitting, for *The Guiding Light* represents the whole panoply of soap opera history. Before we look at the more recent show and the story line summary for forty-four years, let's take a brief look at the early days.

BACKGROUND

Imagine Irna Phillips—who died on December 23, 1973 after fifty years of achievement in radio and television broadcasting—as a smart looking, career-oriented young woman who was one of the two creative centers of a whole new form of entertainment. Imagine a swarm of actors, producers, directors and New York advertising executives descending on post-Depression Chicago in 1937, all getting in on a runaway new daytime radio product that had mysteriously developed there. Imagine dozens of radio-studio rooms abuzz with twenty-five daytime soap operas: actors huddling around live microphones with scripts in hand; sound effects men simulating doorbells and footfalls; organists sounding ominous chords; announcers waxing ecstatic over detergents, as stories were broadcast daily to forty million radio consoles, while housewives listened.

When *The Guiding Light* began on January 25, 1937, new fifteen-minute serials were starting as fast as writers could dream them up. In the twelve months preceding, fifteen shows were launched, including *Pepper Young's Family, John's Other Wife, Big Sister, Bachelor's Children* and *Aunt Jenny's True Life Stories*. From the start *The Guiding Light* was produced by the Compton Advertising Agency for Procter & Gamble, which did not then own the show but merely leased it from its creator, Irna Phillips. Listeners who had their radios tuned to the NBC Red network always knew when they were about to hear another episode of *The Guiding Light* by those opening dramatic organ chords from Goetzl's *Aphrodite*.

In the beginning, Irna had not thought of the Bauer family, which came later on in the late 1940s. Originally, *The Guiding Light* was about the life of Dr. Rutledge, pastor of a church in the city of Five Points (Anywhere, U.S.A.), and the lives of the members of his family and parish. The show had a rather religious tone, with a theme that faith brings happiness. Whole episodes were frequently devoted to a single sermon by Dr. Rutledge. In fact, this minister had given so

210

many sermons on the show that they were eventually published in a book that sold 290,000 copies. Each year on Good Friday Dr. Rutledge would give the traditional Good Friday message, "Seven Last Words," which was repeated on the show, year after year, even after the Rutledges were gone and the Bauers had replaced them. In a way, *The Guiding Light* has always been "a religious" story—minister or no minister—for its core families have always displayed faith and togetherness.

The original cast on the show was as follows:

ARTHUR PETERSON (Dr. John Rutledge)
RUTH BAILEY (Rose Kransky)
MERCEDES MCCAMBRIDGE (Mary Rutledge)
ED PRENTISS, later JOHN HODIAK (Ned Holden)
GLADYS HEEN (Torchy Reynolds)
RAYMOND EDWARD JOHNSON (Mr. Nobody from Nowhere)

The Guiding Light of those days, like most of the radio soaps of the thirties, would strike us today as obvious and unsophisticated. There would be more organ music connected with each episode than a band of angels could endure, plus the endless cash-prize giveaways that required the purchase and label-cutting of four or five boxes of Procter & Gamble soap. The stories themselves, although often inspirational, were painfully slow and simple. Each day the announcer would introduce the story with a long statement that framed the characters and situations for viewers. In the late thirties an episode of *The Guiding Light* (this one dealing with one of its many subplots) would begin thusly:

Organ Music.

ANNOUNCER: *The Guiding Light.*

More organ music.

ANNOUNCER: The country's biggest-selling laundry soap brings you (*sound of a cash register*) the biggest contest in value of cash and prizes any soap has ever offered.

More organ music.

ANNOUNCER: Well, friends, here's wonderful news for you—
WOMAN: Just a minute. If you say one more word about all those people who won all that money in your contest I'll just—I'll—well, I don't know what I'll do!

ANNOUNCER: You sound as if you're jealous.
WOMAN: I'm plenty jealous. I'd like to win some of that big money myself. But I forgot all about entering . . .
ANNOUNCER: Now don't worry . . . here's good news for you. Starting today, another big P&G Soap contest gets under way. And again, a thousand-dollar bill, five five-hundred-dollar bills and fifty Electrolux refrigerators must be won this week!
WOMAN: Wonderful!
ANNOUNCER: Now remember, just add twenty-five words or less to the statement "I like P&G Soap because . . ."
WOMAN: I like the way P&G helps cut grease on dishes and gravy. P&G is so economical, and yet my yellowish-looking sheets and tablecloths turn out a clear, snowy white!
ANNOUNCER: Well, everyday experiences like that can win. All you have to do is finish the statement "I like P&G Soap because . . ." and send it along with four P&G Soap wrappers to *The Guiding Light*, Cincinnati, Ohio. Entries judged for sincerity, originality, and aptness of thought. Judges' decision final.

More organ music.

ANNOUNCER: And now . . . *The Guiding Light* . . . (*announcer softens voice*) There are times in our lives when we seem to have lost all sense of direction, all sense of identity, when we as individuals seem suspended in midair . . . when living seems hopeless, without objective. It was an apathetic, listless young woman who returned to her apartment in San Francisco this morning. Not even the flowers that had been sent by Martin Kane on her arrival seemed to arouse her from a feeling of detachment. Not even during the rehearsal at the studio later in the day, or during her evening broadcast, was she aroused from the almost dead sadness that had taken possession of her.

Martin Kane, sensitive to the mood of the young woman, suggested that they go to a quiet restaurant right after the broadcast. Seated across the table from the girl whom he hopes someday to marry, he suddenly loses patience with her apparent disinterest in him, and says—
MARTIN: Snap out of it, Mona.
MONA: Is there anything to snap out of, Martin?

MARTIN: It seems to me there is . . . look here, you're not being very fair.

MONA: You don't think so?

MARTIN: No, I don't.

MONA: I told you that I preferred to go home right after my broadcast. I told you that I pouted. You insisted that I needed a little recreation. I really wanted to go home.

MARTIN: Don't you think you owe a little something to your friends?

MONA: At this moment I don't feel anything. I haven't since I got back.

MARTIN: Your divorce . . . it did that to you?

MONA: I don't want to talk about the divorce. It's over.

MARTIN: But not as far as you're concerned.

MONA: Please believe me, Martin, it's over as far as I'm concerned. As far as everyone is concerned. And I don't want to talk about it.

MARTIN: Don't you think you can rouse yourself from your own thoughts long enough to at least be . . . well, human . . . to someone who's trying to help you over a rather tough spot.

MONA: It's very nice of you to help me over what you believe is a tough spot. But the tough spot is in your imagination. Oh, Martin, I get constantly out of patience with you. You make me feel that I have to be on the alert, constantly enthusiastic . . . you want me to be something I'm not. Just because you want it to be that way . . .

* * *

By no stretch of the imagination could this be considered a well-written scene. It is excruciatingly slow, somewhat unreal and ponderously makes the single point that Mona is depressed after her divorce and that Martin Kane cares for her. But you should hear, rather than merely read, this old excerpt from *The Guiding Light*. Somehow the enthusiastic announcer, all the churchy commentary from the organist, that wordy opening statement setting a mood and the actors' breathy reading of sudsy dialogue all combine to transcend the obvious literal flaws. Within minutes you are captured by the intimacy. The hushed way Martin and Mona are talking takes hold of your imagination. You feel as if you are eavesdropping. Instantly you understand how twenty million housewives were involved in a radio show that had so little polish.

A few years after *The Guiding Light* began, it was

moved to Hollywood and then, in 1949, to New York, as were many radio serials. Once In New York, the whole show was revamped, and the Rutledge family was replaced by the Bauer clan. They included Papa and Mama Bauer, their son Bill (called Willie), and daughters Trudy and Meta. The Bauers were first- and second-generation German-Americans who managed to stay together despite many adversities. They believed in the old-fashioned virtues of love and marriage and of doing whatever was best for one's children. In effect, Dr. Rutledge's religious beliefs were being tested on an everyday basis by the Bauer family.

When the Bauers came on, the show's locale was moved from Five Points to Selby Flats, a mythical suburb of Los Angeles (inspired by the show's move from Chicago to Hollywood). In fact, that's how Cedars Hospital—where Ed Bauer, Justin Marler and all their doctor friends in the city of Springfield now practice medicine—came into being. Cedars Hospital was supposed to remind people of the famous Cedars of Lebanon Hospital in Los Angeles, and it was later miraculously relocated in Springfield (Anywhere, U.S.A.), where the characters in the story moved some time after the show made the transition to television.

All these moves were effected by the writers and producers for one reason alone: to give the characters bigger, more urban settings to move around in. Ten years after the premiere, listeners still heard the announcer proclaim the same serial title, but everything else about the show—with the exception of its underlying theme of family togetherness, which has always been the same—had changed. The organ music was shortened to a few brief chords; there were no more big-money prizes, only a curt message from the sponsor; and the plots were now rather "adult," dealing with insanity, morbid deaths, drawn-out tragedies, disastrous love affairs and unwanted pregnancies.

* * *

In 1950, well after the radio show had made its stylistic transition, Charita Bauer joined the fictional Bauer family as Bert Bauer, Bill Bauer's young wife. (It was a mere coincidence that her own last name and her character's were the same.) She is still on the show, thirty-four years later and, along with Mary Stuart and Larry Haines of *Search for Tomorrow*, has the distinction of being one of the three actors who have remained in their soap opera roles longest. At the time she came on *The Guiding Light*, she had already played every conceivable kind of heroine and heavy on radio soaps like *Young Widder Brown, Just Plain Bill, Rose of My Dreams* and *Ma Perkins*. "There were so many I couldn't remember them all. I remember that I used to love to play sexy gun molls and criminals. It was more fun to be mean." As she sits in her New York living room discussing her years on *The Guiding Light*, she displays a perky smile—the same one that she must have had when she was a child actress on the stage. Moments later the expression changes to mature interest.

"When I first came on *The Guiding Light*, the show had just moved to New York from Hollywood, like so many of the other ones. Our show was fun in those days. It seems to me it was more colorful. We were on radio, and so you used your imagination more when you heard the show than you do today. Our writers weren't confined to specific sets, and actors didn't have to look their parts. Today it seems that more happened on the old radio program—but then, I don't know. The past always seems to be more interesting than the present, somehow." Of course, when Charita played a young wife in her early days with the show, she got involved in more complex and dramatic entanglements than she does today, playing essentially a "recap" character: Bert Bauer, the middle-aged head of the Bauer family, who usually now only sympathizes when her relatives and friends get into trouble.

"I was only on a few years before the producer told us that we'd be going on television. Our first day was June 30, 1952. We were all so happy and excited. For the first time people would see what we looked like—instead of just hearing our voices—and we were going to make more money, since we would still be doing the radio show at the same time. In the morning I'd go over to Liederkrantz Hall to do the live TV show, and later, at a quarter to two, I'd rush across town to read the same script for the live radio show. For four years we did this! If you missed a show on television, you could catch it the same day on radio.

"Naturally television was a lot more work. In radio, you just read your script in front of a microphone after a few hours of rehearsal. In television you had to memorize all your lines, and to do just one show on the air took a whole half day. When the show went to television, we were directed by Ted Corday, and most of the radio cast came right onto TV. On TV we were produced by Dave Lesan. Jone Allison left after six

months and was replaced by Ellen Demming as Meta; and after a few years on television Ed Bryce replaced Lyle Sudrow as Bill. But of course Theo Goetz was still Papa Bauer. We really were a tightly knit little group then—much more than today. We used to help each other out in so many ways. Now there are just too many actors on the show for your relationship with them to be that close. But there's always been a good feeling among the actors."

In 1956 the radio segment was discontinued, four years before the last radio soaps faded into oblivion. "I was sad when the radio show stopped. It was the end of an era—and besides, we were going to lose that extra forty dollars a show!"

Little Michael Bauer was born shortly before the show went to television. While Charita was still playing the pregnant Bert Bauer, she went to Irna Phillips and asked her if the child was to be a boy or a girl. The show's writer said it was to be a boy. Then Charita asked if Irna wouldn't make life a whole lot simpler for Charita by naming the new arrival Michael. Her own son, Michael, had just been born and Charita was afraid of becoming confused over the names of her two children. Irna agreed and (the fictional) Michael Bauer received his name.

Charita now shuts her eyes and thinks back, and a warm smile comes to her lips as she remembers one story in particular concerning her two sons. "Glenn Walken [he's now called Christopher Walken, the movie star] played the first Michael on the TV show. He was only seven years old, and my Michael was six. Now, my Michael had seen Glenn on television, and he knew that the little boy had the same name in the story and how he'd gotten the name, and it didn't seem to bother him much. One day I took my son on a shopping trip to Best and Company and we ran into little Glenn Walken and his mother. We stopped and talked for a while, and then I started home with Michael. He suddenly grew very quiet. 'What's the matter, dear?' I said. Then he said 'Mommy, who do you love more—the real Michael or the make-believe Michael?' I was stunned. 'You, darling! Of course I love you more!' I've never forgotten that; I was just so touched. I guess finally seeing Glenn Walken in person suddenly made the other Michael seem real."

After thirty-four years of work on a serious soap opera, Charita recalls occasions on the live show that were not so serious. "One Thanksgiving we were supposed to be at Meta's and we were all sitting around the dining table. Ted Corday, our director, wanted the camera to pan around Theo Goetz's head, but there was just no way of doing it without Theo coming into the camera lens. Ted told Theo, 'Could you slip under the table and then come back after the camera pans.' Ellen Demming was convulsed, but Ted, who didn't always have such a great sense of humor, didn't think it was funny. I remember Theo would roll his eyes when he went under the table . . . And then there was the time when Susan Douglas was pregnant, but her character, Kathy, wasn't. She had to be shot from the shoulders up or while seated. But invariably the director would decide to take her in full profile, and he'd ask her, 'Could you hold your tummy in?' . . . I remember once Ted Corday, who died ten years ago, went wild because he kept hearing some strange clock ticking all the way through a scene during dress rehearsal. It turned out that the crew was just playing a joke on Ted. Ted didn't laugh."

* * *

Like all long-lived soaps, *The Guiding Light* has had its share of declines in story quality and poor ratings, but the show, mostly because of the dedication of the Compton Advertising Agency and Procter & Gamble, has always made gallant comebacks. In the early seventies, there was a good deal of hand-wringing at both companies over a prolonged period of weakness in the show, which went deep into its structure. In an attempt to preserve the original theme of old-fashioned family virtues, the writers found themselves contrasting the wholesome togetherness of the Bauers with unstable, eccentric behavior in characters outside the family, like Ken Norris and Roger Thorpe. For newer, younger viewers who were responding to the youthful fantasies on *The Young and The Restless, The Guiding Light* seemed a little arch. In 1975 Bridget and Jerome Dobson took over as head writers and began struggling with the hard problem of how to update the show without destroying its center. By 1977, when it went to an hour, the Dobsons had created an appealing glamorous structure around the Bauers, incorporating all the new, trendy elements: Young Love (Ben and Amanda), amoral wealthy people (the Spauldings) and characters involved in intricate sexual fantasies (the Marlers). While injecting youth and glamor into the story, the Dobsons also brought back the old presumed-dead character of Bill Bauer, as a way of counteracting all the new razzle-dazzle with something that reminded viewers of the past. But those same loyal fans who remembered the old show objected to Bill's being portrayed as a weakling, and the writers quickly eliminated the character.

The Dobsons had thoroughly revived *The Guiding Light* (part of the change was renaming the show to just *Guiding Light*), keeping it fresh for viewers during that critical period when many older soaps were being streamrollered by ABC competition, especially *General Hospital*. In 1980, P&G made a clever move, fighting fire with fire. It hired Doug Marland as the head writer after he had been dismissed as the head writer of *General Hospital* (following a dispute with Gloria Monty). He then continued the Dobsons stories and introduced the poor Reardon family and the wealthy Chamberlains, and generally gave more weight to younger story lines, such as the Kelly Nelson/Morgan Richards love story, which brought the show into consistent third place behind *General Hospital*.

Like most soaps, *The Guiding Light* has had many elaborate location sequences in the past few years, including Santo Domingo (where Roger Thorpe was killed), Tenerife (part of the Canary Islands) and St. Croix.

THE STORY ON RADIO

The Bauer saga has been going on for 35 years, and there have been hundreds of subplots centering about the family. However, in all that time there has been only a handful of major stories involving the family. At the start, Papa Bauer (Theo Goetz) and Mama Bauer (Addie Klein) had come over from the old country and settled in Selby Flats, California, a seaport town. Their three American-born children—Bill Bauer (Lyle Sudrow, and later Ed Bryce on television), Meta Bauer (Jone Allison, and later Ellen Demming on television), and Trudy Bauer (Charlotte Holland)—were all young adults when the Bauer story began.

Bill Bauer married Bert (played the first year on the New York show by Ann Shepherd and for the next thirty-four years—up to the present—by Charita Bauer) shortly before Mama Bauer died, leaving Papa

Bauer as the sole family head. Bill was a hard-working young man. But Bert, who is today a sympathetic character as head of the Bauer family, was then selfish and unsympathetic as his materialistic young wife. There were many marital conflicts. One of them, for example, centered around Bert's constant obsession with getting Bill to buy a house even though they couldn't afford it.

Trudy Bauer married a man named Clyde and eventually waltzed off with him to find a life in New York City. Although the character was important to the story during the early radio era, Trudy lasted only briefly on television (played then by Lisa Howard, and Helen Wagner) and is never talked about by the Bauer family these days.

Meta was the most colorful member of the Bauer family for many years, as well as being a pivotal character on both radio and television. Meta had burst out of the tightly knit family, running away to the big city to become a model. She soon got involved with the reprehensible Ted White (Arnold Moss), became pregnant by him and married him. After their son Chuckie (Sarah Fussell) was born, Meta and Ted White were divorced, and Ted won partial custody of their son. He was an overbearing father, however, insisting that his timid son become tough and learn to box. Meta kept objecting to his unreasonable treatment of Chuckie. One day, while Chuckie was being forced to box, he had a freak accident and was killed. Meta went out of her mind and shot and killed Ted. While she was on trial for the murder of her ex-husband, a newspaperman named Joe Roberts (Herb Nelson) fell in love with her, believing she had killed her ex-husband only as a result of temporary insanity. After he helped gain her acquittal, they were married.

THE STORY ON TELEVISION

Meta and Joe Roberts had a sound marriage, although it was strained when Joe became overprotective of his grown daughter, KATHY ROBERTS (Susan Douglas). Kathy had married BOB LANG, who was killed in an automobile accident after Kathy learned that she was pregnant. Anxious for her child to have a father, she immediately married DR. DICK GRANT (James Lipton), an ambitious young doctor from a wealthy family. Kathy gave birth to a baby girl, ROBIN

(last played as an adult by Gillian Spencer), making Dick believe he was Robin's father. But with the advice of wise REV. DR. KEELER (Ed Begley, Melville Ruick), Kathy admitted the truth and Dick and Kathy's marriage was annulled.

When Joe Roberts tragically died of cancer, his widow, Meta, and his daughter, Kathy often argued; Kathy resented her stepmother's advice-giving. Their relationship worsened when they both fell in love with handsome MARK HOLDEN (Whitfield Connor), a business associate of Bill Bauer. He wound up marrying Kathy and adopting her daughter, Robin, who became a troublesome teenager. Then Kathy was critically injured in a car accident and died in her wheelchair! Meta and Mark were thrown together, out of their mutual concern for motherless Robin, but it was DR. BRUCE BANNING (Les Damon, Barnard Hughes, among others) whom Meta finally wed. She would remain happily married to him for many years.

Dick Grant had always been in love with Kathy Roberts. For a while, long before her death, he was pursued by a man-hungry nurse named JANET JOHNSON (Ruth Warrick, Lois Wheeler), but he couldn't forget Kathy. Dick became so jealous when he learned that his colleague at Cedars, DR. JIM KELLY (Paul Potter), was running after Kathy, that Dick froze during surgery, then ran to New York where he began living in a rooming house. There he met MARIE WALLACE (Lynne Rogers), an easygoing artist, and brought her back to Los Angeles where they married. But they encountered years of interference from his snobbish mother LAURA GRANT (Alice Yourman).

The marriage of Bill and Bert Bauer weathered numerous storms. Bill frequently succumbed to alcoholism and Bert often connived for material things, which Bill was unable to give her. Then they had to face a new generation of conflicts after their two sons became adults. They were MICHAEL BAUER (played as an adult by Gary Pillar, Bob Pickering and for the last fifteen years by Don Stewart) and WILLIAM EDWARD BAUER (Bob Gentry, for twelve years Mart Hulswit and currently Peter Simon). Michael, the eldest, had a way with women which displeased Bert no end. His first love was Robin Holden, Meta's ward, whom Bert disliked intensely. Robin's stepfather, Mark, married his housekeeper, RUTH JANNINGS (Louise Platt, Virginia Dwyer), who had a son, KARL JANNINGS (Richard Morse). Michael and Karl were friends until they found themselves in a contest over Robin. One night

Karl started a fistfight with Mike and accidentlly fell to his death! Mike stood trial and was acquitted. Mike then married Robin, but Bert forced an annulment. Bill and Bert were constantly at odds over her interference in their sons' lives.

Meanwhile, DR. PAUL FLETCHER (briefly Michael Kane, then for thirteen years Bernard Grant), a hard-working man from a poor family, came on staff at Cedars Hospital. He became friendly with Dick and Marie Grant, then married ANNE BENEDICT (Joan Gray, Elizabeth Hubbard), a debutante who had become his patient. Her mother HELENE (Kay Campbell) approved the marriage, but her powerful father HENRY BENEDICT (John Gibson, John Boruff, Paul McGrath) snubbed his nose at his once poor son-in-law. The marriage was rife with class conflicts, which were aggravated when Paul opened a clinic in a rough section of town. Anne pouted when he made the clinic building their home. She bought a gun for protection and pulled it on DORIS CRANDALL (Barbara Becker), an alcoholic Paul was trying to rehabilitate. Paul struggled with Anne over the pistol and Anne was accidentally shot to death! Paul was tried for murder and found innocent.

The source of Doris Crandall's alcoholism was her ex-husband, rich womanizer ALEX BOWDEN (Ernest Graves), owner of the famed Bowden art galleries. Alex had an eye for young women and was especially interested in Robin Lang. With Bert's approval and eager prodding, Alex and Robin married, but the union wasn't good and ended in divorce; soon after, Alex left Springfield. Robin then fell in love with Paul Fletcher, who was raising his young son JOHNNY FLETCHER (played as an adult by Don Scardino and Erik Howell) under the watchful eye of Paul's half-sister JANE (Chase Crosley). Jane had a string of failed romances, which caused her to overcompensate by becoming a possessive caretaker to little Johnny, creating problems for Paul and Robin. Eventually Jane married understanding attorney GEORGE HAYES (Philip Sterling), and soon after Paul and Robin were happily wed.

* * *

Dick Grant discovered he was sterile but refused to adopt a child with his wife Marie out of manly pride. Dick and Marie were on the verge of a divorce when they befriended a young waif named PHILLIP COLLINS (Carson Woods) and adopted him. The three

left Springfield. Marie's admirer, JOE TURINO (Joseph Campanella), sought solace with Marie's friend, AMY SINCLAIR (Joanne Linville).

Young Mike Bauer worked as a law clerk under the tutelage of lawyer George Hayes and soon became involved with George's secretary, pretty JULIE CONRAD (Sandra Smith). When Julie discovered she was pregnant, Bert and George persuaded Mike to marry her, but after their daughter HOPE (now played by Elvera Roussel) was born, Julie suffered a mental breakdown and committed suicide in a mental hospital. Bert became such a domineering grandmother to Hope that Mike spirited his daughter away to Bay City, Michigan, where he became involved in a destructive romance with PAT RANDOLPH, the wife of another attorney. (See the *Another World* story line.)

Bert's preoccupation with Hope practically ruined her marriage to Bill, who went back to alcohol and started an affair with his understanding secretary, MAGGIE SCOTT (June Graham). Later, Maggie's es-

Papa's daughter, Meta Bauer (Jone Allison, right), married newspaperman Joe Roberts (Herb Nelson, left) after he helped gain her acquittal from the charge of murdering her husband, Ted White. Kathy Roberts (Susan Douglas, next to Nelson) was Joe's daughter from a previous marriage and figured prominently in the story until the mid-fifties. Lyle Sudrow (seated) was Bill Bauer.

tranged husband BEN (Bernard Kates) returned to Springfield and rebuilt his relationship with his and Maggie's daughter, PEGGY SCOTT (Fran Myers). After teenage Peggy discovered her mother's affair with Bill Bauer, she grew upset and became involved with Paul Fletcher's son, Johnny, which so angered Ben that he suffered a heart attack and died. For a long time guilt feelings over Ben's death kept Johnny and Peggy apart. After Maggie Scott also died, Bert and Bill, who had reconciled, took orphaned Peggy into their home.

The Fletcher family was thrown into endless turmoil. After Paul's old friend, DR. SARA MCINTYRE (Patricia Roe, Jill Andre, Millette Alexander), came to Cedars Hospital, Robin became neurotically jealous over Paul and Sara's friendship. Then Robin was killed by a speeding truck which swerved to avoid hitting a child! Paul became more and more attracted to Sara, whose forthrightness was in marked contrast to Robin's immaturity, but Sara was unwilling to settle down into a relationship. Suddenly a young girl showed up claiming to be TRACY DELMAR (Victoria Wyndham, Melinda Fee), Sara's niece. Johnny Fletcher was awed by Tracy's worldliness and married Tracy, breaking Peggy Scott's heart. On the rebound, Peggy married spoiled MARTY DILLMAN (Chris Wines), a smooth, rich kid involved in crime. Marty knew that Tracy was actually CHARLOTTE WARING, a schemer who had assumed the identity of the *late* Tracy Delmar to get her hands on Sara's money! Marty was killed, leaving Peggy to stand accused of the crime. But with Mike's help and Charlotte's admission about her true identity, Peggy was acquitted and the real killer turned out to be FLIP MALONE (Paul Carpinelli), Marty's criminal accomplice. Johnny divorced Charlotte and married Peggy. But Peggy had been left with a child she had by Marty, young BILLY, and had to endure the interference of Marty's overbearing mother, CLAUDIA DILLMAN (Grace Matthews). Johnny's career as a doctor at Cedars was cut short when the pressure of following in his father Paul's footsteps caused him to have a

Kathy Roberts married Dr. Dick Grant (James Lipton) but the marriage was annulled when Dick learned that Kathy was pregnant by her first husband, Bob Lang. She gave birth to a baby girl whom she named Robin.

Ellen Demming (left) became the new Meta Bauer Roberts in January, 1953, with Susan Douglas still playing Kathy and Tarry Green (right) playing Joey Roberts, Kathy's brother from a previous marriage.

nervous breakdown and be put in a sanitarium. Soon after, Paul Fletcher moved to Washington, D.C.

* * *

Ed Bauer went to medical school and became friends with DR. JOE WERNER (last played by Anthony Call). Originally a heel, Joe mellowed and married Dr. Sara McIntyre after the accidental death of LEE GANTRY (Ray Fulmer), a greedy husband who tried to kill her for her money. Ed was the protégé of DR. STEPHEN JACK-SON (Stefan Schnabel), Chief of Surgery at Cedars Hospital. Dr. Jackson, a widower (or so everyone thought), was frightened that his only daughter, LESLIE (Lynne Adams), would marry the wrong man; and so, fond of Ed, the well-meaning Dr. Jackson encouraged them to marry. After a time, Ed and Leslie did marry, but it wasn't a good union. Leslie pressured Ed for them to have a baby, and Ed began to drink heavily and beat up Leslie in alcoholic rages.

Meanwhile, handsome lawyer Michael Bauer re-turned to Springfield with his daughter, Hope. Mike was again falling in love with another married woman. But this time it was far worse for Mike, for the woman was Leslie Bauer—the wife of his brother, Ed. Both Mike and Leslie were torn by guilt feelings and tried to keep their love for each other a secret. But with Ed's drinking problem destroying what little was left of her marriage to him, Leslie was finding it harder to keep Mike out of her life and thoughts.

When Cedars Hospital could no longer keep Ed on staff because of his drinking, he ran off to Tarry-wood, where he had an affair with an attractive secretary, JANET MASON (Caroline McWilliams). Leslie found out, and finally this persuaded her to openly admit her love for Mike. But Ed's sudden return from Tarry-wood and his begging her forgiveness made her break off with Mike and resume her life as Ed's wife. She intended to divorce Ed later on, when he was better rehabilitated.

Michael Bauer, Bill and Bert's son, was just an infant when the TV program started, but by 1954 he was played by seven-year-old Glenn Walken. Ed Bauer (originally called "Billy") wasn't born yet. Glenn later changed his name to Christopher Walken, today a famous stage and film actor.

By 1957, Kathy had wed Mark Holden (Whit Connor) and was having problems with her daughter, Robin Lang (Zina Bethune), now twelve. After Kathy was killed in an auto accident in 1958, The Guiding Light's production office was swamped with letters of grief and protest.

Mike was distraught when he learned that Leslie was pregnant with Ed's child, and he turned for comfort to scheming Charlotte Waring and married her. Leslie, devastated by Mike's marriage, left Ed for good this time and got a divorce. When their son was born she named him FREDERICK (now played as an adult by Michael O'Leary), after Ed and Mike's wonderful, good-hearted grandfather, PAPA BAUER (Theo Goetz). Leslie, now alone, met millionaire STANLEY NORRIS (William Smithers) and allowed herself to become entranced by his glittery life-style. Against her father's objections, she became Mrs. Stanley Norris.

At this point the elaborate saga of the Norris family began to unfold. Stanley's insecure and immature daughter, HOLLY NORRIS (Lynn Deerfield, Maureen Garrett), attempted to revive her relationship with her wealthy, power-lusting father, who had been alienated from her and from his son, KEN NORRIS (Roger Newman), a lawyer, and from his (Stanley's) ex-wife,

BARBARA NORRIS (Barbara Berjer), who wrote a syndicated cooking column.

Ken fell in love with Janet Mason, Ed Bauer's old affair. She returned his love and—despite her misgivings about their relationship because of his fanatically jealous temperament—finally married him. His sister, Holly, met ROGER THORPE (Mike Zaslow), an employee of her rich father's, and had an affair with him, convinced that Roger would marry her. But Roger, a lascivious type, only had eyes for Janet Norris, Ken's wife. Meanwhile, Barbara Norris met and fell in love with Roger's father, ADAM THORPE (Robert Milli), as good and decent as his son was irresponsible.

Within a short period of time, all the Norrises were touched by tragedy and mishap. Stanley Norris was murdered in cold blood, and Leslie was accused of the murder when her fingerprints were found on the murder weapon. Holly Norris was struck by a car after running into the street in a daze on seeing her

The company, Christmas, 1958, included, from left, top row: Kay Campbell, Lin Pierson (Alice Holden), Zina Bethune, Whit Connor, Louise Platt (Ruth Holden, Mark's new wife), Bernie Grant (Paul Fletcher), Theo Goetz, Charita Bauer, unidentified actress, wardrobe mistress Flossie Richard. Bottom row: producer Erwin Nicholson, director Jack Wood, James Lipton, Joan Gray (Anne Fletcher), production assistant Peter Andrews, Lynn Rogers (Marie Wallace) and set decorator Elwell.

lover, Roger Thorpe, leave the apartment of her sister-in-law, Janet Norris, wiping lipstick off. And, to complete this tragedy of errors, Ken left Janet when his hospitalized sister told him about seeing Roger Thorpe leaving Janet's apartment. However, what really happened was that Roger had forced his way into her apartment and Janet had successfully repelled his advances.

* * *

With Leslie accused of murdering her husband, Stanley Norris, none other than Mike Bauer defended her in court. Mike had by now realized what a conniving, hardhearted schemer Charlotte really was—interested only in being the wife of a prominent attorney rather than in being a real wife and mother. After it was proved that Stanley Norris was murdered by his secretary's mother, MARION CONWAY (Kate Harrington), Leslie was acquitted. In love with Mike more than ever before, Leslie now had to leave town—for the man she loved was married to another woman.

But Mike had already taken Hope and moved away from Charlotte. One night, Flip Malone, once sent to prison with her help, tried to shoot her. But he mistakenly shot Mike, who just happened to be walking into the house. Leslie, hearing that Mike had been seriously wounded, rushed to be with him at the hospital. At long last, they decided to marry.

But Charlotte wouldn't have it. She thought of every scheme she could to keep the court from granting Mike a divorce so that he could marry Leslie—even telling the court the outright lie that she was carrying Mike's child. The court wouldn't buy it and granted the divorce.

But Leslie's father, Dr. Jackson, *did* buy it—or at least the idea that the adverse publicity Charlotte and Mike's divorce was creating would sour a marriage between Mike and his daughter. When Leslie and Mike both told him that they would marry despite his objections, he suffered a heart attack and kept on suffering one at each and every suggestion of a marriage between his daughter and her ex-husband's brother. Eventually Mike and Leslie had to call off their wedding once again.

Joseph Campanella played artist Joe Turino who in 1959 became romantically involved with Amy Sinclair, played by Joanne Linville.

Ed Bryce became the new Bill Bauer in 1959 and kept the role for a decade, until the character presumably died in a plane crash. In 1978 Bill (still played by Ed Bryce) turned up alive and briefly returned to Springfield.

A rejected Charlotte began to seek other prey— this time Dr. Joe Werner. In love with his wife, Dr. Sara McIntyre, but temporarily fascinated by Charlotte, Joe had a brief, guilt-ridden affair with her. However, the mentally disturbed KIT VESTED (Nancy Addison), a hospital volunteer working with Joe, had already become infatuated with him. When she discovered that Charlotte, whom Kit believed to be her friend and confidante, was seeing Joe on the side, she felt betrayed by Joe *and* Charlotte and so invented a scheme to get even. One night she slipped a number of sleeping pills into Charlotte's drink and then called Joe Werner to come over to the house, saying merely that Charlotte had passed out after a fall. Joe proceeded to treat her simply for a concussion, and when Charlotte died of an overdose instead, an investigation was held and he was asked to leave his post as chief of staff. His peers felt that he should have recognized the symptoms of an overdose of barbiturates. Suffering from guilt and self-castigation, he ran away and took to the bottle. Kit had her revenge.

* * *

While young, overwrought Holly Norris was being treated at Cedars by the handsome Ed Bauer, she began to forget she was betrayed by Roger Thorpe and fell in love with her doctor instead. And Ed— feeling sorry for himself because he was a thirty-year-old man living with his mother while his ex-wife, Leslie, was about to marry his brother —began to see a lot of Holly. One night he got drunk and married her; they spent the night in a motel. The next morning Holly claimed, falsely, that they had consummated the marriage, and so he was forced to accept her as his wife. Ed's mother, Bert Bauer, shed her old interfering ways and became a supportive mother-in-law to Holly. But Meta Banning rightly sensed that her nephew was in for trouble.

A happier event was the marriage between Mike and Leslie. Her father, Dr. Jackson, finally gave his consent to their marriage, and an elaborate wedding was held in Bert's house. The waiting all these years was over for Mike and Leslie.

But the surprises for them weren't over. It suddenly turned out that her father hadn't been a wid-

The colorful villain Alex Bowden (Ernest Graves) ran an art gallery in 1960 and had a "fondness" for young girls. He married Robin Lang Holden (now Abigail Kellogg). Graves stayed until 1966.

By 1962, Sandy Smith played Julie Conrad and Gary Pillar played the adult Michael Bauer. Julie was the mother of Hope, conceived out of wedlock. After Julie and Michael finally wed, Julie went insane and died in an asylum. Michael left Springfield and suddenly popped up as a character in Another World's *Bay City.*

ower at all, as everyone believed. Her mother, VICTORIA BALLENGER (Carol Teitel), showed up in Springfield, having deserted Dr. Jackson years before when Leslie was just a baby. A cunning woman, Mrs. Ballenger wormed her way into living with Leslie and Mike and made a pretense of love for Steve Jackson. However, she failed in her attempt to cause a rift between Mike and Leslie, and ran off with an old lover—but only after telling Leslie that Steve was not her real father! Leslie found out that the story was true, and for a while it caused serious problems between her and Steve.

The disturbed Kit Vested's fantasies of a love affair with Joe Werner were, strangely, becoming fulfilled when Kit found him sick with pneumonia in a hotel and brought him to her brother's cabin in the woods. While he recuperated, Kit viciously intercepted all the letters he sent to his worried wife, Sara. Believing now that Sara was happy without him, he had a lawyer ask her for a divorce on his behalf. Sara said she'd consent only if a face-to-face meeting with

Joe were set up. Kit, realizing that all her lies were about to be uncovered, prepared to murder Sara the same way she had murdered Charlotte. She failed when Joe found the drugged Sara in the nick of time. Kit shot him, and was in turn shot and killed herself while she and the wounded Joe struggled with the gun. After the ordeal, Joe recuperated from the bullet wound, and he and Sara were at last happy again.

Ed Bauer tried to make a go of his "accidental" marriage to Holly, but Holly proved far too immature to be a responsible wife to a doctor, often accusing him of neglecting her to handle emergencies at the hospital. After many arguments, Ed demanded a separate-bedrooms arrangement until things became better in their marriage. Then Roger Thorpe suddenly showed up again in Springfield, and Holly, out of loneliness, had an affair with this philandering young man who had once caused her so much pain. When

Chase Crosley joined the show in 1964 as the sister of Paul Fletcher (Bernie Grant), nurse Jane Fletcher, and stayed in the part for five years. Jane was withdrawn and unhappy until she met George Hayes, who drew her out and later married her. In 1966, Chase became pregnant and played out her own pregnancy in the story.

Bernard Kates and June Graham were featured in the electric story of an unstable married couple, Ben and Maggie Scott. Maggie worked as Bill Bauer's secretary and had an affair with Bill, which nearly broke up his marriage.

Holly found herself pregnant, it *had* to be Roger's child, because she hadn't been having sexual relations with Ed. Desperate to cover up her child's real parentage, Holly ingratiated herself with Ed, enough so that he believed she had changed, and they resumed sexual relations. Holly felt safe now in announcing that she was pregnant by her own husband.

Roger, of course, had only been using Holly, as he had most women. Yet he was changing for the better, and sincerely fell in love with nurse Peggy Fletcher. Ironically, when at last he felt emotionally secure enough to ask a woman to marry him, Peggy couldn't marry Roger—because she was still legally married to Johnny Fletcher, who had left Springfield several years before. Several brutal loan sharks, from whom Roger had borrowed money to rescue his failing business, severely beat Roger up when he couldn't pay them back—and also threatened to harm Peggy and her young son, Billy. Peggy was beginning to wonder if perhaps she hadn't become involved with the wrong man.

Meanwhile, Ken Norris's old neurotic jealousies were revived when he began to believe, wrongly, that his wife Janet and Ed Bauer were having an affair. Suddenly, the jealousies became pathological and Ken's mind snapped. He felled Ed with a bullet in the chest one night. The bullet severed a pulmonary vein, and Ed almost died under Dr. Joe Werner's scalpel. Ed lived, but his left hand was paralyzed, which meant the end of his surgical career. Ken, obviously a very sick man, was placed in a sanitarium and eventually settled in California, once cured. Janet took baby Emily and went to live with her mother in San Diego.

* * *

Ed suffered a severe depression when he learned that the partial paralysis would be permanent. The only thing that helped lift his spirits was the birth of "his" daughter, whom he and Holly named CHRISTINA. Although Holly felt relief that Ed believed Christina to be his own, Holly was still neurotically in love with

Gillian Spencer took the role of Robin in 1965. Robin married Paul Fletcher after he accidentally caused the death of his previous wife, Anne. Ben and Maggie Scott had died, leaving behind their winsome fourteen-year-old daughter, Peggy Scott (Fran Myers). Afterward, Peggy was virtually adopted by the Bauer family.

Ed Bauer, Bert's youngest son, was a surgeon by 1967 and was played by Bob Gentry. He married Leslie Jackson (Lynne Adams), which began one of the best-remembered love triangles on the show—involving alcoholic Ed, sweet Leslie and his brother Michael. Lynne Adams won her part over nine hundred other actresses.

Roger and even tried to keep Roger and Peggy apart, to hold on to him. Then Christina became sick and needed a transfusion. Ed's blood, naturally, wasn't the right type (Roger finally gave his anonymously), and Holly became frantic that Ed would learn the truth. In the end Holly felt she couldn't continue the lie, and confessed the whole tawdry story of her affair with Roger. Horrified, Ed instantly broke with Holly and made sure that the whole family, as well as Peggy Fletcher, found out. Peggy, to be sure, was disturbed, but believed that Roger loved her. When her divorce from Johnny Fletcher came through, she wed Roger in a small ceremony, with only Roger's father, Adam, and Bert Bauer as witnesses. Ed, with both his surgical career and his marriage wrecked, became more despondent than ever, and would probably have become an alcoholic again had not RITA STAPLETON (Lenore Kasdorf), a beautiful nurse at Cedars who had fallen in love with him, offered him comfort and friendship. Meanwhile, two other people at the hospital suffered because of Rita's interest in Ed: DR. TIM RYAN (Jordan Clarke), who was so in love with Rita that when she began seeing Ed his work at the hospital became shoddy; and PAM CHANDLER (Maureen Silliman), a pretty young hospital employee who loved Tim and blamed Rita for all his troubles. With their love lives unresolved, both Pam and Tim eventually left Springfield.

Hope, Mike Bauer's daughter, was blossoming into a beautiful young woman. Inexperienced in the game of love, she made numerous romantic mistakes, which usually worried Mike. For instance, when she came back to Springfield during a recess from her college in California, she told Mike that she

Don Stewart succeeded Bob Pickering as Michael Bauer in 1968 and is still in the role. Elissa Leeds, several years later, played his daughter Hope (from his union with the late Julie Conrad) as a young teenager.

Mart Hulswit replaced Bob Gentry as Ed Bauer in 1969. After Ed's drinking got him fired from Cedars Hospital, he ran off to Tarrywood and had an affair with Janet Mason, while his wife Leslie and brother Michael were secretly falling in love. Mart Hulswit played Ed Bauer for a full decade.

was in love with one of her professors—an ALEX MCDANIELS (Keith Charles)—and that, once back at school, she intended to move in with him. Mike went to see Professor McDaniels, a married man, and forced him to break off with Hope. Angry at Mike's interference, she went to live with her grandmother Bert and began working at the Metro nightclub. There she became interested in a singer named CHAD RICHARDS (Everette McGill), who used to be in love with Hope's stepmother, Leslie Bauer. Chad began having mysterious blackouts and seizures and became violent. It was found that his behavior was caused by a benign brain tumor, which was excised. Cured but ashamed of himself, Chad left Springfield. Later, Hope again worried Mike when she fell in love with ex-convict BEN MCFARREN (Stephen Yates), who was pressuring her to move in with him.

Mike and Leslie Bauer's first year of marriage was for the most part happy. Lawyer Mike took on a new client, ANN JEFFERS (Maureen Mooney), who wanted Mike to investigate the whereabouts of her husband,

SPENCE JEFFERS (John Ramsey), and son JIMMY. She had left Spence years before, and now wanted custody of Jimmy. The "Sam Spade" work brought Mike first to Alaska, then to California—but he finally located Spence. It turned out that Spence had already killed one man; he now came to Springfield in a rage, threatening both Ann and Mike at Mike's house. After knocking Mike unconscious, Spence stormed out of the house, and a minute later the screech of wheels, then a scream, could be heard. Ann rushed out the door, and to her horror, Leslie was lying in a pool of blood near the garage. In his psychotic state, Spence had run over poor Leslie with his car. She was rushed to Cedars. For a while everyone thought that she would recover despite her internal injuries. But Leslie suspected she was near the end. She asked to see Mike, and told him she loved him. Mike held back his grief long enough to bring Spence Jeffers to justice.

Wealthy Dr. Sara McIntyre (Millette Alexander, center) was wooed into matrimony by unscrupulous Lee Gantry (Ray Fulmer), who was in league with Mildred Foss (Jan Sterling) to murder Sara so that Gantry would inherit her money. The scheme was foiled in the nick of time and Gantry and Miss Foss were killed.

Leslie married wealthy Stanley Norris (William Smithers) on the rebound after she divorced Ed and then learned that Michael, with whom she was in love, had been duped by vicious Charlotte Waring into marrying her. The story had, in effect, replaced the antagonist in the original love triangle with two evil characters, a typical way in which soap writers like to prolong their love stories.

Mike had waited so long to marry Leslie, and now, after only two years of happiness together, she was lost to him forever.

* * *

By the time their divorce came through, Holly had matured and was beginning to see that her love for Ed was much deeper than she had ever suspected. However, Rita was anxious to marry Ed and tried her best to keep Ed and Holly apart. Then, Rita was accused of murder! The happiness of not only Rita, but Ed, Roger and Peggy as well, became threatened by revelations made during Rita's trial. Years before, both Rita and Roger Thorpe had an involvement in Abilene, Texas. Mike Bauer had a tough time defending Rita because she wouldn't be specific about her past in Abilene—to protect Roger's marriage to Peggy and, most of all, to keep Ed's love. In the end, it was disreputable Roger who gained her an acquittal by testifying on Rita's behalf. Roger's motivation: to become a hero in Rita's eyes and win her away from Ed.

Roger continued to be a catalyst in the breakup of marriages. His own marriage to Peggy ended when she thought twice about the man she married. After divorcing him, she moved with little Billy to Boise, Idaho. Holly still loved Ed, but agreed to step aside when she saw that it was Rita he now cared for. Barbara Thorpe so blamed Roger for the breakup of Holly's marriage to Ed, that there were continual arguments between Barbara and Adam over Roger, and they were forced to divorce.

Sara and Joe Werner filled the emptiness in their lives by adopting a ten-year-old boy called T.J. (played as a child by T. J. Hargrave—see cast list for adult actors), found sick and starving on the streets by the police. The only specter which now threatened the happiness of Sara and Joe was the heart condition he

The Mike-and-Leslie story ended in 1976 when Leslie was hit by a car and killed. By 1978 Mike was involved with Jackie Marler (Cindy Pickett, left) and her friend Elizabeth Spaulding (Lezlie Dalton), the wife of wealthy and profligate Alan Spaulding. Jackie was hiding the deep secret that Elizabeth's son, Phillip, was really Jackie's son.

Stephen Yates and Janet Grey played artist Ben McFarren and Eve Stapleton in 1977. Ben married Eve, even though a neurological disorder had caused her to become blind. Later they divorced over a misunderstanding.

developed after he was shot during his life-or-death struggle with insane Kit Vested several years before. Suddenly, on assignment in India, Joe died of a heart attack! Sara was shattered—her only comfort now was T. J.

The lives of the Bauers were suddenly thrown into turmoil when Bill Bauer turned up alive! Everyone believed that he had been killed ten years before in a plane crash. Instead, he had tried to run away from his alcoholism by turning his back on his family, taking on a new identity as "Bill Moray," and beginning a new relationship in Canada with a woman named SIMONE KINCAID (Laryssa Lauret). A series of events brought Bill back to his family. Simone's daughter HILLARY (Linda McCullough, currently Marsha Clark), a student nurse at Cedars of Springfield, had an emergency appendectomy at the hospital. Wearing a beard as a disguise, Bill came to Cedars to see Hillary, but then spotted his son Mike being hon-

ored as Springfield's Man of the Year. He was overcome by old emotions and gradually revealed himself to his wife and sons. Bert and Mike accepted the situation as best they could; but Ed became so upset that he went back to drinking. Anxious to right the wrongs he committed, Bill helped Ed conquer alcoholism once and for all, then moved to Chicago, since Simone had left him for another man. Before he left, the Bauers discovered another secret: Hillary was Bill's own daughter. Hillary, Mike and Ed, all half-brothers and half-sister, in time grew close.

For years hidden pasts and the deepest of ruinous secrets had been brewing well outside the boundaries of Springfield. Now, as if drawn by a common purpose, they suddenly emerged in and around Cedars Hospital. Handsome, tempestuous DR. JUSTIN MARLER (Thomas O'Rourke) began practicing there. Years before, in Chicago, he had been engaged to Dr. Sara McIntyre, but had jilted her for a more prestigious marriage to JACKIE SCOTT (Cindy Pickett, Carrie Mowery), the daughter of Justin's superior, DR. EMMET

Alan Spaulding (Chris Bernau) married Mike's daughter Hope Bauer (Elvera Roussel) at Bert's house in 1980. They had become lovers during an exciting sequence in which they were trapped on an island together.

Springfield's wholesome young heartthrob, Kelly Nelson (John Wesley Ship), fell in love with Morgan Richards (Kristin Vigard) in 1981. Before they could marry, they had to wend through an elaborate triangle involving trouble-making Nola Reardon. By now most soaps were prominently featuring teen-agers in complex love stories.

SCOTT (Peter Turgeon). The marriage was a mistake and ended in a bitter divorce. Alone now, Justin was falling in love with Sara all over again.

Jackie Scott arrived in Springfield, too, and widower Mike Bauer began to see a lot of her. Jackie seemed to go out of her way to become friendly with fragile ELIZABETH SPAULDING (Lezlie Dalton), who had also just come to town with her wealthy, demanding husband ALAN SPAULDING (Chris Bernau) and their eight-year-old son PHILLIP (Jarrod Ross). Slowly, Sara and Mike were drawn into a web of dreadful secrets involving Justin, Jackie and the Spauldings. Eight years before, Jackie had been pregnant with Justin's child before she divorced him. She had gone to Europe to have an abortion but, unknown to Justin, had had their baby in a clinic. Meanwhile, at the same clinic, Elizabeth Spaulding had just lost her own baby. Without telling Elizabeth, her husband Alan and the clinic's head made a deal with Jackie to substitute Jackie's baby boy for Elizabeth's dead baby. That baby boy was Phillip. However, Alan never knew Jackie's identity. Now, Jackie began going to great lengths to get close to young Phillip. Oddly, his real father, Justin, began treating him for a congenital heart condition and became quite close to the boy, without knowing that Phillip was his own son!

Mike Bauer became the legal counsel for Alan Spaulding's company, and soon fell in love with Alan's wife, Elizabeth. Elizabeth had been growing weary of her husband's domineering selfishness and philandering. When he insisted on hiring as his secretary a beautiful schemer named DIANE BALLARD (Sofia Landon), with whom he obviously planned an affair, Elizabeth threw up her hands and filed for divorce. After it was granted, Alan gave in to the charms of beautiful Jackie and married her, without realizing that she only wished to get closer to her son Phillip. Mike comforted Elizabeth and represented her in a

Amanda Wexler (Kathleen Cullen) joined Guiding Light *in 1979 as the shy daughter of manipulating Jennifer Wexler. Later she was proven to be the illegitimate daughter of Alan Spaulding and began running Spaulding Enterprises with him. In 1982 she became involved with scheming Mark Evans (Mark Pinter).*

Nola Reardon (Lisa Brown, center) began working for mysterious archeologist Quinton McCord (Michael Tylo, right). In a sequence filmed in St. Croix in 1982 (which included George Kappaz, left, as Gunther Lugosi), there were underwater scenes. Quinton turned out to be Sean Ryan, rich Henry Chamberlain's illegitimate son.

long legal battle against Alan for custody of Phillip, which she won. During all this family disruption, Phillip's heart condition kept flaring dangerously, stopping Mike and Elizabeth from openly declaring their love for each other.

Justin wanted to marry Sara, who still had feelings for him but found it hard to forgive his having jilted her to marry Jackie. To think things over, she went to the tropics, then returned to Springfield with a new husband! He was corrupt attorney DEAN BLACKFORD (Gordon Rigsby), who became Alan's new lawyer. After Dean Blackford murdered the man he and Alan had bribed to falsely testify at Phillip's custody hearing, Sara had her new husband investigated, and he plotted to kill her. Mike Bauer got to Dean just as he was about to fling Sara off a cliff. In the ensuing struggle, Dean was killed.

* * *

EVE STAPLETON (Janet Grey) was Rita Stapleton's younger sister and the roommate of Hillary Bauer. Eve was innocent and unselfish, quite Rita's opposite. After Hope Bauer broke off with young artist Ben McFarren, Eve fell in love with him and was just about to marry him when she contracted a rare brain disorder, which caused her to become blind. Eve tried to call off the wedding, but Ben insisted that they marry. Afterward, her illness disappeared. While struggling to make ends meet from Ben's art commissions, they moved to a cottage on a parcel of land owned by eccentric LUCILLE WEXLER (Rita Lloyd), who lived nearby in a dank, cold mansion with her reclusive teenage daughter AMANDA (Kathleen Cullen). Vicious Lucille had a sick hatred of men. Sensing that her sympathetic daughter, Amanda, loved Ben, she plotted to throw the two of them together so that Eve would finally leave him and Ben would ultimately wind up as Lucille's household slave! Part of the plan worked; on cue, Eve walked out on Ben, then divorced him. Amanda and Ben grew closer.

Meanwhile, Alan was trying to make a go of his marriage to Jackie, who was the strongest-minded woman he had ever known. Jackie became pregnant, hoping that a child by Alan would compensate for their losing custody of Phillip. Alan still resented Mike Bauer for having stolen his wife and having helped her take his son away from him. Therefore, when Hope, who had become an interior decorator, began to decorate a villa Alan had purchased for Jackie,

Alan gave her a tough time as a way of getting even with her father Mike. Suddenly Alan and Hope were in a plane accident and found themselves stranded on a deserted tropical island where they made passionate love! Through the power of young Hope's love, Alan began a slow transformation from a moneymaking entity to a caring human being. After they were saved and brought back to Springfield, Jackie realized that she had lost Alan to Hope. The baby died and she divorced him.

There was still another terrible secret involving the Spauldings, yet to be uncovered. Ben and Amanda were dumbstruck when Alan's rich father BRANDON SPAULDING (John Wardwell) died and left her a sizeable part of Spaulding Enterprises. No one knew why. After investigating, Ben discovered that Lucille Wexler, Amanda's mother, had been Brandon's mistress. By now Ben knew too much and the disturbed Lucille made several attempts on his life. Ben and Amanda suspected that she had been fathered by Brandon, but the truth was quite different: Amanda was the daughter of one Jane Marie Stafford and Alan himself! Only Brandon and Lucille, who adopted Amanda, knew the truth, which Lucille had been trying to hide for years for fear that she would lose Amanda's love. Alan gracefully accepted Amanda as his new business partner and Ben and Amanda were married, to Lucille's dismay. Soon a mysterious woman named JENNIFER RICHARDS (Geraldine Court) came in answer to an ad Lucille had placed for someone to manage her household staff. In time Jennifer developed a deep friendship with Amanda. Lucille resented the relationship and discovered that Jennifer was really Jane Marie Stafford, Amanda's natural mother! She suddenly pulled a knife on Jennifer, but in a scuffle Lucille fell on it herself and was killed. Of course, Jennifer had known all along that Amanda was her daughter. Jennifer was tried and cleared of murder after she reluctantly admitted on the stand that Amanda was her own daughter by Alan Spaulding. The shock of learning her parentage caused Amanda, who had become pregnant by Ben, to lose her baby and withdraw into herself. She also suspected that Ben still loved Eve. She gave him his freedom to return to her, but Ben insisted on standing by his wife.

* * *

Ed, Rita and Holly all continued to be haunted by the incubus of Roger Thorpe, who still used his sexuality as a weapon. After Rita and Ed became engaged, Roger felt rejected and raped her brutally one night. She kept silent about the assault, fearful that the rape would harm her relationship with Ed, whom she finally married. Then Roger proposed to Holly, intending to legitimize their daughter Christina. Having lost Ed to Rita and failed in a new relationship with DR. PETER CHAPMAN (Curt Dawson), Holly, against her mother's better judgment, married unstable Roger. The marriage was a nightmare from the start, as Barbara Thorpe had feared. Holly would not sleep with her new husband, who accused her of continuing to love Ed. Then Roger raped her. But unlike Rita, she refused to keep silent and pressed charges against her own husband. He was defended by ROSS MARLER (Jerry ver Dorn), Justin's unscrupulous younger brother. During the course of the trial, Ed and Roger had a violent confrontation and Roger pulled a gun on Ed. While the men were struggling, Holly walked in on them, grabbed the gun and shot Roger! Badly wounded, Roger blackmailed Alan Spaulding—with damaging information about the bribed witness—into sending him to the Spaulding Clinic in Puerto Rico. Later, the head of the clinic, DR. GONZALO MORENO (Gonzalo Madurga), notified Adam Thorpe that his son was dead. Holly was sent to jail to await trial for murder.

Ed, his family and his friends were made constantly aware of Rita's selfishness. She finally did admit that Roger had raped her, but not soon enough to help Holly's case. Rita was sorely relieved when Mike gained Holly's release on grounds of temporary insanity, for Rita had been growing restless with the burden of caring for Christina. She was becoming bored, in fact, with her whole marriage to Ed and with the Bauer family. Feeling trapped, she had an affair with DR. GREG FAIRBANKS (David Greenan), a slippery womanizer. Ed found out and separated from her. When Rita became pregnant, she wasn't sure who the father was.

Of course, Roger had not died at Alan's Puerto Rican clinic but had, with the help of Alan and his money, become a fugitive from justice. He went to Paris and had an affair with a plastic surgeon, DR. RENEE DUBOIS (Deborah May), who saw the gentle side of him. Longing to live with his daughter Christina, Roger made plans to kidnap her and raise her without interference from Barbara or the Bauers. He returned to Springfield, donning a beard and masquerading as

an elderly professor and taking up residence in a boarding house owned by BEA REARDON (Lee Lawson). Quite unbalanced by now, Roger wound up kidnapping Rita and taking her to a deserted cabin while she was still pregnant. Brothers Ed and Mike saved her, but in the ordeal she lost the baby. She and Ed reconciled. But Roger was still at large. After it was learned that he had murdered his lover, Dr. Renee Dubois, the Bauer brothers tracked him to the Caribbean. In a struggle with Ed, Roger fell off a cliff to his death.

Enigmatic Roger had changed so many lives and, in a way, was still changing them. Barbara, who had divorced Roger's father Adam because of Roger, tried to restore their relationship. But he had already fallen in love with Sara McIntyre, and Adam and Sara married. Now that Roger was dead and Ed had gone back with Rita, Holly decided to take Christina and leave town. Barbara would have been left quite alone, were it not for the arrival of ANDREW NORRIS (Barney McFadden, Ted Leplat), one of her sons. A journalist, Andrew set out to write a biography of Alan Spaulding, whose life surely would have made a steamy best seller.

* * *

Ed Bauer's honest, decent godson KELLY NELSON (John Wesley Shipp) moved to Springfield and became Ed's houseguest while he continued his medical studies. He was a wonderful young man with an abiding faith in the goodness of everyone, and at least three lovely young women became enamored of him. One was NOLA REARDON (Lisa Brown), one of poor Bea Reardon's seven children—a girl who dreamed of romance and luxury. She was as much taken with Kelly's good looks as with his future potential as an upper middle class doctor. Hillary Bauer (as she now called herself), however, fell deeply in love with Kelly only for himself. For a while Kelly grew close to her. But it was with MORGAN RICHARDS (Kristen Vigard, Jennifer Cooke), Jennifer's stubborn daughter, that Kelly had physical relations and fell in love. The lovers didn't have an easy time getting together. Kelly felt guilty about abandoning Hillary, and Morgan found it hard to drop her boyfriend "Tim" (T.J.) Werner, Sara's adopted son who was also Kelly's best friend. Eventually Hillary accepted the loss of Kelly gracefully, but Tim, after finding out about Morgan and Kelly, took to liquor and only conquered his problem with the help of fellow alcoholic Ed Bauer. But the greater threat to the lovers was grasping Nola, who engineered one plot after another to confuse Kelly and Morgan's communications and foil their romance. Nola got Kelly drunk one night and in her bed, making him believe that they had had relations. After she became pregnant by her eager boyfriend FLOYD PARKER (Tom Nielsen), a member of the Cedars custodial staff, she claimed that Kelly was the father. Noble Kelly would have married Nola had her mother not come forward to tell everyone that Floyd had to be the father. Kelly and Morgan finally wed in a beautiful ceremony at Laurel Falls. Nola was just about to say "I do" to Floyd when it came out as "I can't." She couldn't go through with a marriage which would have been a lie.

Although Elizabeth Spaulding, following her divorce from Alan, was deeply in love with Mike Bauer, she was frightened of what her marriage to Mike would do to her son Phillip's heart condition. Meanwhile, Justin, who had no idea that Phillip was his own son, continued to treat the boy and grew so fond of him and Elizabeth that he finally asked her to marry him. For Phillip's sake, Elizabeth married Justin but continued to see and love Mike. Then the inevitable happened: Jackie told Justin the truth, that she and he were Phillip's real parents. Jackie and Justin grew much closer to each other and to Phillip, completely unnerving Elizabeth and forcing her to receive psychiatric treatments. She grew much stronger with her therapy, and in time discovered the truth about Phillip herself. She divorced Justin, leaving Phillip with his real parents so that she could get further therapy in Zurich. Justin realized that he had loved Jackie all along and married her.

Alan and Hope were happily married with Mike Bauer's grudging blessing, although Mike secretly continued to try to prove that Alan had helped the late Roger Thorpe become a fugitive. Alan became heavily involved in business affairs and before long his marriage to Hope was in trouble. Ed and Rita, who lived next door to Alan and Hope's mansion, were also having problems, mostly concerning Rita's extravagance and selfishness. Rita began a secret affair with Alan. Meanwhile, Barbara's son, Andrew Norris, still wanted to write a scandalous biography of Alan Spaulding. He raided the files of Dr. Sara McIntyre, who had been guarding many local secrets gathered from her new sex therapy sessions—including Rita's affair with Alan. Andrew began blackmailing all of the people mentioned in Sara's confidential files. The outcome was that Andrew was caught and incarcer-

ated, a shocked Barbara left Springfield to join her daughter Holly, and Rita was so shamed by the exposure of her extramarital affair with Alan that she left Springfield as well. Hope and Alan reconciled and had a little boy, ALAN MICHAEL. Soon after, however, Mike's obsession with proving that Alan was a criminal led him to Diane Ballard, who was murdered by Ross Marler's schizophrenic wife CARRIE (Jane Elliot), and to her secret tape recordings which showed that Alan had obstructed justice by aiding Roger Thorpe. After Alan paid for his crimes with a short prison term, he returned to Hope's arms and even became friends with Mike.

Just when Hope had given birth to her son, Jackie Marler, now wonderfully happy with Justin after so many years, gave birth to a new daughter, SAMANTHA. But Jackie and Justin's happiness was woefully short-lived, for Jackie was killed in a plane crash. Justin had, to face raising his two children alone.

Amanda became quite involved in her work as part owner of Spaulding Enterprises and had several professional run-ins with her father, Alan. Ben McFarren, confused about himself, decided to divorce her to pursue his artistic career in Florence. Meanwhile, Kelly and Morgan also divorced because of his jealousy over JOSH LEWIS (Robert Newman), a sly young man who was attracted to her. And Ed Bauer, finally over Rita, married MAUREEN REARDON (Ellen Dolan), Nola's sensible older sister.

Nola finally matured when she fell for a handsome but mysterious archeologist, QUINTON MCCORD (Michael Tylo). Their lives were briefly endangered by Quinton's evil arch enemy, SILAS CROCKER (Benjamin Hendrickson), but in time Silas was killed. Quinton then revealed he was the illegitimate son of HENRY CHAMBERLAIN (William Roerick), Alan's longtime business associate and former mentor. Henry, a powerful man, nonetheless had a heart of gold and began keeping company with the downtrodden Bea Reardon. Henry's spoiled daughter, VANESSA (Maeve Kinkead), had an affair with Bea's macho son, TONY (Gregory Beecroft), until he tired of her childish ways. Since Tony's rejection of her, Vanessa deplored her family's connection with the poor Reardon's—particularly when her newfound brother Quinton changed his name to Chamberlain and married Nola!

CAST

THE GUIDING LIGHT
CBS: June 30, 1952–

Bertha Bauer	Charita Bauer (P)
Bill Bauer	Lyle Sudrow (P)
	Ed Bryce*
	Eugene Smith
Papa Bauer	Theo Goetz (P)
Meta Roberts Banning .	Jone Allison (P)
	Ellen Demming*
Joe Roberts	Herb Nelson (P)
Kathy Roberts Holden .	Susan Douglas (P)
Dr. Dick Grant	James Lipton (P)
Laura Grant	Alice Yourman (P)
Joey Roberts	Tarry Green
Rev. Keeler	Ed Begley
	Melville Ruick
Sid Harper	Philip Sterling
Elsie Franklin	Ethel Remey
Trudy Bauer	Lisa Howard
	Helen Wagner
Michael Bauer	Glenn (Christopher) Walken
	Michael Allen
	Paul Prokopf
	Gary Pillar
	Robert Pickering
	Don Stewart*
Dr. Ed Bauer	Pat Collins
	Robert Gentry
	Mart Hulswit*
	Peter Simon
Janet Johnson	Ruth Warrick*
	Lois Wheeler
Peggy Regan	Patricia Wheel
Dan Peters	Paul Ballantyne
Dr. Jim Kelly	Paul Potter
Leila Kelly	Nancy Wickwire
Dr. John Brooks	Charles Baxter
Mrs. Laurie	Lois Wilson
Marie Wallace Grant ...	Lynne Rogers*
	Joyce Holden
Mark Holden	Whitfield Connor
Robin Lang Fletcher ...	Zina Bethune
	Judy Robinson
	Abigail Kellogg
	Nancy Malone
	Ellen Weston
	Gillian Spencer
Dr. Paul Fletcher	Michael Kane
	Bernard Grant*
Anne Benedict Fletcher	Joan Gray*
	Elizabeth Hubbard
Henry Benedict	John Gibson
	John Boruff*
	Paul McGrath
Helene Benedict	Kay Campbell
Marian Winters	Katherine Meskill
Dr. Bruce Banning	Les Damon
	Barnard Hughes*
	Sydney Walker
	William Roerick
Alice Holden	Sandy Dennis
	Diane Gentner
	Lin Pierson
Ruth Jannings Holden ..	Louise Platt
	Virginia Dwyer*
Karl Jannings	Richard Morse
Joe Turino	Joseph Campanela
Amy Sinclair	Connie Lembcke
	Joanne Linville
Philip Collins	Carson Woods
Alex Bowden	Ernest Graves
Doris Crandall	Barbara Becker
George hayes	Philip Sterling
Jane Fletcher Hayes ...	Pamela King
	Chase Crosley*
Dr. John Fletcher	Sheldon Golomb
	Daniel Fortas
	Donnie Melvin
	Don Scardino
	Erik Howell
Julie Conrad Bauer	Sandra Smith
Hope Bauer Spaulding .	Jennifer Kirschner
	Paula Schwartz
	Elissa Leeds
	Tisch Raye
	Robin Mattson
	Katherine Justice
	Elvera Roussel*
Andrew Murray	Dana Elcar
Lt. Carl Wyatt	Gerald S. O'Loughlin
Dr. Stephen Jackson ...	Stefan Schnabel
Leslie Jackson Bauer ..	Lynne Adams*
	Kathryn Hays
	Barbara Rodell
Peggy Scott Thorpe ...	Fran Myers

Maggie Scott	June Graham	Dr. Tim Ryan	Jordan Clarke
Ben Scott	Bernard Kates	Tim ("T.J.") Werner	T. J. Hargrave
Martha Frazier	Cicely Tyson		Kevin Bacon
	Ruby Dee*		Christopher Marcantel
Dr. Jim Frazier	Billy Dee Williams		Nigel Reed
	James Earl Jones	Andrew Norris	Barney McFadden
Dr. Joe Werner	Ben Hayes		Ted Leplat*
	Ed Zimmermann	Chad Richards	Everett McGill
	Berkeley Harris	Ann Jeffers	Maureen Mooney
	Anthony Call*	Rita Stapleton Bauer ...	Lenore Kasdorf
Dr. Sara McIntyre	Patricia Roe	Eve Stapleton McFarren	Janet Grey
	Jill Andre	Ben McFarren	Stephen Yates
	Millette Alexander*	Jerry McFarren	Peter Jensen
Charlotte Waring Bauer	Victoria Wyndham*		Mark Travis
	Dorrie Kavanaugh	Viola Stapleton	Sudie Bond
	Melinda Fee		Kate Wilkinson*
Claudia Dillman	Grace Matthews	Spence Jeffers	John Ramsey
Marty Dillman	Robert Lawson	Malcolm Granger	Ed Seamon
	Christopher Wines*	Georgene Granger	Delphi Harrington
Flip Malone	Paul Carpinelli	Raymond Shafer	Keith Aldrich
Ira Newton	Sorrell Booke	Dr. Justin Marler	Thomas O'Rourke
	Larry Gates	Jackie Marler	Cindy Pickett*
Janet Mason Norris	Caroline McWilliams		Carrie Mowery
Deborah Mehren	Olivia Cole	Dr. Emmet Scott	Kenneth Harvey
Lee Gantry	Ray Fulmer		Frank Latimore*
Mildred Foss	Jan Sterling		Peter Turgeon
Barbara Norris Thorpe .	Augusta Dabney	Alan Spaulding	Chris Bernau
	Barbara Berjer*	Elizabeth Spaulding	
Stanley Norris	Michael Higgins	Marler	Lezlie Dalton
	William Smithers*	Phillip Spaulding	Jarrod Ross
Ken Norris	Roger Newman		Grant Aleksander
Holly Norris Thorpe ...	Lynn Deerfield	Katie Parker	Denise Pence
	Maureen Garrett*	Hillary Kincaid Bauer ..	Linda McCullough
Kit Vested	Nancy Addison		Marsha Clark*
David Vested	Peter D. Greene	Simone Kincaid	Laryssa Lauret
	Dan Hamilton*	Dr. Peter Chapman	Curt Dawson
Linell Conway	Christine Pickles	Max Chapman	Ben Hammer
Marion Conway	Lois Holmes	Brandy Shellooe	Sandy Faison
	Kate Harrington*		Jobeth Williams*
Roger Thorpe	Michael Zaslow	Diane Ballard	Sofia Landon
Adam Thorpe	Robert Gerringer	Dean Blackford	Gordon Rigsby
	Robert Milli*	Dr. Mark Hamilton	Burton Cooper
Karen Martin	Tudi Wiggins	Amanda Wexler	
Charles Eiler	Graham Jarvis	Spaulding	Kathleen Cullen
Betty Eiler	Madeleine Sherwood	Lucille Wexler	Rita Lloyd
Victoria Ballenger	Carol Teitel	Gordon Middleton	Marcus Smythe
Dr. Wilson Frost	Jack Betts	Maya Waterman	Sands Hall
Mrs. Hoffmann	Lilia Skala	Whitney Foxton	Joseph Maher
Pam Chandler	Maureen Silliman	Clarence Bailey	Philip Bosco

Ross Marler . . . .   Jerry ver Dorn
Lainie Marler Bowden .   Kathleen Kellaigh
Floyd Parker . . . .   Tom Nielsen
Brandon Spaulding . . . .   David Thomas
                                  John Wardwell
Dr. Gonzalo Moreno . . .   Gonzalo Madurga
Dr. Greg Fairbanks . . . . .   David Greenan
Dr. Renee DuBois . . . . . .   Deborah May
Dr. Paul Lacrosse . . . . .   Jacques Roux
Jennifer Richards Evans   Geraldine Court
Morgan Richards Nelson   Kristen Vigard
                                  Jennifer Cook
Kelly Nelson . . . .   John Wesley Shipp
Nola Reardon . . . .   Lisa Brown
Bea Reardon . . . .   Lee Lawson
Carter Bowden . . . .   Alan Austin
Lt. Larry Wyatt . . . .   Joe Ponazecki
Dr. Ingrid Fischer . . . . . .   Taina Elg
Vanessa Chamberlain . .   Maeve Kinkead*
                                  Anna Stuart
Henry Chamberlain . . . .   William Roerick
Joe Bradley . . . .   Michael J. Stark
Logan Stafford . . . .   Richard Hamilton
Chet Stafford . . . .   Bill Herndon
Duke Lafferty . . . .   Gary Phillips
Derek Colby . . . .   Harley Venton
Trudy Wilson . . . .   Amy Steel
Trish Lewis . . . .   Rebecca Hollen
Tony Reardon . . . .   Gregory Beecroft
Gracie Middleton . . . . . .   Lori Shelle
Carrie Todd Marler . . . .   Jane Elliot
Quinton McCord . . . . . .   Michael Tylo
Violet Renfield . . . .   Beulah Garrick
Josh Lewis . . . .   Robert Newman
Lesley Ann Monroe . . . .   Carolyn Ann Clarke
Mark Evans . . . .   Mark Pinter

Maureen Reardon . . . . .   Ellen Dolan
Lucian Goff . . . .   Andreas Katsulas
Ron Kennedy . . . .   Matthew Barry
Helena Manzini . . . .   Rose Alaio
Silas Crocker . . . .   Benjamin Hendrickson
Ivy Pierce . . . .   Deborah May
Brian Lister . . . .   Richard Clarke
Mona Enright . . . .   Leslie O'Hara

Creator: Irna Phillips
Head Writers: Irna Phillips, Agnes Nixon, Julian Funt and David Lesan, Theodore and Mathilde Ferro, John Boruff, James Lipton, Gabrielle Upton, Jane and Ira Avery, Robert Soderberg and Edith Sommer, James Gentile, Robert Cenedella, Bridget and Jerome Dobson, Douglas Marland, Pat Falken Smith, L. Virginia Browne
Executive Producers: Lucy Ferri Rittenberg, Allen Potter
Producers: David Lesan, Richard Dunn, Peter Andrews, Harry Eggart, Charlotte Savitz Ciraulo, Leslie Kwartin, Joe Willmore
Directors: Ted Corday, Walter Gorman, Jack Wood, Gary Delmar, John Neukum, Joseph K. Chomyn, Nick Havinga, Leonard Valenta, Peter Miner, John Litvack, John Sedwick, Allen Fristoe, Harry Eggart, Lynwood King, Jeff Bleckner, John Tracy, John Pasquin, Bruce Franchini, Randy Winburn, Michael Gliona, Robert Schwarz, Bruce Barry, Jill Mitwell
Organists: Burt Buhrman, John Gart, Charles Paul
Musical Director (later): Charles Paul
Packager: Procter & Gamble

LOVING

BACKGROUND AND STORY

Every executive in the soap world is holding his breath. If *Loving* turns out to be a success, the ad agencies will buzz with sudden conferences, the telephone wires between producers and head writers will burn hotly. Co-created by the strong team of Agnes Nixon and Douglas Marland, *Loving* premiered on June 26, 1983 and was the first new soap to attempt to appeal to the same young audience that *All My Children* and *General Hospital* generated in the seventies. Doug Marland, in fact, was the head writer of *General Hospital* in 1978, expanding the Scotty Baldwin/Laura Vining story, which captured the fancy of millions of teenagers. Mrs. Nixon, of course, created and wrote *All My Children*, loved by millions of college students.

What the soap world badly wants to know now, and *Loving* may give it the answer, is how much more youth appeal daytime serials should have than they already have. With its university backdrop, the focus of the new show is on young love in a highly contemporary setting. One of the three families in the story is wealthy and one is lower middle-class, revealing a "classic soap opera" structure, but with references to contemporary topics such as liberal priests, the media revolution, campus rebellion, even President Reagan's austere budget cuts and the terrifying new contagious disease, AIDS.

This is Agnes Nixon's third serial creation for ABC (following *One Life To Live* and her hugely successful *All My Children*) and Doug Marland's first. (See the story on Mrs. Nixon preceding the *All My Children* story line summary.) Young, easygoing Doug Marland lives and works in Connecticut. He first had contact with the soap world as an actor on shows like *The Brighter Day* and *As The World Turns*. In the early seventies he began working as a script writer for Harding Lemay, who was the head writer of *Another World*. Doug Marland's talent was unmistakable and in 1976 he became the head writer for *The Doctors*, scripting the show with an eye toward a young audience. Two years later Jacqueline Smith, head of daytime in New York for ABC, aware of the youthful energy Marland had injected into *The Doctors*, hired him to do the same for *General Hospital*. Doug's brilliant scripts and Gloria Monty's revolutionary producing made that show top-rated. In 1980 he became head writer for *Guiding Light* and later created his own continuing serial for cable TV's Showtime called *A New Day In Eden*, about the love lives of young adults.

He and Agnes Nixon began working on their new soap, which was taped in New York, six months prior to its premiere from a basic story that Agnes had written. She has said that one of her objectives in the creation of *Loving* was to write a soap for the college audience which first discovered her *All My Children*. *Loving*'s first few months were high-rated, as many viewers quickly took to Doug Marland's inspired scripts, his energetic characters, and the show's excellent direction and production values.

235

THE CHARACTERS

Loving centers on three families connected with Alden University in the eastern seaboard town of Corinth, within driving distance from New York, Philadelphia and Washington, D.C. MERRILL VOCHEK is a young, attractive, ambitious anchorwoman on WCN television in Corinth. Her brother, JIM VOCHEK, is a progressive young priest. Their sister, NOREEN VOCHEK DONOVAN, is a nurse (who works with AIDS patients) married to policeman-Vietnam vet MIKE DONOVAN. Mike's father, PATRICK DONOVAN, is a retired policeman who now heads campus security at Alden University; Mike's mother is ROSE, a seamstress. Their other son, DOUGLAS DONOVAN, is a professor of drama and communications. The youngest, STACEY, will soon be a student at the university.

ROGER FORBES is the new president of Alden University, in love with Merrill Vochek, and his wife, ANN, is the daughter of society people CABOT and ISABELLE ALDEN. Cabot is the chairman of the board at Alden; his grandfather founded the institution. Roger and Ann have two children: JACK FORBES, a sophomore and popular athletic figure on campus, and LORNA FORBES,

soon to be a freshman. Isabelle and Cabot have another grandson, CURTIS.

Two other smaller family groups serve in a supporting capacity. GARTH SLATER, Dean of the University, is the husband of JUNE and father of LILY, a high school senior. BILLY BRISTOW heads the athletic department and is married to flirtatious RITA MAE. They are both southerners.

PREMIERE CAST

Merrill Vochek	Patricia Kalember
Father Jim Vochek	Peter Davies
Noreen Vochek Donovan	Marilyn McIntyre
Mike Donovan	James Kiberd

Loving, which began on June 26, 1983, was about three families in the university town on Corinth. The Donovan family included, from left: Marilyn McIntyre as Noreen, Mike's wife; Teri Keane as Rose, their mother; Bryan Cranston as Douglas, a college professor; and James Kiberd as Mike, a policeman who lost his job because of government cutbacks.

The wealthy family of the story were the Forbeses, which included, seated: Susan Walters (left) as Lorna Forbes, Shannon Eubanks as Ann. Standing, John Shearing (left) as Roger Forbes, the president of Alden University, and Perry Stephens as star athlete Jack Forbes.

Rose Donovan	Teri Keane	Lily Slater	Jennifer Ashe
Patrick Donovan	Noah Keen	Billy Bristow	Tom Ligon
Douglas Donovan	Bryan Cranston	Rita Mae Bristow	Pamela Blair
Stacey Donovan	Lauren-Marie Taylor		
Roger Forbes	John Shearin		
Ann Alden Forbes	Shannon Eubanks		
Jack Forbes	Perry Stephens		
Lorna Forbes	Susan Walters		
Cabot Alden	Wesley Addy		
Isabelle Alden	Augusta Dabney		
Curtis Alden	Chris Marcantel		
Garth Slater	John Cunningham		
June Slater	Ann Williams		

Creators: Agnes Nixon and Douglas Marland
Head Writer: Douglas Marland
Producer: Joseph Stuart
Directors: Andrew D. Weyman and Robert L. Scinto
Musical Director: Michael Karp
Packager: Dramatic Creations, Inc.
Musical Director: Michael Karp
Packager: Dramatic Creations, Inc.

ONE LIFE TO LIVE

IN late 1967 ABC asked Agnes Nixon (see her career story in the section preceding the *All My Children* summary) to devise a daytime serial for the network. What she came up with in her debut as a soap creator was an intriguing saga of romances and intermarriage between different classes, ethnic groups and, even in one story, between different races. "It was certainly a risk," said Agnes. "As long as I can remember, the networks and producers have always had a parochial philosophy about daytime serials: 'Stay away from anything controversial.' As a writer I got tired of all the putdowns by the critics of the serials who said we never did anything relevant."

On July 15, 1968, *One Life To Live* was born. In the first two years' story line, a poor Polish-American auto mechanic fell in love with the unstable daughter of a wealthy WASP, while the same daughter fell in love with an Irish-American, whose sister had married a Jew, while another daughter of the wealthy WASP fell for the doctor brother of the Polish-American mechanic, whose devoted hard-working sister eventually became involved with a middle-aged doctor who had once fallen in love with a black woman. It was all endlessly wonderful and beautifully written, bringing in high ratings for the network.

Agnes carefully researched her stories, trying out new devices, such as her split-personality story involving Victoria Lord, and a tasteful tale of a light-skinned black woman who, for the show's first four months, was thought by the audience to be white. Before involving the character, Carla Gray, in a love story with a black man, Agnes spoke to the actress, Ellen Holly, at length about the problems that light-skinned blacks have with whites and other blacks. The outcome was a believable story in which the family of the black doctor with whom Carla Gray fell in love rejected her because of her light skin.

Agnes Nixon's theme in her *One Life To Live* was clear and simple: despite misunderstandings arising out of differences between various economic, cultural and ethnic groups, we are all alike inside. In 1970, as part of the show's mission of raising social consciousness, the character of Cathy Craig became involved with drugs and joined New York's Odyssey House, a real-life rehabilitation center for teenage addicts. The show filmed Cathy in therapy sessions with the actual boys and girls of the center. Later, the same character wrote an article for the town's newspaper, the *Banner*, dealing with the subject of venereal disease. Viewers were asked to write in for free copies of the article, which Agnes Nixon carefully researched and wrote with the aim of helping people obtain necessary information about a taboo subject.

Notwithstanding such services to the public and the show's greater relevance than other soaps, *One Life To Live* did not gain popularity with viewers because of its social awareness but because of the drama itself. Agnes Nixon's characters, her method of intertwining story threads and the day-to-day plotting revealed her as a master storyteller, as she remains today with the show she still writes, *All My Children*.

By the mid-seventies, *One Life To Live* veered

away from interethnic stories and became a more traditional soap opera, even though the characters still had ethnic-sounding last names: Riley, Wolek, Siegel. No doubt management realized that tales of romances between members of different social groups could not be sustained indefinitely. In 1975, to boost sagging ratings, the story focused on a new villainess, Dr. Dorian Cramer, and a new hero and heroine, liberated Pat Kendall and adventurer Tony Lord—played by Jacquie Courtney and George Reinholt, who had been the popular Steve and Alice on *Another World*. These characters brought small Llanview a more worldly flavor and moved the show even further away from its earlier story lines.

During the renovation that ABC did on its house soaps in 1978, *One Life To Live* was reshaped into a far more glamorous show, offering much of the "adult" fare that was succeeding on nighttime soaps such as *Dallas*. There was now a new interest in prostitution—not the seamy kind, but the sort that French *auteur* filmmakers love, about a beautiful young wife who secretly turns tricks to make extra spending money. There was also a handsome pimp who later attempted to redeem his debauched life by pretending to be his deceased twin, a doctor. In 1980 the story was dominated by a wealthy but morally bankrupt Texan and his handsome sons, with lots of sexual blackmail and a scandal concerning the Texan's presumed deceased wife. *One Life To Live* had become unmitigated story, pure entertainment. In the current story line only two of Agnes Nixon's original characters are left: Vicky Lord, now married into the Texas Buchanan family, and Dr. Larry Wolek, her brother-in-law and dear friend.

One sad note: In 1980 Nat Polen, who for many years had played Dr. Jim Craig, died of cancer. For some time he had known that he was terminally ill but chose to continue in his role until the last. In respect for Polen's memory, the role was not recast.

THE STORY

Among Llanview's most prominent families were the Lords, headed by VICTOR LORD (Ernest Graves, lastly Shepperd Strudwick), wealthy owner of Llan-

When One Life To Live *premiered on July 15, 1968, one of its few WASP families were the Lords of Llanview. Wealthy widower Victor Lord (Ernest Graves) had hoped for a son but wound up with two daughters. Frustrated, he raised his healthier daughter, Victoria Lord (Gillian Spencer), as he would a son, making her prideful and ambitious. Eventually she developed a severe case of split personality.*

Joe Riley (Lee Patterson) and his sister, Eileen Riley Siegel (Patricia Roe), had been brought up in a poor Irish-American family. She was married to a Jewish lawyer named Dave Siegel. Vicky's attraction to Joe, a fellow reporter at the Banner, *only worsened her schizophrenia.*

view's newspaper, the *Banner*. A widower, Victor had been blessed with two daughters, but he had always really wanted a son to carry on his name. So he did the next best thing: He began to treat his older daughter, VICTORIA LORD (Gillian Spencer, currently Erika Slezak), as if she were the son he never had—dominating her and instilling in her a sense of duty and family pride. She grew up to be a beautiful, strong-minded woman, and a great asset to Victor as the *Banner's* bright chief business executive. But because of her upbringing, Vicky fell deeply out of touch with herself and would not admit how much she needed a man. She began to exhibit signs of bizarre emotional breakdown: a split personality began to emerge. At times she was Victoria and at times she was a mysterious persona called "Nikki Smith," the pliant part of Vicky who openly sought love from a man. Unknown to Vicky's family, or Vicky herself, "Nikki" would wander around Llanview.

The Woleks, Polish-Americans, were even poorer than the Rileys. Vince Wolek (Antony Ponzini) fell in love with "Nikki Smith," who used to come into the garage where he worked, but had no idea that she was really the alter ego of wealthy Victoria Lord. When the truth finally came out, and Vince realized that she was socially beyond his reach, he turned to his sister, Anna Wolek (Doris Belack), for comfort.

When JOE RILEY (Lee Patterson) first came to work at the *Banner*, Vicky was immediately attracted to this hard-living, hard-drinking loner with an enormous talent for writing. They were both reporters at the time and competed with each other for stories, all in great fun. Her attraction to Joe, however, was worsening her schizophrenia, which was eventually uncovered and cured by psychiatrist DR. MARCUS POLK (Norman Rose). Now able to accept her love for Joe, Vicky and he were at last married. He was everything Vicky had ever longed for in a man.

Their idyll ended, however, with the sudden screech of automobile wheels. Joe was in an auto crash and presumed dead, and Vicky's world was shattered. She turned for comfort to a fellow executive at the *Banner*—stable, conservative STEVEN BURKE (Bernard Grant).

Vicky's younger sister, MEREDITH LORD (Lynn Benesch), was frail, suffering from a debilitating blood disorder. Meredith fell in love with DR. LARRY WOLEK (Mike Storm), whose different background—he was a poor Polish-American from the wrong side of the tracks—caused her father to disapprove of a union between the two. Meredith, he felt, had been brought up properly and could never be happy with someone like Larry. But the couple persisted, and eventually Victor Lord, a sensible man at heart, was forced to accept the situation. After their wedding, Victor, knowing that Larry didn't have much money, generously asked them to live with him at Llanfair, the family estate, but Larry wanted to remain independent of his domineering father-in-law, so he and Meredith instead moved into a garage apartment on the estate.

Later, Meredith became pregnant—against doctor's orders—and she had twins. Only one, DANNY WOLEK (played as an adult by Tim Waldrip), lived. The death of one of her babies, and the warning of doctors that she should never risk childbirth again, sent her into a postpartum depression. At this point it was thought wise for her to undergo pyschiatric counseling—and she was successfully treated by none other than DR. JOYCE BROTHERS (playing herself).

Larry's family, the Woleks, were an amazing example of the American Dream come true—no matter how poor you are, with enough hard work you can become as successful as the next man. There were three Wolek children: ANNA WOLEK (played longest by Doris Belack), the oldest; VINCE WOLEK (played longest by Antony Ponzini); and Larry. At first, all the Wolek children, whose parents were dead, lived together and gave one another a helping hand. Vince, tough on the outside but with a heart as big as California is long, owned the B&W Trucking Company and put his younger brother, Larry, through medical school. Anna, a wise and wonderful woman, would do anything to help her brothers out of difficulty.

As a youngster, Anna Wolek was in love with Joe Riley, and in that regard she was no different from any other woman with whom Joe later came into contact. Later Anna entered Llanview society (just like Larry), when she married DR. JAMES CRAIG (Nat Polen), a widower with a daughter, CATHY CRAIG (Amy Levitt, Dorrie Kavanaugh, Jennifer Harmon). Cathy had a severe adjustment problem as an adolescent and was by that time becoming a drug addict. With the help of her parents, and therapy sessions at Odyssey House—a real rehabilitation center for young addicts—Cathy

kicked her habit.

Joe Riley's sister, EILEEN (last played by Alice Hirson), fell in love with DAVE SIEGEL (Allan Miller), a lawyer. The fact that he was Jewish and she was a Gentile posed certain problems for the two, which they worked out in time. They had a son, TIMMY SIEGEL (last played by Tom Berenger), and a daughter, JULIE SIEGEL (Lee Warrick, Leonie Norton), an oversensitive girl who became involved in an unhappy affair with callous JACK LAWSON (Jack Ryland). When Julie tried to kill herself over the affair, she was saved in the nick of time by handsome DR. MARK TOLAND (Tommy Lee Jones). Soon Mark and Julie became romantically involved and were wed.

Julie loved Mark but was still haunted by her guilt feelings over her affair with Jack Lawson. Julie's subconscious began working overtime, making her frigid with Mark. When her lack of sexual responsiveness began to wreak havoc on her marriage, Julie started

The three Wolek children had lost their parents. Anna and Vince slaved to put their young brother, Larry Wolek (Paul Tulley), through medical school. Nurse Karen Martin (Niki Flacks) seduced Larry, became pregnant, then forced him to marry her. But it was frail Meredith Lord (Trish Van Devere), Vicky's sister, whom Larry really loved, ever since she had stood by him during Larry's trial for the murder of Dr. Ted Hale.

seeing Dr. Polk, a psychiatrist, to help her overcome her sexual coldness toward Mark.

At first, her mother, Eileen, didn't think that seeing a psychiatrist was any way for Julie to solve the problem. But then, Eileen Siegel hadn't been thinking clearly since her husband, Dave Siegel, had died of a heart attack. An "up" person at heart, but always on the verge of hysteria when faced with the distress of those around her, Eileen was finding herself overcome by emotional burdens, among them the loss of her husband and the problem of her daughter, Julie. She began taking tranquilizers and pep pills to get through her day. It wasn't long before she was addicted to them.

Making Eileen's emotional state worse was the sudden death of her close friend, Meredith Wolek. Always fragile, suffering from a blood disorder, Mer-

edith was assaulted by burglars who had broken into her house. After they knocked her down. she suffered a cerebral hemmorhage and later died in the hospital. Her husband, Larry Wolek, was shocked and devastated. He and his son Danny, moved in with his sister, Anna, and her family.

Joe Riley was not dead, after all! A lovable waitress in a Llanview restaurant, WANDA WEBB (Marilyn Chris), had fallen in love with him, although neither she nor he knew at the time that he was Joe Riley. After the auto crash Joe suffered amnesia and had been wandering ever since. Suddenly Joe collapsed in her restaurant from an aneurysm, and when he was rushed to the hospital, everyone in Llanview—including Vicky, now Mrs. Steven Burke—knew that Joe Riley was alive.

Vicky didn't know which husband she wanted— Joe Riley or Steve Burke. In a way, she loved them both, but each for different reasons. Her decision was to stay with Steve—even though she still loved Joe, perhaps even more than Steve. Joe's presence at the

The problem of Vicky's split personality had been uncovered and corrected by Dr. Polk, enabling Vicky to marry Joe Riley in 1969. Soon after, he was presumed killed in an auto accident.

Ellen Holly appeared as Carla Gray, a light-skinned black woman who was attempting to "pass" in white Llanview society. While engaged to black Dr. Pryce Trainor with the approval of her mother Sadie, she also became involved with Dr. James Craig (Robert Milli), using the name "Benari."

Banner, where he was once again working as its top writer, was sending Steve Burke into a panic over the fate of his marriage and was making Vicky more and more uncomfortable about the decision she had made. Finally, Vicky asked Steve for a divorce to marry Joe.

Joe Riley was now Vince Wolek's roommate. Vince, who gave up the trucking business to become a policeman, was falling head over heels in love with Wanda Webb. Vince, the perpetual bachelor, and Wanda were married in a beautiful wedding.

Vince's black friend and fellow police officer was LIEUTENANT ED HALL (Al Freeman, Jr.), who at long last was marrying CARLA GRAY (Ellen Holly), Dr. Jim Craig's pleasant secretary. A light-skinned black, Carla for a long time would not admit to being black, and even rejected her mother, the Woleks' former neighbor SADIE GRAY (Lillian Hayman), in order to pass for white. Carla now accepted her blackness and was proud of it. Carla and her new husband were making plans to adopt JOSHUA WEST (Laurence Fishburne), a rebellious boy who was involved with youth gangs. For Carla, the adoption of a young black "alter ego" was yet another way of reconciling herself to her own painful past.

A newcomer to the Llanview Hospital was DR. DORIAN CRAMER (Nancy Pinkerton, Claire Malis, Robin Strasser). She lived with her sister, MELINDA (Patricia Pearcy, Jane Badler), who had been crippled in a riding accident. Attractive Dorian, who had become an overprotective keeper of her sister, had made up her mind never to marry because of Melinda. Nevertheless, she began an affair with Dr. Mark Toland, who was sexually frustrated because of his wife Julie's frigidity. When Melinda discovered that her sister and Mark were cohabiting secretly in a rented apartment, she became even more deeply disturbed but refused to tell either Dr. Polk or Larry Wolek, her only real friend in Llanview.

There was yet another dark secret in Llanview. While Joe Riley desperately hoped that Steven Burke would grant Vicky her divorce so that she might once again become Mrs. Joe Riley, he was unaware that Cathy Craig was pregnant with his child. Before Vicky had given Joe reason to hope that they might be reconciled, he had gone to New York with Cathy to try to

Mike Storm became the third Larry Wolek and Lynn Benesch was the new Meredith. Larry and Meredith finally wed by 1969 but had scant happiness. Mery suffered from a severe blood disorder which required her to be hospitalized periodically.

Peggy Wood made a guest appearance as Dr. Kate Nolan, Dr. Jim Craig's mother-in-law from his previous marriage. Now played by Nat Polen, Jim Craig had just married Anna Wolek (in 1970). At left is Jim's grown daughter Cathy Craig (Amy Levitt), who was to become a focal point in the story.

help her write her first novel, not realizing that Cathy was deeply attracted to him. Lonely and distraught, Joe allowed Cathy to seduce him into a brief affair. Now, with Vicky again in Joe's life, Cathy decided that she would suffer the terrible burden of her pregnancy alone.

* * *

An endless swirl of complicated events, touching the lives of everyone in Llanview, began with the deceptively simple tragedy of RACHEL WILSON (Nancy Barrett). Rachel, terminally ill, generated great compassion in her doctor, Larry Wolek. He wanted to help his patient face death with dignity, but her husband, BEN FARMER (Rod Browning), insisted on subjecting her to heroic would-be cures at another hospital. Larry fought Ben for "custody" of Rachel, who was begging to be granted her own "right to die." Suddenly she was found dead from an overdose of potassium chloride and Larry was arrested on a charge of murder (there is no such thing as a charge of "mercy killing"). After

a prolonged trial, Larry was convicted. Then, Dorian Cramer confessed that she and her secret lover, Dr. Mark Toland, had caused Rachel's death. Through a series of oversights at the hospital, they had both given Rachel the same dose of her normal potassium chloride injection, killing her. After Dorian's revelation, Larry was cleared, Dorian was fired from Llanview Hospital, and Mark Toland, who had committed manslaughter, fled town. Melinda Cramer, already verging on breakdown, became institutionalized.

Steve Burke, realizing that his marriage was hopeless, gave Vicky her divorce so that she could wed Joe Riley, and eventually left Llanview. Joe and Vicky were happy about their forthcoming remarriage; then Joe suddenly learned from his sister, Eileen Siegel, that Cathy Craig was carrying his baby. Joe nobly offered to marry Cathy, even though he loved Vicky, but Cathy didn't want a marriage based only on a pregnancy. In the end, however, Cathy swallowed her

1970. When Dr. Craig discovered that his daughter, Cathy, had become a drug addict, he insisted that she join New York's Odyssey House, a real-life rehabilitation center for teenage drug addicts. One Life to Live filmed Amy Levitt and Nat Polen in scenes with the actual boys and girls at the center.

Vicky (now Erika Slezak, daughter of Walter Slezak), turned to Steve Burke (Bernie Grant) after Joe was presumed dead in 1971. On the day Vicky married Steve, Joe turned up alive. For many months Vicky was torn between the two men.

pride and decided to accept Joe's repeated proposals of marriage—but before she could tell Joe, he had already run off and married Vicky.

Cathy gave birth to MEGAN CRAIG RILEY, who became Cathy's whole life. Not long after Megan's birth it was learned that she had a heart defect which threatened her life. Joe began spending many hours with Cathy and their unhealthy little girl, neglecting Vicky. After surgery was performed on Megan's heart, her doctors—Larry Wolek and Jim Craig—realized that the child would only live a few years at the most. They also told Vicky that Megan's condition was inherited from Joe's genes, making it dangerous for him to father another child. Fearing that this terrible news would destroy her marriage, Vicky made Larry and Jim promise not to tell Joe.

Mark Toland, now hiding from the police in San Francisco, accidentally spotted Victor Lord in the same city. Mark found out that Victor had been looking for his long-lost illegitimate son and then discovered the son's identity from his mother, DOROTHY RANDOLPH. When Mark returned to Llanview to sell the new information to Victor, Dorian involved Mark in another moneymaking scheme. She had accidentally stumbled upon hospital records which showed that

Joe Riley was the carrier of the genes responsible for Megan's terminal illness. She gave the information to Mark for him to blackmail Vicky. He asked her for $50,000, threatening to tell Joe the truth if he was not paid. Vicky agreed, but later kept going to Mark's room at the Llanview Motel with Larry Wolek to beg for more time to raise the money.

Mark Toland was suddenly found murdered. Lieutenant Ed Hall discovered Julie Toland's fingerprints in Mark's motel room, but before she could be arrested her brother, Tim, confessed to the murder to protect Julie. Finally, nurse SUSAN BARRY (Lisa Richards) solved the mystery of Mark's death. She had been desperately in love with Larry Wolek and driven to alcoholism because of his rejection of her. One night she had gone to Mark's motel room, where she believed Larry and Vicky were consummating an affair, and, in a drunken rage, began struggling with Mark, who had a gun. The gun went off and Mark was killed. Later, she came back to the scene of the crime and, when a stranger opened the door, Susan be-

Wanda Webb (Marilyn Chris) was a lovable waitress who fell in love with Joe Riley when she discovered him in her restaurant in 1971. A triangle began when Vince found himself in love with Wanda. Marilyn Chris and Antony Ponzini had many splendidly acted comic scenes together.

Julie Siegel (Lee Warrick) married Dr. Mark Toland (Tommy Lee Jones) in 1973, but they were unhappy from the start because of Julie's mysterious frigidity. Jane Alice Brandon (left) was the new Cathy Craig.

lieved he was the ghost of Mark, became terrified, ran into the street and was hit by a motorcycle. As she lay dying, she confessed the incredible story to the police.

TONY HARRIS LORD (George Reinholt, Philip MacHale, Chip Lucia) was that stranger in the motel room, soon to play an even more important part in this onrush of fate. For a number of years, Tony had been living the life of a soldier of fortune, ending up in Vietnam, where he ran a nightclub in Saigon. He had smuggled a valuable piece of jade to his mother—who was Dorothy Randolph. Tony was Victor Lord's son! After she died, Tony followed Mark Toland back to Llanview, assuming that Mark had stolen the jade. But then Mark was murdered.

Meanwhile, Dorian Cramer and MATT MCALLISTER (Vance Jeffries), Victor Lord's protege, were both caring for Victor Lord, who had suffered a heart attack. The two began scheming ways of acquiring Victor's fortune. A duped Victor married Dorian, who expected him to die soon, leaving her a wealthy widow. Before long Victor and Tony learned that they were father and son and saw one another. But because Dorian had told Tony lies, turning him against Victor, he lambasted his father, rejecting all the values that the Lords stood for. Aghast, Victor cut Tony out of his will. When Victor finally learned the truth about Dorian's plotting, the shock was too much and he died of a stroke before he could change his will. Through her cunning, Dorian had become a wealthy widow.

* * *

Young Tim Siegel died in one of Llandview's most senseless tragedies. He had been in love with pretty and proper JENNY WOLEK (Kathy Glass, now Brynn Thayer), a cousin of the Woleks' who came to Llanview as a novitiate nun taking nursing courses at the hospital. Tim's mother, Eileen Siegel, didn't approve of the relationship because she felt it had been the cause of Tim's giving up law school; Vince Wolek was also vehemently opposed to the romance between Tim and his niece, because in his eyes Jenny was already a nun (novitiates are in training, and aren't nuns until they take their final vows). After Jenny experienced much heartache over whether she wished to be married to God or to Tim, she decided to become Tim's wife. Furious over her decision, Vince and Tim got into a heated argument on the stairs of Llanview Hospital. Tim lost his balance and fell, hitting his head and becoming critically injured. Jenny

Eileen Siegel (Alice Hirson) and members of the Wolek family pleaded with her son Timmy (Tom Berenger) to stop seeing Jenny Wolek, a novitiate nun, in 1975. Jenny finally married him just before he died following a fall down a flight of stairs.

Dr. Dorian Kramer (Nancy Pinkerton) treated heart patient Victor Lord (Shepherd Strudwick), then married him for his money. She viciously kept from him the truth that he had a long-lost son. When Victor died, Dorian became his wealthy widow.

and Tim were married in his hospital bed only minutes before he died.

Strong-minded PAT KENDALL (Jacqueline Courtney) came to Llanview with her son BRIAN (Steve Austin) to work as an editor at the *Banner*. Some years before she had had an affair with Tony Lord in Rio de Janeiro. Unknown to Tony, Pat became pregnant and had his son, Brian. Although Pat was still in love with Tony, she refused to tell him the truth, even now, because she believed that her husband, a fugitive and a radical, was still alive. At first Pat pretended to be interested in Tony again only as a friend, while Brian began to look upon him as a kind of a father.

Meanwhile, Joe and Cathy's child, Megan, was killed in a terrible accident! Megan had been having a respiratory attack and Vicky, in a panic, drove her to the hospital. The car crashed, killing Megan and putting Vicky in a coma for months. Cathy developed a psychopathic hate for Vicky, although Joe knew that the accident wasn't Vicky's fault.

After she recovered, Vicky was shocked to learn that she was pregnant with Joe's child. Vicky had to choose either to have an abortion and lose her love child, or risk having a baby born like Megan. She decided to have the baby. Then vicious Dorian, seeing a chance to hurt Vicky, her arch enemy, told Joe the truth, that Megan had inherited a terminal disease from him. Deeply hurt at Vicky's web of lies, Joe refused to make love to his wife and the marriage was nearly finished. Making matters worse, Larry Wolek, who had been Vicky's only source of comfort, realized that he was falling in love with her.

Tony Lord had been growing impatient with Pat's strange indecisiveness and allowed himself to become involved with Cathy Craig. He married her, without realizing that she was becoming mentally unbalanced. She began seeing psychiatrist DR. WILL VERNON (Farley Granger, Bernie McInerney, Tony George) about her morbid fantasies concerning her dead daughter. After Vicky gave birth to frail, slightly premature KEVIN, Cathy went insane and believed that he was really her baby. She took it from Llanview Hospital to a place far from town, while Vicky, Joe, Jim Craig and all their friends became frantic. The baby was eventually discovered by a detective hired by Dorian. Overjoyed at Baby Kevin's return, Vicky and Joe found happiness again. Cathy Craig came back to

George Reinholt and Jacqueline Courtney were fired from their roles as Steve and Alice on Another World *in 1975 and were quickly hired by* One Life To Live *to play the lovers, Tony Lord and Pat Kendall. The move was obviously made to attract fans of rival* Another World.

Movie star Farley Granger originated the 1976 role of psychiatrist Dr. Will Vernon, who was treating the mentally disturbed Cathy Craig (Jennifer Harmon). Will's children, Brad and Samantha, later became prominent in the story.

Llanview, was greatly helped by psychiatrist Will Vernon, and divorced Tony Lord, who was still in love with Pat. Then Cathy found herself drawn to Larry Wolek. But when Larry married Jenny's pretty young sister, KAREN WOLEK (Kathy Breech, Judith Light)—his "kissing cousin"—Cathy went off to Arizona and California to finish a novel, which became a great success. She decided to stay out west.

Pat finally learned that her husband, PAUL KENDALL (Tom Fuccello), had indeed been killed and now she wanted to grow closer to Tony. Then Paul Kendall showed up! It turned out that he had been an FBI undercover agent. For Brian's sake, Pat tried to take up her life with Paul again, but her love for Tony was too strong and she divorced Paul.

* * *

Prostitution and pornography suddenly came to sedate Llanview. Larry Wolek's new bride, Karen, was an immature spendthrift who refused to live on Larry's hospital salary. She began turning tricks with older businessmen for extra money to buy dresses and jewelry. Larry, of course, had no idea. Then, MARCO DANE (Gerald Anthony) showed up in Llanview. An old lover of Karen's from a commune, lowlife Marco had gone into pimping and pornography. After discovering that Karen was a housewife-turned-prostitute, he forced her to accept him as her pimp. Meanwhile, Vicky Riley's sweet teenage godchild, TINA CLAYTON (Andrea Evans Massey), came to town and began living with Vicky. Marco offered naive Tina Clayton a job as a "model," which she accepted. After obtaining legitimate photographs of young Tina, he superimposed a photo of her head on the body of another girl who was nude and then showed the fake photo to a horrified Vicky. He threatened to distribute the photo unless Vicky paid him off, and for a while she considered giving in to the blackmail.

Karen's childish behavior soon began to ensnare everyone in a web of tragedy. After Pat Ashley Kendall divorced Paul Kendall, she decided to tell her son Brian that Tony Lord, and not Paul, was his real father. After she said the words, he was so upset that he ran into the street. At that moment, Karen was a passenger in a speeding car driven by TALBOT HUDDLESTON

Karen Wolek (Judith Light) married Larry Wolek, who had no idea that she was turning to prostitution to earn extra spending money. Slick Marco Dane (Gerald Anthony) became her pimp in 1978.

Edwina Lewis (Margaret Klenck, standing), a reporter at the Banner, *loved fellow reporter Richard Abbott (Luke Reilly), but because of her crass ambition lost him to the much sweeter Becky Lee Hunt (Jill Voigt), a country singer.*

(Byron Sanders), a shady businessman with whom Karen had been tricking. The car struck Brian, killing him, and sped away. No one knew who the hit-and-run driver was. After a grief-stricken Pat told Tony why Brian had run into the street, Tony couldn't handle his guilt and left Llanview to think things over.

Some time after the accident Vicky decided to go to Marco Dane's studio to tell him that she refused to accept his blackmail, only to find him murdered! Vicky was accused of his murder. At her trial, KATRINA KARR (Nancy Snyder), one of Marco's prostitutes, came forward to say that she saw Talbot Huddleston kill Marco. It seems that after he ran over little Brian Kendall that day with his speeding car, Marco found out, began blackmailing him, and Talbot murdered Marco. Vicky was exonerated and Talbot was arrested, but not before Karen Wolek was forced to testify about her own disgraceful career as a prostitute. She and Larry broke up.

After the trial Vicky and Joe Riley believed that they could finally settle down and be happy. There had been one heartache after another. Now they were delighted when Vicky found out that she was once again pregnant by him. But before the child was born,

Joe learned the terrible news that he had a brain tumor. He settled his affairs and faced death bravely. After Joe died, Vicky gave birth to a beautiful baby boy, JOEY.

Jim Craig almost died himself when escaped convicts held him hostage. The stress caused him to suffer a heart attack and his recovery took many months.

After Brian died and Tony Lord fled Llanview, unhappy Pat buried herself in her new work as hostess of her own television talk show, "The Pat Ashley Show." Rich financier ADAM BREWSTER (John Mansfield) saw her on television and came to Llanview to court her. She became involved with him, not knowing he had epilepsy. Later, when Pat found out that he

Dorian Cramer Lord (Claire Malis, right) tried to break up the romance between her backward sister, Melinda (Jane Badler), and Dr. Peter Janssen (Jeff Pomerantz) in 1979. After Peter married Melinda, Melinda went insane and tried to kill Jenny Wolek.

Tina Clayton (Andrea Evans), Vicky's sweet godchild, became the innocent victim of one evil moneymaking plot after another. First Marco Dane tried to blackmail Vicky with faked pornographic photos of Tina; then Tina was kidnapped; then unwittingly used by her criminal father to fleece Vicky. She is seen here (in 1979) with Greg Huddleston (Paul Joynt).

was dealing in violence and gun money, she broke off with him.

* * *

When NAOMI VERNON (Teri Keane)—the jealous, self-pitying wife of psychiatrist Will Vernon—took an overdose of sleeping pills, she fully expected to be found in time. But Naomi miscalculated and died. Will and Naomi's son, BRAD VERNON (Jameson Parker, Steve Fletcher), had fallen in love with sweet Jenny Wolek. Now, deeply upset over how his mother died, he felt he needed to sleep with Jenny before they were married. When Jenny refused he resumed an affair with an old girl friend, LANA MCLAIN (Jackie Zeman), who became pregnant by him. Suddenly Lana died of a drug overdose, like Brad's mother, and Brad was booked on suspicion of murder and jailed. After he was released, Jenny forgave his indiscretion and the two were wed. But Jenny would soon find that Brad's pattern of seeking sexual release with other women during times of crisis would cause her endless heartache.

Will's pretty young sister SAMANTHA ("SAM") VER-NON (Julie Montgomery, Susan Keith, Dorian LoPinto) was devastated when the car in which she was a passenger crashed, killing DR. PAMELA SHEPHERD (Kathleen Devine), who had been seeing Will romantically. She turned to Tony Lord, who came back to Llanview for a few months. Tony, realizing that he was the first man she had ever slept with, was going to marry Sam. But she knew he didn't return her love and called the wedding off. More experienced now, but not for the better, she began to live with Jim Craig's nephew MICK GORDON (James McDonnell), an Olympic speed skater who was immature about relationships. After Brad came out of jail, Sam began to help her brother rebuild his health club business, and Mick Gordon complained that Sam was neglecting him. The affair broke up but Sam had still not learned how to choose her men.

Two new reporters at the *Banner* were Vicky's cousin RICHARD ABBOTT (played longest by Luke Reilly) and EDWINA LEWIS (Margaret Klenck). They were in love but Richard Abbott objected to Edwina's crass ambition and materialism. He turned to BECKY LEE HUNT (Jill Voigt, now Mary Gordon Murray), a country

When Joe Riley died, strong-minded Clint Buchanan (Clint Ritchie) took over as publisher of the Banner *in 1980. He was attracted to Joe's grieving widow, Vicky, who at first wouldn't permit herself to return his interest—until he saved Tina Clayton from her kidnappers.*

Texas millionare Asa Buchanan (Philip Carey) came to Llanview to be near his son Clint, and tried to run everyone's lives. Kristen Meadows (left), played Mimi King, Asa's mistress, and Arlene Dahl played Lucinda Schenk, Mimi's mother.

singer who was as sweet as Edwina was grasping, and married her. For a long time Edwina tried to win Richard back, but eventually she fell in love with DR. MARIO CORELLI—Marco Dane's twin brother! However, just before their wedding he confessed to her the astonishing fact that he wasn't Mario but Marco Dane, who everyone thought had been murdered! After Mario had been mistaken for Marco by Talbot Huddleston and killed, Marco swore that he would atone for Mario's fate by virtually becoming him and doing his medical work (Marco had had medical training). After the hospital and the authorities found out about the impersonation, Marco was sent to prison for four weeks. When he was released he vowed that he would really become a doctor and entered medical school, while continuing a stormy romance with Edwina.

But before the Marco/Mario scandal was revealed, another one was in the making. Jenny Vernon had become pregnant, and while she was bedridden in the hospital Brad lustfully sought out other women, including Jenny's sister, Karen Wolek. When Karen refused to have relations with him, Brad raped her. Jenny found out and told Brad that their marriage was over.

Two women were about to give birth on the same day at Llanview Hospital—Jenny Vernon and Katrina Karr, who had been one of Marco's prostitutes and had fingered Talbot Huddleston as Mario's murderer. Kat told everyone that she would give up her baby after it was born. When Jenny's baby girl died, Karen begged Marco/Mario not to tell Jenny, who had suffered so much already, but to substitute Kat's new baby girl and pretend that it was Kat's baby that had died. Marco went along with the baby switch. Jenny named her new baby girl MARY, since Kat said that she was going to name *her* baby Mary if it had lived!

* * *

Edwina Lewis never knew that the father who

Bo Buchanan (Robert S. Woods) came to Llanview with his father Asa and fell in love with Pat Kendall. Asa schemed to break them up. For a while Bo was led to believe that Asa wasn't his natural father.

Pretty Katrina Karr (Nancy Snyder) had been one of Marco Dane's prostitutes and figured prominently in the show's long baby-switch story: her own illegitimate baby girl had been switched for Jenny Vernon's baby, which had died right after his childbirth. In 1981 Kat fell in love with Marcello Salta (Stephen Schnetzer).

had deserted her years before was DR. IVAN KIPLING (Jack Betts), who came to work at the hospital with his wife FAITH (Mary Linda Rapeleye). A brilliant brain surgeon but emotionally troubled, he visited prostitutes almost every night and outfitted them in sultry black negligées. One of them was Karen Wolek, the wife of his colleague Larry Wolek! When Faith found out and left Ivan, he went temporarily insane and tried to kill Karen by pushing her down the stairs. Before the law could catch up with him, he ran off with Faith to Rio de Janeiro.

Another deeply disturbed individual was Melinda Cramer, Dorian's younger sister, who had been having problems for years. DR. PETER JANSSEN (last played by Denny Albee), a fine doctor and well-liked by everyone (he had once been in love with Jenny in St. Carlos where she did missionary work), became engaged to Melinda. Domineering Dorian was convinced that Melinda was too much of a weakling to marry any man and plotted to break up the romance, but Melinda and Peter did marry. Melinda, however, became deeply depressed when she was told by a maestro that the injury to her arm would make it impossible for her to resume her career as a concert pianist. She was sent to the Compton Clinic, a mental

In 1982, Dorian (Robin Strasser) had to contend with the sudden arrival of her teenage illegitimate daughter, Cassie Howard (Cusi Cram). The two began a stormy relationship.

hospital, for nine months. Meanwhile, a lonely Peter found himself newly attracted to Jenny Wolek, who had separated from Brad.

The situation grew complicated. Peter treated Jenny's baby girl, Mary (Kat's baby girl), for a blood disease and thereby discovered that Mary could not have been Jenny's biological child. Brad also found out that Mary wasn't his daughter and told Peter that he would tell Jenny the truth, unless Peter stopped seeing her. Then Melinda came out of the Compton Clinic and, learning that she had lost Peter to Jenny, tried to kill Jenny. Melinda was put back in the clinic and Peter had his marriage to her annulled. Throughout all of this, Jenny still loved Brad!

On the day Peter and Jenny were finally married, Brad sent Jenny a vicious wedding present: a tape recording that Brad had made of Peter's confession to a priest of the terrible secret about Mary. Jenny refused to listen to the tape. Then Katrina Karr found out the truth herself and went to Jenny's, intending to air the whole situation. Desperate to stop Kat, Peter got in his car and drove toward Jenny's on an icy road, suddenly crashing to his death! The tragedy had been so unnecessary, for later Jenny listened to the tape recording and learned what no one wanted her to know. Bravely, she gave up Mary to Kat, on the condition that she could see the baby any time, and began to see more and more of Brad.

* * *

The fabulous and elaborate tale of the Texan Buchanan family began to unfold. Handsome and fiercely independent CLINT BUCHANAN (Clint Ritchie) came to town to take over the *Banner* from the dying Joe Riley. He had been estranged from his multi-millionnaire father, ASA BUCHANAN (Philip Carey), for years. Next, Asa Buchanan came to Llanview, to get to know his son Clint once again, and with him came an entourage of relations and friends. Among them was his other son, BO BUCHANAN (Robert Woods), who fought the influence of his super-domineering father.

Pat Ashley began seeing Clint Buchanan. Soon after Pat's twin sister MAGGIE (also Jacqueline Courtney) showed up in Llanview and became terribly jealous of Pat's accomplishments. Then she kidnapped Pat and locked her in the basement. Donning a wig like Pat's own hairdo and wearing Pat's dresses, Maggie started to date Clint Buchanan. But Clint became suspicious that this woman wasn't Pat. Fearing that she would be exposed, Maggie rushed into the basement, where Pat was still locked up, intending to shoot Pat with a gun. Then, during a struggle between the two sisters, the gun went off, killing Maggie. Pat was saved, but her relationship with Clint was short-lived. Pat and Clint argued over Maggie's death and broke up, and Pat turned to the less mature Bo Buchanan.

Bo's interest in Pat Ashley began a dramatic chain of events. Asa, despising strong, defiant women like Pat Ashley, tried to break up Bo and Pat by forcing Asa's own mistress, MIMI KING (Kristen Meadows), to seduce Bo. That scheme failed. Bo and Pat went to Paris together and met a woman calling herself NICOLE BANNARD (Taina Elg), who, as soon as she saw Bo, knew that he was her son. Nicole Bernard was really OLYMPIA BUCHANAN, Asa's wife and the mother of Bo and Clint. Years before, Olympia had had an affair with YANCY RALSTON (William Andrews) and became pregnant. During a stormy argument over whether to tell Asa, she had killed Yancy. When Asa found out the truth, he had Olympia banished, forcing her to take an assumed name and pretend to be dead in return for Asa's financial support. Now, after seeing her grown son Bo, Olympia came to Llanview with Bo and Pat and was determined that her two sons should know their mother again.

Asa reacted by having Olympia locked up in his creepy mansion, Moorecliff. He assigned his nephew, RAFE GARRETSON (Ken Meeker), to guard her. But Rafe felt sorry for her and began sending Pat Ashley notes with clues to the missing Nicole's (Olympia's) whereabouts. Meanwhile, Asa became engaged to Samantha Vernon, giving her a dazzling emerald ring. But Clint recognized it as the emerald ring that his mother Olympia had been buried with! When he opened up Olympia's crypt he found the body of a man. Asa married Sam and threw a masquerade ball at Moorecliff in her honor. Driven insane by her imprisonment, Olympia, lurking about the mansion during the ball, confronted Bo with the awful truth that she was his mother. Moments later, the crazed Olympia tried to kill Samantha, but in the violent struggle fell to her own death over a balcony. Soon after, Bo told off his father, taking his real father's name, "Ralston," and Sam divorced Asa. Bo took the name, "Ralston," after the mad Olympia led him to believe Ralston was his real father.

Clint Buchanan, now the publisher of the *Banner*, was falling in love with his predecessor's widow, Vicky Lord Riley. But Vicky was too distraught to face an involvement with him—although his vitality was very much like the late Joe's. Then her godchild, Tina Clayton, was suddenly kidnapped! Vicky, who was now quite wealthy through various trust funds left to her by her father, Victor Lord, was forced to pay a $500,000 ransom. When Clint rescued Tina and helped get Vicky's money back, Vicky realized she really did love Clint. Soon the larcenous TED CLAYTON (Keith Charles, Mark Goddard) came to town. The father of Tina Clayton, having deserted her years before, he pretended to be interested in reconciling with his daughter, but he was really interested in getting his hands on Vicky's great wealth. Whenever Ted Clayton visited Tina at Vicky's, he would slip Vicky a mind-altering drug that robbed her of all will. It made her forget her love for Clint and accept Ted's proposal of marriage. Clint tried to prove that Ted was a fraud.

But it was policeman Vinnie Wolek, who uncovered information proving that Ted was in cahoots with a ring of counterfeiters. Before he could tell what he knew, Vinnie Wolek was murdered by Ted Clayton! Ted had given him a dose of poison from a ring on his finger that made Vinnie's death seem like a heart attack. Karen Wolek, who had gone straight, now pretended to go back into prostitution to catch Ted. After Tina discovered that Ted had been drugging Vicky all along, Ted kidnapped Vicky and took her up to his cabin. Eventually Ted was captured, sent to prison and later shot to death by Ed Hall (now promoted to Captain). Clint almost died trying to rescue Vicky, who, freed from her ordeal, accepted his proposal of marriage. Tina, ashamed that she had had such a father, left Llanview.

Mean-spirited Dorian Cramer had gone from one affair to another, but finally chose to marry HERB CALLISON (Anthony Call), the ambitious district attorney who had tried Vicky for murder. Then Dorian's sixteen-year-old daughter, CASSIE HOWARD (Cusi Cram), came to Llanview and began living with Dorian and Herb, who adopted her. For years the girl had believed that Dorian was dead. Cassie started growing far closer to Herb than her mother. After Herb Callison won the governorship of the state, he learned that Dorian, with Asa Buchanan's help, had virtually bought the election. Herb then gave up the governorship, broke up with Dorian and moved out of Llanview with Cassie. The three of them, however, had a shaky reconciliation until DAVID REYNOLDS (Michael Zaslow), Cassie's real father, showed up.

After Bo and Pat Ashley broke up, Tony Lord came back to town and married Pat, at long last, in a wonderful wedding. Bo, meanwhile, began handling Becky Lee Abbott's singing career and dealing with his real father's relations: EUPHEMIA RALSTON (Grayson Hall), Bo's aunt; DELILAH RALSTON (Shelly Burch), her daughter; and DREW RALSTON (Matthew Ashford), her nephew. Bo took it upon himself to lavish the Ralstons with gifts and money, until he discovered his own mother had lied to him. Bo was Asa's son after all! Once Bo learned that Euphemia had known the truth about his parentage and had said nothing, Euphemia left town in disgrace. Bo then fell for Delilah, whom he knew not to be a blood relation, but she married Asa. Bo, distraught, had an affair with Becky Lee after her divorce from Richard. Then Delilah divorced Asa and married Bo. At the same time Becky found herself pregnant with Bo's child. To legitimize the child and to spite Bo, Asa then married Becky!

CAST
ONE LIFE TO LIVE
ABC: June 15, 1968

Victoria Lord Buchanan	Gillian Spencer (P)
	Joanne Dorian
	Erika Slezak*
	Christine Jones
Dr. Larry Wolek	Paul Tulley (P)
	James Storm
	Michael Storm*
Meredith Lord Wolek ..	Trish Van Devere (P)
	Lynn Benesch*
Victor Lord	Ernest Graves* (P)
	Syndey Walker
	Shepperd Strudwick
Anna Wolek Craig	Doris Belack* (P)
	Kathleen Maguire
	Phyllis Behar
Dr. James Craig	Robert Milli (P)
	Nat Polen*
Vincent Wolek	Antony Ponzini* (P)
	Jordan Charney
	Michael Ingram[1]
Joe Riley	Lee Patterson (P)
Eileen Siegel	Patricia Roe (P)
	Frances Sternhagen
	Alice Hirson
Dave Siegel	Allan Miller (P)
Sadie Gray	Lillian Hayman* (P)
	Hilda Haynes
	Esther Rolle
Dr. Price Trainor	Thurman Scott (P)
	Peter DeAnda*
Lt. Jack Neal	Lon Sutton (P)
	Jack Crowder*
Dr. Henry Stanton	Leon Stevens (P)
Dr. Ted Hale	Terry Logan (P)
Dr. Marcus Polk	Donald Moffat (P)
	Norman Rose*
Bill Kimbrough	Justin McDonough (P)
Karen Martin Wolek ...	Niki Flacks (P)
Cathy Craig Lord	Catherine Burns
	Amy Levitt
	Jane Alice Brandon
	Dorrie Kavanaugh
	Jennifer Harmon
Julie Siegel Toland	Lee Warrick*
	Leonie Norton
Tim Siegel	William Fowler
	William Cox
	Tom Berenger
Carla Gray Hall	Ellen Holly
Grace Trainor	Frances Foster
Amy	Jan Chasmar
Tom Edwards	Joseph Gallison
Dr. Kate Nolan	Peggy Wood
Millie Parks	Millee Taggart
Artie Duncan	John Cullum
Stan Perlo	Martin Meyers
Marcy Wade	Francesca James
Steve Burke	Bernard Grant
Bert Skelly	Wayne Jones
	Herb Davis*
Jack Lawson	David Snell
	Jack Ryland
Dr. Mark Toland	Tommy Lee Jones
Wanda Webb Wolek ...	Marilyn Chris*
	Lee Lawson

[1]This is not the same Michael Ingram who appears in other cast lists.

Capt. Ed Hall	Al Freeman, Jr.*
	David Pendleton
Josh West Hall	Larry Fishburne*
	Todd Davis
Hubcap	Scott Jacoby
	Lenny Bari
Dr. Dorian Cramer Callison	Nancy Pinkerton
	Claire Malis
	Robin Strasser
Melinda Cramer Janssen	Patricia Pearcy
	Jane Badler*
John Douglas	Donald Madden
Ben Howard	Albert Hall
Earl Brock	Kevin Conway
John Douglas	Donald Madden
Rachel Wilson	Nancy Barrett
Ben Farmer	Rod Browning
Susan Barry	Lisa Richards
Laszlo Braedeker	Walter Slezak
Danny Wolek	Neail Holland
	Eddie Moran
	Tim Waldrip
Mrs. Gordon	Ethel Barrymore Colt
Henry Simmons	Eli Mintz
Dr. Alex Blair	Peter Brouwer
Matt McAllister	Vance Jefferis
Jenny Wolek Janssen	Katherine Glass
	Bryann Thayer*
Sheilah Rafferty	Christine Jones
Sister Margaret	Dorothy Lyman
Bernice Munson	Kelly Houston
Michiko Kita	Lani Gerrie Miyazaki
Tony Harris Lord	George Reinholt*
	Philip MacHale
	Chip Lucia
Pat Kendall Lord	Jacqueline Courtney
Brian Kendall	Stephen Austin
Dr. Peter Janssen	Jeff Pomerantz*
	Robert Burton
	Denny Albee
Karen Wolek[2]	Kathryn Breech
	Judith Light*
Brad Vernon	Jameson Parker
	Steve Fletcher*

[2]There were two characters named Karen Wolek, each married to Larry.

Samantha Vernon	Julie Montgomery*
	Susan Keith
	Dorian LoPinto
Dr. Will Vernon	Farley Granger
	Bernie McInerney
	Anthony George*
Naomi Vernon	Teri Keane
Lana McClain	Jacklyn Zeman
Marco Dane	Gerald Anthony
Mary McGruder	Nancy Franklin
Frank McGruder	Frank Hamilton
Paul Kendall	Tom Fuccello
Rebecca Lee Hunt	Jill Voigt
	Mary Gordon Murray*
Richard Abbott	Luke Reilly*
	Keith Langsdale
	Robert Gribbon
Ina Hopkins	Sally Gracie
Edwina Lewis	Margaret Klenck
Dr. Pamela Shepherd	Kathleen Devine
Talbot Huddleston	Byron Sanders
Adele Huddleston	Lori March
Greg Huddleston	Paul Joynt
Dr. Jack Scott	Arthur Burghardt
Aldo Pierson	Berkeley Harris
Luke Jackson	Marshall Borden*
	Peter Matthey
Bonnie Harmer	Kim Zimmer
Herman Cantrell	Edmond Genest
Irene Clayton	Kate McKeown
Tina Clayton	Andrea Evans-Massey
Dick Grant	A. C. Weary
Gwendolyn Abbott	Joan Copeland
Adam Brewster	John Mansfield
Gretel Cummings	Linda Dano
Dennis O'Reardon	Rudy Hornish
Katrina Karr	Nancy Snyder
Herb Callison	Anthony Call
Dr. Ivan Kipling	Jack Betts
Faith Kipling	Mary Linda Rapeleye
Fran Gordon	Barbara Britton*
	Willi Burke
Mick Gordon	James McDonnell
Ellen Snow	Breon Gorman
Maggie Ashley	Jacqueline Courtney
Clint Buchanan	Clint Ritchie
Bo Buchanan	Robert S. Woods
Asa Buchanan	Philip Carey
Mimi King	Kristen Meadows

Chuck Wilson	Jeremy Slate
Jud Benson	Jamie Phillips
Jamie Rumson	Phillip Casnoff
Johnny Drummond	Wayne Massey
Scooter Burdette	Gordon Russell
Ted Clayton	Keith Charles
	Mark Goddard
Marcello Salta	Stephen Schnetzer
Lloyd Dieter	James Chesson
Olympia Buchana	Taina Elg
Rafe Garretson	Ken Meeker
Steve Piermont	Robert Desiderio
	Richard K. Weber
Pamela Chaffee	Judy Tate
Cassie Howard Callison	Cusi Cram
Meg Winter	Robin Morse
Chip Warren	Sammy Davis, Jr.
Lucinda Schenk	Arlene Dahl
Yancy Ralston	William Andrews
Blanche Ralston	Margaret Gwenver
Georgina Whitman	Ilene Kristen
	Nana Tucker Visitor*
Jimmy Whitman	Gregory Marc Schaffer
Astrid Collins	Marilyn McIntyre
Darryl Simon	Stuart Cohen
Renee Traynor	Sabrina Moore

Ariel Crane	Penny Campbell
Gary Corelli	Jeff Fahey
Kyle Dickenson	Peter Coleman
Karl Eberhardt	John Cunningham
Helen Murdoch	Marie Masters
Euphemia Ralston	Grayson Hall
Drew Ralston	Matthew Ashford
Delilah Ralston Buchanan	Shelly Burch
David Reynolds	Michael Zaslow

Creator: Agnes Nixon
Head Writers: Agnes Nixon, Paul Roberts and Don Wallace, Gordon Russell, Sam Hall and Peggy O'Shea
Executive Producer (first few months): Don Wallace
Producers: Doris Quinlan, Joseph Stuart, Jean Arley
Directors: Don Wallace, Walter Gorman, Jack Wood, Del Hughes, Neil Smith, David Pressman, Peter Miner, Gordon Rigsby, Al Freeman, Jr., Norman Hall, Lynwood King, Joseph Stuart, Ray Hoesten, Allen Fristoe, Larry Auerbach
Musical Direction: Aeolus Productions, Jack Urbont
Packagers: Creative Horizons, Inc., ABC-TV

RYAN'S HOPE

THE most remarkable aspect about the early *Ryan's Hope* was its great dignity. In a story about a large lower-middle-class Irish American family living in New York City, the writers found compassion for the point of view of every family member. Old-fashioned Johnny and Maeve Ryan wanted the best for their grown children, whose love lives were influenced by the changes in modern society. The likable, staunchly Catholic parents struggled to understand their children's behavior. Each of the children—Mary, Frank and Pat—made deeply painful choices in their personal lives, always respectful of their parents' feelings. As the moral universes of parents and children continually clashed, viewers were upset and enthralled by the truth of it all.

The creators were Claire Labine and Paul Avila Mayer. After ABC executives had seen the miracle that Labine and Mayer had performed as head writers of the badly failing *Where The Heart Is* and *Love of Life*, the network offered them their own serial. *Ryan's Hope* premiered July 7, 1975, and within a short time became ABC's second most highly rated serial.

The roots of *Ryan's Hope* went deep into the oldest traditions of soap opera, to Irna Phillips's family soaps, her tentpole characters, as far back as her radio show *Today's Children* and Carlton E. Morse's *One Man's Family*. What is astonishing is that those forty-five-year-old ideas, given the freshness of new writing talent, were as up-to-date as ever. Labine and Mayer had put their finger on what soap opera was all about.

In 1982 they left the show and a new writing team, facing the end of a number of old story lines involving the Ryan family, emphasized other characters beside the Ryans. The strong moral world of the Ryans seemed to be disappearing, which disheartened many of the show's fans. After the ratings remained down for months, Labine and Mayer returned to their brainchild and quickly brought the story back to its earlier point of view, even reinstating some of the show's old love triangles. *Ryan's Hope* seemed more like its old self.

THE STORY

Shortly after policeman FRANK RYAN (currently played by Geoffrey Pierson) began his campaign to represent the Ryan's community as city councilman, a mysterious tragedy occurred. Frank was found lying on the bottom of one of Riverside Hospital's back staircases with a broken neck. No one knew how the accident happened. For weeks all the Ryans were in torment as Frank's life hung in the balance. While in a semicoma, Frank mumbled, cryptically, the words "Delia" and "pushed." Frank's wife, DELIA RYAN (Ilene Kristen, Randall Edwards, now Kristen again), was frantic to find out what Frank meant. Later, when Frank's life was out of danger, his loving parents, JOHNNY RYAN (Bernie Barrow) and MAEVE RYAN (Helen Gallagher), were still desperately worried when their friend DR. ED COLERIDGE (Frank Latimore) told them that Frank might be in a wheelchair for the rest of his life. Frank, despite his affliction, bravely decided to resume his campaign for the local election.

Meanwhile, there were many questions which Frank either refused to answer or tried to cover up with lies. After Frank had been found unconscious at the bottom of the stairs by DR. ROGER COLERIDGE (Ron Hale), Dr. Ed Coleridge's son, it was discovered that the $6,500 which Frank had on him was missing, and he wouldn't say how he had fallen. Reporter JACK FENELLI (Michael Levin), skeptical of Frank's saintlike image during the campaign, thoroughly investigated all the mysteries surrounding Frank's accident, and wrote a damaging article.

The mystery of Frank's affairs slowly unraveled.

Frank had to confess to members of his family that he was originally carrying the $6,500 to pay off a blackmailer. Roger Coleridge had found out Frank's shameful secret and threatened to reveal it unless Frank gave him the cash, which Roger needed to pay off his gambling debts. When Roger found Frank after Frank "fell," he searched his pockets and took the $6,500. What was Frank's shameful secret? He had been having an affair with JILLIAN "JILL" COLERIDGE (Nancy Addison), Roger's sister. Conservative Maeve and Johnny Ryan, good Catholics, had no idea that Frank's marriage was so bad that he was forced to seek love in the arms of another woman—and one who was an old friend of the family. The idea of divorce and remarriage in the Ryan clan was unthinkable. Frank now

Ryan's Hope has always dealt with the strivings of one family, the closely knit Ryans of New York City. When the show premiered on July 7, 1975, tavern owners Maeve and Johnny Ryan (Helen Gallagher and Bernie Barrow, sitting) were the family heads. Their children were, behind them, from left: younger son Pat Ryan (Malcolm Groome), an intern; Delia Reid Ryan (Ilene Kristen), wife of Frank; older son Frank Ryan (Michael Hawkins); and daughter Mary Ryan (Kate Mulgrew).

went to the City Council and withdrew, offering as his reason that he had had an extramarital affair and was being blackmailed. However, Delia, terrified of a divorce, followed Frank to the meeting of the City Council and got up and declared that she and Frank had reconciled, convincing them not to accept Frank's resignation. What Delia would not tell anyone, however, was that *she* was the one who pushed Frank down a flight of stairs! She had pushed him in anger after Frank told her he wanted a divorce to marry Jill Coleridge. Frank still wanted to marry Jill even now, but Jill, unwilling to be the cause of wrecking Frank's political career, told him that their relationship had to end so that he could return to his wife. Pressured by his parents and his own political ambitions, Frank began having sexual relations with Delia for the first time in months.

* * *

During Frank's convalescence, campaign, and eventual election to the City Council, MARY RYAN (Kate Mulgrew, Mary Carney, Kathleen Ryan Tolan, Nicolette Goulet) had fallen in love with Jack Fenelli, the reporter who had made himself odious to the Ryans with his damaging article about Frank. When Maeve and Johnny learned that their daughter was sleeping with Jack, they were shocked and informed Mary that he would not be welcome in their home. Mary promptly moved out of the house and in with Jack. But Mary, a traditional Catholic at heart, soon realized that she really wanted marriage after all. Jack, however, had grown up in an orphanage, which left him too emotionally insecure for a long-term commitment like marriage. Finally, Jack forced Mary to move back with her parents. But when Mary took a job as a reporter for the local TV news station, Channel R, Jack became jealous of the relationship between Mary and her boss, SAM CROWELL (Dennis Jay Higgins). After much soul-searching, Jack asked Mary to be his wife and, apart from continual quarrels over Jack's selfishness and Mary's attachment to her family, the two settled down to normal married life.

DR. NELL BEAULAC (Diana Van Der Vlis) came to work at Riverside Hospital, after separating from her husband, DR. SENECA BEAULAC (John Gabriel). She had left him because she didn't want him to find out that she was suffering from two cerebral aneurisms (blood vessels in the brain that have become so weakened

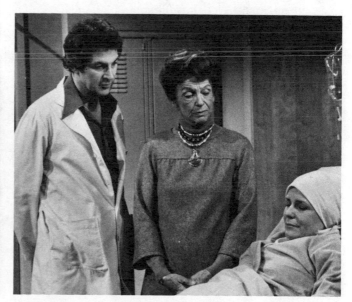

Mary Ryan, just out of college, fell in love with reporter Jack Fenelli (Michael Levin) and had an affair with him. A shocked Maeve and Johnny insisted that the couple marry. The mores of the older Ryans would continually clash with the modern social values of their children.

Dr. Nell Beaulac (Diana van der Vlis) was dying of neurological aneurisms in 1976 and made her husband, Dr. Seneca Beaulac (John Gabriel), promise to let her die with dignity. After she became permanently comatose, Seneca pulled the plugs on her life support machines, then had to face a murder trial. At center is Gale Sondergaard as Marguerite Beaulac.

that they may burst, causing massive stroke), one inoperable and the other terminal. Seneca followed her to Riverside Hospital, where he stayed on to become chief of neurosurgery, hoping to win her back. After he found out the terrible truth of Nell's condition, he convinced her to live with him again, but they both knew it would happen: Nell's aneurisms burst and she was left severely brain damaged, kept alive only by machines. Seneca pleaded with the hospital to pull the plugs, since Nell had told him that she didn't want to live like a vegetable. When they refused, he pulled them himself. Jill Coleridge, a fine lawyer, defended him against a charge of murder. It looked bad for Seneca, until some of Nell's letters were found in which she clearly stated her wish that she not be kept alive by extraordinary means. The judge sentenced him to a mere one week in jail. Soon after, Jill and Frank grew close and had a brief affair at her beach house in the Hamptons. But Jill realized that she could never forget Frank Ryan and broke off with Seneca.

FAITH COLERIDGE (currently played by Karen Morris Gowdy), Jill and Roger Coleridge's sister, was an intern at Riverside Hospital. Another intern, BUCKY CARTER (Justin Deas), millionaire-heir to the Carter Shoe Company and nephew of the deceased Nell Beaulac, fell in love with Faith. But it was his best friend, PAT RYAN (Malcolm Groome), that she really loved. Pat began seeing Faith; when she began growing excessively possessive, he tried to break off the relationship as gently as he could, but she was nevertheless deeply hurt. Meanwhile, KENNETH CASTLE (Ty McConnell), who had been hired by Seneca to look after Nell before her death, fell in love with Faith—but young Kenneth was a mental case. He terrorized Faith, first by imprisoning her in the basement of the hospital, then by sneaking around her apartment building. In a desperate attempt to catch the crazed Kenneth, Dr. Ed Coleridge fell from the roof of Faith's building to his death. His children, Faith, Jill and Roger, were grief stricken.

* * *

Vicious Roger Coleridge, antagonistic toward the Ryans and his sister, Jill, decided to cause trouble by seducing Delia Ryan. Delia had never really been in love with Frank; in fact, she had originally loved his brother Pat, but when he wouldn't marry her she married Frank to spite him. Soon the extramarital fling

![image](Frequent visitors to Ryan's Bar were Dr. Clem Moultrie (Hannibal Penney Jr., left) and Delia's brother, Bob Reid (Earl Hindman).)

Frequent visitors to Ryan's Bar were Dr. Clem Moultrie (Hannibal Penney Jr., left) and Delia's brother, Bob Reid (Earl Hindman).

Seneca Beaulac had an affair with Jill Coleridge (Nancy Addison), the lawyer who won him an acquittal on the charge of murdering his wife Nell. She broke off the affair to marry Frank Ryan, with whom she had been in love, and then discovered that she was pregnant with Seneca's baby, thus creating a major triangle.

was in full flower, complete with colorful lies. Delia claimed to be going to a Chinese cooking school (to become a more interesting wife for Frank!) and that she had made a new friend at the school, "Sheila," who was showing her all sorts of marvelous new cooking tricks, which naturally kept Delia away from Frank and Little John for hours at a time—while in reality she and Roger were having a grand time on his huge, exotic bed. But the truth came out when Frank followed her to Roger's apartment and found them making love. Frank immediately asked for a divorce. In another act of lavish fakery, Delia climbed onto the ledge of a high hotel window and threatened to jump unless Frank promised not to divorce her. Frank promised, but after Dee was safe he went ahead with his plans to rid himself of her and marry Jill. Staunch Catholic Maeve Ryan still wouldn't hear of it. Jill was crushed when she heard that her future mother-in-law would always resent her.

Then to Jill's utter shock, she learned that she was pregnant—not by Frank, but by Seneca Beaulac! The pregnancy was the result of the brief tryst Jill and Seneca had, during the period when Frank and Dee had reconciled. Jill couldn't bring herself to tell Frank the truth, leading him to believe the unborn child was

his. Frank went to the Dominican Republic to obtain a quicky divorce from Dee—after the courts awarded temporary custody of Little John to Johnny and Maeve Ryan—and was just about to wed Jill, when he learned that Seneca was the father of Jill's baby. He demanded that Jill give total custody of the baby to Seneca as a condition of their marriage. The idea was unthinkable. Jill and Frank broke up.

* * *

After the divorce from Frank, Delia tried to lure his brother Pat Ryan into marriage by seducing him. When she learned she was pregnant, she told Maeve and Johnny that the baby was Pat's. They insisted that he do the moral thing: break up with his fiancée, Faith Coleridge, and marry Dee. Then Roger Coleridge performed a blood test and discovered that *he* was the father of the unborn infant. With nowhere else to turn, destructive Delia married conniving Roger. Later, their baby died.

Meanwhile, Jack Fenelli was in a terrible automobile accident on the New Jersey Turnpike, with broken bones throughout his body. During his recov-

By 1978 Delia Ryan (now Randall Edwards) had divorced Frank and married Dr. Roger Coleridge (Ron Hale), by whom she had become pregnant. Flighty and immature, Delia divorced Roger, too, after having beginner's luck with business investments.

The Ryans in 1978 were, from left, behind Bernie Barrow and Helen Gallagher: Sarah Felder as Siobhan Ryan, the youngest daughter who had recently returned to New York; John Blazo as Dr. Pat Ryan; Daniel Hugh-Kelly as Frank Ryan; and Kathleen Ryan Tolan as Mary Ryan Fenelli. Frank was now running for the Senate.

ery, his wife Mary Ryan Fenelli told him what she thought would be joyous news, that she was expecting a baby. Jack, who had grown up in an orphanage, hated the idea of having children, and his hostility toward the expected child created such continual marital disputes that Jack finally asked for a divorce and the couple separated. Neither one of them, of course, really wanted to live apart, but their prideful, argumentative natures kept them from expressing their feelings to each other. TOM DESMOND (Tom McGreevy), a fine man who handled public relations for Riverside Hospital, began to fall in love with Mary. But when he realized that she still loved Jack, he entered into a little conspiracy of the heart with Maeve Ryan to get Mary and Jack back together. They arranged for Mary and Jack to be locked overnight in the cellar of Ryan's Bar and by morning the feuding lovers were reconciled. They took their marriage vows again and spent a glorious second honeymoon in Ireland.

When they returned, SIOBHAN RYAN (Sarah Felder, Ann Gillespie, Marg Helgenberger), Mary's younger sister, showed up at Riverside after having traveled on her own for several years. Fiercely independent, Siobhan had rejected the rigid moral system of her parents, to Maeve's and Johnny's dismay. Her Irish wolfhound, FINN MCCOOL, virtually symbolized her free spirit. Siobhan was strongly attracted to her sister's

husband, Jack Fenelli, who was beginning to feel neglected by Mary, now working night and day as a television reporter for Channel R. Jack was interested in Siobhan, but not seriously, although one night he almost made love to her. However, Jack did become annoyed when Siobhan fell in love with mysterious JOE NOVAK (Richard Muenz, Roscoe Born), an attractive fisherman who owned his own boat.

That simple romance of Siobhan's was soon to involve the Ryans in the worst tragedy ever to befall them and to link their lives to the evils of the underworld. At first no one knew that Joe Novak's charming uncle, TISO NOVOTNY (Dan Clarke), was a kingpin in the local mob, which also had a ring in Joe's nose. Mary found out, through her investigative reporting work for her television station, that Joe and Uncle Tiso were involved in the mob's dope-smuggling operation. To keep her quiet, Tiso rigged Mary's car so that it would crash. Mary suffered dreadful injuries and died in Jack's arms. The Ryans were devastated. Although Johnny and Jack had never been friendly before, their obsession with proving that Joe Novak had caused Mary's death brought them together. Siobhan had gone ahead and married Joe. But shortly after the wedding Tiso died, leaving control of his piece of the

Siobhan Ryan had become involved with Joe Novak (Richard Muenz, left), who had ties to a crime syndicate through his uncle, Tiso Novotny (Dan Clarke, right), in 1979. After Mary gathered evidence on the mob, Tiso had her killed.

A bizarre 1980 triangle involved wealthy Rae Woodard (Louise Shaffer, middle), reporter Michael Pavel (Michael Corbett) and Rae's illegitimate daughter Kim (Kelli Maroney, right). Both mother and daughter were horrified to learn, at different times, that they were sleeping with the same man. The triangle was resolved when Michael was murdered.

mob to Joe. When Siobhan found out that Joe was secretly doing mob business, she left him and Riverside.

* * *

After Delia married Roger Coleridge, Delia became preoccupied with investing in businesses. Although she was reckless, she had beginner's luck and successfully parlayed her investments until she could buy the Crystal Palace restaurant. Through continual contact with the immature Delia, Roger lost some of his brashness and began to beg her to join him in a more settled sort of life. That only bored her and she divorced him. Meanwhile, Roger began having a secret affair with attractive RAE WOODARD (Louise Shaffer), the ruthless, power-thirsty wife of WILLIAM WOODARD (Shepherd Strudwick, Wesley Addy), an aging newspaper tycoon. One day William's plane crashed near Riverside Hospital. As he lay dying in his hospital bed, he confronted his wife with her affair with Roger, then expired, leaving her the powerful and wealthy owner of his newspaper.

Jillian Coleridge had her baby, whom she called EDMOND. Although the infant was Seneca's and Seneca wanted to marry her, she still loved Frank and thought he loved her back. Rich Rae Woodard became infatuated with Frank and succeeded in getting him elected to the U.S. Senate with her money and political influence. During the campaign Jill found them together in a hotel room, believed Frank now wanted Rae, and abruptly married Seneca. Soon afterward Jill was severely injured in a gas explosion at her beach house, which tragically killed little Edmond. Despondent, Jill felt she couldn't keep up the sham of her marriage to Seneca and prepared to leave town. Just then, fate intervened, for Jill and Frank found themselves trapped in an elevator. They told each other anew how much they loved one another. When Rae realized that she had lost Frank to Jill, she decided to make him pay. She manipulated Frank into an influence-selling scheme, which forced him to resign his seat in the Senate. Undaunted, Frank and Jill became partners in a law firm as well as newly engaged. Frank took a case in St. Louis for several months, but returned and decided to try politics again.

But the course of Jill and Frank's love seemed

Seneca Beaulac became interested in Barbara Wilde (Judith Barcroft) in 1981. Barbara was a soap opera actress (in the story) who was being treated by Seneca for a feigned illness in an effort to increase the ratings of her show.

An elaborate 1981 masquerade party included almost all of the show's young leads. They were, from left, kneeling: David Rasche (Wes Leonard), Roscoe Born (Joe Novak), Earl Hindman (Bob Reid), Maureen Garrett (Elizabeth Jane Knowles). Standing: Gordon Thompson (Aristotle Benedict-White), Karen Morris Gowdy (Dr. Faith Coleridge), Mackenzie Allen (Sgt. Jim Speed), Nancy Addison, Ron Hale and Nicolas Surovy (Orson Burns).

doomed, as one problem after another interfered. Jill became caught up in the troubles of her new client, KEN GEORGE JONES (Trent Jones), a successful rock star who suffered from terminal cancer. Partly out of pity she had an affair with him, and later, when his condition caused unbearable pain, she agreed to pull the plug on his life support system—just as her old lover and client Seneca had done for his wife Nell. And just like Seneca she was tried for murder and exonerated. Meanwhile Frank, during Jill's involvement with Ken George Jones, began seeing Jill's sister, Faith Coleridge. Faith had long since broken up with Pat Ryan, had an unhappy marriage to public relations man Tom Desmond, and now needed to succeed in this new relationship with Frank. But there was too much against it. First LITTLE JOHN RYAN (Jadrien Steele), who resented Faith, did everything he could to subvert the match. Then one day Frank was hit by a car and superficially hurt. Jill ran to Frank and the two de-

clared their love again. Having failed so often to find love with a man, Faith became an alcoholic.

Siobhan Ryan returned to Riverside after a year's absence and joined the police department. Joe Novak also came back to New York and began working for Delia, managing her Crystal Palace restaurant. Although legally separated, Siobhan and Joe couldn't keep away from each other now that they were both back in the city. Joe had long since helped the police capture Mary's murderers but his connections to the mob were far too strong and he began doing business with them again. Siobhan and Joe once again broke up over the same problem. But he refused to give up on their love, even protectively following her when she was used as a prostitute decoy in a police department stakeout.

Delia Ryan Coleridge next became involved with slick ladies' man BARRY RYAN (Richard Backus), the nephew of Johnny Ryan and the late Ken George Jones's manager. But this time the shoe was on the other foot, for Barry Ryan began to see other women behind Delia's back. One night Delia happened to find Faith Coleridge quite drunk and gave her a lift in her car. While behind the wheel Delia spotted Barry on the street kissing young actress LILLY DARNELL

Marg Helgenberger became the new Siobhan Ryan Novak in 1982, playing opposite Roscoe Born as her on-again-off-again husband, Joe Novak. They tried numerous reconciliations, but continually had to part because of his ties to the crime syndicate. She became involved in her new work as a policewoman.

After many years rich Rae Woodard resumed her romance with even richer Hollis Kirkland (Peter Haskell), who turned out to be the father of Kim. The only problem: he had an uppity society wife, Catsy, who refused to give him a divorce. The Kirklands all left Riverside.

(Christine Ebersole), who had been infatuated with him, and in a jealous rage Delia ran him over. Afterward she swore that drunken Faith had caused the accident. But Delia's disgraceful lie (which Roger, Faith's brother, eventually exposed) actually did a lot of good. Barry made a bargain with Faith: if she gave up drinking he wouldn't press charges. Faith dried out, but once again it looked as if she was headed for a big romantic disappointment. She was falling in love with police detective MITCH BRONSKY (James Sloyan), who returned her interest but was also attracted to his police co-worker, Siobhan Ryan Novak—while, of course, Joe Novak was still in love with his wife.

ELIZABETH JANE RYAN (Maureen Garrett), Johnny Ryan's niece, came to New York and took a job working as an assistant to Rae Woodard at her newspaper. Elizabeth Jane fell in love with Roger Coleridge and the two announced an engagement. But she never told Roger that she was still married to OX KNOWLES (Will Patton), a racecar driver who was currently fleeing South American despots. Roger's and Elizabeth Jane's wedding day arrived, but just before the two were married, Elizabeth Jane spotted Ox Knowles among the wedding crowd and refused to go through with the ceremony. She tried getting back together with Ox, but when that didn't work, left town. None other than grasping Delia soon became attracted to international, glamorous Ox Knowles.

* * *

Rae Woodard's life became troubled and complicated when her illegitimate daughter, KIMBERLY HARRIS (Kelli Maroney), a fledgling actress, suddenly came to New York. Neither Rae nor her daughter realized at first that they were both having a liaison with the same man, MICHAEL PAVEL (Michael Corbett), one of Rae's newspaper reporters whose late father had nefarious connections to Tiso Novotny. When Kim learned the shocking truth, she accepted the much older Seneca Beaulac's proposal of marriage. But after marrying Seneca, she was still attracted to Michael and continued having sexual relations with him. When Rae finally found out about Michael and her daughter, she was horrified and confronted the two of them *in flagrante delicto* on a houseboat. There was terrible rage, a gun pulled, a struggle, a shot and suddenly Michael was dead. Rae willingly took the blame for his murder, for fear her daughter

would be accused, but it was later proven that Michael was really shot to death by SAL BROOKS, a mob figure who had shot Michael Pavel a second time, fatally. Disgusted by the whole immoral mess, Seneca divorced Kim, who found herself carrying his baby. After fighting with her mother over custody of the child, Kim took her newborn daughter, ARLY, and fled New York.

Meanwhile, fabulously wealthy HOLLIS ("KIRK") KIRKLAND (Peter Haskell), an old lover of Rae Woodard's, arrived in New York with his disturbed young daughter, AMANDA KIRKLAND (Mary Page Keller, Ariane Munker). After twenty years, Rae and Kirk renewed their love and decided to wed. But his current wife, CATSY KIRKLAND (Christine Jones), a bitchy society type, refused to agree to a divorce. Moreover, she was dead set against the budding romance between poor, sweet Amanda and Pat Ryan, her therapist. Kim, while out of town, learned that Hollis Kirkland was her father, and quickly came back to New York to enter her wealthy father's life. In time, Kirk and Catsy reunited and left Riverside after Pat Ryan began to unearth some dubious Kirkland family skeletons. To get back at Pat, Rae paid beautiful con artist CHARLOTTE GREER (Judith Chapman) to announce that she had been married to and jilted by Frank in St. Louis.

CAST
RYAN'S HOPE
ABC: July 7, 1975

Maeve Ryan	Helen Gallagher (P)
Johnny Ryan	Bernard Barrow (P)
Frank Ryan	Michael Hawkins (P)
	Andrew Robinson
	Daniel Hugh-Kelly*
	Geoffrey Pierson
Dr. Patrick Ryan	Malcolm Groome* (P)
	John Blazo
	Robert Finocceli
	Patrick James Clark
Mary Ryan Fenelli	Kate Mulgrew* (P)
	Mary Carney
	Kathleen Ryan Tolan
	Nicolette Goulet
Jack Fenelli	Michael Levin (P)
Delia Ryan Coleridge	Ilene Kristen* (P)
	Robyn Millan
	Randall Edwards

Dr. Roger Coleridge	Ron Hale (P)		Marg Helgenberger
Jillian Coleridge Ryan ..	Nancy Addison	Kevin McGuinnes	Malachy McCourt
	Altman (P)	Annie Colleary	Pauline Flanagan
Dr. Faith Coleridge	Faith Catlin (P)	Ethel Green	Nell Carter
	Nancy Barrett	Thatcher Ross	Patrick Horgan
	Catherine Hicks	Wes Leonard	David Rasche
	Karen Morris Gowdy	Poppy Lincoln	Dianne Thompson Neil
Dr. Ed Coleridge (P) ...	Frank Latimore	Dr. Adam Cohen	Stan Birnbaum
Dr. Nell Beaulac	Diana van der Vlis (P)	Joe Novak	Richard Muenz
Dr. Seneca Beaulac	John Gabriel (P)		Roscoe Born*
Dr. Bucky Carter	Justin Deas (P)	Tiso Novotny	Dan Clarke
Dr. Clem Moultrie	Hannibal Penney, Jr. (P)	Dan Fox	Peter Ratray
Ramona Gonzalez	Rosalinda Guerra (P)	Kimberly Harris Beaulac	Kelli Maroney
Dr. Marshall Westheimer	William Kiehl (P)	Michael Pavel	Michael Corbett
Bob Reid	Earl Hindman (P)	Chester Wallace	Robert Lupone
Little John Ryan	Jadrien Steele (P)	Barry Ryan	Richard Backus
Nick Szabo	Michael Fairman (P)	Elizabeth Shrank-Ryan .	Pamela Blair
Reenie Szabo	Julia Barr	Ken George Jones	Trent Jones
Jumbo Marino	Fat Thomas	Lilly Darnell	Christine Ebersole
Kenneth Castle	Ty McConnell		Kathryn Dowling
Marguerite Beaulac	Gale Sondergaard	Domenick Bernardi	Vince Pasimeo
	Anne Revere	Amy Morris	Kay Delancey
Sam Crowell	Dennis Jay Higgins	Rose Melina	Rose Alaio
Diana Carter	Sally Chamberlain	Matthew Pearse	Tom Aldredge
Sister Mary Joel	Sylvia Sidney	Claudius Church	Charles Cioffi
	Nancy Coleman	Elliot Silverstein	Joe Silver
	Natalie Priest	Dr. James Ross	James Congdon
	Jacqueline Brookes	Crimmins	Ron Tomme
Martha McKee	Tovah Feldshuh	Edgar Daniels	Malachi Throne
	Dorrie Kavanaugh	Orson Burns	Nicolas Surovy*
Anne Burney	Jody Catlin		Robert Desiderio
Dr. Alex McLean	Ed Evanko	Lt. Oliver Jones	Louis Zorich
Bernard Levine	Bruce Weitz	Sgt. Jim Speed	Mackenzie Allen
	Jerrold Ziman	Alexei Vartova	Dominic Chianese
Cathleen Thompson ...	Nancy Reardon		Leonardo Cimino
Art Thompson	Gregory Abels	Elizabeth Jane Knowles	Maureen Garrett
Alicia Nieves	Ana Alicia Ortiz	Barbara Wilde	Judith Barcroft
Tom Desmond	Thomas McGreevy	Spencer Smith	Lester Rawlins
Miriam George	Rosetta LeNoire	Aristotle Benedict-White	Gordon Thomson
	Frances Foster	Yvonne	Patricia Triana
	Minnie Gentry	Ox Knowles	Will Patton
Rae Woodard	Louise Shaffer	Hollis Kirkland	Peter Haskell
Bill Woodard	Wesley Addy	Amanda Kirkland	Mary Page Keller
Dave Feldman	Joseph Leon		Ariane Munker
Nancy Feldman	Lisa Sutton	Carol Baker	Lori Cardille
	Megan McCracken	Leopold Osquillo	Ernesto Gonzalez
	Nana Tucker Visitor*	David Newman	Robert Brown
Siobhan Ryan Novak ...	Sarah Felder	Sydney Galloway	Marilyn McIntyre
	Ann Gillespie	Mitch Bronsky	James Sloyan

Catsy Kirkland . . . . Christine Jones
Leigh Marshall . . . . Felicity LaFortune
Charlotte Greer . . . . Judith Chapman

Creators: Claire Labine and Paul Avila Mayer
Head Writers: Claire Labine and Paul Avila Mayer, Mary Ryan Munisteri
Assistant Head Writers (for Mary Ryan Munisteri): Roger Crews and Eugene Price

Executive Producers: Claire Labine and Paul Avila Mayer, Joseph Hardy
Producers: George Lefferts, Robert Costello, Ellen Barrett, Felicia Minei Behr
Directors: Lela Swift, Robert Myhrum, Jerry Evans, Bruce Minnix, Tom Donovan, Lynwood King, John J. Desmond, Michael Gliona, Stephen Wyman
Musical Directors: Carey Gold, Charles Paul
Packagers: Labine-Mayer Productions, ABC-TV

SEARCH FOR TOMORROW

ASK any long-term daytime fan who her favorite soap opera heroine is and the answer will surely be Joanne of *Search for Tomorrow*. The show is important not only because millions of people have either grown up or grown older with Joanne, but because its rare continuity has kept viewers directly linked to the show's beginnings and to one sustaining moral point of view. Much of the credit for that achievement must go to Procter & Gamble and to Mary Stuart, who for thirty-three years fought to keep her character, Joanne, the same noble human being, despite the many writers who have been tempted to change her.

BACKGROUND

Search's history began early in 1951 when Mary Stuart, an ex-MGM starlet who had made numerous "B" movies, found herself sitting with a complete stranger, Roy Winsor, while they waited for her fiancé to join them for lunch. "I really didn't know what to say to him," said Mary, "so I just started making haphazard conversation. He was involved with television producing and I just happened to say that I felt that television wasn't satisfying the needs of women. Radio wasn't either. 'Women are too perfect on radio and television shows,' I said. 'Women can't see themselves. Why can't television do something real for them?' I don't even think I was all that sure of what I

was talking about, but I had to say something. Roy then said to me, 'You should play the lead in that kind of television program.'"

Winsor, a vice president in charge of radio and television production for the old Biow advertising agency, was already in the process of talking with Procter & Gamble about a new afternoon television serial that P&G would sponsor. Roy Winsor says today that he was deeply impressed with Mary Stuart during that first meeting and had her in mind for the lead of the new serial from the start. "And why not?" says Roy. "Mary Stuart had all the qualifications: she was attractive, and I knew that she had the experience and was a hard worker. Obviously that first meeting brought us all tremendously good luck. I don't think we could have come up with a more perfect Joanne if we had searched the world."

Mary was hired and agreed to a salary of $500 a week. Shortly before the first live air date, Roy Winsor and Procter & Gamble finally hit upon the title they wanted for the series. *Search for Happiness* had been rejected as being too saccharine. The first P&G products to be advertised on the program were Spic & Span and Joy dishwashing liquid, which Winsor says caused him to wonder if there wouldn't be some obvious conflict between the serious nature of the drama and the happy-go-lucky sound of the commercials. (Today's viewers are more used to the inane contrasts between the commercials and the drama.) Agnes Eckhardt (later Nixon) was hired by Winsor as the first head writer but was replaced after thirteen weeks by Irving Vendig, a master of melodrama who wrote the show for the next seven years.

On September 3, 1951, viewers first saw *Search for Tomorrow* on CBS-TV in a 15-minute live broadcast. It's doubtful whether any of the viewers who saw it recognized that sweet young housewife—her hair done up in a plain bun at the back, a loose fitting housedress buttoned up to the neckline, walking around in the plainest sort of kitchen set—as the same sexy, bare-shouldered movie queen who appeared in twenty adventure films and countless lusty Hollywood publicity stills.

The story at first was simple. Joanne and Keith Barron were happily married; they had a little daughter, Patti, and were somewhat hovered over by Keith's possessive parents. After six weeks Keith was killed in an automobile accident, and so began Joanne's troubles as a young, widowed mother. About two months after the show started, Marge and Stu Bergman came into the story as Joanne's next door neighbors. They had a young daughter, Janet.

The show's appeal for viewers was almost instantaneous. It had a taste of real life about it: quiet scenes between a mother and child, typical in-law problems, the helplessness that families feel when confronted with sudden death. Some light comedy was supplied by Larry Haines and Melba Rae as the Bergmans who were always around with a smile, a joke, and an outstretched hand when things got a bit rough for Jo. This touch distinguished Winsor's new serial from so many of the unrelieved ones that had preceded it on radio.

"But essentially, we did get the idea for *Search* from radio," Winsor says today. "I wrote the original presentation for the serial and saw Joanne as a kind of young Ma Perkins, the sort of woman who cared about her neighbors' problems, who would offer help to others and who could face her own personal troubles with dignity."

Mary Stuart's portrayal of Joanne was so skilled, compelling and realistic that after a while she became the show, at least for viewers. She had somehow learned, overnight—and obviously without too much help from the kinds of films she'd done in Hollywood—how to quietly project emotions that viewers realized were probably unbearable for the character. When Jo's first husband was killed, for example, the realism of Mary's somewhat underplayed grief was stunning. After a while, millions at home began to hope and pray that she truly would find the "tomorrow" she sought.

"I'm positive that's why *Search for Tomorrow* became so popular and stayed that way . . . it was Mary," says Lynn Loring, the show's first Patti, today an executive at Aaron Spelling Productions and the wife of actor Roy Thinnes. "After a while it wasn't just acting for Mary. Six months after the show started, she *became* Joanne. That's how the character became so real. I remember when I first met Mary she was a gorgeous, young, and vibrant woman—she couldn't have been, oh, much more than twenty-two. I remember when I was a girl I saw a painting of her with that lovely oak-blond hair falling down over her shoulders. Then slowly, as she got into the part, Mary started looking older, wearing dresses like Joanne. But I think that was only because Mary took her work so seriously. You know, she was so concerned about the program and the character that she used to go out and do the marketing for Joanne's refrigerator herself! That's unheard of in television work. Because of Mary, a television show, for the first time, had a kitchen that really resembled a kitchen. She decided what it would look like, the kind of food that she would chop during a scene, how she would do it. It was her worrying over details like that that made *Search for Tomorrow* more real for the viewers."

In the beginning, when the show was done live from Liederkrantz Hall, Roy Winsor was producing *Search* with a budget of $8,073.75 a week; that wouldn't even pay for a day's taping now. Many of the sets were merely suggested or improvised. Black backdrops, instead of walls, were employed, and rooms were only hinted at with door frames hung in thin air and paintings dangled from ceiling wires. One time, when Jo's mother-in-law, Irene Barron (played by Bess Johnson), had lost her custody suit to get Patti away from Joanne, the old lady went berserk and kidnapped Patti. A chase scene in the woods was aired using "just a little patch of woods no wider than a living room," and branches attached to music stands—with the director, Charles Irving, cutting from the branches to a face going by, then to feet. "It was exciting to watch the way the whole thing was improvised," says Mary.

* * *

Search for Tomorrow remained extremely popular for several decades. Although each of the show's many writers had a slightly different focus during that period, essentially they kept Joanne at the center of the story, concentrating on her problems and the problems of characters whose stories revolved around hers. If these other characters were not directly threatening Jo's happiness, they at least needed her constant advice to find happiness of their own. The show was about "the world's oldest ingenue," as Mary would kid.

In the early seventies, at a time when the daytime ratings wars were becoming brutal, *Search for Tomorrow* was beginning to slip in the ratings. The truth was that all of the soaps that began in the fifties, including the unbeatable *As The World Turns*, were in trouble. Younger viewers were beginning to watch the soaps, but not necessarily the ones their mothers watched, and especially not a show about an old-fashioned heroine. To try to recapture the audience, *Search*'s writers began layering the show in terms of distinct age groups, with the aim of keeping loyal older viewers while attracting new, younger ones. Joanne was kept important but not constantly at the center, while young romances were introduced, such as those of Liza and Steve Kaslo (Meg Bennett and Michael Nouri) and Amy and Bruce Kaslo (Anne Wyndham and Joel Higgins). The writers also used thirtyish stories, such as those of Scott and Kathy Phillips (Peter Simon and Courtney Sherman), and fortyish stories like Joanne's and Stu Bergman's. In modern day statistical jargon, the show had been altered "demographically." The changes brought substantial improvements in the ratings.

Again there were problems, this time by the late seventies, when millions of new viewers, especially teenagers, began taking to the soaps. The writers tried to appeal to them but in the process many older, loyal viewers were put off by the show's young story lines. In 1978, Joyce and Bill Corrington became the head writers and cleverly introduced a group of characters from New Orleans, including Travis Sentell, members of his family and Martin Tourneur, who was Jo's new love interest. Liza was paired romantically with Travis and their love story (played out by Sherry Mathis and Rod Arrants) became a great hit with viewers. Press releases began to describe *Search for Tomorrow* as "the story of Liza and Travis Sentell" and writers who came after the Corringtons deemphasized Joanne's love life, once again to the displeasure of loyal viewers.

But Jo was not Helen Trent, who on radio could get away with remaining a thirty-five-year-old ingenue for twenty-eight years. Millions of viewers have seen Jo grow older on television and one would naturally expect that she would slow down after four husbands, merge into the problems and triumphs of her friends and family and become less the center of attention. In a way, Joanne's present status on the show as a happy matriarch fulfills *Search for Tomorrow*'s original promise of realism.

The show was moved to NBC in 1981, only the second time a television soap opera has switched networks. (*The Edge of Night* was the first when it went from CBS to ABC in 1975.) Since then, and just before the move, Procter & Gamble has made of Joanne's Henderson a splendid town, whose boundaries have been expanded with sensational location shootings in places like New Orleans, Rome, even Hong Kong. By May, 1983, the Liza/Travis story was in full bloom as writers continued to seek a new contemporary identity for the show.

THE STORY

At first Henderson's JOANNE GARDNER BARRON (Mary Stuart) wondered how she could keep on going after the sudden death of her husband, KEITH BARRON (Johnny Sylvester), in an automobile accident. But she could not permit herself to wallow in grief, for she had a six-year-old daughter, PATTI BARRON (played as a child by Lynn Loring, see cast list for others), to look after. Courageously, the young widow took a job in Henderson Hospital as the only means she had of supporting her little girl.

Of course, she could have turned to Keith's wealthy parents for help, but Joanne knew that IRENE BARRON (Bess Johnson) wanted to take Patti now that her son was dead. Her conviction that she and her husband, VICTOR BARRON (Cliff Hall), could provide for Patti better than Joanne grew into an obsession. She tried everything she could to win Patti's affections despite Victor's admiration for Joanne. Later, after Irene tried but failed to gain custody of her granddaughter, she lost her mind and kidnapped the little girl. The law finally made Irene return Patti to Jo, but not before she took flight with the child and led everyone on a long chase through the woods.

Jo's best friends were STU and MARGE BERGMAN

(Larry Haines and the late Melba Rae), a good-natured couple who always knew how to laugh, even when the going got rough. Marge and Stu spent many hours in Jo's kitchen, having coffee with her and talking over personal problems. Priceless friends, they were always around when Jo needed them. They had two young children: JANET (played as a child by Ellen Spencer, then by Sandy Robinson until 1961, and by Fran Sharon until 1966; then Marian Hailey continued the role, and Millee Taggart took over in 1971) and JIMMY (Peter Lazer). Jimmy Bergman, however, was really the son of Stu's dead brother, and he was later taken by the brother's second wife and her new husband. Janet Bergman became Patti's best friend. Later, Marge and Stu had another child, TOMMY BERGMAN (currently an adult played by Robert LuPone).

After Patti was once again safe at home, Joanne met ARTHUR TATE (played from 1955 to 1966 by Terry O'Sullivan, except for six months in 1956 when Karl Weber took the role) at Henderson Hospital, where she was working, and the two soon fell in love. Arthur's lawyer and friend, NATHAN WALSH (George Pe-

trie), also found himself deeply attracted to Joanne, but he put aside his feelings when he realized that Jo was in love with Arthur. Later, Walsh became one of Jo's most trusted allies.

Jo and Arthur, in ten years of courtship and marriage, certainly endured enough crises to last any other couple a lifetime. On the day of their wedding, for instance, a mysterious woman named HAZEL (Mary Patton) came to Joanne Barron's Motor Haven—which Jo and Arthur jointly owned and ran as a business—and claimed to be his wife. She looked exactly like the wife Arthur believed died years before, but of course, this wasn't Hazel Tate at all, but rather her twin sister, SUE. She had been hired by the local syndicate to upset Jo and Arthur's marriage plans so that they could gain control of the Motor Haven, to use as a front for a dope-peddling operation.

Jo and Arthur were stymied by Hazel's apparent

At the premiere of Search for Tomorrow on September 3, 1951, Mary Stuart played Joanne Barron, a young wife and mother. Johnny Sylvester played Keith Barron and Lynn Loring their little girl, Patti. Johnny Sylvester (now known as John Sylvester White) recently appeared as the comic Mr. Woodman in the sitcom Welcome Back, Kotter.

Melba Rae and Larry Haines became regulars as Marge and Stu Bergman, Joanne's best friends in 1952. They had appeared briefly in December 1951. Producer Charles Irving so liked the warmth and sense of fun they brought to their characters that he kept them on. Ellen Spencer played the first Janet Bergman, Stu and Marge's little girl. Melba Rae died suddenly in 1971. Larry Haines is still on the show.

return from the dead, until Nathan Walsh discovered her true identity. To trick her into admitting the truth, Arthur, Jo and Nathan faked a fire and hired an actress to impersonate the dead twin sister, Hazel. Distraught on "seeing" her dead sister, Sue rushed out into the woods, where she was later found murdered. The D.A. immediately accused Joanne of the murder, and she might have stood trial if Arthur and Nathan hadn't discovered the identity of the real killer. In the process, however, Arthur was shot in the heart and nearly killed. For a long time, he was an invalid. Depressed that in his condition he couldn't be a real husband to Joanne, he refused to go ahead with their original wedding plans.

Meanwhile, the syndicate wasn't about to give up their efforts to gain control of the Motor Haven. Their next ploy was to send to Henderson a woman named ROSE PEABODY (Lee Grant, Nita Talbot and finally Constance Ford), who was supposed to gain the friendship of Arthur and Jo and then figure out some way of ruining Jo's reputation so that she would have to sell the Motor Haven.

To win Jo and Arthur's friendship, Rose pretended to need help with her mute brother, WILBUR (Don Knotts). Soon she and Wilbur were staying at the Motor Haven as guests of the people she was supposed to destroy. One day Rose poisoned the soup that Jo would be serving to a group of workers, but at the last moment she couldn't go through with the horrible deed and poured the soup down the drain. Eventually, psychiatry proved that Wilbur had become mute as a reaction to the shock he'd endured many years before after almost killing their foster father, who had tried to sexually molest Rose. When Wilbur was made to realize why he became mute, he suddenly found his voice again. The happy brother and sister then left Henderson.

* * *

Joanne finally convinced Arthur to marry her despite the complications caused by the gunshot wound. But shortly after the wedding fate had more trouble in store for them. Joanne became pregnant at about the same time that Arthur was having severe financial troubles with the Motor Haven. He was forced to turn for help to his wealthy aunt, CORNELIA SIMMONS (Doris Dalton). She moved to Henderson

After Keith died in an auto accident, his mother, Mrs. Irene Barron (Bess Johnson) tried to take Patti away from Joanne—first by cunning, then with a custody suit, finally by kidnapping little Patti. In the early days the show was almost entirely focused on the problems of widowed Joanne.

By 1954, Jo was running the Motor Haven motel to support her little girl. Lawyer Nathan Walsh (George Petrie) was a good friend. Rose Peabody (Nita Talbot, who succeeded Lee Grant) was sent by the mob to force Joe to close the Motor Haven. The props and sets were extemely simple: everything was pushed up against mere cardboard or black velour walls.

and, like Jo's previous in-laws, became Jo's enemy. Aunt Cornelia would have liked nothing better than a permanent separation between Jo and Arthur.

DUNCAN ERIC, Jo and Arthur's son, was born, but later was killed when he ran into the street and was struck by a car. As if things weren't bad enough, Jo's mother died and her father, FRANK GARDNER (Eric Dressler and later Harry Holcombe) and newly widowed sister, EUNICE (played first by Marion Brash and lastly by Ann Williams), arrived in Henderson to further complicate the lives of the Tates.

Eunice—an unstable, selfish woman—was attracted to Arthur, who returned her attentions. They had an affair. Later, Eunice suffered pangs of guilt and told Joanne the whole story. Taking this turn of events as an opportunity to separate Jo and Arthur forever, Aunt Cornelia offered Arthur a job in Puerto Rico, where she had most of her business interests. Torn by shame because of his unfaithfulness to Jo, Arthur accepted the offer. Cornelia married a younger man, REX TWINING (Larry Hugo), but he soon found himself drawn to Eunice.

Arthur returned to Henderson to find some startling occurrences. Aunt Cornelia was found murdered. Eunice and Rex were tried and found guilty. But the real murderer was found by ALLISON SIMMONS (Ann Pearson)—Aunt Cornelia's daughter—to be her mother's housekeeper, HARRIET BAXTER (Vicki Viola). After they were exonerated, Eunice and Rex were married and moved to Puerto Rico. Jo's father, Frank Gardner—who had been managing the Motor Haven in Arthur's absence—also found happiness by marrying Stu Bergman's widowed mother, thus making Jo and Stu sort of relatives.

* * *

Best friends Janet Bergman and Patti Tate, by now in their late teens, were having adult problems of their own.

Janet fell in love with BUD GARDNER (George Maharis), Jo's cousin. They were married and had a son, Chuck. When Bud left home and was later reported to have died in an accident, Janet allowed herself to fall in love with DR. DAN WALTON (Martin Brooks, Philip Abbott and finally Ron Husmann). Janet married Dan, not realizing that Bud was still alive. While she and

Joanne met Arthur Tate (Terry O'Sullivan) in 1952 and married him, after an extended courtship, on May 18, 1955. Mary Stuart was eight months pregnant at the time and had to be photographed above the waist during the ceremony. To date she has played her part longer than any other actor on a television soap.

Jo's sister Eunice (Marion Brash, right) suddenly showed up in Henderson in 1957. After having an affair with Arthur, Eunice became involved with Rex Twining (Larry Hugo) and then had to stand trial for murder with him. The real murderer was uncovered by Arthur's cousin, Allison Simmons (Nina Reader, left). Eunice finally married Rex.

Dan were still on their honeymoon, Bud returned to Henderson. Out of his mind with jealousy and anger on hearing of the marriage, Bud tried to force his way into the Bergmans' home. Later, in a chase with the police, he was injured in a car crash and would have died had Dan Walton not gotten to him in time to save his life. Janet, realizing that she was still legally Bud's wife and that he needed her, returned to him, even though she now loved Dan.

Bud soon got into a fight with Stu Bergman, who came to his apartment and pleaded with Bud to give Janet up. Stu was knocked unconscious. When he finally came around, Bud's body was lying dead on the street, many floors below the apartment, and the police booked him for homicide. Later Joanne discovered a drainpipe that Bud had pulled from the side

of the building in his attempt to flee the apartment without being seen, having thought he had killed Stu. With this evidence it was shown that Bud had died an accidental death, and Stu was cleared. Janet and Dan Walton then left Henderson so that Dan could practice medicine in Chicago.

Patti went to visit her grandparents in Arizona, where she had an unhappy involvement with an older married man. She returned to Henderson, deeply depressed. She soon became romantically involved with young, devil-may-care TED ASHTON. One night when Ted was driving wildly, he and Patti were in a serious accident, and Patti wound up in a wheelchair. Doctors could find nothing medically wrong with her, however. Her paralysis was caused by all the emotional traumas she had suffered. One day Ted Ashton, wild

On April 8, 1959, the cast celebrated its 2000th show. From left: Ann Pearson, Vicki Viola (as Harriet Baxter), Larry Hines, Terry O'Sullivan, Mary Stuart, Frank Overton (as Nathan Walsh), Lynn Loring, Tony Ray (as Bud Gardner), Marion Brash and Larry Hugo.

as ever, broke into the Motor Haven and threatened Jo with a gun. Seeing her mother endangered was the shock Patti needed. She got out of her wheelchair and walked over to Ted Ashton in an attempt to save Jo's life. Distracted by Patti, Ted dropped the gun; Jo retrieved it and called the police. Patti was cured.

* * *

Alcoholism suddenly began to plague Henderson. Arthur, distraught over the past and over his inability to cope with Tate Enterprises, began to drink. So did FRED METCALF (Tom Carlin, Donald Madden and David O'Brien), Allison's newspaperman husband. Arthur's drinking and his frustrations at work combined to cause a serious heart attack. Fred Metcalf, an emotionally insecure man who was intimidated by both his wife's money and his domineering mother, AGNES METCALF (Katherine Meskill), drank his way to a divorce, despite the help he was receiving from Alcoholics Anonymous.

While Arthur was recuperating from his heart at-tack, a woman from Puerto Rico named MARION GILL (Jane McArthur) filed a paternity suit against him, but later admitted that another man had fathered her child. Marion fell in love with Fred Metcalf, and he thought he also loved her. However, he knew he really still loved Allison, his ex-wife, and it turned out that she also still loved him. Fearful of making a mistake, Fred suddenly left Henderson for Chicago just before he was supposed to marry Marion. But JOHN AUSTIN (Frank Schofield), a good friend to both Fred and Allison, realized they still loved each other and brought Fred back to Henderson. So, despite all of their past difficulties, Fred and Allison were finally able to find happiness together.

Patti continued to follow a self-destructive life pattern. She fell in love with an older, married doctor named EVERETT MOORE (Martin Brooks) and, after spending one night with him, became pregnant. When Everett's wife ISABELLE (Lenka Peterson) committed suicide, Patti would probably have married him—but only for the sake of her child. She had be-

Depressed after an affair with an older man in 1961, Patti (still Lynn Loring) was in a car crash that left her in a wheelchair, although the doctors found nothing physically wrong with her. Then, when Jo's life was threatened by a gun-wielding young man, Patti suddenly got up from the wheelchair to save her mother.

Allison Simmons (Ann Pearson) in 1964 married Fred Metcalf (Tom Carlin), a reporter whose insecurities turned him into an alcoholic. The Allison-Fred story went on for several years, introducing the audience to the importance of Alcoholics Anonymous. Over the years Search *has featured many story lines involving male alcoholics.*

gun to realize that her attraction to this older man was neurotic. However, she was in an automobile accident and suffered a miscarriage, so she no longer had to consider marriage to Everett. The accident also made it impossible for her to bear another child.

* * *

Arthur Tate dropped dead of a heart attack. Joanne was once again a heartbroken widow, so DR. BOB ROGERS (Carl Low) of Henderson Hospital offered her a job as a librarian there to help take her mind off Arthur. Dr. Rogers soon became a close, dear friend of Joanne's.

The story of SAM REYNOLDS (Bob Mandan from 1964 to 1969, briefly George Gaynes and finally the late Roy Shuman) now began to interweave into the fabric of the life of Joanne, her family, and her friends. Sam Reynolds was a business tycoon who, before Arthur Tate's death, had started acquiring some of Henderson's business firms. One of the businesses he had taken over was Tate Enterprises, much against Arthur's will. This caused Arthur much grief and may have contributed to his untimely death. Jo therefore

held a grudge against Sam Reynolds, who was nonetheless irresistibly attracted to her. Sam would have given anything to undo the pain he had caused her and for a whole year tried in vain to win her favor.

Finally, after Sam suffered a near-fatal stab wound in the liver while saving Patti from a knife-wielding dope fiend at the hospital, Jo allowed herself to return Sam's affections and the two declared their love for one another. But Sam sadly admitted that he wasn't free to marry because his scheming wife, ANDREA WHITING REYNOLDS (Virginia Gilmore, later Joan Copeland), refused to give him a divorce even though they had been separated for many years. So ruthless was Andrea that she had turned their son against him—going so far as to convince the boy to use *her* maiden name. Everyone in Henderson knew the young man as LEN WHITING (Dino Narizzano, Jeff Pomerantz), never suspecting he was Sam Reynolds's son.

While Jo and Sam were trying to straighten out their own lives, their children were becoming romantically involved. They had met at Henderson Hospital, where Patti worked as a nurse and Len was a bright

Search for Tomorrow's *greatest romance, begun in 1965, was between Joanne and business tycoon Sam Reynolds (Bob Mandan). Arthur had just died of a heart attack and Jo, blaming Sam, resisted his advances. But after Sam risked his life to save Patti's, the romance was on. It caused the ratings to soar and lasted four memorable years.*

A young Ken Kercheval played Nick Hunter, who fell in love with Emily Rogers (Pamela Murphy) in 1967. Emily was expecting a child by another man but agreed to marry Nick to give her baby a name.

young intern. Finally a wedding date was set. Jo and Sam and all their friends were deliriously happy about the forthcoming marriage—happy, that is, until Andrea Whiting arrived on the scene and schemed to break up the relationship.

Sam, in a last desperate effort to break free in order to marry Jo, threatened to sue Andrea for divorce on grounds of deception. Andrea decided to kill him rather than let him marry Jo. She already knew that Sam, as a result of his stab wound, had developed a rare blood condition and was dependent upon an experimental (and fictitious) drug, Hemadol, which became lethal to the patient if he imbibed liquor. Inviting him over for a drink, Andrea intended to slip him a cocktail composed of liquor and a few drops of the drug, but the drinks got mixed up, and Andrea almost died. Sam was then tried for attempted murder. The trial was spectacular and suspenseful, climaxed by Andrea's breaking down on the witness stand and admitting that she had had an affair with another man, LARRY CARTER (Hal Linden), while married to Sam and that she was to blame for the death of Len's twin brother. One night, instead of taking care of the child at home, Andrea had been out cavorting with Carter; a fire had started and killed the little boy.

After the trial, Andrea received psychiatric help and voluntarily granted Sam Reynolds the divorce he had been seeking for years.

Although the court's decision was good for Jo and Sam, who could now marry, Andrea's revelation was shocking for Len. Not a strong-willed or emotionally secure man anyway (in fact, quite like Patti), Len went into a depression, giving up medicine and his plans to marry Patti. He began doing manual labor in a factory, trying to forget the horrors he had heard during the trial. After a while, however, he met a girl named GRACE BOLTON (Jill Clayburgh), who was dying of a brain tumor. Inspired once again to renew his Hippocratic oath, Len saved the girl's life with an impromptu piece of surgery—he removed a fish bone from her throat with a bent spoon! He also had an affair with her. The relationship was temporary, however, and soon afterward Grace left for California.

At the hospital where Len was again practicing, he and Patti continually ran into each other. After saving the life of a sick child together, they declared their love again and were married. Meanwhile, Grace, who never told Len that she was pregnant with his child, died in childbirth in California. Patti, who had suffered another miscarriage, became depressed over

Jill Clayburgh, in 1969, played Grace Bolton, a young girl dying of a brain tumor. Carl Low played Jo's good friend at Henderson Hospital, Dr. Bob Rogers.

Patti (now Leigh Lassen) married Len Whiting (Dino Narizzano), the son of Sam Reynolds, in 1969, not knowing that a girl named Grace Bolton had just had a child by him. Notice how Search's *love stories were changing, now often involving some dilemma of parentage rather than mere affairs.*

losing her baby and began taking addictive pep pills. Finally, Len and Jo talked her into adopting a child—Grace and Len's child, whom Jo had been taking care of secretly. Neither Len nor Jo told Patti that she would be adopting Len's own son, who was eventually named Chris.

* * *

Jo's sister, Eunice, who returned from Puerto Rico after her divorce from Rex Twining, now married lawyer DOUG MARTIN (Ken Harvey) and became much more stable and unselfish. When Eunice married Doug, neither she nor he knew that the young Vietnam veteran named SCOTT PHILLIPS (Peter Simon, Peter Ratray) was in reality Doug's illegitimate son. After Scott's parentage was revealed, father and son eventually became close. Meanwhile, Scott, by now a law student, made the mistake of marrying a materialistic girl named LAURI (Kelly Wood), and later divorced her. Lauri took her illegitimate son, ERIC LESHINSKY (Chris Lowe), and became involved with an unhappily married professor, JIM MCCARREN (Michael Shannon). Meanwhile, Scott fell in love with a fellow law student, pretty KATHY PARKER (Courtney Sherman, Nicole Goulet). A born careerist, Kathy desperately wanted to become a successful lawyer. When she learned that

she was pregnant with Scott's child, she secretly had an abortion. Later, she and Scott were married.

Just before Sam and Jo were to be married, Sam was asked to go to Africa on a special assignment for the United Nations. He was gone longer than Jo expected. While Sam was absent, Jo was the victim of a catastrophic automobile accident—caused by her sudden realization, while driving, that Len was the father of Grace Bolton's baby. DR. TONY VINCENTE (Anthony George) saved her life at Henderson Hospital, but at the time he could do nothing about the total blindness that the injury had caused. While all of Jo's family and friends worried over her condition, news came that Sam Reynolds had died in Africa. Fearful of what the shock would do to her in her present state, Jo's family held back the news. In time, however, she found out and suffered a dreadful depression.

Jo's blindness was finally cured, after which she sought to take her mind off Sam by working as a volunteer at the Rec House, a center for underprivileged teenagers, where Dr. Tony Vincente also worked. At first mutual troubles made Jo and Tony seek solace in each other's company. In Tony's case, he was unhappily married to MARCY (Jeannie Carson),

Janet Bergman (Millee Taggart) was over her youthful romantic problems by 1971 and married wealthy psychiatrist Wade Collins (John Cunningham). For the next ten years the characters supplied humor and stability to the story.

Scott Phillips married fellow law student Kathy Parker in 1972, and for the next decade they played sleuths with numerous personal problems. The real-life actors, Peter Simon and Courtney Sherman, met while playing their parts and married.

a spoiled rich girl who used a pretense of being crippled and confined to a wheelchair to hold on to him. In Jo's case, first it was the news of Sam's death, then her worry when she learned that Patti had been taking drugs as a result of the emotional shock of losing her baby. So Jo and Tony had good reason to turn to each other. And their relationship did not remain platonic.

But Tony was already married, and both of them felt torn by guilt. Then Tony learned that Marcy had been faking her confinement in a wheelchair and could walk. Tony divorced his wife. It looked as if he and Jo could find happiness together.

They weren't in each other's arms very long before Sam Reynolds turned up—on the eve of their engagement party. The report that her fiancé had been killed in Africa had been erroneous, to say the least! Jo, of course, loved Tony Vincente, but Sam still loved her and wanted to marry her. Prodded by his need for her, as well as by the urging of her family and friends, Jo broke off with Tony and made plans to marry Sam. But then a strange thing happened. Her blindness returned—this time, a psychosomatic

symptom of her inner conflict over her love for Tony versus her desire not to hurt Sam. Jo began seeing a psychiatrist to cure her blindness.

When their wedding day arrived, Jo was still blind, but Sam—who knew that she loved another man and whose African ordeal had caused severe, near-psychotic personality changes in him—insisted that they not put off their marriage. At the office of the justice of the peace, Jo suddenly changed her mind and begged Sam to take her home. He pretended to agree, but then kidnapped her and drove her to her brother-in-law's deserted cabin in the woods, calling her family in Henderson to assure them that they were now on their honeymoon. Jo, confused and stunned, was even more confused when a strange young couple, GEORGE JOSLYN (Kipp Osborne) and SARAH FAIRBANKS (Susan Sarandon), broke into the cabin and shot Sam with a gun they found. Later, after they had fled, Jo, still blind, was found in a state of hysteria, hovering over Sam's body.

Back in Henderson, the family was growing concerned because they hadn't heard from the honey-

After Eunice (Ann Williams) became a widow in 1972, she was courted by her boss, wealthy lawyer John Wyatt (Val Dufour) and married him. For several years, earlier, Eunice's story had concerned her desire to have a career against her husband's wishes and was obviously influenced by the Women's Liberation movement.

Jo took her third husband Dr. Tony Vincente (Tony George), in 1972, after Sam Reynolds was killed at the climax of a wildly melodramatic story line involving psychosomatic blindness, psychotic jealousy and kidnapping.

mooners. Tracing Sam's phone call to Doug's cabin, Tony Vincente and Doug Martin went up to the cabin and found Sam dead and Jo unconscious after a bad fall in the woods. When she awoke, her sight had miraculously returned. Later, the murderers were apprehended. Tony and Jo were finally able to walk down the aisle together.

With her mother now out of danger, Patti should have been happy with her husband, Len, and little Chris. But EMILY HUNTER (Louise Shaffer, then Kathryn Walker), the neurotic daughter of Dr. Bob Rogers, started trying to break up Len and Patti's marriage because of her attraction to Len and a mysterious vendetta against Patti. By using her pretended friendship for both of them, she was able to cause them to separate. Then Emily began arranging "mistakes" for Patti to commit in her role as a mother, hoping to cause Patti to lose custody of Chris. Finally, after Len

and Patti were reunited, Emily kidnapped Chris. The house Emily took Chris to was set afire, but Len and Patti, with the help of Andrea, arrived just in time to save Chris. Emily, the Iago-like villainess, was consumed in the flames. After things had quieted down, Patti and her husband decided to start fresh in Seattle. Andrea, too, became happier, because, by saving Chris's life, she had settled the score with her own guilt for having caused the death of Len's twin brother years before. Soon after the departure of Len and Patti, she too left town.

*   *   *

Henderson suddenly became a sad place the day that Marge Bergman died. She and her husband, Stu Bergman, had been Joanne's best friends for more than twenty-three years.

Deeply affected by the untimely death of his wife, Stu tried to pick up the pieces of his life and become, if he could, both father and mother to his son, Tommy. Eventually he hired a housekeeper, ELLIE HARPER (Billie Lou Watt), a close friend and cousin of Scott Phillips. Stu and Ellie began growing fond of each other. Obviously she wouldn't mind becoming Stu's next wife.

Young composer Steve Kaslo (Michael Nouri) began living with Liza Walton (Meg Bennett), Janet's teenage daughter by Dr. Dan Walton. Steve suffered from leukemia. By 1975, the show was putting a great deal of emphasis on young love.

David Sutton, alias David Sloan (Lewis Arlt), a U.S. marshal sent to Henderson in 1976, fell in love with deceitful Stephanie Wilkins (Marie Cheatham), who came into the story two years earlier as an old flame of Tony Vincente's. Both characters became important to the show's major stories.

It was really a double tragedy that struck Stu's family. Dan Walton, the husband of his daughter, Janet, also died, leaving her to care for their teenage daughter, LIZA (Kathy Beller, Meg Bennett, currently Sherry Mathis), and their son GARY (Tommy Norden, Rick Lohman, lastly Stephen Burleigh). After a respectful period of mourning, Janet took up her life again, and she fell in love with handsome, wealthy psychiatrist DR. WADE COLLINS (John Cunningham). Liza, however, considered the relationship between her mother and Wade a betrayal of her dead father's memory. After bringing her mother to the point of nearly breaking off with Wade, Liza finally accepted him as her stepfather after he skillfully forced her to examine her own motives in objecting to her mother's remarriage. Janet soon after became Mrs. Wade Collins. Later, Stu sold his house and moved with his son, Tommy, into Janet and Wade's huge house.

Handsome, well-to-do lawyer JOHN WYATT (Val Dufour) came to Henderson, indirectly causing all sorts of trouble. The very first thing John did was to buy a failing magazine, previously owned by KARL DEVLIN (David Ford), who had built the magazine up from scratch. Karl, remaining on the magazine as a figurehead boss, deeply resented the young executive, FRANK ROSS (Andrew Jarkowsky), whom John Wyatt had placed in the office. Karl also didn't much care for the new freelance writer John hired—Jo's own sister, Eunice Martin. Eunice's husband, Doug Martin, wasn't keen on the idea of her new job, either, for it threatened his identity as breadwinner and he feared that John Wyatt was more interested in his wife's affections than in her writing. After many arguments over Eunice's new job, Doug moved to a hotel.

At the same time, Karl Devlin was becoming rather psychotic with suspicion that the younger executive, Frank Ross, would push him out of his job. In the heat of fury, Karl killed Frank. He immediately

Jo and Stu opened the Hartford House in 1976. Among their guests are, at left rear table: John and Eunice Wyatt (Val Dufour and Ann Williams). Center table, mid-ground: Jennifer Pace (Morgan Fairchild) and Bruce Carson (Joel Higgins). At front table, second from left, is Ellie Harper (Billie Lou Watt).

became paranoid and thought Eunice had seen him commit the murder. When she announced that she was going up to John Wyatt's cabin to think through her problems with Doug, Karl Devlin, now completely insane, decided to follow her up there and do away with her as well.

Meanwhile, Jo convinced Eunice's husband, Doug, that there was nothing between Eunice and John and that he should return to his wife. She told him that Eunice had gone to the cabin, so Doug decided that he'd follow her up there too. Both men, Karl Devlin and Doug Martin, were beaten to their destination by MARIAN MALIN (Pat Stanley)—John Wyatt's secretary—who got to Eunice first in order to warn her not to become involved with John Wyatt. Marian said that she loved him and wanted him for herself. Eunice, who never wanted John in the first place, agreed and said she was going back to Doug; she would let Marian wait for John at the cabin.

The whole episode reached a climax when Karl, mistaking Marian for Eunice, murdered Marian, and later, when Doug Martin arrived, tried to kill him, too. Doug didn't die, but the shot he received paralyzed him from the waist down. Karl Devlin was caught and pronounced criminally insane.

Kathy Phillips, being "liberated," was still adamant about not having children and was furious when her husband, Scott, agreed to adopt Eric Leshinsky when his mother, Lauri, was killed in an auto accident on the first night of her honeymoon. Since everyone considered Kathy practically a villainess for not wanting Erik, she acquiesced and made a reluctant attempt to be his mother. Meanwhile, she was working as a lawyer in John Wyatt's office. John's plans to win Eunice Martin's love were aided, ironically, by Doug Martin himself. Realizing that he would be confined to

After Wade Collins was murdered by kidnappers, wealthy widow Janet Collins was pursued by several fortune hunters. By 1982 she had fallen in love with corrupt builder Ted Adamson (Wayne Tippit). Some months later she left Henderson but, as in the past, the character will most probably return.

Search *paired Liza Kaslo (Sherry Mathis) with wealthy Travis Sentell (Rod Arrants) in 1978 and put the two in one exotic adventure story after another. In 1982 they were shipwrecked on a Caribbean island, where Liza almost drowned.*

a wheelchair indefinitely, Doug forced Eunice to divorce him. Eunice loved Doug but reluctantly started giving in to John Wyatt's attentions. When Doug suddenly left Henderson, Eunice accepted John Wyatt's proposal of marriage—more out of fear of being alone at this low point in her life than out of love for John.

* * *

All of Jo's attention was suddenly turned to Patti's new problem. Although the doctors had warned her that she would be risking her life if she ever attempted to have another child, Patti was overjoyed that she had become pregnant again and decided that she would not have her pregnancy aborted. She was brought to Henderson Hospital, with nurse STEPHANIE WILKINS (Marie Cheatham) assigned to look after her. However, it turned out that Stephanie Wilkins—a beautiful, though cunning, woman—had had an affair with Tony Vincente. Still in love with him, she began to use Satanic subterfuge to win him from unsuspecting Joanne. This was the beginning of much heartbreak for Jo. Stephanie brought to Henderson her stepmother, RANEY WESNER (Katherine Squire) and daughter WENDY WILKINS (Andrea McArdle, currently Lisa

Peluso), claiming she was Tony's child, born after the old affair had ended. Tony, as Stephanie had hoped, began spending much time with little Wendy, as well as with Stephanie. When Jo discovered that Wendy was really the daughter of DAVE WILKINS (Dale Robinette), Stephanie's ex-husband, Jo realized that Stephanie was scheming to steal her husband from her, but didn't tell Tony for fear he would be hurt. She did plead with him continually not to spend so much time with Stephanie and her little girl. Believing that Jo was unreasonable, Tony left her; soon he and Stephanie had resumed their old affair. But Dave Wilkins refused to perpetuate Stephanie's vicious lie about his own daughter. After Dave told Tony the truth, Tony was so shocked that he suffered a heart attack. He told Stephanie to get out of his life. Even though Jo

The show went to Hong Kong in 1981 for one of the most ambitious location sequences ever taped for a soap. Maureen Anderman played evil Sylvie Descartes, who forced singer Zack Anders (Shawn Stevens) into helping her kidnap Travis and Liza in Hong Kong for the fabulously expensive jade necklace given to Liza by Travis.

Joanne married gambler-playboy Martin Tourneur (John Aniston), her fourth husband. Her divorce from him became Jo's first divorce ever, a slight departure from her ultra-conservative image for more than thirty years. "I'm the world's oldest ingenue," laughs Mary.

had been dreadfully abused by Tony, she forgave the man she loved and took him back.

Meanwhile, Len joined Patti in Henderson. They had many painful arguments about her stubborn decision to endanger her life by having her baby. Because of her delicate condition, they couldn't have sexual relations, and Len became even more bitter, finally taking to drink. One night, while intoxicated, he drove his car wildly out of Henderson, and hit another car, which was entering town. Len had no idea of the identity of the other driver, who was severely injured in the crash. Len had the decency to call an ambulance for the other driver, but cowardly fled the scene before help came.

That other driver happened to be Doug Martin!

Beautiful teenager Suzie Wyatt (Cynthia Gibb), the late Eunice Wyatt's daughter, took up with beautiful teenager Warren Carter (Michael Corbett) in 1982, but was really in love with Brian Emerson: a story typical of the new teen love triangles.

Doug, finally able to function after many months in a wheelchair following the paralysis caused by the bullet wound, had been on his way back to Henderson from Washington, where he had resumed his law practice. The auto accident caused by Len made Doug a total paraplegic—paralyzed this time from the neck down! Eunice Wyatt, never fully able to rid herself of guilt feelings that she had somehow betrayed Doug by divorcing him and marrying John Wyatt—was shattered to hear that Doug would be a hopeless invalid for the rest of his life. She immediately left John to take an apartment near the hospital, where she could look after Doug.

By the time Scott learned of this terrible second tragedy that had befallen his father, Doug, his marriage to Kathy was foundering. Scott kept insisting that Kathy spend less time with her legal duties in John's law office and more time with him and little Erik. Kathy went off on an extended business trip to California, and Scott, feeling abandoned, began to give in to the wiles of Gary Walton's beautiful coed girl friend, sexy JENNIFER PACE (Morgan Fairchild). When Kathy returned to Henderson and found Scott involved with Jennifer, Kathy and Scott separated.

Meanwhile Doug, kept alive by extraordinary mechanical devices, begged his son to "pull the plug." Someone did pull the plug, and Scott, found with his father's dead body in the hospital room, was charged with murder. And it was none other than Kathy who defended him. Scott, along with all of their friends, were astonished at how energetic, clever and meticulous Kathy was in attempting to prove her husband innocent. Her dazzling courtroom technique during the murder trial finally resulted in Jennifer Pace, Scott's lover, going to pieces in the witness chair and confessing that it was she and an accomplice, HAL CONRAD, who pulled the plug on Doug. Jennifer believed that if she pulled the plug, then Scott couldn't be prosecuted for Doug's murder. But Hal Conrad was strictly a murderer who was afraid that Doug would expose him as an embezzler. After Scott was exonerated, Hal held Kathy, little Erik and Ellie at gunpoint. Meanwhile, Len Whiting, after having harbored for months the secret that he was the hit-and-run driver who made Doug a paraplegic, was just then on his way to Kathy's to confess the truth. When he entered the house, he courageously lunged for the gun and was shot. Seconds later the police came in the door and arrested Hal Conrad. Len, now a hero, was only sentenced to work in a poverty area for two years. He and Patti—who had lost her baby—left Henderson to begin repaying society.

Jennifer went to prison. Although by now Scott had fallen in love with his wife, Kathy, all over again, he didn't dare tell Jennifer until her release from prison; he felt she had gone through enough. But then Jennifer discovered that she was pregnant with his baby. Kathy, believing that she had lost Scott for good, divorced him and an unhappy Scott married Jennifer after she was freed on probation. Jennifer, however, knew that Scott still loved Kathy, and her frustration caused arguments and bitterness in the new marriage. Scott became an alcoholic. During one of these marital disputes, Jennifer accidentally fell through a glass door. Not only was her fetus killed, but she suffered terrible scars on her beautiful face. During her many months of plastic surgery, which eventually did restore her face, Jennifer suffered severe depression, which made her impossible to live with. Scott left her; he hit the bottle worse than ever, then left Henderson altogether.

Tony Vincente was warned that he could have another coronary seizure if he didn't take it easy. With Jo once again his chief support, Tony returned to his medical duties at Henderson Hospital. He became concerned with the plight of a patient there, ROBIN KENNEMER (Lane Binkley), a prostitute whose life was being threatened by the syndicate. Apparently Robin knew too much for her own good. One night the syndicate sent someone to "take her for a ride." Tony rushed to her defense. During his fight with the awful yegg, Tony suffered another heart attack and died. Joanne became desperately grief stricken—so depressed she couldn't even talk to friends.

Tony at least lost his life in preventing the death of another, for Robin was temporarily saved from violence at the hands of the syndicate. She went to supersleuth Kathy Phillips for help, now putting Kathy's life in danger. By now, Scott was back in Henderson and realized that Kathy was soon to be killed if he didn't find her. Just before she was about to be slain, Scott walked in the door and saved her life. Robin's employers were put behind bars. Scott, jumping at his chance for a happy life with Kathy again, went to Alcoholics Anonymous to help him dry out. He and Kathy remarried. She became a good mother to Erik.

Jo had a grown ward by the name of BRUCE CARSON (Robby Benson, Joel Higgins), who first fell in love with Liza Walton, then became involved with Jennifer Phillips, then had a brief affair with AMY KASLO (Anne Wyndham) on the rebound. Bruce didn't love Amy, and the relationship ended.

Liza Walton had broken off with Bruce because she fell in love with Amy Kaslo's brother, STEVE KASLO (Michael Nouri). For a while Liza and Steve lived together without being married, which upset Liza's parents, Janet and Wade Collins. Eventually Liza and Steve were married, but not long afterward their marriage became mired in tragedy. Steve was hospitalized with leukemia—thought terminal at first. After further tests, Steve's doctor, Gary Walton—Liza's brother— told Amy Kaslo that she could save her brother's life by permitting a bone-marrow transplant from her to Steve. But Amy was pregnant with Bruce Carson's baby! She was told that the operation might well kill her unborn child. It was either her baby's life or her brother's life. She made the agonizing decision to wait until her baby was born before submitting to the transplant. Miraculously, Steve was able to hang on to life by a thin thread until the birth. After the transplant was performed, Steve was cured. He and Liza were happy again. Soon, however, conflict over their respective careers as song-writer and high-fashion model, began to threaten their marriage.

Bruce begged Amy, before and after the birth of their baby—whom they called TORY (short for Victoria)—to marry him. He didn't love Amy, but he was deeply fond of her, and a wife and child were more important to him than the kind of insecure love affairs he had been having. Amy didn't want the sort of marriage that Bruce was offering—but in the end agreed to a simple loveless arrangement. They would live together as man and wife, for the sake of Tory, but not have sexual relations. Bruce became frustrated, for indeed he wanted to learn to love Amy. Later he turned to fellow writer GAIL CALDWELL (Sherry Rooney), for a physical relationship, just as Amy had decided she loved Bruce and wanted relations with him. Bruce realized, when he had to make a choice that he truly loved Amy, and the two agreed to live a normal married life.

Joanne, trying to find something to take her mind off Tony's death, opened an inn, called the Hartford House, with her best friend, Stu Bergman—shades of the old days, when she and Arthur Tate used to run the Motor Haven. A mysterious stranger who called himself CHRIS MILLER (Paul Dumont) took a room at the inn. He kept to himself constantly, claiming that he was a writer and needed privacy. Chris began to fall in love with Jo and see her a great deal, despite the objections of the new bartender, DAVID SLOANE (Lewis Arlt)—who at first appeared to be some sort of accomplice. Stu and all of Jo's other friends began to suspect that the two men were criminals and warned Jo against becoming further involved with Chris. In reality, Chris was named Chris Delon and was supposed to testify against notorious gangsters, and David Sloane was a U.S. Marshal named David Sutton assigned to protect Chris until the big trial. Although Chris tried to warn Jo about the danger, she persisted in seeing him. One of the gangsters broke into his room, pulled out a gun and shot just as Jo walked in the door. She took a bullet in the stomach and went into a coma for a week; she almost died. All of her friends were worried sick. Chris was guilt-stricken. When the coma lifted, Dr. Bob Rogers told Jo she might never walk again. After Chris testified in California he came back to Henderson for Jo, who was confined to a wheelchair. Chris wanted to marry her, but Jo, not wanting to burden him, refused. Then, when Chris's ex-wife came to Henderson and it was found that she had only two more years to live, Jo made Chris realize that he had to make his wife's last years happy ones by reconciling with her and taking her back to California. Alone, with the prospect of never walking again, Jo became deeply depressed.

While Jo faced a life of perpetual invalidism, Stu's years of unhappiness since Marge's death ended when he married Ellie Harper. She had become so distressed by her love for Stu—who, for the longest time, saw her only as a friend—that she had left Henderson. However, after Jo was shot she rushed right back to be by Jo's side, and Stu suddenly realized that he had been in love with Ellie all long. He declared his love, and these two lonely, wonderful people were married.

Eunice became mysteriously frigid with her new husband, John Wyatt. Unable to understand the cause, John had an affair with Jennifer Phillips. When Eunice found out, she forced John to move out of their house, although she still loved him. Jennifer realized that her hold on John was tenuous, and so she carried out a clever scheme devised by her cunning friend, Stephanie Wilkins. She invented a story about a mysterious rapist who had attacked her and was harassing her with phone calls. She and Stephanie even messed up Jennifer's place, making it look as though the fictitious rapist had been there. John, feeling protective—as Jennifer and Stephanie knew he would—moved in with Jennifer, naturally destroying any possibility of a reconciliation between John and Eunice. Then, when Jennifer couldn't keep her lies straight in her stories to both John and the police, Stephanie became alarmed. She and David Sutton had been having an affair, and she feared that she would lose him when the truth came out. Jennifer also feared she would lose John. The truth did come out, and John walked out on Jennifer and reconciled with Eunice. But the Wyatts' happiness was all too brief. Always unstable, Jennifer now became insane and murdered Eunice! Jennifer made John Wyatt look like the killer, and he was tried and convicted. Meanwhile, WALTER PACE (Tom Klunis)—Jennifer's father—had married Stephanie Wilkins for her money (acquired in a previous brief marriage to Wade's late brother Clay), and attempted to hide his knowledge of his daughter's crime. Stephanie finally forced Walter to make Jennifer confess and exonerate John. Jennifer was placed in an asylum.

A love triangle soon emerged. Stephanie fell in love with John; John, reminded by Jo of his beloved Eunice, fell in love with Jo; Jo fell in love with a new arrival, DR. GREG HARTFORD (Robert Rockwell), once connected with Hartford House. Stu hated Greg Hartford because, many years earlier, he had made Stu's sister, Louise, pregnant before she drowned in Crystal Lake. Stu believed that Greg had deliberately allowed her to drown to avoid marrying out of his class. Jo accepted Greg's explanation about the accident but found it hard to deal with Greg's unstable teenage daughter MEREDITH (Tina Orr), who concocted devious schemes to discredit Jo and undermine her engagement to her father, whom she didn't want to share. Greg finally left Henderson to take his daughter to New York to undergo psychiatric treatment.

* * *

Wade Collins was kidnapped and brutally murdered! The evil ransom plot had been created by Wade's best friend, DR. ALLEN RAMSEY (Conard Fowkes), and Ramsey's paramour, FAY CHANDLER (Kathleen Devine), who were finally destroyed. Janet, almost killed herself by the kidnappers, was devastated but had to face the fact that she was now a vulnerable wealthy widow. Several smooth fortune hunters pursued her. Not long after, another tragedy struck her family: Steve Kaslo's leukemia had not been arrested as everyone had hoped. He tried to keep Liza from finding out about his deteriorating condition and swore her brother, Gary, to secrecy, before going to New York to record a song he had written for her. Although a doctor there warned him to rest, Steve pushed himself, and collapsed before finishing the recording. He died not long after. Liza went into deep, bitter mourning, retreating from the world around her.

Jo had to face a sticky legal problem. The title to Hartford House was being challenged by a corrupt builder named TED ADAMSON (Wayne Tippit). Stephanie, who had finally gotten John Wyatt to marry her, was jealous of John's affection for Jo, and secretly helped Ted Adamson try to acquire the title of Jo's inn, to get her to leave Henderson. The scheme backfired when John cleared Jo's title and Ted revealed that Stephanie had been the one who "donated" land where Jo could relocate her inn. Then John and Ted became political rivals when they ran against each other for city council. However, when Ted's unscrupulous daughter LAINE (Megan Bagot) began looking for skeletons in John's closet to damage his credibility, John decided to withdraw to protect his stepdaughter, SUZI (last played by Cynthia Gibb), Eunice and Doug Martin's daughter. He talked Jo into running in his place. But John's wife, Stephanie, continued to help Ted Adamson against Jo, and had an affair with him. Unable to bear Ted any longer, John went crazy and attacked Ted. In the struggle, John was accidentally shot and killed! Jo adopted little Suzi.

Meanwhile, Liza Kaslo was determined to keep Steve's memory alive in the movie that would feature Steve's song, "You Can Love Again." Production had been halted when the money ran out. Liza's mother's company, Collins Corporation, denied funding for the film on the advice of legal counsel. Desperate to see the film made, Liza took the advice of her new roommate, Laine Adamson, and sold her ten percent interest in Collins Corporation to unscrupulous Ted Adamson, who hoped eventually to take over the company. TRAVIS TOURNEUR SENTELL (Rod Arrants), the wealthy

and handsome grandson of the founder of Tourneur Instruments, came to Henderson to meet with Ted Adamson and became enchanted with the beautiful young widow. He secretly put up money for Liza's movie.

Liza slowly began to accept Travis's friendship and love, but his mother MIGNON (Anita Keal), widowed many years, resented her involvement in her son's life. Meanwhile, Travis's enemies were plotting his annihilation. The mob sent NICK D'ANTONI (Jerry Lanning) to Henderson to kill Travis. When bombing attempts were unsuccessful, Nick kidnapped Liza, who was rescued by Travis and Nick's brother MARC D'ANTONI (Chris Goutman). Later, a new storm arose when Travis discovered that his late father, Travis Sr., had had a wartime affair with a woman who had given birth to a daughter, Travis's half-sister. Travis, Liza and investigator David Sutton went to Italy, where Liza and Travis were married, and started a search for his half-sister. She turned out to be a fragile ex-nun named RENATA CORELLI (Sonia Petrovna). David had tracked her down, fallen in love with her and later married her in Henderson. However, Travis's mother, Mignon, became severely unbalanced when she learned that the husband she worshipped had fathered an illegitimate child. In her insanity Mignon believed that Liza herself had been her husband's paramour. With the help of evil Nick's friend, a psychic fraud named TANTE HELENE (Jane White), Mignon tried but failed to murder Liza.

* * *

During a period when Kathy and Scott Phillips's marriage went briefly sour, Kathy had had a one night stand with David Sutton. She quickly reunited with Scott, but when she learned she was pregnant she became tormented that David, not Scott, might be the father. The uncertainty caused her to have a nervous breakdown. She was infinitely relieved when blood tests on her newborn baby DOUG showed the child to be Scott's. Later a lab technician discovered that there had been a mistake, but Dr. Gary Walton and his wife, psychologist CAROLYN HANLEY (Marilyn McIntyre), persuaded David Sutton not to reveal that Doug was his own son. But the truth came out anyway when Doug was in a car accident and needed a blood transfusion. Hurt beyond belief, Scott began drinking again and raged against David. When David was run down by a car, Scott was tried for attempted murder, but Kathy's brilliant defense cleared him and the Phillips family left Henderson for a fresh start elsewhere. Some time later Kathy divorced Scott and returned to Henderson with Dougie and married a temperamental artist, GARTH TAPER (David Gautreaux), who was eventually killed in a car crash.

After years of being on the loose, David settled down with his new bride, Renata, while they eagerly awaited the birth of their own baby. Suddenly, their happiness was cut short: Renata was killed in a fire in their apartment in Henderson Towers. Her baby, MIA, was born just before she died. Two irresponsible people had caused the fire: MARTIN TOURNEUR (John Aniston), Travis's gambling, alcoholic playboy uncle, who had been smoking in bed before he passed out in a stupor; and JIM RAMSEY (Ralph Byers), who worked for Adamson Construction Company and had cut corners in the Henderson Towers fire system. Ramsey drowned in Emerald River after a confrontation with Ted. Martin Tourneur fell in love with Jo and, although she spurned him at first, in time she gave in to his charms and married him, only to discover that he was so addicted to gambling and liquor that their marriage couldn't last. She eventually divorced him.

Ted Adamson and widowed Janet Collins were in love and about to marry, when Scott's half-sister JAMIE LARSEN (Patricia Estrin) blackmailed Ted into marrying her instead! She knew that he had been responsible for Jim Ramsey's death. But Jamie was wanted by the FBI and later disappeared. Janet left Henderson to start a new life with her young son in California. Ted left town separately to be near his daughter, Laine, who had become pregnant by Gary Walton after an extramarital affair. Completing this flurry of departures, Gary and his wife Carolyn also moved out of Henderson.

* * *

Ted Adamson had another daughter named SUNNY (Marcia McCabe), who resented her father's dirty dealings and had tried to help Jo fight him. Travis Sentell's cousin, LEE SENTELL (Douglas Stevenson), came from New Orleans to join the family business in Henderson and fell in love with Sunny. However, a young waitress named CISSIE MITCHELL (Patsy Pease) also loved Lee, seduced him, then became pregnant. Realizing he loved Sunny, she reluctantly

gave her baby up for adoption and, as fate would have it, Liza and Travis, who couldn't have a child of their own, became the baby's new parents. At first Cissie, who babysat for the Sentells, had no idea that their new baby boy was really hers—but realized his identity when she spotted a birthmark on the child's hand. After a bitter custody suit Cissie and Lee were awarded joint custody. Lee's new preoccupation with little ROGER LEE interfered with Sunny and Lee's plans to marry. Then Sunny discovered that she had a malignant brain tumor and fell under the spell of a quack, DR. WINSTON KYLE (Nicholas Cortland), who convinced her that for a sizable sum he could cure her with health foods and herbs. But the man was quite deranged and held Sunny, now blind from the tumor, a prisoner in Jamaica, where Lee and Travis finally found her. Kyle was institutionalized and Sunny received medical treatment. Afterward, Lee, who became increasingly involved with Cissie and his small son, married Cissie. But when Lee continued to remain close to Sunny, Cissie fled Henderson with their baby. Lee wanted a reconciliation and joined them many months later. Sunny began a romance with DANE TAYLOR (Marcus Smythe), Travis Sentell's longtime friend.

After the agonizing loss of their newly adopted baby in the custody battle with Cissie, Liza and Travis began to have trouble in their marriage. Because she couldn't give Travis a child, Liza felt she wasn't a complete woman. They decided to try to revive their marriage with a cruise on the *Queen Elizabeth II*, during which Travis bought Liza a beautiful and expensive jade necklace that two other passengers—a singer named ZACH ANDERS (Shawn Stevens), and his manager SYLVIE DESCARTES (Maureen Anderman)—were determined to acquire, by murder if necessary. The jade necklace became the center of a malicious, complex plot against the Sentell family, resulting in the murder of Mignon and the kidnapping of Travis and Liza in Hong Kong. After Zach and Sylvie were exposed, Liza and Travis experienced further travails: Tourneur Instruments' top secret project, called Operation Sunburst, continued to make the young couple targets for those who wanted to sabotage it. But perhaps the most stunning event was the return from the dead of TRAVIS ("RUSTY") SENTELL, SR. (David Gale), who turned out to be the mastermind of an international gun-running syndicate. He became determined to win the affection of his long lost son and to destroy his marriage to Liza in favor of a union with his young goddaughter AJA DOYAN (Susan Monts), who was already in love with Travis. Rusty became so devious that he ended up murdered, and Aja was discovered to be the perpetrator.

* * *

Henderson's younger generation had its own heartaches. Stephanie's daughter Wendy had fallen in love with a young man named SPENCE LANGLEY (Timothy Patrick Murphy) who claimed to be "Brian Emerson," Stephanie's longlost illegitimate son. Spence had only been interested in Stephanie's money, but when he began to fall in love with Wendy—who was now calling herself "Dawn"—Spence had to tell Stephanie that he wasn't really her son. Later, after Wendy and Spence broke up, Wendy and her mother were at odds over her new involvement with young but poor KEITH MCNEIL (Craig Augustine). Stephanie wanted her daughter to marry into wealth.

Eventually the real BRIAN EMERSON (Jay Acavone), Stephanie's illegitimate son, came to Henderson, trying to salvage a professional boxing career. He fell in love with Suzi Wyatt, but when an injury caused him to go blind he didn't want to burden her and broke off the relationship. Still in love with Brian, young Suzi began seeing a secret gun-runner, WARREN CARTER (Michael Corbett), while his more aggressive sister KRISTEN (Susan Scannell) quickly took up with Brian and became pregnant by him. Brian, who had regained his sight, loved Suzi but married Kristen out of obligation, unaware that before the wedding she had suffered a miscarriage. Suzi married Warren Carter, and began drinking to mask her unhappiness while her best friend Wendy married Keith. But the marriages proved immature: Warren and Wendy had a hot, steamy affair.

For quite a few years Stu Bergman's life had been settled and happy. He had been comfortably married to Ellie and enjoyed running the inn with Jo. As always he worried a great deal about the people around him, especially his son Tom, who had recently taken a legal position in Washington. Suddenly Ellie left Stu and ran off with the inn's temperamental chef; later, the inn burned to the ground. Undaunted, Stu convinced Jo to be his partner in a new venture. They bought and renovated an old riverboat, turning it into a most appealing nightspot, where friends and family congregated, along with the customers. There he met DR. BARBARA MORENO (Olympia Dukakis), a psychiatrist who struck his fancy. Stu's uncanny rapport with Barbara's withdrawn son, JOSH (Josh Freund, Damion Scheller), gradually won her over.

CAST
SEARCH FOR TOMORROW
CBS: September 3, 1951 to March 26, 1982
NBC: March 29, 1982

Joanne Barron Tourneur	Mary Stuart (P)
Patti Barron Whiting . . .	Lynn Loring* (P)
	Abigail Kellogg
	Gretchen Walther
	Patricia Harty
	Nancy Pinkerton
	Brooke Bundy
	Melissa Murphy
	Melinda Plank
	Trish van Devere
	Leigh Lassen (a.k.a. Natalie Israel)
	Tina Sloan
Keith Barron	John Sylvester (P)
Irene Barron	Bess Johnson (P)
Victor Barron	Cliff Hall (P)
Louise Barron	Sara Anderson (P)
Dr. Ned Hilton	Coe Norton
Stu Bergman	Larry Haines
Marge Bergman	Melba Rae
Janet Bergman Collins .	Ellen Spencer
	Sandy Robinson
	Fran Sharon
	Nancy Franklin
	Marian Hailey
	Millee Taggart*
Arthur Tate	Terry O'Sullivan*
	Karl Weber
Sue	Mary Patton
Nathan Walsh	George Petrie*
	Frank Overton
	Richard Derr
	Mark Lenard

Rose Peabody	Lee Grant	Dr. Nick Hunter	Burr DeBenning
	Constance Ford		Ken Kercheval*
	Nita Talbot		Stephen Joyce
Wilbur Peabody	Don Knotts		Terry Logan
Eunice Webster Wyatt	Marian Brash	Andrea Whiting	Virginia Gilmore
	Ann Williams*		Lesley Woods
Frank Gardner	Harry Holcombe		Joan Copeland*
	Eric Dressler	Cal Foster	Colgate Salisbury
Jessie Bergman Gardner	Joanna Roos	Walter Haskins	Douglass Watson
	Nydia Westman		Ernest Graves
Allison Simmons Metcalf	Nina Reader	Tom Bergman	Peter Broderick
	Anne Pearson*		Ray Bellaran
Cornelia Simmons Twining	Doris Dalton		John James
			Mitch Litrofsky
Rex Twining	Laurence Hugo		Robert Lupone
Pearl March	Isabel Price	Althea Franklin	Dody Goodman
	Sylvia Field	Doug Martin	Kenneth Harvey
Bud Gardner	Tony Ray	Ellie Harper Bergman	Billie Lou Watt
	Anthony Cannon	Ida Weston	Vera Allen
	George Maharis	Scott Phillips	Peter Simon*
Harriet Baxter	Vicki Viola		Peter Ratray
Slim Davis	Wayne Rogers	Jill Carter	Barbara Baxley
Fred Metcalf	Tom Carlin	Larry Carter	Hal Linden
	Donald Madden	Grace Bolton	Jill Clayburgh
	David O'Brien	Dr. Peter Murphy	Charles Siebert
Agnes Metcalf	Katherine Meskill	Lauri Lawson Phillips	Kelly Wood
Hester Walsh	Kay Medford	Magda Leshinsky	Lilia Skala
Dr. Dan Walton	Martin E. Brooks	Erik Leshinsky	Christopher Lowe
	Philip Abbott	Dr. Tony Vincente	Anthony George*
	Ron Husmann		Lawrence Weber
Jimmy Bergman	Peter Lazar		Robert Loggia
Monica Bergman	Barbara Baxley	Marcy Vincente	Jeanne Carson
Marion Gill	Jane McArthur	Agnes Lake	Anne Revere
Sue Knowles	Audra Lindley	Al Franklin	Al Fann
Dr. Brad Campbell	George Kane	John Burroughs	Adam Wade
Dr. Everett Moore	Martin E. Brooks	Dick Hart	Michael Zaslow
Isabel Kitteridge Moore	Lenka Peterson	Claire Hart	Peggy Whitton
Dr. Lawson	House Jameson	Kathy Parker Taper	Courtney Sherman Simon*
Geoffrey Crane	Geoffrey Lumb		Nicolette Goulet
Helen	Sandy Duncan	Jim McCarven	Michael Shannon
Dr. Len Whiting	Dino Narizzano*	Bruce Carson	Robby Benson
	Jeff Pomerantz		Michael Maitland
Sam Reynolds	Robert Mandan*		Gary Tomlin
	George Gaynes		Steve Nisbet
	Roy Shuman		Joel Higgins
Dr. Bob Rogers	Carl Low	Dr. Gary Walton	Tommy Norden
Emily Rogers Hunter	Pamela Murphy		John Driver
	Louise Shaffer*		Richard Lohman
	Kathryn Walker		

	Robert Bannard	Gwen Delon	Barbara Babcock
	Stephen Burleigh	Nancy Craig	Melanie Chartoff
Liza Walton Sentell	Denise Nickerson	Gail Caldwell	Sherry Rooney
	Kathleen Beller	Kitty Merritt	Donna Theodore
	Meg Bennett	Cindy French	Allison Argo
	Hope Busby	Dr. Greg Hartford	Robert Rockwell
	Sherry Mathis	Meredith Hartford	Tina Orr
Dr. Wade Collins	John Cunningham	Evelyn Reedy	Lenka Peterson
Helen Collins	Natalie Schafer	Dr. Allen Ramsey	Conard Fowkes
William Collins	Ralph Clanton	Fay Chandler	Kathleen Devine
George Joslyn	Kipp Osborne	Bill Mendell	Robert Heitman
Sarah Fairbanks	Susan Sarandon	Donna Davis	Leslie Ray
John Wyatt	Val DuFour	Chance Halliday	George Shannon
Dr. Matt Weldon	Robert Phelps	Kylie Halliday	Lisa Buck
Melissa Hayley Weldon .	Linda Bove	Ted Adamson	Malachi Throne
Karl Devlin	David Ford		Wayne Tippit*
Frank Ross	Andrew Jarkowsky	Laine Adamson	Megan Bagot
Marian Malin	Pat Stanley	Sunny McClure	
Jennifer Pace Phillips . .	Robin Eisenman	Adamson	Marcia McCabe
	Morgan Fairchild*	Marc D'Antoni	Christopher Goutman
Stephanie Wilkins Wyatt	Marie Cheatham	Nick D'Antoni	Jerry Lanning
Wendy Wilkins McNeil .	Andrea McArdle	Travis Sentell	Rod Arrants
	Lisa Peluso*	Mignon Sentell	Anita Keal
Suzi Martin Carter	Kristan Carl	Gen. Roger Tourneur . . .	William Robertson
	Amy Arutt	Martin Tourneur	John Aniston
	Stacey Moran	Sharon Peterson	Verna Pierce
	Cynthia Gibb	Buck Peterson	Christopher Loomis
Dr. Walter Osmond	Byron Sanders	Tante Helene LeVeaux .	Jane White
Paula Markham	Sharon Spelman	Lee Sentell	Douglas Stevenson
Ralph Haywood	James O'Sullivan	E. N. Sentell	Jay Garner
	Drew Snyder*	Tod Adamson	Kevin Bacon
Dave Wilkins	Dale Robinette	Simon D'Antoni	Gregory Sutton
Walter Pace	Wayne Tippit	Renata Corelli Sutton . .	Sonia Petrovna
	Edward Grover	Prince Antonio Stradella	Robert Desiderio
	Tom Klunis	Beau Mitchell	Danny Goldring
Hal Conrad	Ben Hammer	Cissie Mitchell Sentell .	Patsy Pease
	Vince O'Brien	Spencer Langley	Timothy Patrick Murphy
		Brian Emerson	Paul Joynt
Dr. Carolyn Hanley			Larry Joshua
Walton	Gayle Pines		Gene Pietragallo
	Marilyn McIntyre*		Jay Acovone
Amy Kaslo Carson	Pamela Miller		
	Anne Wyndham*	Dr. Jamie Larsen	
Steve Kaslo	Michael Nouri	Adamson	Patricia Estrin Arrants
Clay Collins	Brett Halsey	Jim Ramsey	Ralph Byers
Karen Dehner	Kathleen Dezina	Dr. Winston Kyle	Nicholas Courtland
Danny Walton	Neil Billingsley	Dr. Max Taper	Don Chastain
Robin Kennemer	Lane Binkley	Garth Taper	David Gautreaux
David Sutton	Lewis Arlt	Sylvie Descartes	Maureen Anderman
Chris Delon	Paul DuMont	Zach Anders	Shawn Stevens

Dane Taylor	Marcus Smythe
Aja Doyan	Susan Monts
Jenny Deacon	Linda Gibboney
Warren Carter	Michael Corbett
Kristen Carter	Susan Scannell
Keith McNeil	Craig Augustine
Andie McNeil	Stacey Glick
Ringo Altman	Larry Fleischman
Rusty Sentell	David Gale
Dr. Barbara Moreno . . .	Olympia Dukakis
Josh Moreno	Josh Freund
	Damion Scheller

Creator: Roy Winsor

Head Writers: Agnes Eckhardt (now Agnes Nixon), Irving Vendig, Charles Gussman, Frank and Doris Hursley, Julian Funt and David Lesan, Leonard Kantor and Doris Frankel, Lou Scofield, Robert Soderberg and Edith Sommer, Ralph Ellis and Eugenie Hunt, Theodore Apstein, Gabrielle Upton, Ann Marcus, Peggy O'Shea, Irving and Tex Elman, Robert J. Shaw, Henry Slesar, Joyce and John William Corrington, Linda Grover, Harding Lemay, Don Chastain, David Cherrill, Gary Tomlin

Executive Producers: Roy Winsor, Woody Klose, Mary-Ellis Bunim, Fred Bartholemew, Joanna Lee

Producers: Charles Irving, Myron Golden, Everett Gammon, Frank Dodge, Robert Driscoll, John Edwards, Bernie Sofronski, Mary-Ellis Bunim, Robert Getz

Directors: Charles Irving, Ira Cirker, Hal Cooper, John Frankenheimer, Dan Levin, Bruce Minnix, Ned Stark, Burt Brinckerhoff, Nick Havinga, Joseph Stuart, Richard T. McCue, Robert Schwarz, Don Wallace, Robert Nigro, Paul Lammers, Seth Glassman, Mel Shapiro, John Pasquin, Andrew D. Weyman, Henry Kaplan, Richard Dunlap, Robert Rigamonti

Organists: Chet Kingsbury, Bill Meeder, Ashley Miller

Musical Direction (later): Elliot Lawrence Productions

Packager: Procter & Gamble

THE YOUNG AND THE RESTLESS

IT is difficult to guess what daytime television would be like today if *The Young and The Restless* had never premiered. Would there have been that revolution in story structure and production values beginning in 1978? Would soap operas have failed to become immersed in the current climate of sexual liberation and the cult of youth? No one knows. But one thing is established fact: after creator William Bell and executive producer John Conboy premiered their watershed show on March 26, 1973, head writers and producers all over the soap world came under tremendous pressure to introduce young, physically appealing characters in their stories and to be less cryptic about sexual matters. Many soaps in the mid-seventies solved the problem by building elaborate swimming pool sets and filling them with luscious nymphets and handsome young men with bulging pectorals. *The Young and The Restless* had very little of that kind of seminudity, but the show did seem suggestive to viewers because of John Conboy's sensuous lighting effects on his voluptuous young actors, who played out William Bell's deeply romantic plots. There was also little talk after the first years about sex, as removed from the mystique of romanticism. But *The Young and The Restless*'s image as a high-rated soap about erotic young people who brought viewers close to their sexual world nevertheless was the dominant one that influenced all other daytime dramas.

For more about the extraordinary style and content of the early years of *The Young and The Restless*, see page 43.

During its eleven-year history, *The Young and The Restless* has had a stable, slowly evolving story line, with a relatively small number of major characters—a sign of masterful soap opera writing. In the late seventies and early eighties, however, both the story and the production went through a series of dynamic changes. The show went to an hour (which William Bell had been resisting for several years) and H. Wesley Kenney succeeded John Conboy as executive producer. Wes Kenney was not especially fond of his predecessor's dark lighting, and its slow and sensual fantasy mood, both factors in *The Young and The Restless*'s great success. Instead, the new producer bathed his actors and sets with lots of light ("My God!" exclaimed a soap watcher friend of his, "You have sets!") and speeded up the individual scenes, as most soaps were doing at the time in response to the ABC threat. The old, leisurely romantic style had sadly gone by the wayside.

Meanwhile, William Bell began moving the emphasis away from the Brooks and Foster families and making two other families prominent: the wealthy and glamorous Abbotts, and the poor, down-to-earth Williamses. What the writer seemed to be doing was to remake his original rich/poor families into ones which would express even more youthful appeal. With both the Abbotts and the Williamses came a string of gorgeous new teenage characters, all with their own special sexual natures. Bell's new character of Victor Newman also seemed to be a replacement for the old Brad Eliot, as the new male arrival who

293

deeply affects the emotional lives of the women around him. The show has been engaging Victor, a rude but compelling man (wonderfully played by Eric Braeden), in a series of unusual erotic stories with women of different ages and backgrounds. The result is that Bell has pushed the boundaries of the show's televised fantasies beyond anything that could have been imagined in March 1973.

ABOUT WILLIAM BELL

William Bell is one of the elite creators of current soaps who are still writing their own shows. Of that handful (which includes Agnes Nixon, Claire Labine and Paul Avila Mayer, and Douglas Marland), he has the most unusual background, having begun his career as a young lawyer in Chicago. One of his clients had been Irna Phillips and the two soon became good friends. She asked him to write dialogue for her show, *The Guiding Light*, which by now, the mid-fifties, was on television. The close working relationship continued and he wrote *As the World Turns* with her and later, in the mid-sixties, *Another World* as well as the short-lived nighttime soap, *Our Private World*.

Bell's real reputation in daytime began in 1967, when he took over as head writer of *Days of Our Lives*, which had had such poor ratings that cancellation was imminent. His stories for the Horton clan (see summary) combined fantasy and clinical psychology in a way that captured viewers' imaginations and the ratings soared.

He stayed with *Days of Our Lives* for six years and then began to devise the concept for a soap opera of his own creation for CBS. It took him about three weeks. Originally he had in mind a story about four sisters and a mysterious stranger who comes to town, reminiscent of William Inge's *Picnic*. Then he began to introduce the poor Foster family for contrast. But the main story revolved around young people. Said Bill Bell, "I knew I wanted a broad base of wholesome, identifiable young people in situations that reflected a segment of contemporary life." At first he was going to call his show *The Innocent Years* but later changed the title to the more explicit *The Young and The Restless*.

William Bell is married to Lee Phillip Bell, who aided him in the creation of the show. He still lives and works in Chicago.

THE STORY

Chicago psychiatrist-neurosurgeon BRAD ELIOT (Tom Hallick) suddenly gave up medicine and left town, just minutes after the son of his financée died under his scalpel. He was torn by the idea that he had killed the boy. Later on, after he wandered into Genoa City and began working on a newspaper, *The Chronicle*, he saw a news report come in on the wires: DR. BRAD ELIOT OF CHICAGO HAS BEEN KILLED IN AN AUTO CRASH. Brad realized that the man who had stolen his car and identification papers as he was leaving Chicago had been killed in a crash in that car. Here was the perfect way to "die" and start his life all over.

The paper he worked on was published by STUART BROOKS (Robert Colbert), husband of once ravishingly beautiful JENNIFER BROOKS (Dorothy Green) and the highly moralistic father of four exceptionally attractive daughters: LESLIE (Janice Lynde, Victoria Mallory), LAURALEE (Jaime Lyn Bauer), CHRIS (Trish Stewart, Lynn Topping Richter) and young PEGGY (Pamela Peters Solow, Patricia Everly). Stuart Brooks had taken a liking to Brad from the first moment he met him in a Genoa City restaurant. He not only offered him a job on his paper, but introduced him to his oldest daughter, Leslie, an aspiring concert pianist. It was indeed a strange act of trust and intuition on the part of Stuart, for Brad insisted on keeping his background a mystery, which should have put Stuart off. But then, Brad had a mysterious, unexplainable effect on most people. He instilled trust, and he was always eager to help others.

Leslie Brooks was shy and socially backward when she first met Brad. She had spent so much time studying to be a concert pianist that she had completely neglected her social life. With Brad's attentive help, she began to feel more attractive, more feminine, and she grew to love him deeply.

Chris Brooks, Stuart's second-youngest daughter, was the one who gave her father painful misgivings. Eager that his extremely trusting daughter marry the right man—and not be taken advantage of by *any* male—Stuart became dead set against her interest in "SNAPPER" FOSTER (William Gray Espy, David Hasselhoff), a medical student from a poor family. It was Snapper's seeming indifference to his daughter—even more than his low-class background—that angered Stuart Brooks.

And Snapper Foster didn't seem to know himself

what he felt toward Chris. His main concern, before his personal happiness, was getting through med school and helping his mother, LIZ FOSTER (Juliana McCarthy), put his younger brother, GREG FOSTER (James Houghton, Brian Kerwin, Wings Hauser, Howard McGillin) through law school. Liz's husband had deserted the family seven years before, leaving her to work in a factory and her two sons and daughter, JILL FOSTER (Brenda Dickson, Bond Gideon, Deborah Adair), to fend for themselves. Somehow Liz managed, though often at the expense of her health. Jill had helped out by working as a beautician, although she would have liked to chuck it all and become a glamorous model. Liz wanted nothing more than to see her two sons professionally successful and married to smartly brought-up girls—like Chris Brooks.

Snapper thought Chris wasn't ready for marriage. Instead, for a physical relationship, he turned to SALLY MCGUIRE (Lee Crawford), a young waitress at Pierre's, a popular night spot in Genoa City. Sally was Chris's opposite. Her mother had committed suicide and her

father had died an alcoholic; she'd already had an illegitimate child. In love with Snapper, her only path to a better life, she tried to hold onto him by conceiving his child. When Chris first found out about the affair from her irate father, she became confused and self-doubting, deciding to leave her father's house to take her own apartment. She did try to have premarital relations with Snapper, as Sally had, but couldn't go through with it. Snapper understood and respected her all the more. One night a stranger, GEORGE CURTIS (Tony Geary), broke into her apartment and raped her brutally! She felt ashamed and shattered. To help her get over the degradation of her first experience with sex, Snapper proposed marriage. Meanwhile, Chris pressed charges against her attacker, but in vain, for there were no witnesses, and the rapist was set free. Although Chris now feared sex with any man, Snapper showed such patience and understanding during their first uneasy weeks of marriage that Chris was finally able to make love with him.

Crushed after hearing of Snapper's marriage to Chris, the pregnant Sally McGuire had no one to turn to and tried to kill herself. After Brad Eliot saved her life, she told PIERRE ROLLAND (Robert Clary), the owner of the club where she worked, that she was pregnant. Pierre, in love with her from the start, asked her to marry him and told her that no one else need know

On March 26, 1973, when The Young and The Restless *began, Stuart and Jennifer Brooks (Robert Colbert and Dorothy Green) headed the story's well-to-do family. They had four beautiful daughters just emerging into womanhood. Stuart owned the Genoa City* Chronicle.

Liz Foster (Julianna McCarthy) was the hard-working matriarch of the second, poorer family. Her husband had deserted her years before. She and her three children—law student Greg (James Houghton), medical student Snapper and hairdresser Jill—had to struggle to make ends meet.

that the child she was carrying wasn't his. After they were married, however, Pierre's sister, MARIANNE ROL-LAND (Lilyan Chauvin), became jealous of Sally and, after making a few educated guesses, accused her of carrying another man's child. She then confronted Pierre with her suspicions, and he admitted she had guessed the truth. A short time later, Pierre was attacked by a mugger and died in the hospital. Sally, still expecting Snapper's baby, was feeling more alone than ever.

* * *

Lauralee "Laurie" Brooks finally came home from college and took a job on her father's newspaper, working closely with Brad Eliot. Snobbish and immature, Laurie set her sights on Brad, even though her sister, Leslie, was deeply in love with him. At every opportunity Laurie would attempt to undermine Leslie and Brad's relationship, failing to deliver important messages from one to the other. Soon Laurie had

Leslie believing that Brad was losing interest in her, and Brad believing that Leslie's career as a concert pianist would suffer if he pursued her.

Now that Sally needed his help, Snapper, with his wife's consent, began to spend a great deal of time with her. He had already been told of her past suicide attempt, and feared what she would do to herself if she were left too much alone. After Sally gave birth to little CHARLES PIERRE, Snapper confessed to Chris that he was the boy's father. Chris, now pregnant, became so tortured by doubts about her marriage that she aborted. To "find" herself (once again), she separated from Snapper and took a job as a social worker in legal aid for brother-in-law Greg Foster. Meanwhile, Sally began a new life for herself and her baby in Chicago. After a time, Chris gained new independence, and she and Snapper resumed their marriage.

Up until now, Greg had felt romantic affection for only one woman—Chris, his sister-in-law. Now he fell in love with a client, beautiful GWEN SHERMAN (Jennifer Leak). There was nothing about flame-haired Gwen to suggest that she was, in fact, a prostitute. When Greg found out through his brother, he was terribly upset and called off the planned wedding. A kindhearted

Snapper Foster (William Gray Espy) had a sexual relationship with hard-luck girl Sally McGuire (Lee Crawford) while engaged to Chris Brooks, Stuart's daughter, because Chris wouldn't have premarital sex. It was the first time a soap had ever talked so directly and extensively about sex.

After becoming pregnant by Snapper, Sally McGuire wed Pierre Roland (Robert Clary) in 1974, hoping that she could make him happy. Brad Eliot (Tom Hallick, second from left) had been the mysterious stranger who arrived in Genoa City at the premiere, acting as a catalyst in everyone's lives.

man, Greg simply couldn't leave Gwen in the lurch, and he offered to help her reform. Gwen vowed she would, and Greg began to feel that there was yet hope for an eventual marriage, but when Gwen's violent pimps threatened to kill Greg for interfering, she was forced into accepting clients again. Hurt, Greg cursed at her—"Tramp!"—and she tried to kill herself. When Snapper told Greg that she was being coerced into remaining a call girl, Greg convinced Gwen to press charges against these dreadful pimps, and for the first time Gwen was beginning to discover the joys of chastity and integrity. She turned toward God and joined a convent.

A strange series of events led to the near fulfillment of all of Jill Foster's fantasies of love, glamor and wealth. Rich KAY CHANCELLOR (Jeanne Cooper) was a steady client at the beauty salon where Jill worked. Mrs. Chancellor, an aging dipsomaniac, took a fancy to Jill and asked her to come work for her as her personal girl Friday. Jill anxiously accepted the job and became thoroughly infatuated not only with Mrs. Chancellor's manner of living, but also with PHILLIP CHANCELLOR (Donnelly Rhodes), Kay's soft-spoken husband. After Phillip announced his love for Jill, a moral girl, she refused to sleep with him until they could help alcoholic Kay stand on her own two feet. Jill struggled to keep her rival away from gin bottles and stable boys. (Kay needed them for sexual outlet—Phillip had refused to have relations with her for several years.) Nothing seemed to help Kay—until one day she found Phillip and Jill in each other's arms. The shock of realizing she would lose Phillip made her go on the wagon. She began to devise ways of breaking up Phillip and Jill.

Scheming Laurie Brooks finally did shatter the growing tender romance of Brad Eliot and her sister,

The compact cast of The Young and The Restless *in 1975 included, from left, top row: Lee Crawford, Donnelly Rhodes (Phillip Chancellor), Jeanne Cooper (Kay Chancellor). Middle row: James Houghton, William Gray Espy, Trish Stewart (Chris Brooks), Jaime Lyn Bauer (Laurie Brooks). Bottom row: Brenda Dickson (Jill Foster), Juliana McCarthy, Robert Colbert, Dorothy Green and Janice Lynde (Leslie Brooks).*

Leslie Brooks. Because of Laurie's continual plotting to make Les think that Brad no longer cared for her, Les became deeply upset. When Les wrote Brad a letter begging him to join her in Detroit for her big concert appearance, Laurie made sure Brad never received the love letter, then seduced Brad herself and proposed marriage. Believing Les no longer needed him, Brad accepted. Leslie began showing severe symptoms of manic-depression: she went to New York, was found wandering blankly in Central Park, and was admitted to a psychiatric hospital, her identity unknown. When her identity was discovered, Brad learned the truth of what Laurie had done and broke their engagment. Les, with Brad's help, had a complete recovery, and a wedding date was set. Meanwhile, Les bought Pierre Rolland's nightclub from his widow, Sally, and renamed it the Allegro, where Les began singing as a way of learning how to express her personality more fully. Brad told Les the truth of his own past: how he had been a Chicago neurosurgeon who had had an affair with a nurse called BARBARA ANDERSON (Diedre Hall), who had his son, who even-

tually died while Brad was operating, causing Brad such guilt that he ran from Chicago and gave up medicine. Leslie said that she would keep the story a secret, and she and Brad were wed.

BILL FOSTER (Charles Gray), the husband who deserted his wife, Liz, and their three children nine years before, was living in another town. Snapper had finally gotten Liz to agree to have Bill declared legally dead, so that she might be free to remarry. Then Liz met a fine man, SAM POWERS (Barry Cahill), and he and Liz became engaged. Meanwhile, Bill Foster, knowing that he was dying of lung cancer, wrote to his family and came to Genoa City. Since Bill was dying, everyone, except Snapper, forgave him for the heartbreak he had caused the Fosters, and Liz agreed to have him move into the house for his last months—not sleeping with his wife, of course. Bill, a completely reformed man, encouraged Liz to marry Sam Powers for her own good, but in the end Liz decided to send Sam away. In her mind, she was still a married woman. Secretly Jill and Greg hoped that their parents would rediscover their love for each other.

BROCK REYNOLDS (Beau Kayzer), Kay Chancellor's

The youngest of the Brooks girls, Peggy (Pamela Peters), was also the most sensitive. She was shattered when her mother, Jennifer, announced that she intended to divorce Stuart to marry an old flame. Later, like her sister Chris, Peggy was raped and afterward couldn't face having sex with any man.

In 1976 John McCook played wealthy businessman Lance Prentiss, who was first attracted to Leslie but then fell in love with her sister Laurie (Jaime Lyn Bauer). The show had some main characters, like Lance and Laurie, suddenly break out into song while on balconies or dancing under chandeliers.

estranged son, came back to Genoa City. He was a handsome, exotic young man who had recently given up his profligate ways—which included a sex-and-drugs "trip" with Laurie while they were both living in Paris—to become a self-styled evangelical religious reformer. Brock took a platonic interest in Jill, who confessed that she loved Phillip but wanted to end the relationship because it was killing Kay. Kay then offered Brock a part of her fortune to seduce Jill and marry her. Brock agreed, because he believed it was the only way to end the agony for Jill and his mother. To give herself a way out of a messy situation, Jill accepted Brock's proposal. Brock insisted on performing the ceremony himself, and they lived in a cabin in the woods, without having physical relations. Phillip was shocked when he found out. Then Jill learned she was pregnant from the one night she had spent with Phillip! After Jill told him that she was carrying his child, he vowed to divorce Kay and marry her. Phillip flew to the Dominican Republic for a Reno-type divorce, but Kay swore that Phillip would never marry Jill. Kay met him at the airport and, on the pretext of giving him a friendly lift, got him into her car and drove off a cliff. Kay survived, but Phillip was on his deathbed at the Genoa City hospital, where he insisted on marrying Jill, telling her that he wanted their child to be the heir to his fortune. When Phillip died, Jill's grief was soon replaced by her hatred of Kay Chancellor for what Kay had done.

Many months of anguished bitterness followed the tragedy. Jill, as Phillip's widow, now possessed his money and his property, including the house where Jill had been Kay's servant. Jill insisted that her entire family move into the house, but they weren't used to having servants do for them and felt strange at first; with Jill's prodding, they grew to like being "wealthy." Meanwhile, Kay was driven by only one impulse: to prove that Phillip and Jill weren't really married and to get back her house. During a messy courtroom battle, Kay told how she had been "coerced" into signing divorce papers while too drunk to know what she was doing, and won the case not only reacquiring the estate, but making Phillip's baby illegitimate. The thought that Jill was carrying Phillip's baby preyed on

Lance's mother Vanessa (K. T. Stevens) first appeared as a mysterious veiled figure in Lance's house after Laurie married him. Vanessa, who had been horribly disfigured in a fire years before, sensed that Laurie was her rival for Lance's affections and plotted to destroy her.

Lucas Prentiss (Tom Ligon), Lance's seafaring brother, arrived in 1977 and helped create a wonderfully complex triangle. Lucas fell in love with Leslie (Victoria Mallory, left), who loved Lance and was carrying his baby. But Lance was already married to Laurie, Leslie's sister. Leslie wed Lucas to give her baby the Prentiss name, while Vanessa (K. T. Stevens, right) used Lucas to hurt Laurie.

Kay's mind and Kay offered Jill one million dollars if Jill would give Kay legal custody of the child. Jill agreed, but after little Phillip, Jr., was born, she couldn't go through with the "sale" and decided, instead, to sue Mrs. Chancellor for part of the estate on behalf of Phillip, Jr., but the court denied Jill's petition. Jill broke down in hysterics, vowing this time to get even with Kay Chancellor.

Jill devised a plot. She came to Mrs. Chancellor and, as if no time had passed, began to talk about Phillip as still alive and about the need for Kay to give up drinking. Kay already *had* given up drinking after Phillip died. Kay thought she was going insane, just as Jill had hoped, and began drinking from the liquor bottle that Jill left in a paper bag. When Liz Foster found out that Jill had turned Kay back into an alcoholic, in order to kill her, Liz begged her daughter to stop the scheme. Finally Jill came to her senses and told Mrs. Chancellor the truth, but by now Kay was already back on the booze.

* * *

Dennis Cole became the new Lance Prentiss in 1978, here accompanying Victoria Mallory as Leslie to her reception at the Royal Palace in London and the grand ball given in honor of her concert artistry.

Jennifer Brooks, feeling unneeded now that her children were grown, and taken for granted by Stuart, was about to ask Stuart for a divorce to marry her old lover, DR. BRUCE HENDERSON (Paul Stevens), when Stuart collapsed of a heart attack. Guilt stricken, Jen decided to wait until Stuart had recovered before asking for a divorce. The family was in turmoil and deeply divided in their opinions. Worldly Laurie was the most sympathetic of the three girls to her mother's plan for a new life, while the younger Peggy hated Jen so much that she had to move out of the house. True to her word, Jen asked Stuart for a divorce when he was well and, although filled with guilt, flew to Chicago to begin a life with Bruce. Immediately afterward she discovered a lump in her breast. It was malignant, and a mastectomy was performed. Jen then refused to marry Bruce *or* return to Stuart, who still wanted her. But Stuart continued to love his wife, and in time Jen got over her feeling of being too disfigured for a man to love, and they were reconciled.

Jen also had to face another crisis. Laurie—after a romance with married JED ANDREWS (Tom Selleck)—fell in love with Bruce Henderson's son, MARK HENDERSON (Steve Carlson). Mark was the big love in Laurie's life, the one man who allowed her to abandon that shell of protection which made her appear hardened.

The Young & The Restless *introduced a bold teenage storyline in 1980 that featured Doug Davidson (right) as Paul Williams, who had fathered the baby of young April but at first refused to marry her. Later, both Paul and Greg Foster (now Wings Hauser, left) became rivals for her.*

Jen was stunned when Laurie and Mark announced their engagement—for all these years Jen had been harboring a secret. Bruce, not Stuart, had been Laurie's father! Therefore Laurie and Mark were half-brother and half-sister. When Mark heard the truth from Jen, he was dazed, and immediately left town. A bewildered Laurie finally heard the whole story too. She blamed Jen for robbing her of her birthright *and* her man.

Peggy Brooks, the youngest and most melancholy of the four daughters, fell in love with her college teacher, JACK CURTIS (Anthony Herrera). When Peggy found out that Jack's real name was Jack Curtzynski—a married man interested in other women because his wife, JOANN (Kay Heberle), had recently grown overweight—Peggy's whole world fell apart. Jack said that he wanted to divorce Joann to marry Peggy, but Peggy soon learned that Joann had built her whole life around Jack and would be destroyed by a divorce. Peggy found herself in the agonizing position of sending the man she loved back to Joann, and even helping the woman gain back her self-confidence. Then Peggy, a virgin, was raped! It had been by a man she couldn't see very well. Chris became convinced that the rapist was RON BECKER (Dick De Coit), a young man, with a wife and baby, who had previously been charged with rape. Peggy, during a most painful trial, accused Ron of being her rapist, without being absolutely sure, because Chris was so sure that he was her attacker. After he was acquitted, his wife NANCY (Cathy Carricaburu) discovered that he *was* the rapist and went into schizophrenic withdrawal, leading to her commitment. Chris tried to adopt the Becker's little girl, KAREN (Brandi Tucker), despite Snapper's warning that it would cause heartache for Chris. After Nancy Becker recovered, she fought for and regained custody of her child, then left town with her husband.

* * *

Leslie Brooks Eliot had no idea why her husband, Brad, was avoiding her concerts, walking out

In 1980, Eric Braeden originated the compelling character of Victor Newman, whose coldness alienated his wife Julia (Meg Bennett). Since divorcing Julia, he has been involved with several other beautiful women, all of whom have found him emotionally inhospitable.

Eve Howard (Margaret Mason, left) had had an illegitimate child by Victor and so hated him that she planned to murder him so that her son would inherit his money. Jill (Deborah Adair) befriended Eve when she came to Genoa City in 1982.

on dinners and behaving quite as if he had lost interest in her. Brad hadn't. He had found out that he was going blind, because of incurable nephritis of the optic nerve, and was avoiding Leslie to keep her from learning the truth. He feared that if she knew she would give up her concert career to care for him. When his eyesight was nearly gone, he left Leslie completely. Laurie began looking after him in her apartment. In time, Brad saw doctors who were able to cure his blindness, but by then Brad believed that his prolonged separation from Leslie had done irreparable damage to their marriage and he left Genoa City for good.

A severely depressed Leslie, meanwhile, found that she had an admirer. Wealthy businessman-playboy LANCE PRENTISS (John McCook, Dennis Cole) followed Leslie from concert to concert, professing his ardor. Trying to forget Brad, she had an affair with Lance, but broke it off when she thought she could never love any other man but Brad. So Lance turned to her sister, Laurie, wining and dining her in New York, Paris and London. It was "just one of those things" at first, but soon they began to fall in love. Lance was forgetting his original infatuation with Leslie, and Laurie was beginning to get over the awful hurt of losing Mark. Yet Laurie had no idea why Lance would not permit Laurie to enter a certain room in his house, or what those scarves, thrown about, with a monogrammed "V" meant. The initial was for VANESSA PRENTISS (K. T. Stevens), Lance's possessive mother. She had saved her son's life from a fire, but in the process her face was so brutally disfigured that she now had to wear a veil and hide from the world. Vanessa was jealous of any new woman who entered her son's life. After Laurie discovered the secret, she convinced Vanessa to undergo plastic surgery, which miraculously restored Vanessa's face. By then, however, she had developed a deep hatred of Laurie.

Genoa City's only happy event at this time was the remarriage of Bill and Liz Foster. But Bill only had a year of life left. When the inevitable happened and Bill began to suffer terribly while he was kept alive with extraordinary mechanical devices, he begged Liz to "pull the plug." At last, she did—and completely forgot that she had done it, after suffering a mild stroke. Snapper was accused of killing his own father, but with the legal help of his brother, Greg, he was acquitted. Meanwhile, Jill Foster found herself attracted to DAVID MALLORY (Robert Gibson), the handsome young man who had been blind until a cornea transplant restored his vision. The eyes he now bore had been the late Bill Foster's!

Joann, Jack Curtis's ex-wife, had become the protégé of Kay Chancellor, who showered her with gifts, clothes and much affection; feeling newly secure, Joann shed weight and became attractive and self-confident. The growing attachment, however, between Joann and Kay was, as Brock warned Kay, unnatural. Kay felt married to Joann and resented any interest Joann had in a man. Just before the two were to leave for a trip to Hawaii, Brock broke up the relationship by shaming Joann with the truth about Kay's feelings for her. Peggy Brooks, meanwhile, had married Jack Curtis, but was so disgusted with sex after having been raped by Ron Becker that she left Jack and moved back with her parents. Jack realized that he still loved Joann, especially now that she had become an utterly new, thin person, and remarried her.

Stuart Brooks and all four Brooks girls were distraught over the death of Jennifer from cancer. After a time, widower Stuart began to take an interest in widow Liz Foster, whom he had always admired and with whom he had much in common.

* * *

From her brief affair with Lance Prentiss, Leslie was now carrying his child! She was in love with Lance—but he was already married to her sister, Laurie. Rather than upset her sister's marriage, Leslie chose to suffer in silence. Suddenly, bearded seaman LUCAS PRENTISS (Tom Ligon), the brother whom Lance hadn't seen for years, arrived in Genoa City. He fell deeply in love with Leslie and, even though he knew she loved Lance, offered to marry her to give her baby the Prentiss name. Leslie, who found herself responding to Lucas's simple sweetness, married him, then had a baby boy which she named BROOKS. But the pressure of secretly loving Lance, not being able to tell him of the child she bore him, and being married to a man she didn't love, caused Leslie to decide to leave Genoa City. She arranged to leave Brooks with Laurie and Lance. But just before her departure, Leslie had a blowup with Laurie, who knew all about Brooks's true parentage. This had been the final shock and caused Leslie to suffer a severe nervous breakdown, which resulted in almost total amnesia. She wandered off to a neighboring community and found herself at Jonas's Bar, where the owner, JONAS (Jerry

Lacy), a Humphry Bogart-like rogue, fell madly in love with her. But after a time Leslie regained her memory and went back to Genoa City, followed by Jonas. Soon Lucas Prentiss, her husband, and Jonas began competing for her affections. In love with neither man, Leslie threw herself back into her work and started a concert tour of Europe.

Jill Foster, penniless once again, had gone back to hairdressing to support herself and Phillip Jr. She found herself attracted to her co-worker—handsome, blond, muscular hairdresser DEREK THURSTON (Joe LaDue). When Kay Chancellor, Jill's eternal rival, met Jill's blond Apollo, naturally she also wanted him, and offered to buy him his own salon, the Golden Comb, if he married her and lived with her for at least one year. Jill protested Derek's accepting the offer, but Derek assured her he only wanted Kay's money. However, after Derek married Kay, Jill was stunned when he told her that he took his wedding vows to Kay seriously, if only for one year. Feeling rejected, Jill set her sights on none other than well-to-do widower Stuart Brooks. While Jill knew that he had fallen in love with her mother, Liz Foster, she felt that her own future came first. During a trip to Las Vegas, Jill seduced Stuart and later trapped him into marriage by claiming to be carrying his baby. When Stuart later found out that she was not pregnant, he demanded that she divorce him. At first Jill refused.

Meanwhile, Derek's ex-wife, SUZANNE LYNCH (Ellen Weston), deadly as a venus fly trap, showed up and began devising vicious schemes to win Derek back. She falsely befriended Kay and began offering her chocolates spiked with powerful drugs that caused her to behave so bizarrely that she had to be committed to a sanitarium. There Kay's hospital roommate ate some of Suzanne's funny candy and, in a frenzy, set fire to their room. The woman was burned to death beyond recognition. Kay then slipped her wedding ring on the corpse's finger, making everyone believe that Kay had died in the fire. Now quite sane and heavily veiled, Kay attended her own funeral and began to haunt poor, dreadful Suzanne, who thought she was seeing Kay's ghost all over the Chancellor mansion. Suzanne went temporarily mad and swore to repent. Jill, believing that she could now marry Derek, gave Stuart his divorce. But just as her wedding to Derek had begun, Kay revealed herself. Jill, hungry for either love or money, now had neither. Stuart and Liz married happily, and were a source of strength to

their respective children for a long time to come.

Despite his greed, Derek loved Kay in his own way. He agreed to go with her on a second honeymoon cruise, which turned into a disaster. On the ship, Kay ran into DOUGLAS AUSTIN (Michael Evans), an old flame who was now a con man pretending to be a wealthy socialite. Derek became so jealous that he left the ship and flew back to the mainland. Believing that she had lost him forever, Kay threw herself overboard but, instead of drowning, she washed ashore on a nearby island. She was saved by a macho Cuban named FILIPE RAMIREZ (Victor Mohica), who dominated Kay as no man ever had, and she fell in love with him. Kay and Filipe went back to the mainland so that she could get treatment for her injured foot in a hospital. There she ran into Douglas Austin again, and this time it was Filipe who misunderstoood the relationship and went back to his island without her. Her sexual fantasy ended, Kay returned to Genoa City, where she gave Derek his walking papers.

Laurie Brooks Prentiss's life continued to be dominated by her mother-in-law Vanessa's hatred of her. To punish Lance for having married Laurie, Vanessa removed him as head of Prentiss Industries and made Lucas the president. At first Laurie and Lance enjoyed their new freedom from work, traveling to gambling and drinking palaces in Monte Carlo, Rome, Greece, the Bahamas. But when Lance's gambling and drinking became self-destructive, Laurie gave in to Vanessa's cruel, secret demand that she leave him, so that he could continue as head of the family company. Lance moved to Paris without Laurie. But Vanessa felt she had suffered too much at the hands of Laurie and wanted greater revenge. Learning from her doctors that she had only two months to live, she devised a sick plot. She came to Laurie's place unannounced one day, and walked out onto the balcony with Laurie, while Lucas was upstairs with little Brooks. She started screaming, "Don't push me!", and leaped off the balcony. The police arrived and charged Laurie with Vanessa's murder. Later, after little Brooks found some writing of Vanessa's proving that she was devising her own death, Laurie was set free.

* * *

A number of very young people in Genoa City faced difficult sexual dilemmas.

Policeman CARL WILLIAMS (Brett Hadley) and his

wife, MARY WILLIAMS (Carolyn Conwell), were good, simple people who only wanted their children to grow up properly. They were disturbed at the promiscuous behavior of their son, PAUL WILLIAMS (Doug Davidson), especially when they found out he had impregnated teenager APRIL STEVENS (Cynthia Eilbacher) and wouldn't take responsibility for her situation.

Pretty NIKKI REED (Erika Hope, Melody Thomas) was the sister of DR. CASEY REED (Roberta Leighton), who practiced at the clinic where Snapper Foster worked. Nikki had caught gonorrhea from Paul Williams and was treated for it by DR. SCOTT ADAMS (Jack Stauffer), who began dating her. Deep trouble arrived for Nikki when her perverse, incestuous father, NICK REED (Quinn Redeker), came to live with her. When he tried to rape Nikki, as he had her sister Casey many years before, Nikki killed him. Greg Foster became her lawyer and gained an acquittal for her on a charge of murder. Afterward the two grew close and married. But Greg was troubled by Nikki's tendency to act independently and run around town, and the two soon separated. Then Nikki met JERRY "CASH" CASHMAN (John Gibson), a professional male stripper, who convinced her to join him in a strip act at a club called the Bayou. The act became the sensation of Genoa City.

Meanwhile, VICTOR NEWMAN (Eric Braeden), a successful but ruthless businessman, came to Genoa City to run Chancellor Industries for Kay Chancellor. His wife, JULIA NEWMAN (Meg Bennett), hated his coldness and felt like another piece of his property. Because she wanted to find her own identity, she agreed to become a photographer's model for Jabot Cosmetics and photographer MICHAEL SCOTT (Nick Benedict). After an argument with Victor, Julia turned to honorable, compassionate Michael Scott, and the two made love. Then Julia became pregnant. Ice-cold Victor had already had a secret vasectomy, specifically to test his wife's fidelity. He therefore believed Julia's baby to be Michael's. Seeking revenge, he prepared his basement fallout shelter, complete with television cameras and torture devices, then imprisoned Michael there, periodically torturing him. After a while Julia spotted Michael on one of Victor's television monitors and tried to free him. During a terrible struggle, Julia fell down a flight of stairs and miscarried. Michael got away. Then Victor ironically discovered that *he* was the father of Julia's baby, for the vasectomy had not taken properly. When Julia

became gravely ill, Victor vowed that if she recovered he would grant her the divorce she wanted. She did recover and Julia and Michael Scott left Genoa City together. Victor became a lonely and rejected man.

He began to concentrate on business matters. Laurie Prentiss, after a quarrel with Lance, had foolishly turned over company proxies to unscrupulous Victor, giving him full control of Prentiss Industries. Then, finding himself attracted to Nikki Reed, Victor bought the Bayou, the club where she and Cash performed their strip act. Soon Victor talked Nikki into moving into his house so that he could help her become a fine lady. Separated from his emotions, he couldn't admit to himself or her that he loved her, although he had sexual relations with her. When she became pregnant, she did not dare to say it was Victor's, for fear of his heartless reaction, and so pointed to handsome architect KEVIN BANCROFT (Christopher Holder) as the father. Kevin loved Nikki and married her, despite the furious objections of his mother, ALLISON BANCROFT (Lynn Wood), who wanted him to marry her own choice, CAROLYN HARPER (Mimi Maynard). Scheming Allison set out to prove that Nikki's baby could not have been her son's by gaining evidence that Victor Newman's vasectomy had been a fraud.

Kay Chancellor, after she rid herself of Derek, became infatuated with Nikki's new strip-act dancing partner, Cash. She lavished him with presents and trips. When she discovered that he was in desperate trouble with evil creditors, she hurriedly made plans to move to Europe with him. But suddenly tragedy struck. Near the Bayou, where he and Nikki performed, he was stabbed in a dark hallway. He and Kay professed their love for each other in a hospital room, just before he died. Kay then turned to her old college flame, EARLE BANCROFT (Mark Tapscott), Kevin's father. Earle hated his loveless marriage to Allison, but for the sake of propriety she refused to give him up.

* * *

Jill, always drawn to wealth and glamor, went to work for Jabot Cosmetics, where playboy JACK ABBOTT (Terry Lester) worked. His rich father, JOHN ABBOTT (Brett Halsey, Jerry Douglas), owner of Jabot, continually worried about Jack's unwholesome womanizing, hoping that his son would settle down to marriage. Jill dated Jack for a time, but when she realized that John Abbott was falling in love with her, she began a campaign to marry him and also to advance herself at Jabot. Jack, who saw her as a cruel opportunist, fired her. Jill fought back with a lawsuit claiming sexual discrimination. When, at long last, she got John Abbott to marry her, she feared that Jack, her perpetual antagonist, was plotting to ruin her marriage. To stop that, she convinced her old boyfriend, bartender ANDY RICHARDS (Steven Ford, the son of ex-President Gerald Ford), to bug Jack's office at Jabot. Jill hoped to protect her own marriage by destroying Jack.

Jack Abbott himself fell in love with underage PATTY WILLIAMS (Tammy Taylor, Lilibet Stern), the daughter of protective Carl and Mary Williams. They forbade her from marrying the irresponsible Jack, but they couldn't fight nature and in time the two were married. Glad to see his son settled, John Abbott gave him the presidency of Jabot Cosmetics as a wedding present, but Jack was already beginning to cheat on Patty with a young model, DIANE JENKINS (Alex Donnelley). With her bugging device, Jill now knew about the illicit affair.

Jack and his wife Patty, Jill and John Abbott all lived uneasily in the fabulous Abbott home, where John's two daughters, ASHLEY (Eileen Davidson) and TRACI (Beth Maitland), had just returned. Beautiful Ashley, just graduated from college, didn't trust Jill, sensing that she intended to cause trouble between her brother and her father, which was true. Beth developed a crush on cute singer DANNY ROMALOTTI (Michael Damian), who returned her interest, but her serious weight problem caused her to feel insecure about the romance. Danny's sister, singer GINA ROMA (Patty Weaver), just released from prison, did her best to help along her brother's romance with the wealthy Abbott girl.

Lance Prentiss, Leslie and Laurie all left Genoa City. After Laurie was acquitted of murdering Vanessa, she and Lance attempted a reconciliation, but then argued bitterly over Laurie's having given Victor Newman control over Prentiss Industries. They broke up again. By now Lance knew that he was Brooks's real father and also that Leslie had been in love with him from the start. Leslie and Lance planned to marry, but when Brooks, who had until now thought of Lucas as his father, refused to accept Lance as his father, Lance became discouraged and left town. Not long after, Leslie fell in love with the brilliant lawyer, ROBERT LAURENCE (Peter Brown), who had defended Laurie. But

Robert had a grown daughter, ANGELA (Liz Keifer), who thoroughly resented Leslie and wanted her father to reconcile with her mother CLAIRE (Suzanne Zenor). When Leslie realized she had lost Robert to his family, she decided to leave Genoa City too. Her sister Laurie felt she had to do one last thing for Lance. Victor, alone again, had fallen in love with Laurie and she agreed to marry him. On their wedding day, Victor gave control of Lance's company back to Laurie. Just before the ceremony, she went to the ladies room and slipped away, leaving Victor's ring behind and turning Prentiss Industries back over to Lance before she, too, left town.

For the last five years, Chris and Snapper Foster had had a marriage that was often quite shaky. After they adopted a baby, it looked as if they would settle into a more peaceful union. Then Sally McGuire showed up in town! Her son by Snapper, now called CHUCKIE (Marc Bentley), was a victim of an incurable kidney disease. Snapper offered his own kidney to his son. To prevent Snapper from getting further involved with Sally and Chuckie, Chris invited Sally's boyfriend, Stan, to come to town. The plan worked. Sally married her ex-flame, and together with Chuckie left Genoa City for good. Unfortunately, Stuart and Liz separated when Stuart disapproved of Snapper's concern for Chuckie. This initially superficial conflict soon brought the true cause of the marital problem to light: Liz felt alienated in Stuart's upper-middle class world. She moved back to her old home, and Stuart found himself attracted to the provocative Gina Roma.

Promiscuous Paul Williams finally married the girl he impregnated, April Stevens, for the sake of their little girl HEATHER. Although April loved Paul, she found herself torn between him and her newly found, well-to-do twin sister, BARBARA (Beth Scheffel). When Barbara promised to give April everything she wanted and to reunite their scattered family far from Genoa City, April left town with Barbara and her parents, leaving Paul alone. Meanwhile, Paul's father, Carl Williams, had been unfairly suspended from the police force. He had been trying to get evidence against a syndicate boss, PETE WALKER (William H. Bassett), but before he could, had been framed by hooker PAM WARREN (Kristine De Bell) who was rubbed out by goons. Paul was determined to vindicate his father and went undercover, pretending to become a henchman of Pete Walker's. In time Paul cleared his father, vanquished the mob and became engaged to reformed hooker CINDY LAKE (Deanna Robbins).

EVE HOWARD (Margaret Mason), an old paramour of Victor Newman's, came to Genoa City, obsessed with revenge for hurts of the past. After Victor acknowledged that he had fathered her son CHARLES and made him a beneficiary in his will, Eve began plotting Victor's murder. Julia sensed this and warned Victor, who faked death in order to entrap baleful Eve.

The entire Abbott family went into shock when a mysterious newcomer to Genoa City, wealthy MADAM MERGERON (Marla Adams), who was attempting to buy Jabot Cosmetics, revealed herself to be DINA ABBOTT, the wife who had deserted John Abbott years before and the mother of Jack, Ashley and Traci. Once again, Jill had to fight for her marriage to John Abbott, for Dina begain scheming to win him back.

CAST

THE YOUNG AND THE RESTLESS
CBS: March 26, 1973

Liz Foster Brooks	Julianna McCarthy (P)
Stuart Brooks	Robert Colbert (P)
Jennifer Brooks	Dorothy Green (P)
Leslie Brooks Prentiss .	Janice Lynde (P)
	Victoria Mallory*
Chris Brooks Foster ...	Trish Stewart (P)
	Lynne Topping Richter
Dr. Snapper Foster	William Gray Espy (P)
	David Hasselhoff*
Greg Foster	James Houghton (P)
	Brian Kerwin
	Wings Hauser
	Howard McGillin
Jill Foster Abbott	Brenda Dickson (P)
	Bond Gideon
	Deborah Adair
Peggy Brooks	Pamela Peters Solow* (P)
	Patricia Everly
Dr. Brad Eliot	Tom Hallick (P)
Sally McGuire Rolland .	Lee Crawford (P)
Pierre Rolland	Robert Clary (P)
Barbara Anderson	Deidre Hall* (P)
	Laura Saunders
Frank Martin	Jay Ingram
George Curtis	Tony Geary
Warner Wilson	Rick Jason

Lauralee Brooks Prentiss	Jaime Lyn Bauer
Gwen Sherman	Jennifer Leak
Mitchell Sherman	Fred Beir
	William Wintersole*
Kay Chancellor	Jeanne Cooper
Phillip Chancellor	John Considine
	Donnelly Rhodes*
Sam Powers	William Mims
	Barry Cahill*
Jed Andrews	Tom Selleck
Marianne Rolland	Lilyan Chauvin
Teresa	Ann Morrison
Jeff	Rod Arrants
Brock Reynolds	Beau Kayzer
Dr. Bruce Henderson ..	Robert Clarke
	Paul Stevens*
Regina Henderson	Jodean Russo
Dr. Mark Henderson ...	Steve Carlson
Maestro Ernesto Fautch	Karl Bruck
Jane Hayes	Alexandra Morgan
Jerry Frazier	Michael Gregory
Bill Foster	Charles Gray
Sister Teresa	Carmen Zapata
Fran Whittaker	Susan Brown
Ruth Hicks	Vivian Brown
Jack Curtis	Anthony Herrera
Joann Curtis	Kay Heberle
Lance Prentiss	John McCook*
	Dennis Cole
Vanessa Prentiss	K. T. Stevens
David Mallory	Robert Gibson
Nancy Becker	Cathy Carricaburu
Ron Becker	Dick DeCoit
Karen Becker	Brandi Tucker
Derek Thurston	Caleb Stoddard
	Jeff Cooper
	Joe LaDue
Cynthia Harris	Lori Saunders
	Heather Lowe
Jodie Conway	Cynthia Eilbacher
Tom Bennett	Mark Montgomery
Candace Weber	Stacy Lande
Doris Weber	Vanessa Brown
Lucas Prentiss	Tom Ligon
Dr. Casey Reed	Roberta Leighton
Nikki Reed Bancroft ...	Erica Hope
	Melody Thomas*
Linda Larkin	Susan Walden

Larry Larkin	Gary Giem
Patty Minter	Carol Jones
Scott Adams	Jack Stauffer
Suzanne Lynch	Ellen Weston
Nick Reed	Quinn Redeker
Paul Williams	Doug Davidson
Rose DeVille	Darlene Conley
Vincent Holliday	Alex Rebar
Walter Addison	Paul Savior
Jonas	Jerry Lacy
Max	Billy Curtis
April Stevens Williams .	Janet Wood
	Cynthia Eilbacher*
Carl Williams	Brett Hadley
Mary Williams	Carolyn Conwell
Steve Williams	David Winn
Patty Williams Abbott .	Tammy Taylor
	Lilibet Stern*
Victor Newman	Eric Braeden
Julia Newman	Meg Bennett
Douglas Austin	Michael Evans
Michael Scott	Nicholas Benedict
Filipe Ramirez	Victor Mohica
Dr. Sebastain Crown . . .	Edgar Daniels
Edith Mills	Jeanne Bates
Matthew	Thomas Havens
Rebecca	Cindy Fisher
Sumiko	Helen Funai
Judy Wilson	Loyita Chapel
Dorothy Stevens	Melinda Cordell
Wayne Stevens	William Long, Jr.
Eve Howard	Margaret Mason
Jack Abbott	Terry Lester
John Abbott	Brett Halsey
	Jerry Douglas*
Jerry Cashman	John Gibson[1]
Simone Vauvin	Anita Jodelsohn
	Jean-Celeste Ahern
Danny Romalotti	Michael Damian

Andy Richards	Steven Ford
Karen Richards	Jeanna Michaels
Chuckie Rolland	Marc Bentley
Barbara Harding	Beth Scheffel
John Harding	Lee Dubroux
Robert Laurence	Peter Brown
Claire Laurence	Suzanne Zenor
Angela Laurence	Liz Keifer
Kevin Bancroft	Christopher Holder
Earle Bancroft	Mark Tapscott
Allison Bancroft	Lynn Wood
Carolyn Harper	Mimi Maynard
Ashley Abbott	Eileen Davidson
Traci Abbott	Beth Maitland
Capt. Alex Morgan	Ben Hammer
Pete Walker	William H. Bassett
Pam Warren	Kristine DeBell
Cindy Lake	Deanna Robbins
Frank Lewis	Brock Peters
Joe Blair	John Denos
Brian Forbes	Jay Kerr
Gina Roma	Patty Weaver
Dina Abbott	Marla Adams

Creators: William J. and Lee Phillip Bell
Head Writers: William J. Bell and Kay Alden
Executive Producers: John Conboy, H. Wesley
Kenney, William J. Bell
Producers: Patricia Wenig, Edward Scott
Directors: Herbert Kenwith, Richard Dunlap, Bill
Glenn, Howard A. Quinn, Rick Bennewitz,
Susan Orlikoff Simon, Merrily Mossman,
Lilyan Chauvin, Frank Pacelli, Dennis
Steinmetz, Rudy Vejar
Musical Directors (together): Don McGinnis, Jerry
Winn and Bob Todd
Packager: Corday Productions for Screen Gems and
Columbia Pictures Television

[1] Not the same John Gibson who appears in the
other lists.

Part Three

PAST FAVORITES

INTRODUCTION

A soap opera that has lasted for twenty years and is canceled leaves a big heartache and many memories. Here is a selection of shows that were either favorites for many years or of historical importance. *Love of Life* and *The Secret Storm* were both: long-lived and at the center of the soap world.

Many pages are devoted to the story line summary of *Love of Life*, and for a special reason. It was one of the first soaps on television, with a storyline spanning three decades. Within its wonderfully flowing plot line, moving from tiny Barrowsville to New York City to suburban Rosehill, one detects the heart of the soap world changing as society changes. The character of Vanessa is a barometer of the values of the housewives who watched *Love of Life* for twenty-nine years. When she divorced Bruce in the late sixties, it was earth-shattering: she was perceived as a certain kind of flawless heroine, derived partly from radio. Obviously the world had changed since 1951; but Van's divorce also meant that divorce was becoming such an accessible option for daytime viewers that Vanessa was allowed to have one too. In this volume, the story line of *Search for Tomorrow* is also summarized in detail. Together with *Love of Life*, both summaries represent an extraordinary view of the evolution of the daytime serial.

The Brighter Day was a forerunner to *As The World Turns* and was important as a television serial. *From These Roots* is still remembered for its first-rate writing, directing and acting. *The Doctors* was tremendously popular in the sixties. *Love Is A Many Splendored Thing* didn't last long but had a great influence on the modern soap world. *Texas* is included for people who saw the show and may be curious about the continuity of the story line—as well as how it ended.

Read the cast and credits lists in this section as in the earlier part of the book. An asterisk (*) next to an actor's name indicates he played his role longer than any other actor. The symbol (P) indicates the actor was in the premiere cast.

LOVE OF LIFE

ROY WINSOR had a very distinct theme in mind when he started *Love of Life*. The story was to be an allegory concerning modern-day morality. Vanessa was the pure sister always searching to do the right thing; her *modus vivendi*, for the most part, was to keep others from being hurt. Margaret, or "Meg," was the villainous sister who, like Milton's Satan, felt that it was "better to reign in hell than serve in heaven." She preferred the easy road to riches to the harder road to dignity. Vanessa, on the other hand, fought in the cause of good—comforting her nephew Beanie when her sister abandoned him, trying to keep Meg from hurting their parents, always slow and careful about her own romantic involvements. Van's hard-earned reward was the self-respect that Meg never earned.

The theme and story of the early years of *Love of Love* was relentless and occasionally heavy-handed. Humor was hard to find. Because Van and Meg were personifications of ideas, they tended to be written in one-dimensional, black-and-white ways, although Peggy McCay and Jean McBride, the original Van and Meg, fleshed out the moralistic writing with superior performances. Said Hildy Parks, who played Ellie, Van's roommate, "Peggy was a dedicated actress. I don't know how she put up with all that nobility, but she did. She made Van less obviously long-suffering than the way the story was written."

The organ music was live, like the rest of the fifteen-minute show, and used to introduce the pro-gram as the title-logo appeared over the actors' faces and Charlie Mountain announced: "*Love of Life*: The story of Vanessa Dale in her courageous struggle for human dignity." Minutes before this rather arch beginning, the organist would play something funny and the actors would all break up.

Meg was written out of the show in 1957, and new writers, tired of the relentless single-theme approach, changed *Love of Life* into a story about a great many people rather than just two people on the opposite poles of human dignity. The show fared well for a few years, but by late in the sixties, faced with competition from dramas like *Days of Our Lives* and the aberrant psychology of newer soaps, *Love of Life* lost ratings. It began to try to compete, with frequent stories of divorces, love triangles involving pregnancy and drug use by young characters, but succeeded only in turning away loyal habitues of the show. There was talk of cancellation.

In 1973 an energetic producer named Jean Arley took over *Love of Life*. With the help of writers Claire Labine and Paul Avila Mayer, she reinstated the character of Meg as well as the theme of the war between good and evil personified by the Dale sisters. Ms. Arley also threw in a good portion of Young Love, took out the archness of the early story without removing its significance and proceeded to make *Love of Life* far more vital. She also instilled far more elaborate production values, rivaling those of *The Young and The Restless*. Unfortunately too many older viewers had given up on Van and Bruce when the story veered from the sanctity of family life in the late sixties, and not enough young viewers ever took to the revamped show. CBS canceled *Love of Life* on February 1, 1980. It was the second oldest soap, running for more than twenty-nine years on television. Many long-term fans were devastated.

Note: Although *Love of Life* is recalled by millions of loyal viewers, the scope of its story line now threatens of be lost. Therefore, a detailed summary is given here, to preserve it for viewers, for students of soap opera and for researchers. Special thanks go to Larry Auerbach, *Love of Life*'s director for its entire run, for supplying most of the early story line.

THE STORY

Neither elderly WILL DALE (Ed Jerome) nor his wife, SARAH DALE (Jane House, Joanna Roos), could comprehend how their two daughters managed to be such temperamental opposites. Even when the girls were infants, Will and Sarah noticed how little Vanessa would always smile placidly while little Margaret had screaming tantrums. After graduating from high school in Barrowsville, New York—where the family had always lived—proper VAN (Peggy McCay, Bonnie Bartlett and Audrey Peters, who played the part the longest) went to art school. Her sister, MEG (Jean McBride, Tudi Wiggins), announced her intention of marrying for money. Wealthy and respectable CHARLES HARPER (Paul Potter) fell for beautiful but immoral Meg and, unfortunately for him, married her.

When the story began, Van and Meg continued to live on opposing ends of the moral spectrum. Van was in her early twenties and unmarried, forever concerned with Meg's neglect of her small son BENNO "BEANIE" HARPER (played longest by Dennis Parnell, then as an adult by Christopher Reeve and Chandler Hill Harben). Poor Charles Harper complained bitterly to Van about his wife's unethical behavior; Van, along with the girls' parents, Will and Sarah, had to lecture Meg all the time about what her selfishness

Love of Life premiered on September 24, 1951, with Jean McBride playing the bad sister, Meg Dale Harper. Paul Potter played wealthy Charles Harper, whom Meg married only for his money, and Dennis Parnell was Benno Harper ("Beanie"), their son. Like all soaps then, the show ran only fifteen minutes a day.

Peggy McCay (center) was the first Vanessa Dale, the good sister who searched for human dignity. Van loved only one man in the early years, lawyer Paul Raven, played by Richard Coogan (right). Van's roommate was Ellie Crown, played for five years by Hildy Parks (standing next to Richard Coogan). Ellie was a colorful character whose amoral attitude toward life often shocked virtuous Van. For years Ronald Long (left) was Evans Baker, a lawyer who helped prove Meg innocent of the murder of her criminal boyfriend.

was doing to the whole family. Unpredictable Meg was always getting involved in some kind of unsavory activity, with the idea of getting something for nothing.

After Charles took Meg and Beanie to New York City, he became desperately unhappy over Meg's infidelities with attractive, shady men. Van was forced to move to New York herself to keep an eye on her devil-may-care sister, and especially to look after unloved and abandoned nephew Beanie. By now Will had died and Sarah was left alone in Barrowsville—but Vanessa kept going home for short visits, keeping her mother informed of what new troubles Meg had gotten herself into. In New York, Van had a roommate named ELLIE CROWN (Hildy Parks), a colorful young woman who was not quite as careful as Van when it came to involvements with the opposite sex. Ellie, like everyone else, was shocked (and often titillated) to hear all the talk of Meg's incorrigible escapades. Van, to support herself, got a job as an artist in an advertising agency which produced television shows.

One of Meg's underworld paramours in New York City was MILES PARDEE (Joe Allen, Jr.). Meg was bedazzled by Miles's fabulous estate in an exclusive part of Long Island—which was used as a front for Miles's huge smuggling operation. Meg, one night, was out at the big Long Island house, drinking, while Miles Pardee awaited the arrival of a shipment of contraband. While the tension of waiting mounted, Miles was suddenly murdered. Meg, found drunk by the police, was arrested as the murderess. Her whole family, including respectable Charles, was mired in scandal—which Meg unabashedly flaunted in their faces.

Van, with the help of a lawyer turned FBI agent, PAUL RAVEN (Richard Coogan, later Martin Brooks), cleared Meg by uncovering the real killer, a member of the smuggling gang who had a grudge against

Family confrontations, like this one in 1952, were always caused by Meg's dangerous escapades, which of course provided the story interest. Jane Rose and Ed Jerome played Sarah and Will Dale, parents of Meg and Van.

Steven Gethers, as corrupt casino-owner Hal Craig, punches an unidentified actor as Meg and Beanie look on in 1953. Most of the action took place in Barrowsville, a mythical town in upstate New York. A divorced Meg had become involved with Craig, while Van, who worked as a reporter for the Barrowsville Times, *helped expose Craig and his crooked Halfway House.*

Miles Pardee. Charles Harper by now was completely fed up with Meg. After divorcing her, he moved to Europe. Meanwhile, Van was slowly falling in love with Paul Raven.

Unused to the idea of romance, Van suddenly gave up her job at the ad agency and went back to Barrowsville. Paul was unwilling to let Van get away so easily, and moved to Barrowsville himself. He set up a law practice there with fellow lawyer COLLIE JORDAN (Carl Betz), and continued to court Van, who had taken a job with the Barrowsville *Times*. Meg, now husbandless, also came back to her home town with her son. Her return, of course, meant new complications for sister Vanessa—for Meg soon became involved with a corrupt gambler named HAL CRAIG (Steven Gethers). The relationship started when Meg was hired as a cashier at Hal Craig's Halfway House. Van then helped the *Times* do an exposé on Craig and his gambling activities, naming crooked banker HAMILTON BROWN (Tom Shirley) and the ne'er-do-well SENATOR ED DEAKINS (Joseph Boland) as Hal Craig's accomplices. Meg fought constantly with Van, trying to stop her from continuing the exposé articles. Then Hal Craig bought a nightclub in Barrowsville called the Steeplechase Room, and put it in Meg's name to protect himself. The purchase seemed corrupt and Paul Raven was hired to investigate it, again infuriating Meg and turning sister against sister.

Vanessa felt that she and Paul Raven had waited long enough, and they were finally married in Barrowsville. Van, a virgin, looked appealing in her white-as-snow wedding dress during the elaborate ceremony. She and Paul attempted to have a baby, but when Van found that she was unable to conceive she talked with Paul about adopting a child. Then she and Paul found six-year-old CAROL (Tirell Barbery), a deaf

Joanna Roos (right) was Althea Raven, Paul Raven's sympathetic mother. Virginia Robinson came on the show in 1956 as Judith Lodge Raven, Paul's insane first wife, who tried to cause trouble between Paul and Vanessa. Althea tried to protect her son's marriage to Van against his unstable first wife. Fourteen years later, Joanna Roos came on the show again, this time as Van's mother Sarah, the role originated by Jane Rose.

Bonnie Bartlett (center) took the role of Van in 1955. Vanessa, in 1958, met and fell in love with Bruce Sterling (Ron Tomme), a teacher at Winfield Academy in Rosehill, New York. She moved to Rosehill to marry him, but soon ran into problems with Bruce's large family, which included his two children from a previous marriage, Alan and Barbara Sterling (Jimmy Bayer and Nina Reader, at left), and his former in-laws, Vivian and Henry Carlson (Helene Dumas and Tom Shirley, at right).

mute who won their hearts, even though she seemed, perhaps because of poor treatment in the past, to resist their love. She was a rather wild little girl.

After Van and Paul decided to adopt Carol, a strange woman came to Barrowsville. She was forever watching Carol—from a discreet distance. Then she confronted Paul and Van. To Paul's shock, the woman was his former wife, JUDITH LODGE RAVEN (Virginia Robinson). Van was upset that Paul had kept his previous marriage a secret. And little Carol turned out to be Paul's child by Judith! After their marriage had ended, Judith, unknown to Paul, was pregnant and gave birth. She later gave the child up for adoption, but now wanted her back. Judith had, since her divorce from Paul, gone insane, and was being cared for by Paul's mother, ALTHEA RAVEN (Joanna Roos). When Judith ran away to look for her daughter, Althea Raven traced her to Barrowsville, came to town, and fought with her to leave Carol Raven with Paul and Van.

Suddenly Sarah's house burned down, and Judith

was found murdered in the charred mess. Since Van's fingerprints were on the murder weapon, a cane which had been used to bludgeon the victim, Van was charged with the murder. EVANS BAKER (Ronald Long), the lawyer who had previously defended Meg in the Miles Pardee murder trial, was called to Barrowsville to handle the defense, with Paul assisting. Van was nearly convicted and sentenced—when it was discovered that the murderer was BEN RAVEN (David Lewis), Paul's brother. Ben hated Judith, who had ruined him in their home town of Marlton.

Hal Craig was now threatening little Carol Raven's life. Carol had been taken in by Hal Craig's twin brother, before her adoption by Van and Paul, and had been mistreated terribly. Hal Craig's brother had been murdered. When Carol looked into a locket belonging to Hal Craig, she had a sudden fit. It was a mystery why Hal wanted to kill Carol. Van and Paul

Audrey Peters (center) became the third Van in 1959 and remained in the part for the next twenty-one years. Barbara Sterling's first marriage was to impetuous Dr. Tony Vento (Ron Jackson). Spoiled by her rich grandmother, Vivian, Barbara had always been attracted to hotheaded young men and was a trouble to her father. From left: Nina Reader, Ron Jackson, Audrey Peters and Ron Tomme.

Link Porter (Gene Pellegrini) arrived in Rosehill in 1960 with his wife, Maggie Porter (Joan Copeland, left). Maggie knew she was terminally ill and tried to encourage a match between Van and Link, hoping that they would marry after her death.

took her into hiding; then Paul, Collie Jordan and Meg went to New York, looking for Craig. They found him, and he confessed to murdering his twin brother, whose picture Carol had seen in the locket. Apparently Carol had witnessed the murder. Now that she was being treated kindly, she was beginning to speak and hear again. Her grandmother, Althea, took her back home with her.

* * *

All the scandal that Van and Paul had suffered in Barrowsville made life there no longer tolerable for them, and the couple moved to New York City once again, where Paul took a job in a law firm and Van resumed her old job with the advertising agency. Meg, too, was in New York, after selling the Steeplechase Room, which Hal Craig had signed over to her. Now moderately wealthy, Meg asked Paul to invest her money. Paul, intending well, made the mistake of getting involved with shady land speculators, who sold him worthless land in Mexico. JACK ANDREWS (Donald Symington) was one of the swindlers. Suave and good looking, Jack immediately interested Meg. He married her, mainly to acquire what was left of her money after his cohorts had bilked her and Paul out of the rest. Paul insisted on inspecting the land, and, accompanied by a few of the double-dealers, took a Bee-Line air-charter plane, heading toward the land site. Before reaching Mexico, the plane crashed, and all aboard were presumed killed. Jack Andrews immediately fled from New York with the money. Meg suddenly became a pauper, and Van a widow.

Putting aside her grief, Van took on the responsibility of supporting Meg, Beanie and herself—and she quickly advanced in her job at the ad agency. The agency produced a television variety show called *The Starship*, emceed by TAMMY FORREST (first Scotty McGregor, then Ann Loring). NOEL PENN (Gene Peterson), the executive producer of the show, suddenly found he had a crisis on his hands. Tammy, an alcoholic, was becoming too "sick" to continue as emcee. Noel had a brilliant flash. He had been noticing Van,

Lee Lawson became the new Barbara Sterling Vento in 1961 and Paul Savior played the first Rick Latimer, the brash young son of a wheeler-dealer who was trying to acquire Henry Carlson's paper mill. Despite the objections of her father, Bruce Sterling, she married Rick.

Robert Alda played opposite Eileen Letchworth in 1966 as her husband Jason Ferris. Neurotic Sharon tried to wreck Van's marriage. Later Sharon and Jason left Rosehill for good.

and a certain charisma about her, and so had Van replace Tammy. Tammy naturally resented Van, but in time grew to like her, for Van was helping Tammy to quit the booze. Meanwhile, HARLOW SCOTT (Martin Rudy), was falling in love with Van. But when Van discovered that he was a married man with two children (one of whom was played by the young Warren Beatty), she sent him back to his wife. Then Meg learned that her husband, Jack Andrews, had been killed by other members of his gang for the remainder of Meg's money—*and* that she was pregnant! She had been having an affair with attorney TOM CRAYTHORNE (Lauren Gilbert); not wanting to admit that her child had been conceived with Jack Andrews, she foisted a paternity suit on Tom Craythorne, who was finally

proven innocent of fathering Meg's new child. Naturally, Van again lectured her sister on her unending immorality. Unable to bear any more of Van, New York City or Barrowsville, Meg took Beanie and left for parts unknown.

* * *

Tom Craythorne and Van became friends. He introduced her to a friend of his, widower BRUCE STERLING (Ron Tomme), who taught at Winfield Academy, a boys' prep school in Rosehill, New York. Bruce and Van fell in love, and not long after were married in Rosehill, Van's new home.

When Van first arrived in Rosehill, she was surprised, to say the least, at the complicated domestic situation that surrounded Bruce. His two nearly grown children, BARBARA STERLING (Nina Reader, then Lee Lawson, and finally Zina Bethune) and ALAN STERLING (Jimmy Bayer, then Dan Ferrone, Dennis Cooney, and finally John Fink), were being cared for—and spoiled—by the rich parents of Bruce's dead wife, VIVIAN CARLSON (Helene Dumas) and HENRY CARLSON (Tom Shirley, then Jack Stamberger). Their daughter, Gaye Sterling, had been killed in an automobile acci-

In 1967, Jonathan Moore and Diane Rousseau came on as Van and Bruce's next-door neighbors, Charles and Diana Lamont. They were forever having marital troubles, but remained the Sterlings' best friends. Important new characters on the serials have seldom been "next-door neighbors" of the main characters. The Lamonts were an exception.

Meg returned to Love of Life *in 1973, now played by Tudi Wiggins (left). The character hadn't been seen for seventeen years. She was as grasping as ever. Her son Beanie, now called Ben, was now grown and was played by Christopher Reeve (right) several years before he became an instant movie star in* Superman. *Ben had become a young scoundrel, marrying Betsy Crawford (Elizabeth Kemp, center) only to get a gift of money from his rich mother.*

dent, but there was always some suspicion that Gaye had actually committed suicide. In any event, Vivian had erected a shrine, as it were, to her dead daughter's memory, and was aghast that Bruce could be so heartless as to remarry. Vivian immediately launched a custody suit against Bruce for Barbara and Alan, but lost. The war was mostly snobbish Vivian's, for her dominated husband, Henry, grew to like Vanessa.

Barbara started a little war of her own against Vanessa after a certain incident. Barbara and her boyfriend, KEN SHEA (Roger Stevens), were out driving one night and ran over DR. TONY VENTO (Ron Jackson), the handsome son of a cleaning woman, MRS. VENTO (Agnes Young). Soon Barbara fell in love with Tony, and confided in Van that she was planning to elope with him. Van revealed Barbara's secret to Bruce, for her own good, and the planned marriage was stopped. Barbara never forgave Van for interfering.

While Vivian imagined her deceased daughter Gaye to have been nothing less than a saint, Van discovered that Gaye had been anything but. She learned that Gaye had had an affair with JOHN DENNIS (Coe Norton), the headmaster of Bruce's school, and that Dennis was the real father of Alan Sterling. Van, considerate of everyone's feelings, kept her knowledge a secret.

* * *

Around this time, a young rapist, GLENN HAMILTON (Bert Convy), was terrorizing Rosehill girls. While trying to stop Glenn from molesting SANDY PORTER (Bonnie Bedelia), Bruce was struck down and taken to the hospital in a coma. When he recovered consciousness, he was paralyzed. Although Van had persuaded John Dennis not to reveal to young Alan that he was his real father, Bruce's complete helplessness made John feel that he would make a better father, and so he confronted Bruce with the truth. John did give up his attempt to win custody of Alan, but not before Henry and Vivian Carlson had learned the truth about Gaye's infidelity. Vivian was so shocked that she became hysterical and had to be hospitalized. Van stayed with Vivian, continually reassuring her, until Vivian got a grip on herself. Vivian wound up grateful to Van for her emotional support, and the two became friends.

Barbara, however, was still bitter against Van for stopping her elopement with Dr. Tony Vento. She took charge of nursing her father back to health, and began to suggest to Bruce that his physician, DR. HERB SALTZMAN (Walter Brooke, then Robert Gerringer), was having an affair with Van behind his back. Although Dr. Saltzman eventually did fall in love with Van, Van remained faithful to and in love with her husband. Bruce, who was nearly recovered, began to believe his daughter's insinuations, and confronted Van with his suspicions. When Van realized that she simply couldn't convince Bruce of her love for him, she went to Reno for a divorce. After Van had left, Bruce realized what a fool he had been and instantly followed Van to Reno. He found her there before the divorce had gone through, begged her forgiveness and brought her back to Rosehill.

That was just the beginning of the Sterlings' marital troubles. Henry Carlson owned the Carlson Paper Company in Rosehill and offered Bruce an executive position there. A little tired of teaching at an all-boys school, Bruce took the job. A scoundrel by the name of GUY LATIMER (John Straub) had been trying to persuade Henry Carlson to sell his company to him. When Henry refused, Guy Latimer devised a scheme to steal the company's patent for no-tear paper and thereby force Henry to sell. Guy made a secret pact with GINNY CRANDALL (Barbara Barrie), the ambitious wife of Winfield Academy teacher BILL CRANDALL (Stratton Walling), to pry the formula out of Bruce with her charms. She became Bruce's secretary and indeed did have an affair with him—Bruce had already been attracted to her at the school. Ginny succeeded in obtaining the formula. When Bruce realized what he had done to Henry's paper company, he resolved to expose Guy Latimer for the crook he was. After taking a job as an "undercover agent" in another company Guy wanted to own, Bruce made his evidence public, and Latimer was ruined.

But Bruce's marriage went temporarily on the rocks when Van discovered that her husband had had an affair with Ginny Crandall. Van left him and moved into an apartment with Alan. LINK PORTER (Gene Pelligrini), a businessman from Scarsdale, New York, had already moved to Rosehill with his wife, MAGGIE PORTER (Joan Copeland), and daughter, Sandy—the girl Bruce was trying to protect when the young rapist felled him. Link Porter worked for the Carlson Paper Company, and the Porters now knew the Sterlings. Maggie found out that she had leukemia, with only six months to live, and feared that Link would marry the wrong woman after she was gone. Maggie admired

Love of Life (1951–1980)

Van's character. Knowing that Van had separated from her husband, Maggie attempted to create a love match between Link and Van.

Tammy Forrest, the alcoholic actress whom Van had first replaced and then befriended in New York, was also living in Rosehill now. She fell in love with Link. After Maggie's death, Link wed Tammy Forrest. Then Maggie's twin sister KAY LOGAN showed up (still Joan Copeland, wearing a blond wig) and viciously tried to break up Link and Tammy. After Link and Tammy endured many travails, Link eventually died of cancer.

* * *

Bruce and Van patched things up and were once again a happy couple, much to Barbara Sterling's dismay. Barbara had wanted Bruce all to herself. She did eventually marry Dr. Tony Vento, but the marriage quickly ended in divorce and Barbara became deeply neurotic, refusing to leave her father's side for long periods of time. Then Barbara met RICK LATIMER (played the longest by Jerry Lacy), swindler Guy Latimer's rebellious son. Van perceptively saw that Barbara was far too unstable for this new relationship with a rather maverick young man, and once again tried to stop Barbara from marrying before it was too late. Unwilling to take any advice from Van, Barbara married Rick, and the union was a disaster. Well before their son, HANK LATIMER (see cast list on p. 326) was born, Barbara and Rick had split up. On the verge of a nervous breakdown, Barbara came back to live with the Sterlings. Rick sued for custody of his son and won, and Barbara, an emotionally drained and pitiful girl, left Rosehill.

Bruce and Van moved to a new house and found themselves living next door to NELL SALTZMAN (Ruth Baker), whose husband, Dr. Herb Saltzman (who had cared for Bruce and fallen in love with Van). The Sterlings also became friends with a troubled couple named JASON (Robert Alda) and SHARON FERRIS (Eileen Letchworth). Nell Saltzman continued to hold a grudge against Van (who had never returned the deceased Herb Saltzman's affections). Nell began having a torrid affair with Jason Ferris, in a very public manner, while disguising herself in a blond wig to look like Vanessa! Sharon Ferris, thinking that Van was stealing her husband, homicidally loathed Van. Then Jason told Sharon that it was Nell with whom he was sleeping, and Sharon went temporarily in-

sane and tried to shoot Nell Saltzman. In the end, Jason and his wife reconciled and left town, and Nell went too.

Van and Bruce's new next-door neighbors soon became their best friends and confidants. They were CHARLES LAMONT (Jonathan Moore), owner of a bookstore, and his wife, social psychologist DIANA LAMONT (Diane Rousseau). Charles's college-aged son by a previous marriage, BILL PRENTISS (Gene Bua), a sensitive, musically talented boy, fell in love with TESS KRAKAUER (Toni Bull Bua), a beautiful but immature girl who didn't know exactly who she was or what she wanted. Tess returned his love and married him.

The college romance had been complicated, however, by another college-aged girl, SALLY BRIDGEMAN (Cathy Bacon), who was unstable and fell wildly in love with Bill. When the campus love triangle ended with Bill's marriage to Tess, Sally went off the deep end and started taking drugs. Through her addiction she met a college radical, also on drugs, named JAMIE ROLLINS (Ray Wise), who suddenly sobered up to the reality of drug danger when Sally took an overdose and wound up with aphasia (the loss of the ability to speak). For a while Sally listened to Jamie's warnings and kept away from drugs, but when she learned that her mother, tavern owner CLARE BRIDGEMAN (Renee Roy), was having an affair with Jamie's father, RICHARD ROLLINS (Larry Weber), who was married at the time, she went into a deep depression and ran away from home.

Tess and Bill were having severe marital troubles, mainly because of their youth and Tess's lack of maturity. Wealthy industrialist JOHN RANDOLPH (Byron Sanders) took a shine to Tess and lured her away from Bill by dangling the bait of travel and luxuries in front of her eyes, and Tess divorced Bill for the glamor that John Randolph could offer. Then, thinking she wanted love, not riches, she divorced John and went back to Bill. Then she divorced Bill again and went back to John—then finally back to Bill, this time a much more grown-up, determined young lady. But the police did not think much of the motives of Tess or Bill when John Randolph was suddenly found murdered. Tess and Bill were both tried, but it turned out that Richard Rollins, Jamie's father and John's employee, was the killer.

* * *

The attorney who defended Tess and Bill called

himself "Matt Corby." He had suffered amnesia following a plane crash years before and still couldn't remember a thing about his previous life. He was now strangely in love with Van. Once, during a conversation, he called her "Meg." Van was absolutely dumbfounded! Meg had never been to Rosehill. Then suddenly, as Matt continued talking with Van, memories from his previous life came flooding back to him. He was Paul Raven! Vanessa hadn't recognized him because of the extensive plastic surgery performed on his face after the crash (actor Robert Burr now supplied Paul's changed face). Van realized she was married to two men and was in shock. Paul still wanted her as his wife.

Fatefully, Van and Bruce had only recently separated, because of a brief fling that Bruce had with DR. JENNIFER STARK (Joan Bassie), a beautiful Briton who aggressively pursued Bruce after he became the Dean of Admissions at State University. Van was torn between her two husbands—which one did she really love, Paul or Bruce? After much soul-searching she finally divorced Bruce—less over the question of Paul than because of the affair with Jennifer. She was about to remarry Paul Raven when it was suddenly revealed that as Matt Corby he had been married to EVELYN CORBY (Lee Kurty) and had had a daughter, STACY CORBY (Cindy Grover), with his new wife. But Evelyn Corby had been mysteriously murdered. Paul Raven, alias Matt Corby, was unmasked as his wife's murderer and went to prison. Later he was killed while trying to arbitrate a prison riot, à la Attica. So Van, once with two husbands, now wound up without any husband at all. Little Stacy Corby, however, did stay with her.

By now Sally Bridgeman, rehabilitated by a psychiatrist, learned that she was pregnant with Jamie's child. Jamie wanted to marry Sally, but, afraid that the burden of a baby would interfere with his plans to become a lawyer, asked her to have an abortion. An angry and now responsible Sally refused both the offer of marriage and the abortion, but later, when their daughter, DEBBIE, was born, she relented and married Jamie.

Shortly after Sally left the drug scene, Stacy Corby, Van's ward, became involved in it. This time it was Sally who was giving Stacy advice to give up drugs, and also to give up the wild bunch of destructive kids she was hanging around with. Eventually she straightened out and was even able to accept the re-

marriage of Van and Bruce (by now publisher of a Rosehill newspaper, the *Herald*), which she had secretly opposed. At Van and Bruce's big, fancy wedding, the two of them, and Stacy, were the picture of happiness.

Tess and Bill Prentiss had been acquitted of murder only to face yet another horror—Bill developed a serious blood disorder, leukocytemia, and died after receiving bizarre treatments from a quack.

At the hospital Bill had also been treated by two accredited doctors: DR. JOE CORELLI (Paul Michael Glaser, Tony LoBianco), who fell in love with Tess, and DR. DAN PHILLIPS (Drew Snyder), who was dating KATE SWANSON (Sally Stark), a singer working at the Club Victoria, owned by Rick Latimer. Rick was distraught because his wife, Barbara Latimer, had deserted him for parts unknown, leaving him with their son, Hank Latimer. While Joe Corelli was getting nowhere with his plans to marry Tess because she couldn't forget Bill, Dan was more successful with Kate. He married her, and she became pregnant. Rick Latimer, who wanted Kate for himself, thought Kate might be carrying his child, for one night he had raped her. A blood test, however, revealed that the baby was really Dan's. Rick, ready to sink to outright deceit to get Kate, remained silent when he discovered that Dan's nurse, CANDY LOWE (Nancy MacKay, Susan Hubly)—jealous of Kate and in love with Dan herself—had faked the blood test report to show that the baby was Rick's. After Candy gladly showed it to Dan, he divorced Kate.

* * *

Tess was tried for the murder of BOBBY MACKEY (Richard Cox), Sally Bridgeman's cousin, a con man who had tried to bilk Tess out of her son Johnny's trust fund. Jamie, just at that time, was passing his bar exam to become a lawyer. His whole career, he felt, was ruined because it was exposed that he had let his wife, Sally, persuade him to back her up in a lie to the police concerning her cousin Bobby's innocence before being killed. One day, after Sally and Jamie, had argued a lot about her responsibility in the affair, she walked out on him, telling him in a note: "I'm taking our baby Debbie and leaving town." Months later, Sally sent Jamie a tragic telegram informing him that Debbie had drowned.

Kate Phillips gave birth to a beautiful little girl, REBECCAH, and was on the verge of marrying the deceitful Rick Latimer to give the baby a father. Then Dan, realizing that he still loved Kate and that he had divorced her out of false pride, begged Kate to come back to him, vowing that he would now accept Rebeccah as his own daughter. After Candy Lowe confessed that Rick was not Rebeccah's father after all, Kate remarried Dan. For a while things looked bright for the couple—until Kate, still singing in Rick's Club Victoria and starting to achieve great success with her first record album, became stricken with what seemed to be throat cancer. Although Kate survived her illness, her life was touched with tragedy when Dan and Rebeccah were both killed in a dreadful car accident.

After Tess Prentiss was acquitted of the murder of Bobby Mackey, she felt so emotionally drained that she left her son Bobby with his grandparents, Charles and Diana Lamont, and went on a "vacation" to Mexico. Later she wrote to the Lamonts that she didn't intend to return.

The responsibility of having to care for their grandson on a permanent basis began to cause a rift between Charles and Diana, who were never a completely stable couple anyway. Soon Charles began to react to his increasing marital problems with a classic case of impotence. Diana talked him into seeking help at the Clinic for Sexual Dysfunction (a sex-therapy clinic), run by a DR. TED CHANDLER (Keith Charles). Charles resisted treatment, and Diana, feeling frustrated, began a brief but painful affair with the younger Jamie Rollins. Soon afterward, Kate fell in love with Dr. Ted Chandler and left town with him.

* * *

Van's mother, Sarah, became inconsolable after the death of her second husband, ALEX CALDWELL (originally the late Fred Stewart, later Charles White). Soon she herself was stricken with a brain abscess and seemed close to death. As she bided what she thought were her final hours and Van sat at her bedside, she asked to see her estranged daughter, Meg, who had been away for seventeen years. Van and Bruce investigated and discovered that Meg had last married a man named Eduoard Aleata. After they wrote her a letter, a young girl named CAROLINE "CAL" ALEATA (Deborah Courtney, Roxanne Gregory) turned up at Van's doorstep. She said she was Meg's daughter! It turned out that Cal was a love-starved girl who, like her stepbrother, Beanie Harper, had been much

neglected by her mother and had run away from home. She had read Van's letter to Meg and thought that she'd find love in Rosehill with her aunt.

Sarah Caldwell had a miraculous recovery after brain surgery. She was of course happy to see Meg, who came to Rosehill looking for her daughter, but sad that Meg's character hadn't really changed. Meg was still a troublemaker and still attracted to corrupt, devious men. Her decision to remain in Rosehill, in fact, was colored by the sudden romantic interest in her on the part of the town's politically corrupt mayor, JEFF HART (Charles Baxter). After Van and Cal discovered that Jeff had been responsible for horsemeat being served in Cal's school cafeteria, Jeff tried to have them killed. Meg had an affair with this monster and married him. Once again, she and Van were at loggerheads over morals.

Then, Jeff Hart and his henchman PHIL WATERMAN (Michael Fairman) discovered that Assistant District Attorney Jamie Rollins was having a secret affair with Diana Lamont. They threatened to expose the affair unless Jamie stopped his investigation of Jeff's corrupt administration. Instead, Jamie quit his post in the D.A.'s office and persuaded Diana that her husband, Charles, had to be told the truth. When Charles found out, he had a heart attack, and Diana dared not ask him for a divorce. Later, when Charles was recovering, he stubbornly refused to grant her a divorce. Then Charles began to grow close to FELICIA FLEMMING (Pamela Lincoln), little Johnny Prentiss's teacher. When Charles realized he was now in love with Felicia, he began to talk of marriage with her, and gladly granted Diana her divorce. Diana, now pregnant by Jamie, started living with him; marriage for the moment was impossible, because Jamie was still legally wed to Sally Rollins, and had to find her before he could divorce her. Without benefit of matrimony, Diana grew terribly insecure in her relationship with the younger Jamie, despite his repeated vows of love. Charles was also having problems with his intended, Felicia—who kept putting off their wedding date because she was neurotically terrified of sexual relations. (By now Charles had overcome his impotence.) When Charles finally found what her problem was, he refused to believe that she wouldn't respond to him once they were married. He was wrong, however, for on their wedding night Felicia withdrew from him in utter horror. Charles, confused, decided that the two of them should sleep in separate bedrooms.

Ben "Beanie" Harper joined his mother, Meg, and sister, Cal, in Rosehill. Meg's neglect of him during his formative years had warped his character. He was now a handsome ski bum, living mostly off his mother's extensive fortune (from the death of a previous husband) and the attentions of susceptible women. Since Meg had decided to cut Ben off without a penny until his manner of living had improved, Ben, in his desperation for money, became secretly employed by Jeff Hart as a spy in the Sterling family. As part of his job, Ben took pictures of Bruce Sterling and a pretty reporter, BETSY CRAWFORD (Elizabeth Kemp, Margo McKenna), who worked for Bruce's paper, the *Herald*. The photos were then faked into a composite, showing Bruce in bed with Betsy, and circulated around town. At the time, Bruce was running against Jeff in a mayoral election. Because of the faked photos, Jeff won reelection.

DAVID HART (Brian Farrell), Jeff's over-dominated son, fell in love with Meg's daughter, Cal, after Meg and Jeff were wed. It was easy for them to meet, since they lived in the same house, with their parents. Both David and Cal, along with the Sterlings, had known for months that Jeff was corrupt—but Meg refused to believe their stories about Jeff's activities. However, when Ben told her that Jeff had threatened his life, Meg finally realized that her husband was a monster and left him. She helped David acquire evidence that showed how Jeff had cheated the city of Rosehill out of millions of dollars. Jeff made preparations to leave the country pronto, but just before he left he tried to rape Cal. Jeff suddenly walked in and, in a rage, shot and killed his father. In shock after having committed patricide, David had to be sent to a mental hospital.

* * *

Ben Harper began wooing reporter Betsy Crawford. But Ben was only using Betsy to convince his mother that he had reformed, so that she would agree to finance his new business venture with Rick Latimer, an elaborate resort called the Beaver Ridge Complex. Meg was so overjoyed that Ben had become involved with wholesome Betsy, that she promised to give him half a million dollars outright if he married her. However, no one knew that he was already married to ARLENE LOVETT (Birgitta Tolksdorf). For a share of his half-million, Arlene was persuaded to keep quiet while Ben committed bigamy.

Meg, forever interfering in her children's lives, at

first tried to discourage her daughter Cal from marrying "a sick boy like David Hart," who was still in a psychiatric hospital. Meg even went to see David and told him that Cal was being unfaithful to him. Meanwhile, Rick Latimer, quite as greedy as Ben, became Meg's lover in order to insure her investment in his Beaver Ridge Complex. When Meg became suspicious that Rick was falling in love with Cal, she decided that Cal and David should marry after all. Meg again went to the hospital and told David that there was absolutely nothing wrong with his mind and that he should just walk out! But he was still quite ill. He left the hospital. After seeing Cal and Rick together, David assumed, from what Meg had told him about Cal's infidelity, that they were having an affair and refused to see Cal. In a rage, David set fire to Rick's place, the Club Victoria, not realizing that he was trapping Arlene Lovett, who played piano there. After David rescued Arlene, they became friends and he soon became romantically attached to her. Cal, disturbed by David's odd coldness and new association with Arlene, asked Meg one night if she had arranged for his untimely release from the hospital. When Meg admitted how she had lied to David about Cal's fidelity and had schemed to get him released, Cal was beside herself with anger and rushed out into the night. She screeched her car frenziedly away from the house, while Rick, who had observed the whole argument, worriedly followed her in his own car. Cal drove through a guardrail and over an embankment; Rick called an ambulance. He was half out of his mind with grief, for he had fallen deeply in love with Cal. While Cal—who had suffered a broken back in two places—was recovering, Rick hardly left her bedside.

* * *

At Van's request, EDOUARD ALEATA (John Aniston), Meg's ex-husband, came to Rosehill to look after Cal during this crisis in her life. For a while he was attracted to Van, who was being neglected by Bruce, Rosehill's new and overworked mayor. Then Eddie grew fond of Felicia Lamont, Charles Lamont's new wife. Felicia was suddenly terrorized by a young rapist named ARNIE LOGAN (Richard Dow), who followed her everywhere, and sent Charles letters stating that Felicia was having an affair with Eddie. Indeed, Charles had already become annoyed at the close friendship developing between Felicia and the handsome, cultivated Latin. One night Arnie attempted to attack Felicia in her own home. It was quite dark. Felicia grabbed the gun she had just bought and fired it at a figure she believed to be her attacker. Instead, she had shot Charles! He became permanently paralyzed. Out of guilt, Felicia vowed to become his life long nurse.

Rick Latimer was suspected of trying to burn down his own nightclub in order to collect the insurance money, but then David Hart broke down and confessed that he had been the arsonist. Arlene, who had grown quite fond of David and was sincerely interested in his welfare, tried to quiet his fears during his nervous collapse at the police station. Soon after, David voluntarily went to a sanitarium, knowing full well that it would be some time before he would become emotionally adjusted to reality.

Jamie Rollins, as David Hart's attorney, investigated Arlene Lovett's past, discovering that she and Ben had been married, but Ben denied it had ever been legal. At first Jamie was reluctant to go to Ben's new wife, Betsy, with the damaging news, for she was now carrying Ben's child. In an attempt to stop Jamie from investigating further, Ben pretended to be Jamie's friend and got Jamie drunk one night. After Jamie passed out, Ben took pictures of him and Arlene partly undressed in bed together. Then Ben sent the photos to Diana Lamont, convincing her that Jamie and Arlene were having an affair. She became doubly depressed, for in the previous months she had been experiencing mounting anxiety in her marriage. Bruce Sterling, as mayor of Rosehill, had appointed her to the important position of Director of the Family Assistance Program. But leading citizens of Rosehill—shocked that a woman in her position should be unmarried, pregnant and living with a much younger man—had demanded that Bruce fire Diana. Then, Diana found out that Jamie's divorce from his estranged wife, Sally, wouldn't be final until after the birth of her baby. It was just too much for Diana, who was already past normal child-bearing age. She went into premature labor and lost her baby. After she recovered from the distress of her loss, she began to reevaluate her relationship with Jamie.

Fearful that Ben was really falling in love with Betsy, Arlene Lovett went to her with the whole story of Ben's bigamy and chicanery. After Ben admitted that Arlene's story was true, Betsy told him that she would never allow him to see their baby after it was born. Her brother, DR. TOM CRAWFORD (Richard K. Weber, Mark Pinter), had just arrived from Europe, and saw his sister through the storm of breakup. Ben fled Rosehill to think things out, while the whole family met with shattered Meg to ferret out blame and seek solutions. On his own, Ben returned and confessed his crime to the authorities—taking all the blame on himself. He was sentenced to from one to four years in prison. Because Ben had portrayed Arlene as an unwilling accomplice, she was not imprisoned. Ben was totally reformed and contrite, intending to convince Betsy to return to him with their child once he was released. Meanwhile, Betsy, drained, had to face a husbandless childbirth.

Betsy's best friend, Cal, was having no easier a time of it. After Cal was fully recovered from injuries sustained in the auto accident, Rick proposed marriage and she accepted. Meg, still in love with Rick, cruelly told her daughter that while he had been seeing Cal he had been sharing her mother's bed! Rick shamefully admitted that Meg's story was true, but added that he loved Cal. Cal couldn't bear any more shocks. She told her mother that she never wanted to see her again, and made preparations to leave Rosehill for good. Meg now believed she had won Rick. To insure her hold on him, she completed her financial backing of the Beaver Ridge Complex. But Rick threw it all back in Meg's face, found Cal, begged her forgiveness and asked her to marry him immediately. Cal came back to Rosehill to marry Rick. Meg, refusing to see the man she loved married to her daughter, hired loan shark/racketeer RAY SLATER (Lloyd Battista) to make sure that Rick had an "accident" before the wedding day. The wedding took place, but Meg continued to scheme to break up Meg and Cal.

* * *

Arlene Lovett, was now attempting to abandon her old scheming ways, just as Ben had, to lead a more decent life. Her only thought now was to pay for the serious heart operation needed by her mother, CARRIE JOHNSON (Peg Murray). Ironically, Carrie's doctor became Tom Crawford, Betsy's brother—who was drawn to Arlene. To pay for the operation, Arlene went to crooked Ray Slater, who was willing to supply the money only if Arlene went into his "employ." Pimping beautiful girls to wealthy, sophisticated men happened to be one of his sidelines. Through Ray, Arlene became involved with suave, married IAN RUSSELL

(Michael Allinson) who showered her with expensive presents. Arlene was torn between Ian, who was the answer to all her financial troubles, and Dr. Tom Crawford, whom she truly loved.

Diana Lamont made the noblest move of her life: she came to the decision that her own emotional makeup would make a life with the younger Jamie Rollins impossible. Noticing that Jamie had befriended Betsy, who was facing difficult days, Diana attempted to promote a match between them. At first Jamie was angry, but he understood better when Di explained what her state of mind was now like, after losing the baby, and having a hysterectomy. She was finding peace within herself thanks to her prolonged stay at a convent, and did not love Jamie any more. Religion was supplying the comfort to her that marriage couldn't.

* * *

Ben was released from prison, and was intent on both winning Betsy back and making it on his own without help from his mother. It looked as if Ben would find himself, when he became involved in a hit-and-run accident. He believed he had killed Jim Marriott, the beloved son of DR. ANDREW MARRIOTT (Richard Higgs, Ron Harper) and MIA MARRIOTT (Veleka Gray). Andrew had lost all interest in life when his son died, and, with Mia's encouragement, Ben found himself in the strange position of becoming a substitute son for Andrew to help the doctor get back on his feet. Ben lived in perpetual fear that Andrew would discover that indeed he, Ben, had killed Jim. After Betsy decided to leave Rosehill permanently with their newborn girl, SUZANNE, Ben became more involved with Mia and had an affair with her. When Andrew found out, he left her. Finally Ben confessed that he was their son's inadvertent killer, but he was exonerated.

Felicia Lamont, while still caring for her wheelchair bound husband, Charles, discovered that she was carrying Eddie Aleata's child. Only Van knew of Felicia's secret. She had a healthy baby boy but, tragically, Felicia died in childbirth. Eddie told Charles that he was the real father and insisted on custody of his son, but Charles, desperate to hold on to any living memory of his dead wife, refused to hand over the baby. Eddie engaged a sharp woman attorney named DORY PATTEN (Sherry Rooney); however, before the case could reach the courts, Charles had a change of heart and surrendered the child to Eddie. Both men continued to cherish poor Felicia's memory.

Wealthy Ian Russell was suddenly murdered and Arlene Lovett, his paid paramour, had to stand trial. Because she still loved Dr. Tom Crawford, she avoided giving evidence that would have implicated him. She was sentenced to twenty-five years in prison, but was soon freed when the killer was shown to be one of Ian Russell's partners in crime. Meanwhile, Arlene discovered she was pregnant by the murdered Ian and hoped that she could finally find happiness with Tom. But her dreams of a better life were shattered when Tom selfishly refused to raise Ian's child. During all of this, Arlene's former pimp, Ray Slater, had given up his crooked ways and fallen deeply in love with beautiful Arlene. He married her, even though he knew she loved Tom Crawford. Arlene took a long time before agreeing to sleep with Ray, but when they did finally consummate their marriage they became quite a happy couple and good parents to little APRIL JOY SLATER, the child Ian had conceived. The Slaters also became co-owners of Rick Latimer's Beaver Ridge Complex and friends to a down-and-out young girl named BAMBI BREWSTER (Ann McCarthy), who once had a crush on Ray when they worked together at the Key Club. When Bambi became briefly ill, Arlene and Ray went to her hometown in Iowa to learn of her medical history and discovered that she was the daughter of a minister and had been a victim of child abuse. While in the town, Arlene grew friendly with a detective named HAL CARSON (W. T. Martin), who fell in love with her. Ray became insanely jealous of their relationship until Hal eventually convinced him that Arlene had never returned his love. Young Bambi Brewster developed romantic problems of her own. She became engaged to the cook at Beaver Ridge, TONY ALFONSO (Peter Gatto), but on their wedding day he disappeared after a mysterious phone call from beautiful KIM SOO LING (Irene Yaah-Ling Sun), a Vietnamese girl with whom he had had an affair during his Vietnam war days. Kim informed Tony that he was the father of her son. Nevertheless, Bambi and Tony later went on with their plans to marry.

Bruce Sterling learned that he had aplastic anemia, a serious blood disease, and that his days were possibly numbered. Rather than face Van with the truth, he began promoting a friendship between Van and Andrew Marriott, whom Bruce greatly admired and hoped would marry Van after his death. Andrew, still separated from his wife, Mia, did indeed fall in love with Van, who was perplexed at Bruce's sudden disinterest. When Bruce's blood disorder turned out to be nonterminal, Bruce told Van about it and once again became her loving husband. In time the disease went into complete remission, and Andrew remained a friend to the Sterlings. Then Bruce accepted a post as a law professor at the university, and he and Van moved into a charming old house owned and still inhabited by old PROFESSOR TIMOTHY MCCAULEY (Shepperd Strudwick). Timothy and Van's widowed mother, Sarah, grew enchanted with one another and, deciding to spend their twilight years together, married.

Meg was still trying to break up Rick Latimer and her daughter Cal, who were now happily married. When a quiet, mysterious young man named MICHAEL BLAKE (Richard Council) became a boarder in Rick and Cal's garage apartment, Meg began pushing Michael and Cal together at every turn and Michael soon fell in love with Cal. Then Meg arranged for Rick to find Cal and Michael together at a lakeside cabin, hoping that he would assume the worst. During the confrontation Meg's plan backfired and Michael was killed in a boating accident. Afterward Rick and Cal, realizing that Meg would always be poisonous, took young Hank Latimer and left Rosehill for good. Meg tried to ease her conscience by turning her attention to Ben, and to his affair with Mia, which she considered wrong.

Betsy and little Suzanne, who had been in London, returned to Rosehill—with ELLIOT LANG (Ted Leplat), her new husband! He was a pompous, possessive young lawyer whom she had met in London. Soon it became clear that both Ben and Betsy still cared for one another, and Elliot and Ben's lover, Mia, conspired to keep them apart. But Betsy's marriage to Elliot Lang was a hopeless arrangement which led to Elliot's savage rape of her, causing her to become pregnant again. Betsy fled to the same lakeside cabin where Michael Blake had died, to think things through. Ben followed her there, hoping that they could straighten out their lives. Suddenly a snake threatened Betsy's life. Ben fought it off with a boat paddle, but in the process seriously injured Betsy and caused her to lose her baby. While Betsy lay in the hospital in grave condition, her husband, Elliot, now Rosehill's new district attorney, had Ben arrested and tried for assault. Ben was defended by Bruce (who, as

a law professor, became Rosehill's chief supersleuth). Just as it looked as if Ben would be convicted, Betsy got up from her hospital bed, rushed into the courtroom and cleared Ben of all blame. Then Betsy fainted. Her doctors indicated that her prognosis wasn't good and Ben suffered terribly with the thought that she might die.

Van and Bruce took in a ward, teenaged alcoholic LYNN HENDERSON (Amy Gibson), who was being counseled by DR. JOE CUSACK (Peter Brouwer), a friend of Tom Crawford. When Andrew's philandering son ANDY MARRIOTT (Chris Marlowe) came to Rosehill, Lynn fell in love with him. Andy, however, became interested in Charles's therapist, MARY JANE OWENS (Corinne Neuchateau), and the two left Rosehill happily together. Lynn Henderson, saddened by the loss of Andy, her first love, also left town. Dr. Joe Cusack became involved with WENDY HAYES (Elaine Grove), assistant to Eddie Aleata's lawyer, Dory Patten. Then Joe Cusack was killed in a car accident. Dory Patten married Eddie and closed her Rosehill practice, moving out of town with him and his small son. Wendy, completing this exodus, also departed.

Bruce's teaching job at the university involved the Sterlings with the problems of young students. One student, an ex-con named STEVE HARBACH (Paul Craggs), formed an inordinate attachment to Van. Then another student, AMY RUSSELL (Dana Delany), became friendly with Van and Bruce and seduced Steve. Amy had been harboring a secret, which she was now ready to reveal: the identity of the man who had fathered her illegitimately. He was none other than Bruce Sterling!

CAST

LOVE OF LIFE
CBS: September 24, 1951 to February 1, 1980

Vanessa Dale Sterling ..	Peggy McCay (P)
	Bonnie Bartlett
	Audrey Peters*
Meg Dale Hart	Jean McBride* (P)
	Jane Wenman
	Tudi Wiggins
Sarah Dale McCauley ..	Jane Rose (P)
	Joanna Roos*
	Valerie Cossart
Will Dale	Edwin Jerome (P)
Charles Harper	Paul Potter (P)

Benno ("Beanie")
Harper . . . . Dennis Parnell* (P)
                     Tommy White
                     Christopher Reeve
                     Chandler Hill Harben
Ellie Hughes Crown . . . . Hildy Parks* (P)
                     Mary K. Wells
                     Lenka Peterson
                     Bethel Leslie
Miles Pardee . . . . Joe Allen, Jr. (P)
Mrs. Rivers . . . . Marie Kenney (P)
Evans Baker . . . . Ronald Long
Paul Raven . . . . Richard Coogan*
                     Martin E. Brooks

(when known as Matt
    Corby during
    amnesia) . . . . Robert Burr
Judith Lodge Raven . . . . Virginia Robinson
Althea Raven . . . . Joanna Roos
Ben Raven . . . . David Lewis
Hal Craig . . . . Steven Gethers
Collie Jordan . . . . Carl Betz
Grace Jordan . . . . Patricia Sales
Carol Raven . . . . Tirrell Barbery
Jack Andrews . . . . Donald Symington
Tom Craythorne . . . . . . Lauren Gilbert*
                     Charles Braswell
Noel Penn . . . . Gene Peterson
Tammy Forrest Porter . . Scotty McGregor
                     Ann Loring*
Bruce Sterling . . . . Ron Tomme
Barbara Sterling Latimer Nina Reader
                     Lee Lawson*
                     Zina Bethune
Alan Sterling . . . . Jim Bayer
                     Dan Ferrone
                     Dennis Cooney
                     John Fink
Vivian Carlson . . . . Helene Dumas*
                     Eleanor Wilson
Henry Carlson . . . . Tom Shirley
                     Jack Stamberger*
John Dennis . . . . Coe Norton
Ken Shea . . . . Roger Stevens
Mrs. Vento . . . . Bess Johnson
                     Agnes Young*
Dr. Tony Vento . . . . Ron Jackson
                     Jordan Charney
Rick Latimer . . . . Paul Savior

                     Michael Ebert
                     Edward J. Moore
                     Jerry Lacy*
Guy Latimer . . . . John Straub
Ginny Crandall . . . . Barbara Barrie
Bill Crandall . . . . Stratton Walling
Dr. Herb Saltzman . . . . . Walter Brooke
                     Robert Gerringer*
Nell Saltzman . . . . Adele Ronson
                     Ruth Baker*
Judson Williams . . . . . . Frank M. Thomas
Link Porter . . . . Gene Pellegrini
Maggie Porter . . . . Joan Copeland
Sandy Porter . . . . Bonnie Bedelia
Julie Murano Latimer . . Jessica Walter*
                     Jane Manning
Loretta Murano . . . . . . Josephine Nichols
Connie Loomis . . . . Irene Kane
Philip Holden . . . . David Rounds
Glenn Hamilton . . . . . . Bert Convy
Kay Logan . . . . Joan Copeland
Lynn Nelson . . . . Andrea Martin
Ace Hubbard . . . . Jed Allan
Dr. Kenneth Wannberg . Frederick Rolf
Elizabeth Wannberg . . . Sybil White
Collette . . . . Mildred Clinton
Jonas Falk . . . . Roy Scheider
                     Ben Piazza
Jeffrey Carlson . . . . William Bogert
Hank Latimer . . . . Justin Sterling
                     David Carlton
                       Stambaugh*
Lauri Krakauer . . . . Claudette Nevins
Mickey Krakauer . . . . . . Alan Yorke (a.k.a.
                       Feinstein)
Anna Krakauer . . . . Jocelyn Brando
Tess Krakauer Prentiss . Toni Bull Bua
Bonnie Draper . . . . Carol Walker
                     Karen Grassle
Kate Swanson Chandler   Leonie Norton
                     Sally Stark*
Charles Lamont . . . . Jonathan Moore*
                     Stan Watt
Diana Martin Lamont . . Diane Rousseau
Toni Prentiss Davis . . . . Frances Sternhagen*
                     Louise Larabee
Paul Davis . . . . Vincent Carroll
Bill Prentiss . . . . Gene Bua*
                     Philip Clark

John Randolph	Barton Stone
	Byron Sanders*
Amanda Randolph	Margaret Barker
	Carol Bruce
	Joan Lovejoy
Miguel Garcia	Raul Julia
Alex Caldwell	Fred Stewart
	Charles White
Lester Mullett	Conrad Bain
Clare Bridgeman	Renee Roy
Ed Bridgeman	Hugh Franklin
	Russell Gold
Sally Bridgeman Rollins	Catherine Bacon
Jamie Rollins	Donald Warfield
	Ray Wise*
Dick Rollins	Lawrence Weber
Sue Rollins	Louise Troy
Dr. Jennifer Stark	Joan Bassie
Victoria Randolph	Melinda Fee
Link Morrison	George Kane
	John Gabriel*
Stacy Corby	Cindy Grover
Evelyn Corby	Lee Kurty
Dr. Dan Phillips	Drew Snyder
Dr. Joe Corelli	Tony LoBianco
	David Little
	Michael Glaser
Loretta Allen	Jeannette DuBois
Judy Cole	Marsha Mason
Dr. Otto Kreissinger . . .	Barnard Hughes
	Leon Stevens*
Arden Delacorte	Geraldine Brooks
Bobby Mackey	Richard Cox
Beatrice Swanson	Jane Hoffman
Vinnie Phillips	Nancy Marchand*
	Beatrice Straight
Dr. Lloyd Phillips	Douglass Watson
Dr. Carl Westheimer . . .	Mason Adams
	Philip Sterling
Betsy Crawford Lang . .	Elizabeth Kemp*
	Margo McKenna
Caroline ("Cal") Aleata Latimer	Deborah Courtney
	Roxanne Gregory
Jeff Hart	Charles Baxter
David Hart	Brian Farrell
Felicia Flemming Lamont	Pamela Lincoln
Phil Waterman	Michael Falrman
Dr. Ted Chandler	Keith Charles
Arlene Lovett Slater . . .	Birgitta Tolksdorf
Carrie Johnson	Peg Murray
Edouard Aleata	John Aniston
Arnie Logan	Richard Dow
Jim Crawford	Kenneth McMillan
Dr. Joe Cusack	Peter Brouwer
Lynn Henderson	Amy Gibson
Ray Slater	Lloyd Battista
Ian Russell	Michael Allinson
Bambi Brewster	Ann McCarthy
Mia Marriott	Veleka Gray
Dr. Andrew Marriott . . .	Richard Higgs
	Ron Harper*
Michael Blake	Richard Council
Dr. Tom Crawford	Richard K. Weber*
	Mark Pinter
Dory Patten Aleata	Sherry Rooney
Wendy Hayes	Elaine Grove
Mary Jane Owens	Corinne Neuchateau
Andy Marriott	Chris Marlowe
Elliot Lang	Ted Leplat
Tony Alfonso	Peter Gatto
Dr. Leann Wilson	Mary Ann Johnson
Steve Harbach	Paul Craggs
Amy Russell	Dana Delany
Wes Osborne	Woody Brown
Kim Soo Ling	Irene Yaah-Ling Sun
Hal Carson	W. T. Martin
	Also: Warren Beatty

Creator: Roy Winsor
Head Writers: John Hess, Harry Junkin, Don Ettlinger, John Pickard and Frank Provo, Lillian and Martin Andrews, Loring Mandel (a.k.a. Christopher Bell), Robert Soderberg, Robert J. Shaw, Roy Winsor, Eileen and Robert Mason Pollock, Ray Goldstone, Paul Roberts and Don Wallace, Esther and Richard Shapiro, Claire Labine and Paul Avila Mayer, Margaret DePriest, Paul and Margaret Schneider, Gabrielle Upton, Jean Holloway, Ann Marcus
Executive Producers: Roy Winsor, Bertram Berman, Darryl Hickman
Producers: Charles Schenck, Richard Dunn, Ernest Ricca, Al Morrison, John Green, Robert

Driscoll, Joseph Hardy, Tony Converse, Freyda Rothstein, Tom Donovan, Jean Arley, Cathy Abbi

Directors: Larry Auerbach, Earl Dawson, Burt Brinckerhoff, Art Wolff, Jerry Evans, John J. Desmond, Portman Paget, Gordon Rigsby, Robert Myhrum, Heather H. Hill, Dino Narizzano, Rick Bennewitz, Joseph K. Chomyn, Lynwood King, Robert Nigro, John Pasquin, Robert Scinto

Organists: John Gart, Charles Paul, Eddie Layton, Carey Gold (on synthesizer)

Musical Director (later): Charles Paul

Packagers: Roy Winsor Productions for American Home Products, Inc., CBS-TV

THE BRIGHTER DAY

THE BRIGHTER DAY, which had successful versions on both radio and television, was an early Irna Phillips creation which would show future soap writers how to structure their stories. Substitute doctors for her clergymen and you see the makings of most of the well-known soaps from the late fifties on.

The Brighter Day, which first appeared on radio in 1948, was the story of the Dennis family of the town of Three Rivers. The family was headed by Reverend Richard Dennis, a widower with five children: Liz, the mother figure in the family; Althea, a neurotic who wed rich Bruce Bigby for materialistic reasons; Grayling, the only son; Patsy, a typical teenager; and Babby, the youngest.

The television version was added some five years later, on January 4, 1954, on CBS, with both the radio and television shows running simultaneously until the radio version was discontinued in 1956. (If you missed the show on television, you could turn your radio on later in the afternoon and catch the same episode.) However, 1956 was a good year for *The Brighter Day*, and in two years it had become one of CBS's highest rated serials. Associated with the show were such soap-producing giants as Ted Corday, Allen Potter and Terry Lewis; outstanding directors such as Walter Gorman; and superb acting talents, including Hal Holbrook and the eleven-year-old Patty Duke.

The writers were equally good, but were so diverse in their individual approaches that around 1960 the show finally lost its hold on the audience. Irna

When The Brighter Day *premiered on television on January 4, 1954, running simultaneously with the radio show, the Dennis family and some of their friends had moved to the town of New Hope after their homes had been washed away by a horrendous flood. From left: Lois Nettleton as Patsy Dennis, Hal Holbrook as Grayling Dennis, Bill Smith as the Reverend "Poppa" Richard Dennis, and Mary Lin Beller as Babby Dennis. Liz, the oldest, had married and left the fold. Another daughter, Althea, had a breakdown and was institutionalized shortly after the show went to television.*

329

Phillips, who could have rescued it, was too involved with her other television soaps, especially the more modern *As the World Turns*, to give much time to *The Brighter Day*, which she had written splendidly for radio. P&G dropped the show in 1961 and CBS took over.

There had already been several jarring changes in the show's setting. When *The Brighter Day* first went to television, the Dennis family and their friends moved from Three Rivers to New Hope, Pennsylvania, following a flood. Then the family, in the late fifties, moved to the college town of Columbus. After CBS moved the show, in 1961, from New York to Hollywood's Television City, causing numerous cast changes, the audience dwindled and *The Brighter Day* was canceled on September 28, 1962.

CAST
THE BRIGHTER DAY
CBS: January 4, 1954 to September 28, 1962

Rev. Richard Dennis . . . Bill Smith
Blair Davies*

Gloria Hoye played Sandra Talbot, Grayling's love interest. Sandra was at first mysterious, but later the family learned that she had been hiding a past involvement with Grayling's business partner. Grayling and Sandra married. He had a drinking problem, but later overcame it. Blair Davies, left, had replaced Bill Smith as the Rev. Richard Dennis in 1956.

In 1957, Lori March, right, played Lenore Bradley, the spoiled rich sister of Lydia Canfield (Murial Williams, left), a newspaper man's wife. The warm and loving life that Lydia, her husband Max, and the Dennis family led helped Lenore change into a more sympathetic person. Lori March was with the show a year and a half.

Mary K. Wells, right, played Sandra during the later, more troubled years of her marriage to Grayling, beginning in 1960. Margaret O'Neil was Althea, Grayling's sister.

Althea Dennis	Brooke Byron
	Jayne Heller
	Margaret O'Neill
	Anne Meacham
Grayling Dennis	Hal Holbrook
	James Noble
	Forrest Compton
Sandra Talbot Dennis	Ann Hillary
	Gloria Hoye
	Diane Gentner
	Mary K. Wells
	Nancy Rennick
Babby Dennis Nino	Mary Linn Beller
	Nancy Malone
Patsy Hamilton	Lois Nettleton
	June Dayton
Dr. Randy Hamilton	Larry Ward
Emily Potter	Mona Bruns
Max Canfield	Herb Nelson
Lydia Harrick Canfield	Murial Williams
Donald Harrick	Walter Brooke
Lenore Bradley	Lori March
Tom Bradley	Robert Webber
Crystal Carpenter	Vivian Dorsett
Steven Markley	Peter Donat
Ellen Williams Dennis	Patty Duke
	Lanna Saunders
Peter Nino	Joe Sirola
Mitchell Dru	Geoffrey Lumb
Maggie Quincy	Patsy Garrett
Yvonne Sorel	Eva Soreny
Walter Dennis	Paul Langton
Mort Barrows	Benny Rubin

Also: Jack Lemmon, William Windom, Santos Ortega, Charles Baxter, Judy Lewis, William Post, Jr., Sam Gray, Robert Rockwell, Douglas Marland

Creator: Irna Phillips
Writers: Doris Frankel, James Cavanagh, John Haggert, Eileen and Robert Mason Pollock, Sam Hall, Irna Phillips, Barry Lake, David Davidson, Hendrik Vollaerts
Executive Producer (briefly): Ted Corday
Producers: Mary Harris, Bob Steele, Therese Lewis, Allen Potter, Leonard Blair
Directors: Ed Kogan, George Bartholemew, Del Hughes, Jack Wood, Walter Gorman, Allen Potter, Marvin Silbersher, Portman Paget, Herbert Kenwith, Hal Cooper
Organists: Dick Leibert, Arlo Hults
Packagers: Procter & Gamble, CBS-TV

THE SECRET STORM

THE SECRET STORM was the most literary serial to emerge from the fifties and well ahead of its time. It was like Eugene O'Neill's *Strange Interlude*, with all the members of one family withdrawing into their own private worlds of despair, while endless personal frustrations surfaced. The show was also a kind of morality play. In fact, in the mid-sixties, it added these closing remarks, incredibly similar to the old radio soap epigraphs: "You have been watching *The Secret Storm*, the story of the Ames family and of deep-rooted human emotions, and how these emotions are stirred up into becoming 'the secret storm.' All his life Peter had believed in honesty, kindness and justice—qualities which have brought him into conflict with both members of his family and friends. The children are grown and married now, and they often turn to Peter and Valerie for advice—but ultimately it is the individual alone who must solve his own problems . . ."

At this time, the mid-sixties, *The Secret Storm* was at the top of the Nielsens. When CBS bought the show (along with *Love of Life*) from American Home Products in 1969, Roy Winsor, who created *The Secret Storm* and had produced it ever since it premiered on February 1, 1954, departed as producer. CBS's own management took over and various writers, each determined to script the show in his own way, wrote off important members of the Ames family. By 1970, the show's focus went askew, and CBS executives, unskilled as soap producers, didn't know what to do. As Jada Rowland, who was Amy Ames until the end, says, "By this time, new viewers didn't even know who the Ames family were." Only Amy Ames and Susan Ames Dunbar were left from the original family, and Susan was no longer written as the same strong character she had been.

The Secret Storm was now in a good deal of trouble, as was *Love of Life*, which was also losing its audience. In 1972, Joe Manetta became producer and tried to save the show by leading it into more contemporary, controversial areas: a priest gave up his frock to marry; Amy had herself artificially inseminated; there was talk of impotency. The ratings improved, but only slightly, and cancellation came on February 8, 1974, twenty years and a week after *The Secret Storm* began. It was a great tragedy, because the show had been so vital for so many years. For several years afterward, viewers kept writing to the network, asking for the show to be brought back, and indeed there was some discussion about reviving the show. But it was just talk.

THE STORY

The sudden screech of automobile wheels set off a tragic chain of events in Woodbridge. ELLEN AMES was taken to the hospital in critical condition, and she died two days later. Her whole family—husband PETER AMES (Peter Hobbs, then Cec Linder, and later

332

Ward Costello and Larry Weber), eighteen-year-old daughter SUSAN AMES (Jean Mowry, most recently Judy Lewis), sixteen-year-old son JERRY AMES (Robert Morse, later played for several years by Wayne Tippit), and nine-year-old daughter AMY AMES (Jada Rowland)—was devastated by the loss of Ellen. But it was Peter and Jerry who took the blow hardest. Young Jerry, overcome by anger and grief, made an attempt on the life of the man who caused the automobile accident that took his mother's life. Jerry was sent to a reform school. Peter began to show symptoms of temporary insanity. Everyone in the Ames family felt they had to look after him.

Susan Ames became the new mother figure, and as time went on she became bossy, domineering and fearful of any changes in the status of the family—especially concerning any possible remarriage plans

of her handsome father. Ellen Ames's sister, PAULINE HARRIS (Haila Stoddard), also resented any plans Peter might make toward marriage—unless, of course, *she* was to be part of his new marriage plans. Pauline had at one time been engaged to Peter, before he shocked her by eloping with her sister, Ellen. Pauline resented their marriage and continued to love Peter.

So when Peter became interested in the housekeeper JANE EDWARDS (Virginia Dwyer), Susan did everything she possibly could to prevent a marriage from happening. And Aunt Pauline did even more. She turned up with BRUCE EDWARDS (Biff McGuire), Jane's long-lost husband, thought to have been dead, but really marooned on a desert island, and this naturally threw a monkey wrench into the romance of Peter and the housekeeper. Later, when Jane and Bruce reconciled, Peter fell in love with beautiful MYRA

Tragedy struck the Ames family of Woodbridge on the first day of The Secret Storm, *February 1, 1954. Ellen Ames, the wife of Peter Ames (Peter Hobbs), was critically injured in an auto accident and soon died. Their children were (from left) teenager Jerry (Robert Morse), the already grown Susan (Jean Mowry) and nine-year-old Amy (Jada Rowland). For many months viewers felt the dreadful impact of the Ameses' grief.*

After the storm of sorrow had passed, Peter fell in love with his new housekeeper, Jane Edwards (Virginia Dwyer, right), in 1955, and wanted to marry her. But the late Ellen's sister, Pauline (Haila Stoddard), loved Peter herself and broke up the marriage plans. For many years "Aunt" Pauline had been a catalytic character in the story.

LAKE (Joan Hotchkis, June Graham) and married her. But Myra's and Peter's families mixed like oil and water, and the marriage was short-lived.

By the time Amy was a high-school senior, she had fallen in love with rebellious KIP RYSDALE (Don Galloway, David O'Brien, Ed Griffith), son of the wealthy ARTHUR RYSDALE (played longest by John Baragrey), who had recently become Pauline's new husband. Amy's father and Kip's family both wanted them to get married, but it turned out that Kip was already involved with NINA DI FRANCISCO (Nita Talbot) the daughter of his high-school Spanish teacher. After Kip accidentally killed the girl and had to go to prison, Amy said she forgave Kip for being unfaithful and would wait for him. But while Kip was in prison she wasn't able to keep her promise. Now a freshman at Woodbridge University, she was attracted to her history professor, PAUL BRITTON (Nick Coster). Paul returned her interest but was already married, although

unhappily, to TERRY BRITTON (Marion Brash). He said he was staying married to Terry, only for the sake of their son. Amy then threw caution to the wind and had an affair with Paul, resulting in her pregnancy. When Paul found out, he offered to divorce his wife and marry Amy, but she refused him, saying she wanted a marriage based on love, not on forced circumstances. Amy swore she'd raise her baby alone.

But that wasn't to happen. Kip Rysdale came out of prison, learned of Amy's condition, and asked her to marry him, if only to give her baby a name. Amy, now fearful of going it alone, accepted the proposal. After becoming Mrs. Rysdale, however, her true love for Paul Britton came back to haunt her, and she couldn't have sexual relations with her new husband. Finally, after Paul returned to Woodbridge newly divorced from his wife, he convinced Amy not to continue with her sham marriage but to marry him instead. Amy divorced Kip, and she, Paul, and their little

Rachel Taylor replaced Jean Mowry as Susan Ames in 1957. Susan fell in love with Alan Dunbar (James Vickery), a golf pro and originally a shady character with criminal connections. Later Alan turned sympathetic and married Susan, giving up golf to become an investment banker. Much later he became a reporter on Peter's newspaper.

By 1963, Ward Costello was the new Peter Ames, who married Valerie Hill (Lori March), a wealthy widow with a troublemaking daughter and a son who was first played by Roy Scheider, now a movie star.

daughter, LISA BRITTON (Judy Safran), became a happy family.

*   *   *

Amy's father, Peter Ames, also found happiness with his third wife, VALERIE (Lori March), who had a grown daughter, JANET HILL (Bibi Besch), now divorced. Peter's marriage was happy—until tragedy again struck the family and Peter died of a heart attack while away on a business trip. The family's presence in Woodbridge was slowly diminishing. Jerry Ames had gone off to Paris to live with his wife, HOPE (Pamela Raymond), a talented painter.

For a long time Amy Ames's best friends were married couple KEN (Joel Crothers) and JILL STEVENS (Barbara Rodell). Ken fell in love with LAURI (Stephanie Braxton)—a weak, piano-playing, neurotic type—and he later married her, after divorcing Jill, who married wealthy HUGH CLAYBORN (Peter MacLean). Jill gave birth to Ken's child, CLAY (Steven Grover). Then Jill and Hugh Clayborn were killed in a plane crash. Ken also died. Instead of tearing her apart, Ken's death brought about a drastic change in Lauri's character. She was suddenly a new person: stronger, better able to cope with life. She gladly took up the job of becoming the mother of Ken's son.

Amy Britton was now to encounter her sharp-fanged archrival, BELLE CLEMENS (Marla Adams). Beautiful Belle had had a daughter, ROBIN (Marya Zimmet), who died in a boating accident in which Amy was also involved. Belle blamed Amy for her illegitimate daughter's purely accidental death, and she swore that she'd get even with Amy by stealing the affections of Amy's husband, Paul Britton. Since Paul had once been married to a blonde who looked just like Belle, he was easy bait for this scheming viper, and Amy was

Diana Muldaur played Ann Wicker, a scheming businesswoman who worked for Peter Ames' newspaper in 1965. Ed Griffith was Kip Rysdale, with whom Amy Ames had fallen in love.

Jada Rowland (center) was a young woman of twenty by 1965 and still playing Amy, who was now torn between Kip and a married professor at Woodbridge University. Judy Lewis (left) became the new Susan Dunbar and James Vickery (right) continued to play her husband Alan, who was being seduced by Diana Muldaur as Ann Wicker. Diana Muldaur and Jim Vickery actually did fall in love on the show and later married and moved to California. Judy Lewis is Loretta Young's daughter.

no match. After Paul divorced Amy, Belle soon became Mrs. Paul Britton.

Amy was literally dumbstruck by what Belle had done to her. People worried about her when she began to have hallucinations, to play with dolls and pearls and the like. Amy had to see a psychiatrist, a DR. IAN NORTHCOTE (Gordon Rigsby, Alexander Scourby), who cured her and eventually married Amy's stepmother, Valerie Ames.

Attention was also being paid to the problems of Amy's sister, Susan, whose husband, ALAN DUNBAR (Jim Vickery, Liam Sullivan), was listed as killed in action. Susan then married newspaperman FRANK CARVER (played longest by Larry Luckinbill). To her shock, it turned out that Alan Dunbar had not been killed at all but had been a P.O.W. and was now back in Woodbridge, warped by his war experiences. Alan got involved in a drug ring headed by DAN KINCAID (Bernard Barrow), who was running for governor of the state at the same time. Belle Britton, who by now

was becoming bored as the wife of a professor, met Dan and suddenly saw herself as a wealthy governor's wife. And Dan was spellbound by Belle. Belle divorced Paul Britton and married the man she thought would turn out to be the state's next governor.

Amy now became the daughter-in-law of her hated rival, Belle. Amy had fallen in love with Dan Kincaid's lawyer son, KEVIN KINCAID (David Ackroyd), and married him. But despite her new, forced kinship, Amy and Belle continued to be archenemies.

All Belle's plans to become First Lady collapsed when Dan's underworld connections were revealed and he was sent to prison. But Amy and her sister, Susan, were also drawn into the wreckage when Amy's husband, Kevin, was shot by one of his father's Mafia friends and paralyzed from the waist down. Susan was accused of murdering her first husband, Alan Dunbar—who was actually killed in a general shootout with Dan's drug-dealing friends. During the trial Susan's husband, Frank Carver, stood by her. After her acquittal, the Carvers left Woodbridge.

Before her husband, Kevin, had become a paraplegic and impotent as a result of the shooting, Amy

Joan Crawford filled in for her daughter, Christina, when she became ill for three days in 1968. Joan played Joan Borman, a gold-digging, confused woman. Joan Crawford is here in a scene with Jeffrey Lynn, as Charlie Clemens, who tried to take over the Herald, *Peter's newspaper. Years later, after her mother's death, Christina Crawford wrote* Mommie Dearest, *a book portraying her mother as a child-abuser.*

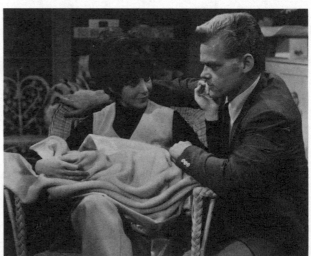

In 1970, Barbara Rodell and Peter MacLean played Jill and Hugh Clayborne, who had a child; Jill was Amy's best friend. When the popular couple were killed in a plane crash in the story, hundreds of faithful viewers sent angry, complaining letters to the show.

Kincaid mistakenly thought that she was pregnant and had told Kevin the good news. Now, with Kevin in a wheelchair, and not wanting to depress him further with the news that she wasn't carrying his child after all, Amy asked her friend, DR. BRIAN NEEVES (Jeff Pomerantz, later Keith Charles), to arrange for her to be artificially inseminated. He agreed but, because he fell in love with her himself, he supplied his own semen. It was to have been a secret, but nurse MARTHA ANN ASHLEY (Audre Johnston), a cohort of Belle's, told Belle, and she in turn threatened to tell Kevin unless Amy forked over enough cash. Amy came up with the blackmail money, which Belle needed to keep her dashing new lover, ROBERT LANDERS (Dan Hamilton), happily supplied with racing cars, his great passion. Little did Belle suspect that Robert Landers was really Dan's illegitmate son. The only person who had that information was Belle's one-time ward, JOANNA MORRISON (Audrey Landers, Ellen Barber), who was in love with Robert herself. It was becoming apparent that Dan and Robert, now enemies because of Belle's affair with Robert, would soon have to confront the reality of their father-son kinship.

On February 8, 1974, The Secret Storm *aired for the last time, with most of the show's stories ending happily. Amy had wed Kevin Kincaid (David Ackroyd), who was recovering the use of his legs after having been paralyzed by a gun-shot wound. The accident had been caused by his criminal father, Dan Kincaid (Bernie Barrow, left), who finally turned straight after paying his debt to society.*

Kevin, however, had already found out that Amy had been artificially inseminated with Dr. Brian Neeves's sperm. He forced Amy, who was just having her baby, whom she called Danielle, to move out of the house and in with her stepmother, Valerie, and her husband, Ian. Kevin, thinking only of Amy's happiness, made her divorce him and began trying to encourage her to marry Brian, the real father of the child. Amy—confused and unhappy—began having an affair with Brian.

* * *

After the death of her husband, Ken, Lauri Stevens couldn't believe it but she was falling in love with a priest. His name was FATHER MARK REDDIN (David Gale), who, despite his devotion to the Church, found himself drawn to Lauri. The two fought their feelings for a while, but finally Mark decided he wanted to be Lauri's husband (and the father of her stepson, Clay Stevens) more than he wanted to stay in the priesthood. Mark and Lauri were wed and seemed happy—yet Mark couldn't seem to forget his vows to the Church. He seemed to be torn between two worlds, though Lauri at first had no suspicion that he wasn't completely satisfied with their life together. Subconsciously, however, she may have felt it, for soon after, when they moved into an old house, Lauri became obsessed with the idea that it was haunted by its previous owner, Georgina—and even thought that *she* was Georgina's reincarnation. Her delusions were fed by a young handyman, ERIC KOVAC (David Wilson), who was psychotic and had murdered Georgina and her children years before.

Mark, too, was showing signs of deep emotional stress: he was becoming an alcoholic, rather than face his true desire to return to the Church. One terrible night, all of Lauri's and Mark's problems were resolved by a scourge of death and violence. Mark had gone to pay a call to his old church superior, MONSIGNOR QUINN (Sydney Walker), and found him on his deathbed; Mark, despite himself, was miraculously transformed into a priest again as he prayed all night for the soul of the dying prelate. Meanwhile, young Eric, the psychopath, had broken into Lauri's bedroom and saw the image of his past victim, Georgina, coming at him through a big standing mirror. He jumped through it and was gashed to death by the broken glass. The horrible violence of that night brought Lauri to her senses; she was able to see that

Mark really belonged with the Church. Mark was also transformed by his own ordeal and knew that he had to return to the frock. As they parted, they vowed that they would never forget what they had given each other.

Robert Landers finally discovered that he was the son of Dan Kincaid and the brother of Kevin Kincaid. He then went to Italy in pursuit of an important racing Grand Prix so that his new prestige would make Dan feel proud of him. Before the race, however, he stopped off in London to give moral support to his brother, Kevin, who was secretly undergoing a dangerous operation on his legs. Although Kevin, who now knew of Robert's real parentage, had previously rejected him, Robert was determined to prove that he could be both a good brother and a good son.

Meanwhile, Amy, who found out why Kevin went to London so abruptly, refused to marry Brian. She realized that she would never be able to love anyone else but Kevin. Brian was hurt, but not destroyed. One afternoon, shortly after turning Brian down, Amy came home to find Kevin sitting in her living room. He begged her not to come to him; he got up on his own feet and walked toward her. He almost made it, but fell on the floor a few feet away. Amy, deliriously happy at Kevin's return, fell down with him, hugging and kissing his face. Moments later, Valerie came in, followed by Amy's daughter, Lisa. They, too, fell to the floor, forming a circle of happiness. Kevin, Amy, Lisa and little Danielle would never again be parted.

At Kevin's mysterious urging, Dan Kincaid paid a visit to Robert Landers and his pregnant bride-to-be, Joanna Morrison. When Robert told his one-time rival, Dan, that he was his illegitimate son, Dan was stunned. He looked into his son's eyes, and they both realized that they had many years to make up for. Dan was now blessed with two sons, and although his wife, Belle, was leaving him and Woodbridge to take up a glamorous singing career, it was apparent that he was destined to remain a most happy man indeed.

CAST

THE SECRET STORM
CBS: February 1, 1954 to February 8, 1974

Amy Ames Kincaid	Jada Rowland* (P)
	June Carter
	Beverly Lunsford
	Lynne Adams
Peter Ames	Peter Hobbs* (P)
	Cec Linder
	Ward Costello
	Lawrence Weber
Susan Ames Carver	Jean Mowry (P)
	Rachel Taylor
	Norma Moore
	Mary Foskett
	Frances Helm
	Judy Lewis*
	Mary McGregor Jackson
Jerry Ames	Robert Morse (P)
	Warren Beringer
	Ken Gerard
	Wayne Tippit*
	Peter White
	Stephen Bolster
Pauline Harris Rysdale .	Haila Stoddard (P)
Grace Tyrell	Marjorie Gateson* (P)
	Margaret Barker
	Eleanor Phelps
J. T. Tyrell	Russell Hicks (P)
Dr. Spence Hadley	Jay Jostyn
	Roy Poole
	George Smith
	Addison Powell
Bart Fenway	Whitfield Connor
Jane Edwards	Barbara Joyce
	Virginia Dwyer*
	Marylyn Monk
Bruce Edwards	Biff McGuire
	Ed Bryce
Skip Curtis	Martin E. Brooks
Myra Lake Ames	Joan Hotchkis
	June Graham
Ezra Lake	Wendell Phillips
	Don McHenry
Bryan Fuller	Carl King
Lucy Stokes	Joyce Barker
Alan Dunbar	James Vickery*
	Liam Sullivan
Joe Sullivan	James Broderick
	Frank Sutton
Father Farrell	Barnard Hughes
George Hewlett	Otto Hulett
Nancy Hewlett	Barbara Lord
	Jane McArthur
Nick Cromwell	Byron Sanders
Kate Lodge Ames	Polly Childs

Jeff Nichols	James Pritchett
Arthur Rysdale	Lester Rawlins
	John Baragrey*
	Frank Schofield
Kip Rysdale	Don Galloway
	David O'Brien
	Ed Griffith
Eduardo DeGama	Cal Bellini
	Joseph Della Sorta
Nina DiFrancisco	Nita Talbot
Paul Britton	Nicolas Coster*
	Jed Allan
	Edward Kemmer
	Ryan MacDonald
	Conard Fowkes
	Linden Chiles
Terry Britton	Marion Brash
Julian Dark	Jordan Charney
Evelyn Dark	Lesley Woods
Katie	Margaret Hamilton
	Mary Boylan
Valerie Hill Northcote . .	Lori March
Peter Dunbar	Michael Kearney
	Mark Kearney
	Donnie Melvin
Casey Arnold	Konrad Matthaei
Rocket	Donna Mills
Stone	Stephen Elliott
Ann Wicker	Diana Muldaur
Hope Crandall Ames . . .	Pamela Raymond
Matthew Devereaux . . .	John Colicos
Carol Devereaux	Lois Markle
Felicia Stringer	Elizabeth Wilson
Janet Hill Porter	Bibi Besch
Dr. Tony Porter	Arlen Dean Synder
Wendy Porter	Rita McLoughlin
	Julie Mannix*
Brooke Lawrence	Julie Wilson
George Bennett	Dan Frazer
Marian Bennett	Gloria Hoye
Freddy Fay	Dennis Patrick
Bob Hill	Roy Scheider
	Justin McDonough
	Edward Winter
Frank Carver	Lawrence Luckinbill
	Jack Ryland
	Robert Loggia
Mary Lou Carver	Joanna Miles
Wes Glenway	Clifton James

Erik Fulda	George Reinholt
Charles Clemens	Jeffrey Lynn
Karen Clemens	Beverly Hayes
Robin Clemens	Marya Zimmet
Belle Clemens Kincaid .	Marla Adams
Nick Kane	Keith Charles
Joan Borman	Christina Crawford
Archie Borman	Ken Kercheval
Judge Sam Stevens	Terry O'Sullivan
Ken Stevens	Gordon Gray
	Joel Crothers*
Jill Stevens Clayborn . . .	Audre Johnston
	Irene Bunde
	Barbara Rodell
Laurie Hollister Reddin	Linda DeCoff
	Stephanie Braxton*
Nola Hollister	Rita Morley
	Rosemary Murphy
	Mary K. Wells*
Wilfred Hollister	Barnard Hughes*
	Alexander Clark
Lisa Britton	Diane Dell
	Terry Falis
	Judy Safran
Aggie Parsons	Jane Rose
Irene Sims	Jennifer Darling
R. B. Keefer	Troy Donahue
Dr. Ian Northcote	Gordon Rigsby
	Alexander Scourby
Owen Northcote	Gordon Rigsby
Mary Lou Northcote . . .	Clarice Blackburn
Hugh Clayborn	Peter MacLean
Didi Clayborn	Judi Rolin
Clay Stevens	Steven Grover
Cory Bocher	Terry Kiser
Kitty Styles	Diana Millay
	Diane Ladd*
Kevin Kincaid	Dennis Cooney
	David Ackroyd*
Dan Kincaid	Bernard Barrow
Joanna Morrison	Audrey Landers
	Ellen Barber*
Ursula Winthrop	Jacqueline Brookes
Martha Ann Ashley	Audre Johnston
Alden	Cliff DeYoung
Polly	Susan Oakes
Mark Reddin	David Gale
Stace Reddin	Gary Sandy
Jessie Reddin	Frances Sternhagen

Monsignor Joseph
　Quinn .... Sydney Walker
Dr. Brian Neeves ...... Jeff Pomerantz
　　　　　　　　　　 Keith Charles
Niele Neeves .... Betsy von Furstenberg
Doreen Post .... Linda Purl
Julius Klekner .... Philip Bruns
Dr. Ira Bromfield ...... George Rose
Eric Kovac .... David Wilson

Creator: Roy Winsor
Head Writers: William Kendall Clarke, Henry
　　　　　 Selinger and Harrison Bingham,
　　　　　 Stanley H. Silverman, Lou Scofield,
　　　　　 Will Lorin, Max Wylie, Orin Tovrov,
　　　　　 Carl Bixby, Jane and Ira Avery, John
Hess, Don Ettlinger, Gillian Houghton
(a.k.a. Gabrielle Upton), Gerry Day
and Bethel Leslie, Robert Cenedella,
Frances Rickett
Executive Producers: Roy Winsor, Charles Weiss
Producers: Richard Dunn, Ernest Ricca, Tony
　　　　　 Converse, Robert Driscoll, Robert
　　　　　 Costello, Joseph D. Manetta
Directors: Gloria Monty, Neil Smith, Michael
　　　　　 Onofrio, Portman Paget, David Roth,
　　　　　 Robert Myhrum, Joseph L. Scanlan
Organists: Charles Paul, Eddie Layton, James Leaffe,
　　　　　 Carey Gold (on synthesizer)
Packagers: Roy Winsor Productions for American
　　　　　 Home Products, Inc., CBS-TV

FROM THESE ROOTS

FROM THESE ROOTS is still remembered by many viewers as one of the most polished of all serials. Created by John Pickard and Frank Provo, the show was clearly not from the midwestern school of soaps, with characters that materialize in a vacuum, but instead stressed a definite time, place and culture. Introduced by Procter & Gamble on NBC on June 30, 1958, *From These Roots* was based on the large Fraser family in the New England town of Strathfield. The heroine, Elizabeth Fraser, wrote fiction and eventually married a playwright, David Allen. Her father, Ben Fraser, owned a newspaper. Eventually Liz had to fight a scheming alcoholic actress, Lynn Franklin, for the love of her husband. It was wonderfully sophisticated, incorporating the flavor of the Eastern theatrical world with the usual love triangles. At one point, in fact, *From These Roots* featured a production within a production, when Barbara Berjer, as the actress Lynn Franklin, played the title role in a "live" television production of *Madame Bovary*. Backstage dressing room jitters, the director's anxiety in manning the control room, and the actress's quick costume changes were all blended into Lynn's romantic dilemma between David Allen and Tom Jennings (played by Bob Mandan and Craig Huebing).

These were, however, unfamiliar situations to the average daytime viewer in the late fifties, who was not used to so much culture being mixed into the soap medium. That seems the only reason for the eventual failure of a show that was beautifully written and di-

At the premiere of From These Roots *on June 30, 1958, Elizabeth Fraser (Ann Flood), a fiction writer, had just returned to Strathfield, a New England town, to rejoin her father, Ben Fraser (Rod Hendrickson), and work as a reporter on his newspaper, the* Record. *Ben was the patriarch of the large, well-to-do Fraser family.*

341

rected by such pros as Paul Lammers, Don Wallace and Lenard Valenta, and employed the acting talents of some of the best performers around, including Ann Flood, Henderson Forsythe, Julie Bovasso, Byron Sanders, Bob Mandan, Billie Lou Watt, Craig Huebing, Millette Alexander, Barbara Berjer, and Vera Allen. Procter & Gamble sold *From These Roots* to NBC, which later withdrew it on December 29, 1961.

CAST

FROM THESE ROOTS
NBC: June 30, 1958 to December 29, 1961

Liz Fraser Allen	Ann Flood*
	Susan Brown
Ben Fraser	Grant Code
	Rod Hendrickson*
	Joseph Macaulay
Emily Benson Teton . . .	Helen Shields
Jim Benson	Henderson Forsythe
Lyddy Benson	Sarah Hardy
Tim Benson	John Stewart
Peggy Tomkins Benson .	Mae Munro
	Ellen Madison*
Laura Tomkins	Audra Lindley
Nate Tomkins	Ward Costello
Ben Fraser, Jr	Frank Marth
Rose Fraser	Tresa Hughes
	Julie Bovasso
Dan Fraser	Dana White
Myra Fraser	Nancy R. Pollock
Mildred Barnes	Sarah Burton
	Doris Dalton
	Violet Heming
Fred Barnes	Tom Shirley

Ben's son, Ben Fraser Jr. (Frank Marth), wed Rose Corelli (Julie Bovasso). They represented the less "cultured" branch of the family running a farm and eschewing the family newspaper.

From These Roots, in 1959, had a sophisticated love triangle. Liz Fraser had married fellow writer David Allen (Bob Mandan, center) and their marriage began to suffer because of a conflict in their literary careers. Alcoholic actress Lynn Franklin (played by Barbara Berjer, right) was married to theatrical director Tom Jennings (Craig Huebing, left), but was really in love with David Allen and tried to break up his marriage to Liz. By the time the show was cancelled in 1961, Liz and David had decided to stay together and achieved success as writers.

	Lauren Gilbert
Kass	Vera Allen
Dr. Buck Weaver	Len Wayland
Maggie Barber Weaver	Billie Lou Watt
Bruce Crawford	Byron Sanders
Enid Allen	Mary Alice Moore
David Allen	Robert Mandan
Luisa Corelli	Dolores Sutton
Artie Corelli	Frank Campanella
Ahmed	Hal Studer
Stanley Kreiser	Leon Janney
Lynn Franklin Jennings	Barbara Berjer
Tom Jennings	Craig Huebing
Jimmy Hull	John Colenback
Frank Teton	George Smith
Hilda Furman	Charlotte Rae

Richard	Richard Thomas
Jamie	Alan Howard
Don Curtiss	Clarke Warren
Jack Lander	Joseph Mascolo
Gloria Saxon	Millette Alexander

Creators: John Pickard and Frank Provo
Writers: John Pickard and Frank Provo, Leonard Stadd, John M. Young
Executive Producer (briefly): John Green
Producers: Don Wallace, Paul Lammers, Eugene Burr
Directors: Don Wallace, Paul Lammers, Joseph Behar, Leonard Valenta
Organist: Clarke Morgan
Packagers: Procter & Gamble, NBC-TV

THE DOCTORS

THE DOCTORS, which lasted nearly twenty years, had an unusual beginning for a serial. For a few months following its premiere on April 1, 1963, it was a half-hour anthology series of daily stories centered around life at Hope Memorial Hospital. Each episode had a title, like "Whatsoever House I Enter," "We Know Not What," and "One Too Many," and featured only one of the show's four leading players: Fred J. Scollay as hospital chaplain Sam Shafer, Jock Gaynor as Dr. William Scott, Margot Moser as Dr. Elizabeth Hayes and Richard Roat as Dr. Jerry Chandler. Jim Pritchett, who was eventually to become the show's doctor star, was first introduced on June 20, 1963, as a corporation president. The show liked him so much that three weeks later he was brought back as the familiar stethoscope-bearing "tentpole" character, Dr. Matt Powers. Around that time, *The Doctors* began running one story a week.

Orin Tovrov, who had written *Ma Perkins* on radio for two decades, created *The Doctors* for Colgate-Palmolive and was the first head writer. Anthology soaps have never been successful on television, and so on March 2, 1964, Tovrov turned his show into a continuing serial with regular characters with whom viewers could relate over a stretch of time.

Like *General Hospital*, which premiered on the same day, *The Doctors* was a great success in the sixties. It's strong stories employed complicated medical equipment, behind-the-scenes doctors and nurses and advanced television technology, imparting authenticity, heightening the drama. The hospital atmosphere was new to daytime and kept viewers fascinated. The writing, especially the depiction of romantic relationships in a hospital, was excellent. During one long story line of the late sixties, involving the brilliant invention of hot-blooded Italian neurosurgeon Nick Bellini and his romance with well-bred Dr. Althea Davis—charismatically performed by Gerald Gordon and Liz Hubbard—*The Doctors* became a must-see and ratings soared.

By the early seventies, the appeal of the hospital milieu began to wear thin. The audience was growing tired of brain operations and the personal dilemmas of a handful of doctors at a time when other shows were offering the alternative of youth and glamor. Colgate-Palmolive, in a predictable maneuver, changed management and writers and introduced many new characters in an attempt to revivify the show. For brief periods the ratings improved. But *The Doctors* never did again achieve the excitement it had had in the preceding decade, not because it was badly written but because the hospital idea itself was worn out. The same thing happened to *General Hospital*, which was able to save itself only by being reborn into an alien entity, a show with only vague connections to its old hospital self. *The Doctors* was cancelled on December 31, 1982.

344

THE STORY

People at Hope Memorial Hospital always felt comfortable coming to hospital head DR. MATT POWERS (Jim Pritchett) with their troubles because of his easy armchair manner and solid character. So did a new doctor at the hospital, DR. MAGGIE FIELDING (Ann Williams, Bethel Leslie, Lydia Bruce). But neither Matt nor Maggie was especially happy, despite their strong characters, for they each lacked love and marital security. Matt had had an unhappy marriage with his last wife, Grace, and had to care for his sixteen-year-old son MIKE POWERS (see cast list on p. 350). Maggie was unhappily married to ALEC FIELDING (Charles Braswell, Joseph Campanella). Slowly, Maggie and Matt began falling in love. Then a great irony occurred. One of the reasons Maggie's marriage was unhappy was that Alec was suffering from impotency, which was curable through an operation. Bravely putting his own feelings aside, Matt agreed to perform the operation so that his patient could have sexual relations with the woman Matt loved! Alec was cured, but shortly after the operation was killed in an accident. But Matt now refused to marry Maggie because his first wife had committed suicide, possibly because Matt had neglected her so much for his work, and Matt secretly feared that the same thing would happen to Maggie.

After being mysteriously rejected by Matt, Maggie married vicious KURT VAN ALEN (Byron Sanders), who made her utterly miserable and then deserted her. She discovered she was pregnant with Van Alen's child but couldn't marry Matt because she was still married to Van Alen. After she gave birth to GRETA (played as a very young girl by Eileen Kearney and later by Jennifer Houlton), Kurt Van Alen was reported stabbed to death in a low dive in the South Seas, and a relieved Matt and Maggie were preparing to marry. Suddenly, Kurt's sister, THEODORA ROSTAND (Carmen Matthews), came to Hope Memorial seeking custody of Greta because she was the heir to her late father's fortune. Just to rid themselves of Theodora, Matt and Maggie signed over Greta's fortune to her, kept custody of Greta and finally, after three painful years, were able to marry.

Meanwhile, young Mike Powers had become a medical student and had fallen in love with beautiful

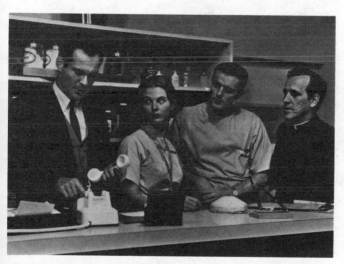

After six months of anthology stories, The Doctors became a continuing serial in 1964 about life at Hope Memorial Hospital. The stars were Jim Pritchett (left) as Dr. Matt Powers, head of the hospital; Ann Williams as Dr. Maggie Fielding; Richard Roat and Fred J. Scollay, from the original anthology cast, as Dr. Jerry Chandler and hospital chaplain Sam Shafer. Jim Pritchett remained on the show for its entire run.

Major cast members in 1965 included, from left: Adam Kennedy as wealthy cattle baron Brock Hayden; Ellen MacRae as Dr. Kate Bartok; Elizabeth Hubbard as Dr. Althea Davis; and Gerald O'Loughlin as Pete Banas, the hospital custodian. Ellen MacRae is now known as Ellen Burstyn, the academy-award winning movie star.

LIZ WILSON (Pamela Toll), whose neurotic mother HARRIET (Meg Myles) had tried to keep her from having normal romantic relationships with boys. Mike, a precocious student, believed he had developed an important new drug. Liz, who loved and believed in Mike, took the drug, which had a dreadful psychedelic effect on her. Made temporarily insane, Liz climbed onto the ledge of a high window at Hope Memorial. She was saved by a board member, PHILIP TOWNSEND (Ralph Purdom) who promptly kidnapped Liz because he loved her. After much ado, Liz was rescued and back in Mike's arms.

DR. ALTHEA DAVIS (Elizabeth Hubbard), born Althea Hamilton, was the beautiful new head of the outpatient clinic at Hope Memorial. She divorced stuffy DAVE DAVIS (Karl Light), with whom she had two children, PENNY (Julia Duffy) and BUDDY, and for a while became engaged to Matt Powers, before he married Maggie. Then she met DR. NICK BELLINI (Gerald Gordon), a brilliant brain surgeon who was raised in a Chicago ghetto. The difference in their backgrounds, she of proud, Puritan, New England stock, and he rough and earthy, caused sparks to fly. Their love affair reached the heights, but was also stormy and unpredictable because of opposing temperaments and clashing pride. Early in their relationship, they went away for a weekend of bliss, only to return and find that her son Buddy had contracted spinal meningitis. He suddenly died. After temporarily breaking up over the tragedy, Nick and Althea married and lived with her teenage daughter Penny, who adored her new stepfather. But Nick and Althea's immovable temperaments inevitably caused a breakup and the two divorced. Blaming her mother for losing Nick, Penny went to live with her father, Dave Davis, in California.

A brash, girl-chasing intern named DR. STEVE ALDRICH (David O'Brien) came to Hope Memorial and instantly started creating havoc. He seduced neurotic DR. KAREN WERNER (Laryssa Lauret), made her pregnant

Matt's teenage son Mike Powers (Harry Packwood) and the popular Liz Wilson (Pamela Toll) provided the show with a story of young romance in 1967. Liz almost fell to her death from a hospital ledge after taking a psychedelic drug that Mike had made as an experiment.

Brain surgeon Nick Bellini (Gerald Gordon) and Dr. Althea Davis were wed late in 1968. Theirs became the longest, most involving love story on The Doctors. *Viewers loved the idea of a romance between a brilliant though brash roughneck surgeon from Chicago and a sophisticated lady physician brought up in the finest New England schools.*

and, after she attempted suicide, married her. They eventually divorced and Karen attempted to return to Germany with their son, ERICH ALDRICH (Keith Blanchard), but the plane crashed. Erich survived and later began to live with his father. Through all of this a happy-go-lucky, self-effacing gal Friday to Matt Powers, nurse CAROLEE SIMPSON (Carolee Campbell for many years, then Jada Rowland), loved Steve from a distance. After Steve began to pay serious attention to her, she had an affair with him and became pregnant—but, because of jealousy and misunderstanding, never told him. Instead, Carolee married DR. DAN ALLISON (Richard Higgs), for the sake of the baby, but Dan was a psychopath who knew he was dying of a heart condition. Vowing to take revenge on Steve for the love Carolee still bore him, Dan Allison took his own life, making it appear that Steve had murdered him. Just before Steve was to be sentenced for the crime, the late Allison's son, BILLY ALLISON (see the cast list on p. 350), found his father's diary and Steve was exonerated. Steve and Carolee were married.

Althea went on an extended European trip and met a suave psychiatrist, DR. JOHN MORRISON (Patrick Horgan), who followed her back to Hope Memorial and married her. John's sole purpose in life became one of keeping Nick and Althea apart, since he knew that they still loved one another. He manipulated people, gave unethical psychiatric advice, faked a wheelchair paralysis and even caused the death of a young nurse—all to hold onto Althea. She herself had discovered his chicanery, but had an auto accident and became comatose before she could tell anyone. Nick performed a brilliant brain operation on her and saved her life. Eventually John Morrison was murdered by one of his patients.

After his teenage crush on Liz Wilson, young Mike Powers had had several romances, but nothing quite as serious as with TONI FERRA (Anna Stuart), a pretty new lab technician. After several people, including her estranged mother and her mother's old lover, showed up at the hospital and meddled with Mike and Toni's relationship, they finally married. But soon Mike, who had always tried too hard to live up to his father's expectations, took to dangerous

David O'Brien joined the show in 1969 as Dr. Steve Aldrich, a complete heel with the ladies. Carolee Campbell was introduced a few months later as gentle and shy nurse Carolee Simpson (the actress's own first name was considered so interesting that it was used for her character). Steve and Carolee fell in love and had an affair. Then she became pregnant and married someone else. The Steve and Carolee story went on for years.

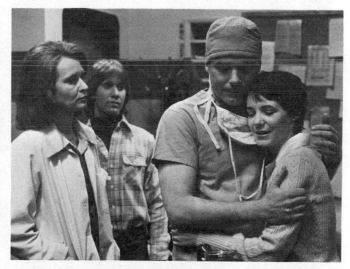

In 1976, Jada Rowland (right)—whom viewers had watched grow up on The Secret Storm *as Amy Ames—joined as the new Carolee Aldrich, just released from a mental hospital. Lydia Bruce (left) had been playing Dr. Maggie Powers since 1968. Next to her is Shawn Campbell as Billy Allison, Steve and Carolee's adopted son.*

amphetamines, or "pep pills," for courage. Unable to practice medicine properly and with his marriage endangered, he ran away to work as a ship's doctor. Soon after, his frantic wife, Toni, realized she was pregnant. Meanwhile, Matt Powers's nephew, DR. ALAN STEWART (Gil Gerard), joined the staff of Hope Memorial. Unhappily married, Alan was drawn to Toni, who had already heard the terrible news that Mike had been killed in an explosion aboard ship. She let herself fall in love with Alan. After Alan's jealous wife, MARGO (Mary Denham), died from a gynecological infection, Toni and Alan were married. Suddenly Mike showed up! The explosion hadn't killed him, but it had mutilated his face, and after plastic surgery his looks were completely changed. Hurt that Toni refused to leave her new husband, Mike demanded custody of their newborn boy, MICHAEL PAUL; then Mike agreed to give up the baby if she would at least live with him for three months. In the end, Toni chose Mike, and Alan left the hospital for good. Then Toni broke up with Mike to move to California to care for her sick mother.

DR. ANN LARIMER (Geraldine Court), one of Steve Aldrich's ex-wives, became engaged to Nick Bellini when Nick and Althea realized they were better off as friends than lovers. But Ann caught Obonda fever (a fictitious disease) which prevented her from having sexual relations, and so she couldn't marry Nick. After she recovered in Arizona and broke up with Nick, she returned to Madison and began to live with Steve and Carolee as their guest. One day Carolee found Steve in Ann's arms, assumed the worst, ran off

The entire cast of The Doctors *posed for its fifteenth anniversary in 1978. From left, front row: Jim Pritchett, Kathleen Turner (Nola Aldrich), Glenn Corbett (Jason Aldrich), Meg Mundy (Mona Croft, Steve's mother), Lauren White (M. J. Carroll), Shawn Campbell (Billy Allison), Pamela Lincoln (Doreen Aldrich), Jada Rowland and David O'Brien. Top row: Larry Webber (Barney Dancy), Lydia Bruce, Thor Fields (Erich), Frank Telfer (Luke Dancy), Dorothy Fielding (Sara Dancy), Phillip English (Dr. Colin Wakefield), John Shearin (Dr. Mike Powers, Matt's son) and Jennifer Houlton (Greta Powers, Maggie's daughter). The show left the air late in 1982.*

to New York and had a complete mental breakdown there. Desperate to hold onto Steve, and to keep him and Carolee apart, Ann Larimer went to New York and found Carolee in a hospital. Moments before Steve arrived there, Ann spirited Carolee off to an institution, where she intended to keep her forever. Steve now married Ann, but when he found out the shocking truth, he divorced her and remarried poor Carolee, who recovered. Later Ann had a child by Steve in Brazil.

The poor Dancy family came to Madison. They included four grown children, JERRY DANCY (Jonathan Hogan), NOLA DANCY (Kathryn Harrold, Kathleen Turner and finally Kim Zimmer), LUKE DANCY (Frank Telfer), SARA DANCY (Dorothy Fielding) and JOAN DANCY (Peggy Whitton). Each of the Dancys reacted differently to their prior poverty and, in the process, became involved with people connected with Hope Memorial. Jerry Dancy married Althea's daughter, Penny, but they had troubles because of Penny's desire for materialistic comfort and Jerry's lack of funds. Meanwhile, his sister JOAN DANCY, a junkie, became Matt Powers's patient and suddenly had her respirator plug pulled. Matt was tried for the murder and defended by JASON ALDRICH (Glenn Corbett), Steve's lawyer brother, newly arrived in Madison. Eventually Jason forced the real murderer, DR. PAUL SUMMERS (Paul Carr), to confess. Jerry Dancy also spent much time seeking his sister's murderer and put a further strain on his marriage to Penny. She left him and moved to Japan, where Althea followed, but Penny later died. Shattered by the news, Althea returned to her friends at Hope Memorial.

Nola Dancy, tired of being poor, pursued Jason Aldrich, who was on the verge of a divorce from his first wife, DOREEN (Pamela Lincoln). Nola finally schemed her way into marrying Jason, but after he learned she had been unfaithful to him, he left town. Afterward, Nola learned that she was pregnant. Jason returned to Madison after her baby, JESSICA, was born and had blood tests performed, proving that he was not the father. Furious at the discovery, Jason once again left town, but later MONA ALDRICH CROFT (Meg Mundy), Steve and Jason's mother, found out from a birthmark that Jessica was his child after all. When Jason was suddenly reported killed, Mona first tried to gain custody of the child, then kidnapped her and took her to Italy. Eventually, Jason turned up alive and Mona returned with the baby to Madison, but then

Jason really did die when he was shot by a homocidal girl who had loved him.

Luke Dancy was also determined to live in style by romancing two wealthy older women. Then he fell in love with pretty young MISSY PALMER (Dorian LoPinto), who had been raped by her father and was now afraid of sex. Luke and Missy became a happy twosome after they successfully made love. They soon ran into problems, however, with hospital medical inspector VIVECA STRAND (Nancy Pinkerton), who was determined to have Luke as her lover. In the end, Luke and Missy married, but soon afterward Missy was taken hostage by the psychopathic leader of a cult and shot to death.

Mike Powers also had a relationship which ended in tragedy. He married Sara Dancy, who had already had an affair with DR. COLIN WAKEFIELD (Philip English) and had trouble forgetting his lovemaking. (Mike was stunned when he discovered Sara's "goodbye" tape recording for her old lover. On it she said that she would think of him whenever she was in bed with her new husband!) After Mike was injured in an auto crash and almost died, Sara realized how much she loved Mike. Then Sara learned she had only a few weeks to live and died in Mike's arms.

Greta Powers, Maggie's daughter by the late Kurt Van Alen, and Billy Allison, Steve and Carolee's ward and eventually adoptive son, were older teenagers now and fell in love. Greta became pregnant and gave birth to their child, LEE ANN. Billy, however, turned unpredictable, spending his days getting high on alcohol and drugs, and he and Greta parted. Billy moved out West, but came back to Madison desperate to reconcile with Greta when he learned of the large inheritance she was about to receive from her aunt, Theodora Rostand. Greta and Billy briefly reconciled, but when she realized he had not changed his ways she divorced him and married THEO WHITNEY (Tuck Milligan) and moved with him and Lee Ann to California. Later, Billy was murdered.

A series of grave robberies in Madison unleashed a plague from the Aldrich crypt. Although a serum was developed it was too late for Mona Croft, who died from the disease. After that, a newcomer to Madison, ADRIENNE HUNT (Nancy Stafford), who appeared to be a pretty young girl, was revealed to be a sixty-year-old woman, Felicia, who was the mother of the *real* Adrienne. She was being kept young with the use of a mysterious elixir of youth.

Matt and Maggie Powers had been having serious marital problems for several years. At one point Matt developed heart trouble and grew terrified of making love to Maggie, fearing that the exertion might kill him. Matt became infatuated with Carolee's cousin M.J. MATCH (Lauren White); meanwhile, he had no idea that Maggie was pregnant with their baby. Matt and Maggie divorced, and soon after Maggie became seriously ill and lost the baby. Matt rushed to her side and they grew close once again. When Matt almost died himself from aplastic anemia, Maggie knew she still loved him. He proposed and she accepted.

Note that there are two separate casts for *The Doctors*, one for the short-lived anthology show, one for the continuing story line which began in 1964.

CAST
THE DOCTORS
(as an anthology serial)
NBC: April 1, 1963 to February 28, 1964

Dr. William Scott	Jock Gaynor (P)
Dr. Jerry Chandler	Richard Roat (P)
Dr. Elizabeth Hayes	Margot Moser (P)
Rev. Sam Shafer	Fred J. Scollay (P)
Dr. Johnny McGill	Scott Graham
Dr. Matt Powers	James Pritchett
Dr. Maggie Fielding	Ann Williams
Alec Fielding	Charles Braswell
	Joseph Campanella
Dr. George Mitchell	Staats Cotsworth
Nora Harper	Muriel Kirkland
Martha Liggett	Jean Sullivan
Ma Thatcher	Madeleine Sherwood
Pa Thatcher	John Cullum
Michael Powers	Rex Thompson

Creator, Head Writer and Executive Producer: Orin Tovrov
Producer: Jerry Layton
Directors: Carl Genus, H. Wesley Kenney, Herbert Kenwith
Musical Director: Robert W. Cobert
Packager: Colgate-Palmolive

An asterisk (*) next to an actor's name indicates that he or she played the part longest. The symbol (P) means member of the premiere cast.

CAST
THE DOCTORS
(as a continuing story)
NBC: March 2, 1964 to December 31, 1982

Dr. Matt Powers	James Pritchett (P)
Dr. Maggie Fielding Powers	Ann Williams (P)
	Bethel Leslie
	Lydia Bruce*
Dr. Michael Powers	Rex Thompson (P)
	Harry Packwood
	Robert LaTourneaux
	Peter Burnell
	Michael Landrum
	Armand Assante
	John Shearin
	James Storm
	Ashby Adams
	Stephen Burleigh
Rev. Sam Shafer	Fred J. Scollay (P)
Brock Hayden	Adam Kennedy (P)
Nora Hansen Lloyd	Joan Anderson (P)
Dr. Steve Lloyd	Craig Huebing (P)
Judy Stratton Lloyd	Joanna Pettet (P)
Edie Barclay	Patricia Harty (P)
Nurse Brown	Dorothy Blackburn (P)
Mrs. McMurtrie	Ruth McDevitt (P)
Dr. Althea Davis	Elizabeth Hubbard*
	Virginia Vestoff
Edna Hamilton	Joanna Roos
	Florence Williams
	Margaret Barker
Dave Davis	Karl Light
	Josef Sommer*
	Richard Clarke
Penny Davis Dancy	Christopher Norris
	Jami Fields
	Julia Duffy*
Pete Banas	Gerald S. O'Loughlin
Dr. Kate Bartok	Ellen McRae (a.k.a. Burstyn)
Jessie Bartok	Jocelyn Somers
Stowe Phillips	Edward Kemmer
Jackie	Louise Lasser
Kurt Van Alen	Byron Sanders
Tia Mahala	Victoria Racimo
Theodora Rostand	Carmen Matthews
	Clarice Blackburn
	Augusta Dabney

Liz Wilson . . . . Pamela Toll
Keith Wilson . . . . Morgan Sterne
Harriet Wilson . . . . Meg Myles
Dr. John Rice . . . . Terry Kiser
Polly Meriwhether . . . . . Betty Walker
Dr. Bill Winters . . . . James Noble
Ruth Winters . . . . Anne Whiteside
Dr. Nick Bellini . . . . Gerald Gordon
Dr. Rico Bellini . . . . Richard Niles
      Chandler Hill Harben
Dr. Karen Werner . . . . . . Laryssa Lauret
Dr. Steve Aldrich . . . . . . David O'Brien
Carolee Simpson Aldrich   Carolee Campbell
      Jada Rowland
Martha Allen . . . . Sally Gracie
Philip Townsend . . . . . . Ralph Purdom
Shana Golan . . . . Marta Heflin
Nancy Bennett . . . . Nancy Donahue
Paul Bennett . . . . James Shannon
Anna Ford . . . . Zaida Coles
Cathy Ryker . . . . Carol Pfander
      Nancy Barrett
      Holly Peters
Dr. Dan Allison . . . . Richard Higgs
Billy Allison Aldrich . . . Bobby Hennessey
      David Michael Elliott
      Shawn Campbell
      Alec Baldwin
Greta Powers Aldrich . . Eileen Kearney
      Ariane Munker
      Jennifer Houlton*
      Jennifer Reilly
      Grace Harrison
      Lori-Nan Engler
Toni Ferra Powers . . . . . Anna Stuart
Barbara Ferra . . . . Nancy Franklin
Dr. Vito McCray . . . . Paul Henry Itkin
Dr. John Morrison . . . . . Patrick Horgan
Dr. Hank Iverson . . . . . . Palmer Deane
Lauri James Iverson . . . Marie Thomas
Dr. Ann Larimer . . . . Geraldine Court
Mona Aldrich Croft . . . . Meg Mundy
Dr. Winston Croft . . . . . Philip Sterling*
      Daniel Keyes
      Richard Whiting
Dr. Rolf Krilling . . . . Michael Ebert
      Brian McKeon
Erich Aldrich . . . . Keith Blanchard
      Thor Fields

Sgt. Ernie Cadman . . . . . George Smith
Dr. Alan Stewart . . . . Gil Gerard
Margo Stewart . . . . Mary Denham
Elinore Crane . . . . Patricia Wheel
Luke McAllister . . . . Alex Sheafe
Dawn Eddington . . . . . . Roni Dengel
Dr. Tom Barrett . . . . Anthony Cannon
Rex Everlee . . . . Matthew Tobin
Iris Fonteyn . . . . Tanny McDonald
Andy Andersson . . . . . . Lloyd Bremseth
Stacy Wells Summers . . Leslie Ray
Big Jack Bradley . . . . . . Jack Urbont
M. J. Match Carroll . . . . Lauren White
      Carla Dragoni
      Katherine Glass
      Amy Ingersoll
Emma Simpson . . . . Katherine Glass
Scott Conrad . . . . George Coe
Eleanor Conrad . . . . Lois Smith
Wendy Conrad . . . . Fanny Spiess
      Kathleen Eckles
Dr. Paul Summers . . . . . Paul Carr
Dr. Jerry Dancy . . . . Jonathan Hogan*
      Terry O'Quinn
Joan Dancy . . . . Peggy Whitton
Nola Dancy Aldrich . . . . Kathryn Harrold
      Kathleen Turner
      Kim Zimmer
Sara Dancy Powers . . . . Antoinette Panneck
      Dorothy Fielding*
Luke Dancy . . . . Frank Telfer
Virginia Dancy . . . . Elizabeth Lawrence
Barney Dancy . . . . Lawrence Weber
Jason Aldrich . . . . Glenn Corbett
Doreen Aldrich . . . . Jennifer Wood
      Pamela Lincoln*
Tom Carroll . . . . James Rebhorn
      Jonathan Frakes*
Kyle Wilson . . . . Wayne Tippit
      Gene Lindsey
Harold Kingston . . . . . . Daniel Keyes
Ted Kingston . . . . Philip Kraus
Ricky Manero . . . . Jason Matzner
Dr. Jesse Rawlings . . . . . Petronia Paley
Dr. Colin Wakefield . . . . Philip English
H. Sweeney . . . . Peggy Cass
Missy Palmer Aldrich . . Dorian LoPinto

Ian Ziering
Mark Andrews

Viveca Strand . . . . Nancy Pinkerton
Dr. John Bennett . . . . . . Franc Luz
Ashley Bennett . . . . Valerie Mahaffey
Dr. Jack Garner . . . . Ben Thomas
Brad Huntington . . . . . . Nicholas Walker
Darcy Collins . . . . Nana Tucker
Alan Ross . . . . Richard Borg
Lillian Foster . . . . Beatrice Winde
Dr. Terri Foster . . . . Caroline Byrd
Calvin Barnes . . . . Larry Riley
Dr. Claudia Howard . . . . Doris Belack
Natalie Bell Dancy . . . . . Laurie Klatscher
                               Jane Badler*
Catherine Shaw . . . . Lisabeth Shean
Kevin Shaw . . . . Jeff Allin
Danny Martin . . . . John Pankow
Katy Whitney . . . . Maia Danziger
Theo Whitney . . . . Tuck Milligan
Dr. Jeff Manning . . . . Michael J. Stark
Philip Manning . . . . Alvin Epstein
                               James Douglas*
Adrienne Hunt . . . . Nancy Stafford
Ivie Gooding . . . . Chris Calloway
Kit McCormick . . . . Hilary Bailey
Lt. Paul Reed . . . . Mark Goddard
Dr. Murray Glover . . . . . Rex Robbins
Dr. Jean Marc Gauthier . Jean LeClerc
Hollis Rodgers . . . . Donna Drake
Ken Lucia Robinson . . . Fred Burstein
James Langley . . . . John Rixey Moore
Marilyn Langley . . . . Barbara Lang
Elizabeth Harrington . . Brooke Shields

Creator: Orin Tovrov
Head Writers: Orin Tovrov, Ian Martin, James Lipton, Rita Lakin, Rick Edelstein, Ira Avery and Stanley H. Silverman, Eileen and Robert Mason Pollock, Robert Cenedella, Margaret DePriest, Douglas Marland, Ethel and Mel Brez, Linda Grover, Elizabeth Levin and David Cherrill (a.k.a. C. David Colson), Ralph Ellis and Eugenie Hunt, Lawrence and Ronnie Wencker-Conner, Harding Lemay, Barbara Morgenroth and Leonard Kantor
Executive Producers (later years): James A. Baffico, Robert Costello, Gerard T. Straub
Producers: Jerry Layton, Bertram Berman, Allen Potter, Joseph Stuart, Jeff Young, Charles Weiss, Doris Quinlan, Joe Rothenberger, George Barimo
Directors: H. Wesley Kenney, Paul Lammers, Herbert Kenwith, Robert Myhrum, Hugh McPhillips, Norman Hall, Stan Zabka, Gene Lasko, Jeff Young, Gordon Rigsby, Dino Narizzano, Dick Feldman, Ivan Curry, Gary Bowen, Tony Giordano, John J. Desmond, David Handler, Stephen Wyman, Henry Kaplan, Gregory Lehane, Robert Scinto
Musical Direction: Robert W. Cobert, Score Productions
Packagers: Colgate-Palmolive, NBC-TV

LOVE IS A MANY SPLENDORED THING

LOVE IS A MANY SPLENDORED THING was originally adapted by Irna Phillips as a sequel to the
novel and motion picture of the same name, about a
love affair between war correspondent Mark Elliott
and a Eurasian woman doctor. Irna had envisioned
her new serial taking place years after Mark Elliott had
died and revolving around his Eurasian daughter Mia,
who wished to become a physician just like her
mother. As in the novel and movie, the main love story
would be interracial—daytime's first. However, right
after the show premiered on September 18, 1967, CBS
began to have misgivings, not only about the interracial love story between Mia and Dr. Jim Abbott, but
also about Irna's other story involving a novitiate nun
who falls in love with her sister's boyfriend. This was
of course back in the days when the networks were
much more concerned with giving offense to different
segments of the audience. Fred Silverman, head of
programming, ordered Irna to send Mia away and
have Laura, the novitiate nun, abandon her habit.
Angered, Irna left the show.

As noted on page 38, the story under the new
writers, the Averys, concentrated on romances among
young people, with the incidental characters of Mark
Elliott (nephew of the late Mark Elliott) and sisters
Laura and Iris Donnelly now becoming all important.
After David Birney took over the role of Mark Elliott,
the ratings became impressive, proving for the first
time that young actors could carry a soap.

But casting troubles caused other writers to de-
emphasize the theme of Young Love, which had made
the show popular, and instead veered toward political
intrigue, replete with dirty tricks, espionage and
murder. Mark, Iris and Laura remained as characters,
but became unwholesome in their dealings with each
other (see the following story line) and less interesting to the audience. *Love Is A Many Splendored Thing*
was canceled on March 23, 1973.

THE STORY

MIA ELLIOTT (Nancy Hsueh), the Eurasian daughter
of the late war correspondent Mark Elliott, was
headed for San Francisco, where she was to study
medicine and join her aunt and uncle, PHIL (Len Wayland) and HELEN ELLIOTT (Grace Albertson, Gloria
Hoye), and their closest friends, the Donnelly family.
On board ship Mia met newsman PAUL BRADLEY (Nicholas Pryor), whom she dated in San Francisco, but
she soon fell in love with DR. JIM ABBOTT (Robert Milli)
and broke up with Paul. After several months, however, Mia discovered that Jim Abbott had performed
an illegal abortion which resulted in the death of a
woman, and she left San Francisco. Following a mal-
practice suit, Jim was barred from practicing medicine and had to turn to research.

MARK ELLIOTT (Sam Wade, David Birney, Michael
Hawkins, Tom Fuccello), the son of Phil and Helen
Elliott, a talented young architect, became interested

353

in IRIS DONNELLY (Leslie Charleson, Bibi Besch), the fiercely independent daughter of widowed pathologist DR. WILL DONNELLY (Judson Laire). Iris's softer sister, LAURA (Donna Mills, Veleka Gray, Barbara Stanger), was a noviatiate nun, called Sister Cecilia. When Laura realized that she was falling in love with Mark, she refused to take her final vows. Laura and Iris fought bitterly over Mark.

Their older brother, First Lieutenant TOM DONNELLY (Robert Burr, Albert Stratton), lived with his son, RICKY (Shawn Campbell). Tom's wife, MARTHA (Beverlee McKinsey), had deserted him and Ricky and had become an actress, changing her name to Julie Richards. She now returned to San Francisco with her no-good boyfriend JIM WHITMAN (Berkeley Harris), who was later murdered. Tom was accused and stood trial, but it was eventually proven that scheming Julie had accidentally killed him, and she left town.

Mark wed Laura after she gave up the idea of becoming a nun. For a while her sister, Iris, became involved with Dr. Jim Abbott. Jim, however, accepted a position at Lansing Medical Center and left San Francisco. Iris then took a job with a senatorial candidate named SPENCE GARRISON (Edward Power), and

they fell in love. Spence had a domineering father, an asthmatic daughter and a troublesome wife, NANCY (Susan Browning), who wouldn't give him a divorce. Iris and Spence flew in his private plane to Lake Tahoe, intending to have a tryst; the plane crashed, causing Iris to sustain brain injuries which led to her eventual blindness.

Meanwhile, Mark and Laura's marriage broke up after Laura learned that he had been unfaithful. However, Laura's loyal sister, Iris, while blind, persuaded Laura to return to Mark after he was exonerated on a charge of murder. Volatile DR. PETER CHERNAK (Vincent Baggetta) operated on Iris with a new laser-beam technique and cured her blindness. Iris and Spence were married.

One night, while drunk, Mark raped Iris, believing, in the darkness, that she was his wife, Laura. Iris became pregnant with Mark's child but told her husband, Spence, that it was his. Spence was again running for senator. The incumbent, ALFRED E. PRESTON (Don Gantry), was "owned" by millionaire WALTER TRAVIS (John Carpenter). JOE TAYLOR (Leon Russom), a former employee of Walter's, accidentally taped a conversation which revealed that the father of Iris's

At the premiere of Love Is A Many Splendored Thing, September 18, 1967, Mia Elliott (Nancy Hsueh, pronounced "Shay") met serviceman Paul Bradley (Nicholas Pryor) on a ship coming from her country to San Francisco, and they had a brief courtship. Soon after the show began, the theme of interracial love was dropped and Mia left the story.

By 1968, Love Is A Many Splendored Thing's new story of Young Love made the show extremely popular. It was also well ahead of its time. Two sisters, Laura (Donna Mills, left) and Iris Donnelly (Leslie Charleson), fought over the same young man, Mark Elliott. Their father, Dr. Will Donnelly (Judson Laire, center), tried to intercede.

Love is a Many Splendored Thing (1967–1973) **355**

baby, little MAGGIE, was really her brother-in-law, Mark Elliott. Joe eventually gave the tape to Travis, who tried to use it against Spence during the campaign. But Iris by now had told Spence about the rape and, although he was tormented, their marriage remained intact. Despite the tape, Spence was elected.

For a while sisters Iris and Laura were on the outs. Dr. Jim Abbott came back to San Francisco and tried to win Iris back. Laura took advantage of Jim's interest in her sister and conspired with him to prove Iris an unfit mother of little Maggie and thereby win custody of the child herself; Laura knew that Maggie was really her husband's daughter and was desperate because she couldn't conceive herself. In the end, Iris and Spence kept Maggie, and Laura and Mark adopted a child.

CAST

LOVE IS A MANY SPLENDORED THING
CBS: September 18, 1967 to March 23, 1973

Iris Donnelly Garrison .	Leslie Charleson
	Bibi Besch
Mark Elliott	Sam Wade
	David Birney
	Michael Hawkins
	Vincent Cannon
	Tom Fuccello
Laura Donnelly Elliott .	Donna Mills
	Veleka Gray
	Barbara Stanger
Tom Donnelly	Robert Burr
	Albert Stratton*
Helen Elliott Donnelly .	Grace Albertson
	Gloria Hoye*
Dr. Will Donnelly	Judson Laire
Ricky Donnelly	Shawn Campbell
Mia Elliott	Nancy Huseh
Phil Elliott	Len Wayland
Dr. Jim Abbott	Robert Milli*
	Ron Hale
Paul Bradley	Nicholas Pryor
Spence Garrison	Michael Hanrahan
	Ed Power*
	Brett Halsey
Nancy Garrison	Susan Browning
Margaret Garrison	Flora Campbell

David Birney became the second Mark Elliott in 1969 and the ratings soared. The story was conventional soap opera—Mark had a murder trial, cheated on Laura, comforted his blind sister-in-law, Iris—but the performers had great charisma and the scripts were lively. David Birney and Donna Mills went on to stardom in nighttime television.

In 1972, widower Dr. Will Donnelly (Judson Laire) wed Lily Chernak (Diana Douglas), mother of Betsy Chernak (Andrea Marcovicci, right). Tom Donnelly (Albert Stratton, left) was Will's son. The show went off the air the following year.

Chandler Garrison .... Martin Wolfson
                        William Post, Jr.*
Jean Garrison .... Jane Manning
Andy Hurley .... Don Scardino
                        Russ Thacker
Steve Hurley .... Paul Stevens
                        Mark Gordon
Nikki Cabot .... Jody Locker
Angel Allison Chernak . Susan Kaye Stone
Dr. Peter Chernak ..... Michael Glaser
                        Michael Zaslow
                        Vincent Baggetta*
Lily Chernak Donnelly . Diana Douglas
Dr. Betsy Chernak Taylor Andrea Marcovicci
Dr. Sanford Hiller ...... Stephen Joyce
Marion Hiller .... Constance Towers
Julie Richards .... Beverlee McKinsey
Jim Whitman .... Berkeley Harris

Sen. Al Preston .... Don Gantry
Walter Travis .... John Carpenter
Joe Taylor .... Leon Russom
Simon Ventnor .... David Groh

Creator: Irna Phillips
Head Writers: Irna Phillips, Jane and Ira Avery, Don Ettlinger, James Lipton, Ann Marcus
Executive Producers: Joseph Hardy, Charles Weiss
Producers: Tom Donovan, Joseph Hardy, Charles Weiss, John Conboy, Linda Fidler Wendell
Directors: Tom Donovan, Peter Levin, John J. Desmond
Musical Director: Wladimir Selinsky
Organist (later): Eddie Layton
Packager: CBS-TV

TEXAS

JOYCE and Bill Corrington, who created *Texas* along with Paul Rauch, the executive producer, had originally suggested another sort of show to both Procter & Gamble and NBC. They had devised a daytime historical romance called *Reunion*, which was to take place in New Orleans at the end of the Civil War. The Corringtons felt that viewers were becoming sated with contemporary soaps and that something different, a costume drama, would have a better chance of attracting an audience. P&G approved the idea, but NBC, already suffering from the lowest daytime ratings, was frightened of such a dramatic departure. The network suggested a spinoff from the time-tested *Another World*. Then its producer, Paul Rauch, thought of the Texas theme, with NBC quickly approving the "bible"—the written proposal—perhaps because, as Bill Corrington believes, the nighttime *Dallas* was so successful.

Other moves were made to try to insure the success of the new soap. One of *Another World*'s most popular characters, Iris Carrington Bancroft, played by Beverlee McKinsey, was moved from Bay City to Houston, where she became the focus of *Texas*. After *Texas*'s premiere on August 4, 1980, however, a serious problem with the character began to emerge. The audience had loved the old, vicious, scheming Iris on *Another World*; but the writers would have had trouble basing their new show on such a mean-spirited woman, and so quickly transformed her into a warm, understanding type. The plot excuse for the change was Iris's meeting and settling down with the one man she had always loved. But the audience distinctly did not like the new Iris, who lacked the vituperative and glamorous excitement of the old. With the new show's ratings in great peril, the writers killed off Iris's new husband and chased her out of town.

From that point on, bad went to worse. A succession of head writers came and went, each changing the show's already over-manipulated focus. Viewers were forced to spend a good deal of their time watching major characters leave town, while new romances were introduced. The ratings stayed down. In the show's last months, however, after one of *Texas*'s own actresses, Pamela Long Hammer, took over as head writer, *Texas* was beginning to have the kind of look and sound that might have made it a winner, if other circumstances had been right. Ms. Hammer had decided to concentrate at least half the show on the love lives of teenagers, giving it a new youthful appeal. But all of these drastic changes and experiments on a new serial, in a daytime block of soaps that were also low-rated, finally forced its cancellation on December 31, 1982.

One might add that this was not a case of good riddance. Many viewers were distraught at the show's abrupt departure. The performers on *Texas* had been, from its beginning, top notch and its directors were among the best in Procter & Gamble's stable. P&G's new writing discovery, Pamela Long Hammer, has since gone on to become the head writer of *The Guiding Light*, with former *Texas* co-writer, Richard Culliton.

357

THE STORY

Wealthy IRIS CARRINGTON BANCROFT (Beverlee McKinsey) moved to Houston to be near her only son, DENNIS CARRINGTON (Jim Poyner), who had just opened an art gallery. Iris had spent years in Bay City where she had tried one evil scheme after another to break up the marriage of her father, Mackenzie Cory, and his younger wife, Rachel. In Houston, she suddenly met oil magnate ALEX WHEELER (Bert Kramer), the only man she had ever loved but whom she hadn't seen for twenty-five years. The last time they had seen one another, when they were both very young, they had spent three passionate days together on her father's yacht. Alex, afraid to tell her that he was nothing but a penniless seaman, abruptly vanished, planning to

Texas, *which began on NBC on August 4, 1980, was originally about wealthy Iris Carrington, who had relocated to Houston from* Another World's *Bay City (see photo on page 49). But after the first year, Iris departed and other characters became prominent, including scheming Reena Cook (Carla Borelli, center) who wed ranch foreman Max Dekker (Chandler Hill-Harben, left). At right is oilman Justin Marshall (Jerry Lanning), Reena's former lover. The show was canceled December 31, 1982.*

find her again when he was rich and powerful. The young Iris, embittered by Alex's betrayal of her, became selfish and guileful. Now, after she and Alex rediscovered one another and exchanged vows of love, Iris softened into a caring and sensitive woman. She told Alex the secret she had been hiding for years: that her son Dennis was really Alex's son. Her ex-husband, ELIOT CARRINGTON (played on this series by Daniel Davis), never knew that Dennis wasn't his own.

Eliot, a war correspondent, was believed to have been killed in Vietnam several years before, but now showed up in Houston to be near Dennis, whom he still believed to be his son. When he heard the truth, he was horrified and deeply angered. On the day of Alex Wheeler's marriage to Iris, minutes after the ceremony, Alex was shot by an unknown assailant! Luckily, he survived. After an investigation, his attacker turned out to be Eliot, who now hated Alex for stepping into his role as father.

At first, however, everyone thought that good-looking, ambitious JUSTIN MARSHALL (Jerry Lanning) had shot Alex. Justin blamed Alex for the suicide of his father, MIKE MARSHALL (Stephen D. Newman), another oil tycoon, whose company had gone under when Alex failed to lend him sufficient funds to save it. Another of Mike's sons, BARRETT MARSHALL (Stephen D. Newman, who had played the father), was reported missing in action in Vietnam. His wife, GINNY MARSHALL (Barbara Rucker), believing he was dead, had an affair with RYAN CONNOR (Phil Clark), Alex's nephew, and became pregnant. Barrett, however, was still alive and returned to Houston. Ginny was torn between Ryan, the father of her unborn baby, and Barrett, her husband. Then, when Barrett learned that his wife was pregnant by another man, Barrett went into a physical rage and caused Ginny to lose her child. Devastated by what he had done and sensing that his years in Vietnam had changed him, Barrett left Houston to seek therapy. Ginny and Ryan were wed, but shortly afterward Ryan was tragically killed in a plane crash.

Dennis fell in love with DAWN MARSHALL (Dana Kimmell), Barrett's sister. Since the Marshalls hated Alex, she was beside herself when Dennis revealed that he was Alex's son. Then she was raped by ex-con BILLY JOE WRIGHT (John McCafferty), and she finally left town. Alone now, Dennis fell for the poisonous charms of Dawn's older, more wordly sister, PAIGE MARSHALL (Lisby Larson), a golddigger who was attracted to the oil fortune that Dennis would inherit from his father, Alex. After Dennis married grasping Paige, he found out about her former life as a star of porno movies as well as her various schemes to get her hands on his money, and left her. Meanwhile, Alex Wheeler had learned of criminal activities involving his company and the Texas mob. Fearing he knew too much, the mob murdered him! A shattered Iris turned her energy toward helping her son, who began heading for a nervous breakdown when he learned that his one-time father, Eliot Carrington, and his estranged wife, Paige, were having a romance. After Paige and Dennis were divorced, mother and son left Houston for good.

Beautiful but tempestuous REENA COOK (Carla Borelli) was unhappily married to DR. KEVIN COOK (Lee Patterson), a moral man who had trouble dealing with his wife's temper tantrums. He found himself falling in love with an attractive interne, Dawn and Paige's sister COURTNEY MARSHALL (Catherine Hickland), whom he planned to marry after his divorce from Reena. But Courtney soon became interested in JEB HAMPTON (Kin Shriner), Ginny's younger brother, who had just come to town, and was torn between Jeb and the older Kevin. Believing that Jeb would be better for Courtney, Kevin left Houston, but then her romance with Jeb didn't work out and she also left town. Determined to find her, Jeb soon departed as well.

Newly divorced Reena married hard-working, youthful MAX DEKKER (Chandler Hill Harben, Jay Hammer), foreman of the Marshall ranch and one of the four closely knit Dekker children. With macho Max she became less temperamental and more loving. But their happiness was short-lived. Max became convinced that Marshall Oil, now owned by Justin Marshall, was illegally erecting oil wells and sabotaged one, only to be killed in an explosion. Meanwhile, Reena and her mother, VICKY BELLMAN (Elizabeth Allen), owner of television station KVIC-TV, were stunned to learn that Vicky's husband, lawyer STRIKER BELLMAN (Clifton James), was really a bigamist who had another family in Mexico! Husbandless, Vicky developed a relationship with HUNT WESTON (Michael Longfield), a sensitive, caring man who eventually revealed that he was a priest. Hunt offered to marry her, but Vicky convinced him he belonged to the church.

Spirited Reena had always been rather attracted to Justin Marshall, but she now blamed him for the death of her husband, Max Dekker, who died trying to undo Justin's oil rigs. Reena landed an important job at World Oil, now run by the late Alex's brother, GRANT WHEELER (Donald May). She made a flippant bet with Justin that she would either put his company, Marshall Oil, out of business in six months, or else she would sleep with him—even though he was already married to pretty ASHLEY LINDEN (Pam Long). While working at World Oil, Reena and Grant Wheeler were attracted to one another. Grant begged her to forget her self-destructive urge for revenge on Justin and Marshall Oil, but to no avail. When she lost the bet with Justin, she did sleep with him but without much joy. Soon after, she and Grant ended their new romance.

Justin also broke up with his wife, Ashley, who later realized that she was carrying his baby. During this trying time, Ashley's only solace was her ten-year-old cousin, GREGORY (Damion Scheller), and her sister ALLISON LINDEN (Elizabeth Berridge, Terri Garber), who had moved in with Ashley and Gregory following her aunt's death. What only Ashley knew was that Gregory was really her son by T. J. CANFIELD (David Forsyth), an old flame who was now an executive at World Oil. The romance between Ashley and T.J. originally broke up because of his parents, well-to-do MILDRED and BURTON CANFIELD (Lori March and Larry Weber), who didn't think that Ashley would be suitable as their daughter-in-law. T.J. had recently been romancing Paige Marshall, but when he discovered that Gregory was his son, he thought that he, Paige and Gregory should now become a family. Ashley, however, was still in love with Justin. When Ashley suddenly disappeared following a raging storm, Justin was devastated. He had finally realized how precious she was to him, and he now set about becoming a doting father to Gregory, whom he had already adopted with Ashley. T.J. decided against launching a custody suit, realizing Gregory already had a father he loved. It was Gregory's unwavering faith that eventually brought his mother home, after everyone thought she had died. Ashley had been suffering from amnesia and had found shelter with a mysterious, angelic man, who finally brought her back home just as she was about to go into labor. She gave birth to little KATHERINE PAIGE. Just then, however, T.J. was becoming interested in Paige Marshall all over again.

Billy Joe Wright, the ex-con who had raped Dawn Marshall, decided to turn straight after he was nearly arrested for murder. He tried to make a go of his marriage to sweet NITA WRIGHT (Ellen Maxted), who gave birth to their son. But things didn't work out for them and she moved to New York. Hurt, Billy Joe began to see ELENA DEKKER (Caryn Richman), Max's youngest sister, who had always been attracted to him.

Trying to forget his love for Reena, Grant Wheeler immersed himself in the problems of his children: LACEY (Lily Barnstone), BRETTE (Harley Kozak) and his playboy son MARK (Michael Woods). Mark became involved with RUBY (Dianne Thompson Neil), the sister of Billy Joe Wright, and Brette began seeing Elena's brother RIKKI DEKKER (Randy Hamilton), a local television personality. Soon both couples found themselves in great danger from the Texas mob after they found a map to a hidden oil reserve. Hearing that her children were in trouble, Grant's haughty estranged wife, JUDITH (Sharon Acker), arrived in town and began trying to worm her way back into his life. In time the two couples were saved, but during the peril, Rikki's friend, easygoing tour guide JOEL WALKER (Charlie Hill), was shot and blinded. Ruby's best friend, sweet, naive LURLENE HARPER (Tina Johnson) nursed him back to health and they married. Mark couldn't make up his mind between Ruby and Allison Linden, but eventually chose Ruby, and they eloped. Afterward, Ruby became pregnant. Brette and Rikki, however, broke up when he was offered a job in California. Judith, realizing that Grant would never love her the way he did Reena, agreed to give him a divorce so he could marry Reena but plotted to sue him for stewardship of World Oil.

CAST
TEXAS
NBC: August 4, 1980 to December 31, 1982

Reena Cook Dekker	Carla Borelli
Striker Bellman	Robert Gerringer
	Clifton James*
Victoria Bellman	Elizabeth Allen
Iris Carrington Wheeler	
	Beverlee McKinsey
Alex Wheeler	Bert Kramer
Dennis Carrington	Jim Poyner
Paige Marshall	
Carrington	Lisby Larson
Justin Marshall	Jerry Lanning
Kate Marshall	Josephine Nichols

Mike Marshall	Stephen D. Newman
Barrett Marshall	Stephen D. Newman
Ginny Marshall Connor	Barbara Rucker
Ryan Connor	Philip Clark
Dr. Courtney Marshall . .	Catherine Hickland
Dawn Marshall	Dana Kimmell
Max Dekker	Chandler Hill Harben
	Jay Hammer
Terry Dekker	Shanna Reed
Rikki Dekker	Randy Hamilton
Elena Dekker	Caryn Richman
Maggie Dekker	Shirley Slater
Billy Joe Wright	John McCafferty
Nita Wright	Ellen Maxted
Dr. Kevin Cook	Lee Patterson
Dr. Bart Walker	Joel Colodner
Samantha Walker	Ann McCarthy
Clipper Curtis	Scott Stevenson
Jasmin Cehdi Connor . .	Donna Cyrus
Sheik Cehdi	Mitch Gred
Col. Ahmed Al Hassin . .	Maher Boutros
Ralph Whalen	James Harper
Steven Marshall	Gregory Sutton
	Damien Miller
Jeb Hampton	Kin Shriner
Eliot Carrington	Daniel Davis
Shelly Leigh	Pamela Lewis
Bernie Stokes	Michael Medeiros
Chris Shaw	Benjamin Hendrickson
Peter Parnell	Ned Schmidtke
Joe Foster	Tom Wiggin
Jim Lawrence	John Horton
Vivien Gorrow	Gretchen Oehler
Ashley Linden Marshall	Pamela Long Hammer
Ruby Wright Wheeler . .	Dianne Thompson Neil
Lurlene Harper Walker .	Tina Johnson
Grant Wheeler	Donald May
Lacey Wheeler	Lily Barnstone
Brette Wheeler	Harley Kozak
Mark Wheeler	Ernie Garrett
	Michael Woods*
Bubba Wadsworth	Stephen Joyce
Phil Roberts	Berkeley Harris
T. J. Canfield	David Forsyth
Beau Baker	Robert Burton
Miles Renquist	Philip English
John Brady	James Rebhorn
Allison Linden	Elizabeth Berridge
	Terri Garber

Gregory Linden
  Marshall . . . . Damion Scheller
Mr. Hannibal . . . . Richard Young
Gretchen Randolph . . . . Natalie Campbell
Joel Walker . . . . Charles Hill
Hawker Barnes . . . . William Andrews
Boots Boudreaux . . . . . . Robert Nichols
Roger Benton . . . . Luke Reilly
  Richard Manchester
Hunt Weston . . . . Michael Longfield
Judith Wheeler . . . . Sharon Acker
George St. John . . . . Christopher Goutman
Mildred Canfield . . . . . . Lori March
Burton Canfield . . . . Donald Crabtree
  Lawrence Weber*
Mavis Cobb . . . . Dody Goodman
Christine Rush . . . . Claire Timoney
Stella Stanton . . . . Virginia Graham

Margaret Ellington . . . . Mady Kaplan
Doris Hodges . . . . Mary Pat Gleason

Creators: Joyce and John William Corrington and
    Paul Rauch
Head Writers: Joyce and John William Corrington,
      Dorothy Ann Purser and Samuel D.
      Ratcliffe, Paul Rader and Gerald
      Flesher, Pamela Long Hammer
Executive Producers: Paul Rauch, Gail Kobe
Producers: Judy Lewis, Bud Kloss, Wendy Dalton,
    Robert Calhoun, Christine Banas
Directors: Andrew D. Weyman, John Pasquin, Kevin
    Kelly, Frank Gaeta, John Driver, Bruce
    Minnix
Musical Direction: Score Productions, Elliot
    Lawrence Productions
Packager: Procter & Gamble

APPENDIX A
Casts for Selected Radio Soaps

In the lists which follow, the main source for the casts alone was *The Big Broadcast* by Frank Buxton and Bill Owen. Dates, writers, theme music and sponsors, for the most part, came from *The Serials* by Raymond William Stedman, as did some of the epigraphs. Story themes of some of the less well-known radio soaps were obtained from a variety of other sources, including soap expert John Kelly Genovese.

All dates refer to a soap's life on daytime radio.

VIC AND SADE
NBC Blue: 1932 on

Not really a soap, but a forerunner; the two had bubbly conversations about their friends and neighbors.

Vic Gook	Art Van Harvey
Sade Gook	Bernardine Flynn
Rush Gook	Billy Idelson
	Johnny Coons
	Sid Koss
Uncle Fletcher	Clarence Hartzell
Dottie Brainfeeble	Ruth Perrott
Chuck Brainfeeble	Carl Kroenke
Russell Miller	David Whitehouse
L. J. Gertner	Johnny Coons

Writer: Paul Rhymer
Theme music: Chanson Bohémienne by Boldi

BETTY AND BOB
NBC Blue: 1932 to 1940

A boss marries his secretary and they later have marital problems.

Betty Drake	Elizabeth Reller
	Beatrice Churchill
	Alice Hill
	Arlene Francis
	Edith Davis
	Mercedes McCambridge
Bob Drake	Don Ameche
	Les Tremayne
	Spencer Bentley
	Carl Frank
	J. Anthony Hughes
	Van Heflin
Mae Drake	Edith Davis
Bobby Drake	Frank Pacelli
Peter Standish	Francis X. Bushman

Writer: Robert Hardy Andrews
Theme music: Salut d'Amour by Elgar
Sponsor: General Mills

TODAY'S CHILDREN
NBC: 1933 to 1938

Family story about Mother Moran and her children. This was Irna Phillips's first network serial.

Mother Moran	Irna Phillips
Dorothy Moran	Jean McGregor
Patty Moran	Fran Carlon
Eileen Moran	Fran Carlon
	Ireene Wicker
Frances Moran	
Matthews	Bess Johnson
	Sunda Love
Henry Matthews	Raymond Edward
	Johnson
Junior Matthews	Donald Weeks
Nancy Matthews	Harriet Cain
Terry Moran	Fred Von Ammon
Lucy Moran	Lucy Gilman
Bobby Moran	Frank Pacelli
Richard Coles	Bob Bailey
Bob Brewer	Bob Griffin
	Olan Soule
Charlotta Lagorro	
Armour	Gale Page
Liza	Edith Adams

Creator/Writer: Irna Phillips
Sponsor: Pillsbury

JUST PLAIN BILL
CBS, later NBC: 1933 to 1955

He was the famous barber of Hartville, who solved everyone's problems. The show first began on evening radio in 1932.

Bill Davidson	Arthur Hughes
Nancy Donovan	Ruth Russell
Kerry Donovan	James Meighan
Jonathan Hillery	Macdonald Carey
Edgar Hudson	Clayton "Bud" Collyer
Dorothy Nash	Teri Keane
Percy Blivens	Ray Collins
Elmer Eeps	Joe Latham

Creators: Frank and Anne Hummert*
Writer: Robert Hardy Andrews
Sponsor: Kolynos tooth paste (American Home Products)
Theme music: Polly-Wolly-Doodle (banjo and harmonica)
Epigraph: "The real life story of a man who might be your next door neighbor—a story of people we all know."

THE ROMANCE OF HELEN TRENT
CBS: 1933 to 1960

The dressmaker who drove men wild with desire and wound up Hollywood's chief costume designer; the most popular serial during the Depression.

Helen Trent	Virginia Clark
	Betty Ruth Smith
	Julie Stevens
Gil Whitney	Marvin Miller
	David Gothard
	William Green
Cynthia Carter	Mary Jane Higby
Agatha Anthony	Marie Nelson
	Katherine Emmet
	Bess McCammon
Roy Gabler	John Larkin
Karl Dorn	Alan Hewitt
Frank Chase	Whitfield Connor

Creators: Frank and Anne Hummert
Theme music: Juanita (humming)
Epigraph: "And now 'The Romance of Helen Trent': the real-life drama of Helen Trent, who, when life mocks her, breaks her hopes, dashes her against the rocks of despair, fights back bravely, successfully, to prove what so many women long to prove, that because a woman is thirty-five, or more, romance in life need not be over, that romance can begin at thirty-five."

*Frank and Anne Hummert created their many serials through the Blackett-Sample-Hummert advertising agency, and later through their own production company, Air Features. Blackett-Sample-Hummert is today known as the Dancer, Fitzgerald & Sample advertising agency, which has clear links to the Hummerts' earliest soaps.

MA PERKINS
NBC Red: 1933 to 1960

She owned a lumberyard, took loving care of her employees, was wonderfully wise and solved all sorts of hard human problems.

Ma Perkins	Virginia Payne
Shuffle Shober	Charles Egleston
	Edwin Wolfe
Willy Fitz	Murray Forbes
Evey Perkins Fitz	Dora Johnson
	Laurette Fillbrandt
	Kay Campbell
Junior Fitz	Cecil Roy
	Arthur Young
	Bobby Ellis
Fay Perkins Henderson .	Rita Ascot
	Marjorie Hannan
	Cheer Brentson
	Laurette Fillbrandt
	Margaret Draper
John Perkins	Gilbert Faust
Gladys Pendleton	Virginia Payne
	Patricia Dunlap
	Helen Lewis
Tom Wells	John Larkin
	Casey Allen

Creators: Frank and Anne Hummert
Writer: Orin Tovrov

THE STORY OF MARY MARLIN
NBC Red: 1935 to 1945

Strong, brave Mary fought constantly to keep her husband Joe out of trouble.

Mary Marlin	Joan Blaine
	Anne Seymour
	Betty Lou Gerson
	Muriel Kirkland
	Eloise Kummer
	Linda Carlon
Joe Marlin	Bob Griffin
David Post	Carleton Brickert
	Arthur Jacobson
Mac McKenna	John Daly

Oswald Ching	Peter Donald
Philo Sands	Barry Drew
Arnold	Arthur Kohl
	Robert White

Creator/Writer: Jane Cruisinberry
Sponsor: Kleenex
Theme music: Clair de Lune (on piano) by Debussy

MARY NOBLE, BACKSTAGE WIFE
Mutual, then NBC: 1935 to 1959

By the end of this serial, Mary became a great stage star and Larry lost his status as an idol.

Mary Noble	Vivian Fridell
	Claire Niesen
Larry Noble	Ken Griffin
	James Meighan
	Guy Sorel
Lady Clara	Ethel Owen
Marcia Mannering	Eloise Kummer
Maude Marlowe	Henrietta Tedro
	Ethel Wilson
Pop	Alan MacAteer
Ada	Kay Renwick

Creators: Frank and Anne Hummert
Sponsor: Dr. Lyons tooth powder
Theme music: The Rose of Tralee
Epigraph: "The story of Mary Noble, a little Iowa girl who married Larry Noble, handsome matinee idol, dream sweetheart of a million other women, and her struggle to keep his love in the complicated atmosphere of backstage life."

PEPPER YOUNG'S FAMILY
NBC: 1936 to 1959

Drama about a family. It was first called *Red Adams* on evening radio in 1932, but when Beechnut became the sponsor, the company didn't want the title to remind people of its competitor, Adams Gum, and so the title became *Red Davis*. Later the name was changed to *Forever Young*, and finally to *Pepper Young's Family*.

Larry ("Pepper") Young	Curtis Arnell
	Lawson Zerbe
	Mason Adams
Linda Benton Young ...	Eunice Howard
Mary Young	Marion Barney
Sam Young	Jack Roseleigh
	Bill Adams
	Thomas Chalmers
Peggy Young Trent	Betty Wragge
Carter Trent	Bert Brazier
	James Krieger
	Stacy Harris
	Michael Fitzmaurice
	Chester Stratton
	Bob Pollock
Ivy Trent	Irene Hubbard
Horace Trent	Charles Webster
Edie Gray Hoyt	Jean Sothern
Andy Hoyt	Blaine Cordner
Hattie Williams	Greta Kvalden
Nick Havens	John Kane
Hal Trent	Madeline Pierce

Creator/Writer: Elaine Sterne Carrington
Theme music: Au Matin

DAVID HARUM
NBC Blue: 1936 to 1950

David Harum was a conservative but lovable small-town banker and Susan was his longtime sweetheart.

David Harum	Wilmer Walter
	Craig McDonnell
	Cameron Prud'Homme
Susan Price Wells	Peggy Allenby
	Gertrude Warner
	Joan Tompkins
Aunt Polly	Charme Allen
	Eva Condon
Tess Terwilliger	Florence Lake
Lish Harum	William Shelley
Willy	William Redfield

Creators: Frank and Anne Hummert
Theme music: Sunbonnet Sue

BIG SISTER
CBS: 1936 to 1952

Grown sisters Ruth and Sue Evans faced life.

Ruth Evans Wayne	Alice Frost
	Nancy Marshall
	Marjorie Anderson
	Mercedes McCambridge
	Grace Matthews
Dr. John Wayne	Martin Gabel
	Paul McGrath
	Staats Cotsworth
Sue Evans Miller	Haila Stoddard
	Dorothy McGuire
	Peggy Conklin
	Fran Carden
Jerry Miller	Ned Wever
Ned Evans	Michael O'Day
Lola Mitchell	Arlene Francis
Eric Ramsey	Richard Widmark
Richard Wayne	Jim Ameche
Dr. Seabrook	Everett Sloane

Creator/Writer: Lilian Lauferty
Sponsor: Rinso (Lever Brothers)
Theme music: Valse Bluette

MYRT AND MARGE
CBS: 1937 to 1942

Story of two Broadway chorus girls who mostly gabbed to each other about their experiences. The show had been on nighttime radio since 1931. In real life, the players were mother and daughter. The last names of their characters, Spear and Minter, were meant to plug the sponsor's product, Wrigley's Spearmint Gum.

Myrtle Spear	Myrtle Vail
Marjorie Minter	Donna Damerel Fick
	Helen Mack
Clarence Tiffingtuffer ..	Ray Hedge
Thaddeus Cornfelder ..	Cliff Arquette
Tad Smith	Robert Walker
Jack Arnold	Vinton Hayworth
	Santos Ortega

Lizzie Lump	Marjorie Crossland
Jimmy Minter	Ray Appleton
Detective O'Toole	John Daly

Creator/Writer: Myrtle Vail
Theme music: Poor Butterfly

AUNT JENNY'S TRUE LIFE STORIES
CBS: 1937 to 1956

Radio's most popular daytime anthology series. Aunt Jenny was the storyteller.

Aunt Jenny	Edith Spencer
	Agnes Young
Danny	Dan Seymour
Whistling canary	Henry Boyd

Theme music: Believe Me, If All Those Endearing Young Charms
Sponsor: Spry and Rinso (Lever Brothers)

THE GUIDING LIGHT
NBC Red: 1937 to 1956

Originally, a story about the Rutledge family; later in the forties the Bauers became prominent. The show is the longest running soap opera of all time. See page 210.

Dr. John Rutledge	Arthur Peterson
Mary Rutledge	Sarajane Wells
	Mercedes McCambridge
Ned Holden	Ed Prentiss
	John Hodiak
Rose Kransky	Ruth Bailey
	Charlotte Manson
Jacob Kransky	Seymour Young
Mrs. Kransky	Mignon Schreiber
Charlotte Brandon	Betty Lou Gerson
Roy Fencher	Willard Waterman
Meta Bauer White	Jone Allison
Ted White	Arnold Moss
Trudy Bauer	Laurette Fillbrandt
Bill Bauer	Lyle Sudrow
Bertha Bauer	Ann Shepherd
	Charita Bauer

Papa Bauer	Theo Goetz
Mama Bauer	Adelaide Klein

Creator/Writer: Irna Phillips
Sponsor: Procter & Gamble
Theme music: Aphrodite

OUR GAL SUNDAY
CBS: 1937 to 1959

Despite his continual suspicions, Sunday was never unfaithful to Lord Henry.

Sunday Brinthrope	Dorothy Lowell
	Vivian Smolen
Lord Henry Brinthrope	Karl Swenson
	Alistair Duncan
Slim Delaney	Van Hetlin
Oliver Drexton	Santos Ortega
Madelyn Travers	Joan Tompkins
Gann Murray	Hugh Marlowe
Prudence Graham	Anne Seymour
Countess Florenze	Ara Gerald
Lile Florenze	Inge Adams
Lanette	Charita Bauer

Creators: Frank and Anne Hummert
Sponsor: Anacin (American Home Products)
Theme music: Red River Valley
Epigraph: "The story of an orphan girl named Sunday from the little mining town of Silver Creek, Colorado, who in young womanhood married England's richest, most handsome lord, Lord Henry Brinthrope. The story asks the question, 'Can this girl from a mining town in the West find happiness as the wife of a wealthy and titled Englishman?'"

LORENZO JONES
NBC Red: 1937 to 1955

Comic soap about an impractical inventor and his more conservative wife Belle. In later years it experienced a drastic stylistic change. To help the show's sagging ratings, Lorenzo was given amnesia and the comedy was removed, to make the show more like other serious soaps.

Lorenzo Jones	Karl Swenson
Belle Jones	Betty Garde
	Lucille Wall
Irma Barker	Nancy Sheridan
	Mary Wickes
	Grace Keddy
Jim Barker	John Brown
	Frank Behrens
Chester Van Dyne	Louis Hector
Clarence K. Muggins . . .	Roland Winters
	Kermit Murdock
Angus	Art Carney
Judy	Colleen Ward

Creators: Frank and Anne Hummert
Theme music: Funiculi, Funicula
Epigraph: "We all know couples like lovable, impractical Lorenzo and his wife, Belle. Their struggle for security is anybody's story, but somehow with Lorenzo, it has more smiles than tears."

THE ROAD OF LIFE
NBC Blue and Red: 1937 to 1959

The famous hospital soap about Dr. Jim Brent, who married Jocelyn McLeod; the forerunner, by Irna Phillips, to all other hospital and medical soaps. All emergencies were preceded by: "Dr. Brent . . . call surgery . . ."

Dr. Jim Brent	Ken Griffin
	Matt Crowley
	Don MacLaughlin
	David Ellis
	Howard Teichmann
Mrs. Brent	Effie Palmer
Mr. Brent	Joe Latham
John ("Butch") Brent . .	Donald Kraatz
	Roland Butterfield
	Lawson Zerbe
	David Ellis
	Bill Lipton
Francie Brent	Elizabeth Lawrence
Dr. Carson McVicker . . .	Charlotte Manson

Carol Evans Martin	Lesley Woods
	Barbara Luddy
	Louise Fitch
	Marion Shockley
Frank Dana	John Larkin
Jocelyn McLeod	Virginia Dwyer

Creator and first writer: Irna Phillips
Sponsor: Procter & Gamble
Theme music: Pathetique Symphony

WOMAN IN WHITE
NBC Red: 1938 to 1948

About nurse Karen Adams, who married Dr. Kirk Harding, and featuring other doctors, all involved with exciting hospital crises.

Karen Adams Harding . .	Luise Barclay
	Betty Ruth Smith
	Betty Lou Gerson
	Peggy Knudsen
John Adams	Willard Farnum
	Harry Elders
Janet Munson Adams . .	Edith Perry
	Lesley Woods
	Barbara Luddy
Dr. Kirk Harding	Karl Weber
Dr. Lee Markham	Macdonald Carey
	Marvin Miller
Dr. Paul Burton	Ken Griffin
Eileen Holmes	Sarajane Wells

Creator/Writer: Irna Phillips
Sponsor: Pillsbury
Theme music: Interlude by Lucas

JOYCE JORDAN, GIRL INTERNE
(later called *JOYCE JORDAN, M.D.*)
CBS: 1938 to 1948

About the struggle of a young woman to make it in a traditional man's profession.

Joyce Jordan	Ann Shepherd
	Betty Winkler
	Elspeth Eric
	Gertrude Warner

Dr. Clifford Reed	Raymond Edward Johnson
Dr. Alan Webster	Richard Widmark
Granny Hewitt	Ruth McDevitt
Vic Manion	Frank Lovejoy
Ada Manion	Vera Allen
Dean Russell	Larry Haines
Dr. Mildermaul	Ed Begley
Dr. Rheinhardt	Stefan Schnabel

Creator/Writer: Julian Funt
Sponsor: General Mills

VALIANT LADY
NBC Red: 1938 to 1946

One of a number of soaps about strong wives and their weaker husbands. The show was written for Joan Blaine, who had also originated the title role in *The Story of Mary Marlin*, which had the same theme.

Joan Barrett	Joan Blaine
Jim Barrett	William Johnstone
Dr. Truman ("Tubby") Scott	Charles Carroll
	Bartlett Robinson

Creators: Frank and Anne Hummert
Sponsor: General Mills
Theme music: Estrelita
Epigraph: "The story of a brave woman and her brilliant but unstable husband—the story of her struggle to keep his feet planted firmly on the pathway to success."

YOUNG WIDDER BROWN
NBC Red: 1938 to 1956

Ellen Brown ran a tearoom; patient Dr. Anthony Loring waited interminably for her hand in marriage while she solved one sticky problem after another.

Ellen Brown	Florence Freeman
Janey Brown	Marilyn Erskine
Mark Brown	Tommy Donnelly
Dr. Anthony Loring	Ned Wever

Victoria Loring	Ethel Remey
	Riza Joyce
	Kay Strozzi
Maria Hawkins	Agnes Young
	Lorene Scott
	Alice Yourman
Peter Turner	Clayton "Bud" Collyer
Roger Power	Frank Lovejoy
Millie Baxter	Charita Bauer
Mark	Dick Van Patten

Theme music: In The Gloaming
Sponsor: Sterling Drugs

STELLA DALLAS
NBC Red: 1938 to 1955

Based on the novel by Olive Higgins Prouty and preceded by the famous Barbara Stanwyck movie. Stella's rich son-in-law, Dick Grosvenor, 'committed suicide' each year in August for a period of three years. The actor, Macdonald Carey, had a nasal problem which impeded his breathing enough to keep him from the microphone during the height of the hay fever season, so the writers would use this as an opportunity for high drama. After Carey recovered, Dick would always turn up alive.

Stella Dallas	Anne Elstner
Laurel Dallas Grosvenor	Joy Hathaway
	Vivian Smolen
Dick Grosvenor	Carleton Young
	Macdonald Carey
	Spencer Bentley
	George Lambert
	Michael Fitzmaurice
Mrs. Grosvenor	Jane Houston
Stephen Dallas	Frederick Tozere
Helen Dallas	Julie Benell
Ada Dexter	Helen Claire
Gus Grady	Walter Kinsella
Sam Ellis	Mandel Kramer
Nellie Ellis	Barbara Barton

Creators: Frank and Anne Hummert
Sponsor: Phillips Milk of Magnesia
Theme Music: How Can I Leave Thee?

Epigraph: "The true-to-life story of mother love and sacrifice, in which Stella Dallas saw her own beloved daughter Laurel marry into wealth and society and, realizing the differences in their tastes and worlds, went out of Laurel's life."

LIFE CAN BE BEAUTIFUL
NBC Red: 1938 to 1954

One day young Chichi walked into the Slightly Read Book Shop and encountered its wise old Jewish proprietor, Papa David Solomon, who began teaching her his optimistic philosophy of life; thereafter she became his ward. Listeners thrilled to Papa David's unending wisdom. The show was known in the industry as "Elsie Beebe", a pronunciation of the acronym.

Carol ("Chichi") Conrad	Alice Reinheart
	Teri Keane
Papa David Solomon . . .	Ralph Locke
Stephen Hamilton	Earl Larrimore
	John Holbrook
Barry Markham	Richard Kollmar
	Dick Nelson
Nellie Conrad	Agnes Moorehead
Logan Smith	Clayton "Bud" Collyer
Hank Bristow	Ian Martin
Mrs. S. Kent Wadsworth	Adelaide Klein
Gyp Mendoza	Waldemar Kappel
	Paul Stewart

Writers: Carl Bixby and Don Becker
Sponsor: Procter & Gamble
Epigraph: "*Life Can Be Beautiful* is an inspiring message of faith drawn from life."

WHEN A GIRL MARRIES
CBS: 1939 to 1957

A young socialite defies her family and marries beneath her station, purely for love. Most of the show's history concerned Joan's marital problems after she married Harry Davis, although the plot also dealt with the dilemmas of friends and relatives.

Joan Field Davis	Noel Mills
	Mary Jane Higby
Harry Davis	John Raby
	Robert Haag
	Whitfield Connor
	Lyle Sudrow
Anne Davis	Marion Barney
Tom Davis	Bill Quinn
Dr. Samuel Tilden Field	Edwin Jerome
Mrs. Field	Ethel Wilson
Eve Topping Stanley . . .	Irene Winston
Phil Stanley	Michael Fitzmaurice
	Richard Kollmar
	Staats Cotsworth
	Karl Weber
	Paul McGrath
Mrs. Stanley	Ethel Owen
Lillie	Georgia Burke

Creator/Writer: Elaine Sterne Carrington
Sponsor: Prudential Insurance
Theme music: Seranade by Drigo
Epigraph: "Dedicated to everyone who has ever been in love."

THE RIGHT TO HAPPINESS
NBC Blue: 1939 to 1960

Irna Phillips created this show out of a subplot of her *The Guiding Light.* She took the Kranskys of that show and made them the new main characters; then the Kramer family became important, with Carolyn Kramer as the heroine.

Carolyn Kramer Nelson	Claudia Morgan
	Eloise Kummer
Dwight Kramer	Frank Behrens
	Ed Prentiss
	David Gothard
Mr. Kramer	Julian Noa
Mrs. Kramer	Leora Thatcher
Miles Nelson	Gary Merrill
	John Larkin
Dr. Richard Campbell . .	Les Damon
	Alexander Scourby
Ted Wakefield	Jimmy Dobson
	William Redfield
Constance Wakefield . . .	Violet Heming

Rose Kransky . . . . Luise Barclay
                             Ruth Bailey

Creator/Writer: Irna Phillips
Sponsor: Procter & Gamble
Theme music: Song of the Soul by Breil.

YOUNG DR. MALONE
NBC Blue: 1939 to 1960

The famous hospital soap about the Malone family, including Dr. Jerry Malone and his son, Dr. David Malone.

Dr. Jerry Malone . . . . . . Alan Bunce
                             Carl Frank
                             Charles Irving
                             Sandy Becker
Ann Richards Malone . . Elizabeth Reller
                             Barbara Weeks
Robbie Hughes . . . . Richard Coogan
Alice Hughes . . . . Nancy Coleman
Jessie Hughes . . . . Isobel Elsom
Dr. Sewell Crawford . . . . Paul McGrath
Lucille Crawford . . . . . . Janet McGrew
Dr. David Malone . . . . . . Bill Lipton
Jill Malone . . . . Joan Lazer
                             Rosemary Rice
Tracey Malone . . . . Jone Allison
                             Joan Alexander
                             Gertrude Warner
Sam Williams . . . . Berry Kroeger
                             Martin Blaine

Sponsor: Post Bran Flakes (General Foods)

PORTIA FACES LIFE
CBS: 1940 to 1951

All about the brilliant lady lawyer.

Portia Blake Manning . . Lucille Wall
Walter Manning . . . . Myron McCormick
                             Bartlett Robinson
Arline Manning . . . . Joan Banks
Dickie Blake . . . . Raymond Ives
                             Larry Robinson

                             Alastair Kyle
                             Edwin Bruce
Kirk Roder . . . . Carleton Young
Dr. Stanley Holton . . . . . Donald Briggs
Miss Daisy . . . . Henrietta Tedro
                             Doris Rich
John Parker . . . . William Johnstone
Clint Morley . . . . Santos Ortega
Kathy Marsh . . . . Marjorie Anderson
                             Esther Ralston
                             Selena Royle
                             Rosaline Greene
                             Anne Seymour
                             Elizabeth Reller
Meg Griffin . . . . Alison Skipworth

Creator/Writer: Mona Kent
Sponsor: General Foods

THE SECOND MRS. BURTON
CBS: 1940 to 1960

Originally, the story of Terry Burton's struggle to take the place of Stan Burton's first wife and gain acceptance by Stan's family. In the fifties, the show became a light comedy.

Terry Burton . . . . Sharon Douglas
                             Claire Niesen
                             Patsy Campbell
                             Teri Keane
Stan Burton . . . . Dwight Weist
Mother Burton . . . . Evelyn Varden
                             Ethel Owen
Brad Burton . . . . Dix Davis
                             Karl Weber
                             Ben Cooper
                             Larry Robinson
Marcia Burton Archer . . Alice Frost
Lew Archer . . . . Larry Haines
Lillian Anderson . . . . . . Elspeth Eric
Jim Anderson . . . . King Calder
Rev. Cornwell . . . . Bartlett Robinson
Don Cornwell . . . . Robert Readick

Writers: Priscilla Kent, Martha Alexander, John M. Young, and Hector Chevigny
Sponsor: General Foods

PERRY MASON
CBS: 1943 to 1955

Adventures of the world's most famous lawyer, based on stories by Erle Stanley Gardner.

Perry Mason	Bartlett Robinson
	Santos Ortega
	Donald Briggs
	John Larkin
Della Street	Gertrude Warner
	Jan Miner
	Joan Alexander
Paul Drake	Matt Crowley
	Charles Webster
Lt. Arthur Tragg	Mandel Kramer
	Frank Dane
Sgt. Dorset	Arthur Vinton
Peg Neely	Betty Garde
Mary Blade	Mary Jane Higby

Writers: Irving Vendig, Ruth Borden
Sponsor: Procter & Gamble

ROSEMARY
NBC: 1944 to 1955

Secretary Rosemary married her boss, Bill Roberts, and afterward her solid emotional support helped him surmount numerous crises.

Rosemary Dawson	Betty Winkler
Peter Harvey	Sidney Smith
Bill Roberts	George Keane
	Robert Readick
Tommy Taylor	Jackie Kelk
Patti Dawson	Jone Allison
	Patsy Campbell
Mother Dawson	Marion Barney
Lefty Higgins	Larry Haines
Dr. Jim Cotter	Bill Adams
	Charles Penman
Joyce Miller	Helen Choate
Dick Phillips	James Van Dyk

Creator/Writer: Elaine Sterne Carrington
Sponsor: Procter & Gamble

THIS IS NORA DRAKE
NBC: 1947 to 1959

Nora was assistant to the head of a mental clinic and faced numerous personal and professional problems.

Nora Drake	Charlotte Holland
	Joan Tompkins
	Mary Jane Higby
Arthur Drake	Everett Sloane
	Ralph Bell
Charles Dobbs	Grant Richards
Dorothy Stewart	Elspeth Eric
George Stewart	Leon Janney
Dr. Ken Martinson	Alan Hewitt
Peg Martinson	Lesley Woods
	Joan Alexander
	Mercedes McCambridge
Tom Morley	Robert Readick
Andrew King	Roger DeKoven
Suzanne Turrie	Joan Lorring

Writer: Milton Lewis
Sponsor: Toni home Permanent

THE BRIGHTER DAY
NBC: 1948 to 1956

Story of Rev. Richard Dennis, a widower with five children. The television show began in 1954 and ran simultaneously until the radio show was canceled in 1956. This was one of Irna Phillips's many family stories. See also page 329.

Rev. Richard Dennis . . .	Bill Smith
Liz Dennis	Margaret Draper
	Grace Matthews
Althea Dennis	Jay Meredith
Grayling Dennis	William Redfield
Patsy Dennis	Pat Holsky
Barbara ("Babby")	
Dennis	Lorna Lynn
Sandra Talbot	Ann Hilary
Cliff Sebastian	John Larkin
Jerry	John Raby

Creator: Irna Phillips
Writers: Irna Phillips, Orin Tovrov
Sponsor: Procter & Gamble

ONE MAN'S FAMILY
NBC: 1955 to 1959

Had been a popular nighttime radio serial since 1933, before it went to daytime radio in 1955; about the large Barbour family of San Francisco, where the show was first heard on local radio.

Henry Barbour	J. Anthony Smythe
Fanny Barbour	Minetta Ellen
Paul Barbour	Michael Rafetto
Hazel Barbour Murray .	Bernice Berwin
Claudia Barbour Lacey .	Barbara Fuller
Clifford Barbour	Barton Yarborough
Jack Barbour	Page Gilman
Betty Carter Barbour . .	Jean Rouverol
Joan Roberts Barbour . .	Mary Lou Harrington
Nicky Lacey	Bob Dwyer
Penny Lacey	Ann Whitfield
Dan Murray	Bill Bouchey
Hank Murray	Conrad Binyon
Margaret Murray	Dawn Bender
Teddy Barbour	Jeanne Bates

Creator/Writer: Carlton E. Morse
Theme music: Destiny Waltz by Barnes, and Patricia by Paul Carson

By far the majority of daytime television serials that have come and gone lasted less than ten years. The lists of casts and credits that follows were compiled by John Kelly Genovese with the invaluable help of back issues of Daytime TV, Afternoon TV, TV Guide and TV/Radio Mirror; *The Complete History of Soap Operas* (Dee and Zee Enterprises, 1976); conversations with Charita Bauer, Ann Flood, Ella G. Horsley, Allen Potter, Leonard Stadd, Roger Stafford, Leonard Valenta, Billie Lou Watt and Roy Winsor; and past records kindly shown by John Behrens at the CBS Program Information Department, and the NBC Research Department. An asterisk (*) next to an actor's name indicates that he or she played the part the longest.

A WOMAN TO REMEMBER
DuMont: May 2 to July 15, 1947

About television star Christine Baker and her professional and romantic conflicts with another actress, Carol Winstead; the first network television soap.

Christine Baker .... Patricia Wheel
Steve Hammond ...... John Raby
Carol Winstead .... Joan Castle
Bessie Thatcher .... Ruth McDevitt
Charley Anderson ..... Frank Thomas, Jr.

Writer: John Haggert
Producer: Bob Steele

THESE ARE MY CHILDREN
NBC (local Chicago affiliate): 1947

A story about a mother and her children; Irna Phillips's first television serial, probably based on her radio soap, *Today's Children.*

Mother .... Alma Platto
Children .... Jane Brooksmith, George
                      Kluge, Martha
                      McClain, Eloise
                      Kummer, Joan Arlt

Creator/Writer: Irna Phillips

THE FIRST HUNDRED YEARS
CBS: December 4, 1950 to June 27, 1952

A comic soap about married life, centered on newlyweds Chris and Connie Thayer, who reluctantly set up housekeeping in a bat-infested Victorian house given to them by her parents, the Martins. It was CBS's first daytime serial.

Chris Thayer .... James Lydon
Connie Thayer .... Olive Stacey
                       Anne Sargent
Mr. Thayer .... Don Tobin
Mrs. Thayer .... Valerie Cossart
Mr. Martin .... Robert Armstrong

Mrs. Martin . . . .   Nana Bryant
Margy Martin . . . .   Nancy Malone
                                 Mary Linn Beller
                                 Also: Larry Haines, Nat
                                   Polen, Charles Baxter

Creator/Writer: Jean Holloway
Producer: Hoyt Allen
Directors: Everett Gammon, Gloria Monty
Organist: Clarke Morgan
Packager: Procter & Gamble

MISS SUSAN (later titled, *MARTINSVILLE, U.S.A*)
NBC: 1951 to 1952

Susan Peters, a handicapped actress, starred as wheelchair-ridden attorney Susan Martin.

Susan Martin . . . .   Susan Peters
Nurse . . . .   Katherine Grill
Housekeeper . . . .   Natalie Priest
                                 Also: Robert McQueeny,
                                   John Lormer

HAWKINS FALLS
NBC: 1951 to 1955

Billed as a "TV novel"; an often humorous chronicle of folksy, small town gossips emanating from Chicago. It had expensively staged outdoor scenes.

Clate Weathers . . . .   Frank Dane
Lona Corey . . . .   Bernardine Flynn
Dr. Floyd Corey . . . .   Maurice Copeland
Millie Flaigle . . . .   Ros Twohey
Laif Flaigle . . . .   Wyn Stracke
Belinda Catherwood . . .   Hope Summers
Elmira Cleebe . . . .   Elmira Roessler
·Spec Bassett . . . .   Russ Reed
                                 Also: Barbara Berjer,
                                   Sam Gray, Jean Mowry

Creators/Writers: Roy Winsor and Doug Johnson
Producer/Director: Ben Park

THE EGG AND I
CBS: September 3, 1951 to August 1, 1952

Based on the humorous book by Betty McDonald about city slickers who move to a farm. It premiered the same day as *Search for Tomorrow.*

Betty McDonald . . . .   Pat Kirkland
Bob McDonald . . . .   Frank Craven
Ma Kettle . . . .   Doris Rich
Pa Kettle . . . .   Frank Twedell
Jed Simmons . . . .   Grady Sutton
Lisa Schumacher . . . . . .   Ingeborg Theek
Paula French . . . .   Karen Hale

Based on book by Betty McDonald
Writer: Manya Starr
Producer: Montgomery Ford
Director: Jack Gage
Packager: CBS-TV

THE HOUSE IN THE GARDEN (later titled *FAIRMEADOWS, U.S.A.)*
NBC: 1952

Short-lived story about a small town family.

Father . . . .   Howard St. John
Mother . . . .   Ruth Matteson
Children . . . .   Tom Tyler, Hazel Dawn, Jr.,
                                   Mimi Strangin

THE WORLD OF MR. SWEENEY
NBC: 1953 to 1955

A spinoff of a Kate Smith Show segment; featured a general store owner, his daughter and grandson.

Cicero P. Sweeney . . . . .   Charles Ruggles
Kippie . . . .   Glenn Walken
Kippie's mother . . . .   Helen Wagner

THE BENNETTS
NBC: July 6, 1953 to January 8, 1954

About a married couple; emanated from Chicago.

Wayne Bennett	Don Gibson
Nancy Bennett	Paula Houston
	Also: Sam Gray, Jack
	Lester, Viola Berwick

THREE STEPS TO HEAVEN
NBC: August 3, 1953 to December 31, 1954

Concerned Mary Jane ("Poco") Thurmond, a small town girl hitting New York City and its jet set; it was a combination romance and adventure.

Mary Jane ("Poco") Thurmond	Phyllis Hill
	Diana Douglas
	Kathleen Maguire
Bill Morgan	Walter Brooke
	Gene Blakely
	Mark Roberts
Charlotte Doane	Mona Bruns
Chip Morrison	Robert Webber
Vince Bannister	John Marley
Mrs. Cleve	Harriet McGibbon
Jason Cleve	Lauren Gilbert
Jennifer	Lori March
Mike	Joe Brown, Jr.
Alice	Laurie Ann Vendig

Creator/Writer: Irving Vendig
Director: Gordon Rigsby

FOLLOW YOUR HEART
NBC: August 3, 1953 to January 1954

A television version of the radio soap, *When A Girl Marries*, with different character names; about a debutante who marries against her mother's wishes.

Julie Fielding	Sallie Brophy
Mrs. Fielding	Nancy Sheridan
	Also: John Seymour,
	Anne Seymour, Maxine
	Stuart

Creator/Writer: Elaine Sterne Carrington

VALIANT LADY
CBS: October 12, 1953 to August 16, 1957

Concerned Helen Emerson, widow of inventor Frank Emerson and mother of three. This was not a television remake of the old radio serial, *Valiant Lady*, but a completely new story.

Helen Emerson	Nancy Coleman
	Flora Campbell*
Frank Emerson	Jerome Cowan
Mickey Emerson	James Kirkwood, Jr.
Kim Emerson	Lydia Reed
	Bonnie Sawyer*
Diane Emerson Soames	Anne Pearson
	Dolores Sutton
	Marion Randall
	Leila Martin
Hal Soames	Earl Hammond
Bonnie Withers	Joan Loring
	Shirley Egleston
Capt. Chris Kendall	Lawrence Weber
Linda Kendall	Frances Helm
Elliott Norris	Terry O'Sullivan
Joey Gordon	Martin Balsam
	Also: Margaret Hamilton,
	Helen Wagner, Abby
	Lewis

Creator: Allan Chase
Writers: Charles Elwyn, Martha Alexander, Virginia
    and Adrian Spies
Producers: Carl Green, Leonard Blair
Directors: Ira Cirker, Herbert Kenwith, Ted Corday
Organist: John Gart
Packager: General Mills

WOMAN WITH A PAST
CBS: February 1 to July 2, 1954

About New York fashion designer Lynn Sherwood.

Lynn Sherwood	Constance Ford
Diane Sherwood	Felice Camargo
	Barbara Myers
Steve Rockwell	Gene Lyons
Sylvia Rockwell	Mary Sinclair
	Geraldine Brooks

Pegs . . . . Ann Hegira
Gwen . . . . Jean Stapleton

Creator/Writer: Mona Kent
Producer: Richard Brill
Director: Marcella Cisney

ONE MAN'S FAMILY
NBC: 1954 to 1955

A video version of the Carlton E. Morse radio serial, taken from his old radio scripts; about the Barbour family, who faced changing values as they continued to live in their elegant home in the Seacliff section of San Francisco.

Henny Barbour . . . . Theodor Von Eltz
Fanny Barbour . . . . Mary Adams
Paul Barbour . . . . Russell Thorson
Claudia Barbour . . . . . . Linda Leighton
Clifford Barbour . . . . . . James Lee
Jack Barbour . . . . Martin Dean
Hazel Barbour Roberts . Anne Whitfield
Johnny Roberts . . . . Jack Edwards

Creator/Writer: Carlton E. Morse
Musical Director: Paul Watson

PORTIA FACES LIFE (later titled THE INNER FLAME)
CBS: April 5, 1954 to July 1, 1955

Televised version of the radio serial about a lady lawyer and her family.

Portia Manning . . . . Frances Reid
Fran Carlon
Walter Manning . . . . Donald Woods
Karl Swenson
Shirley Manning . . . . Renne Jarrett
Ginger McManus
Dickie Blake . . . . Charles Taylor
Dorie Blake . . . . Jean Gillespie
Tony Farraday . . . . Mark Miller
Kathy Baker . . . . Elizabeth York
Bill Baker . . . . Richard Kendrick

Also: Sally Gracie, Mary Fickett

Writers: Mona Kent, Charles Gussman
Producer: Beverly Smith
Directors: Lloyd Gross, Hal Cooper
Musical Director: Tony Mottola (guitar soloist)
Packager: General Foods

THE SEEKING HEART
CBS: July 5 to December 10, 1954

About a crime doctor, his social-climbing wife and his ambitious female assistant.

Dr. John Adam . . . . Scott Forbes
Grace Adam . . . . Dorothy Lovett
Dr. Robinson McKay . . . Flora Campbell
Also: Audrey Christie, Judith Braun, James Yarbrough

Writer: Welbourn Kelley
Producer: Minerva Ellis
Director: James Yarbrough
Organist: Bill Meeder
Packager: Procter & Gamble

FIRST LOVE
NBC: July 5, 1954 to December 30, 1955

About newlyweds; aired live from Philadelphia.

Lauri Kennedy James . . Patricia Barry
Zachary James . . . . Val DuFour
Tod Andrews
Matthew James . . . . Paul McGrath
Doris Kennedy . . . . Peggy Allenby
Paul Kennedy . . . . Melville Ruick
Mike Kennedy . . . . John Dutra
Judge Kennedy . . . . Howard Smith
Quentin Andrews . . . . . Frederic Downs
Chris . . . . Frank Thomas, Jr.
Amy . . . . Rosemary Prinz

Creator/Headwriter: Manya Starr
Producer: Al Morrison
Packager: Jergens

A TIME TO LIVE
NBC: July 5 to December 31, 1954

Career girl story about roving reporter Julie Byron.

Julie Byron	Pat Sully
Madge Byron	Viola Berwick
Don Riker	Larry Kerr
	John Himes
Carl Sherman	Jack Lester
Greta Powers	Zohra Alton
John Eustice	Will Hussung
Lt. Miles Dow	Dort Clark
Daphne	Toni Gilman
Chick	Len Wayland
Dr. Clay	Dana Elcar

Creator/Executive Producer: Adrian Samish
Writer: William Barrett
Producer/Director: Alan Beaumont

CONCERNING MISS MARLOWE
NBC: July 5, 1954 to July 1, 1955

About aging actress Maggie Marlowe, whose love life began to show promise as her career went on the decline.

Maggie Marlowe	Helen Shields
	Louise Albritton
Bill Cooke	John Raby
Harriet the Hat	Jane Seymour
Linda Cabot	Sarah Burton
Hugh Fraser	Lauren Gilbert
Jim Gavin	Efrem Zimbalist, Jr.
Mike Donovan	Byron Sanders
John Moran	Philip Coolidge
Mrs. Koester	Leora Thatcher

GOLDEN WINDOWS
NBC: July 5, 1954 to April 1, 1955

Storybook serial about the love life of classical pianist Juliet Goodwin.

Juliet Goodwin	Leila Martin
Charles Goodwin	Eric Dressler
Tom Anderson	Herbert Patterson

John Brandon	Grant Sullivan
Mrs. Brandon	Harriet McGibbon
Joseph Kindler	Frank Hammerton
Miss Bigelow	Ethel Remey
Lt. Thomas	Ralph Camargo
Hazel	Barbara Cook
Larry	Dean Harens

Packager: Procter & Gamble

THE GREATEST GIFT
NBC: August 30, 1954 to July 1, 1955

Story of a private medical practice.

Dr. Eve Allen	Anne Burr
Dr. Phil Stone	Philip Foster
Harold Matthews	Martin Balsam
	Will Hare
Betty Matthews	Athena Lorde
Jim Hanson	Jack Klugman
Ned Blackman	Ward Costello
	Gene Peterson
Harriet	Anne Meara
Lillian	Mary K. Wells
Arthur	Frank Maxwell

Creator: Adrian Samish

MODERN ROMANCES
NBC: October 4, 1954 to 1958

Anthology serial narrated by Martha Scott and Mel Brandt; presented a different story every week, taken from Modern Romances magazine.

Writers: Harry Junkin, Bob Corcoran
Producers: Jerry Layton, Wilbur Stark
Director: H. Wesley Kenney

THE ROAD OF LIFE
CBS: December 13, 1954 to July 1, 1955

A continuation of Irna Phillips's famous radio saga of Dr. Jim Brent, his family and their rich adversaries, the Overtons.

Dr. Jim Brent . . . . Don MacLaughlin
Jocelyn McLeod Brent . Virginia Dwyer
Sybil Overton Fuller . . . Barbara Becker
Conrad Overton . . . . Charles Dingle
Hugh Overton . . . . Douglass Parkhirst
Malcolm Overton . . . . . Harry Holcombe
Reggie Ellis . . . . Dorothy Sands
John Brent . . . . Bill Lipton
Francie Brent . . . . Elizabeth Lawrence
Frank Dana . . . . John Larkin
                              Chuck Webster

Creator: Irna Phillips
Writer: Charles Gussman
Producer: John Egan
Director: Walter Gorman
Organist: Charles Paul
Packager: Procter & Gamble

THE WAY OF THE WORLD
NBC: January 2 to October 7, 1955

Anthology soap taken from women's magazines.

Linda Porter (narrator)   Gloria Lewis

Packager: Borden

A DATE WITH LIFE
NBC: October 10, 1955 to June 29, 1956

Anthology serial about life in Bay City. The narrator, Jim Bradley, was editor of the Bay City *News*.

Jim Bradley (narrator) . Logan Field
Tom Bradley (his
  brother, later
  narrator) . . . . Mark Roberts

Producer: Therese Lewis
Organist: John Gart
Packager: Borden

HOTEL COSMOPOLITAN
CBS: August 19, 1957 to April 11, 1958

Anthology soap using a swank hotel as the setting for stories, narrated by Donald Woods.

Creator/Executive Producer: Roy Winsor
Director: John J. Desmond
Organist: Charles Paul
Packager: Roy Winsor Productions for American
              Home Products, Inc.

THE VERDICT IS YOURS
CBS: September 2, 1957 to September 28, 1962

Anthology serial presenting simulated trials without scripts; it featured court reporters and a studio audience which determined the outcome of the cases. Veteran mystery writers, however, outlined the cases.

Court reporters . . . . Jim McKay
                              Bill Stout
                              Jack Whittaker

Producers: Eugene Burr, Bertram Berman
Directors: Byron Paul, Al Rafkin

KITTY FOYLE
NBC: January 22, to September 26, 1958

Based on the novel and movie, which had starred Ginger Rogers as the working girl heroine.

Kitty Foyle . . . . Kathleen Murray
Pop Foyle . . . . Ralph Dunne
Ed Foyle . . . . Bob Hastings
Sophie Foyle . . . . Kay Medford
Mac Foyle . . . . Larry Robinson
Wyn Strafford . . . . William Redfield
Molly Scharf . . . . Judy Lewis
Molly as a girl . . . . Patty Duke
Rosie Rittenhouse . . . . . Les Damon
                              Also: Teri Keane, Arlene
                                Golonka

Writers: Carlton E. Morse, Sarett Rudley
Producer: Charles Irving

TODAY IS OURS
NBC: June 30 to December 26, 1958

Story of school principal Laura Manning, her ex-husband and small son. The show included the character of Dr. David Malone, who was the Manning family doctor. When *Today Is Ours* was discontinued, Dr. David Malone and his own family found themselves the new central characters of *Young Dr. Malone*, which replaced *Today Is Ours*.

Laura Manning	Patricia Benoit
Karl Manning	Patrick O'Neal
Leslie Manning	Joyce Lear
Nicky Manning	Peter Lazer
Glenn Turner	Ernest Graves
	Also: Jean Stapleton,
	John McGovern,
	Audrey Christie

Creators/Writers: Julian Funt and David Lesan
Packager: Procter & Gamble

YOUNG DR. MALONE
NBC: December 29, 1958 to March 29, 1963

Continuation of the radio serial; chronicled the later life of the Malone family and their associates at Valley Hospital in Denison, Maryland. The radio show ran concurrently for a year with the television serial but had a different story line: Dr. Jerry Malone, young David's father, was running the Three Oaks Clinic.

Dr. Jerry Malone	William Prince
Tracey Malone	Virginia Dwyer
	Augusta Dabney*
Dr. David Malone	John Connell
Jill Malone Renfrew	Kathleen Widdoes
	Freda Holloway
	Sarah Hardy
Emory Bannister	Judson Laire
Clare Bannister Steele .	Lesley Woods
Lionel Steele	Martin Blaine
Lisha Steele Koda	Zina Bethune
	Michele Tuttle
	Susan Hallaran

	Patty McCormack
Faye Bannister Koda . . .	Lenka Peterson
	Chase Crosley
Dr. Stefan Koda	Michael Ingram
Dierdre Bannister	Margot Anders
	Elizabeth St. Clair
Laddie Bannister	John Vickers
Dr. Ted Powell	Peter Brandon
Dr. Eileen Seaton	Emily McLaughlin
Peter Brooks	Robert Lansing
Phyllis Brooks	Barbara O'Neill
Ernest Cooper	Robert Drivas
	Nicholas Pryor
Fran Merrill	Patricia Bosworth
Jody Baker	Stephen Bolster
Clara Kershaw	Joyce Van Patten
Larry Renfrew	Dick Van Patten
Gail Prentiss	Joan Hackett
Harold Cranston	William Post, Jr.
Amanda Pennypacker . .	Ruth McDevitt
Gig Houseman Malone .	Diana Hyland
Lillian Houseman	Ann Shoemaker
Sam Langdon	Stephen Elliott
Stretch Collins	Jack Grimes
Dr. Matt Steele	Eddie Jones
	Franklyn Spodak
	Nicolas Coster
Dr. Fred McNeill	Hugh Franklin
Natalie Price	Joan Wetmore
Marge Wagner	Teri Keane
Erica Brandt	Ann Williams

Creator: Irna Phillips
Writers: Julian Funt, Charles Gussman, Harry Junkin, Ian Martin, Richard Holland
Producers: Lucy Ferri, Carol Irwin, Doris Quinlan
Directors: Walter Gorman, James Young, Tom Donovan
Organists: Billy Nalle, Charles Nalle
Packagers: Procter & Gamble, NBC-TV

FOR BETTER OR WORSE
CBS: June 29, 1959 to June 24, 1960

Anthology series of once-a-week stories about marital problems, based on the files of sociologist Dr. James A. Peterson; narrated by Jim Bannon and Dr. Peterson.

Writers: James L. Henderson, Jack Kelsey, Pauline Stone, Mike Cosgrove
Executive Producer: John Guedel
Producer: Hal Cooper
Directors: Hal Cooper, Dennis Patrick
Organist: Kip Walton
Packager: Lever Bros.

THE HOUSE ON HIGH STREET
NBC: September 29, 1959 to February 5, 1960

Anthology series; probation officer John Collier appeared in stories based on actual juvenile cases.

John Collier . . . . Philip Abbott
Also: Judge James Gehrig, Dr. Harris B. Peck

FULL CIRCLE
CBS: June 27, 1960 to March 1, 1961

Concerned wanderer Gary Donovan, who found romance and intrigue in the town of Crowder, Virginia, and fell at odds with the town's founding family; produced in Hollywood.

Gary Donovan . . . . Robert Fortier
Dr. Kit Aldrich . . . . Jean Byron
Lisa Linda Crowder . . . . Dyan Cannon
Loyal Crowder . . . . John McNamara
Virgil Denker . . . . Michael Ross
Ellen Denker . . . . Nancy Millard
Carter Talton . . . . Byron Foulger
David Talton . . . . Bill Lundmark
Beth Perce . . . . Amzie Strickland
Ray Pollard . . . . Andrew Collmar
Deputy . . . . Sam Edwards

Writer: William Barrett
Producer: Norman Morgan
Directors: Bill Howell, Livia Granito
Musical Director: Marty Klein

THE CLEAR HORIZON
CBS: July 11, 1960 to March 1, 1961 and March 8 to June 11, 1962

An experimental drama about astronauts and their wives at Cape Canaveral; from Hollywood.

Roy Selby . . . . Edward Kemmer
Ann Selby . . . . Phyllis Avery
Ricky Selby . . . . Jimmy Carter
Charles Herbert
Greg Selby . . . . Craig Curtis
Lois Adams . . . . Denise Alexander
Col. Theodore Adams . . William Roerick
Harry Moseby . . . . Rusty Lane
Frances Moseby . . . . Eve McVeagh
Lt. Sig Levy . . . . Michael Fox
Mitchell Corbin . . . . Richard Coogan
Betty Howard . . . . Jan Shepard
Dr. Enid Ross . . . . Lee Meriwhether
Col. Tate . . . . Ted Knight

Creator/Writer: Manya Starr
Producer: Charles Pollacheck
Directors: Joseph Behar, Hal Cooper
Organist: Kip Walton
Packager: Colgate-Palmolive

THE ROAD TO REALITY
ABC: October 10, 1960 to March 31, 1961

Highly experimental show featuring members of a psychological encounter group; ABC's first serial.

Dr. Lewis . . . . John Beal
Vic . . . . Robert Drew
Rosalind . . . . Robin Howard
Margaret . . . . Eugenia Rawls
Joan . . . . Judith Braun
Lee . . . . James Dimitri
Chris . . . . Kay Doubleday

OUR FIVE DAUGHTERS
NBC: January 2 to September 28, 1962

Centered on Helen and Jim Lee and their five daughters; replaced *From These Roots* in a late afternoon time slot.

Helen Lee	Esther Ralston		Susan Garrett	Peggy McCay
Jim Lee	Michael Keen		Dan Garrett	Paul Picerni
Anne Lee	Jacqueline Courtney		Ann Reynolds	Susan Brown
Marjorie Lee	Iris Joyce		Walter Reynolds	Michael Mikler
Jane Lee	Nuella Dierking		Lena Karr	Norma Connolly
Barbara Lee	Patricia Allison		Jerry Karr	Pat Rossen
Mary Weldon	Wynne Miller		Liz Forsythe Stevens	Floy Dean
Don Weldon	Ben Hayes		Matt Stevens	Charles Grodin
Uncle Charlie	Robert W. Stewart			Scott Graham
Greta Hitchcock	Janis Young		Irene Forsythe	Constance Moore
George Barr	Ralph Ellis		Roy Gilroy	Barry Russo
Pat	Ed Griffith		Aunt Alex	Irene Tedrow
			Carol West	Susan Seaforth
			Jill McComb	Betty Conner
				Brenda Benet
			Gillespie	Robert Hogan

Creators: Leonard Stadd and Eugene Burr
Writers: Leonard Stadd, Sid Ellis
Producer: Eugene Burr
Director: Paul Lammers
Packager: NBC-TV

Creator: James Elward
Writers: James Elward, Frances Rickett
Executive Producer: Richard Dunn
Producer: Eugene Burr
Directors: Frank Pacelli, Livia Granito

BEN JERROD, ATTORNEY AT LAW
NBC: April 1 to June 28, 1963

Tale of a big-time lawyer's decision to find himself, in a small town, Indian Hill; taped in Burbank, California. This was the first serial to be broadcast regularly in color.

Ben Jerrod	Michael M. Ryan
John Abbott	Addison Richards
Janet Donelli	Regina Gleason
Peter Morrison	Peter Hansen
Jim O'Hara	Ken Scott
Lil	Martine Bartlett
Engle	William Phillips
Lt. Choates	Lyle Talbot

Creator/Executive Producer: Roy Winsor
Writer: William Kendall Clarke
Producer: Joseph Hardy
Director: Fred Carney
Packager: Roy Winsor Productions for American Home Products, Inc.

THE YOUNG MARRIEDS
ABC: October 5, 1964 to March 25, 1966

Story of four suburban couples; from Hollywood.

FLAME IN THE WIND
ABC: December 28, 1964 to June 25, 1965
A TIME FOR US
ABC: June 28, 1965 to December 16, 1966

Originally a story about class conflict in a small town and the problems of young love. *A Time For Us* was the same serial, except that the family name Skerba was changed to the less ethnic Driscoll.

Martha Skerba	Lenka Peterson
Al Skerba	Roy Poole
Linda Skerba	Barbara Rodell
	Jane Elliot
	Beret Arcaya
	Joanna Miles
Jane Skerba Reynolds	Margaret Ladd
	Beverly Hayes*
Steve Reynolds	Gordon Gray
	Tom Fielding*
Roxanne Reynolds	Margaret Hayes
Craig Reynolds	Frank Schofield
Jason Farrel	Walter Coy
Leslie Farrel	Rita Lloyd
Kate Austen	Kathleen Maguire

Chris Austen	Richard Thomas
Louise Austen	Josephine Nichols
Paul Davis	Conard Fowkes

Writer: Don Ettlinger
Producer: Joseph Hardy
Director: Tom Donovan
Story Editor: Irna Phillips

MOMENT OF TRUTH
NBC: January 4 to November 5, 1965

About college professor Robert Wallace; produced in Canada.

Dr. Robert Wallace	Douglass Watson
Nancy Wallace	Louise King
Sheila Wallace	Barbara Pierce
Johnny Wallace	Michael Dodds
Dr. Russell Wingate	Ivor Barry
Monique Wingate	Fernande Giroux
Vince Conway	Peter Donat
Gil Bennett	John Bethune
Linda Harris	Anna Hagan
Barbara Harris	Mira Pawluk

OUR PRIVATE WORLD
CBS: May 5 to September 10, 1965

This prime time, twice-weekly spinoff of *As The World Turns* found Lisa Hughes, now involved with the wealthy Eldredge family, in the posh Chicago suburb of Lake Forest. The show later had the Eldredges overshadow Lisa, disappointing fans of *As The World Turns*.

Lisa Hughes	Eileen Fulton
Helen Eldredge	Geraldine Fitzgerald
John Eldredge	Nicolas Coster
Tom Eldredge	Sam Groom
Eve Eldredge Robertson	Julienne Marie
Brad Robertson	Robert Drivas
Dick Robertson	Kenneth Tobey
Ethel Robertson	Grace Albertson
Sandy Larson	Sandra Smith
Dr. Tony Larson	David O'Brien
Fran Martin	Pamela Murphy

Creators: Irna Phillips and William J. Bell
Writer: Robert J. Shaw
Producer: Allen Potter
Director: Tom Donovan
Musical Director: Wladimir Selinsky
Packager: Procter & Gamble

MORNING STAR
NBC: September 27, 1965 to July 1, 1966

One of two contemporary serials scheduled in late morning time slots; the other was *Paradise Bay*. About New York woman's magazine editor Katy Elliott, her impulsive teenage sister Jan and Katy's love interest, Bill Riley. The cosmopolitan atmosphere did not mix well with the early time slot. Taped in Burbank.

Katy Elliott	Elizabeth Perry
	Shary Marshall
Jan Elliott	Adrienne Ellis
Ed Elliott	Ed Prentiss
Millie Elliott	Sheila Bromley
Bill Riley	Edward Mallory
Dana Manning	Betsy Jones Moreland
Stan Manning	John Dehner
	John Stephanson
Eric Manning	Ron Jackson
Grace Allison	Phyllis Hill
Eve Blake	Floy Dean
Dr. Tim Blake	William Arvin
The man	Vic Tayback

Creator: Ted Corday
Writers: Jan Huckins and Carolyn Weston, James Lipton
Executive Producer: Ted Corday
Producer: Charles Pollacheck
Directors: Joseph Behar, Lamar Casell
Packager: Corday Productions for Screen Gems

PARADISE BAY
NBC: September 27, 1965 to July 1, 1966

Morning Star's other half. Concerned radio personality Jeff Morgan, his wife Mary and their daughter Kitty, who joined a frivolous rock group called the Moonglows, causing intergenerational problems. The setting was a California beach town.

Jeff Morgan	Keith Andes	Rhoda	Patrice Wymore
Mary Morgan	Marion Ross	Frank	John Lupton
Kitty Morgan	Heather North	Alfie	David Watson
Duke Spalding	Dennis Cole	Chet	Tony Dow
Carlotta Chavez	Alice Reinheart	Joy	Robin Grace
Walter Montegomery	Walter Brooke	Tim	Dack Rambo
Lucy Spalding	June Dayton	Jo-Jo	Tommy Rettig
Bertha DeKalb	Lillian Bronson	Barbara	Pat Connolly
Estelle Kimball	K. T. Stevens	Tad	Michael Blodgett
Chuck Lucas	Craig Curtis	Susan	Cindy Carol
Judge Ellis	Mona Bruns		Also: Merry Anders,
Judge Grayson	Frank M. Thomas		Mary Foskett

Creators: Jerry D. Lewis and John Monks, Jr.
Writers: Jerry D. Lewis and John Monks, Jr., Irving
    Vendig and Manya Starr
Producer: Oliver Barbour
Directors: Bill Howell, Dick Darley

THE NURSES
ABC: September 27, 1965 to March 31, 1967

An adaptation of a CBS prime time series, set in Alden General Hospital and focusing on two nurses, Liz Thorpe and Gail Lukas.

Liz Thorpe	Mary Fickett
Gail Lukas Alexander	Melinda Plank
Ken Alexander	Nicholas Pryor
Cora Alexander	Muriel Kirkland
Brad Kieran	Lee Patterson
Hugh McLeod	Arthur Franz
Brenda McLeod	Patricia Hyland
Jamie McLeod	Judson Laire
Donna Steele	Carol Gainer
Pat Steele	Sally Gracie
Jake Steele	Richard McMurray
Dr. John Crager	Nat Polen
Dr. Paul Fuller	Paul Stevens
Vivian Gentry	Lesley Woods

Writers: Ian Martin and Richard Holland
Producer: Doris Quinlan

NEVER TOO YOUNG
ABC: September 27, 1965 to June 24, 1966

Beach Blanket Bingo came to daytime in this story of teens hanging out at a beachside luncheonette.

Musical Director: Ray Martin

CONFIDENTIAL FOR WOMEN
ABC: 1966

Anthology serial narrated by Jane Wyatt and psychologist Dr. Theodore Isaac Rubin; the once-a-week stories were based on cases in his files.

DARK SHADOWS
June 27, 1966 to April 2, 1971

Gothic saga of the creepy Collingwood mansion in Collinsport, featuring charismatic vampire Barnabas Collins. The show was a hit with teens and inspired paperbacks and nostalgia conventions.

Elizabeth Collins Stoddard	
Flora Collins	Joan Bennett
Barnabas Collins	
Bramwell	Jonathan Frid
Victoria Winters	Alexandra Moltke
David Collins	
Tad Collins	David Henesy
Carolyn Stoddard	
Charity	
Letitia Faye	Nancy Barrett
Roger Collins	
Edward Collins	
Daniel Collins	Louis Edmonds
Maggie Evans	Kathryn Leigh Scott
Sam Evans	David Ford
Joe Haskell	Joel Crothers

Willie Loomis	
Desmond Collins	John Karlen
Dr. Julia Hoffman Collins	
Magda	Grayson Hall
Angelique	
Cassandra Collins	
Valerie Collins	Lara Parker
Quentin Collins	David Selby
Burke Devlin	Mitchell Ryan
	Anthony George
Peter Bradford	Roger Davis
Sarah Collins	Sharon Smyth
Mrs. Johnson	Clarice Blackburn
Cyrus Longworth	
Jeb Hawks	
Gabriel Collins	Christopher Pennock
Daphne Harridge	Kate Jackson
Bruno	
Laszlo	Michael Stroka
Amy	Denise Nickerson
Chris	Don Briscoe
Sabrina Stuart	Lisa Richards
Adam	Robert Rodan
Eve	Marie Wallace
Prof. Elliot Stokes	
Count Petofi	
Mordecai Grimes	Thayer David
Rev. Trask	Jerry Lacy
Balberith	
Charles Dawson	Humbert Allen Astredo
Amanda Harris	
Olivia Corey	Donna McKechnie
Samantha Collins	Virginia Vestoff

Creator/Executive Producer: Dan Curtis
Headwriters: Art Wallace, Gordon Russell, Sam Hall
     Hall
Producer: Robert Costello
Directors: John Sedwick, Lela Swift
Musical Director: Robert W. Cobert
Packager: Dan Curtis Productions

HIDDEN FACES
NBC: December 30, 1968 to June 30, 1969

Crime serial similar in spirit to *The Edge of Night*, which was also created and written by Irving Vendig.

Arthur Adams	Conard Fowkes
Dr. Kate Logan	Gretchen Walther
Martha Logan	Louise Shaffer
Nick Capello Turner ...	Tony LoBianco
Sen. Robert Jaffee	Joseph Daly
Mimi Jaffee	Rita Gam
Mark Utley	Stephen Joyce
Earl Harriman	Nat Polen
Grace Ensley	Ludi Claire
Wilbur Ensley	John Towley
Allyn Jaffee	Linda Blair

Creator/Headwriter: Irving Vendig
Producer: Charles Fisher
Directors: Ted Mabley, Norman Hall, Marvin
     Silbersher, Tom Donovan, Richard Dunlap
Packager: NBC-TV

WHERE THE HEART IS
CBS: September 8, 1969 to March 23, 1973

Tale of the wealthy Hathaways in the town of Northcross; used the "classic soap opera" structure.

Kate Hathaway Prescott	Diana van der Vlis
Julian Hathaway	James Mitchell
Mary Hathaway	Diana Walker
Michael Hathaway	Gregory Abels
Allison Archer Jessup ..	Louise Shaffer
Roy Archer	Stephen Joyce
Stella O'Brien	Bibi Osterwald
Arthur Saxton	Bernard Kates
Helen Wyatt	Meg Myles
Ed Lucas	Mark Gordon
	Charles Cioffi
	Joseph Mascolo
Vicky Lucas Hathaway .	Robyn Millan
	Lisa Richards
Christine Cameron	Terry O'Connor
	Delphi Harrington*
Steve Prescott	Laurence Luckinbill
	Ron Harper*
Dr. Joe Prescott	William Post, Jr.
Nan Prescott	Katherine Meskill
Terry Prescott	Douglas Ross
	Ted Leplat
Lois Snowden	Judy Kercheval
	Jeanne Ruskin*

Amy Snowden	Clarice Blackburn
Dr. Hugh Jessup	Rex Robbins
	David Cryer*
Mugger in park	William DeVane
Dr. Bob Charter	David Spielberg
Ellie Jardin	Zohra Lampert
Peter Jardin	Michael Bersell
Loretta Jardin	Alice Drummond
Margaret Jardin	Barbara Baxley
	Rue McClanahan
Laura Blackburn	Marsha Mason
John Rainey	Peter MacLean
Adrienne Harris Rainey	Priscilla Pointer
Elizabeth Rainey	
Hathaway	Tracy Brooks Swope
Athena Stefanopolis . . .	Despo

Creators: Lou Scofield and Margaret DePriest
Head Writers: Lou Scofield and Margaret DePriest,
      Gabrielle Upton, Cornelius Crane,
      Rick Edelstein, Pat Falken Smith,
      Robert and Elizabeth Haggard, Claire
      Labine and Paul Avila Mayer
Executive Producers: Bertram Berman, Charles
      Weiss
Producers: Freyda Rothstein, Joseph D. Manetta,
      Tom Donovan
Directors: James McAllen, Gary Bowen, Bill Glenn,
      Richard Dunlap
Organists: John Gart, John Winters, Eddie Layton
Packager: CBS-TV

BRIGHT PROMISE
NBC: September 29, 1969 to March 30, 1972

Story set in and around Bancroft College, about students, professors and people of the town of Bancroft. After the show's star, Dana Andrews, left his role, the story focused on the town. Produced in Hollywood.

Martha Ferguson	Susan Brown
Bill Ferguson	Paul Lukather*
	John Napier
Ann Boyd Jones	Coleen Gray
	Gail Kobe*
Sandra Jones Pierce . . .	Susannah Darrow
	Pamela Murphy
Stuart Pierce	Peter Ratray

Henry Pierce	Tod Andrews
	David Lewis*
Tom Boswell	Dana Andrews
Jim Boswell	Eric James
Clara Kelzy	Ruth McDevitt
Red Wilson	Richard Eastham
David Martin	David Pritchard
Jennifer Matthews	Nancy Stephens
Chet Matthews	Gary Pillar
George Townley	Nigel McKeand
Fay Kendall	Kimetha Laurie
Prof. Mitchell	Ivor Francis
Prof. Abbot	Harry Townes
Marion Connelly	Marion Brash
Elizabeth Waters	Betsy Jones Moreland
Howard Jones	Mark Miller
Isabel Jones	Lesley Woods
Vince Adams	Forrest Compton
Dr. Tracy Graham	Dabney Coleman
David Lockhart	Tony Geary
Sylvia Bancroft	Anne Jeffreys
	Regina Gleason
Elaine Bancroft	Jennifer Leak
Dr. Brian Walsh	John Considine
Charles Diedrich	Anthony Eisley
Bob Corcoran	Philip Carey

Creators: Frank and Doris Hursley
Head Writers: Frank and Doris Hursley, Rick
      Edelstein, Robert J. Shaw
Producers: Richard Dunn, Jerry Layton
Directors: Gloria Monty, Herbert Kenwith, Frank
      Pacelli, Jay Arnold
Packager: Bing Crosby Productions

THE BEST OF EVERYTHING
ABC: March 30 to September 25, 1970

Based on the Rona Jaffe novel about career girls at a New York magazine.

Violet Jordan	Geraldine Fitzgerald
Joshua Jordan	John Rust
	Peter Harris
Kim Jordan	Katherine Glass
Linda Warren	Patty McCormack
Dr. Eddie Perrone	Victor Arnold
April Morrison	Julie Mannix

Amanda Key	Gale Sondergaard
Dexter Key	James Davidson
Joanna Key	Bonnie Bee Buzzard
Barbara Lamont	Rochelle Oliver
Ken Lamont	Barry Ford
Johnny Lamont	Stephen Grover
Kate Farrow	Mel Dowd
Mike Carter	Jean-Pierre Stewart
Anne Carter	Diane Kagan

Creator/Writer: James Lipton
Executive Producer: Don Wallace
Producer: Jacqueline Babbin
Directors: Jack Wood, Alan Pultz
Musical Director: Lawrence Rosenthal
Packager: 20th Century Fox

A WORLD APART
ABC: March 30, 1970 to June 25, 1971

The original central character, Betty Kahlman, was a soap opera writer who had never married but had adopted two children. The story, written by Irna Phillips's daughter, Katherine Phillips, with story guidance by Irna herself, was apparently based on Irna Phillips's own life and included problems between the generations. The show's other major family, the Simses, were similar to the Hugheses of *As The World Turns*.

Betty Kahlman Barry . .	Elizabeth Lawrence
	Augusta Dabney
Russell Barry	William Prince
Patrice Kahlman	Susan Sarandon
Chris Kahlman	Matthew Cowles
Adrian Sims	Kathleen Maguire
Dr. Ed Sims	James Noble
Becky Sims	Erin Connor
Dr. John Carr	Robert Gentry
T. D. Drinkard	Tom Ligon
Meg Johns	Anna Minot
Jack Condon	Stephen Elliott
Nancy Condon	Susan Sullivan
Matilde	Rosetta LeNoire
Julie Stark	Dorothy Lyman
Oliver Harrell	David Birney
Olivia Hampton	Jane White
Matt Hampton	Clifton Davis
Linda Peters	Heather McRae

Creator: Katherine L. Phillips
Head Writers: Katherine L. Phillips, Richard and Suzanne Holland
Producer: Tom Donovan
Directors: Tom Donovan, Walter Gorman
Story Editor: Irna Phillips
Musical Director: Wladimir Selinsky
Packager: ABC-TV

SOMERSET
March 30, 1970 to December 31, 1976

Originally called *Another World-Somerset* and offered to viewers as the second half of a full hour of *Another World*, which was set in neighboring Bay City. Characters would go back and forth between the old and new programs, even though there were different story lines; it was done to get loyal *Another World* viewers into the habit of watching *Somerset*. Written by *The Edge of Night*'s writer, Henry Slesar, *Somerset* took on the characteristics of a mystery melodrama. Whole story lines began revolving around the slow poisoning of a beautiful young girl by her psychotically jealous rival, the mysterious murder of a millionaire, and the infiltration of a crime syndicate into one of the town's biggest companies. In 1973, Roy Winsor became head writer and attempted to change the show into a more traditional soap opera, as did other writers after him, but had little success in finding a central theme.

Rex Cooper	Paul Sparer
Laura Cooper	Dorothy Stinnette
Tony Cooper	Doug Chapin
	Ernest Thompson
	Barry Jenner
Ellen Grant	Georgann Johnson
Ben Grant	Edward Kemmer
Jill Grant Farmer	Susan MacDonald
David Grant	Ron Martin*
	Thomas Callaway
	Phillip MacHale
India Delaney Hillman .	Marie Wallace
Robert Delaney	Nicolas Coster
Jessica Buchanan Delaney	Wynne Miller
Randy Buchanan	Gary Sandy
Jasper Delaney	Ralph Clanton

Peter Delaney	Len Gochman
Missy Matthews	Carol Roux
Sam Lucas	Jordan Charney
Lahoma Lucas	Ann Wedgeworth
Pammy Davis	Pamela Toll
Gerald Davis	Walter Mathews
Dr. Stan Kurtz	Michael Lipton
Ginger Kurtz Cooper ...	Meg Wittner
	Renne Jarrett
	Fawne Harriman*
Mitch Farmer	Richard Shoberg
Julian Cannell	Joel Crothers
Dr. Teri Martin Kurtz ...	Gloria Hoye
Eve Lawrence Paisley ..	Bibi Besch
Heather Lawrence Kane	Audrey Landers
Dr. Jerry Kane	James O'Sullivan
Ned Paisley	James Congdon
Victoria Paisley	Veleka Gray
Dale Robinson	Jameson Parker
Carrie Wheeler	Jobeth Williams
Sarah Briskin	Dorothy Blackburn
	Molly Picon*
Mac Wells	Lou Jacobi
Steve Slade	Gene Bua

Creators: Lyle B. Hill and Robert Cenedella
Head Writers: Robert Cenedella, Henry Slesar,
        Warren L. Swanson, Roy Winsor,
        Robert J. Shaw, Winifred Wolfe, Don
        Appell, Russell Kubec, A. J. Russell
Executive Producer: Lyle B. Hill
Producer: Sid Sirulnick
Directors: Joseph K. Chomyn, Joseph L. Scanlan, Ira
        Cirker, Jack Coffey, Bruce Minnix
Organist: Chet Kingsbury
Musical Director (later): Charles Paul
Packager: Procter & Gamble

RETURN TO PEYTON PLACE
NBC: April 3, 1972 to January 4, 1974

Daytime continuation of the nighttime series, which was in turn based on the Grace Metalious novel, *Peyton Place*, about seething liaisons in a small New England town.

Constance Carson	Bettye Ackerman
	Susan Brown*

Elliot Carson	Warren Stevens
Eli Carson	Frank Ferguson
Allison McKenzie	Katherine Glass
	Pamela Shoop
Dr. Michael Rossi	Guy Stockwell
Ada Jacks	Evelyn Scott
Rita Harrington	Patricia Morrow
Norman Harrington ...	Ron Russell
Rodney Harrington	Lawrence Casey
	Yale Summers*
Betty Harrington	Julie Parrish*
	Lynn Loring
Leslie Harrington	Stacy Harris*
	Frank Maxwell
Hannah Cord	Mary K. Wells
Steven Cord	Joseph Gallison
Martin Peyton	John Hoyt
Selena Cross Rossi	Margaret Mason
D. B. Bentley	Mary Frann

Head Writers: James Lipton, Robert Cenedella
Executive Producer (first few months): Don Wallace
Producer: George Paris
Directors: Alan Pultz, Frank Pacelli
Packager: FMC Productions

HOW TO SURVIVE A MARRIAGE
NBC: January 7, 1974 to April 17, 1975

An experimental serial about a divorce and its painful ramifications. This was a courageous attempt by the writers, producer and network to create relevant and contemporary situations for daytime viewers. Psychologist Dr. Julie Franklin advised other characters on how to cope with the problems of dating again after a divorce, how to deal with sudden widowhood and the like.

Monica Courtland	Joan Copeland
Chris Kirby	Jennifer Harmon
Larry Kirby	Michael Landrum
	Ken Kercheval
	Michael Hawkins
Fran Bachman	Fran Brill
David Bachman	Allan Miller
Joan Willis	Tricia O'Neil
Peter Willis	Steve Elmore
	Berkeley Harris*

Dr. Julie Franklin	Rosemary Prinz
Dr. Tony DeAngelo	George Welbes
Alexander Kronos	Brad Davis
Rachel Bachman	Elissa Leeds
Moe Bachman	Albert Ottenheimer
Dr. Max Cooper	James Shannon
Maria McGhee	Lauren White
Johnny McGhee	Armand Assante

Creator: Anne Howard Bailey
Head Writers: Anne Howard Bailey, Rick Edelstein, Margaret DePriest
Executive Producers (first few months): Charles W. Fries and Peter H. Engel
Producers: Allen Potter, Peter Andrews, Madeline B. David, Jeff Young
Directors: Peter Andrews, George Chrison, Richard T. McCue, Robert Myhrum, Jeff Young
Musical Direction: Score Productions
Packager: Metromedia

LOVERS AND FRIENDS
NBC: January 3 to May 6, 1977
FOR RICHER, FOR POORER
NBC: December 6, 1967 to September 29, 1978

Had a "classic soap opera" setup; concerned two families, the rich Cushings and the poorer Saxtons, in a Chicago suburb, with emphasis on class conflict. When the show returned under the new title *For Richer, For Poorer*, the character named Rhett was changed to Bill and the story was greatly speeded up.

Josie Saxton	Patricia Englund
Lester Saxton	John Heffernan
	Albert Stratton
Edith Cushing	Nancy Marchand
	Laurinda Barrett
Richard Cushing	Ron Randell
Austin Cushing	Rod Arrants
Amy Gifford Saxton	Christine Jones
Megan Cushing Saxton .	Patricia Estrin
	Darlene Parks
Rhett (Bill) Saxton	Bob Purvey
	David Ramsey
	Tom Happer
Connie Ferguson Saxton	Susan Foster
	Cynthia Bostick
Jason Saxton	Richard Backus
Eleanor Kimball	Flora Plumb
George Kimball	Stephen Joyce
Viola Brewster	Leora Dana
	Patricia Barry
Lee Ferguson	Robert Burton
Dr. Roy White	Dennis Romer
Colleen Griffin	Nancy Snyder
Sgt. Frank Damico	Stephen Burleigh

Creator: Harding Lemay
Head Writers: Harding Lemay, Tom King
Executive Producer: Paul Rauch
Producers: John Wendell and Harriet Wohl Goldstein
Directors: Peter Levin, Jack Hofsiss, Frank Gaeta, Kevin Kelly, Barnet Kellman
Musical Direction: Score Productions
Packager: Procter & Gamble

APPENDIX C
*Colleges Offering Courses in Soap Opera**

The American University
Dept. of Sociology
(Prof. Muriel Cantor)
Washington, D. C. 20016

Boston College
Dept. of Speech & Communications
(Prof. John Henry Lawton)
Chestnut Hill, MA. 02167

Bowling Green State University
Popular Culture Center
(Dr. Ray Browne, Director)
Bowling Green, OH. 43403

Brooklyn College
School of Humanities
Dept. of Television and Radio
(Prof. Brian Rose)
Brooklyn, N.Y. 11210

Monmouth College
Dept. of Psychology
(Prof. Kenneth Haun)
Monmouth, N.J. 07750

Northeastern Illinois University
5500 N. St. Louis Ave.
Dept. of History
(Prof. J. Fred McDonald)
Chicago, IL. 60625

Queens College
Dept. of Communication, Arts and Sciences
(Prof. James Chesebro)
Flushing, N.Y. 11367

San Diego State University
College of Professional Studies and Fine Arts
Dept. of Telecommunications & Film
(Prof. Michael Real and Elizabeth Heighton)
San Diego, CA. 92182-0117

San Francisco State University
Graduate School of Journalism
(Prof. Ronald Compesi)
San Francisco, CA. 94132

State University of New York at Buffalo
Dept. of Communication
539 Christopher Baldy Hall
(Prof. Mary B. Cassata)
Buffalo, N.Y. 14260

University of Oregon
Dept. of Speech, Telecommunications, and Film
(Ellen Seiter and Grant McKearny)
Eugene, OR. 97403

University of Santa Barbara
Dept. of Sociology
(Prof. William Bielby)
Santa Barbara, CA. 93106

University of Wisconsin—Madison
Dept. of Agricultural and Life Sciences
440 Henry Mall
(Prof. Suzanne Pingree)
Madison, WI. 53706

*or related content. Write to individual departments for current offerings.

BIBLIOGRAPHY

BOOKS

Adler, Bill and Alice Edmunds, *The Soap Opera Quiz Book*. New York: Pocket Books, 1977.

Bonderoff, Jason, *Daytime TV 1977*. New York: Manor, 1976.

Bruns Thomas, Mona, *By Emily Possessed*. New York: Jericho, 1973.

Buxton, Frank and Bill Owen, *The Big Broadcast*. New York: Viking Press, 1972.

Denis, Paul and staff of Daytime TV magazine *Daytime TV's Star Directory*. New York: Sterling's, 1976.

Edmondson, Madeleine and David Rounds *The Soaps*. (Reprinted as *From Mary Noble to Mary Hartman*.) New York: Briarcliff Manor, 1973.

Feinman, Jeffrey, *The Soap Opera Trivia Book*. New York: Manor, 1977.

Fulton, Eileen and Brett Bolton, *How My World Turns*. New York: Warner Books, 1970.

Gilbert, Annie, *All My Afternoons*. New York: A&W, 1979.

Grove, Martin, *The Complete History of Soap Operas*. New York: Dee & Zee Enterprises, 1976.

Higby, Mary Jane, *Tune In Tomorrow*. New York: Cowles Education Corp., 1966.

Kutler, Jane and Patricia Kearney, *Super Soaps*. New York, Grosset and Dunlap, 1977.

LaGuardia, Robert, *From Ma Perkins To Mary Hartman: The Illustrated History of Soap Operas*. New York: Ballantine Books, 1977.

LaGuardia, Robert, *The Wonderful World of TV Soap Operas*. New York: Ballantine Books, 1974; revised edition, 1977.

Laub, Bryna, *The Official Soap Opera Annual*. New York: Ballantine Books, 1977.

Lemay, Harding, *Eight Years In Another World*. New York: Atheneum, 1981.

Meyers, Richard, *The Illustrated Soap Opera Companion*. New York: Drake, 1977.

Rogers, Lynne, *The Love Of Their Lives*. New York: Dell Publishing Co., 1979.

Soares, Manuela, *The Soap Opera Book*. New York: Latham, 1978.

Stedman, Raymond William, *The Serials*. Norman, Oklahoma: University of Oklahoma Press, 1971.

Stuart, Mary, *Both Of Me*. Doubleday & Co., 1980.

Thurber, James, *The Beast In Me And Other Animals*. New York: Harcourt, Brace and Co., 1948.

Wakefield, Dan, *All Her Children*. New York: Avon, 1976.

Warrick, Ruth with Don Preston, *The Confessions Of Phoebe Tyler*. Englewood Cliffs, New Jersey: Prentice-Hall, 1980.

Zimmermann, Ed. *Love In The Afternoon*, New York: Bobbs-Merrill, 1971.

ARTICLES

Adler, B., "Great Soap Opera Fan Letters." Good Housekeeping, March, 1977.

Astrachan, A., "Life Can Be Beautiful/Relevant; Social Problems And The Soap Operas." New York Times Magazine, March 23, 1975.

Birnbach, L., "Daze Of Our Lives." Rolling Stone, October 1, 1981.

391

Bosworth, P., "How To Be A Soap Opera Writer: A Closeup." Working Woman, May, 1981.

Bricker, R. and C. Dykhouse, "Do Skin and Sin On the Soaps Affect Viewers? Social Scientists And The Stars Argue It Out." People Weekly, June 14, 1982.

Campbell, B. M., "Blacks In The Soaps." Essence, November, 1978.

Campbell, B. M., "Hooked On Soaps." Essence, November, 1978.

"Daytime Drama; Taping The Final Episode Of How To Survive A Marriage." The New Yorker, May 6, 1975.

DeMuth, P. & E. Barton, "Soap Gets In Your Mind." Psychology Today, July, 1982.

Edmondson, M., "Confessions Of A Soap Addict." Newsweek, August 22, 1977.

Eskow, J., "Edge Of Reality." Feature, March, 1979.

Gold, A., "How I Got A Role In A Soap Opera." Good Housekeeping, April, 1981.

"How ABC Found Happiness In Daytime TV." Business Week. August 24, 1981.

Kerr, J., "Confessions Of A Soap Opera Addict." McCalls, September, 1977.

LaGuardia, R., "Soap Gets In Your Eyes." Saturday Evening Post, August, 1977.

Lowery, Sharon Anne, "Alcoholics In Soapland." Human Behavior, January, 1979.

Morgan, M., "Soap Opera Competition." Americas, March, 1980.

Perloff, M., "Television: Soap Bubbles." New Republic, May 10, 1975.

"Putting Soaps On The Line." Nation's Business, August, 1981.

Rubin, T. I., "Psychiatrist's Notebook; Soap Operas." Ladies Home Journal, January, 1976.

Saltzman, J., "Tune In Tomorrow." USA Today, November, 1980.

"Sex And Suffering In The Afternoon." Time, January 12, 1976.

"She's Behind The Biggest Bubble In Show Biz: Soap Operas." People, December 28, 1981.

"Springboard To Stardom." Teen, August, 1981.

Tepper, A., "Stop Scoffing At The Soaps!" Seventeen, July, 1981.

Uhry, M. and R. Bricker, "As The World Turns, So Do The Lady Killing Louses Who Are Keeping Up The Soaps." People, March 9, 1981.

Viorst, J., "Soap Operas: The Suds Of Time March On." Redbook, November, 1975.

Winsey, V., "How Soaps Help You Cope." Family Health, April, 1979.

"Women Making Money; Scanning The Soaps." Ladies Home Journal, July, 1975.

JOURNALS

Journal Of Communication, Volume 29, Number 4, Autumn 1979.

Cantor, Muriel G., "Our Days And Our Nights On TV," P. 66.

Cassata, Mary B., Thomas D. Skill, and Samuel Osci Boadu, "In Sickness and In Health," P. 73.

Rose, Brian, "Thickening The Plot," P. 81.

Wander, Philip. "The Angst Of The Middle Class," P. 85.

Journal Of Communication, Volume 31, Number 3, Summer 1981.

Greenberg, Bradley, S., Robert Akelman, Kimberly Neuendorf. "Sex In The Soap Operas: Afternoon Delight," P. 83.

Lowry, Dennis T., Gail Love and Malcolm Kirby. "Sex In The Soap Operas: Patterns Of Intimacy," P. 97.

Fine, Marlene G., "Soap Opera Conversations: The Talk That Binds," P. 90.

Buerkel-Rothfus, Nancy L. with Sandra Mayes. "Soap Opera Viewing: The Cultivation Effect," P. 108.

INDEX

Abbott, Ashley, 305
Abbott, Dina, 306
Abbott, Jack, 304
Abbott, Dr. Jim, 38, 353
Abbott, John, 304
Abbott, Philip, 273
Abbott, Richard, 250
Abbott, Traci, 305
Acavone, Jay, 289
Acker, Sharon, 360
Ackroyd, David, 92, 336
Action in the Afternoon, 24
Adair, Deborah, 295
Adams, Dr. Scott, 304
Adams, Julie, 132
Adams, Karen, 20
Adams, Lynn, 218
Adams, Marla, 306, 335
Adamson, Dr. Gail, 203
Adamson, Laine, 287
Adamson, Ted, 287
Addison, Bernice, 88
Addison, Nancy, 221, 258
Addison, Wayne, 86
Addy, Wesley, 237, 263
Agress, Ted, 119
Albee, Denny, 168, 252
Albertson, Grace, 353
Alda, Robert, 150, 319
Alden, Cabot, 236
Alden, Curtis, 236
Alden, Isabelle, 236
Aldrich, Doreen, 349
Aldrich, Erich, 347
Aldrich, Jason, 349

Aldrich, Dr. Steve, 346
Aldrin, Ariel, 125
Aldrin, Greta, 125
Aleata, Caroline "Cal," 321
Aleata, Edouard, 322
Alexander, Denise, 4, 136, 188
Alexander, Millette, 217, 342
Alexander, Nadine, 168
Alexander, Raven, 168
Alexander, Sandy, 100
Alfonso, Kristian, 143
Alfonso, Tony, 324
Alford, Bobby, 106
All My Children, 4, 7, 40, 47, 49, 50,
  61–78
    background, 61–63
    cast, 77–78
    story, 63–77
Allan, Jed, 140
Allen, David, 341
Allen, Elizabeth, 359
Allen, Joe, Jr., 313
Allen, Vera, 342
Allinson, Michael, 324
Allison, Billy, 347
Allison, Cynthia, 175
Allison, Dr. Dan, 347
Allison, Jone, 213, 214
Ameche, Don, 4
Ames, Amy, 30, 42, 332, 333
Ames, Ellen, 26, 332
Ames, Jerry, 333
Ames, Peter, 26, 31–32, 332
Ames, Rachel, 177, 187
Ames, Susan, 333
Ames, Teal, 154, 155

Amos 'n Andy, 9
Anderman, Margo, 149
Anderman, Maureen, 288
Anders, Zach, 288
Anderson, Barbara, 298
Anderson, Bob, 140
Anderson, Mary, 144
Anderson, Phyllis, 140
Anderson, Renee, 204
Anderson, Richard Dean, 195
Anderson, Ruby, 203
Andre, Jill, 217
Andrews, Dana, 40
Andrews, Florence, 188
Andrews, Jack, 316
Andrews, Jed, 300
Andrews, Tina, 146
Andrews, William, 253
Andropolous, Andrea, 123
Andropolous, Nick, 123
Andropolous, Steve, 123
Aniston, John, 288, 322
Another World, 6, 36, 37, 45–46, 49,
  50, 54, 55, 79–104
    background, 79–83
    cast, 102–104
    story, 83–102
Another World-Somerset, 40
Anthony, Gerald, 248
Anton, Bob, 180
Arley, Jean, 311
Arlt, Lewis, 286
Arnett, Terri Webber, 195
Arnold, Mark, 169
Arrants, Rod, 270, 287
Arthur, Indus, 188

393

As the World Turns, 105–129
    background, 105–110
    cast, 126–129
    story, 110–126
Ashe, Jennifer, 237
Ashford, Matthew, 254
Ashley, Ann, 337
Ashley, Maggie, 252
Ashley, Pat, 252
Ashmore, Frank, 150
Ashton, Ted, 274
Atwater, Barry, 187
Atwood, Larry, 147
Augustine, Craig, 289
Aunt Jenny's True Life Stories, 210, 367
Austen, Winter, 168
Austin, Douglas, 303
Austin, John, 275
Austin, Steve, 247
Avery, Ira, 38
Avery, Jane, 38
Ayres, Jerry, 197–198
Ayres, Leah, 169

Bachelor's Children, 210
Bachman, Lisbeth, 132
Backus, Richard, 264
Bacon, Cathy, 319
Badler, Jane, 243
Baggetta, Vincent, 354
Bagot, Megan, 287
Bailey, Anne Howard, 186
Bailey, David, 85
Bailey, Ruth, 211
Baker, Evans, 315
Baker, Jeff, 112
Baker, Ruth, 319
Baldwin, Lee, 177, 188
Baldwin, Meg, 188
Baldwin, Scotty, 181, 188
Baldwin, Stacey, 194
Baldwin, Dr. Tom, 188
Baldwin, Tommy, 189
Ballard, Diane, 228
Ballenger, Victoria, 222
Bancroft, Allison, 304
Bancroft, Brian, 93
Bancroft, Earle, 304
Bancroft, Iris Carrington, 357, 358
Bancroft, Kevin, 304
Bannard, Nicole, 253
Banning, Dr. Bruce, 215
Banning, David, 138
Banning, Scott, 138
Bannon, Natalie, 118
Barber, Ellen, 337
Barbery, Tirell, 314
Barcroft, Judith, 81, 87
Bard, Monica, 195

Barnard, Greg, 94
Barnes, Joanne, 148
Barnett, Eileen, 149
Barnstone, Lily, 360
Barr, Julia, 71
Barrett, Laurinda, 169
Barrett, Nancy, 244
Barrie, Barbara, 318
Barrington, Lawrence, 131
Barron, Irene, 269, 270
Barron, Joanne Gardner, 26, 29, 269, 270
Barron, Keith, 269, 270
Barron, Patti, 269, 270
Barron, Victor, 270
Barrow, Bernard, 257, 336
Barry, Patricia, 76, 135
Barry, Susan, 245
Barstow, Billy, 236
Barstow, Rita Mae, 236
Bartlett, Bonnie, 312
Barton, Fred, 148
Barton, Jean, 148
Bassett, William H., 305
Bassie, Joan, 320
Bauer, Bert, 212, 213, 214–215
Bauer, Bill, 212, 214
Bauer, Charita, 29, 212, 213–214
Bauer, Dr. Franz, 176
Bauer, Frederick, 219
Bauer, Hillary, 230
Bauer, Jamie Lyn, 294
Bauer, Meta, 52, 212, 214
Bauer, Michael, 213, 215
Bauer, Mike, 84
Bauer, Papa, 212, 214, 219
Bauer, Trudy, 212, 214, 215
Bauer, William Edward, 215
Baxter, Dr. Bruce, 109
Baxter, Charles, 86, 321
Baxter, Harriet, 273
Baxter, Tom, 81, 84
Bayer, Jimmy, 317
Beal, John, 80
Beatty, Warren, 317
Beaulac, Dr. Nell, 259
Beaulac, Dr. Seneca, 259
Beck, Donna, 70
Beck-Hilton, Kimberly, 130
Becker, Barbara, 215
Becker, Karen, 301
Becker, Nancy, 301
Becker, Ron, 301
Bedelia, Bonnie, 318
Beecroft, Gregory, 231
Begley, Ed, 215
Behar, Joe, 134
Beir, Fred, 147
Belack, Doris, 240
Bell, Lee Phillip, 294

Bell, William, 6, 37, 43, 135, 293, 294
Bellaver, Harry, 84
Beller, Kathy, 281
Bellini, Dr. Nick, 344, 346
Bellman, Striker, 359
Bellman, Vicky, 359
Ben Jerrod, Attorney at Law, 382
Benedict, Anne, 215
Benedict, Helene, 215
Benedict, Henry, 215
Benedict, Nicholas, 63, 304
Benesch, Lynn, 240
Benet, Brenda, 150
Bennett, Meg, 270, 281, 304
Bennetts, The, 33, 375–376
Benoit, Pat, 112
Benson, Robby, 285
Bentley, Marc, 305
Beradino, John, 175, 184–185, 187
Berenger, Tom, 241
Berg, Dr. Louis, 5
Bergman, Jimmy, 271
Bergman, Marge, 269, 270
Bergman, Peter, 75
Bergman, Stu, 23, 269, 270
Bergman, Tommy, 271
Berjer, Barbara, 111, 219, 341, 342
Berman, Edith, 160
Berman, Jake, 160
Bernau, Chris, 228
Berridge, Elizabeth, 359
Besch, Bibi, 156, 335, 354
Best of Everything, The, 40, 386–387
Bethune, Zina, 317
Betts, Jack, 101, 252
Betty and Bob, 12, 363
Betz, Carl, 314
Beyers, Bill, 132
Big Sister, 210, 366
Bigby, Bruce, 329
Billingsley, Jennifer, 187
Binkley, Lane, 285
Birney, David, 4, 42, 353
Bishop, Loanne, 206
Blackford, Dean, 229
Blair, Pamela, 237
Blake, Jessica, 150
Blake, Mitch, 98
Blanchard, Keith, 347
Blanchard, Susan, 65
Blanks, Mary Lynn, 122
Blazer, Judith, 125
Bliss, Bradley, 99
Blossom, Roberts, 95
Bogard, Kent, 74
Bogard, Lars, 74
Bogazianos, Vasili, 71
Boland, Joseph, 314
Bolen, Lin, 42–43

Bolster, Steven, 87
Bolton, Grace, 277
Borelli, Carla, 359
Borg, Richard, 170
Born, Roscoe, 262
Boruff, John, 215
Boswell, Thomas, 40
Bovasso, Julie, 342
Bowden, Alex, 216
Boyle, Dawn Marie, 71
Braden, John, 95
Bradley, Paul, 353
Brady, Roman, 151
Braeden, Eric, 304
Brandon, Peter, 116
Brandt, Victor, 132
Brash, Marion, 273, 334
Braswell, Charles, 345
Brauner, Asher, 202
Braxton, Stephanie, 168, 335
Breech, Kathy, 248
Breen, Paulette, 68
Bregman, Tracy, 148
Brennan, Franny, 112
Brent, Dr. Jim, 20
Brent, Phillip, 63
Brent, Ruth, 63
Brent, Ted, 63
Breslin, Pat, 188
Brewer, Jessie, 36, 174, 175, 186
Brewer, Dr. Phil, 36, 175, 186
Brewster, Adam, 249
Brewster, Bambi, 324
Bridgeman, Clare, 319
Bridgeman, Sally, 319
Bright, Pat, 160
Bright Promise, 40, 42, 386
Brighter Day, The, 20, 33, 310, 329–331
    cast, 330–331, 372
Brinthrope, Lord Henry, 18, 21
Britton, Lisa, 335
Britton, Paul, 334
Britton, Terry, 334
Broderick, Jim, 31–32
Bronsky, Mitch, 265
Brooke, Walter, 318
Brookes, Jacqueline, 91
Brooks, Anne Rose, 101
Brooks, Chris, 294
Brooks, David Allen, 170
Brooks, Jennifer, 294
Brooks, Laurealee, 294
Brooks, Leslie, 294
Brooks, Mark, 137
Brooks, Martin, 273, 275, 313
Brooks, Peggy, 294
Brooks, Stephen, 150
Brooks, Stuart, 294
Brothers, Dr. Joyce, 240

Brouwer, Peter, 123, 325
Brown, Ellen, 52
Brown, Gail, 91
Brown, Hamilton, 314
Brown, Helen, 52
Brown, Jefferson, 169
Brown, Lisa, 230
Brown, Peter, 140, 305
Brown, Susan, 203
Browning, Rod, 244
Browning, Susan, 354
Bruce, Lydia, 345
Bruder, Patricia, 111
Bruno, Catherine, 170
Bruns, Mona, 24, 25
Bryant, William, 206
Bryce, Ed, 213, 214
Bryce, Scott, 125
Bryggman, Larry, 116
Bryson, Dr. Kenneth, 169
Bryson, Valerie, 169
Bua, Gene, 319
Bua, Toni Bull, 120, 319
Buchanan, Asa, 252
Buchanan, Bo, 252
Buchanan, Clint, 252
Buchanan, Olympia, 253
Bundy, Brooke, 146, 187
Burch, Shelly, 254
Burgess, Frank, 132
Burke, Steven, 240
Burleigh, Stephen, 281
Burnett, Carol, 4
Burns, Cassie, 150
Burns, Lefty, 84
Burr, Anne, 106, 111
Burr, Robert, 354
Burstyn, Ellen, 4
Burton, Warren, 72, 99
By Emily Possessed, 24
Byers, Ralph, 288

Cahill, Barry, 298
Caldwell, Alex, 321
Caldwell, Gail, 285
Calhoun, Rory, 130
Call, Anthony, 158, 218, 253
Callinan, Dick, 167
Callison, Herb, 253
Cameron, David, 170
Campanella, Joseph, 216, 345
Campbell, Carolee, 347
Campbell, J. Kenneth, 99
Campbell, Kay, 215
Campbell, Shawn, 354
Canfield, Burton, 359
Canfield, Mildred, 359
Canfield, T. J., 359
Cannon, Dyan, 4
Capitol, 21, 130–133

Carey, Macdonald, 4, 50, 135
Carey, Philip, 252
Carlin, Tom, 275
Carlson, Gail Rae, 206
Carlson, Henry, 317
Carlson, Steve, 300
Carlson, Vivian, 317
Carmichael, Byron, 150
Carney, Art, 4
Carney, Mary, 259
Carpenter, Gary, 91
Carpenter, John, 354
Carpinelli, Paul, 217
Carr, Paul, 349
Carricaburu, Cathy, 301
Carrington, Blake, 55
Carrington, Dennis, 358
Carrington, Elaine, 21, 33, 52
Carrington, Eliot, 88
Carrington, Iris, 49–50, 83, 88
Carrington, Steve, 55
Carroll, Dee, 146
Carson, Bruce, 285
Carson, Hal, 324
Carson, Jeannie, 278
Carter, Bucky, 260
Carter, Dixie, 162
Carter, Jonathan, 194
Carter, Kristen, 289
Carter, Larry, 277
Carter, Warren, 289
Carver, Frank, 336
Cashman, Jerry "Cash," 304
Cassadine, Helena, 184, 205
Cassadine, Mikkos, 204
Cassadine, Tony, 204
Cassadine, Victor, 204
Cassen, Dr. Doug, 113
Cassmore, Judy, 99
Castle, Kenneth, 260
Catlin, Tom, 132
Caudell, Lane, 151
Cavanaugh, April, 168
Cavanaugh, Brent, 150
Cavanaugh, Denise, 168
Cavanaugh, Dr. Miles, 168
Cenedella, Bob, 82
Chamberlain, Henry, 231
Chamberlain, Jeff, 131
Chamberlain, Vanessa, 231
Chancellor, Kay, 297
Chancellor, Phillip, 297
Chandler, Bobby, 195
Chandler, Carolyn, 195
Chandler, Fay, 287
Chandler, Dr. Jerry, 344
Chandler, Kellam, 150
Chandler, Pam, 224
Chandler, Dr. Ted, 321
Chandler, Tod, 150

Chaplin Jim, 5
Chapman, Judith, 118, 265
Chapman, Dr. Peter, 230
Charles, Keith, 122, 225, 253, 321, 337
Charleson, Leslie, 38, 42, 179, 180, 195, 354
Charney, Jordan, 84, 241
Chase, Allan, 37
Chastain, Don, 177, 188
Chauvin, Lilyan, 296
Cheatham, Marie, 135, 137, 283
Chernak, Dr. Peter, 354
Chris, Marilyn, 242
Christian, Nathaniel, 147
Christopher, Ron, 156, 158
Cioffi, Charles, 97
Clara Lu, 'n' Em, 9
Clark, Cindy, 87
Clark, Mae, 176
Clark, Marsha, 227
Clark, Phil, 358
Clark, Ted, 87
Clark, Virginia, 15
Clarke, Don, 188, 262
Clarke, John, 135, 137
Clarke, Jordan, 224
Clarke, Richard, 156
Clary, Robert, 146, 295
Clayborn, Hugh, 335
Clayburgh, Jill, 4, 277
Clayton, Jack, 146
Clayton, Jeri, 146
Clayton, Ted, 253
Clayton, Tina, 248
Clayton, Trish, 146
Clear Horizon, The, 35, 381
Clegg, Jordy, 130
Clegg, Julie, 21, 130
Clegg, Myrna, 130
Clegg, Sam, 130
Clegg, Trey, 130
Clemens, Belle, 335
Clemens, Robin, 335
Clerk, Clive, 136
Clinton, Brooke, 188
Clogg, Brenda, 130
Coates, Alan, 170
Colbert, Robert, 294
Cole, Dennis, 302
Cole, Kelly, 72
Cole, Dr. Tim, 111
Coleman, Jack, 150
Colenback, John, 112
Coleridge, Dr. Ed, 257
Coleridge, Faith, 260
Coleridge, Jillian "Jill," 258
Coleridge, Dr. Roger, 258
Colgate-Palmolive, 344
Colicos, John, 184, 204

Colin, Margaret, 124, 168
College courses, 390
Collings, Anne, 190
Collins, Beth, 92
Collins, Brent, 125
Collins, Johnny, 146
Collins, Phillip, 216
Collins, Dr. Wade, 281
Colman, Grant, 117
Colman, Joyce, 118
Colton, Zacharay, 100
Compton, Forrest, 155
Conboy, John, 44, 50, 130, 293
Concerning Miss Marlowe, 33, 378
Confidential for Women, 384
Congdon, James, 81
Conger, Eric, 97
Conley, Corinne, 140
Connelly, Paul, 99
Connolly, Norma, 203
Connor, Ryan, 358
Connor, Whitfield, 215
Conrad, Hope, 216
Conrad, Julie, 216
Conroy, Kevin, 99
Convy, Bert, 318
Conway, Marion, 220
Conway, Valerie, 121
Conwell, Carolyn, 304
Conwell, Pat, 164
Coogan, Richard, 313
Cook, Dr. Kevin, 359
Cook, Linda, 155
Cook, Reena, 359
Cooke, Jennifer, 230
Cooney, Dennis, 117, 317
Cooper, Jeanne, 297
Copeland, Joan, 125, 276, 318
Corbett, Glenn, 349
Corbett, Michael, 265, 289
Corbin, Lamont, 206
Corby, Evelyn, 320
Corby, Stacy, 320
Corday, Betty, 134, 135
Corday, Ken, 135
Corday, Ted, 34, 37, 60, 106–107, 134–135, 213, 214, 329
Corelli, Dr. Joe, 320
Corelli, Mario, 251
Corelli, Renata, 287
Corrington, Joyce and Bill, 270, 357
Cortland, Nicholas, 288
Cortlandt, Nina, 75
Cortlandt, Palmer, 75
Cory, MacKenzie, 83, 89
Costello, Ward, 160, 333
Coster, Nick, 90, 334
Council, Richard, 124
Court, Geraldine, 229, 348
Courtney, Deborah, 321

Courtney, Jacquie, 45, 46, 80, 82, 83, 86, 239, 247, 252
Courtney, Liz, 150
Cowles, Matthew, 72
Cox, Richard, 320
Craggs, Paul, 325
Craig, Cathy, 238, 241
Craig, Don, 140
Craig, Hal, 314
Craig, Dr. James, 239, 241
Craig, Tony, 166
Cram, Cusi, 253
Cramer, Dr. Dorian, 239, 243
Cramer, Melinda, 243
Crandall, Bill, 318
Crandall, Doris, 215
Crandall, Ginny, 318
Crane, Dagne, 114
Cranston, Bryan, 237
Crawford, Betsy, 322
Crawford, Christina, 4
Crawford, Joan, 4
Crawford, Lee, 295
Crawford, Maggie, 124
Crawford, Dr. Tom, 323
Craythorne, Tom, 317
Criscuolo, Lou, 162
Crocker, Silas, 231
Croft, Aldrich, 349
Crosely, Chase, 216
Crothers, Joel, 168, 335
Crowell, McLin, 96
Crowell, Sam, 259
Crown, Ellie, 29, 313
Cruisinberry, Jane, 18
Cudahy, Sean, 74
Cudahy, Tom, 73
Cullen, Kathleen, 229
Culliton, Richard, 357
Cummings, Tony, 99
Cunningham, John, 86, 237, 281
Cunningham, Sarah, 80
Curtin, Walter, 81, 82, 87
Curtis, George, 295
Curtis, Jack, 301
Curtis, Joan, 301
Curtis, Dr. Neil, 144
Curtis, Todd, 130
Cusack, Dr. Joe, 325
Cypher, Jon, 123

Dabney, Augusta, 195, 237
Dade, Phil, 132
Dailey, Irene, 84, 157
Dale, Meg, 312
Dale, Sarah, 312
Dale, Vanessa, 26, 28, 311, 312
Dale, Will, 312
Dallas, Johnny, 159
Dallas, Tracy, 164

Dalton, Deborah, 150
Dalton, Doris, 272
Dalton, Lezlie, 228
Dalton, Mark, 74
Daly, Jane, 132
Damian, Michael, 305
Damon, Les, 106, 110, 215
Damon, Stuart, 180, 200
Dana, Leora, 97
Dancy, Jerry, 349
Dancy, Joan, 349
Dancy, Luke, 349
Dancy, Nola, 349
Dancy, Sara, 349
Dane, Marco, 60, 248, 251
Danelle, John, 76
Daniels, David Mason, 131
Dano, Linda, 102, 125
Dante, Dr. Mark, 196
Dante, Mary Ellen "Mellie," 196
D'Antoni, Marc, 287
D'Antoni, Nick, 287
Dark Shadows, 37, 38, 384–385
Darnay, Toni, 112
Darnell, Lilly, 264
Date with Life, A, 33, 379
David Harum, 12, 366
Davidson, Bill, 18
Davidson, Doug, 304
Davidson, Eileen, 305
Davies, Gwen, 151
Davies, Lane, 151
Davies, Peter, 236
Davis, Dr. Althea, 344, 346
Davis, Daniel, 358
Davis, Dave, 346
Davis, Gerald, 89
Davis, Joan, 21
Davis, Nick, 63
Davis, Rachel, 85
Davis, Sammy, Jr., 4
Davis, Terry, 102, 168
Davis, Todd, 199
Dawson, Curt, 100, 230
Dawson, Howie, 191
Dawson, Mark, 63
Dawson, Vicky, 96, 122
Days of Our Lives, 6, 37, 38, 43, 46,
    50, 54, 55, 134–153
    background, 134–135
    cast, 151–153
    story, 135–151
De Bell, Kristine, 305
De Coit, Dick, 301
De Poulignac, Cecile, 100
De Poulignac, Countess Elena, 92
De Witt, Tracy, 99
Deakins, Senator Ed, 314
Deas, Justin, 113, 260
DeBord, Sharon, 191

Deerfield, Lynn, 219
Dekker, Elena, 360
Dekker, Max, 359
Dekker, Rikki, 360
Delaney, Kim, 76
Delaney, Robert, 90
Delany, Dana, 325
Delmar, Tracy, 217
Delubec, Armand, 22
Deming, Carol, 116
Demming, Ellen, 213, 214
Denbo, Jack, 146
Denham, Mary, 348
Denning, Senator Mark, 132
Denning, Sloane, 132
Dennis, Althea, 329
Dennis, Babby, 329
Dennis, Grayling, 329
Dennis, John, 318
Dennis, Patsy, 329
Dennis, Reverend Richard, 20, 329
Dennis, Sandy, 4
Descartes, Sylvie, 288
Desiderio, Dr. Carl, 82
Desmond, Tom, 262
Devereaux, Camilla, 170
Devereaux, Ian, 170
Devine, Kathleen, 250, 287
Devlin, Jay, 71
Devlin, John, 65
Dezina, Kathleen, 71
Di Francisco, Nina, 334
Di Lucca, Roy, 202
Di Mera, Anthony, 151
Di Mera, Stefano, 151
Dickson, Brenda, 295
Diedrickson, Jim, 170
Dillman, Claudia, 217
Dillman, Marty, 217
Dixon, John, 59, 116
Dobson, Bridget, 46, 214
Dobson, Jerome, 46, 50, 110, 214
Dr. Hudson's Secret Journal, 35
Doctors, The, 36, 50, 310, 344–352
    background, 344
    cast, 350–352
    story, 345–350
Dolan, Ellen, 231
Donato, Danny, 132
DonHowe, Gwyda, 99
Donnelley, Alex, 305
Donnelly, Iris, 38, 353, 354
Donnelly, Laura, 38, 353, 354
Donnelly, Martha, 354
Donnelly, Ricky, 354
Donnelly, Tom, 354
Donnelly, Dr. Will, 354
Donovan, Burke, 126
Donovan, Douglas, 236
Donovan, Dustin, 126

Donovan, Mike, 236
Donovan, Noreen Vochek, 236
Donovan, Patrick, 236
Donovan, Stacey, 236
Donovan, Tom, 80, 81, 177, 178
Dorn, Eliot, 168
Dorrance, Eddie, 72
Douglas, Burt, 156
Douglas, Fred, 86
Douglas, James, 88, 117
Douglas, Jerry, 304
Douglas, Kim, 147
Douglas, Noel, 164
Douglas, Susan, 214, 215
Dow, Richard, 322
Downs, Ada, 84
Downs, Ernie, 84
Doyan, Aja, 289
Drake, Adam, 156
Drake, Alfred, 170
Drake, Dr. Noah, 185, 206
Dressler, Eric, 273
Dressler, Lieux, 175, 179, 201
Drew, Wendy, 106, 111
Driver, John, 161
Dru, Mitchell, 37, 80
Dubois, Renee, 230
Dudley, Amy, 99
Duffy, Julia, 346
Dufour, Val, 81, 87, 281
Dukakis, Olympia, 289
Duke, Patty, 329
Dumas, Helene, 317
Dumonde, Lee, 150
Dumonde, Renee, 151
Dumont, Paul, 286
Dunbar, Alan, 336
Dunbar, Susan Ames, 332
Dunlap, Jason, 99
Durham, Christopher, 132
Dusay, Marj, 130
Duval, Karl, 147
Duval, Martine, 169
Duval, Sharon, 147
Dwyer, Virginia, 30, 80, 84, 215, 333
Dynasty, 55
Dysert, Alan, 74

Early, Candace, 70
Easton, Joyce, 138
Ebersole, Christine, 265
Eccles, Ted, 195
Eckhardt, Agnes, 268
Eda-Young, Barbara, 95
Edge of Night, The, 35, 154–173
    background, 154–155
    cast, 170–173
    story, 155–170
Edmunds, Louis, 76
Edwards, Bruce, 333

Edwards, Jane, 333
Edwards, Randall, 257
Egan, Richard, 130
Egg and I, The, 375
Eilbacher, Cynthia, 304
Eisley, Anthony, 132
Elg, Taina, 253
Eliot, Brad, 293, 294
Elliot, Bruce, 113
Elliot, Jane, 201, 231
Elliott, Helen, 353
Elliott, Mark, 38, 353
Elliott, Mia, 353
Elliott, Phil, 353
Ellison, Brian, 120
Ellison, Mary, 120
Ellison, Teddy, 120
Elman, Irving, 177
Elman, Tex, 177
Elstner, Anne, 17, 20, 23
Emerson, Brian, 289
Endicott, Dwight, 170
English, Brooke, 71
English, Peg, 76
English, Philip, 349
Eric, Duncan, 273
Espy, William Gray, 98, 294
Estrin, Patricia, 288
Eubanks, Shannon, 237
Eure, Wesley, 138
Evans, Dr. Marlena, 147
Evans, Michael, 303
Everly, Patricia, 294
Ewing, Blaine, 97
Ewing, Larry, 97

Fairbanks, Dr. Greg, 230
Fairbanks, Sarah, 279
Fairchild, Morgan, 284
Fairman, Michael, 321
Fairmeadows, U.S.A., 375
Falk, Rick, 186
Fallon, Joshua, 150
Faraday, Josie, 165
Faraday, Mark, 165
Faraday, Serena, 165
Faraday, Timmy, 165
Fargo, Danny, 81, 85
Farley, Elizabeth, 160
Farmer, Ben, 244
Farrell, Brian, 322
Farrell, Kit, 99
Farrell, Mike, 138
Farrell, Shea, 132
Faulkner, Cameron, 192
Fawcett, Allen, 169
Fee, Melinda, 217
Feinstein, Alan, 159

Felder, Sarah, 262
Fenelli, Jack, 258
Ferguson, Hank, 71
Ferra, Toni, 347
Ferris, Jason, 319
Ferris, Sharon, 319
Ferro, Mathilde, 174
Ferro, Theodore, 174
Ferrone, Dan, 317
Fickett, Mary, 62, 63
Fielding, Alec, 345
Fielding, Dorothy, 349
Fielding, Dr. Maggie, 345
Fields, Dr. Jim, 159
Fink, John, 317
First Hundred Years, The, 25, 374–375
First Love, 33, 377
Fishburne, Laurence, 243
Fisher, Frances, 168
Fitzgerald, Geraldine, 40
Fitzpatrick, John, 91
Flame in the Wind, 37, 382–383
Flannery, Susan, 136
Flax, Margo, 66
Fleischman, Larry, 71
Flemming, Felicia, 321
Fletcher, Johnny, 216
Fletcher, Dr. Paul, 215
Fletcher, Steve, 250
Flood, Ann, 156, 342
Follow Your Heart, 33, 376
For Better or Worse, 35, 380–381
For Richer, For Poorer, 47
Forbes, Ann Alden, 236
Forbes, Jack, 236
Forbes, Lorna, 236
Forbes, Roger, 236
Forbes, Susan, 156
Ford, Constance, 84, 272
Ford, David, 281
Ford, Paul, 4
Ford, Steven, 305
Forest, Michael, 123
Forman, William, 5
Forrest, Tammy, 316
Forsyth, David, 126, 359
Forsythe, Betty, 112
Forsythe, Henderson, 111–112, 342
Foster, Bill, 298
Foster, Greg, 295
Foster, Jill, 295
Foster, Liz, 295
Foster, "Snapper," 294
Fowkes, Conard, 39, 286
Frame, Diane, 101
Frame, Janice, 97
Frame, Steve, 81, 82, 83, 85
Frame, Vince, 96

Frame, Willis, 91
Frances, Anne, 4
Francis, Genie, 182, 183, 184, 185–186, 194
Frangione, Nancy, 100
Franklin, Hugh, 62, 63
Franklin, Dr. Julie, 43
Franklin, Lynn, 341
Frann, Mary, 144
Franz, Elizabeth, 101
Fraser, Ben, 341
Fraser, Elizabeth, 341
Frazier, Rev. Norman, 125
Fredericks, Ilsa, 99
Freeman, Al, Jr., 243
Freund, Josh, 289
Frid, Jonathan, 37
From These Roots, 35, 310, 341–343
Froman, David, 169
Front Page Farrell, 12
Fuccello, Tom, 248, 353
Full Circle, 381
Fulmer, Ray, 218
Fulton, Eileen, 6, 113
Fulton, Nora, 170
Funai, Helen, 147

Gabet, Sharon, 168
Gabriel, John, 189, 259
Gabriel, Sandy, 71
Gale, David, 167, 288, 337
Gallagher, Helen, 257
Gallant, Felicia, 102
Gallison, Joe, 81, 85, 144
Galloway, Don, 334
Gamble, Duncan, 132
Gantry, Don, 354
Gantry, Joel, 160
Gantry, Lee, 218
Garber, Terri, 359
Gardner, Bud, 273
Gardner, Eunice, 53, 273
Gardner, Frank, 273
Gardner, Jenny, 76
Gardner, Opal, 50, 76
Gardner, Ray, 72
Garfield, Michael, 99
Garland, Beverly, 4
Garretson, Rafe, 253
Garrett, Maureen, 219, 265
Garrison, Nancy, 354
Garrison, Norman, 120
Garrison, Spence, 354
Gateson, Majorie, 31
Gatteys, Bennye, 136
Gatto, Peter, 324
Gautreaux, David, 288
Gaynes, George, 202

Gaynor, Jock, 344
Geary, Tony, 181, 182–183, 184, 200, 295
General Hospital, 3, 4, 6, 7, 36, 41, 46, 48, 49, 50, 51, 54, 174–209
    background, 174–186
    cast, 206–209
    story, 186–206
Genovese, John Kelly, 176
Gentry, Bob, 100, 215
George, Tony, 247, 278
Gerard, Gil, 348
Gerringer, Robert, 318
Gethers, Steven, 314
Gibb, Cynthia, 287
Gibboney, Linda, 75
Gibson, Amy, 325
Gibson, John, 215, 304
Gibson, Robert, 302
Gideon, Bond, 295
Gifford, Allan, 158
Gilbert, Lauren, 154, 317
Gilbey, Simon, 116
Gilchrist, Dave, 92
Gill, Marion, 275
Gillespie, Ann, 262
Gillette, Anita, 101
Gilliss, Gwynn, 63
Gilmore, Virginia, 276
Girardin, Ray, 191
Glaser, Paul Michael, 320
Glass, Kathy, 246
Gleason, Paul, 70
Gleason, Regina, 137
Godart, Lee, 74, 168
Goddard, Louise, 95
Goddard, Mark, 253
Goetz, Theo, 213, 214, 219
Goldbergs, The, 9
Golden Windows, 33, 378
Goodrich, Deborah, 74
Gordon, Beatrice, 91
Gordon, Gerald, 196, 344, 346
Gordon, Mick, 250
Gordon, Olive, 92
Gordon, Raymond, 91–92
Gorman, Mari, 162
Gorman, Walter, 329
Gorney, Karen, 63
Gorshin, Frank, 170
Gothard, David, 16, 23
Goulet, Nicolette, 259, 278
Goutman, Chris, 287
Gowdy, Karen Morris, 260
Graham, June, 217, 334
Granger, Farley, 247
Granger, Shelley, 132
Grant, Alberto, 159

Grant, Alice, 175, 201
Grant, Armand, 174
Grant, Bernard, 215, 240
Grant, Dr. Dick, 53, 215
Grant, Dr. Frank, 76
Grant, Heather, 197
Grant, Laura, 215
Grant, Lee, 4, 272
Grant, Valerie, 146
Graves, Ernest, 216, 239
Graves, Leslie, 130
Gray, Bruce, 168
Gray, Carla, 238, 243
Gray, Charles, 298
Gray, David, 205
Gray, Florence, 190
Gray, Gordon, 190
Gray, Joan, 215
Gray, Melinda, 123
Gray, Sadie, 243
Gray, Veleka, 123, 324, 354
Grayson, Bernard, 125
Greatest Gift, The, 33, 36, 378
Green, Dorothy, 294
Greenan, David, 230
Greer, Charlotte, 265
Gregory, Jay, 161
Gregory, Michael, 195
Gregory, Roxanne, 321
Grey, Janet, 229
Griffith, Ed, 334
Grimes, Sally, 194
Groome, Malcolm, 260
Grosvenor, Dick, 17
Grosvenor, Laurel, 52
Grove, Elaine, 325
Grove, Jerry, 99
Grove, Margo, 99
Grover, Cindy, 320
Grover, Edward, 117
Grover, Jamie, 335
Grover, Stephen, 335
Guiding Light, The, 5, 20, 23, 25, 29, 33–34, 42, 49, 50, 52, 53, 54, 210–234
    background, 210–214
    cast, 211, 232–234
    radio soap, 367
    story, 214–231
Guthrie, Richard, 138
Guthrie, Steve, 168

Hadley, Brett, 303
Haggart, John, 24
Hagman, Larry, 4
Hailey, Marian, 271
Haines, Cynthia, 125
Haines, Larry, 23, 212, 269, 271

Hale, Ron, 258
Hall, Cliff, 270
Hall, Diedre, 147, 298
Hall, Lt. Ed, 243
Hall, Grayson, 254
Hall-Lovell, Andrea, 148
Hallick, Tom, 294
Halliday, Meredith, 116
Halloway, Rick, 99
Halloway, Taylor, 99
Halsey, Brett, 304
Hamill, Mark, 189
Hamilton, Adele, 146
Hamilton, Brooke, 146
Hamilton, Dan, 97, 168, 337
Hamilton, David, 181, 197–198
Hamilton, Glenn, 318
Hamilton, Randy, 360
Hammer, Jay, 359
Hammer, Pamela Long, 357
Hammett, Mike, 88
Hampton, Jeb, 359
Hanley, Carolyn, 287
Hansen, Ellen, 157
Hansen, Peter, 177, 188
Harbach, Steve, 325
Harben, Chandler Hill, 312, 359
Hardy, Dr. Steve, 174, 175, 187
Hargrave, T. J., 226
Harland, Jane, 191
Harmon, Jennifer, 241
Harper, Benno "Beanie," 312
Harper, Carolyn, 304
Harper, Charles, 312
Harper, Dianne, 148
Harper, Ellie, 280
Harper, Josephine, 166
Harper, Lurlene, 360
Harper, Raymond, 167
Harper, Ron, 99, 324
Harrington, Kate, 220
Harris, Berkeley, 354
Harris, Kimberly, 265
Harris, Pauline, 333
Harrold, Kathryn, 349
Hart, David, 322
Hart, Jeff, 321
Hart, Nina, 116
Hartford, Dr. Greg, 286
Hartford, Meredith, 286
Harvey, Joan, 156
Harvey, Ken, 278
Haskell, Peter, 265
Hasselhoff, David, 4, 294
Hastings, Don, 112, 154
Hatch, Richard, 63
Hauser, Wings, 295
Hawkins, Michael, 353
Hawkins Falls, 25, 375

Hawthorne, James, 169
Hayes, Bill, 135, 139, 150
Hayes, Dr. Elizabeth, 344
Hayes, George, 216
Hayes, Susan Seaforth, 134, 135, 136
Hayes, Wendy, 325
Hayman, Lillian, 243
Hays, Kathryn, 116
Heberle, Kay, 301
Heen, Gladys, 211
Heflin, Frances, 66
Heflin, Van, 4
Heineman, Laurie, 92
Helene, Tante, 287
Helgenberger, Marg, 262
Henderson, Benjamin, 231
Henderson, Brandy, 162
Henderson, Dr. Bruce, 300
Henderson, Lynn, 325
Henderson, Mark, 300
Henderson, Quentin, 166
Herlie, Eileen, 69
Herrera, Anthony, 123, 301
Hewitt, Beatrice, 200
Hewitt, Jeremy, 200
Hiatt, Shelby, 191
Hickland, Catherine, 359
Hidden Faces, 39, 385
Higby, Mary Jane, 21, 25, 52
Higgins, Dennis Jay, 259
Higgins, Joel, 270, 285
Higgs, Richard, 324, 347
Higley, Phil, 96
Hill, Charlie, 360
Hill, Janet, 335
Hill, Tiffany, 205
Hillyer, Liz, 159
Hillyer, Orin, 159
Hirson, Alice, 157, 241
Hobart, Deborah, 99
Hobart, Dr. James, 189
Hobbs, Peter, 31–32, 332
Hobson, Charlie, 93
Hobson, Clarice, 91
Hobson, Denny, 101
Hodiak, John, 211
Hoffman, Dustin, 5
Hogan, Bob, 186
Hogan, Johathan, 349
Holbrook, Hal, 4, 329
Holchak, Victor, 148
Holcombe, Harry, 273
Holden, Mark, 215
Holden, Ned, 211
Holder, Christopher, 304
Holland, Charlotte, 214
Holland, Pat, 122
Holland, Richard, 106, 177
Holland, Suzanne, 177
Hollister, Brad, 123

Holly, Ellen, 238, 243
Holmes, Teddy, 189
Hope, Erika, 304
Horan, James, 101
Horgan, Patrick, 168, 347
Horton, Addie, 135
Horton, Alice, 135
Horton, Bill, 54, 135
Horton, Kitty, 137
Horton, Laura, 54
Horton, Marie, 137
Horton, Michael, 138
Horton, Mickey, 135, 137
Horton, Robert, 125
Horton, Sandy, 137
Horton, Dr. Tom, 134–135
Horton, Tommy, 135
Hotchkiss, Joan, 333–334
Hotel Cosmopolitan, 35, 379
Houghton, James, 295
Houlton, Jennifer, 345
House, Jane, 115, 312
House in the Garden, The, 375
House on High Street, The, 35, 381
Houseboat Hanna, 12
Hover, Bob, 120
How to Survive a Marriage, 42–43,
    388–389
Howard, Amanda, 144
Howard, Cassie, 253
Howard, Eve, 306
Howard, Lisa, 215
Howell, Erik, 216
Hoye, Gloria, 353
Hsueh, Nancy, 353
Hubbard, Elizabeth, 215, 346
Hubbard, Jesse, 76
Hubbard, Liz, 344
Hubly, Susan, 320
Huddleston, Talbot, 248
Hudgins, Wayne, 122
Hudson, Gary, 116
Huebing, Craig, 177, 187, 341, 342
Hughes, Arhur, 18
Hughes, Barnard, 215
Hughes, Bob, 6, 106, 112–113
Hughes, Chris, 105, 106, 108, 110
Hughes, Donald, 106, 116
Hughes, Edith, 105, 111
Hughes, Nancy, 111
Hughes, Penny, 105, 111
Hughes, Tom, 113
Hughes, Will "Pa," 105, 106, 111
Hugo, Larry, 155, 273
Hulswit, Mart, 215
Hummert, Anne, 12, 13, 16, 17,
    18–20, 23
Hummert, Frank, 12, 13, 16, 17,
    18–20, 23
Hunt, Adrienne, 349

Hunt, Becky Lee, 250
Hunter, Emily, 280
Hunter, Kim, 168
Hunter, Susan, 136
Huntington, Margo, 168
Hursley, Doris, 36, 174, 175–176, 177
Hursley, Frank, 36, 174, 175–176, 177
Hussman, Ron, 273
Huston, Pat, 135

Inner Flame, The, 33, 377
Irving, Charles, 29, 269
Itkin, Paul Henry, 146, 160
Ivey, Lela, 170

Jackson, Leslie, 218
Jackson, Ron, 318
Jackson, Dr. Stephen, 218
Jacobi, Steve, 76
James, Clifton, 359
James, Francesca, 66, 72
James, Leslie, 148
Jamison, Elly Jo, 159
Jamison, Kevin, 161
Janney, Leon, 80
Jannings, Karl, 215
Jannings, Ruth, 215
Janssen, Dr. Peter, 252
Jarkowsky, Andrew, 88, 281
Jarrett, Christopher, 170
Jeffers, Ann, 225
Jeffers, Spence, 225
Jeffries, Vance, 246
Jenkins, Diane, 305
Jenner, Barry, 94
Jennings, Tom, 341
Jerome, Ed, 312
John's Other Wife, 12, 210
Johnson, Bess, 269, 270
Johnson, Carrie, 323
Johnson, Georgann, 123
Johnson, Janet, 215
Johnson, Poppy, 170
Johnson, Raymond Edward, 211
Johnson, Tina, 360
Johnston, Audre, 337
Johnston, Lionel, 94
Johnstone, William, 106, 111
Jones, Carolyn, 130
Jones, Christine, 97, 265
Jones, Ken George, 264
Jones, Lorenzo, 23
Jones, Tommy Lee, 241
Jones, Trent, 264
Jonvil, Monique, 76
Jordan, Bobbi, 195
Jordan, Collie, 314
Joslyn, George, 279
Joyce, Bill, 150
Joyce, Stephen, 99

Joyce Jordan, Girl Interne, 368–369
Joyce Jordan, M.D., 368
Just Plain Bill, 12, 17–18, 23, 364

Kahmi, Kathy, 73
Kalem, Toni, 92
Kalember, Patricia, 236
Kamel, Stanley, 141
Kane, Erica, 63–64
Kane, Michael, 215
Kane, Mona, 66
Kane, Silver, 74
Karpf, Elinor, 130
Karr, Katrina, 249
Karr, Laurie Ann, 155
Karr, Mike, 154, 155
Karr, Nancy, 155
Karras, Christina, 71
Kasdorf, Lenore, 224
Kaslo, Amy, 270, 285
Kaslo, Bruce, 270
Kaslo, Liza, 270
Kaslo, Steve, 270, 285
Kates, Bernard, 217
Kavanaugh, Dorrie, 241
Kayzer, Beau, 298
Keal, Anita, 287
Keane, Teri, 156, 237, 250
Kearney, Eileen, 345
Keeler, Rev. Dr., 215
Keen, Noah, 237
Keenan, Paul, 150
Keifer, Liz, 305
Keith, Dr. Alex, 123
Keith, Lawrence, 63, 84
Keith, Susan, 100, 250
Keller, Mary Page, 90, 265
Kelly, Daren, 71
Kelly, Dr. Jim, 215
Kelly, Joe, 201
Kelly, Paddy, 206
Kelly, Rose, 206
Kemmer, Ed, 121
Kemp, Elizabeth, 322
Kendall, Brian, 247
Kendall, Pat, 239, 247
Kendall, Paul, 248
Kennemer, Robin, 285
Kenney, H. Wesley, 134, 293
Kennicot, Dan, 71
Kennicott, Mary, 65
Kerwin, Brian, 295
Kibbee, Lois, 158
Kiberd, James, 236
Kilman, Peter, 191
Kimmell, Dana, 358
Kincaid, Dan, 336
Kincaid, Hillary, 227
Kincaid, Kevin, 336
Kincaid, Simone, 227

King, Mimi, 253
King, Tom, 21
King, Woody, 151
Kingsley, Brandon, 73
Kingsley, Sara, 73
Kinkead, Maeve, 92, 231
Kipling, Faith, 252
Kipling, Dr. Ivan, 252
Kirby, Chris, 43
Kirkland, Amanda, 265
Kirkland, Catsy, 265
Kirkland, Hollis ("Kirk"), 265
Kitty Foyle, 15, 35, 379
Klein, Addie, 214
Klenck, Margaret, 250
Kloss, Bud, 80
Klunis, Tom, 286
Knapp, Robert, 136
Knotts, Don, 272
Knowles, Ox, 265
Kobe, Gail, 42
Kositchek, Chris, 148
Kositchek, Jake, 150
Kosloff, Sylvie, 97
Kovac, Eric, 337
Kozak, Harley, 360
Krakauer, Tess, 319
Kramer, Bert, 98, 358
Kramer, Mandel, 156
Kransky, Rose, 211
Kristen, Ilene, 257
Kurty, Lee, 320
Kyle, Dr. Winston, 288

La Tour, Estelle, 71–72
Labine, Claire, 46, 257, 311
Lacy, Jerry, 116, 302–303, 319
LaDue, Joe, 303
LaGioia, John, 159
Laird, Marlena, 179, 181, 182
Laire, Judson, 354
Lake, Cindy, 306
Lake, Myra, 333–334
Lambie, Joseph, 168
Lammers, Paul, 342
Lamont, Charles, 319
Lamont, Diana, 319
Lamont, Vic, 159
Lamonte, Carol, 90
LaMura, Mark, 74
Landers, Audrey, 337
Landers, Robert, 337
Landon, Sofia, 228
Landzaat, Andre, 204
Lane, Harry, 154
Lane, Sara, 154, 155
Lang, Bob, 215
Lang, Elliot, 325
Lange, Jeanne, 90
Langley, Spence, 289

Lanning, Jerry, 287, 358
LaPiere, Georgann, 197
Larimer, Dr. Ann, 348
Larkin, John, 154, 155
Larsen, Jamie, 288
Larson, Lisby, 358
LaRussa, Adrienne, 146
Last Year's Nest, 24
Latessa, Dick, 164
Latimer, Guy, 318
Latimer, Hank, 319
Latimer, Rick, 319
Latimore, Frank, 257
Lau, Lawrence, 76
Laurence, Angela, 305
Laurence, Claire, 305
Laurence, Robert, 305
Lauret, Laryssa, 227, 346
Laverty, Kirk, 97
Lawrence, Elizabeth, 76
Lawson, Jack, 241
Lawson, Lee, 230, 317
Layne, Mary, 170
Lazer, Peter, 271
Le Claire, Robert, 146
Le Page, Walter, 163
Leak, Jennifer, 92, 296
Lear, Norman, 5
Lee, Anna, 200
Lee, Billy, 106
Lee, Roger, 288
Leigh, Janna, 102
Leighton, Robert, 304
Leister, Johanna, 156
Lemay, Harding, 45, 46, 55, 82, 83
Lemmon, Jack, 4
Lenard, Mark, 81
Leplat, Ted, 230, 325
Lesan, Dave, 213
Leshinsky, Eric, 278
Leslie, Bethel, 345
Lester, Terry, 304
Letchworth, Eileen, 66, 319
Levin, Michael, 258
Levitt, Amy, 241
Lewis, David, 200, 315
Lewis, Edwina, 250
Lewis, Elizabeth, 174
Lewis, Josh, 231
Lewis, Judy, 194, 333
Lewis, Terry, 329
Life Can Be Beautiful, 370
Light, Judith, 248
Light, Karl, 346
Ligon, Tom, 237, 302
Lincoln, Pamela, 321, 349
Lindeman, Regine, 95
Linden, Allison, 359
Linden, Ashley, 359
Linden, Gregory, 359

Linden, Hal, 277
Linder, Cec, 157, 332
Lindley, Audra, 80, 84
Lines, Marion, 170
Ling, Kim Soo, 324
Linville, Joanne, 216
Liotta, Ray, 96
Lipton, James, 81, 215
Lipton, Michael, 112
Lipton, Robert, 125
Livingstone, Samantha, 195
Lloyd, Rita, 229
LoBianco, Tony, 320
Locke, Ralph, 24
Logan, Anne, 201
Logan, Arnie, 322
Logan, Kay, 319
Lohman, Rick, 281
Lollie Baby, 17
Lombardo, John, 148
Long, Pam, 359
Long, Ronald, 315
Longfield, Michael, 359
LoPinto, Dorian, 250
Lord, Meredith, 240
Lord, Tony Harris, 239, 246
Lord, Victor, 239
Lord, Victoria, 238, 240
Lorenzo Jones, 12, 18, 23, 367–368
Loring, Ann, 316
Loring, Dr. Anthony, 5
Loring, Gloria, 150
Loring, Lisa, 124
Loring, Lynn, 269, 270
Loughlin, Lori, 169
Love Is a Many Splendored Thing,
  38–39, 42, 310, 353–356
Love of Life, 4, 7, 25, 26, 28, 29, 32,
  24, 53, 310, 311–328
    background, 311–312
    cast, 325–328
    story, 312–325
Lovers and Friends, 46–47, 389
Lovett, Arlene, 322
Loving, 7, 235–237
Loving Friends and Perfect Couples,
  51
Low, Carl, 276
Lowe, Candy, 320
Lowe, Chris, 278
Lowell, Claire, 105, 106, 111
Lowell, Ellen, 105, 106, 111
Lowell, Jim, 106, 110
Lowell, Judge, 105, 106, 111
Lucas, Sam, 84
Lucci, Susan, 63–64
Lucia, Chip, 246
Luckinbill, Larry, 336
Luisi, James, 91
Lum, Myrtle, 69

Lumb, Geoffrey, 80
LuPone, Robert, 271
Lupton, John, 135, 137
Lydon, James, 25
Lyman, Dorothy, 50, 76, 92, 159
Lyman, William, 92
Lynch, Suzanne, 303
Lynde, Janice, 99, 294
Lyons, Philip, 100

Ma Perkins, 12–13, 23, 365
Mac-Hale, Philip, 246
MacDonnell, Ray, 62, 63
MacKay, Nancy, 320
MacKey, Bobby, 320
MacLaughlin, Don, 5–6, 106, 108, 110
MacLean, Peter, 335
MacRae, Elizabeth, 188
Madden, Donald, 275
Madison, Brian, 168
Madison, Nola, 168
Madison, Owen, 168
Madison, Paige, 168
Madurga, Gonzalo, 230
Maharis, George, 273
Maitland, Beth, 305
Malin, Marian, 282
Malis, Claire, 243
Mallory, David, 302
Mallory, Derek, 168
Mallory, Edward, 135
Mallory, Victoria, 294
Malloy, Larkin, 169
Malone, Flip, 217
Malone, Laura, 97
Mandan, Bob, 276, 341, 342
Manetta, Joe, 332
Mannering, Marsha, 22
Mansfield, John, 249
Marcantel, Chris, 237
Marceau, Bill, 156
March, Audrey, 177, 187
March, Lori, 335, 359
March, Lucille, 187
Marie, Lisa, 202
Mark, Flip, 136
Marland, Douglas, 48, 49, 50,
  178–179, 180, 181, 182, 183, 214,
  235
Marler, Carrie, 231
Marler, Dr. Justin, 212, 227
Marler, Ross, 230
Marlin, Joe, 21
Marlowe, Bilan, 126
Marlowe, Chris, 325
Marlowe, Hugh, 83
Marlowe, Miranda, 125
Maroney, Kelli, 265
Marriott, Dr. Andrew, 324
Marriott, Andy, 325

Marriott, Mia, 324
Marshall, Alex, 149
Marshall, Barrett, 358
Marshall, Courtney, 359
Marshall, Dawn, 358
Marshall, Justin, 358
Marshall, Mike, 358
Marshall, Paige, 358
Marston, Joel, 191
Martin, Ann-Marie, 151
Martin, Bruce, 158
Martin, David, 136
Martin, Debbie, 157
Martin, Dick, 121
Martin, Doug, 278
Martin, Jeff, 63
Martin, Joseph, 63
Martin, Lucy, 158
Martin, Marcella, 85
Martin, Mitzi, 170
Martin, Oliver, 151
Martin, Paul, 65
Martin, Stephanie, 157
Martin, Tara, 63
Martin, W. T., 324
Martinsville, U.S.A., 375
Marx, Gregg, 138
Mary Hartman, Mary Hartman, 5
Mary Noble, Backstage Wife, 22, 23,
  365
Mascolo, Joseph, 151
Mason, Janet, 218
Mason, Margaret, 142
Massey, Andrea Evans, 248
Masters, Marie, 115
Masterson, Kylie, 174, 175
Match, M. J., 350
Matheson, Don, 192
Mathews, Walter, 89
Mathis, Sherry, 270, 281
Matthaei, Konrad, 117
Matthews, Alice, 80, 86
Matthews, Bill, 81, 85
Matthews, Carmen, 345
Matthews, Grace, 217
Matthews, Jack, 23
Matthews, Jim, 80, 83
Matthews, Liz, 80, 84
Matthews, Mary, 80, 84
Matthews, Pat, 80, 84
Matthews, Russ, 85
Matthews, Susan, 80, 86
Matthews, Wally, 117
Matthews, William, 83–84
Mattson, Robin, 197
Mauceri, Patricia, 123
Maxted, Ellen, 360
Maxwell, Jason, 65
May, Deborah, 230
May, Donald, 156, 359

Mayer, Paul Avila, 46, 257, 311
Maynard, Diana, 187
Maynard, Mimi, 304
Mays, Dawson, 205
McAllen, Kathleen Rowe, 126
McAllister, Matt, 246
McArdle, Andrea, 283
McArthur, Jane, 275
McBride, Jean, 311, 312
McCabe, Marcia, 288
McCafferty, John, 358
McCambridge, Mercedes, 4, 211
McCandless, Baxter, 130
McCandless, Gillian, 132
McCandless, Matt, 132
McCandless, Thomas, 132
McCandless, Tyler, 21, 131
McCandless, Wally, 132
McCarren, Jim, 278
McCarthy, Ann, 324
McCarthy, Juliana, 295
McCary, Rod, 191
McCauley, Prof. Timothy, 325
McCay, Peggy, 311, 312
McColl, Diana, 125
McColl, Whit, 125
McConnell, Judith, 121, 191
McConnell, Ty, 260
McCook, John, 302
McCord, Quinton, 231
McCullough, Linda, 227
McDaniels, Alex, 225
McDevitt, Ruth, 25
McDonald, Ryan, 138
McDonnell, James, 250
McFadden, Barney, 230
McFadden, Wally, 74
McFarland, Ian, 123
McFarren, Ben, 225
McGee, Jack, 74
McGill, Everette, 225
McGilligan, Judith, 166
McGillin, Howard, 295
McGowan, Gil, 89
McGrath, Kelly, 169
McGrath, Paul, 215
McGreevy, Tom, 262
McGregor, Scotty, 316
McGuire, Biff, 333
McGuire, Maeve, 92, 156
McGuire, Sally, 44, 295
McGuire, Sandy, 114
McInerney, Bernie, 165, 247
McIntyre, Marilyn, 236, 287
McIntyre, Dr. Sara, 217
McKay, Scott, 166
McKenna, Margo, 169, 322
McKeon, Douglas, 165
McKinsey, Beverlee, 50, 83, 88, 96,
   354, 357, 358

McLain, Lana, 250
McLaughlin, Emily, 175, 186
McLaughlin, Rita, 116
McLeod, Augusta, 191
McNaughton, Stephen, 168
McNeil, Kathy, 125
McNeil, Keith, 289
McRae, Elizabeth, 140
McWilliams, Caroline, 99, 218
Meacham, Anne, 95
Meadows, Kristen, 253
Meecham, Wade, 168
Meeker, Ken, 253
Mendels, Rolanda, 96
Mercantel, Christopher, 101
Mergeron, Madam, 306
Merrill, Gary, 4
Meskill, Katherine, 275
Metcalf, Agnes, 275
Metcalf, Fred, 275
Micelli, Danny, 162
Michaels, Corinne, 148
Michaels, Emily, 169
Mickley, Bill, 180
Milgrim, Lynn, 86
Miller, Allan, 241
Miller, Alma, 115
Miller, Chris, 286
Miller, Lisa, 113
Miller, Taylor, 75
Milli, Robert, 74, 86, 219, 353
Milligan, Tuck, 349
Mills, Donna, 38, 42, 354
Mines, Steve, 136
Minor, Michael, 73, 120
Miss Susan, 33, 375
Mitchell, Cissie, 288
Mitchell, James, 75
Mitchell, Ralph, 122
Moar, Andrea, 75
Modern Romances, 33, 378
Mohica, Victor, 303
Moment of Truth, 383
Montgomery, Claudette, 68
Montgomery, Craig, 125
Montgomery, Julie, 250
Montgomery, Lyla, 123
Montgomery, Margo, 124
Monts, Susan, 289
Monty, Gloria, 4, 30–31, 48, 50, 51,
   178–182, 183–186
Mooney, Maureen, 225
Mooney, William, 65
Moore, Demi, 205
Moore, Everett, 275
Moore, Helene, 87
Moore, Isabelle, 275
Moore, Jonathan, 319
Moore, Lenore, 81, 87
Moore, Susan, 206

Moorehead, Agnes, 4
Moreno, Dr. Barbara, 289
Moreno, Dr. Gonzalo, 230
Moreno, Josh, 289
Morley, Chris, 203
Morning Star, 383
Morran, Jay, 96
Morrison, Joanna, 337
Morrison, Dr. John, 347
Morse, Richard, 215
Morse, Robert, 333
Moser, Margot, 344
Moses, Rick, 203
Mowery, Carrie, 227
Mowry, Jean, 333
Muenz, Richard, 262
Mulgrew, Kate, 259
Mullowney, Deborah, 132
Mundy, Meg, 349
Munker, Ariane, 123, 265
Murdoch, Myra, 76
Murphy, Timothy, Patrick, 289
Murray, Brian, 86
Murray, Carol, 189
Murray, Flo, 85
Murray, Kent, 189
Murray, Mary Gordon, 250
Murray, Peg, 323
Myers, Fran, 217
Myles, Meg, 346
Myrt and Marge, 9, 366–367

Nader, Michael, 121
Napier, Hugo, 125
Narizzano, Dino, 276
Needle, Karen, 170
Neeves, Dr. Brian, 337
Neil, Dianne Thompson, 360
Nelson, Cliff, 170
Nelson, Ed, 132
Nelson, Greg, 76
Nelson, Kelly, 230
Neuchateau, Corinne, 325
Never Too Young, 37, 384
Newman, Julia, 304
Newman, Robert, 231
Newman, Roger, 219
Newman, Stephen D., 358
Newman, Victor, 293–294, 304
Nielsen, Tom, 231
Nix, Martha, 148
Nixon, Agnes, 7, 39, 40, 50, 61 63,
   81–82, 235, 238, 268
Noble, Larry, 22
Noble, Mary, 22, 52
Noone, Kathleen, 74
Norden, Tommy, 281
Norris, Andrew, 230
Norris, Barbara, 219
Norris, Holly, 219

Norris, Ken, 214, 219
Norris, Stanley, 219
North, Heather, 137
North, Rebecca, 146
Northcote, Dr. Ian, 336
Northrop, Wayne, 151
Norton, Coe, 318
Norton, Leonie, 87, 241
Norwood, Dr. Gus, 168
Nouri, Michael, 270, 285
Novak, Joe, 262
Novotny, Tiso, 262
Nurses, The, 37, 384

O'Brien, David, 275, 334, 346
O'Leary, Michael, 219
Olsen, Rocky, 95
Olson, Ben, 136
Olson, Julie, 136
Olson, Steve, 136, 139
One Life to Live, 4, 7, 39, 40, 46, 60, 238–256
    background, 238–239
    cast, 254–256
    story, 239–254
One Man's Family, 24, 33, 373, 377
Ordway, Molly, 96
Orman, Roscoe, 70
O'Rourke, Thomas, 227
Orr, Tina, 286
Ortega, Santos, 106, 111
Osborne, Kipp, 279
O'Sullivan, Jim, 63
O'Sullivan, Terry, 271
Our Five Daughters, 35, 381–382
Our Gal Sunday, 12, 18, 21, 23, 367
Our Private World, 383
Owens, Albert, 169
Owens, Mary Jane, 325

Pace, Jennifer, 284
Pace, Walter, 286
Painted Dreams, 11
Palmer, Ken, 92
Palmer, Missy, 80, 85
Palmer, Scott, 150
Palzis, Kelly, 132
Paradise Bay, 383–384
Pardee, Miles, 53, 313
Parker, Dennis, 168
Parker, Floyd, 231
Parker, Frank, 206
Parker, Jameson, 250
Parker, Kathy, 278
Parker, Norman, 170
Parks, Hildy, 29–30, 311, 313
Parnell, Dennis, 312
Parrish, Gwen, 92
Patten, Dory, 324

Patterson, Lee, 240, 359
Patterson, Linda, 142
Patton, Mary, 271
Patton, Will, 265
Pavel, Michael, 265
Payne, Virginia, 13
Peabody, Rose, 272
Peabody, Wilbur, 272
Pearcy, Patricia, 243
Pearson, Ann, 273
Pease, Patsy, 288
Pellegrini, Gene, 318
Peluso, Lisa, 283
Penberthy, Beverly, 81, 84
Pendleton, Wyman, 168
Penghlis, Thaao, 151, 204
Penn, Noel, 316
Pennington, Marla, 195
Pennock, Chris, 181, 202
Pepper Young's Family, 210, 365–366
Perri, Paul, 96
Perrini, Angie, 92
Perrini, Joey, 96
Perrini, Rose, 96
Perry Mason, 372
Peters, Audrey, 312
Peters, Eric, 141
Peters, Dr. Greg, 140
Petersen, Sven, 95
Peterson, Arthur, 211
Peterson, Gene, 316
Peterson, Lenka, 275
Peterson, Melinda, 122
Petrie, George, 271
Petrovna, Sonia, 169, 287
Peyton Place, 54
Phillips, Bryan, 199
Phillips, Dr. Dan, 320
Phillips, Irna, 3, 11–12, 15, 20–21, 23, 33–34, 35, 37, 38, 40, 52, 53, 79–80, 81, 105–106, 107–109, 210, 329–330, 353
Phillips, Jim, 148
Phillips, Katherine, 40, 109
Phillips, Kathy, 270
Phillips, Scott, 270, 278
Pickard, John, 341
Pickering, Bob, 215
Pickett, Cindy, 227
Pickles, Christina, 92
Pierre, Charles, 296
Pierson, Geoffrey, 257
Pillar, Gary, 84, 215
Pinkerton, Nancy, 243, 349
Pinkham, Dr. Henry, 191
Pinkham, Sharon, 191
Pinter, Mark, 323
Platt, Louise, 215
Polen, Nat, 113, 239, 241
Polk, Dr. Marcus, 240

Pollack, Eileen and Robert Mason, 177, 178
Pollock, Cookie, 156
Pollock, Nancy, 156
Pomerantz, Jeff, 276, 337
Ponzini, Antony, 81, 85, 240–241
Porter, Link, 318
Porter, Luke, 119
Porter, Maggie, 318
Porter, Robert J., 97
Porter, Sandy, 318
Portia Faces Life, 33, 371, 377
Post, William, Jr., 163
Poston, Francesca, 70
Potter, Allen, 80, 83, 329
Potter, Paul, 215, 312
Power, Edward, 354
Powers, Dr. Matt, 344, 345
Powers, Mike, 345
Powers, Sam, 298
Poyner, Jim, 88, 358
Prager, Emily, 155
Pratt, Susan, 201
Prentice, Dr. John, 187
Prentice, Polly, 187
Prentiss, Bill, 319
Prentiss, Ed, 211
Prentiss, Lance, 302
Prentiss, Lucas 302
Prentiss, Vanessa, 302
Preston, Alfred E., 354
Prince, Bill, 157
Princi, Elaine, 125, 149
Prinz, Rosemary, 40, 42, 62, 63, 106, 111
Pritchett, Jim, 113, 344, 345
Procter & Gamble, 27, 34, 35, 42, 45, 46–47, 49, 50, 55, 79, 109–110, 155, 210, 268, 341, 357
Prouty, Olive Higgins, 16, 17
Provo, Frank, 341
Pryor, Nicholas, 84, 160, 353
Purdom, Ralph, 346
Pursley, Tricia, 74

Quartermaine, Dr. Alan, 178, 180, 200
Quartermaine, Alexandria, 204
Quartermaine, Edward, 200
Quartermaine, Lila, 200
Quartermaine, Monica, 179
Quartermaine, Tracy, 201
Quinlan, Doris, 80
Quinn, Signor, 337

Raby, John, 25
Radio soaps, 4, 5, 9–23, 210, 214–215
    casts, 363–373
Rae, Melba, 269, 271

Rahn, Patsy, 195
Ralston, Delilah, 254
Ralston, Drew, 254
Ralston, Euphemia, 254
Ralston, Yancy, 253
Rambo, Dack, 76
Ramirez, Filipe, 303
Ramsey, Dr. Allen, 286
Ramsey, Jim, 288
Ramsey, John, 225
Randall, Tony, 4
Randolph, John, 84, 319
Randolph, Lee, 84
Randolph, Marianne, 92
Randolph, Michael, 55
Randolph, Pat, 216
Rapeleye, Mary Linda, 124, 252
Ratray, Peter, 278
Rauch, Paul, 45, 46, 82, 83, 357
Raven, Althea, 315
Raven, Ben, 315
Raven, Judith Lodge, 315
Raven, Paul, 53, 313
Rawlins, Lester, 159
Ray, Leslie, 162
Raymond, Pamela, 335
Reader, Nina, 317
Reardon, Bea, 230
Reardon, Maureen, 231
Reardon, Nola, 230
Reddin, Father Mark, 337
Redeker, Quinn, 149, 304
Redfield, William, 111
Reed, Dr. Casey, 304
Reed, Nick, 304
Reed, Nikki, 304
Reeve, Christopher, 312
Reid, Francis, 135
Reilly, John, 112
Reilly, Luke, 250
Reinholt, George, 45, 46, 81, 82–83,
   85, 239, 246
Remey, Ethel, 115
Rensenhouse, John, 170
Return to Peyton Place, 42, 388
Reunion, 357
Revenant, Claude, 166
Rey, Alejandro, 147
Reynolds, Andrea Whiting, 276
Reynolds, Brock, 298–299
Reynolds, David, 254
Reynolds, Kaye, 160
Reynolds, Kim, 109, 116
Reynolds, Sam, 276
Reynolds, Torchy, 211
Rhodes, Donnelly, 297
Rich, Christopher, 100
Richards, Andy, 305
Richards, Chad, 225
Richards, Jennifer, 229

Richards, Lisa, 245
Richards, Morgan, 230
Richards, Tina, 120
Richardson, Beau, 167
Richman, Caryn, 360
Richter, Lynn Topping, 294
Right to Happiness, The, 20, 23,
   370–371
Rigsby, Gordon, 229, 336
Riley, Craig, 245
Riley, Eileen, 241
Riley, Joe, 240
Ritchie, Clint, 252
Roach, Doris, 193
Road of Life, The , 20, 23, 33, 35,
   368, 378–379
Road to Reality, The, 35, 381
Roat, Richard, 344
Robbins, Deanna, 306
Roberts, Arlo, 147
Roberts, Kathy, 53, 215
Roberts, Mark, 206
Robinette, Dale, 283
Robinson, Chris, 195
Robinson, Sandy, 271
Robinson, Virginia, 315
Roche, Con, 116
Rockwell, Robert, 286
Rodell, Barbara, 84, 118, 335
Roe, Patricia, 217
Roerick, William, 231
Rogers, Bob, 276
Rogers, Gil, 72
Rogers, Lynne, 215
Rogers, Suzanne, 142
Rogers, Tristan, 204
Rolfing, Tom, 96
Rolland, Marianne, 296
Rolland, Pierre, 295
Rollins, Jamie, 319
Rollins, Richard, 319
Roma, Gina, 305
Romalotti, Danny, 305
Romance of Helen Trent, The, 12,
   13–16, 23, 52, 364
Rooney, Sherry, 285, 324
Roos, Joanna, 312, 315
Rose, Brian, 60
Rose, Norman, 240
Rosemary, 372
Ross, Frank, 281
Ross, Jarrod, 228
Rossilli, Paul, 205
Rostand, Theodora, 345
Rousseau, Diane, 319
Roussel, Elvera, 216
Roux, Carol, 80, 85
Rowland, Jada, 30, 42, 332, 333
Rowland, Jeff, 112
Roy, Renee, 319

Rucker, Barbara, 114
Rudder, Alma, 101
Ruick, Melville, 215
Runyeon, Frank, 123
Ruskin, Jeannie, 155
Russell, A. J., 182
Russell, Amy, 325
Russell, Gordon, 182
Russell, Ian, 323–324
Russom, Leon, 91, 354
Rutledge, Dr. John, 20, 210–211
Rutledge, Ruth, 211
Ryan, Barbara, 123
Ryan, Barry, 264
Ryan, Delia, 257
Ryan, Elizabeth Jane, 265
Ryan, Frank, 257
Ryan, Jennifer, 116
Ryan, Johnny, 257
Ryan, Little John, 264
Ryan, Maeve, 257
Ryan, Mary, 259
Ryan, Michael, 84
Ryan, Pat, 260
Ryan, Dr. Rick, 116
Ryan, Siobhan, 262
Ryan, Dr. Tim, 224
Ryan's Hope, 46, 59, 257–267
   background, 257
   cast, 265–267
   story, 257–265
Rydell, Mark, 112
Ryland, Jack, 241
Rysdale, Arthur, 334
Rysdale, Kip, 334

Safran, Judy, 335
Sago, Benny, 71
Saint, Eva Marie, 4
St. Clair, Gunnar, 125
St. George, Louis, 101
Saltzman, Dr. Herb, 318
Saltzman, Nell, 319
Samms, Emma, 186, 206
Sampler, Philece, 151
Sanders, Byron, 249, 319, 342, 345
Sanders, Carrie, 75
Santoro, Dean, 115
Sarandon, Susan, 279
Sargent, Anne, 25
Saunders, Lanna, 135, 137
Savior, Paul, 188
Saxon, Deborah, 168
Saxon, Tony, 166
Saxon, Whitney, 155
Scannell, Susan, 289
Scardino, Don, 216
Scheffel, Beth, 305
Scheider, Roy, 4
Scheller, Damion, 289, 359

Schmidke, Ned, 94
Schnabel, Stefan, 218
Schnetzer, Stephen, 102, 136, 139
Schofield, Frank, 275
Scollay, Fred, J., 93, 344
Scorpio, Robert, 184, 204
Scott, Ansel, 168
Scott, Ben, 217
Scott, Draper, 166
Scott, Dr. Emmet, 228
Scott, Jackie, 227
Scott, Jean Bruce, 150
Scott, Jordan, 99
Scott, Maggie, 217
Scott, Michael, 304
Scott, Peggy, 217
Scott, Sydney, 64
Scott, Dr. William, 344
Scourby, Alexander, 336
Search for Tomorrow, 7, 23, 25, 26,
    32, 42, 50, 53, 268–292
        background, 268–270
        cast, 289–292
        story, 270–289
Second Mrs. Burton, The, 23, 371
Secret Storm, The, 4, 25, 26, 28,
    30–33, 37, 41–42, 310, 332–340
        background, 332
        cast, 338–340
        story, 332–338
Sedgwick, Kyra, 102
Seeking Heart, The, 377
Seligman, Selig J., 174, 175
Selleck, Tom, 4, 300
Sentell, Lee, 288
Sentell, Mignon, 287
Sentell, Travis ("Rusty"), Sr., 288
Sentell, Travis Tourneur, 270, 287
Severn, Maida, 188
Sevingy, Morlock, 161
Sex, in soap operas, 52–55
Seymour, Anne, 200
Shackelford, Ted, 91
Shafer, Sam, 344
Shaffer, Louise, 165, 263, 280
Shannon, Michael, 278
Sharkey, Matt, 169
Sharon, Fran, 156
Shea, Ken, 318
Shea, Kitty, 66
Shea, Loretta, 101
Shea, Michael, 113
Shea, Pete, 101
Shearer, Dr. Dan, 86
Shearer, Julia, 102
Shearin, John, 237
Sheehan, Doug, 201
Sheperd, Ellen, 74
Shepherd, Ann, 214
Shepherd, Dr. Pamela, 250

Sherman, Courtney, 270, 278
Sherman, Gwen, 296
Sherman, Howard, 190
Sherman, Jenny, 194
Sherwood, Molly, 169
Shipp, John Wesley, 230
Shirley, Tom, 314, 317
Shoberg, Dick, 73, 161
Short, Bob, 42
Shriner, Kin, 188, 359
Shuman, Roy, 113, 276
Siebert, Charles, 117
Siegel, Dave, 241
Siegel, Julie, 241
Siegel, Timmy, 241
Sikking, James, 189
Silliman, Maureen, 224
Silverman, Fred, 49, 177, 178, 179,
    353
Simmons, Allison, 273
Simmons, Cornelia, 272
Simmons, Maggie, 142
Simmons, Richard, 185
Simms, Taffy, 162
Simon, Peter, 123, 215, 270, 278
Simpson, Carolee, 347
Simpson, Eileen, 96
Sinclair, Amy, 216
Slater, Garth, 236
Slater, June, 236
Slater, Lily, 236
Slesar, Henry, 40, 155
Slezak, Erika, 240
Sloane, David, 286
Sloyan, James, 265
Smith, Frank, 202
Smith, Jackie, 178, 180, 183–184
Smith, Jennifer, 202
Smith, Pat Falken, 37, 135, 182,
    183–184
Smith, Phoebe, 156
Smith, Sandra, 216
Smithers, William, 219
Smythe, Marcus, 288
Snow, Norman, 169
Snyder, Drew, 320
Snyder, Nancy, 249
Soap, 5
Soderberg, Robert, 106
Solomon, Deborah, 64
Solow, Pamela Peters, 294
Somers, Jocelyn, 148
Somerset, 387–388
Sommer, Edith, 109
Sommerfield, Diane, 146
Spaulding, Alan, 228
Spaulding, Brandon, 229
Spaulding, Elizabeth, 228
Spaulding, Phillip, 228
Spears, Martha, 156

Spencer, Beal, 122
Spencer, Bobbie, 180, 181, 200
Spencer, Ellen, 271
Spencer, Gillian, 76, 116, 215, 240
Spencer, Jane, 123
Spencer, Dr. Laura, 136
Spencer, Luke, 181, 200
Spencer, Sally, 90
Springfield, Rick, 185, 206
Squire, Katherine, 283
Stafford, Nancy, 349
Stallings, Gil, 117
Stallings, Jay, 117
Stamberger, Jack, 317
Stanger, Barbara, 144, 354
Stanley, Pat, 282
Stanwyck, Barbara, 16
Stapleton, Eve, 229
Stapleton, Rita, 224
Stark, Jennifer, 320
Stark, Sally, 147, 320
Starrett, Valerie, 177, 187
Stauffer, Jack, 304
Stedman, William, 53
Steele, Bob, 25
Steele, Jadrien, 264
Stella Dallas, 5, 12, 16–17, 20, 23,
    52, 369–370
Stenbeck, James, 123
Stephen, McNaughton, 168
Stephens, Perry, 237
Sterling, Alan, 317
Sterling, Barbara, 317
Sterling, Bruce, 317
Sterling, Gaye, 317–318
Sterling, Philip, 216
Stern, Lilibet, 305
Stevens, April, 304
Stevens, Clay, 335
Stevens, Jill, 335
Stevens, Julie, 15, 19–20
Stevens, K. T., 302
Stevens, Kaye, 146
Stevens, Ken, 335
Stevens, Paul, 93, 300
Stevens, Roger, 318
Stevens, Shawn, 151, 288
Stevenson, Douglas, 288
Stewart, Dr. Alan, 348
Stewart, Dr. David, 21, 111
Stewart, "Dee" (Dawn), 122
Stewart, Don, 215
Stewart, Duane, 156
Stewart, Ellen, 59, 122
Stewart, Fred, 321
Stewart, Pamela, 157
Stewart, Paul, 109, 115
Stewart, Susan, 115
Stewart, Trish, 294
Stinnette, Dorothy, 168

Stoddard, Haila, 31, 333
Stone, Jeff, 97
Storm, Mike, 240
Story of Mary Marlin, The, 18, 21, 365
Strand, Viveca, 349
Strasser, Robin, 71, 85, 243
Stratton, Albert, 354
Stratton, Dr. Joel, 191
Stratton, Owen, 191
Straub, John, 318
Stroka, Michael, 166
Strudwick, Shepherd, 239, 263, 325
Stuart, Anna, 347
Stuart, Mary, 29, 32, 212, 268, 269, 270
Studer, Hal, 106
Suddenly Last Summer, 54
Sudrow, Lyle, 213, 214
Sullivan, Liam, 336
Sullivan, Maggie, 206
Sullivan, Susan, 40, 87
Summers, Dr. Paul, 349
Sun, Irene Yaah-Ling, 324
Sutton, Charles, 206
Sutton, Holly, 186, 206
Swanson, Kate, 320
Sward, Anne, 123
Sweet, Dolph, 89
Swenson, Karl, 18, 23
Swift, Logan, 168
Sylvester, Johnny, 270
Symington, Donald, 316

Taggart, Millee, 271
Talbot, Elizabeth, 109, 115
Talbot, Nita, 272, 334
Tanner, Cliff, 96
Tanzini, Philip, 200
Taper, Garth, 288
Tapscott, Mark, 140, 304
Tate, Arthur, 53, 271
Taylor, Brian-Robert, 132
Taylor, Dane, 288
Taylor, Elizabeth, 4, 184–185, 205
Taylor, Holland, 168
Taylor, Joe, 354
Taylor, Josh, 148
Taylor, Lauren-Marie, 237
Taylor, Dr. Peter, 187
Taylor, Tammy, 305
Teitel, Carol, 222
Telfer, Frank, 349
Temple, Lorraine, 148
Templeton, Jackie, 205
Templeton, Laura, 205
Texas, 49–50, 83, 310, 357–361
Thayer, Brynn, 246
Thayer, Chris, 25
Thayer, Connie, 25

These Are My Children, 374
Thinnes, Roy, 4, 175, 186
This Is Nora Drake, 23, 372
Thomas, Frankie, 23, 25
Thomas, Melody, 304
Thomas, Richard, 4
Thompson, Kevin, 121
Thompson, Rex, 345
Thorne, Sybil, 75
Thornton, David, 70
Thornton, Dottie, 71
Thornton, Edna, 71
Thorpe, Adam, 219
Thorpe, Roger, 214, 219
Three Steps to Heaven, 33, 376
Thurston, Derek, 303
Time for Us, A, 37
Time to Live, A, 33, 378
Tinder, Paul, 99
Tinling, Ted, 159
Tippit, Wayne, 287, 333
Today is Ours, 35, 380
Today's Children, 11, 364
Tolan, Kathleen Ryan, 259
Toland, Dr. Mark, 241
Tolksdorf, Birgitta, 322
Toll, Pamela, 346
Tomme, Ron, 317
Tompkins, Joan, 23
Tourneur, Martin, 270, 288
Tovrov, Orin, 13, 344
Towers, Constance, 130
Townsend, Ernest, 170
Townsend, Philip, 346
Travis, Ben, 157
Travis, Jody, 169
Travis, Nicole, 156
Travis, Walter, 354
Trent, Helen, 5, 13–16
Triandos, Ari, 124
Trusel, Lisa, 148
Trustman, Susan, 80
Tucker, Brandi, 301
Tuggle, Billy Clyde, 72
Turenne, Louis, 166
Turgeon, Peter, 228
Turino, Joe, 216
Turner, Janine, 186, 205
Turner, Kathleen, 349
Twining, Rex, 273
Tyler, Amy, 40
Tyler, Ann, 63
Tyler, Dr. Charles, 63
Tyler, Chuck, 63
Tyler, Clarissa, 130
Tyler, Damian, 170
Tyler, Judson, 130
Tyler, Lincoln, 63
Tyler, Phoebe, 40, 63
Tylo, Michael, 231

Ulrich, Kim, 125

Valenta, Lenard, 24, 342
Valiant Lady, 12, 33, 369, 376
Van Alen, Kurt, 345
Van Der Vlis, Diana, 259
Van Vleet, Richard, 63
Vane, Lahoma, 84
Varney, Spencer, 170
Vaughn, Heidi, 156
Venable, Mark, 88
Vendig, Irving, 154, 269
Vento, Dr. Tony, 318
Vento, Mrs., 318
ver Dorn, Jerry, 230
Verdict Is Yours, The, 35, 379
Vernon, Brad, 250
Vernon, Naomi, 250
Vernon, Samantha ("Sam"), 250
Vernon, Dr. Will, 247
Vested, Kit, 221
Vic and Sade, 12, 363
Vickery, Jim, 336
Vigard, Kristen, 230
Vincente, Marcy, 278–279
Vincente, Dr. Tony, 278
Vining, Barbara, 194
Vining, Jason, 194
Vining, Laura, 181, 194
Viola, Vicki, 273
Viving, Laura, 49
Vochek, Jim, 236
Vochek, Merrill, 236
Voigt, Jill, 250
Von Furstenberg, Betsy, 113

Wade, Neil, 112
Wade, Sam, 353
Wagner, Gunther, 169
Wagner, Helen, 6, 106, 108, 111, 215
Wainwright, Philip, 91
Wakefield, Dr. Colin, 349
Waldrip, Tim, 240
Walken, Christopher, 213
Walken, Glenn, 213
Walker, David, 189
Walker, Joel, 360
Walker, Kathryn, 280
Walker, Nicholas, 130
Walker, Pete, 305
Walker, Sydney, 337
Walker, Tonja, 132
Wall, Lucile, 176
Wallace, Don, 155, 342
Wallace, Marie, 215
Walling, Stratton, 318
Wallingford, Langley, 50, 76
Walsh, Nathan, 271
Walter, Norman, 125
Walters, Susan, 237

Walton, Dr. Dan, 273
Walton, Gary, 281
Walton, Liza, 281
Ward, Dr. Jeff, 125
Wardwell, John, 229
Waring, Charlotte, 217
Warner, Cliff, 75
Warren, Pam, 305
Warrick, Lee, 196, 241
Warrick, Ruth, 40, 62, 63, 106, 111, 215
Waterman, Phil, 321
Watson, Douglass, 89
Watt, Billie Lou, 106, 280, 342
Watts, Sharlene, 92
Way of the World, The, 379
Wayland, Len, 353
Weaver, Patty, 146, 305
Webb, Wanda, 242
Webber, Jeff, 195
Webber, Rick, 195
Weber, Karl, 271
Weber, Larry, 319, 333, 359
Weber, Richard K., 323
Webster, Evan, 94
Webster, Libby, 170
Wedgeworth, Anne, 84
Welles, Collier, 169
Welles, Orson, 4
Werner, Dr. Joe, 218
Werner, Dr. Karen, 346
Wesner, Raney, 283
West, Joshua, 243
West, Martin, 186
Weston, Ellen, 81, 303
Weston, Hunt, 359
Wexler, Amanda, 229
Wexler, Lucille, 229
Wheel, Patricia, 25
Wheeler, Alex, 98, 358
Wheeler, Brette, 360
Wheeler, Grant, 359, 360
Wheeler, Judith, 360
Wheeler, Lacey, 360
Wheeler, Lois, 215
When a Girl Marries, 21, 370
Where the Heart Is, 39–40, 42, 385–386
White, Charles, 321
White, Jane, 287

White, Lauren, 350
White, Peter, 63
White, Ted, 52
Whiting, Len, 276
Whitman, Jim, 354
Whitney, Colin, 158
Whitney, Geraldine, 158
Whitney, Gil, 5, 16, 52
Whitney, Gordon, 158
Whitney, Keith, 158
Whitney, Schuyler, 169
Whitney, Theo, 349
Whitton, Peggy, 349
Whyland, Stuart, 150
Wickwire, Nancy, 111, 140
Widdoes, Kathleen, 96
Widmark, Richard, 4
Wiggins, Tudi, 73, 312
Wilkins, Dave, 283
Wilkins, Stephanie, 283
Wilkins, Wendy, 283
Wilkinson, Lisa, 76
Williams, Ann, 168, 237, 273, 345
Williams, Carl, 303–304
Williams, Darnell, 76
Williams, Doug, 139, 150
Williams, Dr. Lesley, 188
Williams, Mary, 304
Williams, Mitch, 181, 202
Williams, Murial, 87
Williams, Patty, 305
Williams, Paul, 304
Wilson, David, 337
Wilson, Hector, 170
Wilson, Liz, 346
Wilson, Mel, 205
Wilson, Rachel, 244
Wilson, Smiley, 170
Wines, Chris, 217
Winograd, Dr. Kate, 149
Winslow, Buzz, 97
Winsor, Roy, 25–26, 27–28, 29, 35, 41, 268, 311, 332
Winston, Susan Plantt, 68
Winthrop, Cass, 102
Winthrop, Stacey, 102
Wise, Ray, 319
Wolek, Anna, 240
Wolek, Danny, 240
Wolek, Jenny, 246

Wolek, Karen, 248
Wolek, Dr. Larry, 239, 240
Wolek, Vince, 240
Wolfe, Karin, 144
Woman in White, 20, 61, 368
Woman to Remember, A, 24–25, 374
Woman with a Past, 376–377
Wood, Kelly, 120, 278
Wood, Lynn, 304
Woodard, Rae, 263
Woodard, William, 263
Woodruff, Stephanie, 149
Woods, Carson, 216
Woods, Michael, 74
Woods, Robert, 252
World Apart, A, 40, 109, 387
World of Mr. Sweeney, The, 375
Wright, Billy Joe, 358
Wright, Nita, 360
Wyatt, John, 281
Wyatt, Sharon, 205
Wylie, Gavin, 169
Wyllie, Meg, 193
Wyndham, Anne, 189, 270, 285
Wyndham, Victoria, 85, 217

Yates, Stephen, 225
York, Francine, 148
Young, Agnes, 318
Young, Janis, 88
Young, Jim, 174–175, 176, 177, 179
Young and the Restless, The, 3, 20, 43–44, 46, 49, 54, 55, 60, 293–307
    background, 293–294
    cast, 306–307
    story, 294–306
Young Dr. Malone, 23, 35, 36, 371, 380
Young Marrieds, The, 37, 382
Young Widder Brown, 12, 23, 52, 369
Yourman, Alice, 215

Zaslow, Michael, 219, 254
Zeman, Jackie, 180, 181, 200, 250
Zenk, Colleen, 123
Zenor, Suzanne, 149, 305
Zimbalist, Efram, Jr., 4
Zimmer, Kim, 349
Zimmet, Marya, 335

STELLA DALLAS DAYS OF OUR LIVES THE EDGE
OF NIGHT ALL MY CHILDREN JUST PLAIN BILL
THE ROMANCE OF HELEN TRENT MARY NOBLE
BACKSTAGE WIFE MA PERKINS THE GUIDING
LIGHT YOUNG DOCTOR MALONE LIFE CAN B
BEAUTIFUL VIC AND SADE GENERAL HOSPITA
ALL MY CHILDREN MYRT AND MARGE PORTIA
FACES LIFE WOMAN IN WHITE AS THE WORLD
TURNS ONE MAN'S FAMILY ALL MY CHILDREN
WHEN A GIRL MARRIES ONE LIFE TO LIVE DARK
SHADOWS THE YOUNG AND THE RESTLESS THE
SECRET STORM RYAN'S HOPE JUST PLAIN BILL
LOVE OF LIFE THE GUIDING LIGHT LIFE CAN B
BEAUTIFUL YOUNG DOCTOR MALONE VIC AND
SADE MYRT AND MARGE ONE MAN'S FAMILY